THE WHICH?
BOOK OF
DO-IT-
YOURSELF

THE WHICH?
BOOK OF
DO-IT-
YOURSELF

Published by Consumers' Association
& Hodder and Stoughton

THE WHICH? BOOK OF DO-IT-YOURSELF
is published in Great Britain
by Consumers' Association,
14 Buckingham Street, London WC2N 6DS
and by Hodder & Stoughton,
47 Bedford Square, London WC1B 3DP

First Edition 1981
© Consumers' Association 1981

ISBN 0 340 26237 0

Typesetting by Vantage Photosetting Company Ltd.,
North Baddesley, Hampshire

Colour Separations by Aero Offset Reproductions Limited,
Eastleigh, Hampshire

Printed and bound by Graficromo, SA, Cordoba, Spain

Acknowledgements

Editor
Roger Davies

Design
Turner Wilks Dandridge Limited

Illustrations
Hayward & Martin Limited
Tom Cross

Cover photographs
Peter Higgins

Contributors

Dave Beadle
Terence D Bines
Mike Bird
Stuart L Davey
Quentin Deane
Christian Donovan
Chris Evans
W P K Findlay
Chris Gill
John E Gregory

Ian W L Hendry
Ivan Holgate
Andrew Jarmin
John Kingham
Mike Lawrence
Louella Miles
A J Newman
R W Sharpe
Raymond W Stacey
Garry Taylor

The publishers also wish to thank
The Brick Development Association
The Building Research Establishment
The Cement and Concrete Association

The Editor and staff of Handyman Which?,
and their consultants, provided valuable
assistance throughout
the production of this book

Contents

CHAPTER SEVEN: ROOFS

CHAPTER EIGHT: DOORS AND WINDOWS

CHAPTER NINE: SECURITY

CHAPTER TEN: METALWORKING

CHAPTER ELEVEN: PLUMBING

CHAPTER TWELVE: DAMP, ROT AND WOODWORM

Foreword

There has always been, in this country, a group of people whose way of life is one of self-help. They may mend their own cars, make their own wine, tinker about with radios, convey their own houses (and build bits of them, too) and regard it almost as a personal failure if they have to pay anyone to do anything for them.

Over the last decade or so, this group has become an army – particularly in the field of home improvement, repair and maintenance, activities loosely described as 'do-it-yourself'.

There are two main reasons for this – the increase in the number of people owning their own home and the high cost and difficulty of finding professional labour. Apart from saving money, many people have found a lot of satisfaction in doing things themselves.

This social revolution has been accompanied – and assisted – by a revolution in do-it-yourself products. Emulsion paint has changed the face of home decorating since it is much easier to use and more durable than the old whitewashes and distempers. The introduction of easy-to-hang, easy-to-clean, vinyl wallcoverings has meant that decoration can be more varied and more interesting. The do-it-yourselfer has an unprecedented number of electrically-powered tools at his disposal, from simple electric drills through electrically-powered saws and sanders to wood-turning lathes and welding kits. The availability of sheets of plastic laminate, plasterboard and man-made wood products (particularly plain and veneered chipboard) and the introduction of devices for joining them together have reduced the skill necessary to make things like kitchen units and built-in wardrobes. And so the list goes on.

This book bridges the gap between craftsmen's textbooks and guides for the novice. It has been written for the modern do-it-yourselfer – who is sufficiently intelligent and technically-minded to understand the intricacies of electrical and plumbing work, sufficiently dextrous to hang wallpaper straight and to saw wood without sawing his (or her) thumb, but who lacks the information about materials, techniques, products and building methods necessary to do the job.

There is something in the book for beginners – not least an understanding that do-it-yourself is not all plain sailing and is something that gains with experience and knowledge. Enthusiasts shouldn't be disappointed either – there's a wealth of technical detail and 'tips of the trade' which can be added to their knowledge.

The book draws heavily on the research and testing experience gained by *Handyman Which?* since it was first published in November 1971. Like the magazine, it depends heavily on comments from experts, consultants and professional bodies in the various fields.

The book concentrates on giving information about materials, tools and techniques for doing a wide variety of jobs plus the background technical information necessary. This includes legal aspects with details of Wiring Regulations, Water Byelaws, Building Regulations, planning permission and so on. Although it is the *Which?* Book of Do-It-Yourself, this book cannot tell you which tool or product to buy. To do so would mean repeating a large part of the contents of *Handyman Which?*, for which there is not space. Generalisations, like 'use only tools made by a reputable manufacturer' have been avoided since it has been found through experience that these sorts of statement can be misleading or are too vague to be helpful. As an example, we have found that the best wood-cutting tools (planes and chisels) are generally the more expensive ones made by the well-known established manufacturers. But the best-value panel saws for wood are certainly not the most expensive and the best-value electric drill has usually been the cheapest. The product you buy will also depend on what you intend to do with it: for making lots of small holes in wood, for example, there's little point in buying expensive high-speed steel twist drills when cheap ones will do the job just as well and won't break your heart when they break in two; for drilling holes in steel, on the other hand, you *do* need a decent drill – carbon steel drills won't go through it. In each section of the book, there is a reference to relevant *Handyman Which?* reports.

To be a successful do-it-yourselfer, it is necessary to be able to buy the tools, materials and equipment that you need at the right price – there is rarely the need to pay the full price for anything. So often the main problem is *where* to buy but sometimes the important decision is whether to buy, hire or simply borrow.

There are a wide variety of 'shops' for do-it-yourself: hardware shops, ironmongers and do-it-yourself shops are usually on the expensive side but are often good for advice; do-it-yourself supermarkets and chains of paint and wallpaper shops are cheaper but you're often left to serve yourself; builders' merchants are sometimes the only place for 'heavy' building materials. It's necessary to become familiar with the shops the trade uses – electrical wholesalers, plumbers' merchants, glass and timber merchants, and even quarries for aggregate. With these places, you're expected to know what you want. Sometimes, it's possible to buy things second-hand – doors from demolition sites, for example – and sometimes you may find a builder who is prepared to sell you small quantities of building materials on an informal basis.

Many expensive tools and pieces of equipment – from hammer drills to scaffolding – can be hired, not only from specialist hire shops but also from some builders. One problem with hiring equipment is that it puts pressure on you to get the job finished in a limited time. It's worth calculating the cost of buying a piece of equipment second-hand (scaffolding or a concrete mixer, say) and then selling it after you've finished the job. This may

work out cheaper and it gives you the freedom to cope with unexpected hold-ups, like a sustained spell of bad weather.

In theory, the building industry has now gone metric, but progress has been sporadic. Some things have gone totally metric – like paint tins (litres), brick sizes (mm), electric cable sizes (sq mm) and concrete (50kg bags). Other things, notably timber and wood products, have simply converted the old imperial sizes into metric quantities, giving rise to absurdities like sheets of chipboard measuring 2440mm by 1220mm which is much more difficult to cope with than the old 8ft by 4ft which is, in reality, what it is. Some products – like woodworking chisels, for example – are a mixture: some imperial, some metric and some with both sizes.

Throughout this book, metric quantities are used wherever possible, with explanations, where necessary, of the relationship between the metric sizes and the imperial ones – in plumbing, for example, all new copper pipe that you buy will be metric (15mm, say), but it is sometimes necessary to know whether existing pipe, to which you may be adding fittings, is imperial or metric. Where products are still predominantly imperial, these dimensions have been used on the basis that these are easier to understand and that they are what you're likely to be faced with when buying.

The next decade will see a continuation of the do-it-yourself boom as house prices and the cost of moving continue to rise and more and more people choose to improve and extend the house they're living in rather than move to a bigger one and as abilities, confidence and knowledge become more widespread. This book will be invaluable.

David Holloway
Editor, *Handyman Which?*

DECORATING

Decorating is the most popular d-i-y job with perhaps as many as 90 per cent of people doing at least some for themselves. Most decorating is fairly straightforward and does not require a lot of expensive tools and equipment, though it can be rather tedious.

There are many materials available for decorating. The most popular are paint and wallcoverings but many others can be used – fabrics, wood boarding and a range of tiles, say.

Indoors, the main aim is to produce an environment which is pleasant to live in. Durability of the decorating material is of relatively little importance as it is likely to be changed before it deteriorates. But there are situations indoors where special properties are needed: in kitchens and bathrooms, for example, the decorating material will have to stand up to condensation; in the kitchen it will also have to be easy to clean.

Outside, durability and appearance are of roughly equal importance.

Painting

There are many different paints available which have both decorative and protective properties. Some are suitable for use both indoors and outside, most are available in a large range of colours and some are available in matt, satin or gloss finishes. Special-purpose paints – for radiators, for resisting condensation and so on – are also available.

Usually, paints can be applied by brush, roller, pad or spray and vary widely in their ease of application. Painting inside is quite straightforward and the results are usually good, though painting with emulsion paint is much easier than with gloss. However, painting often takes more time than is originally allowed and is a bit messy. Painting the outside of a house is much more time-consuming and, depending on the weather, generally less enjoyable than painting inside. There is also much more risk attached – particularly when painting upstairs windows, eaves and so on.

Hanging wallcoverings

Wallcoverings are particularly suitable for decorating large flat areas of wall or ceiling but they cannot be used outside. The different types available vary from ordinary wallpapers to much more exotic wallcoverings with flock or metallic finishes. You can buy plain-coloured wallcoverings – rather like paint – as well as ones carrying complicated designs with lots of different colours and textures. By and large, it costs more to use wallcoverings than paint: vinyls, flocks and metallics are the most expensive to use; ordinary wallpapers and woodchip types tend to be the cheapest.

Wallcoverings vary enormously in their resistance to wear-and-tear: most vinyls, for example, are as easy to clean and wear as well as paint when used indoors; ordinary wallpapers, on the other hand, should be used only in areas of minimum wear. You can use a wallcovering to hide walls and ceilings which are in poor condition and the preparation of the surface before hanging need not be carried out quite as painstakingly as before painting, though large irregularities in the surface will show through.

Hanging wallcoverings is not difficult and is a fairly clean job, but it does require patience and a little more knowledge and skill than painting with emulsion paint. Most people are satisfied with their own work but you should allow more time than you expect.

Tiling

Ceramic tiles are most commonly available in square shapes measuring 108×108mm or 152×152mm and with surfaces which vary in finish from a high gloss to a highly-textured matt surface. They are available in both plain colours and patterns and vary tremendously in price. Ceramic tiles are impervious to water and stand up to cleaning with mild abrasives, so they are an ideal choice for areas in kitchens and bathrooms that are often wet – sink surrounds, splash backs and so on. Ceramic tiles resist heat, so they can be used on worktops and, because they wear well, they can be used on floors too.

Many other tiling materials are also available – cork, plastic, mirror and metallic – and these vary in their appearance, ease of application, properties and price.

Putting up wall tiles does not take much knowledge but does need skill – about the same as for hanging wallcoverings. It is a satisfying job that is not particularly strenuous or dirty and only a few cheap tools are needed.

Wallboards

Man-made wallboards are available in large sheets generally measuring 2440×1220mm with finishes varying from plain white semi-gloss melamine to imitation ceramic tiles or wood. Some imitation wood boards have a slight texture to simulate the wood grain. Wallboards are more durable than most wallcoverings and can be scrubbed occasionally with water without suffering damage.

Like ceramic tiles, wallboards are most suitable for flat surfaces and can be used to cover old walls in particularly poor condition.

Natural softwood cladding – often described as 'knotty pine' – is usually available either as individual 2.4m lengths or in bundles containing random lengths. It can be used to hide walls in poor condition but it should be protected with a clear polyurethane seal or varnish.

Both cladding and wallboards can be fixed to the wall by building a framework of battens and then pinning the boards to it. Wallboards can also be stuck with adhesive if the walls are flat. Putting up wallboards and cladding is no more difficult than any other simple woodworking task but it is rather more strenuous than other decorating jobs and more tools are needed.

Paints and painting

The term paint is used to describe a wide variety of coatings which are applied as a liquid and subsequently dry to form a durable, decorative and apparently solid film. Paint is a very versatile coating medium – it can be used on almost any surface no matter how intricate, and can be applied in a number of different ways.

Most paints are mixtures of three main ingredients – a pigment, a binder and a liquid. The colour and opacity of paint are due to the presence of a **pigment**. This can also impart considerable protection to the other ingredients by harmlessly absorbing otherwise destructive ultra-violet light. The simplest paint is whitewash which once applied is merely a coating of pigment – in this case chalk. Whitewash does not offer much protection to the surface beneath it because it does not generally contain a **binder** (sometimes called a film former or resin). A binder holds the pigment together and sticks it to the surface. Binders are normally solids, so to produce a paint which can be spread over an uneven surface the binder is usually broken up into small pieces and suspended in a **liquid**.

A large variety of names have been attached to this finished mixture of ingredients (now a paint) most of which classify it according to:

- **its use** – primer, undercoat, topcoat and so on
- **the binder it contains** – oil, alkyd and emulsion, for example
- **its traditional name** – lacquer and enamel, for instance.

Paints by use

An ideal 'all purpose' paint should satisfy a number of criteria – it should stick strongly to the surface it is applied to, it should cover well, it should leave a decorative and desirable finish, and should last, particularly when used outside. No one paint performs all these functions well and as a result, paints are formulated for specific uses. For example, when painting woodwork, a three-coat *system* is usually needed consisting of a primer (to stick to the surface beneath), an undercoat (to cover well) and a topcoat (to give a pleasing and durable finish).

Primers and sealers These should be used on new or exposed woodwork, brickwork, metalwork, plaster and so on. They will stick firmly to the surface, seal it, and provide a key for subsequent coats of paint. They should also be used when you want to paint over sound old paintwork with a new, completely different, type of paint. In this situation, primers and sealers prevent chemical attack between the different paints, reduce the likelihood of the new paint not sticking to the old one and should stop the colour of the old paint bleeding through the new one.

A primer by itself is not permanent protection for the surface below – it should be painted over with an undercoat or topcoat as quickly as possible.

Undercoats Normally, you use one of these immediately after a primer when building up a paint system, or on old paintwork when you are changing the colour significantly. Undercoats are designed to have: good *opacity* or *hiding power* so that you can cover a dark colour with a lighter one without having to apply many coats of paint; a *high build capability* so that you can put on a thick coat of paint around corners and over sharp edges where paints tend to be spread too thinly; and a *soft finish* which can be rubbed smooth easily with abrasive paper (ready to take the next coat).

As with primers, undercoats provide no more than temporary protection to the surface beneath and should be painted over as quickly as possible.

Topcoats These are dual-purpose paints providing both a decorative and protective final coat. They are often available in a choice of finishes – matt, eggshell, satin and full gloss. The choice of the topcoat affects the overall appearance of the paint system, its durability outside, and its ability to withstand knocks.

Paints by binder

Many of the more familiar binder names – polyurethane, for example – are often incorporated into the brand name of the paint itself.

Paints are also often called **oil-based** or **water-based** according to the liquid used to carry the binder.

Alkyd (oil-based) Traditionally, paints were based on oil such as linseed which dries to form a solid paint film. Nowadays, the linseed has largely been replaced by better synthetic resins called alkyds. These paints are available in matt, satin and full gloss finishes and, as a whole, are more durable than polyurethane paints on exterior woodwork.

Polyurethane (oil-based) Many gloss paints and clear finishes for wood – varnishes, for instance – contain polyurethane binders or urethane-modified alkyds. Most of these paints – in particular the glosses – are *thixotropic*: they are jelly-like in the can but become liquid when shaken or stirred and are less likely to drip than other types. As a general rule, polyurethane gloss paints are not as glossy as alkyd gloss paints but are quicker drying, particularly tough, and have a reputation for excellent abrasion resistance.

Polyurethane varnishes (a varnish is basically a paint without a pigment) come either as one-pack ready-to-use varnishes or as two separate tins which have to be mixed together to start a non-reversible chemical reaction. Two-pack varnishes generally give an exceptionally tough finish and are often sold for use on wooden floors. Some polyurethane varnishes are sold specifically for interior use and others for both interior and exterior use. While exterior varnishes can be used indoors, the opposite does not always apply – exterior varnishes often have chemicals added to reduce the effects of ultra-violet light. But, even so, you should not expect exterior grade polyurethane varnishes to last for long – most degrade rapidly and to prolong their life you should apply a minimum of *four* coats. The rate of de-terioration depends on the type of wood beneath – varnish is likely to last longer on mahogany-type woods such as sapele and utile and on teak and similar woods, such as afrormosia, than on oak and western red cedar.

Emulsion (water-based) These are available in matt, eggshell, satin and full gloss finishes, though the most glossy emulsion finishes do not produce as much shine as polyurethane or alkyd gloss paints. The most popular emulsion paints are based either on a resin called polyvinyl acetate (pva for short) – giving rise to the term *vinyl* which is often found on paint tins – or on acrylic co-polymers. Most emulsion paints can be washed once they are dry and can be used in areas affected by condensation, such as bathrooms or kitchens. Some inexpensive emulsion paints have very poor resistance to water – rubbing these with a damp cloth rapidly removes the paint and condensation can cause the paint film to become brittle and then flake off. Painting over these paints (even with a water-resistant paint) may prove troublesome – the 'new' paint may be difficult to brush out and the original paint may tend to lift off the surface beneath.

Traditional names

Enamel (oil-based) An old fashioned term which when used correctly describes a heat-glazed finish. But nowadays, the term is rather meaninglessly applied to some ordinary gloss paints.

Lacquer (oil-based) A paint that dries by evaporation of the solvent to leave be-hind a continuous surface paint film. Most paints applied by either brush or roller are not lacquers – they dry by a combination of solvent evaporation and chemical action. The most common lacquers are cellulose lacquers for use on repairs to car bodywork.

Varnish (oil-based) A term used to describe any transparent paint and most often applied to wood finishes.

Distemper (water-based) This contains a pigment in an oil binder emulsified with water. Distempers have poor water resistance and are now rarely sold. You may encounter them on walls and ceilings of old unmodernised properties.

Primers and sealers

If you want paintwork to last as long as possible – outdoors, in particular – you must use primers and sealers correctly. For painting woodwork, a general-purpose primer or leadless wood primer is satisfactory; the former can be used on metals too. But for painting other surfaces your choice is not simple – there are many different primers, each formulated for a specific use, and most of them are difficult to find in the shops. Some of these special primers contain lead and could be harmful in some circumstances – see opposite page.

Knotting A shellac-based varnish which is used to seal knots and other resinous areas in softwood. If these areas are left untreated, wood resins may ooze out of the wood, especially when it is warmed by the sun, and may make oil-based paints blister and discolour.

Aluminium wood primer A wood primer containing aluminium particles. It can be used on timber which has been treated with a non-bituminous based wood preservative and on wood surfaces which have been stripped with a blowlamp.

Aluminium spirit-based sealer This is a primer-sealer containing aluminium formulated for sealing surfaces which tend to bleed through most paints. It can be used on bituminous or dry creosoted woodwork; on colours which tend to bleed, such as gold/bronze paints, and over nicotine stains. It dries very quickly and must not be overbrushed.

Zinc chromate primer A primer formulated for use on aluminium alloys and other non-ferrous metals. It can also be used on iron and steel (it inhibits the formulation of rust) and on glazed tiles.

Zinc phosphate primer This can be used for priming ferrous (iron) materials instead of red lead. It can also be used on aluminium alloys, other non-ferrous metals and glazed tiles.

Calcium plumbate primer CONTAINS LEAD The most effective paint for priming galvanised metal – some window frames, for example. Let the galvanised surface weather before use.

Alkali-resisting primer This should be used when you want to prime new surfaces which may contain alkali – cement, concrete, plaster, bricks and some wall fillers. For plastered walls and ceilings, you can use diluted emulsion paint instead. Alkali-resisting primers are not needed beneath masonry paints.

Stabilising primer A sealer for binding together surfaces which are loose, flaking or powdery – some cement, concrete, plaster and stonework, for instance. Stabilising primers are alkali resisting.

Pink primer MAY CONTAIN LEAD This is the name given to traditional wood primers. Modern pink primers generally do not contain lead but check the label. Do not use a lead-based wood primer around the house: use a leadless wood or a general-purpose primer instead.

Red lead primer CONTAINS LEAD This was the original primer for ferrous materials. It should not be used around the house: use zinc phosphate primer instead.

Primer-sealer/undercoat An acrylic co-polymer water-based paint which can be used as a primer-sealer for all unpainted wood and plaster surfaces. It dries very quickly so you may be able to apply two coats of the primer-sealer and a topcoat in one day. Water-based primers raise the grain of unsealed softwoods making it necessary to smooth the wood surface by rubbing it down before you apply the final coat of paint.

Special-purpose paints

Anti-condensation paint You can use this paint indoors in those areas where mild condensation is a problem. It reduces condensation by providing an insulating film between a warm humid atmosphere and a cold surface: it does not absorb the condensation.

Bitumen There are two types: one is a thick brown or black tar-like material used for waterproofing places like the inside of gutters; the other is an emulsion and is used for concrete or roofs.

Creosote A pungent-smelling dark-brown liquid which can be used as an economical single-coat wood preservative outside. It splashes very easily.

Fire-retardant finishes Special fire-retardant paints are manufactured in a wide range of colours. You apply either two coats of a fire-retardant emulsion or one coat of a fire-retardant undercoat, followed by one coat of a fire-retardant topcoat over a conventional primer. You should think seriously about using this type of paint in those areas of your house where the spread of fire is likely to present an exceptional hazard – on a landing, for example, which provides access to a loft conversion. Ordinary oil-based paints are highly flammable: water-based paints are much less so.

Masonry paint An exterior grade emulsion paint which is usually fortified by inert materials such as sand and crushed marble. For use on brickwork, stucco and asbestos cement. The inert materials reduce erosion of paint film by the weather and fill fine cracks.

Using paint safely

Paints contain chemicals some of which could harm you if you ingested enough.

Lead is the most frequently found and most widely publicised toxic material in paint. A number of years ago nearly all primers contained lead – it was considered to be an indispensable ingredient. Nowadays, few lead-based primers are sold and modern primers without lead perform just as well. Calcium plumbate primer is the one major exception to this rule: for priming galvanised metal there appears to be no leadless equivalent with an acceptable performance. Lead-based primers should carry a warning.

To minimise risks when painting you should:

● **always** use paints which comply with the Toys Safety Regulations for painting toys, playpens and other things used by children, particularly when the paint is a brightly-coloured one. If in doubt write to the technical service department of the paint manufacturer

● **always** wear a face mask when abrading old or brightly-coloured paintwork

● **ask yourself** whether you really need to use any paint which claims to contain a fungicide and also warns about keeping it away from children and animals

● **never** use a lead-based primer unless it is absolutely essential and never use one indoors, particularly where a child could chew the painted surface

● **never** use a blowlamp to strip old or brightly-coloured paintwork in areas with poor ventilation

● **never** use paints without adequate ventilation – many give off unpleasant, and sometimes even dangerous, fumes.

Paints for hot surfaces

The two most widely available paints for using on very hot surfaces are heat-resisting matt black and heat-resisting aluminium. They are suitable for temperatures up to 200°C and 400°C respectively and should be put directly on to the bare surface without using a primer beforehand.

Around the home, the need for a heat-resisting paint is generally limited to painting radiators. Fortunately, most alkyd and polyurethane gloss paints and emulsion paints have adequate heat resistance for this job. Typically, a brilliant white gloss paint will start to go yellow at temperatures around 50 to 60°C – this is about the normal surface temperature of a domestic radiator. Emulsion paint is generally even more heat-resistant and displays little discoloration until beyond 90°C. Darkly-coloured paints are even better. In general, the colour a radiator is painted has little effect on its ability to radiate heat, so radiators can be painted to harmonise with an overall room decoration scheme. However, a matt finish should be used in preference to a glossy one when radiation of heat is important – the difference between a dull surface and a glossy one could be as much as 20 per cent.

To prevent early paint failure on surfaces like radiators which are subjected to large temperature changes, make sure that the elasticity of the separate coats of paint is as similar as possible. Do this by using either a zinc chromate or a zinc phosphate primer (in special circumstances you could use a calcium plumbate primer), followed by two coats of finishing paint. Do not use an undercoat.

Surface preparation

Thorough surface preparation is the key to successful decorating and though it might seem a poorly-rewarded chore, it should be approached with vigour and enthusiasm. Surface preparation means the patient and thorough removal of dirt, grease, corrosion and old decaying and unsound paint, and providing a finely abraded surface for maximum key. In the short term, thorough surface preparation will mean the disappearance of all surface blemishes, old paint chips, cracks and

so on when you apply the final coat of paint. But the real reward will not be seen for a number of years – it is a long life for both the paint and the surface you are putting it on. How much this matters depends on whether you are decorating indoors or outdoors. Indoors you may well want to change your decoration scheme before it deteriorates, but outdoors you want to get the longest possible life out of your paintwork.

Preparing new surfaces

Many new surfaces need relatively little work before you paint them – some may need to be rubbed down with abrasive paper and others may need to have surface hollows smoothed out with a filler. The first coat of paint on most new surfaces is a primer – this provides a key for subsequent coats of paint and should stick well to the surface you put it on, perhaps by sinking in slightly. You then follow the primer with whatever undercoats and topcoats you want.

Details of how to prepare different new surfaces are given below.

Softwood This is light in colour, has an open grain and may have knots. It is the most common building wood used inside houses – for making stairs, door frames, skirting and so on. Softwood is often painted or clear varnished. For both, it needs sanding down (rubbing with an abrasive) to provide an even, but microscopically coarse, surface into which the sealing coat of primer or the first coat of varnish can key. The rougher the wood surface, the coarser the grade of abrasive you can use – but always finish with a fine grade paper and always rub *with* the grain.

After rubbing down, fill all cracks and holes before painting or applying a clear finish. For painting, common white filler is satisfactory but if you want to apply a clear finish, choose a coloured filler to match the natural colour of the wood – white fillers will look unsightly through the clear finish.

Never try to remove any stains on new wood by washing it with a cleaner containing water. Wood readily absorbs moisture and this makes the wood grain on the surface swell – so you have to rub it down again. Use white spirit to remove stains or abrade them away. If you want to paint new indoor woodwork, make sure that it is left for a few days in the room where you want to use it with the heating on. This will remove any excess moisture in the wood which, if left, would expand, vaporise and cause the new paint to blister.

Before applying a primer, all knots and areas of resin – recognised by a darker brown stain in wood – must be sealed with one or two thin coats of knotting.

Once the primer is dry, it will need gently rubbing smooth with a fine abrasive before the next coat is applied. Most primers give wood a fairly rough appearance by lifting tiny wood fibres into the paint surface. One coat of primer is sufficient for most new softwood surfaces. However, the end grain should always have a second coat – the first coat will probably sink in.

You may come across grain fillers in the shops. These should be used indoors and then only when you want a superfine finish. Normally, they are a white or beige paste which you rub into the surface of the wood using a circular motion and then lightly abrade the surface smooth once the filler is hard. You can use a fine-textured sanding-grade filler as an alternative.

If you want to give softwood a clear finish, you can stain it to a darker shade or to another colour either by rubbing a

wood stain into the wood surface before varnishing or by using a tinted varnish. The former method generally produces the best results and is more permanent – the colour of the stain remains even if the varnish film is subsequently removed. If you no longer want this colour you can try to remove it by using a bleaching agent, but good results cannot be guaranteed.

External wall cladding and fencing which have been left with a rough sawn finish need little or no surface preparation. This sort of woodwork is often supplied impregnated with a wood preservative. Use a brush to remove all surface dirt before applying an additional coat of wood preservative.

Hardwood This is generally darker in colour than softwood and has a closer, more even grain – oak, mahogany and teak are typical examples. Paints and varnishes deteriorate fairly rapidly on hardwoods and it is always worth thinking about using a non-filming wood preservative rather than paint. Wood preservatives require little or no preparation for re-coating and often enhance the natural beauty of the wood.

For paint (or varnish), rub down the wood surface before priming. With some oily woods, such as teak, the surface oil should be removed by wiping the wood with a rag soaked in white spirit. Some other hardwoods – mainly the more unusual ones – keep exuding an oily resin to which conventional primers will not stick well. Aluminium primer may solve the problem – check by priming a small area of the wood surface and then attempting to scratch it off two days later. If the primer does not stick, a non-filming wood preservative is your most sensible choice.

Hardwoods can be stained in the same manner described for softwoods. Beech looks particularly effective when stained with bright colours and can be used for making brightly-coloured toys.

Chipboard If the chipboard is clean, all you need do is to smooth off any cut edges and lightly abrade the surface of the board before priming. Pre-sealed boards do not need priming. All primers are likely to cause some surface uneveness – equivalent to raising the grain on natural wood. Water-based (acrylic) primers are particularly troublesome. With these, you should not smooth the surface until you have applied the undercoat, otherwise abrading will simply remove all the primer from the high spots leaving them liable to swell again when you apply the next coat of paint.

Hardboard If the surface of the board is clean, lightly abrade it and then apply a primer. There are many different types of hardboard: some need priming, some do not – see page 107.

Softboards As long as the surface is clean no further preparation is required. Because softboards are so absorbent, they are often painted with an emulsion or other water-based paint. A stabilising primer may be needed on very absorbent boards.

Metal Ferrous metals (those containing iron) quickly become coated with a reddish-brown film of rust unless they are painted or coated with a rust-resistant metal. New galvanised surfaces – many window frames and garage doors, for instance – are coated with a corrosion-resistant non-ferrous metallic film of zinc. These, and other similar metal-coated surfaces, should be treated as if they were non-ferrous.

If a ferrous metal surface shows no signs of corrosion, it will need little preparation before priming. But such a situation is very unusual, so you should look carefully to see whether it has an oil or grease coating. If so, degrease it by using a degreasing agent, such as white spirit, or a paint brush cleaner. Wash this off with water; dry the surface as quickly as possible (by wiping down and then using a fan heater or hair drier) and then prime it at once. New ferrous metal surfaces which show no sign of rusting may have

been coated with a clear lacquer – if so, lightly abrade the surface and prime.

Asbestos Never rub down asbestos sheets – asbestos dust can damage your health. On new boards use an alkali-resisting primer.

Plaster Sound dry walls do not need any special preparation. If the walls are still drying out, use emulsion or other water-based paints only. If the walls have efflorescence – a surface deposit of salt crystals which originate deep in the wall (or plaster) and are transported to the surface by moisture escaping from the new plaster and brickwork – brush it off at regular intervals until the formation of crystals stops. Do not try to remove efflorescence with water – you will soak the salts back into the plaster and they will reappear to damage and discolour paintwork at some later date. Do not paint the plaster until efflorescence stops.

Plasterboard This is normally supplied with a different surface on each side. The grey side is for plastering and the beige side is for painting. As long as the surface is clean and dry, no further preparation is required.

Preparing old paintwork

Old paintwork generally falls into one or more of the following three conditions:

• sound, with no flaking, chips or blisters
• in fairly good condition, but with small areas requiring some repair
• in poor condition with extensive flaking, blistering and so on. In this condition there may be some areas which need repair and cannot be made good until the paint has been removed.

Sound paintwork

The first job is to get the paintwork clean and free from dirt and grease. Usually, you can do this by washing it down with a floor-and-wall cleaner, sugar soap, a special paint cleaner, washing soda or

even just detergent. Sugar soaps and some paint cleaners are slightly abrasive. (However, they will not be abrasive enough to provide a key for gloss paint or remove lumps from a painted surface.) Use warm water and a sponge or stiff brush as appropriate.

Some areas of the house need particularly vigorous treatment. They are:

• the kitchen – concentrate your effort high up on the walls and the ceiling where layers of cooking fat may have built up. Paints will not stick well to fatty surfaces

• the ceilings in rooms with coal fires and the areas around ducted hot air outlets. Places like these are generally covered

with a layer of soot or dust which will mix with your new paint and discolour it unless it is washed off beforehand

• the tops of door and window frames. These should be washed down well – the areas on casement window frames which are hidden when the windows are closed need particular attention.

• all external gloss paintwork.

Do not bother to scrub away at nicotine-stained paintwork if the room is going to be used by smokers after decoration – the staining will soon reappear. However, in rooms where nicotine staining is excessive and smoking no longer occurs frequently, all the old sound paintwork can be sealed with an aluminium primer.

The walls and ceilings of bedrooms painted with emulsion paint rarely need extensive washing down. But even here you should wash down any worn areas (which look slightly glossy in reflected light) and areas around sockets, light switches and so on which tend to get greasy and dirty. If the old paint starts to wash off as you are cleaning it and if it is dirty or greasy, you will have to wash off all the old paint. If the paintwork is fairly clean, you should stop cleaning and apply either a dilute coat of emulsion paint (if you intend to finish the surface with wallpaper or emulsion paint) or a coat of stabilising primer (for an oil paint finish). After washing down, thoroughly rinse down the paintwork with clean water. Avoid letting water run down behind electrical fittings such as sockets and wall switches (turn off the electricity at the mains before you start) and cover any furnishings which are likely to be splashed. Do not begin to paint until the paintwork is completely dry.

Walls and ceilings which were coated with emulsion paint need no further attention. But surfaces covered with gloss paint should be rubbed down with a fine grade abrasive – see page 21. Once this is done, remove the dust with a vacuum cleaner, wipe the paintwork over with a soft cloth dipped in white spirit and, as soon as it is dry, start to decorate.

Paintwork in fairly good condition

Wash down all sound paintwork (see above) then:

● fill cracks, holes, dents and so on with filler – see page 24
● fill chips out of the paintwork with either a fine textured filler or with undercoat. Sand flat when dry
● remove the paint over resin stains with a blowlamp or with a chemical stripper – see page 19. Treat only the stained area and when the wood surface is exposed and clean, seal the knots with knotting followed by one or two coats of primer.

(Use an aluminium primer if you burn off the paint)
● use a coarse abrasive paper to remove the paint surrounding small areas where the paint has lifted or is flaking. Follow this with one or two coats of primer
● treat any areas that are showing signs of corrosion – see page 23.

Paintwork in poor condition

You are unlikely to find paintwork in very poor condition indoors – except perhaps where the paintwork is exceptionally old or the paint was totally unsuited to the environment in which it was used. Paint peeling and flaking from walls and ceilings is likely to be old whitewash or distemper. This can be easily removed by washing it down.

Outside, it is a totally different story. Due to the combined effects of wind, rain and sun, no normal paintwork lasts for more than four or five years on wood without showing signs of deterioration. In some situations paint may not last for more than two years outdoors – paintwork facing south is often the first to show signs of deterioration particularly at the bottoms of windows and on plywood door panels. This deterioration is generally due to rainwater getting into or underneath the paint through small cracks. These are particularly difficult to fill permanently in wooden frames because of the considerable movement which takes place in wood as the temperature and the dampness of the air fluctuates. Dry wood readily absorbs moisture and swells and any paint covering it will crack unless the paintwork is fairly new and still sufficiently elastic to cope with the movement. Even worse, when the paintwork is subsequently warmed by the sun the moisture in the woodwork will vaporise and make the paintwork blister or crack much more.

If you have areas of poor paintwork do not be tempted into simply removing the obviously loose cracked and blistered paintwork and then painting over the whole area – the paintwork surrounding the cracked and blistered areas is also likely to be in poor condition, even though it is not obvious, and any paint put on top of it will not last long. Remove the old paint and expose the original surface. It is not necessary to remove all the old paint – strip it as far as a joint or edge where the old paint is sound. For more details, see the opposite page.

The first signs of deterioration – **checking** (slight breaks in gloss coat) and **cracking** (breaks through to bare wood)

Peeling – large areas of paint coming off to leave bare wood exposed, often due to water getting underneath the paint film

The paint on the plywood centre of the panel deteriorated first allowing water to get underneath the paint on the rail

Removing old paint

There are two main methods of removing old paint – burning if off with a blowlamp or using a chemical paint stripper. Both methods work by softening the paint film making it blister and lift, so that it can be removed with a stripping knife or shave hook. In terms of time and trouble, there is not much to choose between the two methods – both are time-consuming and messy. And both methods can be dangerous if you are careless.

You may also remove old paintwork by mechanical means – using some sort of abrasive. This is, however, very time-consuming, hard work (even if you use power tools) and creates a lot of dust. You are most likely to need to use abrasive papers for finishing off a surface just before you paint it – after using a chemical paint stripper, say – or for rubbing down between coats of paint to provide a key for the next coat. Normally, a combination of methods is used.

Blowlamps

A blowlamp is a flame gun which burns paraffin or bottled gas. Using a blowlamp is the most economical method of stripping large areas of oil-based paint (normal gloss paints, say). Other types of paint such as emulsion or cellulose (often found on cars) cannot be removed successfully by flame and a blowlamp is not suitable for stripping paint over materials, such as plastic, which would be affected by the heat.

A blowlamp can remove paint fairly rapidly and is particularly suitable for flat areas, but to avoid burning the surface under the paint the flame must be moved continuously over the paintwork. Edges and mouldings are difficult to strip with a blowlamp and are likely to be burnt. Areas adjacent to glass are also difficult to strip without the glass being cracked by the flame. And you should not use a blowlamp when you want to leave wood with its natural appearance after you have stripped it. In all three of the above situations the best way to strip paint is with a chemical stripper. Do not use a blowlamp outside when it is windy – in these conditions the flame cannot be controlled effectively.

If you have a lot of paint stripping to do, you should choose a lamp which is comfortable to hold and economical to use. Lamps with broad flame burners do not seem to work consistently better than those without them.

Paraffin blowlamps are much more economical than gas lamps. To get an intense flame with paraffin, you have to provide heat to vaporise it, and pressure to force it out of a nozzle. Initially, the heat comes from meths which you burn in a hollow on top of the lamp. After a few minutes, the lamp has to be pressurised by a few strokes of the pump. Once alight, the lamp itself heats the paraffin but you have to keep it pressurised by using the pump from time to time. The pressure controls the power of the flame which is generally diffuse and not very hot – ideal for stripping paint and plumbing work.

Gas blowlamps use a Liquefied Petroleum Gas (LPG) – either butane or propane. You attach a cartridge or cylinder to the burner, open a valve to let out a stream of gas and burn it. Gas blowlamps generally work off cartridges; gas blowtorches (see picture) work off cylinders at the full pressure of the gas inside the cylinder – few have pressure-reducing regulators. The pressure inside the lamp depends on temperature – as it gets colder the blowlamp becomes less effective. Butane lamps will not work below 0°C but propane ones keep going down to −40°C. The pressure inside the lamp does not depend on how much LPG is left. Both gases are more dense than air, so gas leaks flow along surfaces and collect in hollows. Never tilt a gas blowlamp in use until it has been lit for about five minutes. If you do, the lamp may produce a huge flame and drip burning liquid.

Using a blowlamp

First prepare the area by placing a non-flammable sheet underneath to catch

A typical paraffin blowlamp, cheap to run but messy, tedious and hazardous to light

Three gas blowlamps

A gas blowtorch connected to a refillable gas cylinder

19

scrapings (not always necessary outside) and remove extraneous flammable things from the vicinity of the flame. Keep an old washing-up liquid bottle filled with water handy just in case of a small fire. Place a ceramic tile on a horizontal surface within easy reach but well away from anything which could burn. Always stand the blowlamp on this when you are not using it. Before starting to strip, put on tough gloves – burning paint could fall on to your hands and cause a nasty burn.

After lighting the blowlamp, allow it to warm up for a few minutes before using it. Hold the blowlamp in one hand and a scraper in the other. Play the flame (which is invisible in bright sunlight) over the paint from a distance of approximately 150mm. As the paint begins to bubble, pull it off with the scraper. Two passes will probably be required to leave the surface fairly clean. Slight ridges and mottling of dried paint can be abraded off once the surface is cool.

WARNING Never use a blowlamp for stripping old lead-pigmented paint (assume all very old paint is this type) unless the area is well ventilated. Do not use a blowlamp to strip paint on softwood fascia or soffit boards – old birds' nests are very flammable and if one catches alight it could result in a major roof fire. Never use a blowlamp near a thatched roof.

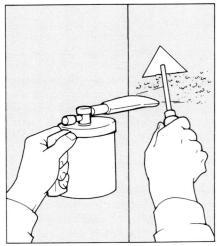

Work downwards with a blowlamp – softening a small area of paintwork at a time and pulling the paint off with a scraper. Keep the blowlamp away from glass

Chemical paint strippers

Chemical paint stripping is the most versatile method of removing old paint and is particularly suitable for use on mouldings; other intricately-shaped painted surfaces, and near glass. Two different types of stripper are commonly used based on either dichloro-methane (solvent strippers) or caustic soda (caustic strippers). All paint strippers may irritate the skin – if you get splashed wash the stripper off immediately and protect your eyes by wearing goggles. (Acciden-

tal splashes in the eyes should be washed out with plenty of water.) When using strippers, wear rubber or plastic gloves and old clothes. Cover up carpets and other floorcoverings well – using polythene sheets in preference to newspapers or dust sheets – and put your scrapings in an old tin rather than letting them fall on the floor.

Solvent strippers are the most common type and can be used on cellulose paint, emulsion paint and oil-based paints, though they work less well on polyurethane paints than on other gloss paints. Most are thick liquids or have a jelly-like consistency and should be applied by brush. After a few minutes the paint should start to blister. Leave it for a few more minutes and then remove it with a scraper. If you wait too long – over 10 minutes – the solvent evaporates and the blistered paint begins to dry making it difficult to remove.

Before applying a primer, all stripped areas must be washed down with water or white spirit – the container label should specify which – and allowed to dry thoroughly. Water soaking into wood can raise the grain, so stripped areas may also need rubbing down.

Caustic strippers can be purchased as a paste which is ready for use or as pellets which have to be dissolved in water first. They can be used on emulsion and oil-based paints but will not strip other cel-

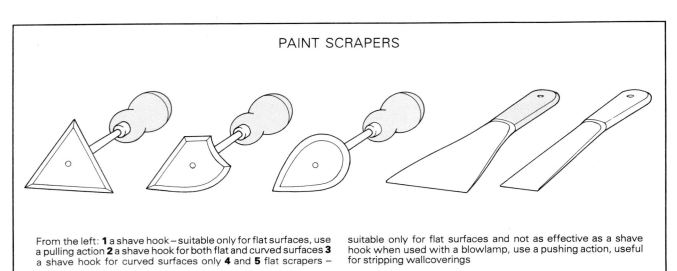

PAINT SCRAPERS

From the left: **1** a shave hook – suitable only for flat surfaces, use a pulling action **2** a shave hook for both flat and curved surfaces **3** a shave hook for curved surfaces only **4** and **5** flat scrapers – suitable only for flat surfaces and not as effective as a shave hook when used with a blowlamp, use a pushing action, useful for stripping wallcoverings

lulose paints or polyurethane paints (or varnishes). Caustic strippers may darken the natural colour of wood quite considerably, so you may need to use a bleach afterwards to restore the colour if you intend to varnish it.

Usually with the paste-type caustic strippers, you have to put on a thick layer, leave it for an hour or two and then scrape away the paste and softened paint. You can use caustic soda pellets dissolved in water as a cheap way of stripping large areas of paintwork or you can immerse objects in the solution. You may need to experiment with the strength of the caustic soda solution to ascertain optimum stripping times for different objects.

When stripping is completed, all surfaces should be washed with copious quantities of water containing a little acid – such as vinegar – and allowed to dry thoroughly before they are abraded flat and a primer is applied.

Most lacquers can be removed by using the solvent for the original paint – cellulose thinners, for example.

Rubbing down

To get the best results from paint or varnish, it should be applied to an even surface which has been very slightly roughened. The process of providing this even surface is known as rubbing down. The usual method is to use an abrasive paper, either by hand or fitted to a mechanical sander. You rub down a surface when you are painting over sound old paintwork, between applying coats of polyurethane varnish and when you are preparing bare woodwork – either new wood or old woodwork which has been stripped and rinsed.

Abrasive papers
Old paintwork used to be rubbed down with either a pumice stone or glass-paper (sometimes called sandpaper). The pumice, and to some extent the glass-paper, have now been replaced by more modern abrasive papers, such as aluminium oxide paper and waterproof silicon carbide paper (often called by its trade name *Wet or Dry*). Both of these papers last longer and clog less than sandpaper but are more expensive. Waterproof silicon carbide paper can be used dry but is more often used wet – the surface being abraded and the paper must be kept wet to reduce clogging. When it is used like this, waterproof silicon carbide paper lasts for a very long time, but the abraded particles remain stuck to the abraded surface and have to be removed by thorough washing down.

Abrasive papers are normally sold in sheets measuring 275×225mm with the grade (coarseness) or grit size marked on the back. They can also be bought in shapes suitable for disc and orbital sanders. The Table alongside shows the most common grades available with the shaded bands indicating the grades which are suitable for surface preparation. If the surface is in poor condition, start by using a coarse grade of paper and finish with a fine grade.

Some abrasive papers are sold as *close coat* with the particles of abrasive very close together, or *open coat* with the particles more widely spaced. Open coat papers clog less readily than close coat ones.

When rubbing down by hand, wrap the abrasive paper around a flat block of cork, rubber or wood. This will ensure that the abrasive paper removes the high spots, dirt particles and so on and will produce a flat finish. An alternative to using abrasive paper is the sanding block. A number of different types are available with either aluminium oxide or tungsten carbide particles as the abrasive. Check the grades of the block and the coarseness of the particles before you buy.

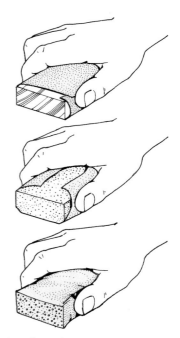

Handsanding using a wood block (top), cork block or integral sanding block (bottom)

ABRASIVE PAPERS		
Abrasive papers	**grades** fine medium coarse	
Glass-paper	00 0 1 1½ F2 M2 S2 2½ 3	
Aluminium oxide	180 150 120 100 80 60 50 40	two different densities available – open and close coat
Waterproof silicon carbide	600 400 280 240 180 150 120 100	can be used wet or dry

Mechanical sanders

The three most common mechanical sanders used for rubbing down are belt sanders, orbital sanders and disc sanders. Before using any of these tools, you should read the instructions and practice on an area of paintwork where any damage you cause will not matter. Do not use a mechanical sander when you are tired, and be particularly careful about using one when you are on a ladder. Mechanical sanders produce a vast quantity of dust, so always wear goggles to protect your eyes and a face mask to avoid inhaling the dust particles.

All mechanical abraders will rub down much more rapidly than you can by hand, so you should approach any new area cautiously using a very light continuous stroking action. Because of the size and shape of mechanical sanders, you should not expect to be able to rub down right into corners, over mouldings and other shaped surfaces – you will have to rub down these areas by hand.

Because sanders work on mains electricity, you should not use a belt or an orbital sander with 'wet' waterproof silicon carbide paper unless the manufacturer of the sander specifically recommends it.

Belt sanders are very useful for rubbing down large horizontal surfaces, such as floors, but they are expensive to buy and it is probably best to hire one when you need it. They have an electric motor which powers a continuous belt of abrasive – different grades are available. Many have their own dust collection system. Belt sanders are fairly heavy and you need to use both hands to operate one.

Orbital sanders are very popular tools for rubbing down. They can be bought as an accessory for an electric drill or as an integral tool, and are often used to prepare a surface for varnishing or polishing. Some manufacturers call them finishing sanders. Any abrasive paper can be attached to the flat bed, but glasspaper tends to tear. Waterproof silicon carbide paper should be used dry and open coat aluminium oxide paper is better than the close coat type.

A **disc** sander attachment can be fixed to an electric drill so that it spins at the speed of the drill. All the types of abrasive papers can be used when they are attached to a special rubber backing pad. A variety of stiffer, non-paper sanding discs are also available but the grades are normally rather coarse. Some of these non-paper sanding discs have an open-mesh design so that the surface underneath can be seen through the spinning disc. Some can be used for cutting through brick and soft metals too.

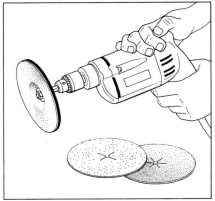

Disc sander fitted to an electric drill – an inexpensive accessory and very useful for removing old paint but care is needed to avoid scratching the surface underneath – make sure only the outer edge of the disc is in contact with the surface

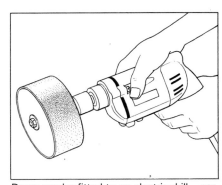

Drum sander fitted to an electric drill – particularly useful as a finishing sander for large, though narrow, flat surfaces, like window frames

MECHANICAL SANDERS

Belt sander – a powerful, heavy sander which is ideal for removing a lot of material from large flat surfaces such as floors. Fitted with a dust collection bag

Orbital sanding attachment for an electric drill – most are less than half the price of integral sanders and are useful for small jobs, though not as quick as integral tools

Integral orbital (or finishing) sander – the front hand acts as a guide: do not exert any downward force as it will not improve the efficiency of abrading

Dealing with mould

If the conditions are right – moisture, still air and poor light – mould can grow almost anywhere, including on porous materials such as plaster and concrete. Excess atmospheric humidity caused by poor ventilation coupled with central heating is the most common cause for mould growth inside houses. Mould is spread by airborne spores or by contact with things which have been previously infected, such as brushes and cleaning cloths. In the conditions it likes, mould can spread very rapidly. Before starting to treat mould, you should try to find out the underlying reasons for the contamination and, where possible, take the appropriate remedial action to reduce the possibilities of re-infection.

First, sterilise all infected and surrounding areas by washing them down with ordinary household bleach diluted in the proportions of one part of bleach to five parts of water. Allow the bleach to soak overnight and then scrape off as much mould and other loose material as possible. Burn all scrapings. Apply a fresh solution of bleach and leave for a minimum of three days before you start to prepare the surface for painting. Bleach will destroy mould but will not prevent re-growth. Special sterilising solutions which contain mould inhibitors – to reduce the likelihood of re-growth – are available. After removing the mould, wash all cleaning equipment in the bleach solution.

A similar sterilising programme can be used for mould on wallpapers. You should remove and burn the infected wallpaper and wash down the wall with bleach solution. Use a fungicidal paste for hanging the new paper.

Corrosion

A metal usually corrodes when it is in contact with both water and oxygen. Some metals corrode faster than others – iron corrodes rapidly while gold hardly corrodes at all. The rate of corrosion can be increased by the presence of chemicals such as salt and sulphur dioxide, by an increase in temperature and by contact with other metals.

Around the home you usually prevent corrosion by painting the metal – so protecting it against water and air. Indoors, it is generally good enough to use a general-purpose or metal primer and to keep the paintwork in reasonably good condition. Outside – on gutters, drainpipes, garden gates and metal window frames, for example – you will have to think about dealing with any corrosion as soon as it appears and using a special corrosion–inhibiting primer.

Corrosion of metals containing iron is usually called *rust* and once it gets a hold it is very difficult to eradicate. All unprotected metals containing iron rust rapidly and you should try to remove all traces of rust before you apply a primer. Painting over rust, even with bitumen, only hides the problem – beneath the paint film corrosion continues and the paint will eventually flake off. Before you start to treat the corrosion, consider whether the rusted item is worth renovating – for example, badly rusted gutters and drainpipes can be cheaply and quickly replaced with plastic equivalents which will need very little maintenance.

Rust can be removed with either mechanical strippers – a wire brush or an abrasive disc fitted to an electric drill – or by hand. Cup brushes and wheel brushes fitted to an electric drill remove surface rust well but, for large areas, you are likely to get the best results with a silicon carbide disc. However, you should be prepared to replace the paper disc quite often. Using a wire brush by hand is a useful method of removing loose flaking rust, but wire wool is better for surface rust. Whatever method you use, internal corners are tricky to get at.

Once all the rust has been removed, carry out any repair work necessary – a glass fibre patch, say – and paint all the exposed metal surface with a zinc chromate primer. Make sure that the primer is thoroughly dry before you paint over it. On metal gutters, you could use a bitumen paint which works by keeping out moisture – so the paint film must be complete. However, you will not be able to paint over the bitumen unless you apply a coat of aluminium spirit-based sealer first.

Rust can be kept at bay only by thoroughly preparing the surface (and removing all existing rust) and using a rust-inhibiting primer followed by an undercoat and one or two topcoats.

Although some metals which do not contain iron – notably aluminium and zinc – can corrode, none do so to a harmful extent. In fact, the corrosive film on some of these metals is beneficial – it becomes a passive protective film over the metal below.

Although you do not need to paint metals such as aluminium or zinc to preserve them, you may want to do so for decorative reasons. To paint aluminium, lightly rub down the oxidised surface layer – use a very fine abrasive paper or steelwool lubricated with white spirit – and then use the appropriate primer.

Do not rub down zinc – this will expose a 'fresh' zinc surface and primers do not stick well to 'fresh' zinc. When you want to paint something which has a zinc coating over iron or steel, avoid any surface preparation (apart from cleaning) prior to painting – any rubbing down may remove some of the zinc plating, especially on edges and corners. Zinc should be primed with a calcium plumbate primer. (CONTAINS LEAD – see page 15.)

Filling holes and cracks

Holes and cracks on the outside of your house – around windows and doors, for example – should always be filled when decorating. If they are left untreated, water may get in behind the paintwork and reduce its life. And filling holes and cracks may help improve the sound insulation of your home. When you use a filler outdoors it has to survive very different conditions from one used indoors.

Fillers for use **outdoors** have to be quite flexible to cope with the movement of building materials which expand and contract according to the weather (wood in particular expands when wet and contracts when dry). They also have to resist extremes of temperature.

Fillers for use **indoors** are much less likely to suffer extremes of temperature and humidity. However, once the job is finished and the paint is on, the filler must be completely unobtrusive. To achieve this, interior fillers should be easy to apply (so that you can leave a good finish) and they should set hard – but not so hard that you cannot abrade them flat.

Most fillers fall into one of two categories: resilient fillers and non-resilient fillers. Resilient fillers – mastics, for example – are useful for filling gaps between dissimilar materials where movement is expected. Non-resilient fillers – those based on plaster and cement, for example – are more suitable for filling cracks in materials which do not move much, like concrete and plaster.

General-purpose fillers should be able to expand and contract to cope with substrate movements yet they should set sufficiently hard to give a good surface for painting over.

Cracks in brickwork and concrete (outdoors)

Cracks often occur in a concrete rendered finish (a concrete finish usually 10 to 15mm thick which is applied to the external side of a brick wall). They may be an early warning that the rendering is starting to lose its adhesion – tap the area around the crack and listen for any hollow sounds. In severe cases, you may need to patch render a considerable area of wall. If you ignore cracks in rendering, rainwater may soak down between the brickwork and the rendering, causing damp inside the house.

Cracks in brickwork and concrete can be filled with a mix of one part of cement to three parts of builders' sand by volume (small quantities can be purchased ready-mixed) or with a cement-based ready-made filler.

First, clean any loose material out of the crack by gouging down it with a suitably-shaped metal tool – a triangular paint scraper, say. If you suspect poor adhesion but you cannot pull the rendering away from the wall with a scraper, carefully knock it away with a hammer and cold chisel (ideally you should use a club hammer and bolster). Thoroughly mix the sand and cement and add water to make a wet paste – just dry enough to retain its shape. Brush water into the crack to wet it thoroughly (unless the instructions on the filler pack warn against this) and then pack in the filler using a filling knife. You could use a wallpaper scraper (or any other flat-edged tool) but a filling knife has a narrower and more flexible blade and makes the job easier. Make sure that you press in the filling material as tightly as possible. With deep and narrow cracks push the filler down into the crack to avoid making a bridge. Fill wide deep cracks in stages, using a depth of filler around 10 to 15mm each time. If possible, allow the filler to dry for two to three days between coats.

Make sure you leave a smooth finish to the final coat as these fillers set too hard to rub down. You can do this by leaving the filler flush with the original surface and then running the wet flat edge of a filling knife along the length of the filler.

Rendering which has cracked away from an external corner needs special treatment. Clean the crack and attach a wood batten vertically so that one straight edge lies along the corner. You can use masonry nails but do not knock them in too far as they will have to be removed later. Mix the filler, wet the area and apply the filler up to the edge of the wood batten. (If a large area has to be filled then use a rendering trowel instead of a filling knife.) Finally, finish off as before. Once the filler is hard, gently remove the wood batten and fill the other side of the crack.

Before painting over the filler, it should be left for a week to dry out and then given two coats of alkaline-resisting primer or masonry paint.

Cracks between wood and brickwork (outdoors)

The gaps normally found around door and window frames (especially on modern houses) are usually very deep. They should be filled any time during a dry spell – do not wait until you next decorate. Mastic is best but you will need to use a lot – so it could be worthwhile hiring a gun. (Mastics can be quite difficult to work with in winter – they become stiff when they are cold.) Try to use one which matches your paintwork so that you will not need to paint over it: an off-white or beige mastic is almost unnoticeable between a white-painted frame and brickwork. Mastics applied by gun will bridge the gap between the wood frame and the brickwork without actually filling it. In most circumstances this is quite adequate, but if you want to force the mastic deeply into wider cracks, use a filling knife. Very big gaps can be packed out with newspaper, leaving a depth of 10 to 15mm for the filler.

Other exterior fillers can also be used but they will be time-consuming. Exterior fillers which say that they *must* be painted over will soften unless they are painted.

Cracks in plaster (indoors)

Most cracks in plaster are due to shrinkage and settlement which takes place soon after a house is built. Once they have been dealt with – an interior general-purpose filler is satisfactory – they are unlikely to require filling again.

Remove any loose material and rake out the crack with a triangular paint scraper.

It is not necessary to wet the crack, just pack the filler into it as tightly as possible. If the crack is deep and wide, fill in layers no deeper than 10 to 15mm each time and allow each layer to dry before putting on the next one. Leave the surface of the final layer just proud of the adjacent plasterwork. When the filler has dried hard, rub it down with a fine abrasive paper over a block of wood or cork, leaving the surface of the filler flush with the plasterwork. The filler will absorb more paint than the adjacent plasterwork, so it must be sealed before the entire wall is painted. Use two coats of a universal primer or emulsion paint over the filled and adjacent area.

A badly-cracked ceiling can be difficult to fill satisfactorily – wallpaper or textured paint may be the best solution.

Cracks in plaster on plasterboard (indoors)

Many interior walls are built by fitting sheets of plasterboard to a timber framework and finishing the plasterboard with a thin coat of a suitable finishing plaster over the whole surface. Plasterboard is also used for ceilings. Cracks can appear in the finishing plaster when individual plasterboard panels move slightly. These cracks are easy to spot – they run in straight lines. But they are very difficult to fill. A general-purpose filler is likely to be too rigid and will soon crack again. A resilient filler such as mastic, could cope with the movement but would produce an unsatisfactory surface finish.

Plasterboard ceilings are often finished with a thick textured paint which is flexible enough to hide fine cracks beneath it. This is a useful way of dealing with a large area of fine cracks. If you wish to retain a flat finish, work textured paint into all the cracks with your finger and smooth the surface off immediately with a damp sponge.

Cracks between ceilings and walls (indoors)

These occur frequently in new houses and are mainly due to the house settling and the plaster shrinking.

Almost all general-purpose interior fillers are too rigid to deal with these cracks and a resilient filler is likely to produce an unsatisfactory finish. Textured paint is worth trying but the gaps are often too wide and the paint comes out as it is wiped over.

If the area between the wall and ceiling is severely cracked or if the crack appears again soon after filling, mask the cracks with a fabric-based self-adhesive tape or cover with coving. Lightweight expanded polystyrene or polyurethane coving can be cut with a tenon saw and stuck in position with a polystyrene tile adhesive. Some manufacturers supply matching corner pieces. Always prime coving with emulsion paint, never use an oil-based primer.

Cracks in wood joints

Gaps often occur in window joints where two pieces of wood have their grains perpendicular to each other.

Outdoors, these gaps can easily vary in size by a factor of two during the course of a year, and there are very few fillers (or paints) that can provide the level of resilience this situation demands.

Your first choice is a mastic. Thoroughly clean out the joint and wait until the wood is dry – ideally at the end of summer – before using the mastic. Work the mastic deep into the open joint leaving the joint slightly underfilled. A more rigid filler will give a tidier finish but do not expect it to be as successful as mastic. Ready-mixed general-purpose fillers seem to be fairly long lasting.

A general-purpose filler should cope successfully with gaps in wood joints indoors. For small gaps, pack the filler in with your finger and smooth the surface off immediately with a damp cloth.

Cracks, knots and problems with wood

Most knots can be painted over with knotting. When part of the knot is missing, use knotting followed by a rigid general-purpose filler. Apply the filler in layers no more than 10mm thick and, if possible, allow two to three days drying time between layers. The filler should be left slightly proud of the surrounding wood and then rubbed down flat.

When attempts to seal knots fail, the offending knot should be drilled out and plugged with dowel rod. Irregular knots should be knocked out with a chisel and filled.

Splits in wood that expand and contract with the moisture present in the atmosphere can be filled with a mastic filler as long as appearance is not important – in barge boarding, for example. Wait until the wood is thoroughly dry before applying the mastic with either a gun (which can be hired) or a tube with a built-in ejection system. Try to force the mastic cleanly into the prepared crack – avoid leaving excess mastic over the crack surface. When the surface finish is important, use a hard finish filler which claims adequate flexibility to cope with wood movements. Underfill the split slightly (again in 10mm layers) and when the filler is dry (two to three days) apply a rigid filler over the top of it. Leave this slightly proud and rub it down flat when it is dry.

Painting...which tool?

Most paints can be applied by a brush, a pad or a roller.

For **emulsion** paint, you should probably use a roller – it is quicker to use than brushes and pads, makes paint go further (on average, a given amount of paint will cover 10 to 20 per cent more surface when it is applied with a roller than with a brush or pad) and generally produces an acceptable finish. But some rollers tend to splatter paint around and you end up with quite a lot of paint left in the roller, so it is not recommended to use one for painting a small area. You will also have to finish the job with a brush or pad – rollers cannot get into tight corners.

For **gloss** paint, your choice seems to be between a pad and a brush. For large surfaces, you could consider a roller but most leave a finish you may not like, tend to shed pile which is a nuisance, and are very difficult to clean. Pads are a little more economical with paint than brushes and do not need re-charging quite as often but, like rollers, they tend to hold on to the paint at the end of the job, are more difficult than brushes to clean, and tend to shed their pile. Brushes shed bristles but these are generally less of a problem to cope with.

Paint brushes

Brushes are generally available in a range of sizes from 13mm to 175mm wide. The smaller ones (up to 100mm) are known as *varnish* brushes and the larger ones (100mm to 175mm) are known as *wal* brushes. Most painting around the home can be done with just three sizes:
- a 25mm brush for applying oil-based paints to narrow sections – windows, say
- a 50mm brush for applying oil-based paints to larger areas such as skirting boards and doors
- a 100m brush for applying emulsion, textured and masonry paints to very large areas such as walls and ceilings.

Paint brushes are usually made in a standard way. They have a wood or plastic handle with a metal band (called a *ferrule*) attached to it. Bristles are glued into the ferrule. Some brushes have wooden filler strips in the ferrule to pack out the bristles. The bristles may be natural – hog, boar or pig's hair – or synthetic (called *filaments* and usually nylon). The smaller sizes of brush (up to and including 50mm) usually have natural bristles and are often the type to buy, even though they be more expensive than brushes with synthetic bristles.

Many manufacturers make three ranges of paint brush. Do not buy from the best (and most expensive) range unless you are a particularly experienced painter – buy from the middle range instead. Avoid buying brushes with short bristles and with excessive filler strips. Instead look for a brush with an even tapered finish (called *bevelling*) and with *flagged* (split) ends to the bristles – these help paint go on more smoothly.

You should always expect some loss of bristle from a new brush. The likelihood of this spoiling the paintwork can be reduced by brushing the bristles backwards and forwards against your hand ('*flirting*') before starting work and by restricting the initial use of the brush to primers and undercoats.

There are two useful special-purpose brushes – a *radiator* brush with an elongated handle and a specially-angled head for painting down behind radiators, and a *cutting-in* brush with angled bristles for painting window bars and getting a clean edge where one wall meets another of a different colour.

Brushes used in emulsion paint and distemper should be washed out in water as soon as you have finished with them – these paints dry very rapidly. Brushes used in lacquers should be cleaned with thinners. With most other paints, brushes should be cleaned with white spirit, paraffin, turpentine substitute or a paint brush cleaner. Finish the job by washing out the brush with soap and water, rinsing it with water alone and then drying it with the bristles loosely held together in the right shape with a rubber band. Brushes used in oil-based paints can be stored for short periods with their bristles just immersed in clean water. Before using them again you should brush out the water on an old piece of board. Brushes can also be stored overnight by putting a few drops of white spirit or turpentine substitute on the bristles and wrapping them in polythene; again brush out before use.

Paint rollers

A roller is basically a handle and a frame which holds a *sleeve* – the part you paint with. Unlike brushes and pads, a roller cannot be used without a paint tray. The most common types of sleeve are: mohair; sheepskin; synthetic fibre; woolpile and sponge (or foam).

Sheepskin rollers are expensive and have the longest pile. They can hold more paint than the other types of roller – typically, enough emulsion paint to cover a square metre of a non-absorbent surface. Sheepskin rollers leave a slightly textured finish when used with emulsion paints, particularly those with silk and satin finishes. They are not suitable for gloss paints – they shed their pile and the roller soon becomes matted and drags in the paint.

Mohair rollers are the best type for gloss paint. But you should not consider using one instead of a brush unless the area you want to paint exceeds four square metres – cleaning a mohair roller is both difficult and expensive. A mohair roller normally applies a thinner coat of paint than a brush and at first the paint appears to have a texture. This soon disappears – the paint flows slightly as it dries. There is no need to wash out a roller between coats of gloss paint – you put a few drops of white spirit on the roller and cover it with polythene.

Foam (sponge) rollers are cheap and can be used with gloss paints but have little else to recommend them. The foam retains too much paint when you have finished, they tend to throw off a fine spray of paint, and can leave small bubbles in the paint surface – with fast-drying emulsion paints these bubbles dry out to small craters.

A roller is an invaluable tool for painting textured walls and ceilings: the length of the pile should be about the same as the height of the texture on the surface you want to cover. Always choose a sturdily-built roller without a raised seam on its sleeve – this could make it difficult to get an even coat. If you want to paint high walls and ceilings, you may want a roller which can take an extension handle – most have a hole in the end of their handle for this. You can use a broom handle as an extension handle, though with some rollers it will need tapering.

There are a few special-purpose rollers:
• radiator rollers have a sleeve about 100mm wide and around 20mm in diameter. They produce quite a good finish but their use is limited by their size
• narrow rollers – about 60mm wide – are available for painting skirting boards and door panels. Do not expect this sort of roller to cut into corners or cope with fiddly pipes.
• pipe rollers with two small sleeves – about 50mm wide – on a flexible frame can be used for painting pipes but they will not paint behind pipes which are close to a wall without getting paint all over the wall itself
• special ceiling rollers with a long handle and a tray (which acts as a paint reservoir) are also available.

Before washing a roller, remove excess paint by rolling it out on newspaper. Most rollers can be dismantled for cleaning (a spanner may be required). Cleaning out emulsion paint is simple – just use plenty of water – but cleaning rollers which have been used in gloss paint is messy and time-consuming. If replacement sleeves are cheap and readily available, you can throw away the old sleeve.

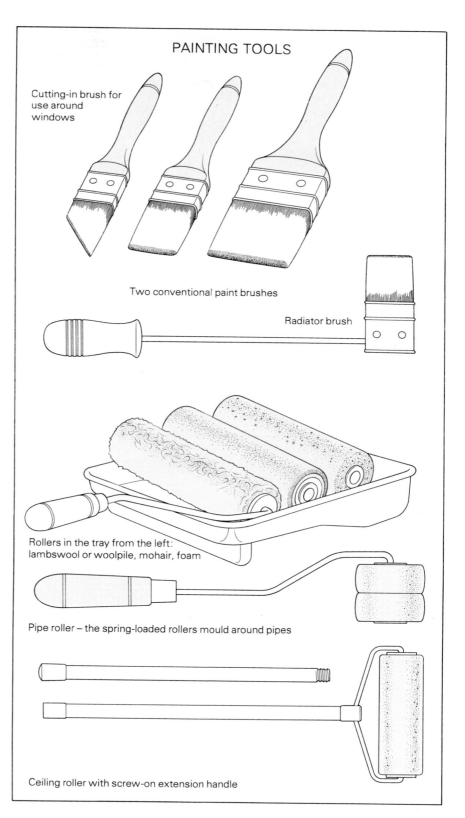

PAINTING TOOLS

Cutting-in brush for use around windows

Two conventional paint brushes

Radiator brush

Rollers in the tray from the left: lambswool or woolpile, mohair, foam

Pipe roller – the spring-loaded rollers mould around pipes

Ceiling roller with screw-on extension handle

Paint pads

A paint pad has a handle, a backing plate, a thin layer of foam and a flat pad of mohair pile which is used to apply the paint. A wide range of sizes and handle styles are available. Standard pads are flat and rectangular and vary in size from about 50×60mm to around 225×100mm. Sometimes pads are sold in sets with a special tray. Pad trays are generally narrower and deeper than roller trays and do not have sloping bases. They also have distinct lips for scraping the pads over to get rid of excess paint. Some pad trays have grooved loading rollers in them: you brush the pad over these to pick up paint.

To use a pad, you dip the pile into the paint and draw the pad across whatever you are painting. Large pads are designed for use with emulsion paint and small pads are more useful for applying gloss or other oil-based paints. Sometimes replacement pads which fit on to the backing plate can be bought. This saves you having to buy a whole new one – or a whole new set – when the pad wears out.

In general, pads are tiring to use and tend to leave a disappointing finish with gloss paint. However, they are particularly splash-free. Recharging a pad can be quite tricky – the pile, not the foam, should be dipped into the paint. As the pile is generally only 6mm thick, you have to be quite accurate, even when using trays with loading rollers.

There are a number of special-purpose pads:
● edging pads can be used for painting areas which are difficult to do freehand. They have small wheels which you run along a corner, say. They are useful for cutting-in between a wall and a ceiling but they will not go right into corners and have to be used with care when painting around things like a light switch. Edging pads are faster to use than conventional brushes but paint must be kept off their wheels and the pile must not be overloaded
● sash and crevice pads come in various sizes. The smallest ones are particularly useful for reaching into awkward places
● long-handled pads are also useful for radiators and other inaccessible places.

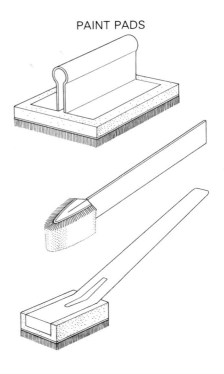

PAINT PADS

Top: standard pad
Middle: touch-up pad
Bottom: sash pad

CHOOSING THE RIGHT PAINT

On most surfaces you have a choice of topcoat. The systems given below are those you are most likely to use. Gloss refers to an oil-based alkyd or polyurethane paint – in most situations, an eggshell or satin paint is also suitable

	PREPARATION	PRIMER	UNDERCOAT	TOPCOAT
WOOD **Bare softwood**	rub down with glass-paper; apply knotting over knots and areas of resin; apply a primer; fill in holes or dents and rub down; touch prime	leadless wood or general-purpose	not always necessary	one coat of gloss (two if no undercoat), more coats outside
Bare hardwood	rub down with glass-paper; wipe oily woods with a rag soaked in white spirit; use a filler to match the timber	leadless wood or aluminium wood primer for oily woods **OR** two coats of preservative or two coats of varnish (indoors) or up to four coats of varnish (outdoors)	not always necessary	one coat of gloss (two if no undercoat), more coats outside
Old paint – sound	wash down well; rub down with glass-paper; wipe over with a rag moistened with white spirit	not needed	advisable when changing colour dramatically	one or two coats of gloss
– unsound	strip off old paint – see page 19 – rub down surface with glass-paper; treat as bare softwood	leadless wood, general-purpose or aluminium wood primer if stripped	as bare softwood	as bare softwood
Man-made boards	some are pre-sealed and do not need priming, others do; rub down unsealed boards lightly	leadless wood or general-purpose	as bare softwood	as bare softwood
METALS **Ferrous – new**	remove all traces of grease and oil with white spirit or a paint brush cleaner; wash; dry with a hairdrier and prime at once	zinc phosphate	not always necessary	as bare softwood
– corroded	remove all traces of corrosion – see page 23 – and treat as new ferrous metal	zinc chromate	not always necessary	as bare softwood
Galvanised – new	let the surface weather before priming it	Calcium plumbate (CONTAINS LEAD)	not always necessary	as bare softwood
– old	clean the surface surrounding but do not use a paint stripper or scratch the surface	Calcium plumbate (CONTAINS LEAD)	not always necessary	as bare softwood
Aluminium alloys	remove excess white deposit with a scraper but do not scratch the metal	zinc chromate	not always necessary	as bare softwood
Copper and brass	clean the surface with steel/wool and white spirit	zinc chromate or zinc phosphate	not always necessary	as bare softwood
STONE/BRICKWORK **– new**	clean with a stiff brush, repoint as necessary	not needed **OR** one coat of thinned emulsion – one part paint to three of water	not needed not needed	two coats of masonry paint two coats of emulsion
– painted	clean with a stiff brush, removing all loose paint, wash, repoint as necessary	not needed	not needed	two coats of masonry paint OR two coats of emulsion
OTHER SURFACES **Asbestos – new**	never rub down	one coat of an alkali-resisting primer	not needed	two coats of emulsion
– painted	brush off loose paint, wash down	seal with thinned emulsion; if porous use a stabilising primer	not needed	two coats of emulsion
Plaster and plasterboard	no special preparation necessary other than making sure the surface is clean and dry	one coat of thinned emulsion	not needed	one or two coats of emulsion

How to paint

There are a number of things to check before starting to paint. Make sure you have:

● **sufficient paint** – painting all the walls in a room can easily consume over five litres of emulsion paint and much more if the walls are absorbent. If you have to use more than one can, do not empty the first one and then start the second – they may be slightly different colours. Instead once the first can is half empty add half of the second can to it and stir thoroughly. Whenever possible start using the new mix of paint at a corner

● **good light** – good light is necessary to achieve a good finish. As far as possible, take the opportunity to paint indoors when the natural light is strong but avoid direct sunlight producing deep shadows in some areas of the room which are difficult for your eyes to adjust to. If artificial light has to be used, fit the highest wattage bulb available without a lampshade

● **no dust** – dust on the final coat of gloss paint will mar the finish. Clean the room, especially the floor, the day before painting, keep dust down during painting by reducing draughts (be careful about limiting ventilation though) and reducing movement within the room – keep out visitors

● **good access** – from a step-ladder you should be able to reach comfortably every nook and cranny you want to paint. If not, improve your access before you begin painting. Pay particular attention to the stairs where you may need to use a stairway platform with your ladder.

Before taking the lid off the paint can, wipe around it to remove dust, grease and so on. Most paints need to be stirred thoroughly before use unless the instructions on the can warn against this. This is done by lifting the bottom layers of the paint up through the top layers for at least three minutes while making sure that no paint solids are left stuck to the bottom of the can. If on opening a can of non-stir jelly-type paint there is a thick layer of liquid on the surface of the paint, it should be thoroughly stirred in and the paint left to re-gel. (The paint could be used in its liquid form.)

Oil-based paints (such as gloss paint) often form a thick skin during storage. This can be removed by carefully cutting around the outside of it with a sharp old knife, lifting it out of the can and throwing it away. The paint can then be stirred.

A can of paint left overnight may grow a very thin skin on the surface of the paint which is difficult to remove without breaking it. The best way to get rid of this is to turn it into a thick skin by leaving the lid off the can for a day or two and then cutting the thick skin away. Overnight skinning can be prevented by gently pouring a tablespoonful of thinners (or solvent) – use white spirit or turpentine substitute for oil-based paints – over the surface of the paint before the lid is put on. The thinners should not be stirred into the paint before it is stored but make sure it is stirred into the paint thoroughly before it is next used. If you are unfortunate enough to end up with bits in paint, try straining these out through a pair of nylon tights – this is not always successful. Other strainers you could try include paper filters from winemaking shops, and kitchen sieves used for flour.

Many emulsion paints and other water-based paints do not form skins but will deteriorate if they are stored in an outside shed and allowed to freeze. The inside of the can may also rust, especially around the inside of the lid – use a spoon to pick off every lump of rust before you use the paint.

Before starting to paint, make sure that everything within splashing distance is covered and that you have some clean rags and a bottle of brush cleaner close to hand.

Painting with a brush

To avoid messing up the paint can and to make getting your brush into the paint easier, transfer some of the paint into a shallow can with a wide top and a handle. A paint kettle is ideal but by no means necessary – any other clean suitably-shaped can will do. Fill about half of the can.

Flick the bristles of the paint brush on your hand a few times to remove dust and loose bristles, dip about one third of the bristles into the paint and gently tap any surplus paint away on the side of the kettle. Repeat twice more. Do not bother removing surplus jelly paint from the brush but try not to have too much paint on the bristles.

How you apply the paint depends on the type of paint and the porosity of the surface.

When using paint that does not dry too quickly (gloss or varnish, for example) over old paintwork (non-porous), apply the paint in small rectangular areas and join these up as you proceed. Start the first area by making a series of dabs of paint approximately 30 to 50mm apart. Do this quickly. Brush out the paint to join the dabs together trying to produce an even layer of paint, but leaving the paint thinner around those edges of the rectangle which border on any surface you will be painting. Brush over the whole area vigorously using criss-cross strokes. Follow this by gently stroking the paint in a vertical direction, then in a horizontal direction and finish up by gently stroking it vertically again. This final stroking is known as laying off. Reload the brush (one or two dips and wipes) and make the next rectangle of blobs adjacent to the area just painted. Join these up as before and work the edge of this new block about 50 to 75mm into the edge of the previous block. Again leave the areas around the edges of the blocks thin on paint – so that you do not put on too much paint when the blocks are overlapped. Finally lay off the paint again.

Make sure that you use only the first third of the bristles when brushing the paint out and when reloading. If you use more, paint will work its way to the top of the bristles and start running over the ferrule and handle. Putting on too much paint by attempting to spread the paint out from one area only instead of using the dabbing technique, may cause the paint to weep, or sag. Near an edge or corner, it may run.

When using paint which dries quickly – emulsion, say – or painting over absorbent surfaces, you will have to modify the block technique. To join painted areas together successfully, you need to keep what is known as a wet-edge. If you work across a large area horizontally using the block technique, you may find that when you come to paint the layer of horizontal blocks directly below the first layer, the bottom edges of the blocks in the first layer have started to dry and you cannot brush the new paint into them. The faster the paint dries or the more porous the surface you are painting, the bigger the problem. You can use the block technique for matt emulsion paints. But with glossy emulsion paints you must work very rapidly and modify the block technique to work radially from a top corner.

It is not necessary to lay-off emulsion paint – simply leave it after using the criss-crossing brush strokes.

Thixotropic or jelly paints should not be brushed out as much as alkyd gloss paints.

Using a roller

To use a roller, you must transfer paint from the can into something the roller will fit into. Special roller trays are available which have a raised back and a ridged surface sloping upwards. The paint should be poured into the base of the tray so that it comes about one third of the way up the sloped surface. Load the roller by dipping it into the paint and then pulling it backwards towards you up the slope of the tray. Push the roller up and down the slope until the paint is evenly distributed throughout the pile – this is particularly important. Do not try to hold too much paint in the roller – it will drip when you lift it from the tray.

Start painting by rolling out a large W (or a similar shape). Then make a series of criss-cross diagonal lines within the W to spread the paint out evenly. Finally finish off with a series of parallel rolls. Make another W alongside the first and carry on as before making sure that each block of paint overlaps the previous one. The edges of each block should be thinly coated to avoid excess paint on the overlaps. Never spin the roller when painting – it causes splashing.

You must use the roller quite quickly with emulsion paint so that you can spread the paint before it dries. But, with gloss and other oil-based paints, you should use the roller much more gently (though just as thoroughly) to reduce the likelihood of making air bubbles in the paint. Preserving a wet-edge is unlikely to be much of a problem with most paints – paint can be applied so quickly with a roller. And even when edges do dry out – with matt emulsion paint – the effect is not likely to be noticed.

One of the snags about using a roller is that you are unlikely to be able to paint any area completely by using the roller alone – rollers are difficult to use near corners, in awkward places, near differently-coloured paintwork, around light switches and so on. So you will have to use a small brush or pad to coat these areas.

Using pads

A new pad can lose a lot of its pile in the paint and on new paintwork: before using one give it a very thorough brushing with a stiff brush and wash it in soapy water. Give it another stiff brushing when it is dry. Even after all this attention think twice about using a new pad to apply oil-based gloss paints – it may still leave pile on the finished paintwork which you will not be able to remove, and which will be very noticeable.

When a pad is new, it is better to use it only for undercoats that you intend to rub down and for putting on emulsion paint in those areas that do not get scrutinised. Once thoroughly run-in, pads are unlikely to shed pile. Unfortunately, most have a limited life – they either become stiff with paint or problems arise with the foam backing.

You should load a pad with paint by dipping its pile into the surface of the paint. Hold the pad flat as the pile is very short and the backing to the pile should not come into contact with the paint. Pads can be dipped into the paint in the can but it is better to use a shallow tray (a deep can lid for example). Drag the loaded pile over the edge of the tray or can lid to remove excess paint and to distribute the paint evenly throughout the pile. Place the loaded pad on whatever you are painting and draw it up and down. Initially this works quite well, but as the pad begins to run out of paint the drag generally increases considerably. At this stage, the pad should be recharged. When using paints that dry quickly or painting over porous surfaces, add a little thinner to the paint to reduce the drag on the pad. Circular motions are often more effective than parallel strokes when painting textured surfaces.

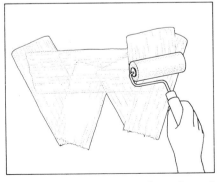

Apply the paint in dabs about 30 to 50mm apart. Brush out the paint to join the dabs together before laying off

Transfer the paint from the roller to the wall by making a large W followed by a series of criss-crossing strokes within the W

Painting walls and ceilings

When painting the walls of a room, there are no strict rules to obey about where to begin, which direction to work and so on, but you should consider the availability of natural light and how long it will take to paint the room. Avoid starting in natural light and finishing in artificial light. Logically, you should start at the top – near to the ceiling – so that any disturbed dust falls on to unpainted areas and so that any drips can be painted out later. But if you are not used to painting, do not learn how to do it by standing at the top of a step-ladder – find somewhere to begin where you will be standing comfortably on the floor. Plan your painting so that you work in horizontal bands from one corner to the next. People who are right-handed will probably prefer working from right to left (and vice versa for left-handed people). Keep the bottom edge of each band fairly uneven to make the overlapped areas less noticeable once they are dry.

When painting ceilings, try to improve access to the ceiling by either running a plank between two step-ladders (or between a step-ladder and a hop-up) or building a small platform tower. You should expect to splash some paint so clear or protect the entire floor area. You should also expect to suffer discomfort from arm and neck strain.

Generally, ceilings are most easily painted with a roller; use a brush where the ceiling meets the walls. Work out from one corner in bands, keeping the edges of the bands fairly uneven. Textured ceilings can be painted with a long-pile roller. Very heavily textured ceilings may have to be painted by stippling paint into the textured finish using a brush.

When using water-based paints, any materials containing iron on the wall surface – nail heads for example – should be given a dab of oil-based paint and allowed to dry before you put on the water-based paint.

When painting over wallpaper with a water-based paint, do not be surprised when small bubbles appear in the paper. This is due to the water in the paint passing through the paper and softening the wallpaper adhesive. Ignore the bubbles – they should nearly all disappear as the paint and paper dry out. Slit any that are left with a sharp razor blade, dab a little wallpaper paste behind and flatten the paper. Leave the area for two days to dry out thoroughly and then paint over the immediate area.

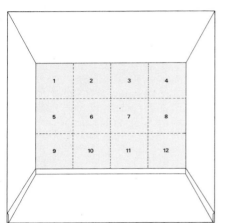

Work across the wall or ceiling as shown in the drawings. Keep the bottom edge of the bands ragged and do not make the squares

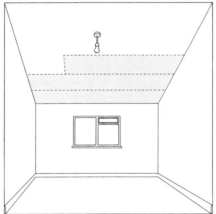

too large. When painting a ceiling, work away from the light sources – like a window – if possible

Painting doors

Painting a large area with gloss paint is not easy – you have to work quickly and evenly and the job can be tiring on the wrist. A door presents one of the largest single areas for gloss painting around the home. The most difficult doors to paint are those which have one large flat, probably hardboard or plywood, surface. Panelled doors are rather easier to tackle. Large areas of gloss paint tend to show surface defects more than any other type of paintwork – before starting to paint, prepare the surface by filling any chipped paintwork with a fine grade filler or undercoat and rub down the whole door surface to a very flat finish. If the door does not close satisfactorily, now is the time to cure its faults – see pages 214 to 215. Doors often become tight through layers of old paint building up on the leading edge. This can be planed off and the bare woodwork rubbed down and primed. Unscrew and remove all fittings apart from the hinges.

If the paintwork is in good condition, there is no need to strip off the old paint. An undercoat will not be needed unless the colour of the door is to be drastically altered. The top edge of a door needs to be painted only when it can be seen. Try to keep paint off bolts and off hinges – hinges move as the door is opened and closed so painted hinges nearly always present an unpainted area to view.

Paint large flat doors in sections – each about 400mm square – using either a 50mm or a 75mm brush.

Painting panelled doors is easier to do but it is a little more complicated. Basically, either the individual panels or the surrounding framework should be painted first – not at the same time. If the panels and framework are to be painted in contrasting colours, paint one colour first – either the framework or the panels

– leave it to dry for about three days and mask it with masking tape before applying the second colour. Do not use masking tape on paint until it is very dry and do not leave it in place for more than a day – it may stick too well. Pull off the masking tape very slowly to avoid pulling off any paint.

Always be very careful when painting internal and external corners and edges. Corners tend to get coated with too much paint and develop a run. The edge at the top of a door also often gets too much paint, but the edges down the side on the other hand often get too little. It helps if you always brush towards edges, not in from them.

If the joint between the door frame and the wall contains filler which is uneven, it is generally more satisfactory to mark a line down the door frame and to finish painting with gloss paint along this line rather than taking the gloss paint on to the uneven filler.

Hardwood doors which are finished with a clear polyurethane varnish will need thorough preparation before they

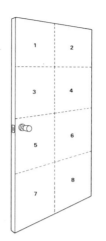 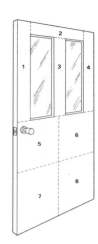 

Paint a large flat door in sections about 400mm square working across the door and then down it in bands. With panelled doors, you can paint either the panels or the framework first. Follow the sequences shown. If the door has glass panels, paint around these first

are redecorated. Use chemical strippers, not a blowlamp, for stripping any flaking varnish off the woodwork – the unavoidable burn marks will ruin the surface. If you want to stain the door, the entire external surface must be stripped back to the bare wood. Use an exterior grade of varnish and apply at least four coats – the life of the finish is proportional to the thickness of varnish applied.

Painting windows

Wash the window frame well, opening it to reach all the mating or sliding surfaces, and make good all defects in the wood or metal – see pages 16 to 25. Cracked, crumbling or broken putty should be removed with a scraping knife or an old chisel, the area primed and new putty applied. Unscrew all fastenings and make sure that they are in good order and ready for refitting when the paint is dry.

The drawings show the order of painting a casement window and a sash window. Remember to open the windows when painting and to make sure that no edges are missed or sills only partially painted.

When using a brush, apply the paint in a series of dabs approximately 60mm apart and join these up. Paint all the narrow sections such as glazing bars by stroking along the grain. There are no quick magical techniques which enable you to avoid accidentally getting paint

on the glass. Masking tape is very successful and certainly worth trying if you are not a very skilled painter, but it is very tedious to apply. Try to keep your hand as steady as possible and use a narrow brush – either a well-used 25mm one or a brush with part of its bristles

taped. If this is not successful, try using a cutting-in brush or a shield pad. Any paint on the glass should be left to dry and then removed with a cutting blade. Outside, overlap the paint about 3mm on to the glass to stop rain-water getting underneath the paint and into the putty.

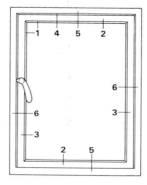 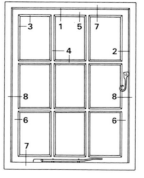 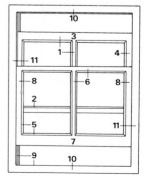

With a casement window, paint the window before the frame. With a sash window, the top and bottom edges of the inner sash should be painted with the same paint type as the inside of the window. Never paint sash cords. Suggested sequences shown

Other painting jobs

Pipes and radiators

The best time to paint radiators is in early summer so that the paint has plenty of time to dry before the central heating is turned on. Special heat-resistant paints are available – but these should be applied to a warm surface. Oil-based gloss and emulsion paints are both generally satisfactory. The colour does not affect the radiation of heat very much but the finish – gloss or matt – may. For further details, see page 15. You should expect new paint to smell when the radiators are turned on but the smell generally goes in time.

There is no need to remove radiators to paint them – surfaces near a wall can be left unpainted if they are out of sight or can be reached with a special radiator brush or roller. Prepare the radiator well and deal with any corrosion before applying the finishing paint.

When painting pipework, start at the top and work downwards. Attempt to paint all around pipes. Where a pipe runs near to a wall, hold a sheet of card between the pipe and the wall to avoid accidentally painting the wall. Do not paint any threads, joints and so on that may need to be undone.

Stonework

It is almost impossible to remove paint from stonework satisfactorily – the decision to paint unpainted stonework needs careful consideration. If you are thinking about applying paint because of a problem with dampness, first consider the possibility of using a clear finish silicone-based water repellent – see page 301.

The first job is to remove any mould – see page 23 – and then brush the surface to remove all loose material. If a lot comes away, apply a sealing coat of stabilising primer. Deal with any large cracks or defects in the stonework – see pages 24 and 25.

Stonework is often rough and finely cracked and is often easier to paint by brush than with a roller or pad. With a brush, you can work the paint into crevices and around any ornamental work. When applying masonry paint, your brushing technique does not need to be as disciplined as for gloss or emulsion paints – brush strokes, texture and overlapping joints are much less likely to show. In general, try to work by using criss-crossing diagonal strokes, paying particular attention to working paint into cracks.

Work in blocks starting at the top of the wall and moving horizontally. Right-handed people will usually find it easier to work from right to left, and vice versa for left-handed people. Keep the horizontal bands uneven, so that the paint overlaps will not be visible.

Avoid applying masonry paint in frosty weather – the paint will be damaged if exposed to frost before it has dried.

Paint spraying

Using a spray gun to apply paint can be quicker and easier than other methods and can give a better finish. Some paints – car body finishes, for example – are specially formulated for spraying; other paints can be sprayed provided that they are 'thinned' with the appropriate solvent.

Successful spraying requires a fair degree of skill and knowledge – both about the paint you're applying and the paint spraying equipment itself.

Types of spray gun

There are two main types of spray gun:

Spray guns with separate compressors These are the conventional design of spray gun. Originally, they had large compressors plus a bulky 'receiver' to balance out fluctuations in pressure. This type of equipment can still be bought (or hired), but the amateur is more likely to be interested in one of the range of smaller guns with separate com-

pressors. The compressor, which is electrically powered, provides a supply of air under pressure to the gun which has a container for the paint. Some of the air passes into the paint container to pressurise the paint, the remainder comes out through the nozzle as a fine stream. When the gun's trigger is pulled back, a needle valve at the back of the nozzle is opened and paint passes up from the container past the needle and into the air flow. The paint mixes with the air flow to provide a fine spray from the nozzle. The amount of paint that flows can be controlled by the trigger – the further that the trigger is pulled back, the more paint that flows – though in practice the amount is limited by the power of the compressor.

Airless spray guns These have all their working parts within the gun unit and have no separate compressor. The paint is forced directly out of the gun by a piston which vibrates backwards and

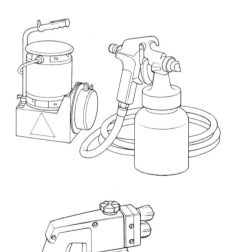

Top: conventional spray gun – connected to air compressor via a flexible hose

Bottom: airless gun

forwards, being driven by an electric armature. It requires considerable pressure to force the paint out of the nozzle and the amount of paint can be varied by adjusting a knob which alters the length of piston stroke, though this is generally a fiddly operation. Obtaining a very fine spray on an airless gun is difficult since the paint has to be pressurised to a certain level to get any spray at all.

Airless guns are more compact and cheaper than separate compressor guns, but they do have disadvantages:
● the vibration of the piston can make an airless gun noisy and uncomfortable to hold
● an airless gun can 'splutter' paint when the level in the container is low. This could ruin a nearly-completed job and it is not particularly easy to see when the paint containers are getting empty. (When spray guns with separate compressors get empty, they simply produce a spray with less and less paint.) Some manufacturers sell larger paint containers or an extension tube to dip into a can of paint.
● because the paint can come out of a gun at extremely high pressure, there is a danger of 'injecting' the skin with paint if you put a finger too close to the nozzle. This is a serious injury as the paint can spread out under the skin. It is difficult to treat, but requires immediate medical treatment – it is important to explain to the person who is treating you exactly what has happened. Most high-pressure airless guns have safety cages round the nozzle to prevent this happening.

For bodywork repairs on cars, small **aerosol** spray paint cans are available. These are used in much the same way as spray guns. Both primers and topcoats are available – it is important to know exactly what colour shade your car is. Although convenient to use, aerosol sprays are an expensive way of covering anything other than small areas.

Using a spray gun

Spray guns are most suited to spraying cellulose paint but can be used for emulsion and oil-based paints as well – sometimes, these require a different nozzle.

Most spray guns can also be used for spraying insecticides and wood preservatives. In all cases, cleaning out the gun thoroughly after use is essential.

In order to get a good finish, a spray gun has to produce a good spray pattern which is broad and even and fades away evenly (and quite sharply) at the top and bottom enabling you to pass along the surface in only slightly overlapping bands. Fan-shaped nozzles tend to produce a more even spray than the usual round ones. The paint must be properly *atomised*, that is have small evenly-sized particles which just blend together to form a uniform coat of paint. How well a spray gun atomises the paint depends partly on the design of the gun, but it is also affected by the *viscosity* (thickness) of the paint being used – the thicker the paint, the more difficult it will be for the gun to break it up into small particles. If the paint is too thin, it may not cover the surface properly.

To get the correct viscosity, the paint has to be thinned – with water for emulsion paint, with white spirit for oil-based paints and with cellulose thinners for cellulose paint. Many spray gun manufacturers provide a *viscosity cup* to check the viscosity – the cup is filled with thinned paint and the time in seconds for it to empty through a hole in the bottom is noted. The paint is thinned until the correct time – usually recommended by the paint manufacturer – is reached.

Spray guns are not ideally suited to emulsion paint – they tend to clog – and it may be almost as quick to use a roller. They are good however for getting oil-based paints into awkwardly-shaped objects like old-fashioned radiators or louvre doors. Because the spray can get on to adjacent surfaces, it is best to take objects to be painted outside or into the garage. On cars, the areas that you do not want to paint have to be masked off with newspaper and masking tape – it is best to start the masking at the edge of a panel or at a ridge in the bodywork so that there is less chance of noticing slight differences in shade.

Safety note Apart from avoiding 'injection' by a high-pressure airless spray

gun, there are precautions which you should take when using any spray gun. The most important precaution is to work in a well-ventilated space – the fine paint mist and fumes can be dangerous. A simple face mask is a sensible addition. Some paints are also inflammable, so spraying should never be done near a naked flame and you should not smoke while spraying.

How to spray
Surface preparation is as important with a spray gun as with any other kind of paint applicator. For car bodies, the paint is rubbed down with Wet and Dry abrasive paper, used wet. For small areas, the edges must blend in with the existing paint work. Where paintwork is rubbed down to bare metal, primer must be used.

Once the areas that you don't want to paint have been masked off, you can start spraying. A spray gun should be kept as horizontal as possible and the nozzle at right angles to the surface being sprayed. For surfaces other than vertical or near-vertical ones, you can get a flexible extension nozzle or an angle nozzle to allow the gun to be used horizontally.

Spraying is carried out in a series of bands, each of which is done in one 'pass' of the gun. It is important to keep the gun at the same distance throughout the pass and that it is moving and spraying as it reaches and leaves the area to be sprayed. This takes a bit of practice which can be done on an old piece of board before starting in earnest.

Common faults with cellulose are:
● **horizontal streaks** caused by passes not overlapping properly
● **rough surface finish** – or 'pinholes' – caused by spraying too far away or when the weather is too hot so that the paint dries before it reaches the surface
● **'orange peel' texture** caused by paint being too thick or the gun not moving fast enough or the nozzle being too close or at an angle to the surface
● **runs** caused by applying too much paint too thickly
Some of these faults can be rectified by spraying over the defect with several light coats of thinned paint.

Wallcoverings

Over the past few years, wallcoverings have improved a lot. They used to be rolls of paper which had to be hung carefully to avoid marking or tearing them and, once hung, they were difficult to clean. Ordinary wallpaper like this is still widely available, but in addition there are many other types. Some have plastic coatings – washables and vinyls – and may be as easy to clean as paint. Others have special surface effects – often with a cloth, flock or metallic finish.

Types of wallcovering

Ordinary wallpaper is paper with a pattern printed on it. The paper surface may be smooth, or it may be embossed to various depths, either in register with the printed design or to give the paper an overall surface texture. There is an enormous range of designs available – more than for any other type of wallcovering. It is sold in rolls of a standard size, measuring about 10m long and 530mm wide.

Hanging ordinary wallpaper is generally easy, although thinner types may tear and heavily embossed ones may stretch. Ordinary wallpapers are generally not very resistant to soiling, particularly where greasy stains are concerned, and can be cleaned only by very gentle wiping. They are easily damaged by knocks and scuffs and tend to lift at the seams in damp or steamy conditions. But they can be cheap to buy (and readily available) and easy to remove when you want to redecorate. The heavily embossed types are also useful for hiding lumps and bumps on uneven walls.

Washable wallpaper is printed wallpaper (like ordinary wallpaper), but with a thin transparent plastic coating over the surface to make it more resistant to stains and marks, and also to make it easier to clean. It is often called vinyl-coated wallpaper, but should not be confused with paper-backed vinyls – see below. Most washable wallpapers have a smooth, glossy surface, although some have matt or embossed surfaces. They are sold in standard-sized rolls, the same as for ordinary wallpapers.

Washable wallpapers are generally less easy to hang than ordinary papers, because they tend to curl up at the edges, and as the base paper is often relatively thin they may tear easily if roughly handled. They are better at resisting stains and scuffs than ordinary wallpapers, and can be scrubbed (gently) instead of just being sponged. They tend to lift at the edges in steamy rooms, but perhaps the biggest drawback of most washable wallpapers is that they are very difficult to strip once hung. However, they do provide a relatively cheap way of covering walls that need regular wiping – children's bedrooms, bathrooms and cloakrooms, for example – and the choice of designs available reflects this intended use. A few are ready-pasted.

Paper-backed vinyls consist of a plastic film (usually of poly*vinyl*chloride, hence the name, although other plastics are sometimes used) into which the printed design is fused, and a paper backing. The surface of the vinyl layer may be smooth or embossed with a variety of textures which may be randomly arranged or in register with the printed design. The range of designs available is very large, and there is also considerable variation in the weight of the paper backing. Rolls of paper-backed vinyls are standard-sized and many brands are available ready-pasted.

Vinyls are generally very easy to hang, with less tendency to stretch or tear than either ordinary or washable papers. A special overlap adhesive has to be used for overlapping joins. They are very resistant to staining and scuffing (although ball-point pen marks can be tricky to remove) and can be scrubbed, but care should be taken to avoid working across the seams. Paper-backed vinyls are very useful for steamy rooms, particularly in kitchens, and are very easy to strip – the plastic layer can be peeled away from the backing paper, which can be left to act as a lining for subsequent paper-hanging. Vinyls are relatively expensive.

Flocks are wallcoverings with a pattern and a raised pile of wool, silk or synthetic fibres. Ordinary flocks have a washable wallpaper base, while vinyl flocks have the pile fused to a paper-backed vinyl base. The patterned areas resemble velvet in feel and looks. Roll sizes are standard, and some brands are available ready-pasted.

Ordinary flocks need great care in hanging, since paste will mark the flocked areas, and the surface can be easily damaged by scuffs and knocks. Vinyl flocks are easier to hang (although paste marks should still be avoided if possible). Once hung, ordinary flocks can be sponged to remove marks, while vinyl flocks can be washed more vigorously (or even scrubbed, depending on the brand). In both cases, however, the pile may become matted or flattened. Both types need brushing lightly from time to time to keep the pile free from dust. Vinyl flocks are easy to strip for redecoration, with the vinyl layer separating from its backing as for paper-backed vinyls; ordinary flocks are more difficult to remove. Both types are expensive.

Foil wallcoverings consist of a metallised plastic film on a paper backing. They may come in a single colour – gold, silver, copper or even bright pop-art – or they may be overprinted with a design fused into the plastic film. The latter may be confused with the so-called light-reflecting vinyls, which are paper-backed vinyls having a metallic paint-like surface embossed with fine lines to produce a light-reflecting design. It is important to distinguish metallised foil wallcoverings (sometimes described as polyester) from light-reflecting vinyls since the foils will conduct electricity and must not be hung where they could come into contact with electric wiring – behind light switches and power points, for example. Most brands of both types are sold in standard-sized rolls, although some metallised foils come in non-standard lengths. Some brands of both types are ready-pasted.

Metallised foils are not particularly easy to hang, especially if heavily embossed. Light-reflecting vinyls are as easy to hang as ordinary paper-backed vinyls. Hanging either type on uneven walls will tend to highlight the bumps. Both types are either washable or scrubbable (but over-vigorous rubbing may spoil the surface effect) and they resist stains and marks well. Metallised foils can be used in humid environments but light-reflecting vinyls tend to lift at the seams. Stripping metallised foils may pose problems, since the protective plastic film and the foil may separate; light-reflecting vinyls are as easy to strip as any paper-backed vinyl. Both types are fairly expensive.

Relief wallcoverings include a number of products with one common characteristic – they have a three-dimensional surface with either a regular or a random pattern that is intended for painting once hung. They are part of the family of *whites* that also includes woodchip paper and lining papers. There are four main types, of which the most widely known is Anaglypta – an embossed paper with a relatively low surface relief. More deeply embossed is Supaglypta, made from cotton linters instead of wood pulp. Vinyl reliefs are paper-backed vinyls with a deeply-embossed solid vinyl surface layer, while blown relief wallcoverings have a surface with a spongy texture reminiscent of expanded foam plastic, again on a flat paper backing. All come in standard-sized rolls; none is ready-pasted.

All the relief wallcoverings are relatively easy to hang, although care must be taken not to flatten the emboss on the thinner Anaglypta types when smoothing the paper into place and butting the seams, and they are heavy – a problem when you want to use them to paper ceilings.

Once hung and painted over, Ana-glypta types can be sponged, while Supaglypta can withstand more vigorous treatment, and the vinyl and blown relief types can be scrubbed. If emulsion paint is used, resistance to stains is only fair, but if an oil-based paint is used resistance to marking and scrubbability are both greatly improved. When it comes to stripping prior to redecoration, vinyl and blown relief wallcoverings can be dry-stripped, but painted Anaglypta and Supaglypta are even more difficult to strip than washable wallpapers. All types are ideal for covering poor surfaces and for disguising lumps and bumps.

Woodchip papers are part of the *whites* family. They are thick pulpy wallpapers into which small chips of wood have been mixed during manufacture to give a wall-covering with a surface texture rather like coarse oatmeal. Coarse, medium and fine grades are available, the texture varying with the size of the wood chips. It is intended for painting over once hung. Rolls are usually standard-sized; few brands are ready-pasted.

Woodchip papers are very easy to hang, but cutting the tops and bottoms is not easy and the papers tear, though any tears will be disguised once the surface is painted. Scuffing and knocks may dislodge wood chips from the surface, which is not very resistant to stains unless decorated with an oil-based paint. Stripping is not easy. However woodchip papers do offer the cheapest way of disguising poor wall surfaces.

Lining paper is a plain wallpaper that is used on walls and ceilings to provide a uniform, even surface over which other wallcoverings can be hung. Double and triplo length rolls are available. It is usually hung horizontally. A special grade called *finished extra white* is intended for painting over – useful as a way of rehabilitating badly-cracked but otherwise sound walls where you do not want the textured or patterned surface that woodchip or other relief wall-coverings would provide. Lining paper usually comes in rolls 11m long and 560mm wide and it is relatively easy to hang.

Fabric wallcoverings consist of a fabric such as hessian, felt, silk or wool stuck to a paper backing for ease of hanging. Paper-backed hessian is the commonest (and cheapest) type; others are available mainly from specialist shops, and can be very expensive. Paper-backed hessian comes in natural and dyed shades; felt comes in a range of colours; and silk, wool and similar fabrics come in a number of designs and colours. Fabric wallcoverings are mostly sold in fabric widths (900mm, for example) and by the metre length rather than by the roll.

Fabric wallcoverings are often hung by pasting the wall, not the wallcovering, and great care must be taken not to get paste on the fabric. Joints may have to be overlapped and then trimmed – follow the manufacturer's instructions. They tend to mark easily but can be cleaned – with dry-cleaning solvents rather than soap or detergent. Stripping is generally fairly easy – the fabric can usually be peeled away from the paper backing.

Foamed polyethylene wallcovering has no paper – the pattern is fused into the surface of the plastic, and the surface is lightly textured to give it a soft, warm feel. It is extremely light, and is hung by pasting the wall, not the wallcovering. Care must be taken not to score or stretch the material as it is hung and to ensure the edges are well stuck down. The surface resists stains fairly well, and can be washed, but not scrubbed. However, the edges tend to lift slightly in hot humid conditions. It is very easy to strip – it simply peels off the wall in one layer. It is broadly comparable in price with paper-backed vinyls, but easier to hang and not so durable.

Strippability

All paper-backed vinyls are designed to be dry strippable – the top plastic layer can be pulled away from the backing paper which can be left to form a lining for the next wallcovering. A few washable and foamed polyethylene wallcoverings are also dry strippable but with these the whole lot comes off.

Buying wallcoverings

Wallcoverings are stocked by a wide range of retail outlets, including paint and wallpaper specialists, d-i-y shops and supermarkets, department stores and builders' and decorators' merchants. Once you have decided what type of wallcovering you want, you then have to find a pattern and colour you like at a price you can afford.

When you go shopping for wallcoverings, you will find that most shops have a number of rolls of various wallcoverings out on display. This applies particularly to *whites* – relief wallcoverings and woodchip papers – and also to a small selection of the best-selling designs in vinyls, washables and ordinary wallpapers. So if you are lucky, you will be able to find something you like and take it home with you. But there are hundreds of designs available and no shop can hope to display more than a small fraction of them. Instead many shops have a number of pattern books containing samples of wallcoverings for you to choose from. These are usually issued to the retailer by the manufacturer, although occasionally a wholesaler (or even the retailer, especially if he is part of a large chain) may make up the pattern books. Books usually contain just one type of wallcovering – usually wallpaper or vinyls, although flocks and foils may also be included. These pattern books are often given a collection name, which may at least help you to narrow down your choice of wallcovering. Wallcovering manufacturers usually alter their collections every two years, though it is unusual for them to change every design in a collection book. Some shops will allow you to take the books home for inspection but you may have to pay a deposit.

Once you have found a pattern you like in one of these books the shop may be able to supply the quantity you need from stock, even if the paper is not on display. If they cannot, they will have to order it, and this may take a few days. The number the shop uses for identifying the pattern is usually on the back of the sample in the book and on the rolls of wallcovering.

When you receive the rolls, check first that you have got the exact design you chose (or ordered). Even if the pattern book number and the numbers on the wallcovering match you may not have the design you chose. Sometimes the numbers on the labels do not match those on the pattern book sample, usually because the book contained a selection of different manufacturers' designs. Rolls also have another number on their labels to tell you when the wallcovering was made. This is the batch number and you should check that all the rolls have identical numbers. If they do not, the shade of each roll may not match. Lastly, check to see that the ends of the rolls are undamaged. Most rolls are shrink-wrapped and the wrapping should be unopened.

Prices

The price of the same wallcovering can vary widely from shop to shop. Manufacturers do not recommend selling prices, and so retailers are governed only by what they have to pay their wholesalers and what profit margin they decide on.

Wallcoverings in pattern books are often divided by manufacturers into a number of price groups and each group is given a price by the retailer.

In general terms, papers on display in shops are priced individually and are cheaper than the same paper in a pattern book. It is also common practice for shops to charge more when they have to order a paper that they do not have in stock. Once you have settled on a particular pattern, especially if it is from a named collection, it may be worth ringing round several stores to find out whether anyone has it in stock at a price lower than the one you would have to pay to order elsewhere.

Quantities

The most accurate way of working out how much you need is to count up the number of widths needed to decorate a given wall or room, add up the lengths and convert this into whole rolls (a standard roll is 10.05 metres long and 530mm wide). If the pattern repeat is large – the size is often given in the pattern book – allow an extra roll.

Less accurate is the simple formula: $n = h \times d \div 5$, where n is the number of rolls you will need, h is the height of each length and d is the distance round the room in metres. Divide by 50 instead of 5 if you measure in feet. Always round the answer up to the nearest whole number. Do not worry about allowing for doors and windows unless they take up a sizeable part of the wall area.

NUMBER OF ROLLS NEEDED												
Wall height from skirting in metres	measurement round room including doors and windows in metres											
	9	10	11	12	13	14	15	16	17	18	19	20
2.0 to 2.2	4	4	5	5	5	6	6	6	6	7	7	8
2.2 to 2.4	4	4	5	5	6	6	6	7	7	8	8	9
2.4 to 2.6	4	5	5	6	6	7	7	8	8	9	9	10
2.6 to 2.8	5	5	6	6	7	7	8	8	9	9	10	11
2.8 to 3.0	5	5	6	7	7	8	8	9	9	10	11	12

To estimate the number of rolls to cover a ceiling measure the length of each strip, count up how many strips will be needed, multiply the two numbers together and divide the answer by 10 if you measured in metres, by 33 if in feet. Round the answer up to the nearest whole number.

ABC of wallcoverings

Anaglypta relief wallcovering intended for overpainting once hung. Regular cellulose adhesive should not be used for ceilings but otherwise any type of adhesive can be used to hang it. Allow the adhesive to dry fully before painting.

Cork wallcovering thinly-sliced veneers of cork stuck to a paper backing, perhaps overprinted with a design as well. A specialist wallcovering, hung with a ready-mixed paste. Expensive, usually sold by the metre.

Felt wallcovering coloured felt stuck to a stout paper backing, awkward to hang because of its weight and the width of the roll – commonly 1830mm wide. Hung with a ready-mixed paste, usually applied to the wall. Expensive, usually sold by the metre.

Flock wallcovering raised pile pattern on paper or paper-backed vinyl base. Use a fungicidal paste for the washable and vinyl types.

Foil wallcovering plastic-coated metallised foil on a paper backing. Use a fungicidal paste (some are ready-pasted); do not hang behind light switches or power points, since the foil conducts electricity.

Friezes and borders friezes are thin ribbons of printed wallpaper usually hung around a room just below the angle between wall and ceiling. Borders are similar but are used to form decorative panels on walls and ceilings, or to frame a doorway or similar feature. They are hung with an ordinary adhesive, and may need trimming along their edges first.

Grasscloth strands of natural grasses woven into a fabric and stuck to a paper backing. A specialist wallcovering, fragile and therefore awkward to hang (use a ready-mixed paste). Expensive, usually sold by the metre.

Hand-printed wallpaper wallpapers printed by hand, not machine. Block printing and screen printing are the most common. When you buy (from specialist suppliers only) check the roll length and width carefully, and also whether the edges will need trimming before the paper is hung. Hang with ordinary adhesive, keeping it off the face of the paper.

Hessian paper-backed fabric wallcovering, sold by the roll or by the metre; usually 900mm wide. Often hung by pasting the wall, using a ready-mixed paste.

Ingrain paper another name for woodchip paper.

Lincrusta a comparatively uncommon relief wallcovering, made from a mixture of linseed oil and fillers applied to a paper backing, hardened and formed into thin sheets simulating natural textures. It comes in standard-sized rolls in a wide range of embossed decorative effects, is hung with its own special adhesive and is usually painted over with an oil-based paint once hung.

Lining paper plain paper used for cross-lining walls prior to hanging other wallcoverings. One grade, called *finished extra white*, can be overpainted once hung. Hang with the paste that will be used for subsequent wallcovering; use ordinary adhesive if overpainting.

Novamura foamed polyethylene wallcovering, hung direct from the roll by pasting the wall. Use a fungicidal paste.

Wet rubbing

Wallcovering can be classified as:
- spongeable – wet adhesive can simply be wiped off its face but the wallcovering can withstand only gentle wiping with a damp cloth or sponge once hung. Wallcoverings in this category may be called acrylic coated
- washable – can be cleaned with a wet soapy cloth but will not withstand mild abrasives
- scrubbable – will withstand washing with a mild abrasive.

Photowalls generic term for enlarged photographic designs intended for use as wall decorations. Sold usually as a series of strips that are hung in sequence like lengths of wallpaper. Hang with a fungicidal paste.

Silk wallcovering plain or patterned silk stuck to a paper backing. A specialist wallcovering, difficult to hang without marking (use a ready-mixed paste). Expensive, usually sold by the metre.

Sisal wallcovering woven fabric wallcovering resembling hessian but coarser and more open in texture. Available in natural or dyed shades, or a mixture of strands, stuck to a paper backing that may be coloured to show through the weave. Hang with a ready-mixed paste.

Supaglypta relief wallcovering intended for overpainting once hung. Use any type of adhesive (but see Anaglypta), allowing it to dry thoroughly before painting.

Vinyl printed plastic film stuck to paper backing. Always hang with a fungicidal paste, and use special overlap adhesive where butt joints are not possible, since ordinary paste will not stick overlaps permanently.

Vynaglypta solid vinyl relief wallcovering on paper backing, intended for overpainting. Hang with a fungicidal adhesive. Sold in standard-sized rolls.

Wallpaper ordinary printed wallpaper. Hang with an ordinary (non-fungicidal) paste. Washable wallpapers must be hung with paste containing a fungicide.

Woodchip wallpaper hang with ordinary paste, allowing this to dry thoroughly before painting.

Woolstrand wallcovering wallcovering consisting of stranded or woven wool on a paper backing. A specialist wallcovering, hung with a ready-mixed paste. Expensive, usually sold by the metre.

Surface preparation

When hanging a wallcovering, the surface should be clean, dry and as flat as possible. Cracks and holes should be filled and the surface made smooth. Screw or nail heads should be sealed with a blob of oil-based paint before filling over them.

Papered surfaces

Walls which have a wallcovering on them should preferably be stripped before another wallcovering is hung. But this is not essential when the original wallcovering is in good condition, clean and firmly stuck as long as it is neither embossed nor has a plastic surface. If a few odd patches of wallcovering have lifted these should be torn away and the rough edges left should be gently abraded smooth with a medium-grade abrasive. If the original surface is in poor condition, do not attempt to hang wallcovering on top of it. The adhesive on the new wallcovering may pull the old one and the new one away from the wall.

Stripping wallcoverings

A few washable wallcoverings and foamed polyethylene ones are dry strippable and can be simply peeled off the wall to leave the original surface beneath. With vinyls, the top layer of plastic can with care be peeled away from its backing paper. If this is done successfully, the new wallcovering can be hung on top of this backing. But if it is only partially successful – if some of the backing paper comes away from the wall – then the whole lot will have to be stripped.

Stripping old wallcoverings often means a lot of hard work. The success of the operation depends on getting water to the original adhesive beneath the wallcovering so that it begins to dissolve and lose its grip. The wallcovering then has to be removed. Sometimes some wallcovering can be removed without wetting it first. With ordinary wallpapers there is relatively little problem – soak the wallpaper with warm water containing a little washing-up liquid or with a special-purpose wallpaper stripper (usu-

ally dissolved in water too). Leave it for a short while to soak through the paper and then scrape off the wallpaper with a flat scraper. This is a messy job – lay polythene sheeting over the floor to catch soggy scrapings as they fall. Stripping is tedious – allow plenty of time to complete the task and keep the wallpaper well soaked. Once all the paper is off, allow the surface to dry and then abrade off any small *nibs* of paper left and wash down the whole surface with a detergent solution. A steam stripper which can be hired will speed up the process but it is hard work to use.

Stripping washables and papers which have been painted is much more difficult – the surface on these is water-resistant and so the diluted washing-up liquid or wallpaper stripper will not be able to do its job until the surface has been removed or broken up. A special-purpose stripping tool with serrated edges can be used to score the surface, or a wire brush or a coarse abrasive – waterproof silicon carbide, grit number 60, for example. If the wallpaper has a particularly stubborn painted finish then it may be necessary to use a chemical paint stripper. In all these cases take care to avoid damaging the surface beneath.

Painted surfaces

If the old paintwork has a matt finish – probably emulsion paint – and is in good condition, it should be washed down with a detergent solution or a paint cleaner, to make sure that all grease is removed. The wallcovering can then be hung when the surface is dry. Sound gloss-painted areas should be washed down too but in addition follow this up by thoroughly rubbing down the whole surface with a coarse grade abrasive. Make good any damaged areas with a filler and when this is dry seal it with wallpaper paste, size or emulsion paint.

Any paint that washes off fairly easily, such as whitewash or distemper, should be removed completely.

Bare surfaces

Bare surfaces should be treated as if they

were to be painted over using the appropriate primer or sealer for the surface – see pages 14 to 17. New plaster or cement which is in sound condition and dry should be painted with a coat of emulsion paint diluted with water. Painting is not essential – size can be used instead – but painting will make it easier to strip the wallcovering at some future date. The wallcovering can be hung as soon as the paint is dry.

Sizing

On very absorbent surfaces, the adhesive applied to a wallcovering may soak into the surface making it difficult to slide the wallcovering into place and producing a less good bond between the wallcovering and the surface beneath.

To stop this happening, the surface can be sealed with a coat of the adhesive before the wallcovering is hung. This is known as sizing.

Very absorbent surfaces – bare plaster and plasterboard – should be sealed and it is also sensible to size a surface before hanging a very heavy or embossed wallcovering. It is not necessary to size painted surfaces or surfaces which have just been stripped. The size should be applied by a brush or roller and allowed to dry before hanging the wallcovering.

A few wallcovering adhesives recommend an animal glue size before using the wallcovering adhesive. But this is rapidly being superseded by using a coat of the wallcovering adhesive itself as a size applied at half the strength recommended for hanging wallcoverings.

When using ready-pasted vinyl wallcoverings use an adhesive containing a fungicide as a size.

Lining paper

Wallcoverings hung straight over uneven walls may crease and stretch; on non-absorbent surfaces such as gloss paint, the adhesive may take a long time to dry and so either stain the new wallpaper or cause it to lift. A lining paper can be used to solve these problems and should prevent joint gaps due to shrinkage.

TOOLS FOR HANGING WALL COVERINGS

A surprisingly large number of tools are needed for hanging wallcoverings. A steel tape measure, a pencil and a pair of scissors are needed to measure each length and cut it before hanging. For pasting wallcoverings, a plastic bucket in which paste can be mixed, a pasting brush to apply the paste to the back of the wallcovering (a 100mm paintbrush is ideal, or even a foamsleeved paint roller) and a table to lay the paper on while it is pasted are all necessary. Fold-up pasting tables can be bought quite cheaply and are worth buying if you do a reasonable amount of paperhanging. Alternatively, a flush door with its handles removed and laid on a stout table or two trestles will do. Have a cloth or sponge handy to wipe the table clean of paste.

When preparing a ready-pasted wall-covering, the bucket, pasting brush and table can be dispensed with. All that is needed is a cardboard soaking tray, usually given away free by the shop where the ready-pasted wallcovering was bought, in which the rolled-up lengths of wallcovering can be immersed. However, a pasting table will still come in useful for laying out and marking up the lengths of wallcovering.

A plumb line is essential for hanging wallcoverings vertically. It can be either bought or improvised using a small flat weight and a length of fine cord. The other essential for hanging most wall-coverings is a paper-hanging brush, which has soft flexible bristles and is used to smooth the wallcovering into place on the wall, butt it into angles and smooth out any bubbles. For vinyls, washable wallpapers and foamed polyethylene wallcoverings, a sponge can be used instead of a paper-hanging brush, since wetting or getting paste on the surface is not so important. Have a clean cloth or sponge handy to remove any paste that does get on the face of the wallcovering, however. Scissors are needed for cutting each length exactly to size once it is hung: long-bladed ones make for more accurate cutting than short ones. Have a sharp knife or a small pair of scissors handy too, for trimming round obstacles such as light switches and pipes. A useful extra to have is a boxwood seam roller, which helps to ensure that seams are well stuck down. It should not, however, be used on wall-coverings with hollow reliefs (Anaglypta, Supaglypta and so on) or on papers with heavy embossing, since the action of the roller will tend to flatten the relief or emboss.

Access equipment is also needed – at the very least a platform step-ladder, and ideally a scaffold board and hop-up or other support, so you can construct a longer working platform. This is vital when papering ceilings.

Paste

Paste is used to stick the wallcovering to the wall. There are several kinds, and it is important to choose the correct type for the wallcovering being hung. Any paste will do for hanging ordinary wallpaper; most are powders for mixing with cold water, although a few hot-water starch pastes and ready-mixed pastes are available. For hanging heavier wallpapers, including relief wallcoverings, the paste can either be mixed to a thicker consistency (the instructions on the packet will give details) or a heavier-duty paste can be used. For washable wallpapers, paper-backed vinyls, metallised foils, vinyl relief wallcoverings and foamed polyethylene wallcoverings, a paste containing a fungicide must be used. Since the face of the wallcovering is impervious to water, the paste will take a long time to dry out and without a fungicide mould might grow behind the wallcovering. You must wash your hands after using fungicidal pastes, and they must be kept away from children and pets. Lastly, for hanging speciality wallcoverings, most manufacturers recommend a ready-mixed paste.

Paste packets generally give details about how much water to add to make up a mix, but do not always specify how many rolls the mix will cover. As a rough guide, allow between 0.5 and 0.7 litres of paste for each roll of wallcovering, more if it is heavily embossed or carries a deep relief, since paste will collect in the hollows.

Size is a paste-like product used for sealing the surface of previously-undecorated plaster prior to paperhanging. It is available from most decorating shops, but a diluted solution of wall-paper paste can often be used instead.

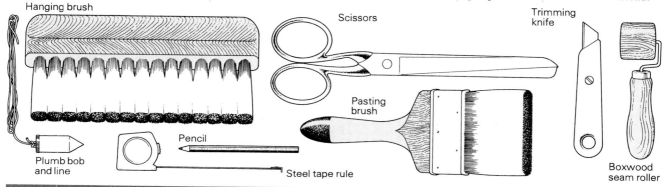

Hanging brush

Plumb bob and line

Pencil

Steel tape rule

Scissors

Pasting brush

Trimming knife

Boxwood seam roller

How to hang wallcoverings

The technique of hanging roll wallcoverings is basically the same for all the different types, although individual materials do need one or two tricks of their own.

The basic techniques

First mix up the paste, following the instructions on the packet. Unwrap the rolls of wallcovering, and look carefully at the design to see which is the top – usually the free end, but if it is not, reverse-wind the roll. Next, check the rolls for colour matching, by unrolling a metre or so of each roll and laying them side by side in natural light. Differences in shade are quite rare with machine-printed wallcoverings as long as the batch numbers are all the same, but some slight shade variation may be noticed on plain-coloured wallcoverings, on vinyls, and on certain paper-backed fabrics. Try swapping the order of the rolls around to get a good colour match along adjacent edges. Lastly, check which type of pattern match the wallcovering has – random, straight (the pattern at any given point on the left-hand edge of the wallcovering is the same as at the right) or drop (the pattern on the left-hand side is different at any point from that on the right).

It does not really matter where you start hanging wallcovering, although it is traditional to start alongside the largest window in the room. The only exception comes when hanging a wallcovering with a large and bold pattern; then it is usual to centre the first length on the chimney breast or other focal point and to work outwards from there in opposite directions round the room.

It is vital that the first length is hung exactly vertically, and a plumb line must be used to mark a vertical line on the wall where the edge of the first length will come. The simplest way of doing this is to make a series of pencil marks alongside the plumb line, and join them up with a long straight-edge. It is useful to have a helper for this.

Measuring and cutting Measure the height of the wall at the point where the first length will be hung, and cut the first length about 100mm longer than this measurement. If the pattern is bold, decide where the first motif will be sited in relation to the ceiling line and cut the paper accordingly. Mark the top of the length on the back of the paper, so you hang it the right way up.

If you are hanging a succession of full lengths, measure and cut further lengths, but watch the pattern match carefully, especially if it is a drop pattern. Continue cutting full lengths until the end of the roll is reached; unless the pattern repeat is very large or your ceilings are very high, a roll should give four full lengths. Shorter leftovers can be used to paper above doors and above and below window openings. When cutting lengths that have a drop pattern, mark the back of the first length cut *1*, and the back of the second length *2*. The third length cut will be an exact match for *1*, the fourth a match for *2* and so on.

Pasting Lay the first length of wallcovering on the pasting table, aligning one end with the end of the table and with one edge fractionally overlapping the table edge. Start brushing on the paste, working from the centre of the length towards the edge and the top. Then move the paper over so its other edge fractionally overlaps the other edge of the table, and paste out towards this edge too. Make sure all areas are pasted. When the top part of the length is completely pasted, fold it over with the pasted area inside, move the paper along the table and paste the remaining part of the length. Fold up the bottom edge in the same way. If you get some paste on the table, wipe it off immediately to avoid transferring it to the front of the wallcovering.

When pasting very long lengths (for ceilings or stairwell walls, for example), the paper may have to be folded concertina-fashion instead.

Some wallcoverings, in particular heavy and embossed types, should be left for a while after pasting to allow the paste to soak in and make the paper more supple. The instructions on the roll label should tell you about doing this.

PAPERING SEQUENCE

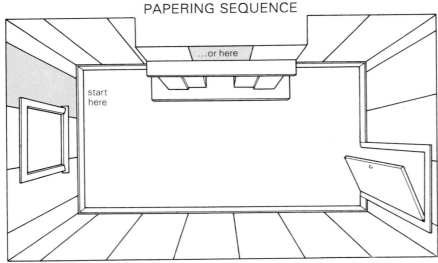

start here

...or here

The order in which you paper a room is not fixed, but you can save a lot of unnecessary trimming – and get the most pleasing results – by following a logical sequence. Papers with large patterns should be centred on a chimney breast (if the room has one) or some other major feature and the paper should be hung working outwards in both directions. Otherwise, start alongside the largest window and work clockwise

MEASURING, CUTTING AND PASTING

Start by measuring the floor-to-ceiling height and add 100mm to the total to allow for trimming. With bold patterns, decide where the first motif down from the ceiling will be

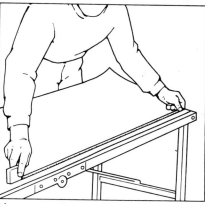

Measure out the overall length of each piece. Remember to allow for trimming

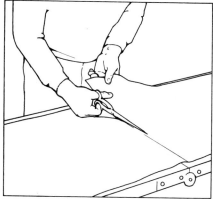

Mark a line across the wallcovering at right angles to the edges and cut carefully along it. If you are cutting a number of full lengths, watch the pattern match carefully

Align one end of the wallcovering with the end of the table and fractionally overlap one edge of the table with the edge of the wall-covering. Start pasting at the centre

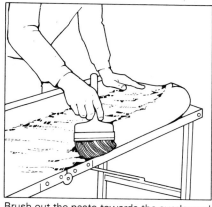

Brush out the paste towards the overlapped edge. Move the paper so that the other edge overlaps the table and brush out the paste in this direction too

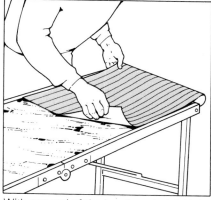

With one end of the length pasted, fold the wallcovering neatly with the pasted area inside; move the wallcovering along the table and paste the other end

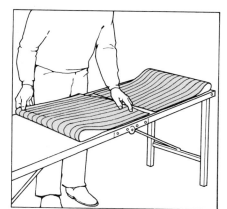

With pasting complete, fold the other end over. Very long lengths – when papering a stairwell, say – may have to be folded concertina-fashion

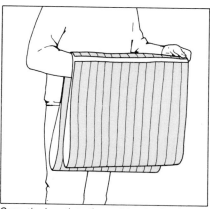

Carry the length to the wall by draping it over your arm

The length should be offered up to the ceiling, alongside your first plumbed line. Allow an overlap for trimming at the top

Hanging Pick up the pasted length of wallcovering over your arm, and carry it to the wall. Climb your steps, and unfold the upper fold in the length, allowing the rest of the length to hang down with the lower fold still in place. Do not let the wallcovering drop suddenly or else it may tear. Holding the top of the length between fingers and thumbs, position the top of the length just below the ceiling line and locate the edge of the length against the plumbed line on the wall. When it is exactly aligned, use a paperhanging brush to press the wallcovering against the wall with a series of long, sweeping strokes to hold it in position, working from the centre towards the

edges to brush out any air bubbles trapped behind the wallcovering. At the top of the length there should be about 50mm of excess wallcovering.

With the top half of the length in place on the wall, unfold the lower part and carry on brushing the wallcovering into place, checking that it is aligned with the plumbed line all the way down. There should be about 50mm of excess wallcovering at skirting board level too.

Return to the top of the length, and use the back of the blade of your scissors to press the wallcovering into the angle between wall and ceiling. Peel the wallcovering away, cut along the crease, wipe off any paste which has got on to

the ceiling and then use the paperhanging brush to dab the trimmed end neatly back into the angle. Brush lightly down the whole length once more, and then repeat the crease-and-trim operation at skirting board level, again wiping off any paste on the skirting board and brushing the trimmed end back into place. Fold up the pasted off-cuts, so you do not tread on them, and paste the second length ready for hanging. Ideally, hanging wallcoverings is a two-person job – one hanging the wallcovering and the other pasting.

Take the second length to the wall, hold it up at ceiling level as before and align its edge carefully with the first

HANGING WALLCOVERINGS

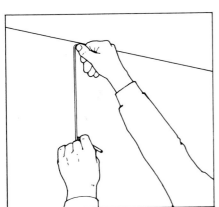
Use a plumb bob and line to mark a true vertical on the wall before hanging the first length – get a helper to hold the plumb bob once it has settled

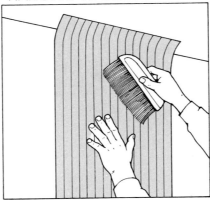
With the length aligned exactly against the plumb line, brush the wallcovering, using firm strokes of a hanging brush – brush from the middle outwards

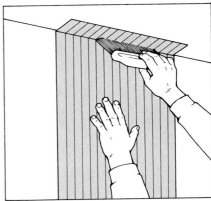
Use the ends of the bristles to dab the wallcovering into angles. Try to avoid getting paste on the ceiling

Crease the wallcovering into angles using the back of the scissor blade, then pull the wallcovering away from the wall and trim

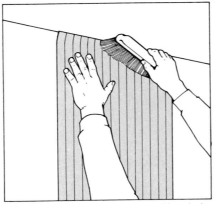
Wipe any paste off the ceiling and brush the wallcovering back into place

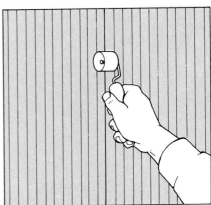
Roll the seams of the wallcovering with a boxwood roller to get good adhesion. You should place a sheet of paper beneath the roller

length, matching the pattern by slipping the length up or down as necessary. When the pattern is matched accurately, brush the length into place and trim at top and bottom as before. Finally, go over the seam between the two lengths to make sure it is firmly stuck to the wall. A seam roller can be run down the seam on flat wallcovering – lay a piece of paper over the wallcovering before using the roller as the roller should not touch the pasted wallcovering. But on embossed or hollow-backed relief wallcoverings a paper-hanging brush should be used instead, dabbing the seam firmly with the ends of the bristles; a seam roller will crush the emboss or relief.

Coping with corners

Room corners are rarely perfectly vertical, so if part of a length of wallcovering is simply folded round a corner, the edge which will abut the next length is unlikely to be a true vertical. To get round this problem, the length that turns the corner should be hung as two strips.

To do this, measure the distance from the edge of the last length to the angle, taking the measurement in several places. For internal corners, add 10 to 15mm to the largest measurement; for external corners, add 30 to 40mm. Mark the measurements on the back of the length, join up the points *before* pasting and cut along the resulting line *after*

pasting. Hang the first part of the length between the last whole length and the corner, matching the pattern carefully. Butt the paper well into internal angles; brush it carefully around external ones. Then hang the second part of the length to a plumb line on the other wall. If the corner is vertical, the pattern will match exactly along the cut edge; if it is not, overlap the second strip slightly over the first. This will not look perfect but will be much less obtrusive than the creasing and the slanted edge that would result if an attempt was made to turn the whole width round the corner.

Wipe any excess paste off the wallcovering surface.

COPING WITH CORNERS

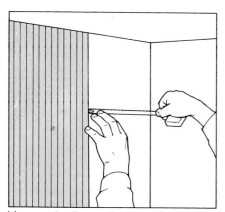
Measure the distance between the corner of the room and the edge of the last length hung. Take measurements at several places

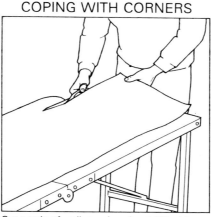
Cut a strip of wallcovering about 10 to 15mm wider than the measured distance

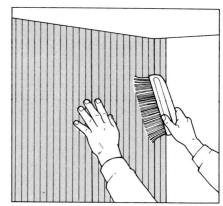
Hang the wallcovering in the usual way, turning the overlap neatly on to the other wall. Make sure that the wallcovering goes well into the corner

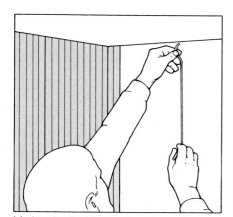
Mark a plumbed line on the other wall

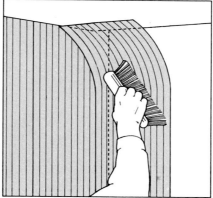
Hang the rest of the length to the plumbed line, brushing it well into the angle. If the corner is true, you may be able to butt-join them

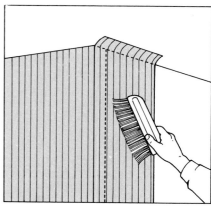
On external corners, turn a slightly larger overlap – 30 to 40mm

Papering around windows and doors

Round a window opening with a reveal, wallcoverings should be hung so that the full length next to the opening has the full width of its top part on the wall over the opening, the full width of its bottom part on the wall under the opening, and has its centre part covering the side of the reveal. Use two scissor cuts to make the centre flap and brush it carefully round the external angle and into the reveal. Crease it and trim it where it meets the window frame. Sometimes this technique of turning the angle causes the wallcovering to crease. Another method is to lap each angle by 10mm and hang strips around the reveal.

Next cut and hang a succession of short lengths of wallcovering on the wall above the window opening, making them long enough to cover the top face of the reveal too. Trim them where they abut the window frame. Do the same below the window sill, until a point is reached where a full length can be hung at the other side of the window opening, in the same way as the full length hung at the first side. Hang this as before covering the side of the reveal.

Two small areas in the top corners of the reveal now have to be patched. Cut these so that they will turn on to the side of the reveal and on to the face of the wall above it. Peel back the edges of the full lengths at each side of the opening, position the patches and then brush the peeled-back flaps into place over the edges of the patch, repasting the flaps if necessary to make them stick (use a vinyl overlap adhesive when hanging vinyl wallcoverings).

Doors can be dealt with by simply creasing the length against the vertical side of the architrave, trimming along the crease and then brushing the wallcovering into place. As with window openings, part of the length will go on the wall over the opening, and it may be necessary to hang a short length over the opening before hanging another full

AROUND WINDOWS AND DOORS

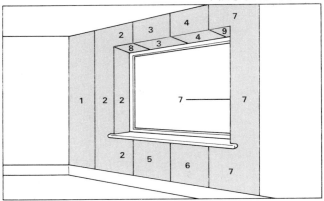

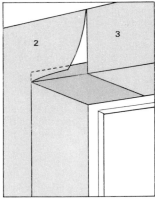

The last full length before the window opening (2) covers the wall above and below it, and the left hand side of one reveal. This is followed by lengths 3 to 6 above and below the window, and another full length 7

Patches (8 and 9 in drawing alongside) complete the job. They should be cut to match pieces 3 and 4. Each patch should be cut slightly larger than the area to be covered and pieces 2 and 7 lifted and brushed down again over the lap

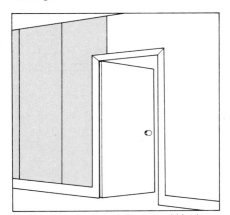

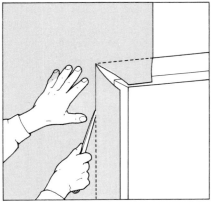

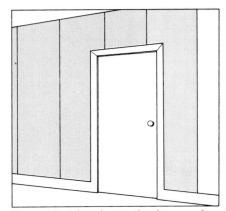

The length next to the door should be hung and trimmed as shown

Cut the wallcoverings into the corner of the architrave, crease it into the angle between the architrave and the wall – using the back of the scissor blade – and trim

Hang a short length over the door opening, and then a trimmed full length at the other side of it

length down the other side.

Where the door is in the corner of a room, the angle above the door is the ideal place to finish hanging the wallcovering, since the inevitable discontinuity in the pattern matching will be noticed least here.

Papering stairwells

In stairwells, the biggest problem is in handling the long lengths involved. Set up a proper working platform in the stairwell first and then measure, cut and hang the longest length, turning about 10mm of it on to the head wall if there is one. Work to a plumb line, as always.

When cutting succeeding lengths, make them longer than the shorter edge of the preceding length, to allow for trimming to the angled skirting board. Usually you can calculate the extra needed.

Hanging long lengths is a job for two people – one person takes the weight of the lower end of the length as the other positions the upper end.

Switches, power points and radiators

To tuck wallcovering behind the faceplates of light switches and power points, make diagonal cuts in the wallcovering from the centre of the faceplate, and

then trim each tongue to leave about 10mm of wallcovering to go behind the faceplate. **Switch off the electricity at the mains**, loosen the screws securing the faceplate, tuck in the tongues neatly behind it and tighten the screws again.

To paper behind radiators, mark the position of the radiator brackets on the top edge of the radiator, and hang the length as normal down to the level of the radiator. Then cut slits in the wallcovering in line with the marks, and poke the narrow strips down behind the radiator with a wire coat hanger wrapped in cloth. Finally, butt-join the strips again underneath the radiator, and trim at skirting board level.

DEALING WITH SWITCHES, SOCKETS AND RADIATORS

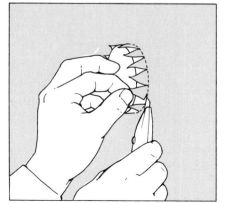

When papering around switches and sockets, make cuts over the switch – as shown – crease the wallcovering neatly and trim

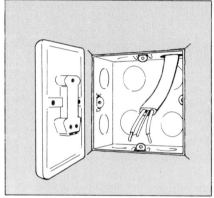

You can tuck the wallcovering behind electrical face plates, but you *must* make sure that the electricity is turned off first

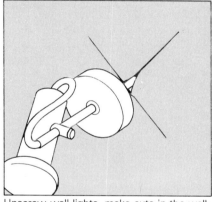

Unscrew wall lights, make cuts in the wallcovering and brush into place before replacing the fitting. Again you *must* turn off the electricity before you start

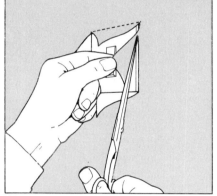

You can trim around circular wall fittings by making a series of cuts – as shown – using a sharp trimming knife

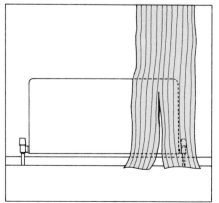

When dealing with radiators, cut a length up from the bottom so that the tongues pass either side of the radiator bracket

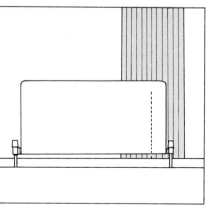

Push the tongues down behind the radiator and trim them off at skirting board level

Papering ceilings

Papering ceilings is far easier than most home decorators think – there are no corners (or hardly ever), no windows and only the occasional obstacle.

Lengths should nearly always be hung parallel to the main window of the room, and the job should be started next to it – this will ensure that the joins are not highlighted. However, if this means wasting a lot of wallcovering, the rule should be ignored. Make a guide-line on the ceiling; cut the first length about 100mm too long to allow for trimming; paste it and fold it up concertina-fashion. Fashion some sort of support for this concertina of paper so that it does not

fold around your arm when you carry it (and while you are hanging it). An old roll of wallcovering is useful.

To hang it, you need to be able to walk across the room at a comfortable working height, so set up a scaffold board on steps underneath the position of the length. Position the free end of the wall-covering in the angle between the wall and ceiling, brushing it into position. Gradually unfold the wallcovering and brush it into place against the guide-line, walking along the scaffold as you proceed. When the length is in place, crease and trim the ends.

Once the first length is in place, successive lengths should be hung parallel

to it with the joints neatly butt-joined. It is unwise to try hanging a wallcovering with a pattern that will have to be matched until you have had some practice at papering ceilings.

Light fittings should be taken down before starting to paper a ceiling, and ceiling roses should be loosened **after switching off the electricity at the mains**. To paper round a ceiling rose, make a hole in the wallcovering, pass the flex through the hole and make star cuts to allow the wallcovering to be tucked neatly behind the rose.

The last length on a ceiling will probably be less than a full width. Trim it before pasting and hanging it.

PAPERING CEILINGS

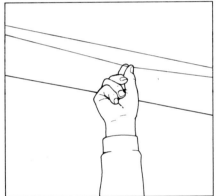

Use a chalked line to mark the ceiling just less than a full width of the wallcovering away from the wall nearest the main window

After pasting, support the folded paper on one hand and brush the end of the length into place. Note the use of a cardboard tube or wooden roller

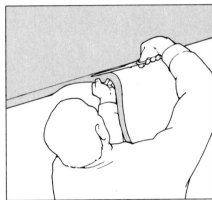

Trim the long edge of the first length to fit neatly along the wall

Alternatively, get a helper to support the folded paper, using a broom, while you brush it into place

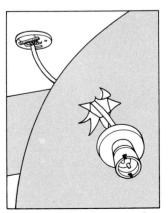

Loosen ceiling roses after switching off the electricity at the mains

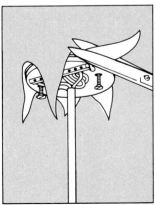

Make star cuts in the paper and trim neatly

How to hang fabrics

As an alternative to using fabric-backed wallcoverings, it is possible to decorate walls using ordinary fabrics bought off the roll from furnishing stores. The fabric should be firmly-woven so that it does not distort on the wall, and should have a surface that will not attract dirt (glazed chintz would be a good selection, a heavily-textured fabric a bad one); it should also be colour-fast, shrink-resistant and moth-proof.

Fabrics can be stuck straight to the wall surface using a thick ready-mixed paste. The paste should be spread evenly on the wall, and the fabric rolled gently into place. This method is best used for fabrics without a definite pattern – pattern-matching is very difficult. Cut the fabric to length, allowing about 25mm at top and bottom for trimming, and roll it up inside out on a cardboard tube. Mark a series of plumbed lines on the wall at intervals about 25mm smaller than the width of the fabric, so the joins can be overlapped and trimmed after hanging. Apply the paste, stopping just short of the plumbed lines, and then unroll the fabric on to the wall. Press it into the angles at wall and ceiling, but leave trimming until the paste has dried in case there is any shrinkage. Hang the next length so that it overlaps the first by about 25mm, and leave until the adhesive has dried. Carry on like this, hanging corner pieces in two parts as for ordinary wallcoverings. When the adhesive has dried, use a sharp knife and a straight-edge to cut through the material at floor and ceiling level, and also to cut through both layers at the overlaps. Peel the waste strips away, apply a little paste beneath the seam and smooth the join carefully back into position.

Fabric can also be stretched over a network of slim battens, a method that

HANGING FABRICS – WITH PASTE

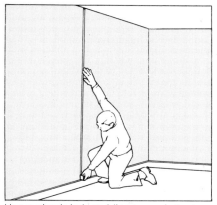

Use a plumb bob and line to mark the true vertical on the wall before hanging the first length

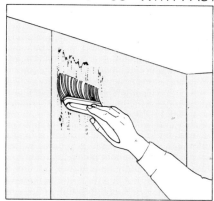

With fabrics, you generally paste the wall, not the wallcovering

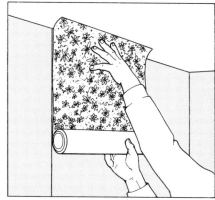

Unroll the fabric to the plumbed line. Note: the fabric has been rolled up inside out on a cardboard tube

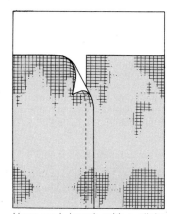

Hang each length with a slight overlap on to the one before

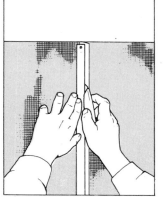

Using a straight edge, trim through both layers with a sharp knife

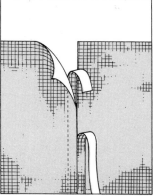

Peel away the waste strips

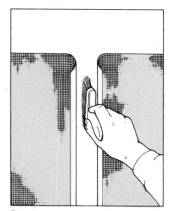

Brush a little adhesive on to the wall, and press the edges back into place

49

allows reasonably accurate pattern matching too. Use slim (25 × 12mm) softwood battens, and a staple gun both to fix the battens to the wall and to staple the fabric to the battens. Cut the first length of fabric and a batten to match the floor-to-ceiling height of the room. Staple the selvedge of the fabric to the batten with a staple every 50mm or so. Staple the batten to the wall against a plumbed line, draw the fabric across the wall and mark on it where the selvedge on the opposite side of the fabric comes. Staple another vertical batten to the wall at this point, again to a plumbed line, and staple the selvedge to it. Repeat the process for the second length, butting the batten tightly against the last batten of the previous length and positioning it so that the pattern coincides as closely as possible. Repeat the process across the whole wall surface; in the opposite corner the fabric will have to be stapled to the face of the corner batten, not to its side, to complete the run. Neaten the edges at ceiling and floor level by pinning lengths of beading to the tops and bottoms of the vertical battens. The seams between lengths will, of course, be more noticeable than with an ordinary wallcovering, but they could be covered with decorative braid or other trim.

A third way of fixing fabric to walls is to use specially-made plastic fabric-mounting track. This should be pinned into place all round the perimeter of the wall to be covered; a self-adhesive strip on the track can then be exposed by pulling off the protective tape, and the fabric pressed into place. The system works best if the lengths of fabric are accurately seamed together first, rather like making up a curtain, into a piece big enough to cover the entire wall. When the fabric has been pressed on to the adhesive strip, the tension can be adjusted so that it hangs without creasing or distortion. The edges of the fabric are then locked into place in a channel in the track, using a special tool sold with the track. The fabric can be easily pulled away from the track for cleaning.

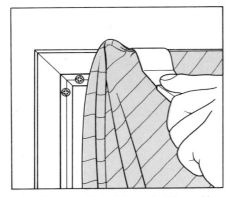

With plastic track, the fabric is held in position with adhesive tape and tucked into the edge with a special tool

HANGING FABRICS – ON BATTENS

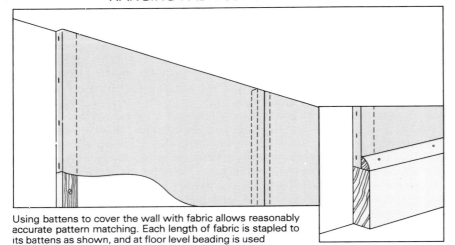

Using battens to cover the wall with fabric allows reasonably accurate pattern matching. Each length of fabric is stapled to its battens as shown, and at floor level beading is used

Wall tiles

Ceramic tiles are just thin pieces of clay, usually with a colour or pattern on the face, covered with a glaze and fired to produce a surface that is extremely hard-wearing, waterproof and stain-resistant. The surface may be smooth or textured.

Tiles come in squares (commonly 108mm and 152mm square), oblongs and a small range of interlocking shapes. Normal tiles are called field or spacer tiles and have square edges. Some manufacturers produce tiles with one or two round edges and some produce border tiles – basically square-edge tiles with the glazing running over one or two edges. Both types are used for finishing off exposed edges of a tiled surface. Special-purpose tiles are also available – heat-resistant tiles for around fireplaces and next to boilers and frost-resistant tiles for unheated outside washrooms, for example.

Fixing tiles is relatively easy, although it can be time-consuming. They should be stuck to the wall with a special ceramic tile adhesive, and the gaps between the tiles should be filled in with a hard-setting waterproof compound called grout. The smaller square tiles often have spacer lugs on the edges to keep them apart as they are being put up. The larger ones, particularly those from continental Europe, do not – matchsticks or card can be used to space them. Once fixed, it is very difficult to remove them without causing extensive damage to the plaster beneath. A tiled surface is a cold one, and so in humid rooms it can cause condensation.

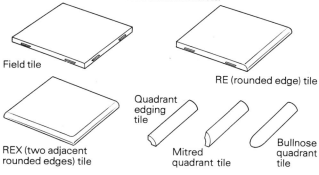

Field tile

RE (rounded edge) tile

Quadrant edging tile

REX (two adjacent rounded edges) tile

Mitred quadrant tile

Bullnose quadrant tile

Cork tiles are made by slicing up pressed layers of the bark of a cork tree to produce thin panels. Most are 300mm square and about 3mm thick but oblong panels are also available, as are thicker panels of softer cork, which are ideal for use as sound insulators or as pinboards.

The surface of cork tiles is warm to the touch, but unless it is sealed (cork floor tiles, for example) it marks easily and is not easily cleaned. Tiles can be stuck to the wall with contact adhesive, which makes them relatively easy to fix but almost impossible to remove later.

Plastic wall tiles are really imitation ceramic tiles. There are two basic size ranges – small ones either 108mm or 152mm square and large ones 304mm square. They are made from thin plastic sheet and generally have hollow backs; some can be fixed to the wall with small double-sided self-adhesive pads, others need an adhesive. Many can be cut to shape with scissors but sometimes a cutting knife gives a better finish. Most can be bent around corners.

Plastic wall tiles are fairly easy to keep clean (but the surface is usually damaged by an abrasive cleaner) and the surface is warm to the touch, unlike ceramic tiles. But they are not as durable as ceramic tiles – in particular they can melt or distort if they get too hot.

Metallic tiles are made from thin metal sheet and have hollow backs. They can be fixed to the wall with double-sided self-adhesive pads or with an adhesive. Like plastic tiles they can be cut to shape with scissors though tin snips may be required for the tougher ones. Metallic tiles can also be bent to shape. The tiles are usually coloured gold, silver or copper and may have a matt or semi-gloss finish. In addition, the metallic effect may be overprinted with a pattern or an individual design. Sizes are the same as for plastic tiles. The durability of metallic tiles varies from brand to brand – some are affected by steam. Most are damaged by abrasive cleaners.

Mirror tiles are small squares of silvered glass, usually 152mm or 230mm square. Most are clear glass. They are usually used for decorating the backs of alcoves and similar small areas, and are fixed to the wall with small double-sided self-adhesive pads. Unless the surface to which they are fixed is perfectly flat and true, a distorted reflection is produced from the surface of the tiles.

Brick and stone tiles are man-made simulations of real brick and stone. Some are actually wafer-thin pieces of pressed stone aggregate, others are plastic. The former can be stuck to the wall with tile adhesive or mortar, the latter with special plastic tile adhesives or a thick wallpaper paste. A wide range of colours, shapes and sizes is available for both types.

Mosaics are tiny pieces of ceramic tile, usually square, though round and interlocking shapes are also available. The pieces are mounted in sheets, held together by an adhesive facing material that is peeled off when the mosaics have been stuck to the wall with ceramic tile adhesive. The gaps between the mosaic pieces can then be filled with grout, as for ceramic tiles. The surface of the mosaics is hard-wearing and easy to clean, although the grouting may gradually become marked.

Mosaics are easy to fix in place, particularly round obstacles, since the sheets can be cut approximately to the desired profile and minor irregularities can be taken up with the grouting, or with cut pieces of mosaic. They are, however, comparatively expensive.

Buying tiles

Ceramic tiles and mosaics are widely sold in d-i-y shops and supermarkets, builders', plumbers' and decorators' merchants and, increasingly, from specialist tile shops (or centres). Most have tiles on display, and you simply ask for the number of tiles you require in the pattern of your choice. If the design you choose is not in stock, it will have to be ordered, and this may take several days.

British-made tiles are often sold in boxes (usually containing either 25 or 50 tiles) as well as singly, so for a large project you may save money by buying whole boxes at a unit price lower than that charged for single tiles or small orders. Continental tiles are normally sold by the square metre or in boxes containing 18 or 36 tiles. It is worth shopping around for tiles as prices can vary by as much as a factor of two from shop to shop.

Check ceramic tiles thoroughly when you get them home. Look for chipped edges, corners or lugs, and differences in colour.

Apart from selecting the tile type you want, you must estimate how many tiles you need. If you know the tile size, this is a matter of simple arithmetic – you count how many tiles are needed to fill a horizontal row from wall to wall and how many rows are needed to tile the wall up to the desired height. However, if you are creating a definite pattern with tiles of different colours or designs, it is worthwhile producing a scale drawing of the area to be tiled, so that you can mark in the pattern and count up how many tiles of each colour or design you need to complete it. Count part tiles as whole ones for estimating purposes. As tiles can vary in colour from batch to batch, you should buy a few extra tiles to allow for breakages in cutting and tiling and some to keep for future use in case some of the tiles crack or fall out.

Count up and order separately the number of special tiles you need to tile external corners and to finish off areas of tiling that do not extend from floor to ceiling. You need tiles with one rounded edge (called RE tiles) or with two adjacent rounded edges (REX tiles).

There are few such problems involved in buying other types of tile. Most are sold in packs, the number depending on the type of tile concerned; some outlets will also break packs to sell you precisely the number of tiles required. Estimate the number you need from the tile size and from the measurements of the area involved. Remember that with the larger tiles, such as cork, you will be able to cut several narrow infill pieces from one whole tile.

Adhesives for tiling

Ceramic tiles should be fixed to the wall with special ceramic tile adhesive, which can be bought ready-mixed in tubs or as a powder for mixing with water. An adhesive spreader usually comes with each tub. To estimate how much adhesive you need, allow roughly one litre of the ready-mixed types for every one to one and a half square metres of tile.

Old tiled surfaces provide a flat firm surface and can be tiled over with few problems. Make sure that the old surface is completely free from grease and dirt and replace any tiles that are loose or have fallen out.

Old plaster must be firm. New plaster should be left for a month to dry out. Apply tiles to finishing plaster only, never to undercoats. (Finishing plasters have a fine texture; undercoats are generally much coarser.) Old brickwork and rendering are also good surfaces for tiling provided they are dry, sound and flat. Leave new brickwork and rendering for at least two weeks before tiling.

Gloss-painted surfaces will take tiles, provided they are sound and clean. Check the adhesion of the gloss paint to the surface beneath by putting strips of self-adhesive tape firmly on it and then ripping them off quickly. If any paint comes off, the surface is not sound. Strip off old wallcoverings and distemper before tiling.

Blockboard, chipboard, plasterboard and plywood can be tiled over as long as the surface is rigid and does not flex. The boards should be backed by a rigid framework. Natural wood expands and contracts as its moisture content changes. Ordinary tile adhesives may

not be able to cope with this movement – use a flexible tile adhesive.

Most ceramic tile adhesives will work on quite hot surfaces but around a fireplace it might be better to use a heat-resistant adhesive especially if tiles are insecure.

At the bottom of a shower, in swimming pools and other places where tiles are in prolonged contact with water, a special waterproof adhesive is needed.

If the surface to be tiled is lumpy or uneven, a thick-bed adhesive can be used to iron it out but using one is not particularly easy.

Once ceramic tiles are on the wall, the gaps between them should be filled with grout – a thick paste which dries hard. It is available either ready-mixed or in powder form; once again the tub or packet should give expected coverage – roughly 0.5kg of powdered grout to every two square metres of tiles. Mosaics need more. Some grouts have fungicides added to prevent mould growth. To apply grout, you need either a rubber squeegee or a sponge.

Cork tiles can be stuck in place with contact adhesive, which must be applied to both the wall surface and the back of the tiles. Non-flammable emulsion types are safer than the strongly-smelling (and highly flammable) solvent-based types.

Plastic, metallic and mirror tiles can be fixed in place either with small double-sided self-adhesive pads, which are sold with the tiles – allow four or five pads per tile – or with an adhesive. Contact adhesives can be used but some tile manufacturers produce special adhesives for their own tiles.

Imitation brick and stone tiles made from fired or pressed material can be stuck to the wall with ceramic tile adhesive or with mortar. Mortar or special grouting powder (available from the tile supplier) should be used to point the gaps between the tiles. Imitation tiles of this type made from plastic can be stuck in place with plastic tile adhesive – the type used for fixing expanded polystyrene ceiling tiles.

Putting up wall tiles

In general terms, decorating with materials in tile form is easier than using materials off the roll, since you are always handling something quite small. But against that is the fact that your setting out has to be done very carefully if the end result is to look right.

Fixing ceramic tiles

It is quite rare for a surface to be tiled to work out at a whole number of tiles in both horizontal and vertical directions. Usually there are a number of narrow strips of cut tile. The golden rule of tiling is to distribute these symmetrically around the edges of the area.

On an unbroken wall, the aim should be to have a border of cut tiles at each side of the area to give visual balance. If the tiled area extends only half-way up the wall, it is more pleasing to have cut pieces at skirting board level, whereas if the wall is tiled from floor to ceiling, then once again a border of cut tiles of equal width should run along the ceiling and skirting board.

Where a wall area is broken by door or window openings, achieving symmetry is more complicated, and it may often not be possible to centre the tiles on the wall without having to cut awkwardly-shaped pieces of tile round the window or door opening. In this case the rule-of-thumb is to regard the door or window opening as the focal point of the room, and to centre the tiles on the opening.

The practical way of achieving a well set out array of tiles is to use what is known as a gauging stick. This is a straight batten of wood about two metres long and marked off into tile widths; use the tile you will be fixing to mark the batten but do not forget to allow for spacer lugs and other gaps for grout. Then use this stick to gauge how many tiles will cover the area, both horizontally and vertically, and to see how the whole tiles will lie on the wall. Measure the width of the cut border tiles that will be needed at the ends of each horizontal row. If each is less than about one-third of a tile width, accurate cutting will be difficult, and in this case the number of whole tiles in the row should be reduced by one so that each border piece will be between one-half and two-thirds of a tile width.

At window openings, use the gauging stick to determine the width of the cut pieces at either side of the window opening; again, try to avoid having to cut narrow pieces of tile, by adjusting the number of whole tiles used to fill the row.

As far as vertical alignment is concerned, the general principle is to centre the tiles vertically over the area to be decorated. Where there is a window opening, apply the same principle to the area between window sill and skirting board, so that there is an equal border of cut tiles top and bottom.

TOOLS FOR TILING

For fixing ceramic tiles, a plumb line and spirit level are needed for setting out the rows to true verticals and horizontals; some slim wooden battens are needed to support the lowest tile rows as work progresses; a notched tile adhesive spreader, a tile cutter and a sponge and some dry cloths are also necessary. With all the other types of tiles, the tool to cut them with varies from type to type – a sharp knife for cork tiles; a pair of old scissors or snips for metallic or plastic tiles; a glass cutter for mirror tiles and a brick bolster and club hammer for pressed imitation brick and stone tiles.

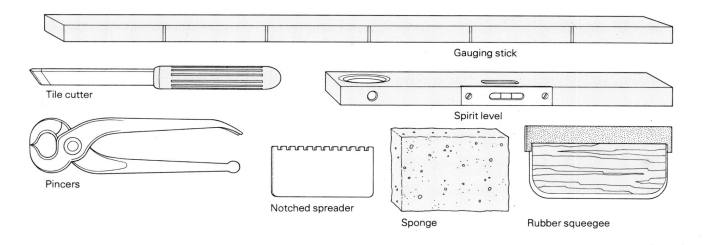

Gauging stick

Tile cutter

Spirit level

Pincers

Notched spreader

Sponge

Rubber squeegee

Finding the level

The next step is to establish an accurately level datum line round the room. Never trust a skirting board to be level – more than likely using a skirting board as a level will mean that horizontal rows will not be truly horizontal, and as tiling is completed by returning to the starting point the rows will not line up.

Mark a line on the wall right round the room with a batten and a spirit level, to coincide with the bottom edge of the lowest row of whole tiles. Along this line pin slim battens to the wall with masonry nails; do not drive the nails home, since the battens will have to be prised off again. If nails cannot be driven into the wall (an old tiled wall, say) get the battens horizontal by placing them on small stacks of tiles. Next, using a plumb line, draw a true vertical line on the wall at the point where tiling is to start – at the edge of the last vertical row of whole tiles (on an unbroken wall) or coinciding with the first row of whole tiles alongside a window or door opening. A vertical batten can be nailed along this vertical line as an extra guide.

Fixing the tiles

Spread the tile adhesive on the wall with a notched spreader, covering an area of about one square metre at a time. Draw the spreader over the adhesive by pressing it down so that the teeth touch the plaster surface beneath; the notches then ensure that the adhesive is spread to a standard depth. Place the first tile on the horizontal batten, line its edge up with the vertical guide line and press it gently but firmly to the wall. Add the next tile alongside the first, with the spacer lugs just touching, and check that its face is level with that of the first tile. If the tiles do not have spacer lugs, use matchsticks or pieces of card between the tiles. Continue along the row until the edge of the area is reached then add a second, third and fourth row, checking all the time that the tiles are accurately aligned with each other. Spread more adhesive along the area above the wall batten, continuing to add whole tiles until the area is covered or until an obstruction such as a door or window is reached. From time to time, use a spirit level on a batten to check that the tiles are truly horizontal.

Cutting tiles

At a window sill, it is usual to tile the reveals and the sill itself with round-edged tiles which overlap the edges of the tiles on the face of the wall round the opening. So the next job is to mark and cut the pieces of tile to go on the wall beneath the window sill. Mark the tile with a felt pen or Chinagraph pencil, and then score the glazed face of the tile with a tile cutter. To snap the tile along the scored line, either press down on either side of the line over a straight edge, or use a pair of tile snappers with angled jaws. If the cut edge is rough, use a tile rubbing stone (a sort of coarse abrasive

STARTING TO TILE

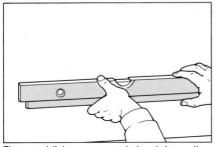

First establish an accurately level datum line round the room using a batten and a spirit level. Nail a batten along this line

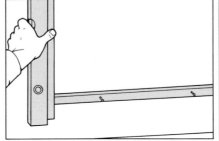

Mark a true vertical at the point where you will start tiling. You can use a spirit level or a plumb bob. Nail a batten down the vertical line

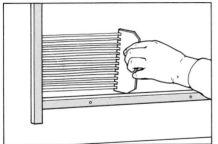

Cover approximately one square metre at a time with the adhesive using a notched spreader pressed down so that its teeth touch the surface beneath

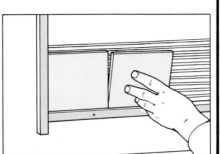

Press the first tiles into place against the battens. If the tiles do not have spacer lugs use matchsticks or pieces of card between them

WINDOW SILLS

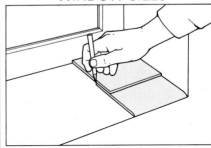

To cut a tile to fit, turn it back to front, mark two points on the sides of the tile where you want the score line to be, turn the tile over, score and cut

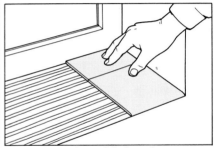

Press the cut piece of tile into place

resembling pumice stone) or an oilstone dampened with water to smooth the tile edges. L-shaped pieces should be scored carefully, and then the waste nibbled away with pincers or tile nibblers. Carry on cutting and fitting the narrow pieces of tile that frame the window opening; then fit the round-edged tiles within the reveal, butting the round edge neatly over the edges of the cut pieces on the face of the wall. Complete the tiling of the reveals with whole tiles or cut pieces as necessary.

Tiling over door and window openings

Fix support battens over door and window openings to carry the first row of cut tiles over the opening. These, and the main support battens near skirting board level, must be left in place until the adhesive has had time to set – for at least 12 hours, and preferably for 24 – or the tiles will slip under their own weight. When they have been removed, cut and fit the border pieces needed to complete

the tiling, buttering adhesive on to the back of each piece before pressing it into place. To cut border pieces turn the tile back to front, mark two points on the sides of the tiles for the position of the score line and then turn the tile over, score it and break it.

Turning a corner

When turning a corner, fix the first vertical row of whole tiles on the next wall before filling in the cut pieces in the angle. With patterned tiles, keep some semblance of pattern continuity by using cut pieces of the same tile to fill the gaps on each side of the angle.

Changes in level

When tiling over existing tiles that stop half-way up the wall, there is a change of level to cope with. If the step is relatively small, fix the last row of whole tiles with their top edges just above the step, and fill the gap behind with plaster, allowing this to harden before carrying on fixing

whole tiles above the step. Steps more than about 12mm deep cannot be disguised in this manner. With these you can either stop tiling at the top of the old tiles and finish off the top of the tiling with a hardwood lipping or slips of cut tile set horizontally, or introduce a visual break in the form of a narrow wooden shelf or the quadrant tiles sold for sealing round a bath.

Grouting

When tiling is complete, the next job is to fill the gaps between the tiles with grout. Apply it with a plastic scraper or a sponge, forcing it well into the gaps between the tiles. Remove excess grout from the glaze as work progresses and smooth over the grout lines with a moistened finger or a small rounded stick – a used lollipop stick is ideal. Do not leave grout to set on the glaze as it may be difficult to get off. When the grout has set, polish the tile surface with a clean, dry cloth to finish the job.

CUTTING TILES

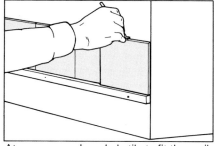

At corners, mark a whole tile to fit the available space – see marking tiles for fitting on to window sills

Score the tile firmly using a tile cutter

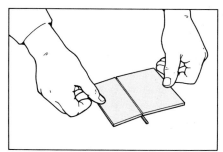

Snap the scored tile over a straight edge – or a matchstick

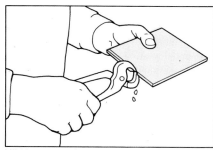

Nibble away at irregular cut-outs with pincers (or pliers)

GROUTING

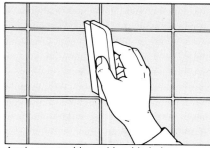

Apply grout with a rubber-bladed squeegee (as shown) brush, sponge or cloth. Run a wet finger or wooden stick along the gaps to finish off

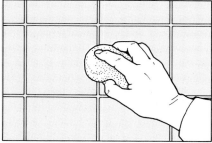

When the grout has set, polish the tiled surface with a dry cloth

Fixing other wall tiles

Cork tiles Setting out is important, but as the joins are far less noticeable and the tiles much larger than ceramic tiles, you will be able to get away with rather less accuracy. Draw true vertical and horizontal guide lines on the wall. Support battens are not needed.

Spread contact adhesive on the wall surface and on the back of the tiles, and leave it for the time specified on the container. Align one edge of the first tile with the vertical plumbed line, and then press it firmly into place. With most contact adhesives the right alignment must be achieved first time as the adhesive will grab immediately and repositioning will be impossible. A few contact adhesives allow some repositioning. Fit subsequent whole tiles by butting the edges tightly against their neighbours.

To cut tiles to fit around the edges of the tiled area, hold a whole tile over the face of the last whole tile fixed. Lay a second whole tile over this one, but butt its edge firmly into the angle of the corner. Mark the tile in the middle of the sandwich along the edge of the tile that is butted into the corner, and then cut along the line with a sharp knife. The exposed part of the middle tile will fit the gap perfectly.

When using the thick, crumbly sort of cork tile, it is a good idea to protect exposed edges such as the corners of chimney breasts by pinning slim wooden beading to the angle before starting to fix the tiles. Tile up to the beading as if it were an internal angle.

A wall tiled in cork can be sealed by brushing on a couple of coats of clear (or coloured) polyurethane sealer.

Mirror tiles These are fixed to the wall with small self-adhesive pads. To put up a single, large tile – on the front of a bathroom cabinet, say – you simply peel off the release paper and squash the pads between the tile and the cabinet. The problem with fixing more than one is that any unevenness in the surface below will cause a distorted image in the tiles. The best way round this is to fix the tiles to a panel of plywood or chipboard first. The completed panel can then be fixed to the wall surface. But even this might not produce perfect results – some tiles do not have straight sides, some may not be perfectly square and some vary slightly in size. Play around with the tiles on the man-made panels before you take the release paper off the self-adhesive pads to see if the irregularities can be cancelled out.

To cut mirror tiles, use a glass cutter to score the surface, and snap the tiles by pressing gently down on either side of the score line over a straight edge.

Metallic tiles These are fixed to wall surfaces with self-adhesive pads, but since the surface of the tiles is not highly reflective it does not matter if the wall surface is slightly uneven. Set out the tiles as described under ceramic tiles, and fix all the whole tiles first. However, in this case, you do not need to worry about cutting small widths as any tiles that need cutting can be trimmed with an old pair of scissors or with tin snips. Tiles can also be bent to turn internal or external angles by nicking the curved edges at each end of the bend line and then bending the tile over the edge of a block of softwood to get a neat fold.

Brick and stone tiles Since imitation brick and stone tiles are less regular in shape than other types of tile, accurate setting out is not so important, but make sure that courses are laid to an accurate horizontal. Some types are fixed with tile adhesive, others with mortar.

When using mortar, it can either be trowelled on to the wall surface and then the tiles can be bedded in the mortar layer, or the mortar can be put on the back of each tile and the tile pressed into place on the wall. With the first method, there is less risk of getting mortar on the face of the tiles when pointing up the gaps, since all that is necessary is to smooth over the exposed mortar.

Ceiling tiles

Tiling a ceiling is an alternative to papering for disguising a ceiling surface that is rough or cracked. By far the most common type of ceiling tile is made from expanded polystyrene. The tiles are about 10mm thick and either about 300mm or 450mm square, and have bevelled edges. They are available in a wide range of designs, which are embossed on to the surface of the tile. Polystyrene adhesive or a thick wallpaper paste should be used to stick the tiles to the ceiling surface. Never use a solvent-based adhesive.

Less common are fibre tiles, made by pressing together a mat of wood or mineral fibres. The tiles are rather thicker than polystyrene ones – up to about 19mm in some cases – and their edges are usually tongued-and-grooved so each tile interlocks with its neighbours. This allows the tiles to be secretly fixed to the ceiling with pins or staples. The surface may be plain or embossed; with sizes again about 300mm or 450mm square.

To complement a tiled ceiling (or for that matter a painted or papered one) cornice or coving can be fixed in the angle between wall and ceiling all round the room. Cornices are ornamental mouldings, while strictly speaking coving is just a quadrant in cross-section, linking the two surfaces together. Both types can be formed *in situ* by plasterers, but nowadays they are sold in prefabricated lengths which can be stuck in place and painted. The cheaper types are made from expanded polystyrene and should be stuck in place with the same adhesive as that used to fix polystyrene ceiling tiles. They come complete with pre-formed corners for turning internal and external angles. The more expensive types are formed from plasterboard, fibrous plaster or even glass fibre. The first two are generally stuck in place with plaster or with a plaster-like adhesive; glass fibre ones are usually pinned into position. With all three, corner mitres have to be cut.

Another type of ceiling tile is used to make illuminated ceilings. These are supported by a framework of slim, lightweight support members criss-crossing the room just below the existing ceiling level and supported on wall battens fixed round the perimeter of the room. The support lattice carries translucent panels that can be lit from above by fluorescent light fittings fixed to the existing ceiling surface. The panels come in a range of colours and embossed patterns, and can easily be lifted out for cleaning or for maintenance work on the light fittings above.

Estimating numbers for ceiling tiles is just a matter of measuring the ceiling dimensions and calculating how many tiles will be needed to cover it; cut tiles are counted as whole tiles for estimating purposes. Coving is sold in standard lengths, usually of 1m, 2m or 6ft; measure the room perimeter and buy sufficient lengths to allow for cutting mitres. If you

are buying an illuminated ceiling (sold chiefly by direct mail from advertisements in home-interest and d-i-y magazines) ask the manufacturer about detailed instructions for measuring up and estimating.

Few, if any, specialist tools are needed for fixing ceiling tiles. For polystyrene tiles, a spreader for the adhesive (usually sold with it), a sharp knife and a straight edge for cutting the tiles to size are all that is needed. For fibre tiles, use a tenon saw for cutting the tiles to size and fix them in place with either a staple gun or a pin hammer. For cornice and coving, a fine saw is needed to cut the material and for accuracy a mitre board should be used. Any slight irregularities can be filled with the adhesive once the length is cut and fixed in position. To install an illuminated ceiling, a hammer for fixing the wall battens, a hacksaw to cut the support battens to length and a sharp knife to cut edge panels precisely to size are needed.

How to tile a ceiling

Whichever type of ceiling tile is to be fitted, setting out is the most important factor, and as with ceramic wall tiles the object of the exercise is to have cut tiles of equal width all round the perimeter of the ceiling.

Polystyrene tiles With polystyrene tiles, begin tiling at the centre of the ceiling. The first job is to find the centre point by linking opposite corners of the walls with string lines. The intersection marks the centre of the room. Obviously, an allowance has to be made for non-rectangular rooms. Next, estimate how many whole tiles will fit in each row across the ceiling;

if the border is ridiculously narrow, better results will be achieved either by fitting coving round the edge of the room to hide the gap, or if this is impossible, by fixing one tile over the centre point instead of four abutting it.

To stick the tiles in place, coat the backs completely with adhesive, and then simply press them into position. They should **not** be stuck up with blobs of adhesive on the backs as this could increase the flame spread hazard. Once all the whole tiles are in place, work round the perimeter of the room cutting and fitting the border pieces. A polystyrene tiled ceiling can be painted with emulsion paint, but gloss, or any other

oil-based paint, must never be used.

Fibre tiles When using tongued-and-grooved fibre tiles, either stick them to the ceiling with panel adhesive (usually used for fixing panels of wallboard to walls) or staple them into place. In either case, start fixing the tiles in one corner of the room, rather than at the centre, so that the interlocking edges can be assembled correctly. So the width of the border tiles must be worked out and the ceiling marked exactly where the first row of full tiles comes.

When stapling the tiles, first pin slim sawn softwood battens to the ceiling at right angles to the joists to provide fixing

ORDER OF FIXING POLYSTYRENE TILES

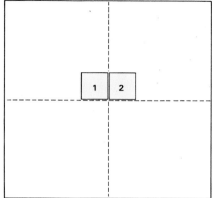

Begin at the centre of the ceiling – you find this by noting the point where the diagonals cross, making allowances for non-rectangular rooms

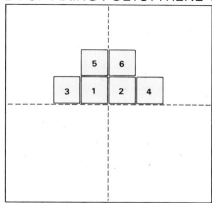

Then add tiles one by one . . .

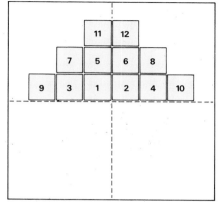

. . . working towards the edge of the ceiling

grounds for the staples – they will not hold in plaster or plasterboard. To do this determine the joist spacing, and mark the ceiling at each joist position. Pin up the first two battens at right angles to the joists, spaced at just the right distance to allow staples to be driven through the tongues of the tiles into the battens. Fix the first row of tiles to the battens with the grooved edges towards the corner of the room, driving the staples through the exposed tongues. Then cover the tongue of one tile with the groove of the next, and so on, to give a secret fixing. With one row completed, add the next row of battens, fix the next row of tiles and carry on in this fashion

until all but the last two sides of border tiles are in position.

Cut border pieces and slip them into position before stapling through them into the battens. Finish off the ceiling by pinning quadrant beading all round the perimeter, driving the nails into the battens.

Illuminated ceilings These come complete with detailed fixing instructions, but the basic principle is the same in all cases. First draw a true horizontal line round the room at the level where the illuminated ceiling is to be installed. Then fix the wall support battens along this line, using masonry nails.

Next, install the required number of fluorescent fittings on the existing ceiling. Cut the T-shaped support battens to length and rest them in place across the room, from one wall batten to the one on the opposite wall. Finally, drop the ceiling panels into place.

Cornice and coving This is simply stuck into place using the appropriate type of adhesive. Where pre-formed corners are available, fix these first, and then add full and cut lengths to complete each wall. Where mitres have to be cut, fix full lengths from each corner out towards the centre of the wall, and then fill in with butt-jointed lengths to complete the run.

FIXING FIBRE TILES

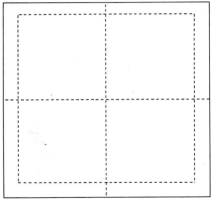

With fibre tiles, you must work out the width of the cut border tiles first and the ceiling must be marked where the first full rows of tiles will be

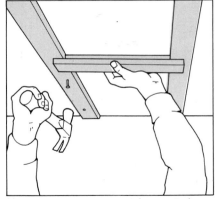

Use a spacer to get accurately repeated gaps between the battens

CUTTING TILES

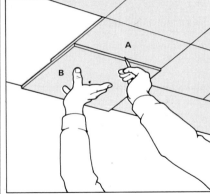

To mark the border tiles accurately, hold tile B over tile A as shown. The uncovered part of A will fill the gap precisely

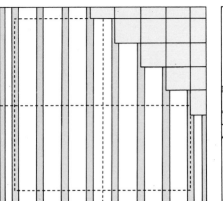

The tiles can be stapled to battens fixed at right angles to the joints, starting in one corner and working in both directions

Staple the tongued-and-grooved tiles to the battens through the tongues

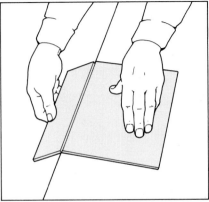

Cut the tile with a sharp knife and snap it over a straight edge

Wallboards

Walls and ceilings can be given the look of natural wood by either putting up planks of tongued-and-grooved softwood cladding (the popular 'knotty pine' look), or fixing sheets of man-made wallboard.

Tongued-and-grooved softwood is machined from planks about 12mm thick and usually 100mm wide, so that the exposed face area of each plank when erected is about 85mm. It is available with a flat or scalloped face, with or without a chamfer down the edge of the face.

Man-made wallboards are sheets of plywood or hardboard with a natural wood veneer or a plastic coating printed to simulate natural wood laminated to one face. There is a wide range of wood finishes to choose from in both types, most of which are manufactured to simulate real tongued-and-grooved cladding. The boards are usually between 4 and 6mm thick, and are sold in sheets measuring 2440×1220mm. Those with natural veneer need sanding and sealing once they are fixed to the wall surface, while plastic-surfaced boards need no finishing.

Both cladding and wallboards can be bought from timber merchants everywhere; in addition, the plastic-faced wall-boards are often stocked by larger do-it-yourself outlets, particularly the do-it-yourself supermarkets. When shopping for tongued-and-grooved cladding, first decide whether you want knotty or relatively clear timber. Then inspect each length to see if it is warped or contains splits or other defects. If possible buy lengths cut slightly longer than your floor-to-ceiling height (or the distance across your ceiling); if not, buy long lengths that will yield two usable pieces with the minimum of wastage. Then work out how many lengths are needed, dividing the exposed face width of the plank into the overall width of the wall to be covered.

Man-made boards generally cost about one-third to one-half less than a comparable area of tongued-and-grooved cladding, although types with natural veneer may be roughly comparable in price to real wood cladding, depending on the veneer type. The board size is convenient, since few ceilings are over 2440mm in height, so to estimate how much is needed to cover a given area you simply measure the wall and calculate how many 1220mm wide panels will cover it.

You will need a selection of ordinary woodworking tools to cut and fit wallboards and tongued-and-grooved cladding.

Fixing tongued-and-grooved cladding

Tongued-and-grooved cladding should be fixed to the wall by nailing it to softwood battens. For vertical cladding, fix horizontal battens (rough-sawn timber 50×25mm is ideal) to the wall with masonry nails at ceiling level and about half-way down the wall. The skirting board can either be used as a fixing batten, or it can be prised off and a softwood batten fixed at floor level instead. If the cladding is to be fixed horizontally, put up battens at each side of the wall and at about 900mm intervals across it. The skirting board can once again be left in place or prised off and replaced when the cladding has been fixed.

Fix the first length of cladding with its grooved edge against the side wall or

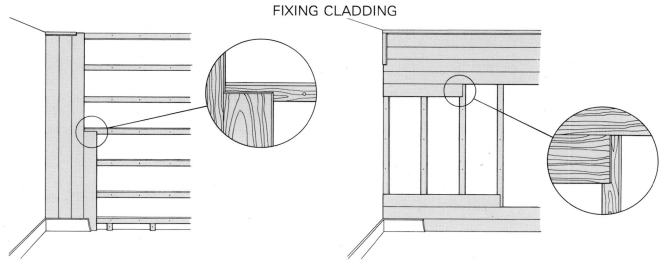

FIXING CLADDING

When fixing vertical cladding, you really need only three battens – one just below ceiling height, one just above skirting board height and one in the middle. But if you have random lengths of cladding, you will need many more

With horizontal cladding, fix the battens 900mm apart and again make sure that all joints in the cladding lie over the battens. The gaps at the ceiling and the side wall can be concealed with beading

ceiling, according to whether it is being installed vertically or horizontally. Drive oval wire nails through the tongue into the battens. Butt up the next length against the first with its grooved edge over the tongue of the previous length and again nail the tongued edge to the battens. Carry on fixing lengths in this way until you reach the last length; this should be cut or planed down to the required width before being pushed into place, and will have to be nailed through the face of the board since the tongue will have been removed. Attach the skirting board over the cladding, and neaten the edges of the area by pinning beading all round the edges to cover the cut ends of the boards.

When fixing cladding to a stud partition wall, there is no need to put up battens. Drive the fixing pins into the wall and ceiling plate of the partition wall at top and bottom, and at points where the horizontal noggins are located within the wall.

To fit cladding round obstacles such as light switches, or to turn it round corners, follow the details shown in the drawings. The simplest way of dealing with flush-mounted switches and power points is to replace them with surface-mounted ones, the face of which will be approximately flush with the surface of the cladding. Once the boards are in place they should be sanded down and sealed to protect the wood surface against dirt and to make it easy to clean. A couple of coats of polyurethane varnish is ideal.

Fixing man-made wallboards

Man-made boards can also be fixed to battens, in much the same way. Again fix horizontal battens at floor and ceiling level, and about half-way up the wall but in addition nail to the wall vertical battens to coincide with each joint between successive panels.

Man-made wallboards can also be stuck direct to the wall surface using special panel adhesives, as long as the wall surface is reasonably true and free from lumps and bumps which would make it difficult to get a good bond. Carefully cut the boards to length, pipe the adhesive on to the back of the boards and on to the wall surface and then firmly press the boards into place. To ensure a good bond, hammer the boards over the glue lines, using a pad of cloth to protect the surface of the boards. As before, finish off the edges of the panelled areas by pinning on beading.

AROUND A LIGHT SWITCH

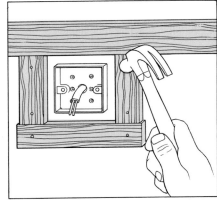

Pin a box of battens around light switches and power points

Trim the cladding to fit neatly . . .

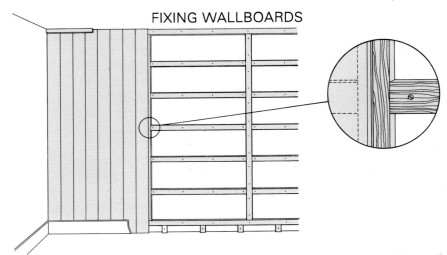

FIXING WALLBOARDS

When fixing wallboards to battens, use vertical battens to support the edges of the wallboards – see insert

. . . and refit the face plate afterwards. This should hide any slight imperfections

CHAPTER TWO

ELECTRICITY

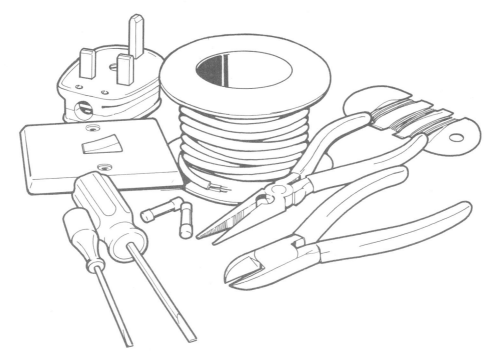

The electrical wiring of the home is thought by many do-it-yourselfers to be out of bounds; the advice 'leave it to a competent electrician' is so widespread that it is easy to get the impression that wiring is hopelessly complicated. It isn't, in fact it is fairly straightforward once the basic principles have been understood. But it is vital that you *do* understand those principles before starting out on any electrical work, the price of making mistakes can be high.

    The early parts of this chapter are designed to help you find out whether you *do* understand how electricity works. If the first five pages leave you baffled, read no further – *do* leave it to a competent electrician.

Understanding electricity and wiring

Electricity, by and large, is useful only when it is allowed to flow. For example, if it flows through a lamp, it produces light and if it flows through a motor, it produces rotation which can be used to drive something. Whatever it flows through, it produces heat – the amount depends on the appliance.

What causes electricity to flow through an appliance is the existence of a difference in electrical 'pressure' between the wire supplying the electricity – the *live* wire – and the wire taking it away – the *neutral* wire. The greater the difference in pressure, the greater the flow. But the flow is also determined by the electrical *impedance* of whatever lies between the live and neutral. If this impedance is low, a given pressure difference will result in a much higher flow than if the impedance is high. You may come across the term resistance as often as impedance; although there is a difference between them, it is not important as far as house wiring is concerned.

The flow of electricity is usually called *current*, and is measured in amperes (amps or A, for short). The pressure difference is strictly called potential difference, but is more often called *voltage* because it is measured in volts (often simply V). Impedance is measured in ohms (symbol Ω). The relationship between the three quantities can be expressed mathematically: impedance is equal to voltage divided by current. This means that if you know two of the amounts involved, you can work out the third.

In practice, a fourth quantity often enters into things: *power*, which is measured in watts (W). The power of, for example, an electrical appliance is a measure of how much electrical energy it consumes in a given period of time. For most practical household purposes, it is equal to the voltage of the supply multiplied by the current that the appliance draws from that supply.

Conductors and insulators

Most materials fall into one of two categories as far as their electrical properties are concerned: they are conductors or insulators.

Conductors allow electricity to flow fairly freely: most metals are conductors, but some more so than others. Copper and aluminium are particularly good, but copper is the conductor most commonly used (though brass – a copper alloy – is used where copper would be too soft, and aluminium where copper would be too heavy or expensive).

Insulators resist the flow of electricity to such an extent that in normal circumstances the flow through a good insulator can be ignored; but any insulator is liable to break down under a sufficiently high voltage, allowing a current to flow. Most non-metals are insulators, but ceramics, rubber and plastics are the main materials used in practice.

Air is also a good insulator and this means that electricity can be distributed around the country through bare overhead wires; only at the points where they are suspended from the pylons or poles do these wires need any insulation. But when the wires come down to ground the electricity has to be kept within them by surrounding the conductor with a layer of insulation. Conductors insulated in this way from one another and from other things make up the **cable** used for the fixed wiring of a house (and underground supplies) and the **flex** (short for flexible cord) which is used to connect appliances to plugs and light fittings to ceiling roses.

Although flex and cable have different constructions and different uses, they are fundamentally similar, and have to be designed and chosen according to the same principles.

The insulation has to be strong enough to prevent the leakage of electricity at the voltage being used in the circuit; insulation which would be adequate for use at very low voltages – the wiring of a battery-operated doorbell, for example – will break down under the greater electrical pressure (usually 240 volts) of a mains-voltage circuit.

The conductors have to be an adequate size for carrying the current of the circuit without generating too much heat (and so getting hot) or impeding the flow to the extent that the voltage at the exit from the conductor is much lower than at the entrance. In practice this means that the higher the current and, to some extent, the longer the circuit, the thicker the conductors have to be. The size of a conductor is expressed by its cross-sectional area – the area of metal visible if the conductor is sliced through at right angles.

There is often (though not always) a need for the different conductors in a flex or cable to be distinguished from one another; for this reason there are standard colour codes which are followed by flex and cable and by appliance makers and which must be followed when you do any wiring work.

The innards of an appliance have quite a lot in common with flex or cable: the electricity flows through conductors and is kept within the conductors by insulation. But the bit of the appliance that does the work – a motor or a heating element or a lamp filament – has a relatively high impedance, compared with that of the cable and flex supplying it.

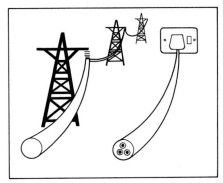

Air keeps electricity within overhead wires; insulation does the job for flex

WARNING: Electricity can kill; read pages 61–66 and disconnect the supply before starting work.

Electricity and shocks

The human body is very sensitive to small currents flowing through it. Mains voltages, although known technically as low voltages, are sufficiently high to cause unpleasant shocks to someone touching a live conductor – even if they are well insulated in other respects from providing a direct route for the electricity to complete its circuit. Someone who touches a live conductor, when another part of them is in good contact with earth, or with earthed metalwork or a neutral conductor, will get a much more serious shock and possibly a fatal one.

The risk is greatest when the body is moist or wet – in these circumstances the shock is almost always fatal. The risk of a fatal shock is also high when the path of the electric current through the body goes across the heart – from one arm to the other, say.

Safety precautions

The first and most fundamental precaution to take before beginning any wiring work is never to start anything you are unsure about, either in theory or in practice; improvisation and bodging may be all right when decorating, but not when wiring. But there are also some procedures which should become part of your routine way of working.

Any circuit that is to be worked on must be dead. This means that it should not simply be switched off, but also isolated from the supply by the removal of the fuse which links the two. Putting the fuse in your pocket reduces the likelihood of someone else reconnecting the supply.

If there is any doubt about which circuit is which (and therefore about whether the one to be worked on has been made dead) the circuit should be tested with some device which reliably indicates the presence of mains voltages – a meter or a purpose made test lamp – these can be bought from electrical wholesalers. Neon mains testers cannot be relied upon in all circumstances.

If there remains any doubt that the circuit is dead and will remain so then switch off the complete electrical installation by the master switch at the meter and check again. Never work on a live circuit.

Before any circuit is made live, all the connections should be double-checked to make sure the right conductors go to the right terminals and that the terminals are tight.

Dealing with shocks and burns

When someone gets a shock by getting hold of something live, the grip of the hand may tighten on to the live object. The first thing to do in this case is to try to turn the supply off. If this is impossible, the aim must be to break the grip without risking shocks yourself. Speed is essential: a wooden implement (a walking stick with a crook handle) or a blanket or a leather strap may be helpful; it may be possible to drag the person out of contact by getting hold of his clothes and avoiding his body. The person should be pulled clear of the electricity supply without delay: if possible, cushion the person's fall. Anyone who has fallen heavily should be moved as little as possible; the fall following the shock may have caused injuries.

A severe shock can cause breathing to stop. In this case, mouth-to-mouth resuscitation should be attempted. Even if the person recovers without such attention, anyone who has collapsed as a result of a shock should see a doctor.

Someone who gets a shock but survives with no serious ill effects should be kept warm and under observation until they are completely back to normal.

Burns caused by electricity should be treated just like any other burns; the immediate aim is to get heat out of the flesh by putting it under cold water as quickly as possible. The damaged tissue should then be covered with a dry clean dressing. Anything other than a slight burn should receive medical attention.

RULES AND REGULATIONS

As with any other sort of d-i-y activity, you could be held responsible for damage to other people's property or for injury to people themselves if it results from your negligence. But there is nothing to prevent the most inexperienced do-it-yourselfer doing wiring if he wants to, and (in England and Wales) no laws about what form the wiring should take.

Although there are no laws, there are rules which professional electricians follow and which every sensible d-i-y electrician should follow as well. These are the *Regulations for the Electrical Equipment of Buildings*, published by the Institution of Electrical Engineers, and more commonly known as the IEE Wiring Regs. Following these rules does not only mean that the installation is safe; it also means that the work is likely to satisfy the Electricity Board when the time comes to have it connected to the supply.

Strictly speaking, the Board's primary interest in the wiring of a house is limited to making sure that its connection to their supply system is unlikely to jeopardise the supply to other houses. But the only way to avoid altogether the possibility of any difficulty with the Board is to be able to convince their installation inspector that the installation has been done in accordance with the Regs.

Earthing and fuses

House wiring is designed to distribute electricity to the points in the home where it is wanted; it is also designed to prevent misuse of the system and to protect users of the system from the results of faults in the wiring or in appliances connected to it. This means that some jobs have to be done simply to keep the system operating, rather than to improve or extend it.

Electrical faults

When something goes wrong with an electrical circuit it is generally because either an insulator or a conductor is not working as effectively as it should. There are four main types of fault.

Fault 1 If the insulation between the live conductor of a flex or cable and the neutral conductor of the same cable is not good, a current can flow from one to the other, bypassing the appliance on the ends of the conductors; if the impedance of the appliance drops to a very low level, the effect is similar. The current flowing through the conductors, instead of being determined by the impedance of the appliance, is limited only by the much lower impedance of the cable and flex supplying the appliance; the resulting current is much higher, generating unhealthy amounts of heat. And the appliance stops working. The increased current will also blow a fuse – either in the plug or the consumer unit.

Fault 2 If the insulation between a live part of the wiring or appliance and the metal body of the appliance is not good (and the body is not properly earthed), the body can become live and give a shock to anyone who touches it.

Fault 3 If the insulation of a live part of the wiring is not good and allows a current to flow to earth, there is the risk that the heat generated by this flow can cause a fire unless the circuit is protected.

Fault 4 If a conductor within the appliance or the wiring is broken, or if a connection comes undone, the appliance will stop working. But if the conductor is only damaged, or if the connection becomes only loose rather than completely undone, a current will continue to flow (and the appliance may continue to operate, perhaps less effectively); the higher-than-normal impedance of the damaged conductor or loose connection will result in the generation of heat, usually causing further damage (to insulation, for instance) and often a fire can result, directly or indirectly.

FAULTS EXPLAINED

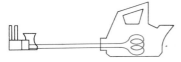

Normally, current flows along the live and neutral conductors, and through the works of the appliance – in this case, a kettle

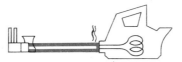

If a 'short circuit' develops, a heavy current may flow, bypassing the element and generating heat – Fault 1

If the insulation of the element breaks down, the whole body of the kettle could become live – Fault 2

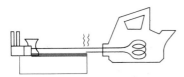

If a failure of insulation allows current to flow to earth, a heavy current may again generate heat – Fault 3

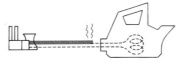

If a poor connection impedes the flow of current, heat will be generated at the point of the high resistance – Fault 4

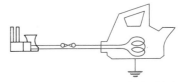

Two steps are taken to deal with these risks: the body of the kettle is earthed, and the live wire is fused

Forms of protection

It is not immediately obvious why electricity should want to flow to earth – see *Fault 3*, above. It does so because the neutral side of the electrical supply from the power station is connected to earth, so there are two alternative paths for the completion of any circuit – down the neutral conductor of the supply cable or via earth. This is why you are liable to get a shock if you touch a live conductor; but it is also the basis of the protection afforded by earthing and fuses.

The principle of **earthing** is that any exposed metalwork on an electrical appliance is connected to earth by a good conductor, with two results. One is that if a fault occurs within the appliance which makes the metalwork live, the voltage on the metalwork cannot rise very high above earth voltage – there is only the low impedance of the earthing conductor keeping them apart; the other is that the current drawn from the supply be-

WARNING: Electricity can kill; read pages 61–66 and disconnect the supply before starting work.

comes very large – there is only the impedance of the supply conductor, the earth conductor and the earth to limit it. This high current is detected by a fuse or circuit-breaker, which will interrupt the flow as a result, and make the circuit wiring and the appliance dead.

Any wiring circuit should have an earth continuity conductor running alongside the main circuit conductors. The earth is connected to any electrical accessories which have an earth terminal; where there is no terminal (eg on a light switch) it goes to a terminal on the steel mounting box (if there is one). All the earths in the house are connected to a central earth point – usually the outer metal sheath of the Electricity Board's underground service cable. Sometimes the Board uses a different form of earthing – called Protective Multiple Earthing. With this system, all the house earth conductors are connected to the neutral of the Board's service cable.

All metal pipework in the house – gas, water, central heating – needs to be earthed, too. The business of connecting these metal systems to the wiring earth is called **cross-bonding.**

Fuses consist of short links of conductor with two well-defined properties: they have a relatively high resistance, so that they generate considerable heat when a fault current flows through them; and they melt when the rate of production of heat exceeds the design level – or, to put it another way, when the excess current which is generating the heat exceeds a certain level.

There are three main circumstances in which a fuse will interrupt the circuit and prevent risks of fire or shock:
● if too big a load is being put on a circuit,

FUSES FOR PROTECTION

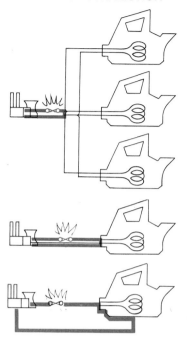

Top: if you overload a properly fused circuit, the fuse will blow
Below: if a short-circuit causes an increase in current, the fuse will blow
Bottom: if a big current leaks to earth, the fuse will blow

perhaps because too many appliances have been connected to it, the fuse should sense that the current being drawn is too high, and cut it off
● if a fault develops which results in a drop in the impedance of an appliance, the fuse should sense the resulting increase in the current being drawn
● if electricity is leaking to earth, either directly or through the earthing conductor to which appliances have their exposed metalwork connected, the total current being drawn will be increased,

and this should be sensed.

Circuit breakers are gadgets which perform the same sort of function as a fuse; miniature circuit breakers (MCBs) are used simply as a substitute for fuses – they have certain advantages of convenience, reliability and precision. But there are also particular types of circuit-breaker which can give protection of a sort that is not possible with fuses. These are earth-leakage circuit-breakers (ELCBs); they detect the flow of very small amounts of electricity from the circuit to earth – amounts which would be nowhere near big enough to blow a fuse but which would be big enough to give fatal shocks. ELCBs cannot do some of the things fuses can do, however – they do not detect faults which result in a large current in the live and neutral conductors but no current to earth; so an ELCB must always be used in conjunction with fuses or miniature circuit-breakers.

The effectiveness of earthing and fuses in cutting off the supply to a circuit or an appliance when its exposed metalwork has become live is very dependent on the effectiveness of the earth connection to the appliance – and this can deteriorate without there being any outward indication. An alternative way of avoiding the risk of live exposed metalwork on an appliance is **double insulation.** In this case, the appliance has no earth connection but has two separate sets of insulation between the live parts and the metal body – or, more often has no metal body at all but has a plastic body which acts as the second, outer layer of insulation between the user and the live parts. Double insulated appliances still need protecting with fuses.

Types of fuse and ratings
There are two basic types of fuse.
Rewirable fuses have a piece of special fuse wire running between two screw terminals; when the fuse blows, melting the wire between the terminals, the remaining bits of wire are removed from these terminals and a new piece of the appropriate rating is fitted in place. Re-

wirable fuses used to be the norm, and there are still many fuse boards fitted with them; you can also still buy the hardware to install them in a new system.

Cartridge fuses are better. With these, the fuse wire is enclosed in a small capsule with metal ends designed to fit into clips; when the fuse blows, a new fuse of

the appropriate rating is fitted in place of the old one. The 3A and 13A fuses to fit in rectangular-pin plugs are of this sort. One of their advantages is that they can be made more precisely than ordinary fuse wire, so they blow at currents which can be more accurately predicted.

In practice, this means that cartridge fuses can be designed to blow at currents which are closer to the *rated* current of the fuse – the current it has to be able to carry without blowing; and this means better protection. A second advantage is that mistakes in replacing a cartridge fuse are less likely than mistakes in re-wiring the other sort; in house wiring, cartridge fuses of different ratings are of different sizes, so they cannot be confused. This is very important, because one of the main things that house-wiring fuses have to do is protect against over-loads of the system, and the wrong fuse could allow an overload to go unde-tected for a long time – perhaps until some damage results.

The fuses in 13-amp plugs and fused spur units are always small cartridge types; they are supposed to be rated as 13A or 3A, but other ratings – 5A, for example – are sometimes found in the shops. All are the same physical size but have a different colour code. In theory you should use 3A fuses for all ap-pliances rated at below 750W, but in practice you do not create any great hazard by using 13A fuses throughout; the main consequence is that there may be slightly more damage to an appliance in the event of a fault, because the 13A fuse will take fractionally longer to blow.

TYPES OF FUSE

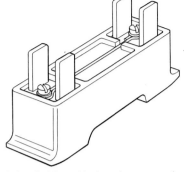

A rewirable fuseholder with the fuse wire in an enclosed insulating tube; to check whether it has blown, tug on the ends with a screwdriver

A fuseholder with the wire exposed – so it's obvious as soon as you pull it out whether that fuse has blown

Cartridge fuses for house wiring (left) are essentially the same as those used in plugs (right), but bigger

The cartridge fuse sits in a holder; to check whether the fuse has gone you need a multimeter or continuity tester

Circuit breakers

The type of circuit-breaker that replaces a fuse is usually called a **miniature circuit breaker (MCB)**. It is much the same size as a fuse-holder, and in some cases is interchangeable in the same consumer units. With some brands, however, the consumer units are different and have different terminals.

MCBs give even more precise protec-tion than cartridge fuses; on the other hand, they cost considerably more. When they blow, they are simply reset instead of needing replacement or rewir-ing; obviously this could represent a sav-ing if faults occurred very often, but in practice they should not, and the main bonus is the convenience of being able to restore the supply without delay, once the fault has been put right. Another advantage is that MCBs can be used as switches to turn off individual circuits.

In some areas it is difficult to provide the house with an earth connection which is good enough to guarantee the efficient operation of fuses and the avoi-dance of shocks. In these circumstances the local Electricity Board will advise on the installation of an **earth leakage cir-cuit breaker** (ELCB); it may be of a type which senses a rise in voltage on the house earth conductor, or it may be of a type which senses any difference be-tween the current flowing in the live and neutral conductors – if there is any cur-rent flowing to earth, there has to be a difference between these currents.

Where an ELCB is being installed as additional protection in a house with an adequate earth connection, it should al-ways be of the second, **current-operated** type. Use a 100mA ELCB for protecting the whole house and a 30mA one for protecting a single circuit.

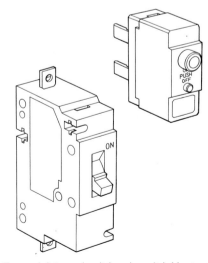

Top: miniature circuit breakers 'trip' instead of 'blowing' – on this type the big button pops out. The smaller button is to test the operation of the breaker

Below: an earth leakage circuit breaker

WARNING: Electricity can kill; read pages 61–66 and disconnect the supply before starting work.

Flex and cable

Electricity is carried around the house to sockets, fixed appliance outlets and ceiling roses by **cable**. Appliances which are permanently fixed in position on the wall, floor or ceiling may be directly served by the house wiring cable if the cable is not subjected to overheating. But most appliances, even the less mobile ones, are usually connected to the fixed wiring by a length of **flex** (short for flexible cord). It gets its flexibility by having conductors made up of many fine strands, whereas cable conductors are thicker and often a single wire.

The two kinds of wire should not be confused; in particular, cable should never be used in a situation where it is not fixed to a support of some kind.

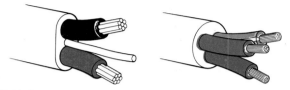

Cable has relatively few, thick strands; flex has more, finer ones

Cable

Cable generally has three conductors – one surrounded by red insulation (normally used as the *live* conductor), one by black (the *neutral*) and the third uninsulated (the *earth continuity conductor*). The three conductors are enclosed in a plastic sheath, with the earth between the two insulated conductors. This sort of cable is called **flat twin and earth** (or two-core and earth).

The complexity of some lighting circuits is such that it is sometimes necessary to use **three-core and earth** cable; the cores have red, blue and yellow insulation. The uses of this are explained in the lighting section starting on page 75. In concrete buildings and in big buildings in general, the wiring is often run in metal or high-impact plastic tubes called **conduit**; in this case, there is no need for a sheath to protect the insulation – the wiring consists simply of a lot of separately insulated **single-core** cable.

Modern cable has plastic insulation and sheathing; but in old houses there may be rubber insulation with rubber or lead sheathing. This sort of cable has not been used for many years, and will now be near (or beyond) the end of its safe working life. There are also other forms of cable available for special applications.

Choosing cable

In practice, most of the wiring in domestic installations is done in just two sizes: 1.0mm^2 for lighting circuits and 2.5mm^2 for socket circuits and many fixed appliances. Only very heavy-loading appliances, such as shower heaters and cookers, or some radial socket outlet circuits, require the use of thicker conductors – see *Special circuits* on page 80.

There are two types of special cable available, one of which is gaining wider applications in domestic wiring. This is **mineral-insulated copper-clad (MICC)** cable with two or more conductors embedded in a heatproof compacted powder, surrounded by a copper tube sheath which acts as the earth conductor. It is used where long life and reduced fire hazard are desired. It is used with a plastic outer sheath underground or where it is likely to be exposed to chemicals which could damage the copper sheath. Underground circuits can also be run in **armoured** cable – much like a conventional cable except that it has a steel wire layer wrapped around the

sheath.

There have been experiments with cables using aluminium instead of copper; a successful version with a copper layer around the aluminium conductors was produced – called Copperclad. The advantage of aluminium is that it is cheaper, the drawback that it has to be bigger to offer the same current capacity: it has not been widely adopted.

Flex

Flex comes in many more varieties than cable. In its simplest form it has only two conductors with insulation of the same colour as the protective sheath; the two conductors may lie parallel, embedded in the same insulation, or may be twisted together. **Parallel twin flex** should have a rib running along the side of one of the

CABLES

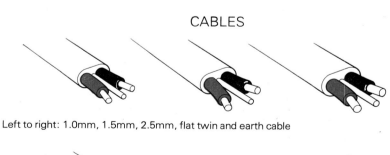

Left to right: 1.0mm, 1.5mm, 2.5mm, flat twin and earth cable

Left to right: 4.0mm, 6.0mm, 10.0mm, flat twin and earth cable

two cores; this core is the one which should be used as the live conductor. **Twisted** flex does not even have this easily-overlooked means of identifying the cores.

More generally useful is **two-core sheathed** flex, with colour-coded insulation on the cores: brown for live, blue for neutral. On appliances sold before about 1970, the code is different: red for live, black for neutral (the same code that is still used for cable).

Where there is a need for an earth connection, **three-core sheathed** flex is used. The insulation of the earth conductor is green and yellow, or just green on older appliances.

Most flex these days has plastic insulation and sheathing; but there are special flexes with rubber insulation or sheathing, or with heat-resistant insulation and sheathing – for use with some heating appliances, for example.

FLEX

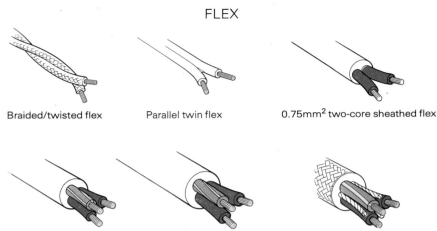

Braided/twisted flex   Parallel twin flex   0.75mm² two-core sheathed flex

1.0mm², three-core sheathed flex 1.5mm² three-core sheathed flex Unkinkable braided flex

Choosing flex

The first thing is to make sure that a flex with the right number of cores is used. This does not only mean using three-core when there is an earth connection to be made; it also means avoiding three-core when there isn't an earth – spare cores make confusion in wiring more likely.

Circular or flat sheathed flex should be used unless the flex is to be used for things like pendant light fittings when twisted cores are acceptable.

The size of conductor to use is determined mainly by the current to be drawn by the appliance being connected. The Table shows the relationship, and also the power of appliance which corresponds to the different current ratings. When using very long flexes – on tools used in the garden, for example – you may need to use a thicker flex than the current rating requires.

Flexes sometimes need to be thicker than the requirements of current capacity and length suggest: where the flex has to stand a lot of handling and battering, bigger conductors make it less likely to be damaged. And the flex used for pendant light fittings needs to be stout enough to support the fitting (unless it is

the very heavy sort with its own supporting chain).

As a rough guide, two-core flex can be expected to support as many pounds in weight as it can carry amps of current.

There are three main sorts of special flex. Where it has to withstand a lot of abuse – in particular, where it may get squashed or rub on sharp edges, the flex should have **tough rubber sheathing (TRS)** which is more resistant to that sort of thing than the usual PVC. Where the flex is used to supply some heaters – storage heaters and immersion heaters, for example – it should have **heat-resistant insulation and sheath**; most domestic heaters (fan heaters, radiant bar fires and so on) are designed so that the flex does not get hot, so ordinary flex will do; but heat resistant insulation is desirable for pendant light fittings, particularly when used with high-power bulbs and for some appliances which have hot external surfaces. The third special flex is called **unkinkable** – it coils neatly and controllably rather than tangling in the way that normal PVC flex tends to (this helps it to keep out of harm's way) and it withstands constant twisting and movement with less likelihood of the core conductors breaking.

Other sorts of wire

All that has been said so far is about cable and flex for use at mains voltages.

The two other sorts of wire used in houses are: flimsy, thinly insulated flex for use at **low voltages** – in wiring a door bell run from batteries or from a low-voltage transformer, for example; and **coaxial aerial cable**, meant to carry the very small signals from a radio or TV aerial down to the set with the least possible loss of signal and pick-up of interference. Neither must be used for mains wiring; there is nothing (apart from cost) against the use of heftier cable or flex in place of low voltage flex, but ordinary twin-core cable is not a substitute for coaxial cable in an aerial lead.

Coaxial cable is strictly for aerial wiring; it's quite different from ordinary cable

FLEX SIZE AND RATING

Flex size mm²	current rating A	appliance power W
0.5	3	720
0.75	6	1440
1.0	10	2400
1.25	13	3120
1.5	15	3600

WARNING: Electricity can kill; read pages 61–66 and disconnect the supply before starting work.

Getting to grips with your wiring

This section looks at how the wiring in a house is actually arranged, and how you should go about deciding what work to do.

The supply to the house

Electricity is generated in power stations and then distributed at very high voltages to sub-stations, where it is transformed to the mains voltage at which it is used. It is fed to individual houses usually through an underground **service cable**; in country areas, it is often brought to the house by means of overhead wires instead.

Once the supply comes into the house, it immediately goes through a single, large **service fuse**, contained in a sealed box. Next, it goes through a **meter**, which measures the amount of electrical energy drawn from the supply. If the house has electric storage heaters, or if off-peak electricity is used for some other purpose, there may be two meters – one for cheaper, off-peak electricity and the other for normal-price electricity (since

1970 it has been usual to install a composite or *white* meter to register both tariff supplies).

Everything up to and including the meter is the property of the Electricity Board; the meter is connected to the household installation by hefty, short pieces of single-core cable called **meter tails**; these belong to the householder but cannot be connected to or disconnected from the meter except by the Board – there are seals on the meter to prevent tampering, or at least to show that tampering has been going on. The service fuse, similarly, can be replaced or repaired only by the Board – but in normal circumstances it should never blow: it is rated at something like 60 to 100 amps, and any fault should blow one of the household fuses and leave the service fuse intact. The fuse is there to give a last line of defence in case the householder somehow manages to render his own fuses inoperative.

The meter tails lead to one or more switches which are in turn connected to the smaller fuses protecting the final

sub-circuits of the installation. In some systems, where not all the wiring between the meter and the sub-circuit fuses matches the rating of the Board's service fuse, there is a suitable consumer's fuse in the circuit between the switch and the fuse-board.

The house fuses and circuits

There are two sorts of circuit found in houses, and it is important to distinguish between them.

In some circuits, a single fuse protects the fixed wiring, the flex to the appliance and the appliance itself; so the cable and flex must have the same current rating as (or a higher rating than) the fuse. In modern British wiring practice, this sort of circuit is used only for lighting circuits and for circuits supplying individual high-power appliances such as immersion heaters or shower heaters. But before the Second World War sockets were wired on this sort of circuit, too.

Each socket usually (though not necessarily) had its own cable leading from its own fuse mounted (along with lots of others) on a large distribution board (more commonly called a fuseboard). To avoid the waste of having low-power appliances being fed by heavy cables and flexes, and to provide the appliances with the best possible fuse protection, houses were wired with circuits and sockets of different current ratings – usually 15A and 5A, and sometimes 2A as well.

The second sort of circuit is that used in modern socket systems; the appliance and its flex are protected by their own local fuse, the fixed wiring circuit by another. The point of this is that the many 5A and 15A circuits of the old system can be replaced by a few (maybe only one) heavier circuit, protected by an appropriately heavy fuse, and that flexes of lower current ratings can be connected to it through lower-rated fuses.

The fuses for the fixed wiring are mounted in a **consumer unit**, which

HOUSE SUPPLIES

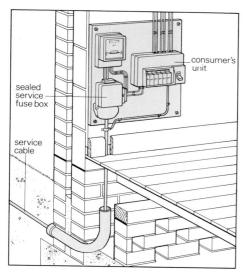

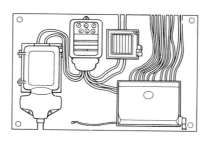

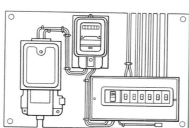

Electricity comes into your house along the service cable and goes through the Board's service fuse and meter before it gets to the individual house circuits

An old system is liable to be a bit chaotic, and may have many circuits emerging from a big fuseboard; modern consumer units tend to have fewer circuits

Left and top: older style plugs and sockets –
5A and 13A. Right: modern 13A plugs

amounts to a small fuse-board with a switch built in to control the whole installation. The smaller local fuses are mounted in the rectangular-pin 13-amp plugs that are used with this sort of circuit, or, for fixed appliances, in special fused connection units.

The heavy cable is usually (though not always) run in the form of a ring, starting and finishing at the consumer unit; this provides two routes for current to flow to any point on the ring. These circuits are often called **ring circuits** (or ring mains).

Old or new installations may have circuits added; so there may be more than one fuse-board or consumer unit. If only one circuit has been added – a single ring circuit, say – this may be wired through a **switchfuse**: a single fuseholder and switch combined.

The differences between old and new lighting circuits are not so profound – there are two common wiring techniques in use, and either may be found in old and new installations. But a modern installation is most likely to use the **loop-in** system and an old installation is more likely to use the **junction box** (or joint box) system.

In the loop-in system, the main circuit runs from the fuse to each ceiling rose in turn, with a cable running out from each rose to the corresponding switch. In the junction box system, the main circuit runs through a series of junction boxes; from each one a cable runs out to the corresponding switch and another goes to the ceiling rose. This is explained in detail in *Lighting circuits* starting on page 75, along with the mysteries of two-way switching (the sort of arrangement that allows the light on the stairs, for example, to be controlled from either upstairs or downstairs).

What's what

Whether you have several antique fuse-boards or a compact consumer unit, there should be labels showing clearly which circuit is which and what rating of fuse should be fitted.

If your system is not marked like this, it is worth working out for yourself what's what and either sticking labels on the fuse carriers or drawing up a chart. Make sure you do the same with new circuits.

Assessing the wiring

First of all, think about any obvious signs that all is not well:
● if fuses blow regularly, is it always the same circuit that's involved or always the same appliance? If a circuit seems to be at fault, it should be looked into without delay – there could be a leakage through poor insulation which carries the risk of fire
● if there is any sign of overheating – warm plugs or switches, charred sockets, suspicious smells – the most likely cause is a poor connection; the screw terminals (or, with 13-amp plugs, the fuseholder) of a plug are more likely to be the source of trouble than the fixed wiring connections.

Next, how fully does the system meet the needs of the household?

OLD WIRING

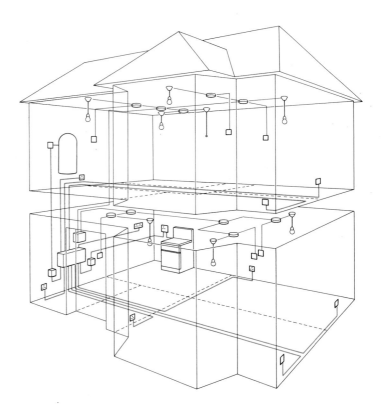

Old wiring will almost always have round-pin sockets often with individual cables running to them. To provide homes with the best possible fuse protection, homes were wired with circuits and sockets of different current ratings. It is likely to use the junction-box system for wiring to lights

WARNING: Electricity can kill; read pages 61–66 and disconnect the supply before starting work.

● there should be no need to use adaptors to provide enough sockets – because they stick out some distance from the wall, adaptors increase the danger of some damage being done to the plug, to socket contacts by a tug on the flex or a blow from a boot

● there should not be long flexes trailing across the floor – apart from the risk of tripping over them, the flex conductors can be damaged by being squashed under chairs and so on.

It is worth trying to determine the type of insulation used in the wiring, and its age: pre-war wiring will have been done with rubber-insulated or lead-sheathed cable, and the rubber will probably have perished by now – particularly where it has been hot (in ceiling roses, for example). More recent rubber insulation (it

was used until the early fifties) may have more life left in it, but not much.

The differences between rubber and plastic are quite pronounced – rubber is dull and matt in appearance, slightly elastic in feel (unless it is perished, when it becomes crumbly); plastic is more shiny and bright. The sheath around a rubber-insulated cable will probably be of rubber itself, oval in cross-section and black in colour; plastic-insulated cable will usually have a flat plastic sheath, grey or white.

The type of sockets used in the house can give only a rough guide to the age of the installation – although post-war wiring will normally have rectangular-pin sockets and pre-war systems round-pin ones, rectangular-pin sockets may have been used to replace round-pin ones

without the wiring being updated.

Look out for signs that the wiring was installed or has been extended without care; if the cable has not been laid and secured neatly, there is some cause for worry about whether connections have been made properly.

Deciding what to do

If you have what appears to be a fairly recent and sound rubber-insulated system, there are two alternative attitudes to adopt. One is to say that the wiring still has some useful life left in it; if the system does not give you enough sockets, it can be supplemented by new additional circuits. The other is to say that the wiring will inevitably need replacing before long, and that since rewiring won't get any cheaper it might as well be done now; by doing so you lessen the risk of dangerous faults developing in the future, can give yourself the benefit of a more convenient system, and possibly increase the value of your house.

Getting help

If you are in doubt about the state of the existing wiring, it makes sense to get help in assessing it. Electricians and Electricity Boards can provide various sorts of help, from a quick look around to a detailed set of electrical measurements and thorough inspections. See *Handyman Which?*, August 1980. Electricity Boards are likely to do the most thorough inspections; electrical contractors on the roll of the NICEIC (National Inspection Council for Electrical Installation Contracting) are also worth contacting. From the standard report form used, it is not always easy to tell what needs to be done to put things right – you may have to ask the contractor.

The total load

If you decide to make any changes which add to the total current which the household can draw from the supply, you need to be sure that the Board's equipment – the service main, the service fuse and the meter – and your own main switch (whether it is separate or part of a consumer's unit) can take the new total current.

NEW WIRING

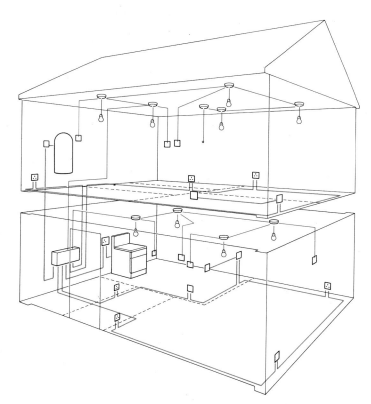

New wiring almost always has ring circuits to serve 13A rectangular-pin sockets with separate supplies for appliances such as an electrical water heater or a cooker. Loop-in wiring to the lights is common. The colours above (and left) do not represent wiring colours – they have been used to illustrate the different circuits

Socket circuits

You can still buy round-pin 5A and 15A sockets, but the advantages of fused plugs make it unlikely that you will want to install new circuits using anything other than rectangular-pin 13A sockets. The Wiring Regs allow four different arrangements with these sockets. The main point about the limitations imposed by the Regs is not that they guarantee safety – for safety, as well as the correct fuse for the cable you have to make sure that the circuit is *installed* safely; the Regs prescribe circuits which are also likely to prove satisfactory in practice – that is, not likely to result in lots of fuse-blowing with the loads most people will put on them. So you might feel able to bend some of the rules to suit your own circumstances; you might, for example, feel justified in stretching the floor area limits given below – the wiring would then, of course, not comply with the Regs.

1 The most common set-up is the **ring circuit**, using 2.5mm^2 cable which starts from the consumer unit or switchfuse, runs from socket to socket around the house and returns to the terminals where it started. The circuit is protected by a 30A fuse.

Ring circuits are allowed to have **spurs** connected to the main ring; each can serve a single fixed appliance, or one or two sockets. A spur can run from the terminals of an outlet on the ring or from the consumer unit, or from a junction box provided for the purpose. Although the biggest current that can in theory be drawn from such a spur is $2 \times 13A = 26A$, it can be run in the same cable as the ring – rated at only 20A. The number of spurs is limited to the number of sockets and fused connection units which are on the ring itself.

There is no limit on the number of sockets or fused connection units which a ring circuit can serve. The logic of this is that the use of many appliances in the home does not imply the use of a lot of power. The reason so many sockets are needed in homes is the number of low-power appliances that people own – TVs, hi-fi, kitchen gadgets, lamps and so on – rather than heaters. What may imply the use of a lot of power (or, at least, the possibility of using a lot of power) is having a lot of space to heat; so the Regs say that one ring can supply no more than 100m^2 of floor space.

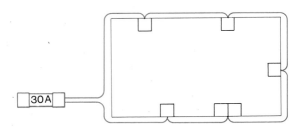

2 Radial circuits are allowed to serve individual rooms only. The same size of cable that is used for ring circuits can be used, but must be protected by a 20A fuse; such a circuit can feed up to six sockets as long as the room is not a kitchen (or a room with water-heating appliances such as a kettle or washing machine) and is not more than 30m^2 in floor area.

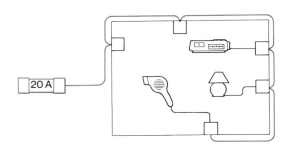

3 A similar radial circuit which is serving a room which *is* a kitchen or a room which is over 30m^2 in area can have only two sockets on it.

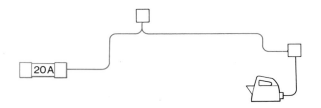

4 A radial circuit serving a kitchen or a bigger room can have up to six sockets if it uses 4mm^2 cable and has a 30A fuse.

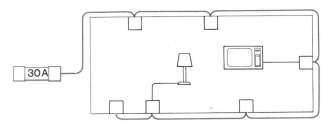

These cable sizes will be satisfactory for most purposes; but if you want to run cables next to one another for a considerable distance, or if the cables are going to have to stand unusually high temperatures, you should use bigger sizes.

WARNING: Electricity can kill; read pages 61–66 and disconnect the supply before starting work.

What you need

The great blessing of the 13A socket system is that having lots of sockets need not cost very much more than having only a few. And since the ownership of electrical gadgets is increasing all the time, it makes sense to install a generous number of sockets when doing any work on socket circuits.

There are published standards for the minimum number of sockets that should be provided in different rooms of the house – but they are not of much help if you want to end up with a genuinely flexible and adequate system. What matters is how you use your rooms, what electrical gadgets you own and how you want to use them.

Start with a rough plan of each floor of the house, and make a list of the things you want to be able to plug in (or connect permanently); then mark the position in which the outlets for those appliances would be most convenient. Think then about alternative arrangements; will you ever want the TV in a different corner, or a different room? Think also about the appliances you do not own but might acquire in the future – hi-fi units needing four or five sockets, more machines in the kitchen?

Be particularly careful about any corners or long stretches of wall where your first plans show no need for sockets; is there really no chance that you will want an outlet there in the future?

Bear in mind, as you plan, that you may save time and effort at the wiring stage if you can install sockets in adjacent rooms back-to-back.

Detailed planning

Once the places where sockets are needed (or may be needed) have been established, it is worth thinking about how they can most easily and economically be wired.

When adding to an existing system with PVC wiring in good condition, use a diagram of the circuit as your starting point. Can extra sockets be wired into the existing circuit? Can they be wired on spurs from existing sockets or from junction boxes? How much can be gained by simply converting existing single sockets to double ones?

If you need new circuits, what would be the most effective arrangement? A single ring for the whole house? Separate rings for each floor? A combination of ring and radial circuits?

THE SOCKETS YOU NEED

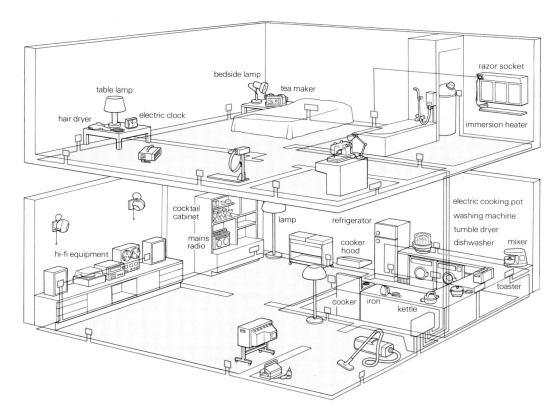

This houseful of electrical appliances may help you put together a full list of the electrical appliances you have around your house. When you have a list, you need to think about which electrical appliances are likely to be used where, which ones will need to occupy a socket full-time and which ones can 'borrow' a socket when you want to use them.

The hardware

Sockets may be surface-mounted or flush-mounted. Flush-mounted ones are not completely flush with the surrounding wall, but they do stick out less and look neater; on the other hand, they take more work to install – a hole in the wall must be made to accommodate the box to which the socket is fixed. Surface-mounted sockets are not particularly stylish, and even when opting for surface mounting you may prefer to use flush-mounted sockets in combination with plastic pattresses.

Sockets are available with and without switches; switched sockets are better – they can be used to turn off appliances which have no switch themselves, or to isolate things like TVs where the normal advice is to unplug them when they are not is use. Sockets are also available with red neon lights to show when they are switched on.

The one essential feature of **fused connection units** is the fuse; they may or may not have a flex outlet in the face or on one edge, or a switch, or a neon indicator light. Which sort you need depends on the particular job you are doing; but switched units are often needed – they should be used unless you plan to install a separate switch nearby to control the appliance.

Flush-mounted accessories have to be mounted in steel boxes fixed in the wall; there are different depths of box, and it is important to have ones which are deep enough for the accessories being used. When working on hard walls, it may be worth choosing a series of accessories which need relatively shallow boxes.

SOCKETS AND ACCESSORIES

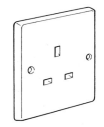 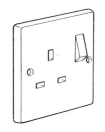

Flush-mounting 13A sockets, in unswitched and switched versions

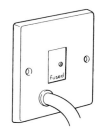 

Fused connection units; you can have any combination of 'extras' – flex outlet, switch and neon – or none at all

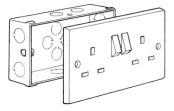

Some brands of socket will fit in a relatively shallow steel box

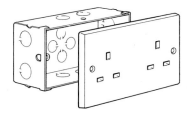

Others have to be used with the standard, full-depth boxes

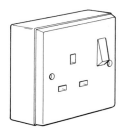

A flush-mounting socket becomes a surface-mounting socket when used with a plastic pattress

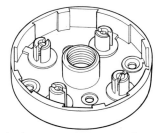

Junction boxes vary in current rating – socket circuits need heftier ones than lighting circuits

Spurs to ring circuits can be wired from the terminals of sockets or fused connection units on the ring itself; but they can also be wired from other points, using **junction boxes** (or joint boxes) – simply a set of screw terminals inside a plastic case. The current rating must be at least 20A.

Bathrooms

You need to be particularly careful about electricity in the bathroom: not only is there usually a lot of metalwork with good connections to earth, but people also immerse themselves in water, which can mean that their bodies provide a good path to earth. The Wiring Regs prohibit ordinary sockets in bathrooms; all that is allowed is special shaver sockets which incorporate a **transformer**. What these achieve in practice is to isolate the shaver from the mains circuit – even when a live part of the shaver and an earthed tap are touched there would not be a complete circuit for a current to flow along.

Shaver sockets are specially designed for use in bathrooms

WARNING: Electricity can kill; read pages 61–66 and disconnect the supply before starting work.

Lighting circuits

The basic circuit that is necessary to make a lamp work is very simple: a live wire with a switch in it and a neutral wire. In practice, sheathed twin-core cable (or two-core and earth in lighting circuits which need to be earthed – see next page) is more likely to be used.

In the **junction-box** (or joint-box) system, a twin cable provides a live and neutral connection to a series of junction boxes – usually one for each switch. Another twin cable runs out of each junction-box to the switch; one core is the live supply to the switch, the other the switched return, which is live or not, according to the switch position. A further twin cable runs out to the ceiling rose; one core is connected to the switched return from the switch, the other to the neutral connection to the junction box.

In the **loop-in** system, the junction box and the ceiling rose are effectively combined. The main live and neutral conductors run from rose to rose instead of box to box.

Either system can have advantages over the other for a particular circuit; the loop-in system has fewer connections, and saves on the cost of a junction box, but the junction-box system can save on cable – and there may be no alternative with some light fittings which do not have all the terminals needed for the loop-in system.

The drawings show red and black insulation on the cores of the switch cables; this is what is often used in practice, but is strictly not allowed by the Regs because it results in a black-insulated core being live when the light is switched on. If you adopt this corner-cutting (to avoid having to buy special all-red cable), do at least put red insulation tape around the black insulation where it is visible – at the ends.

LIGHTING CIRCUITS

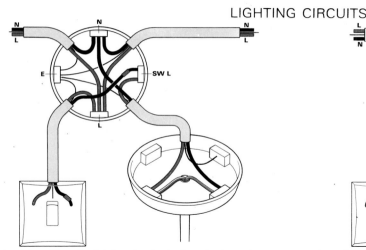

Junction-box wiring of a lighting circuit: the junction box takes most of the connections, and the ceiling rose is simply the point where cable and flex meet. There is one junction box for each switch

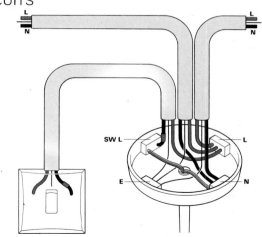

Loop-in wiring of a lighting circuit: the junction box is effectively built into the ceiling rose, which therefore has many more connections. Some light fittings do not have enough terminals for loop-in wiring

Two-way switching

It is quite common to need to be able to switch lights on and off from more than one place – either end of the hall, say, or top and bottom of the stairs, or by the bedroom door and over the bed. Again, it is easiest to see what you are trying to achieve by looking first at how such a circuit could be wired with single-core cable.

Instead of a single on-off switch in the supply line, two switches are needed, each with three terminals instead of the ordinary two. The live supply goes to the common terminal of one switch; the common terminal of the other provides the switched supply to the lamp. The two remaining pairs of terminals are connected by a pair of *strapping* wires. The result

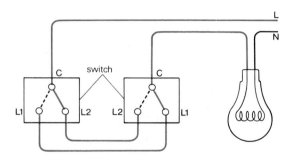

The theory behind two-way switching – the live supply goes to the common terminals (C) on the switches; the remaining terminals (L1, L2) are connected by strapping wires

is that, whatever the position of one switch, the light can always be controlled from the other switch.

In practice, the use of sheathed cable makes the wiring rather more complicated; either the loop-in or junction-box system can be used, but the two switches have to be connected together with three-core cable. The drawing shows how this arrangement works.

Sometimes there is a need for a light to be controlled from more than two places. This is done with special intermediate switches which come between the two two-way switches.

In all of this there has been no mention of earth connections; old lighting circuits often do not have earths, but new ones should have, in case a light fitting is installed which has a metal body and so needs earthing, or in case metal switch plates are used. The drawings show earth conductors throughout. If you are thinking of fitting metal lights or switches to an existing system, make sure it has an earth connection – or install one yourself.

TWO-WAY SWITCHING

In practice, the two-way switching effect as shown on the previous page is achieved by rather more complicated means, using sheathed three-core and earth cable

Cables and fuses

Lighting circuits are normally run with $1.0mm^2$ cable; although this would be adequately protected by a 10A fuse, it is more usual to fit 5A fuses. Allowing for the use of 100W bulbs, you could have up to 12 lampholders on one circuit with a 5A fuse though 10 is more usual. If you do use a 10A fuse so as to be able to run more lights from the one circuit, you may begin to have problems with excessive voltage-drop along the cable: when carrying 10A, the length of $1.0mm^2$ cable should not be more than 15m from fuse to the furthest lamp. The use of $1.5mm^2$ cable allows you to go to about 25m. In practice it makes more sense to install more than one circuit even in a quite small house – then if a fuse blows, there will still be light in part of the house.

How much light, and where?

Lighting a room to make it an efficient workplace is a considerable science; lighting one to make it a welcoming, comfortable place to be in is an equally considerable art.

What follows is no more than an outline of the possibilities.

Light levels

There is a lot of information available on what levels of light are necessary to avoid eye strain when doing certain sorts of activity; but in practice this sort of information is difficult to use in designing a domestic lighting system.

The first thing to decide is the extent to which you want the fixed lighting system (ie the lights fixed to the ceiling or walls rather than lights plugged into sockets) to cope with the different demands you are likely to place on any one room. For relaxing in front of the TV, you may want a very low level of light; for cleaning the carpet, a considerably higher one; for reading the paper, higher still; and for sewing, a very high one. You may decide that the basic room lighting needs to cope with only one of these – carpet cleaning, say. Table lamps could then provide mood lighting (with the main lights off), a standard light could be used for reading, and very directional lighting from an anglepoise-type lamp for sewing. If you want the built-in lighting to be more versatile, it will take a lot more designing.

There are particular things to think about in each room of the house.

Living room Are many different activities (perhaps with conflicting light requirements) going to be happening at one time? Are there particular places in the room where higher-than-normal levels will often be wanted – over the hi-fi, say? Are there particular things

you would like to light relatively brightly – pictures, for example? The more lights you have, and the more directional the light they give, the more likely it is that you will be able to match varying needs.

Dining room Do you want specific light over the dining table, and perhaps the sideboard? Do you want some background lighting for romantic candle-lit dinners?

Bedrooms How bright and how directional do you want your bedside lights to be? Are you likely to want to use the room for another purpose – as a playroom or study, say? Do you want particularly good lighting at the dressing table? What about getting adequate light on to the contents of wardrobes?

Kitchen Are you likely to block out the light from a ceiling fitting when working at the sink, cooker or wherever? Would lights under wall cupboards be a better idea? Or carefully placed spotlights?

Hall, stairs, landing Where could light fittings be best placed to give high overall light levels, but still show up clearly the edges of the stair treads?

Types of light source

Any source of light produces light of a

WARNING: Electricity can kill; read pages 61–66 and disconnect the supply before starting work.

characteristic colour, although the eye rarely recognises the fact unless two sources are compared alongside one another. Ordinary light bulbs produce their light from a hot filament of tungsten; compared to daylight, this is very yellow, warm-seeming. The main other sort of lamp is the fluorescent tube, which produces its light from a coating on the inside of the glass tube – the light is given off as a result of an electrical discharge along the length of the tube. These tubes are available with different coatings which give light of different colours; most are bluer or colder than tungsten light (though some only just so) and there are tubes with an effect very similar to daylight.

Fluorescent tubes are much more efficient than tungsten lamps – for a given power they produce much more light and less heat; in spite of this they are not very popular for domestic lighting, except in kitchens – their colour and shape mean that they are not easy to use to create a welcoming atmosphere.

Switching and dimming

In any room, some thought needs to be given to where switches would be most convenient, and to the desirability of having two-way or intermediate switching so that lights can be controlled from more than one place. Obviously, this need is most acute in rooms with more than one door to them.

If your plan involves having more than one lamp in any room, consider whether it would be valuable to have the different lamps switched separately rather than being all on or all off.

Another way of varying light levels – expensive but giving good control – is to use dimmers. These are switches with knobs which allow you to turn the brightness up and down.

Lamps and fittings

Most light fittings used in the home take ordinary light bulbs – more properly called **general lighting service (GLS)** lamps. The usual sort of lamp in Britain has a bayonet cap; to fit the lamp it

should be pushed into its holder and twisted clockwise a little. On some imported fittings and some special types of lamp the Edison screw (ES) cap is used; it is screwed into the holder.

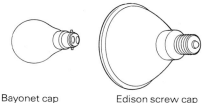

Bayonet cap   Edison screw cap

There is a great range of fittings designed to take ordinary lamps. The simplest are nothing more than lampholders, which leave the bulb exposed unless a shade is fitted. Ones which are meant to be mounted directly on walls or ceilings are called battenholders; many are open at the back and should be used with a backing plate to enclose the terminals. There are two-terminal and three-terminal versions for junction-box and loop-in wiring systems; both have an extra terminal for the earth connection. It is more usual to use pendant lampholders unless space is restricted: these hang by the flex which carries the supply from a rose on the ceiling and they should have lugs built in to them to take the strain of the complete pendant assembly on the flex – otherwise the conductors may get pulled out of their terminals. A third sort of lampholder has a large flex hole with a screw thread on the inside; these are for use in table lamps or other fittings – the screw thread is used for mounting. Some have switches.

Lampholders have a ring or skirt which screws on and off for mounting shades – the shade has to have a hole or ring of the same diameter as the lampholder. Special versions are available with an extended skirt (called a Home Office or HO skirt) to prevent anyone touching the metal lamp cap – these must be used in bathrooms and are a worthwhile precaution where the air is damp or there is a lot of earthed metalwork, such as a kitchen. Lampholders may be made of metal (in which case they must be earthed) or of plastic; where a plastic

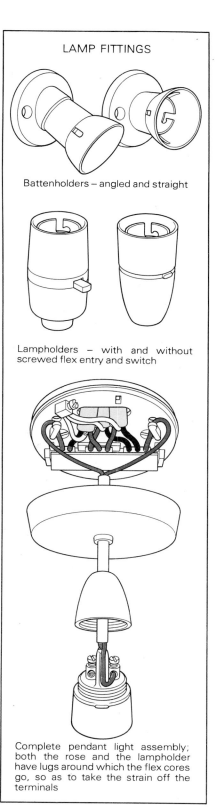

LAMP FITTINGS

Battenholders – angled and straight

Lampholders – with and without screwed flex entry and switch

Complete pendant light assembly; both the rose and the lampholder have lugs around which the flex cores go, so as to take the strain off the terminals

holder is used in an enclosed or poorly-ventilated fitting or shade and is above the lamp, it should be of heat-resisting material.

Most modern ceiling roses are flattish in shape; they consist of a round backplate, which is fixed to the ceiling and which carries the terminals, and a screw-on cover with a central flex exit hole. There are also backless types for use on conduit systems – or in an ordinary system if mounted on a pattress.

The best roses have special lugs built in for the conductors of the pendant flex to go round before going into the terminals; this avoids putting a lot of strain on the electrical connections. The terminals should have separate holes for the different conductors to go in. For joint-box wiring, you need only two terminals plus an earth in the rose; for loop-in wiring, there must be another terminal for the permanently live supply conductors.

Some rose manufacturers make special 'halo' rings to fix behind the rose and increase the area of ceiling covered.

There are some special types of rose available. If you plan to fit a heavy pendant light fitting, you need a rose with a strain terminal to which the supporting wire (separate from the conductors) can

be fixed. If you want to be able to take fittings down easily – useful for cleaning, or in rooms used for different purposes at different times – you can get detachable roses; they cost quite a lot more than the ordinary sort. There are also even more elaborate roses with a mechanism built in to allow the light to be raised and lowered; these are normally sold as a complete assembly with the flex, lampholder and shade.

The shades that are used with ordinary lampholders vary from those which give a uniform diffused light in every direction to ones which give well-defined upward or downward light (or both).

GLS lamps are used in various other sorts of fitting which are fixed directly to the wall or ceiling. Enclosed diffusing fittings are used where even lighting is needed but a decorative fitting is not – and in bathrooms, where exposed fittings might be a hazard. Directional fittings take two main forms – downlighters, which are essentially tubes fixed to or recessed into the ceiling, giving a fairly directional light unless a lens is fitted to diffuse it; and pivoting spotlights, which give beams of varying definition.

To get a better-defined spotlight beam, you have to use a different sort of

lamp. **Internally-silvered (IS)** lamps look rather like ordinary mushroom lamps in shape, but have an internal reflective coating which sends all the light out of the front in a wide beam; most have ES caps, but there are small 40W and 60W versions, the same size as ordinary lamps, with bayonet caps. You can use the smaller IS lamps in ordinary spotlight fittings instead of GLS lamps; bigger ones are used in special fittings to take the ES cap; some fittings leave the body of the lamp exposed, others enclose it.

For the best possible control of the beam, one of two rather more out-of-the-ordinary lamps should be used – either a **parabolic aluminised reflector (PAR)** lamp, with an ES fitting; or a **crown-silvered** lamp (which sends all its light back to the reflector) in conjunction with a parabolic reflector fitting.

Fluorescent tubes are usually mounted in fittings which incorporate a starter to get the discharge in the tube going; there may be a diffuser over the tube, or a reflector along both sides to direct light downwards. There are two main diameters of tubes, with the same two-pin cap at each end; the power depends on length – about 10W a foot.

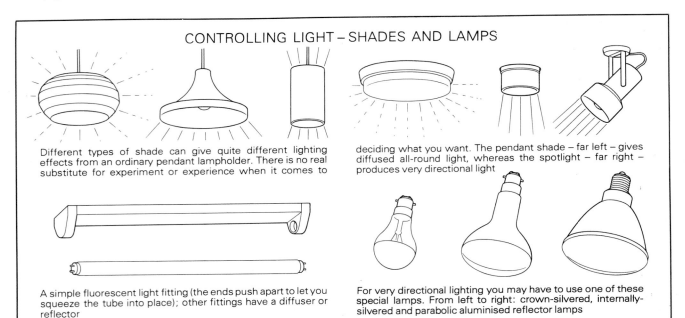

CONTROLLING LIGHT – SHADES AND LAMPS

Different types of shade can give quite different lighting effects from an ordinary pendant lampholder. There is no real substitute for experiment or experience when it comes to deciding what you want. The pendant shade – far left – gives diffused all-round light, whereas the spotlight – far right – produces very directional light

A simple fluorescent light fitting (the ends push apart to let you squeeze the tube into place); other fittings have a diffuser or reflector

For very directional lighting you may have to use one of these special lamps. From left to right: crown-silvered, internally-silvered and parabolic aluminised reflector lamps

WARNING: Electricity can kill; read pages 61–66 and disconnect the supply before starting work.

Switches

Like sockets, lighting switches may be flush-mounted or surface-mounted. The most common sort of flush-mounting switch, called a plate switch, has one or more rockers in the middle of a large flat plate – around 85mm square for one, two, or three-gang switches and double width for four, or six-gang switches. There are plastic pattresses available for surface mounting of plate switches, but normally they are flush-mounted in steel boxes. Some need boxes 25mm deep, others need only 16mm – plaster-depth – boxes. Always allow sufficient space for cable connections.

For places where there is not room to mount a plate switch, architrave switches, which are only about 30mm wide, can be used. They come in one and two-gang versions; the two rockers of the two-gang version are arranged one above the other. There are special steel boxes for these switches.

Most switches are of the two-way variety, so that they can be used in circuits where the light is controlled from two places; some one-gang switches are available in a one-way version, which should be a few pence cheaper than the two-way one. Intermediate switches, for circuits where you want switching from three or more places, are available only in one-gang versions.

Switches are normally made of plastic, but there are also metal ones – modern or traditional in style. They must be earthed. There are also various special sorts of switch with interchangeable plate finishes, and another type with a large flat rocker covering the whole front area of the switch and a detachable transparent cover behind which you can insert wallpaper, say.

Most switches have conventional screw terminals, but some have terminals into which the bare conductor can simply be pushed; they work only with metric-size cable, which has single-strand conductors; earlier, multi-strand conductors need screw terminals.

Lights can be (and in bathrooms usually must be) controlled by ceiling switches with pull-cords. There are one-way and two-way versions. Unless it is being mounted in a conduit box, a ceiling switch will usually need to be mounted on a backplate to enclose the terminals.

Dimmer switches can be used in place of ordinary switches; they go in the same sizes of steel box – though they are often only one-gang, so can take up more room in total. Fluorescent lights need special dimmer switches.

The junction boxes used in lighting circuits are usually round, with four terminals and at least a 5A rating; each terminal normally consists of a single slot into which all the conductors to be connected are put; a screw is then tightened down on to the bundle. Some boxes have knock-out sections in the body so that entries for cables can be made; a better arrangement is what is called selective entry – depending on how the body and the cover of the box are aligned, different numbers of entry holes are produced.

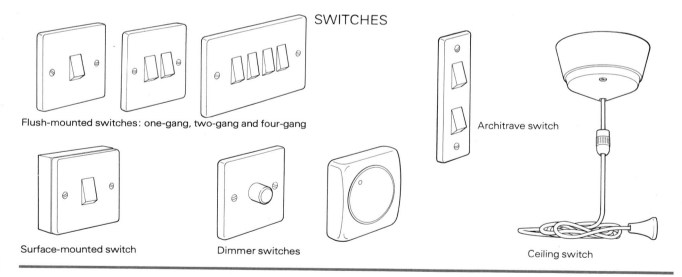

SWITCHES

Flush-mounted switches: one-gang, two-gang and four-gang

Architrave switch

Surface-mounted switch

Dimmer switches

Ceiling switch

Bathrooms

Bathroom lampholders must either have a Home Office skirt fitted or a totally enclosed fitting should be used. Only if the light is more than 2.5m from the bath or shower cubicle can ordinary fittings be used. Wall-mounted switches may be used only if they cannot be reached by someone using the bath or shower; if a light switch cannot be positioned far enough away, a pull-cord type can be used, or a conventional switch mounted just outside the room.

Generally, the safest combination is to use enclosed fittings and ceiling-mounted switches.

Special circuits

It is possible to wire a house with just socket and lighting circuits; but there are some fixed appliances which must have their own circuits – cookers and powerful water heaters, such as those used for showers, for example. It is also common practice to wire immersion heaters on their own circuits, relieving the socket circuit of the major load that it would otherwise carry when the heater is on.

The circuit itself will be straightforward: fuse, switch (mounted close to the appliance) and outlet connected by cable of an appropriate rating. To determine the fuse and cable rating for a heater, you simply divide the power in watts by the voltage. In practice, the voltage will almost always be 240, and you get about the right answer by multiplying the power in kW by four – so a 4kW heater will draw about 16A, a 6kW one about 24A.

The current rating for cooker circuits is arrived at differently. If you add up the total possible power consumption of the oven, grill and rings, it comes to a very large amount; in practice it is very unlikely that you will use the cooker in quite that way – even when you have all the bits switched on, they are unlikely to be drawing their maximum currents all at once. If the theoretical maximum current you have arrived at is Y amps, the circuit should have a rating of $0.3Y+7$; so if Y was 30, the rating would be $(0.3\times30)+7$, which is 16A. Some cooker points have a 13A socket built in as well; for this you should allow an extra 5A – giving a rating of 21A in this example.

The current ratings of fuses go up in 5A jumps – you choose the next fuse rating above the rating you arrive at, and then select the appropriate cable size from the Table below. Any switch in the circuit must also be able to take the current allowed by the fuse. Standard practice for cookers is to use 6mm² conductors protected by a 30A fuse and 30A switch.

Two or more separate cookers can share a supply, as long as the current rating of the circuit to supply them does not work out at more than 30A and each cooker is within 2m of the control switch and in the same room.

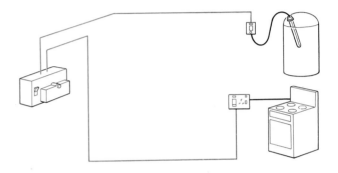

The two most common special circuits – one to an immersion heater and one to a cooker

The hardware

Whatever is being connected to a special circuit will be permanently connected; if the appliance is fixed to the wall, it may be possible to run the cable straight to the appliance terminals; otherwise it will have to be connected by a length of flex to an outlet. Cable is allowed for the final connection to a cooker. See page 68 for types and ratings of flex.

The simplest sort of outlet is simply a point at which the flex and cable are joined, and the flex emerges from the wall; but the outlet can be combined with the switch controlling the circuit. There are switches available for particular uses, with the word *cooker* or *water heater* engraved on the front. Neon indicator lights can be had, too. Cooker switches can have a 13A socket built in, as well; whether this is a good idea depends on precisely where the switch is to be mounted – it is not a good idea to have flexes dangling near the hob.

CABLE SIZES AND RATINGS

Cable size	current rating*		
	i	ii	iii
mm²	A	A	A
1.0	11	12	15
1.5	13	15	17
2.5	18	21	24
4.0	24	27	32
6.0	30	35	40
10.0	40	48	53

*all ratings are for twin PVC sheathed
i   rating for enclosed cables – in conduit, or under floors or loft insulation – used with rewireable fuses
ii rating for exposed cables – in air, surface-mounted or plastered in – used with rewireable fuses
iii rating for enclosed cables used with cartridge fuses or MCBs

Flex outlet to the appliance

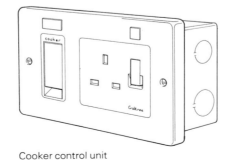

Cooker control unit

WARNING: Electricity can kill; read pages 61–66 and disconnect the supply before starting work.

Getting on with it

The work of installing house wiring mostly has very little to do with electricity – it is chiselling bricks, lifting floorboards, nailing and screwing things in place, and so on. How difficult all this is will depend partly on the construction of the house, and partly on how the circuits to be installed are planned.

The most basic decision is whether the cables are to be run on the surface of the walls or skirting boards, or to be hidden from view. If you take decor at all seriously, you will probably think concealed cables worth the considerable extra effort.

Once a decision to conceal the cables has been taken, it is worth investigating how the construction of the house will aid or impede progress. If the ground floor is a suspended timber type, cables can be run underneath it; on upper floors (again, if they are of timber) it will be much easier to run cables parallel to the supporting joists than at right angles to them; with hollow internal walls it is generally easy to run cables vertically (unless the horizontal studs get in the way), but the vertical timber studs will make horizontal runs awkward; solid wall materials may be very soft, making it easy to chisel out holes for steel boxes, or very hard, making it almost impossible. So before starting the wiring proper it is worth going over your plans in detail to see whether they might be modified to make the work easier.

If you are planning to extend an existing circuit, find out exactly how that circuit is run – the function of every bit of cable that is connected into the circuit must be understood. This can be done partly by simply following the routes of the bits of cable and making up a circuit diagram. But where cables are hidden – in plaster, say – electrical checks will have to be carried out. This means using some device to indicate electrical continuity – see next page. Then, with all connections in the circuit broken (including the ones at the fuse, where the two ends of a ring circuit meet) which cables connect what to what can be established.

Electricity while you work

Small jobs can often be done by daylight or by the light of a torch. But more major ones need the use of electricity either for lighting or power tools. It may be possible to take a supply from one of the house circuits while working on another, but you would have to be completely sure that there was no chance of confusion. If this is not so, or if there are no suitable circuits in the house, a temporary supply will have to be set up. This need be nothing more than a couple of sockets mounted close to the meter and fused – extension leads with multiple sockets can be plugged in to these.

How the supply to these temporary sockets should be arranged will depend on a number of things. If the house has an existing switch and fuse that you do not plan to include in the new wiring, the sockets can be wired into them; when the new wiring is complete, the temporary set-up can simply be disconnected and the new one connected (by the Electricity Board) in its place. If there is no spare hardware, you have a choice: either buy a switchfuse specially to serve the temporary set-up, or use the unit which will eventually serve the new installation and leave the connection of the new installation to that unit until you are ready to lose the temporary supply.

When there is no supply at all to the house or if you have to install a new switchfuse it may be necessary to get the Board to connect the temporary set-up. If you are doing the electrical work yourself, you can sign up for the domestic tariff – even if it is initially only for one or two lights. If an electrical contractor asks the Board for a temporary supply, the Board may charge a special high tariff.

Tools

Some of the tools needed for wiring are general-purpose ones, but some are more specialised.

Screwdrivers are needed for fixing things in place and for tightening connections; it is important to have a range of smallish sizes, with tips in good condition – the terminal screws are made of brass, which is easily damaged. The terminals of some accessories, particularly ceiling roses with lots of terminals in a small space, will accept only the tiniest screwdrivers. Views differ about the desirability of good electrical insulation of the handle of screwdrivers: since you should never be working on live circuits, you do not need insulation – but, on the other hand, insulation means more safety in case of mistakes.

Cable clips are hammered in place; the hammer should have a smooth, clean face to minimise the risk of damaging the very hard masonry pins which the clips use.

Cable has to be cut, and stripped of insulation and sheathing. Although substantial pliers will cope with the cutting, a pair of diagonal cutters will make life easier. A sharp knife is needed to slit and then trim back the sheath; one with a retracting blade has an obvious safety advantage when you are crawling about in confined spaces. The knife can be used for cutting away insulation too, but proper strippers are quicker and less likely to damage the conductors.

It may be that these basic tools will see you through; but any major work is likely to involve drilling and chiselling wood and walls to allow cables to pass or to accommodate or fix accessories; if floorboards need raising it may be worth having some special tools for that, too.

It is possible to complete an entire wiring system without using any electrical tools; but there are some which can help. A continuity tester is useful for finding out whether the conductors form a continuous path from terminal to terminal – see next page. A multimeter is an instrument for measuring all sorts of electrical quantities – usually voltage, current, and resistance; the main value of a meter when wiring is for checking continuity (using the resistance scales) and for checking that a circuit is dead. A multimeter is not of much value in doing the tests that have to be done on the completed system. Checking that a circuit is dead can be done with a neon mains tester; these are usually incorporated in the handle of a small screwdriver, and glow if the top of the driver is in contact with a live conductor while you hold the handle. For a number of reasons, neon testers aren't a particularly good idea. You can get test lamps which give a more reliable indication of the voltage on a conductor – but they may be little or no cheaper than a multimeter.

TOOLS FOR ELECTRICITY

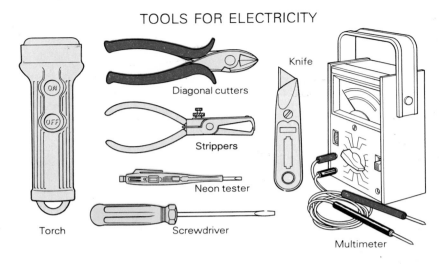

Diagonal cutters

Knife

Strippers

Neon tester

Torch

Screwdriver

Multimeter

MAKING AND USING A CONTINUITY TESTER

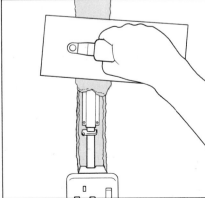

The drawing shows a typical continuity tester – if the clips are brought together, or if they are connected by another conductor, the lamp lights. A bell could be used in place of a lamp.

To chart how a circuit runs, first of all disconnect every conductor from every terminal and from every other conductor. Then, twist together the live and neutral conductors of one cable; now connect the tester to the live and neutral at any point which could be the opposite end of the same cable – when the lamp lights, you know you've found it.

Running cables

Sheathed cable can be run along the exposed surfaces of walls and ceilings. It should be supported by cable clips every 300mm or less when run horizontally, every 400mm or less when run vertically. To make the cable look as neat as possible, it can be straightened by pulling it round a smoothly radiused object (a hammer handle, say) after it has been wound off its drum.

Hidden wiring

If surface wiring is too obtrusive, it can be buried in plaster or, if the construction of the house allows, run in floor spaces and wall cavities. Cables which are going to be plastered over will obviously be at some risk of having nails or screws driven through them at some later date; to minimise this risk the cable should always run vertically to or from the socket or switch or, if necessary, horizontally – never diagonally across a wall. As a precaution against accidental piercing of a cable, fix metal channel over it or enclose it in circular or oval conduit before plastering. If cable is fixed in an unusual fashion – a ring main going around a room at socket height,

RUNNING CABLES IN WALLS

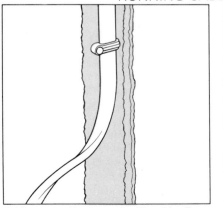

Cable secured in the wall with cable clips – they have hardened pins to penetrate masonry. Make sure you chase out a deep enough channel

Plastering over the cable after it is fixed is relatively simple when it is run in a channel with good surfaces either side

WARNING: Electricity can kill; read pages 61–66 and disconnect the supply before starting work.

for example – it is worth making some kind of record of where the cable runs.

In floor spaces, there must be plenty of slack in the cable to make sure that it is under no mechanical load. Under a suspended ground floor, the cable should ideally be clipped to the joists; if it is not, it should rest on the ground and not hang in loops. In the space under upper floors, it should as far as possible rest on the ceiling of the lower floor – though when run at right angles to the joists it should loop from one joist to the next. In this case, the cable should be run through a series of holes drilled in the joists, at least 50mm down from the top surface. Not only does this avoid the risk that nails will go through the cable when the floorboards are put back – it also does relatively little harm to the strength of the joists. If this is not possible, and cables have to be run in notches cut in the joists, they should be protected by sheets of metal nailed in place over each notch or run in conduit.

Other points to watch
When deciding how to run cables make sure that they do not run alongside central heating pipes. If they are well insulated, no problems should arise from an occasional crossing of paths provided some heat-resisting separator is used – wood battens or something similar are quite satisfactory. Always enclose PVC cable in conduit where it runs alongside or through polystyrene insulation – in a roof space, say.

It is important at the cable-fixing stage to make sure that enough cable is left spare at the points where accessories are to be mounted; how much is needed will vary with the type of accessory and the direction from which the cable approaches it – but remember that the connections have to be made behind the accessory, holding it some distance away from the wall.

Fixing fittings
The techniques of fixing electrical accessories to the surface of walls are no different from those used for other things, and are described in Chapter 4.

Flush mounting of accessories, however, means that steel boxes have to be sunk into the wall. In a solid wall this means that a hole at least as deep as the box has to be chiselled out – it can be a bit deeper with no ill effects – and then the box fixed with screws as usual. In a hollow wall – plasterboard or lath-and-plaster on timber studding – it is not so straightforward; a hole has to be cut out and then a solid mounting point for the box found. Making the hole can be a tricky business in itself; start by boring smaller holes with a brace and bit, and then cut the bigger hole with the point of a general-purpose saw. If the position chosen for the fitting is at or near one of the timber uprights, cut that away to the required box depth and fix the box directly to the upright; otherwise, extend the hole until there is room for a supporting piece of timber to be fixed in place, running from one stud to the next.

Steel boxes have lots of knockouts in the back and sides – circles of metal which are almost (but not quite) detached from the body of the box. Before fixing each box, knock out the circles the cable is to pass through and fit a rubber grommet to each hole to prevent the cable rubbing on the sharp edge of the hole.

The problems with ceilings are slightly different. You are unlikely to be mounting a steel box, because ceiling roses and other ceiling fittings are normally surface mounted. But the fixings that are used for surface mounting on hollow walls are not to be relied on to support the direct downward pull of a light fitting – particularly if the ceiling is made of lath and plaster. So the rose or fitting must be screwed to a proper support – either a joist or a piece of timber which is itself fixed to the joists. This is not difficult to achieve in most houses – quite good access to the back of the mounting can be had by going into the loft or by lifting floorboards on the floor above.

RUNNING CABLE UNDER FLOORS

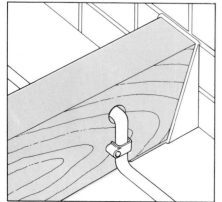

Drilling holes well down in the joists is the best method of running cables at right angles to them – but it may not be easy to do

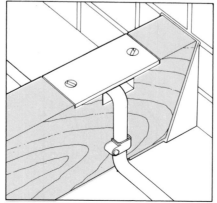

The alternative of cutting notches is no more hazardous if substantial metal plates cover the cables where they cross the joists

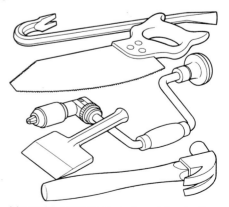

Most wiring jobs involve using a fair selection of ordinary hand tools – such as the jemmy, bolster chisel, brace, hammer and floorboard saw shown here

FIXING ACCESSORIES TO WALLS AND CEILINGS

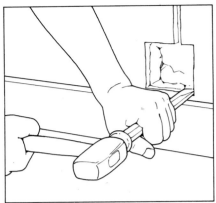

Fitting a flush socket into a solid wall
Chisel out a hole about 7 or 8mm bigger and slightly deeper than the box; aim to get an even 'bottom' for the box to rest on

Mark the positions of two of the screw holes in the back of the steel box, drill the holes and fix the box in place with wood screws and wall plugs

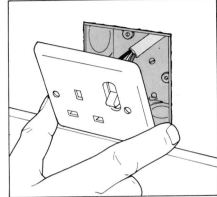

When the connections have been made to the socket, gently guide the wires so that they coil up without being crushed as you push the socket home

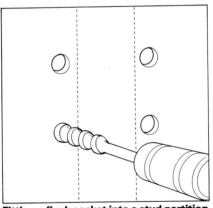

Fitting a flush socket into a stud partition
Start by marking the box position and drilling a large hole at each corner of the marked out square

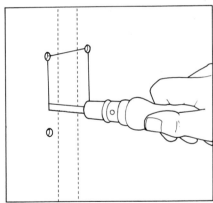

Use a keyhole saw or padsaw to cut out the plasterboard as shown. If the accessory is to be mounted directly over a stud . . .

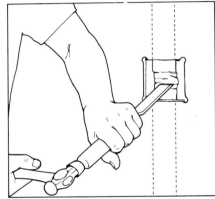

. . . it may be necessary to chisel away some wood to accommodate the steel box; if not, a supporting piece of timber needs to be fixed in place

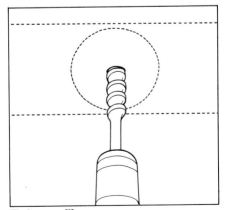

Fitting a ceiling rose
Drilling a hole for the cable from above makes it possible to choose a position where the rose can be fixed direct to a joist

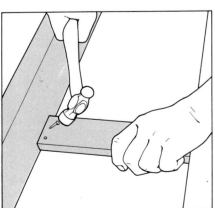

If you cannot fix the rose directly to a joist, fix a cross-piece between two joists with screws – for a not-too-heavy pendant, nailing will do

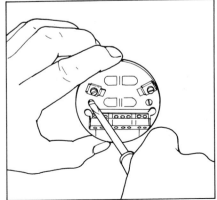

Mark and drill holes for the wood screws to hold the rose in place; knock out the flimsy plastic from the cable entry before fixing in place

WARNING: Electricity can kill; read pages 61–66 and disconnect the supply before starting work.

Making connections

Before connections can be made, the sheath and insulation of the cable have to be stripped back to expose the conductors. The sheath should be removed only from the length of cable which is within the steel box or the accessory itself; carefully slit the sheath along its length with a sharp knife, keeping the cut away from the live and neutral conductors – and keeping the knife pointing away from your hands. Then peel the sheath back and cut off the waste part.

Insulation can be removed with strippers or a knife. The amount to remove will depend on the type of terminal being dealt with; aim to leave virtually no bare conductor exposed once the connection has been made – but make sure there is plenty of conductor for the terminal screw to grip on. This is particularly important where more than one conductor are sharing a terminal.

When installing a ring circuit – or one in which the conductors go on from one accessory to another – it is worth making the effort to remove the sheath and insulation without breaking the continuity of the conductors; then, however bad the connection made at one point, there is still a good, low-resistance path on to the next point in the circuit. The conductors may have to be squeezed into a tight loop with pliers before they will go into the terminals.

The earth continuity conductor has no insulation, but wherever the sheath is removed it should be covered in green and yellow sleeving (previously green), which can be bought for the purpose; this is to prevent accidental contact with the live or neutral terminals when the accessory is screwed into place and to indicate that it is the earthing conductor.

Before the accessory is screwed in place, check that the terminal screws are tight and that all the conductors are firmly gripped. As the accessory is offered up to its box or pattress, help the conductors to bend into a comfortable shape so that they do not get bent too sharply, trapped or pushed up hard against the metal surface of the box.

Testing

No matter how careful you are, it is still possible to make mistakes when wiring. The Board will want to carry out tests on any major new installation before they connect it to their supply; if you have done a job without ever being cut off from the meter – which is possible if you have been extending, adding or renewing circuits without replacing the switch and fuse arrangements – you should still get the new wiring tested by the Board or an electrician. But before you get to that stage it is worth going through your own preliminary tests.

The tests you can do without special equipment are limited; with a multimeter and a backless plug you can check that the polarity of your socket connections is right – that the live conductor goes to all the live holes, the neutral to all the neutrals; you can check that there is an earth connection where there should be; you can check that none of the circuits has a high resistance and that the insulation always does have a high resistance – but what you cannot do is check that the system will still have these desirable qualities under real conditions, with high voltages and large currents.

If you have a friend who knows what to look for, it would be well worth getting him or her to go over the system checking that the right connections have been made, and made properly; then you would both have to make the same mistake before anything could go wrong.

The tests done by the Board before they will connect a new system are essentially designed to ensure that it has adequate insulation resistance; that the earthing is satisfactory; and that it poses no threat to their supply system. The tests do not necessarily tell you whether your installation is safe in other respects; in particular, you want to know whether the earth-leakage protection is up to scratch. The Board (or an electrician) can do extra tests to tell you about this.

CONNECTING UP AN ACCESSORY

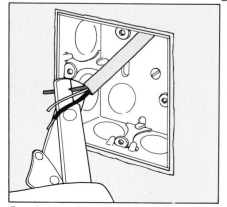

Experience will soon teach you how much cable you need to leave for connecting to the accessory; trim off only as much insulation as necessary

When the conductors are going on to another point, leaving them unbroken ensures that the circuit stays continuous; cut the insulation off with a knife

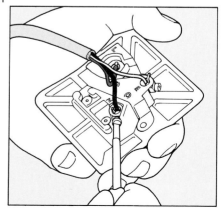

Where there is only one thin conductor to go in a hefty terminal, it is worth bending it double to give the screw plenty to grip

Plugs, fuses and flex

Plugs

The different types of plug you are likely to come across are shown on page 70; they are all essentially the same (except that 13A ones have a fuse inside); but there are variations in detail.

The plug is held together by a screw (on some older plugs, two screws) in the centre of the face. Most plugs also have two smaller screws in the face, near the flex entry; these are part of the cord grip, which is meant to take the strain when there is a pull on the flex.

When the back of the plug is taken off, the terminals are revealed – along with the fuse connected to the live terminal in 13A plugs. There are two types of terminal – one with threaded posts and slotted nuts to tighten down on to the flex conductors, the other with holes into which you poke the conductors and screws to tighten down on to them.

The terminals are always arranged in the same way – as you look at them with the flex entry at the bottom, the earth terminal is at the top, live on the right, neutral on the left. But they should also be marked E, L and N. The live terminal is the one with the fuse.

The stages in wiring a plug are:
● cut enough of the outer sheath off your flex to expose enough of the cores for the earth wire to reach its terminal with a bit to spare; be careful not to cut the insulation of the cores

Plugs vary in how the conductors are connected to the pins, in how the fuse is held and in how the flex is gripped at the entry

● hold the flex against the plug in its proper position, which is with the sheath through the cord grip, and cut the three (or two) cores off to the right length, allowing for them to go round or through the terminals; some plugs come with a paper template to help you with this, and some are specially designed so that all the cores are cut to the same length

● trim away about 10mm of insulation from the end of each core, exposing the conductors, then twist the strands together to make them easier to handle and connect properly
● with the flex held lightly in the cord grip, make the connections to the terminals: with the post type, wrap the conductors clockwise around the post; with the hole type, bend the conductors double before inserting them; tighten the screws or nuts firmly
● secure the flex in the cord grip; this usually means tightening the screws which pull down a fibre or plastic bar on to the sheath but some plugs now have grips into which you simply push the flex
● give the flex a tug to make sure the grip is working, replace the fuse if that is necessary, and replace the back of the plug.

The fuses in 13A plugs are always of the replaceable, cartridge type; you simply lever the old one out with a screwdriver (if you do not need a screwdriver to get the fuse out, the clips in which it's mounted are probably too weak for safety); then push a new one in (having checked, if you are in doubt, that the old one has blown – you need some sort of tester because the cartridges are opaque).

WIRING A PLUG

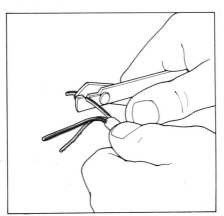

Once the three (or two) conductors have been cut to the right lengths, the same amount of insulation needs to be stripped from each

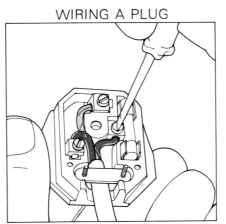

With the flex gripped lightly in the cord grip, connect the conductors securely to the three pins – brown to live; blue to the neutral; and green/yellow to earth

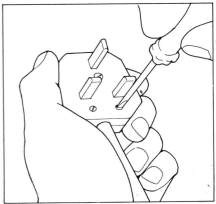

Slacken the grip slightly and push the flex into the plug a bit so that there is no strain on any of the conductors. Then tighten the grip fully

WARNING: Electricity can kill; read pages 61–66 and disconnect the supply before starting work.

Fuse-boards

Modern 'fuse-boards' – consumer units – may have circuit breakers instead of fuses; if one of these trips, you can simply reset it by pressing the button on the front – turn off the supply first. Or they may have cartridge fuses; if one of these blows you have to replace it with a new one. They're like the little fuses inside 13A plugs (except that they're bigger). The fuses are marked with their rating, and are colour coded; they are also different sizes to prevent one of the wrong rating being fitted.

Older fuse-boards and many consumer units have rewirable fuses: check that the fuse has blown by pulling on the fuse wire. To rewire, first of all remove the two ends of the old wire, then replace it with wire of the proper rating – the rating should be marked on the fuse-holder or elsewhere on the fuse-board; if it is not you can try to establish the correct rating by looking at the sort of circuit the fuse is protecting. It is not such a good idea to simply match the old wire to some new – someone may have used the wrong wire before.

Try to avoid getting the new fuse wire kinked or otherwise damaged – you will make it liable to blow easily.

Never replace a fuse with something improvised.

CHECKING AND CHANGING FUSES

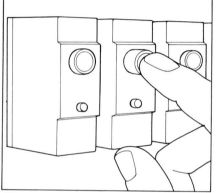

When miniature circuit breakers of this type 'trip', the big button pops out. Switch off the whole system before pushing the button back in

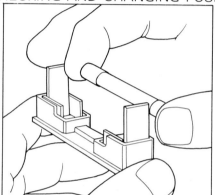

With cartridge fuses, there is no sign of whether the fuse has blown – to be sure, you need a meter or continuity tester. The fuse is replaced as a whole

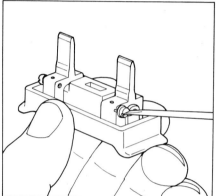

With rewirable fuses, it is easy enough to check whether the wire is intact; a new length of wire is needed to run between the two terminals of the holder

Replacing and extending flex

Replacing

The procedure for replacing the flex on an appliance will obviously vary with the appliance, but it is usually fairly clear which bits of the device you need to dismantle in order to get at the flex terminals.

The main points to watch are:
● use the right sort of flex – see page 68
● make sure that the flex is properly secured by whatever cord grip arrangement the appliance has, and that you replace any special grommet or support at the flex entry.

Extending

Flex can be permanently extended by using an enclosed connector. Fitting one of these is not unlike fitting a plug – but of course there are two sets of connections to make instead of one.

Making an extension lead

An extension lead is a convenient way of temporarily extending the flexes of any appliances you want to use some way from the nearest socket.

Extension leads should always be

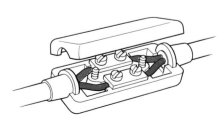

A flex connector is simply a way of joining the conductors of one length of flex to the conductors of another

made with three-core flex rated at 13A or 15A or more, with the heftiest sheathing you can find – the lead is likely to be used in all sorts of places where it will be twisted, trapped and rubbed, and the heavier it is the less likely it is to be damaged.

Fit the appropriate plug one end; at the other, you have a variety of socket devices to choose from. They provide from one to four sockets from the one flex and are usually made of rubber or some other resilient material. They may have an indicator light built in, but do not usually have switches.

The connections to the 'floating' socket are essentially like those to a plug – look for markings to tell you which terminal is which. Never make up an extension lead with a plug at both ends – if you do, one will have live exposed pins.

Replacements and modifications

If the basic wiring of a circuit is in satisfactory condition, you may be able to bring your installation up to scratch by doing no more than replacing the hardware which is connected to it – though it's by no means the case that this process is always easier than installing new circuits.

Sockets

On the front of sockets you will find a pair of screws. On flush-mounted sockets, these hold the socket in place; when they are removed, you can pull the socket forward and get at the connections which are behind. On a surface-mounted socket, the screws hold a front cover on to the main body of the socket; when this is removed, the connections to the socket are exposed; a pair of wood screws holds the body of the socket to the wall.

If the old socket is damaged, it is a straightforward job to fit a replacement: the screw holes should be the same spacing. But do not throw away the old screws – new ones may not fit the threads of your old steel or plastic box. And make sure you do not buy a socket that needs a deeper box than the old one.

When you come to fit the new socket, do not assume that the connections will be arranged in the same way as on the old one – check that you are connecting live to the terminal marked L, and so on. If the cable behind the socket has been cut very short, it is possible (though unlikely) that the conductors might not reach to the terminals on a different brand of socket.

An existing single 13A socket can be

converted to a double quite easily. With surface-mounting ones, it is simply a matter of substituting a double socket for the single one. With flush-mounting ones, you have a choice – make a bigger hole in the wall to accommodate a double-size steel box, or fit a surface-mounting pattress over the existing box, and mount the new socket in that. Check that there is enough cable to reach the new terminals before you attempt this.

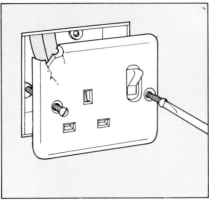

Make sure the circuit is dead before removing the old socket by loosening the screws; keep the screws in case your new ones are different

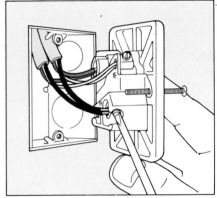

When there is more than one cable connected to the socket, all cores of the same colour should be connected together – use pliers to twist them firmly

Lighting

Replacements and modifications to lighting can be tricky, for two reasons. One is that lights get hot, with the result that the wiring to them is inclined to deteriorate; you may set about doing what you think is a small job, only to find that by disturbing the old, fragile wiring you have made it unsafe and created a much bigger job. The second is that the wiring to lights can be complicated, and you may find a selection of wires behind a ceiling rose or switch with very few clues about what goes where. So do not start unless you are prepared for complications.

Replacing a lampholder is quite straightforward, as long as the flex is in good condition. The top half of the body

screws off (sometimes after a bit of a tussle) to reveal the two terminals; there is no live-neutral distinction, but do make sure the conductors go around the prongs of the lampholder which are meant to take the strain of the flex.

The main difficulty in replacing the flex of a pendant lampholder is that the cover of the ceiling rose may be gummed up with paint, making it difficult to unscrew – particularly if it's an old porcelain type. When the cover is off, note which terminals the flex cores go to (unless there are only two) before disconnecting them. See page 68 for advice on the type of flex to use. If the rose has lugs to take the strain of the flex, make sure you use them.

If an old ceiling rose is damaged, or

too hideous to be left in place, you can replace it with a new one. But if the wiring behind it is old, rubber-insulated cable you run the risk of making the insulation crumble, at least close to the rose where it will have been heated by the lamp. Your new rose needs to have at least as many terminals as the old one. And if there are several wires involved you need to be quite clear about which ones should be connected together when you install the new rose. Make sure that the new rose has a secure mounting even if the old one did not have.

There are lots of sorts of ceiling lights that you might want to fit in place of the usual rose/flex/pendant lampholder arrangement: fittings which have rigid stems instead of the rose and flex; en-

WARNING: Electricity can kill; read pages 61–66 and disconnect the supply before starting work.

closed diffusing fittings; downlighters; **spotlights; track lighting** or fluorescent tube fittings. Obviously, with anything which does not mount in a fashion similar to a rose – ie with a couple of screws quite close together – you may have to take steps to provide something secure for the new fitting to be fixed to. But there may be wiring difficulties, too: fittings of this sort rarely have more than three terminals provided (either as part of the fitting itself or in the form of a floating 'chocolate bar' connector). If the rose you are replacing has the switch return, neutral and earth wires going to it, there is no problem – you can simply connect them to the new fitting; but if it is a loop-in arrangement – see page 75 – there will be a pair of permanently live wires to deal with too. In this case you will have to provide a fourth terminal to give these wires a secure and safe home. Another possible problem is that many of the fittings you are likely to be thinking of putting up will have metal bodies, which should be earthed; in an old house it is unlikely that the lighting circuits will have an earth conductor – so you would have to run one specially from the fuseboard.

WIRING LIGHT FITTINGS

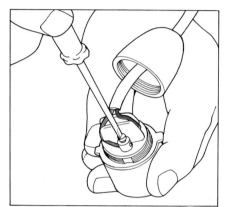

Most pendant lampholders are made of plastic and have only two terminals; the wires can go to either. Metal ones should have an earth terminal as well

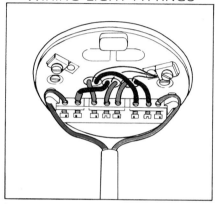

In loop-in wiring, all the connections are made in the rose, which needs three terminal blocks plus the earth block

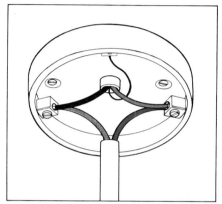

In junction-box wiring, the rose is simply a meeting point between the cable and flex; the rose needs two terminal blocks plus the earth block

Switches

Switches have quite a bit in common with sockets: they all have screws on the front; in the case of flush-mounted ones these release the whole unit, and the terminals are found behind; with a surface-mounted one they release a cover, which conceals the terminals, and there are further screws inside to hold the switch to the wall.

Simple replacement is quite straightforward. As with sockets, the screw holes of flush switches will be at a standard spacing but the screws themselves can vary and you have to be sure that your new switch is not too deep for your old steel box. There is however the further complication with switches that there are different types – mainly, one-way, two-way and intermediate; and if there are two or more switches in the same unit there will be a number of wires which you must identify clearly before you disconnect them from the old unit. Do not worry if there are unused terminals on the old switch – particularly on two, three or four-gang units; it means that the switch is a two-way one but is in a one-way circuit.

A dimmer switch is as easy to fit as a replacement ordinary switch since it usually has instructions.

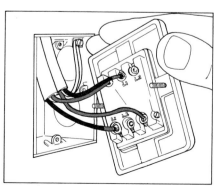

On a multi-gang switch, the terminals are in groups, three to each switch; for two-way wiring you use all three, for one-way just C and L1

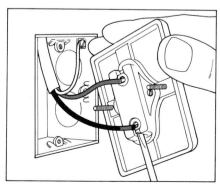

On a one-gang switch, there may be three terminals (to allow two-way switching) or only two. If there are two terminals the wires can go either way round

Extending and installing wiring

So far, this section has dealt only with replacing existing fittings – either with a new version of what was there before, or with something which does a slightly different job. But you will often find that the improvements you can bring about in this way are not enough – you want lights or sockets in places where they do not exist at present.

If your existing wiring is both sound and close to the places where you want additional fittings, you may be able to extend it so as to supply the new things. If the wiring is suspect, or nowhere near, or if the thing you want to fit draws a heavy current, you will need to install a completely new circuit.

Extensions

Whether it is a socket circuit or a lighting circuit you want to extend, the principle is the same: what you are basically trying to do is run a cable with live, neutral and earth conductors from some point on the existing circuit to your new socket point or light point (or, if you plan to use the junction box wiring system for a light, to the place where you plan to mount the junction box).

The easiest way to achieve this may be to run the cable from the terminals of an existing socket, ceiling rose or junction box. The main thing to check, if this looks like the appropriate solution, is that the terminals of the point you are going to use have space for the extra conductors. If they do not, or if there is no convenient point, you will have to break into the existing wiring and install a junction box from which your new extension can run. In a lighting circuit, this box can act as the junction box you connect the switch and rose to, or you can take the supply to another box or a rose with 3 terminals and an earth.

An extension to a lighting circuit can serve as many lights as are allowed by the overall limits discussed on page 76. An extension to a ring circuit constitutes a spur off the main ring, so it can carry only two sockets (two single sockets or one double one) or one fixed fused connection unit.

New circuits

If an extension won't do, you need a new circuit starting from a fuse near the meter. If you have a consumer unit with spare ways in it, it can be connected to this. If not, you have the option of fitting a single switchfuse to provide for just the one circuit or a consumer unit to provide for several; in either case, you will have to get the Board to connect the unit to the meter when you have wired it up.

The fuse and cable rating you need to use depends on the function of the circuit – see the earlier sections on the theory of socket, lighting and other circuits. In a consumer unit, the neutral conductor of your new circuit goes to a solid bar with a row of terminals on it; the earth conductor goes to another solid bar; and the live conductor goes to one side of the fuse way (the other side will be connected by a solid conductor to the switch controlling the whole unit). The conductors of all the circuits running from a unit should be connected to the row of fuseways and the rows of neutral and earth terminals in the same order.

EXTENDING YOUR WIRING

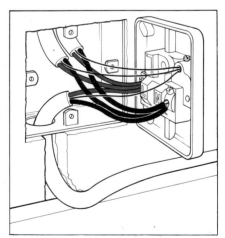

To wire a spur from a ring circuit, remove the socket, feed your new cable into the space behind it and connect the conductors to the socket terminals. If there is only one set of three conductors, the socket must be on a spur or radial circuit. If there are three sets, the socket must be at the root of an existing spur. In either case, try elsewhere

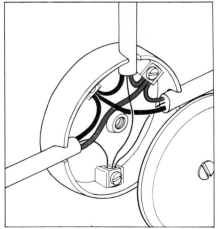

Where there is no convenient socket (or fused connection unit) into which a spur can be connected, a junction box is fitted and the ring circuit led through it. Make sure that the cable you are planning to break into is part of a ring. Junction boxes to be used in exposed places should be of a type with the cover held in place by a screw

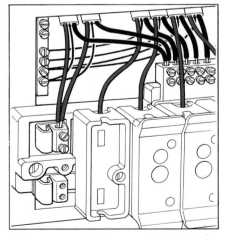

Where a completely new circuit is to be installed to a spare fuse-way in the existing consumer unit, the neutral and earth conductors of the new circuit are connected to spare terminals in their respective terminal blocks, but the live has to be connected to its own fuse-way. The circuit will need an appropriate fuse

WARNING: Electricity can kill; read pages 61–66 and disconnect the supply before starting work.

Installing fixed appliances

Any fixed appliance which can be supplied via a fused connection unit could equally well be supplied via a plug and socket – provided the appliance is not in a bathroom, and does not require a separate double-pole switch – such as a wall heater or water heater.

On the other hand, there is something to be said for treating many appliances as 'fixed' when actually they are not. Washing machines and driers are often left in a fixed position; they take a heavy current over long periods and by wiring them through fused connection units instead of plugs and sockets you avoid any possibility of overloaded contacts leading to overheating.

Wall heater

The simplest way to wire a wall heater is through a fused outlet on a socket circuit. If the heater has a cable/flex entry close to the wall, you can use an outlet without a flex hole, and do all the wiring in cable. There must be a double-pole switch in the circuit (a pull-cord type in a bathroom) unless the heater has one built in. The heater and fused connection unit must not be mounted within reach of the bath or shower.

The fuse you need in the connection unit will be 13A; the cable from the outlet to the heater must be able to take the heater current.

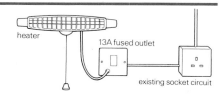

A bathroom wall heater can be wired like this only if the fused connection unit is out of reach from the bath or shower

Heated towel rail

A heated towel rail can be supplied from a switched fused connection unit (with a 13A fuse) wired into a socket circuit. In a bedroom, the connection unit can be next to the towel rail, but if the towel rail is in a bathroom, the switched connection unit must not be mounted so that it can be reached from the bath. This probably means putting it outside and wiring it to a simple flex outlet mounted inside the bathroom. It is best to use heat-resisting flex to connect the towel rail to the flex outlet.

An alternative way to wire a heated towel rail in a bathroom is to use a non-switched fused connection unit – again probably outside – with a ceiling-mounted double-pole switch inside the bathroom.

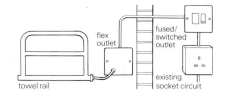

For heated towel rails in bathrooms, the switched fused connection unit will usually be mounted outside with only a simple flex outlet inside

Immersion heater

Although you can wire an immersion heater of 3kW or less from a socket circuit, you should do so only if you plan to make very little use of it (if you intend to heat your water from the central heating, say). If the heater is going to be used a lot, its considerable power will effectively halve the capacity of the socket circuit to provide current for less constantly-used appliances. The more sensible plan is to give the heater a circuit of its own. If it is more than 3kW there's no alternative.

The main part of the circuit, from the consumer unit to an outlet close to the hot water cylinder, should be run in 2.5mm^2 cable for a 3kW heater, with a 15A fuse protecting it. The final part of the circuit, from the wall to the body of the heater, must be in flex, of a heat-resisting type. There should be a double-pole switch close to the heater (with an appropriate current rating), and the simplest arrangement is to use one which has a flex outlet in the front; it should also have a neon indicator.

You may want to be able to switch the heater on and off without walking to the hot-water cylinder every time; in this case, you should still have a switch close to the heater, but wire a second switch in the circuit at the point where it is most convenient; by leaving the 'local' switch 'on', you can control the heater from the 'remote' one.

There are immersion heaters available with two elements – a long one and a short one; when mounted at the top of a cylinder, these allow you to choose between heating the whole contents of the cylinder or (in the interests of economy) just the top part. If the heater does not have its own switch built in, the two elements will have to be supplied separately. But this does not mean separate circuits – a switch should be used which allows you to turn on one element or the other, but not both at one time.

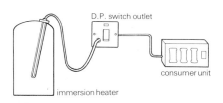

This is a single-element vertically-mounted heater, controlled by a single switch. There are horizontally-mounted types too – fitted at the bottom of the cylinder

Shower heater

Electric shower heaters work by heating cold water as it flows through on its way to the shower head; in order to heat the water 'instantly' like this, the heater has to be high-powered – usually about 7kW – and so cannot be wired to a socket circuit.

There are less powerful water heaters for use at sinks and so on, and ones of 3kW or less *can* be connected to a socket circuit via a fused connection unit and double-pole switch. The rate at which these heaters produce hot water is low, and these low-powered heaters are generally best avoided.

The cable you need for a circuit to supply a shower heater depends on the power of the heater, of course; but most will need 6mm^2 protected by a 30A fuse which can deal with up to 7kW. It will usually be possible to connect the heater directly to the cable; if this is not so, the outlet and flex must be of similar rating.

There must be a double-pole switch in the circuit with an appropriate rating (usually 30A); if it's within reach of the shower, it must be of the ceiling-mounted pull-cord type; it is a good idea to have one with a neon indicator.

These heaters need a large 'head' and so must almost always be plumbed into mains-pressure water supply rather than supplied from the house cistern.

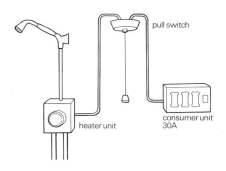

Shower heaters are one of the few fixed appliances which always need their own circuit run from the consumer unit

Shaver outlet

The only type of socket outlet allowed in bathrooms is a shaver supply unit conforming to BS3052. These have a transformer built in to isolate the shaver from the mains supply (and so avoid the risk of serious shock should a fault occur) and a current-limiting device to prevent other more powerful appliances being run from the socket.

In rooms other than bathrooms, a shaver socket outlet conforming to BS4573 may be used – these incorporate a current-limiting device, but no transformer.

The shaver supply unit or outlet imposes very little load, and may be connected to any convenient circuit – either a socket circuit or a lighting circuit. Using a bathroom lighting circuit has the attraction that it's likely to be close at hand – there will be no socket circuit in the room – and that the unit is always switched off when the light is off.

There are combined shaving lights/shaver outlets available; these too need to conform to the relevant British Standard.

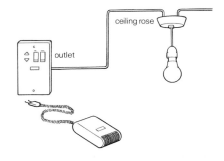

A supply unit wired to the room's lighting circuit; this is not the only possibility – see text

Door bell

Door bells operate at relatively low voltages – so the wiring to the outdoor switch doesn't need to be done with any special care. Some bells get their power from dry batteries, but others have a transformer to convert the mains voltage to the lower voltage the bell uses. This sort obviously has to be connected to the house wiring. The transformer can be simply connected to a lighting circuit (fused at 5A) or connected via a fused connection unit (with a 3A fuse fitted) to a socket circuit.

Be sure that the transformer you buy has a secure insulating cover over the mains-voltage terminals. The transformer may have several different output voltages – be sure to use the one your bell needs.

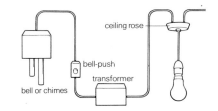

The bell transformer can be connected to a socket circuit instead of the lighting circuit shown here

Clock point

Clock connectors are special outlets which can provide the small current an electric clock draws, without taking up much space; they take special cartridge fuses.

Clock connectors can be installed on a power circuit or a lighting circuit. The connector's terminals may be rather small to accommodate more than one conductor, so it may have to go on the end of a spur or radial circuit rather than part way along a ring circuit.

The clock connectors are a form of plug and socket, but they are not interchangeable with other ones.

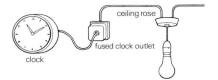

A clock point wired to a lighting circuit; if it is more convenient, a socket circuit can be used

WARNING: Electricity can kill; read pages 61–66 and disconnect the supply before starting work.

Extractor fan

Extractor fans can be fitted in windows or in walls. Those fitted in windows will always need an external flex to supply power; those fitted in walls *can* be supplied by cable buried in the wall. Either sort can be supplied from a fused connection unit.

For a simple one-speed extractor, the supply can be taken direct to the fan. If it does not have a switch built in, there will have to be a switch in the connection unit or between the unit and the fan. The fan *may* have different terminals so that it

can be used to blow in instead of sucking out: the instructions should explain which to use.

Some fans can be used with special control units so that the user can switch the fan to blow or suck, and can choose different speeds. With these, the supply goes to the control unit, and separate wiring goes from the control unit to the fan. The instructions should show you what is needed.

If there is a lightly-loaded lighting circuit nearby, it may be more convenient to wire your fan to that.

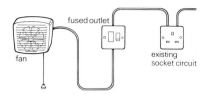

This is the simple set-up with a fan to be used at one speed. in one direction. More elaborate schemes use special control units

Central heating

The complexity of central heating controls varies a lot; but a typical system might have the pump and boiler supplied through a time switch and a thermostat; a more complex system might have a programmer (a more versatile time switch), two or more thermostats for different parts of the system, and motor-driven valves to control the flow of water in different parts of the system.

The various components should have wiring instructions with them; but the

basic scheme of things for our 'typical' system is that the supply goes to the timer, then on to the thermostat, then on to the boiler and pump.

The Confederation for the Registration of Gas Installers require that the system be supplied through a plug and socket; but a switched, fused connection unit can be used instead. Alternatively, the central heating can have its own supply from the fuseboard or consumer unit – this means that failure of the socket circuit does not affect the heating.

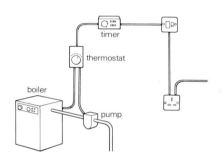

Heating control systems vary a lot – this is only one example (and a fairly simple one)

Cooker point

There are some sorts of cooking appliance which draw relatively small currents, and they can be operated from a socket circuit – either through a plug and socket or a fused outlet. But a full-size cooker – oven, grill and rings – (or a collection of several separate appliances which add up to the same thing) needs its own circuit. The way to calculate the rating of the circuit is explained on page 80; once you have arrived at the current, you know what cable to use - the next size up (with corresponding fuse).

The circuit must have a switch in it, within reach of the cooker, and this normally takes the form of a switch and flex outlet combined, labelled 'cooker'; it may also have a socket built in, when it is called a cooker control unit. The Wiring Regs make an exception of cookers: although most are strictly speaking movable, you are allowed to use cable rather than flex to make the connection from the wall to the cooker.

One suitably-rated unit can supply two cookers if they are within two metres and in the same room.

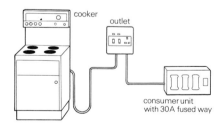

The drawing shows a 30A fuse, which will often be what you need – but don't assume that's so – see text

---

Reports in Handyman Which?

Installing lights

The main ways of wiring lights and different types of light fitting are covered in *Lighting circuits* starting on page 75.

When putting in a whole new lighting circuit, the Wiring Regs require you to use a twin-core and earth cable; when adding to an existing lighting circuit without an earth wire, you will need to supply a separate earth. All exposed earth wire –

inside roses, junction boxes and switches – should be protected with green/yellow sleeving.

Individual lights *can* be connected to a socket circuit – via a fused connection unit (with a 3A or 5A fuse) and a switch: remember that the light will be live when the main lighting circuit fuses are removed.

Wall lights

For several reasons, it makes sense to use the junction-box wiring system when installing wall lights: the existing supply cable is unlikely to run close to the points where you want the lights; you probably want one switch to control more than one light; and the fittings themselves are very unlikely to have the terminals you need for the loop-in system.

You can take the supply to the junction box from any point on the main supply cable of your existing lighting circuit, normally using 1mm² cable (but see page 67). From the junction box you then need to run a two-core and earth cable to the switch, and a cable to the light. If there is to be more than one

light, you can either run separate cables to each one or run a single cable round.

If you're adding wall lights to an old

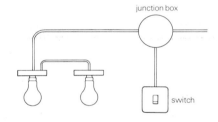

If the lights are close together and some way from the switch, this scheme of wiring may be best

system, be sure that there's an earth conductor – wall lights are likely to include metal, and are easily touched.

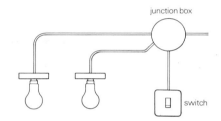

If they're not, separate cables from the junction box to each light may be more economical

A loft light

A loft light can be purely functional, and the simplest sort of fitting to use is a battenholder – it can be screwed to a roof support, keeping the bulb well out of harm's way.

Although you can treat the installation of a loft light like any other lighting circuit, and provide a switch either on

the landing below or just inside the hatch, you could decide to wire the battenholder directly from the landing light, with no additional switch; the loft light would then be on whenever the landing light was on, but with a low-power bulb the electricity you waste won't amount to much. If you use a separate switch, mark it 'LOFT'.

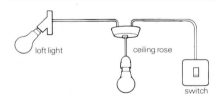

Wiring the light without its own switch only makes sense if you intend to use a low-power bulb

An outside light

The installation of a light mounted on the outside wall of a house is much the same process as the installation of an interior wall light, except that the fitting you use needs to be weatherproof and that you have to devise some means of getting a cable through the wall from inside. The junction-box system is clearly the one to go for; the switch can be outside if it is of a suitable weatherproof type, though an indoor switch will normally be more appropriate.

Installing a light in an outside garage or workshop which is detached from the house is more complicated. You will need to take a separate supply to the out-building from its own mains switch and fuse close to the meter (this supply could also be used for sockets).

The supply can be taken overhead – using a separately-earthed catenary wire at least 3.5m high to support the PVC cable – or underground, using special cable (such as armoured cable) buried at least 500mm deep.

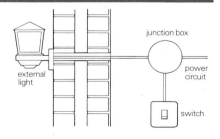

A light on an outside wall connected to a junction box on the lighting circuit

WARNING: Electricity can kill; read pages 61–66 and disconnect the supply before starting work.

CHAPTER THREE

WOODWORKING

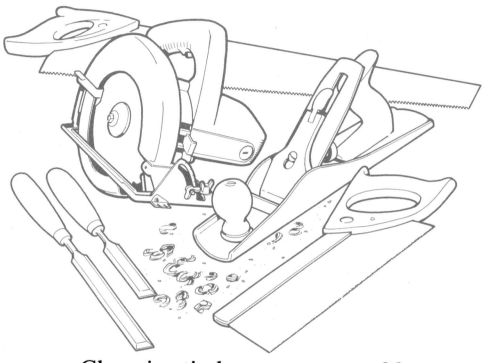

The hundreds of different timber species, which vary widely in their appearance and properties, are usually classified into two broad groups – hardwoods and softwoods. Hardwoods come from broad-leaved trees such as ash and oak. Softwoods come from coniferous trees which mostly have needle-like leaves – Norway spruce, for instance. This is a botanical classification and the terms are only a general guide to the hardness of the woods – balsa, for example, is probably the softest wood available yet it is classified as a hardwood, whereas yew, a hard wood, is classified as a softwood.

Traditionally, softwoods are cheap, easily-worked timbers used in house construction – for flooring, rafters, joists, windows and doors. They are often painted. Hardwoods, on the other hand, are generally more expensive and are considered to be more durable, and more difficult to work. They are used for making furniture and sometimes finished with stain and then polished or varnished to bring out their natural decorative features of grain and texture. However, in recent years, there have been two important changes which make it necessary to forget the traditional approach and to select timbers individually on the basis of their appearance, working properties, durability, strength and so on. First, the high cost of converting trees into timber and the cost of transportation have narrowed the price differential between many hardwoods and softwoods. In fact it is possible to buy hardwoods which are less expensive than some softwoods. Secondly, new hardwoods are being introduced into the UK from the tropical regions of Africa, the Far East and South America. Some of these 'new' timbers are easier to work than the more traditional hardwoods.

Conversion and seasoning

A tree which has just been felled contains a lot of moisture. To make it into timber which can be used, it has to be sawn and dried. These processes are known as conversion and seasoning.

Sawing

Timber is generally sawn:
● **through-and-through** (sometimes called plain-sawn or slash-sawn). In this method the log is cut into planks by simply slicing through the tree. Most of the growth rings make an angle of less than 45 degrees with the surface. The moisture content of a tree is greater around the outside than at the centre, so when through-and-through sawn wood is dried all the planks, apart from those which are cut directly through the centre of the tree, have a tendency to warp. The planks have to be planed flat after drying

● **quarter-sawn.** Timber has growth rings at an angle of 45 degrees or more to the surface of the board. It is often more expensive than through-and-through sawn timber but much less likely to warp.

TIMBER CUTS

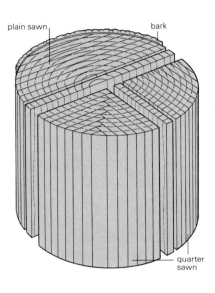

The far side of the log shows through-and-through (plain-sawn) boards. The two nearest quarters of the log show different methods of quarter sawing. The one on the left is used for small logs

Drying

Timber is dried by either stacking it in the open air or by drying it in a kiln. Drying makes timber stronger, more resistant to fungi and better for painting and varnishing.

Once timber has been dried it can still gain and lose moisture – it shrinks as it loses moisture and expands as it gains moisture. Timber which has been stored in the open will shrink when brought indoors, particularly into a centrally-heated room. The effect this has on the timber depends on how the timber was sawn – through-and-through sawn timber tends to warp whereas quarter-sawn timber tends to shrink evenly. Whenever timber is moved between environments which are likely to have very different humidities, it is important to allow time for the timber to come to equilibrium with its new surroundings. This may be as little as a few days for small sizes but well over a week for larger ones.

Wood sizes

Timber merchants sell most of their wood in standard pre-cut sizes. The standard **lengths** for softwoods start at 1.8m and increase in multiples of 0.3m to a maximum of 6.3m, although longer and shorter lengths can be obtained. With hardwoods the situation is much more complicated and as it is likely that a timber merchant will stock relatively few sizes, it is worth checking with him before deciding on what lengths to buy. In very general terms, hardwoods start at 1.8m in length and increase in units of 0.1m, though shorter lengths are often available.

The standard **widths** and **thicknesses** available depend on whether the timber is left rough sawn or planed smooth.

For softwood, three finishes are widely available.

Sawn The timber is cut to standard sizes in both width and thickness by large power saws. Sawn timber is sold by its *nominal* size – as cut from the log. After drying, timber shrinks slightly so the size of sawn timber when it is bought is slightly less than its nominal size.

Planed all round (PAR) This is sawn timber which has had all its sides smoothed and made parallel by planing. A PAR size is usually around 3.5mm less than the nominal sawn size.

Planed both sides This is sawn timber which has had its two largest faces smoothed and made parallel by planing but has its two narrow faces left sawn.

Quality grades

Wood comes in a number of different quality grades depending, among other things, on the number of knots and other faults present – roughly, the fewer the faults the better the quality.

Most softwoods are imported from Brazil, Canada, Scandinavia and the USSR. Each country has its own grading system.

Softwoods, such as European red-wood, from Scandinavia and the USSR are sometimes available in two quality grades – *unsorted* and *fifths*. Unsorted is the better grade and includes all grades originally sorted by the country of origin as better than fifths. However, most timber merchants in this country sort their wood into three grades: *best joinery* (the best of the unsorted grade), *standard joinery* (the rest of the unsorted grade plus some of the better fifths) and *building grade* or *carcassing* (the rest of the fifths). Best joinery should be used when the wood is to be finished with stain or polish; standard joinery can be used for battens and frameworks; and carcassing grade can be used for concealed work. Softwood may also be stress graded – either by machine or visually. The grading marks are usually GS (general structural) and SS (special structural) when visually graded, and MGS and MSS when machine graded.

Timber from Canada may be graded as *clears* and *merchantable.* Clears are better quality than unsorted from Scandinavia and the USSR.

Parana pine (from Brazil) is not usually graded by timber merchants but it is possible to find *No1* and *No2* grades – both are equivalent to Canadian clears.

Hardwoods are not usually graded but it is possible to find boards available at reduced prices which have been wrongly planed or are faulty.

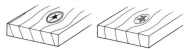
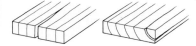
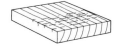

WIDELY AVAILABLE SIZES OF SOFTWOOD

Key		Thickness in mm.													
sawn	Width in mm.	9	12	15	16	19	21	22	25	28	34	38	46	50	63	70
PAR	21														
	25							~				~			
	34														
	38							~		~					
	46														
	50											~			
	150-300	~	~		~		~					~			

Hardwood is usually sold planed all round. The most common sizes are: 21×21mm, 34×21mm, 34×34mm, 46×21mm, 46×46mm and boards which vary in width from 150 to 300mm in standard thicknesses of 6, 9, 12, 15 and 21mm. Timber merchants may stock other sizes and may be willing to place a special order for large quantities. Some timber merchants will plane hardwood to special sizes if given a few days' notice.

Buying timber

Timber can usually be bought from d-i-y shops, some hardware stores and iron-mongers, builders' merchants and, of course, timber merchants. The smaller shops and many builders' merchants do not stock hardwoods but most towns have at least one timber merchant or saw mill selling softwoods and hardwoods.

Timber merchants are often cheaper than other shops, particularly for large quantities, and tend to know more about wood – how to use it and how to treat it. But the larger ones are often busy supplying the trade and will generally expect a fairly large order presented in a knowledgeable manner. Many will not cut softwoods to size – they deal in the standard metric sizes only.

Small timber merchants who rely heavily on d-i-y customers and builders' merchants mainly stock softwoods. The timber can vary in quality so it is essential to choose it carefully yourself and not to order it by telephone. However, by careful choice, it is possible to buy small quantities of good quality timber cheaper than from many large timber merchants. From time to time, small timber merchants obtain limited quantities of new or reclaimed hardwoods. If you have much call for hardwoods, it may be worthwhile making frequent visits and to buy materials for future use.

Many d-i-y shops carry a stock of standard size softwoods and will often cut wood to size, though the cost may be fairly high.

Timber prices can vary widely so it is worth shopping around before you buy. Stockists generally work out their timber prices on the basis of its cost a cubic metre. What this means is that 1.8m length of 50×50mm softwood generally costs twice as much as a 1.8m length of 50×25mm. Very small sizes (which involve a lot of work for their volume) and very large sizes (which may be difficult for the timber merchant to get) often work out more expensive than you would expect. Many timber merchants price their softwood by the metre but sell it in the standard metric lengths. Hardwoods are sometimes priced by the square metre.

Some timber stockists use a sliding scale for working out their discounts – the more you order the less expensive it is a metre. Others have a simple cut-off point – quantities up to 100m are one price a metre, quantities over 100m are cheaper, so it can work out less expensive to buy 56 standard 1.8m lengths of softwood (100.8m) than 55 (99m). Most stockists deliver timber but charges and distances vary.

WOOD TERMINOLOGY

Annual or growth rings These can be seen when a tree is cut across its axis. Each ring represents one year's growth and consists of two parts – springwood (the inner part) and summerwood (the outer part). In many climates rapid growth occurs in spring and so springwood is generally softer than summerwood. Tropical timbers grow all year round but they still produce annual rings showing the extra growth which occurs in the rainy season – these rings are often much less visible.

Hardness A hard timber is one which is difficult to dent on the surface and on the end grain. It should not be confused with hardwoods and softwoods which refer to botanically determined groups. Hardness is a quality needed for furniture, particularly in legs and rails.

Hardwoods These come from broad-leaved trees. The trees shed their leaves in autumn in temperate climates but may remain evergreen in the tropics.

Heartwood This is obtained from the middle part of a tree. It is generally much darker than the sapwood and more resistant to decay or insect attack. It often contains resin, gum or tannin. The heartwood nearly always provides the part of the tree sold as timber.

Sapwood This is the outer layer of a tree which has not yet hardened. It is usually discarded by the woodworker as it is softer than heartwood and is prone to attack by fungi and insects.

Softwoods These come from coniferous trees which generally have needle-like leaves. They include the firs, larch, pines and spruce.

Toughness A wood is tough if it resists splitting and bends considerably before it breaks – for example, ash.

Grain and texture

Wood consists of numerous fibres which generally lie along the axis of the tree. The thickness of the fibres, their arrangement, colour and so on decide the appearance of the *grain* and the *texture* of the timber.

Close grain The annual rings are narrow bands caused by slow compact growth.

Coarse or open grain The annual rings are wide bands caused by rapid growth.

Cross grain This is a fault which occurs when the tree is being converted into timber. When timber has cross grain the fibres do not lie in line with the axis of the timber even though the timber is straight grained.

Interlocking grain The grain spirals around the tree axis and changes in direction during different growth periods. This produces a very complex grain pattern which makes timber very difficult to finish smoothly.

Short grain The fibres lie in such a manner that the timber can snap or fracture without splintering.

Straight grain The fibres lie parallel to the surface to be cut. Chair legs and rails of furniture should be made from straight-grained timber.

Coarse textured The fibres are long and wide apart.

Even textured The fibres are all very similar and there is very little difference between springwood and summerwood.

Fine textured The fibres are small and closely packed together.

Choosing timber

European redwood (often called Scots pine or deal) is one of the cheapest and easiest woods to buy. It is suitable for nearly all d-i-y jobs both inside and, with suitable preservative treatment, outside. It can, however, be fairly knotty. Spruce, which is lighter in colour than redwood and sometimes called whitewood or white deal, is occasionally offered instead of redwood, particularly in Scotland.

Douglas fir, parana pine and western hemlock come from much bigger trees than redwood and these woods are often available in large sizes and free from knots.

Western red cedar, which contains natural preservative oils, is a good choice for use outside but it is expensive and may not take varnishes well – to keep its natural appearance it needs treating with a cedar preservative.

The properties and appearance of hardwoods vary much more than softwoods. They are more difficult to buy but for many jobs are well worth considering.

The summaries give details of the more widely available softwoods and hardwoods including:

● **price rating (££)** giving an indication of the relative prices of different timbers. Prices vary from stockist to stockist and from time to time with the availability of a particular timber
● **colour** of the heartwood – the colour may vary from tree to tree and most timbers darken on exposure to light
● **strength** based on a number of individual properties such as bending, crushing, splitting and so on
● **natural durability** based on the ability of the untreated heartwood to resist fungal attack outside. Timbers with good natural durability should last for more than 25 years; those with poor natural durability may last less than five years. Many of the woods with poor natural durability absorb preservatives fairly well
● **working properties** based on the ease of sawing, planing, nailing and so on.

Softwoods

Douglas fir British Columbian pine, Columbian pine, Oregon pine
● *price rating* **££**
Grows mainly on the west coast of North America, particularly British Columbia. The sapwood forms a narrow band around the tree and is lighter in colour than the heartwood which is generally a light reddish brown. The timber has distinctive figuring when plain sawn and, because the tree is so large, it is possible to produce individual planks half a metre square by 30m in length.

Douglas fir is stronger and more durable outside than redwood. It has an even texture which makes it fairly easy to work, but to get the best results tools need to be regularly sharpened. Care should be taken when joining timber as it is very straight grained and liable to split. The timber can be glued, nailed or screwed and finished satisfactorily with stain and polish.

The timber has a great variety of uses and can be used in structural house work, flooring, furniture and window frames. Commercially it is used for things like telegraph poles and ship masts. Bought timber is often free from knots and other defects and it is one of the best softwoods available.

Parana pine
● *price rating* **££**
Grows in South America, mainly Brazil.

The timber is a creamy brown colour, often with reddish streaks. It is even textured with a straight grain and can often be obtained as wide boards free from knots. When buying this timber select the straightest boards and use it immediately to avoid twisting. If this is not possible, it should be stored flat and weighted evenly until it is needed.

Parana pine is an easy timber to work and a smooth finish can be produced. It glues, stains, polishes and paints well. It takes screws well but care is needed when nailing, especially at bowed edges, if splitting is to be avoided. It is not naturally durable and should not be used outdoors and should be kept away from direct sunlight.

The timber can be used for interior joinery and worktops. Commercially it is used as a plywood veneer.

Redwood Scots pine, European redwood, red deal, yellow deal
● *price rating* **£**
Grows in many parts of Europe and northern Asia. Wood grown in Great Britain is known as Scots pine but the majority, which is imported from the USSR and Scandinavia, is known as redwood. The colour of the sapwood varies from creamy-white to yellow; the heartwood from honey to deep reddish brown. It is a strong resinous timber with clearly visible annual rings.

The timber is fairly light and moder-

ately hard (for its weight). It is generally easy to work, takes nails and screws well and can be glued, painted, stained and varnished satisfactorily, though the quality of finish and ease of working depend upon the amount of resin and knots present. The timber is occasionally stained by a fungus which produces blue-grey streaks in the wood. This fungus does not affect the strength of the wood but makes it less likely to take paint well. The timber is not naturally durable and when used outdoors it should be treated with preservative.

Redwood is the most widely available softwood and can be used for do-it-yourself work involving both joinery and construction. It is widely used in plywood and, by the building trade, for house building including flooring and window and door frames.

Spruce European whitewood, whitewood
● *price rating* **£**
Grows in many parts of Europe, including the British Isles, and in Canada and the USA. The sapwood and heartwood are the same colour and vary from almost white to pale yellowish brown. The timber has a straight grain and a fine texture. Its growth rings are not as pronounced as those of redwood.

The timber has about the same exterior durability and strength as redwood but it does not take preservatives well and this restricts it to interior use. Provided the timber is dry, it is as easy to work as redwood (although tools do need to be kept very sharp) and can be painted, stained and varnished satisfactorily. It does not readily split and can be easily joined with nails, screws or glue. Its main advantages over redwood are its light colour (which does not darken on exposure to light) and its fine lustre.

Spruce can be used for general joinery, flooring, ceilings and furniture. It is also used as a veneer for plywood.

Western hemlock

● *price rating* **£**

Grows in Canada – mainly British Columbia – and the USA. The timber is pale brown, has a distinctive grain pattern (less prominent than Douglas fir) when plain sawn and a slight lustre. It has a straight grain, a fine and uniform texture and can be got as long wide boards.

The timber is about as strong as redwood, it can be glued, screwed or nailed (when nailing near the ends of dried boards, holes should be pre-bored to prevent splitting) and painted, stained or varnished. It also polishes well. It is not naturally durable and does not take preservatives well.

Western hemlock can be used in general joinery and construction including doors, flooring and panelling. Commercially it is used in plywood.

Western red cedar

● *price rating* **£**

Grows mainly in north-west North America, particularly Canada. The sapwood forms a narrow band around the tree and is white in colour. The heartwood is generally a deep reddish brown. The timber has a fairly coarse texture and a noticeable growth-ring figuring. The tree is the largest of the American cedars and can be converted into large boards virtually free from defects and knots.

The timber is very easy to work along the grain and a silk-like finish can be obtained. However the wood is quite soft and the end grain tends to tear or crush unless extremely sharp tools are used. The timber is much lighter and less strong than redwood and tends to mark easily but it does contain an aromatic oil which can keep it free from attack by insects and fungii and so makes it outstandingly durable outdoors. In time, the action of the weather turns untreated timber to a silver grey colour. The timber is acidic and attacks unprotected ferrous metals – corroding the metal and staining the wood. Screws and nails used outdoors should either be of a corrosion- resistant metal, like brass, or covered with a protective coating.

The timber is particularly useful outside – for external cladding, sheds, greenhouses and fence posts, for example. It can withstand high temperatures without warping or twisting and is therefore useful near radiators.

European hardwoods

Some of the hardwoods listed below also grow outside Europe and some timber merchants may offer these non-European woods in place of, or in addition to, the European woods. Japanese oak, American oak and Japanese elm are frequently-found examples. Non-European timbers are usually similar in appearance to the descriptions given below but they are often easier to work. Because of the shortage of home-grown oak, Japanese oak and Tasmanian oak are often imported – Japanese oak is slightly lighter, weaker and less durable than the home-grown wood.

Ash

● *price rating* **££**

Grows in Europe, including Great Britain, and in western Asia and north America. The sapwood and heartwood are both generally a pale creamy colour. The timber has a long straight grain and varies in texture.

Ash is about as strong as oak but is more resistant to splitting and it bends well. It is easily worked and a smooth finish can be obtained. The timber can be glued, stained and polished. It is not naturally durable.

Ash can be used for making furniture, particularly if the wood has to be bent, but avoid any heartwood which is a brown colour. Commercially, it is commonly used as handles for tools and gardening equipment.

Beech

● *price rating* **££**

Grows mainly in central Europe and Great Britain. Generally there is very little difference between the colours of the sapwood and heartwood – both vary from a very pale brown to a reddish brown. The timber has a very straight grain and a fine even texture.

Beech is hard and very strong. Its ease of working depends on how it grew and was dried, though provided sharp tools are used, a smooth finish can be obtained. The timber does not easily splinter and can be glued, stained or polished. It is not naturally durable and is mainly suitable for indoor use.

Beech can be used for interior joinery and construction and for making furniture. Commercially, it is used extensively for making chairs and high quality toys. It is also used for making tools, tool handles and benches.

Elm

● *price rating* **££**

English elm grows mainly in England and Wales; Dutch elm grows throughout the British Isles and was introduced from the Netherlands. Elms were one of the most common of native timbers until the attack of Dutch Elm Disease. Although the disease destroys the living tree, it has no effect upon the quality of the converted timber. The heartwood is a light dull brown colour and shows irregular growth rings.

Both elms have similar strength properties and are exceedingly tough. The timbers are cross grained which makes them very difficult to split and they are almost imperishable in water. They also have an open and coarse grain which makes them very difficult to work but, with care, it is possible to produce a cleanly-finished surface. The timbers can be glued satisfactorily and take nails without splitting. They can also be stained, polished or waxed. The timbers are fairly durable outdoors and take preservatives fairly well.

Elm is traditionally used in farm buildings and on boats. It can also be used for weatherboarding, flooring and furniture – chair seats, for example. More recently it has become a popular wood for making garden furniture.

Lime

● *price rating* **££**

Grows in Europe, including Great

Britain. Both sapwood and heartwood are a light creamy colour. The timber has a straight grain and a fine uniform texture.

Lime probably has about the same strength as oak and resists splitting well, but it is fairly soft. It can be cut evenly in any direction but tends to be woolly and sharp tools must be used to get a smooth finish. It can be nailed and stained and polished very well. It is not naturally durable outdoors.

Lime is an excellent timber for carving and turning kitchenware such as dishes and bowls.

Oak
● *price rating* **££££**
Most oaks are found in the temperate regions of the northern hemisphere. British oak is the straightest and most durable of all the oaks. The sapwood forms a fairly narrow band around the tree and is lighter in colour than the golden brown heartwood. When plain-sawn, the growth rings produce very attractive markings; when quarter-sawn, the surface is figured with rays. The timber is a pale colour when first worked but darkens with age.

The timber is very strong and naturally durable outside. In general, it is not easy to work because of its hardness and coarse grain. The ease of working often depends on the amount of cross grain present and how well the timber has been dried but, as a general rule, tools used need to be sharp, and kept sharp, to produce the best finish and reduce the effort involved. The timber can be glued satisfactorily and takes nails and screws well, except near edges where it should be pre-bored. Oak is acidic and tends to accelerate the corrosion of metals. It is also stained by metals containing iron.

The timber can be used for a wide range of purposes because of its all-round strength – for example for furniture, door and window frames and sills, beams, posts, gates, fencing, boats, and as a veneer. Oak used outdoors is often 'green' to make it cut and nail easily. On drying, its surface will crack and the wood will bleach. Oak bought for indoor use (for furniture, say) should be thoroughly dry when bought.

Non-European hardwoods

Many traditional imported hardwoods, such as teak, are still available but their supply is limited and they can be very expensive. Some of the timbers listed below may have very unfamiliar names but they are in common use today as substitutes for the traditional imported hardwoods. For instance, iroko is often decribed as a teak substitute or African teak when it is used in furniture making.

Agba moboron, tola
● *price rating* **££**
Grows in West Africa. The sapwood and heartwood are very similar in colour and vary from yellowish pink to reddish brown. It has a straight grain and looks like a lighter-coloured mahogany.

The wood has a fine texture and generally works easily but it can sometimes be a little difficult to saw because of its gumminess. The timber can be joined easily – it takes glues, nails and screws well – and can be given a good final finish with stain and polish. Planks may be marked with small holes (produced by a tree beetle that dies when the wood is converted). The timber is very resistant to decay even without preservative treatment.

The timber can be used for furniture, joinery, panelling and flooring. It is a useful general-purpose timber, especially where wood-working properties and natural durability are important. But it has a slight resinous odour which makes it unsuitable for use in situations where it is likely to come into contact with food. Commercially, it has many uses, particularly as plywood and as a veneer.

Idigbo emeri, framiré
● *price rating* **££**
Grows in many parts of Africa. The colour of the timber varies from pale yellow to light brown. It has a uniform fairly straight grain, a fairly coarse and uneven texture and sometimes has figurings which look like plain-sawn oak.

The timber is similar to oak for many of its strength properties but splits more easily and does not resist shock so well. It can be worked easily and given a smooth finish. It takes glue well, can hold screws and nails fairly well and can be stained and finished with polishes and varnishes. Idigbo is naturally durable outside.

Idigbo is a very useful timber for fine carpentry, joinery, construction work, flooring and door and window frames. Commercially, it is used as a veneer for plywood. In damp situations, avoid using idigbo near fabrics – it may leach a yellow stain – and avoid contact with ferrous metals which may stain the wood and may be corroded.

Iroko
● *price rating* **££**
Grows in many parts of tropical Africa. The heartwood has a superficial resemblance to teak being a golden brown with yellowish streaks. It usually has an interlocked grain and a coarse, but even, texture.

A strong, hard and very durable wood. In spite of its open texture and interlocked grain, it works well with sharp tools (but tools do tend to blunt faster than average). It can be given a good finish, particularly if the grain is filled. It can be glued, nailed and screwed.

It can be used as a substitute for teak when making furniture.

Another substitute for teak is *Freijo* (££), which is grown in Brazil.

Jelutong
● *price rating* **££**
Grows mainly in Malaysia. The sapwood and heartwood are both initially creamy white but darken to a straw colour after exposure to air. The timber has a straight grain, an even fine texture and a lustrous surface.

Jelutong is a weak, brittle and soft timber which is easy to work and can be given a very smoothly finished surface. It can be joined satisfactorily with glues, nails and screws and takes stains, polishes and varnishes well. It is not naturally durable outside but readily takes preservatives.

The uses of Jelutong are restricted by latex canals which occur at intervals of about a metre along its length and mean that perfect timber comes in short pieces only. It is one of the 'newer' timbers and so it may not be widely available.

Mahogany
There are two basic types of mahogany – the original mahogany from Central

America traditionally known as American mahogany or Honduras mahogany, and the more recently introduced timber with broadly similar properties known as African mahogany. Both types cover a variety of timbers under the mahogany umbrella.

Mahogany (African)
● *price rating* **£££**

A name which covers all species of *Khaya* found in many parts of Africa. The species are similar in colour to the American mahoganies but their texture is usually more coarse and their grain more interlocked.

All African mahoganies are similar in strength to American mahoganies but are more resistant to splitting. They can all be glued satisfactorily, take nails and screws well and can be polished. All are moderately durable outdoors.

African mahoganies can be used for furniture, high quality joinery, panelling and flooring. They were at one time cheaper than the American mahoganies and were often used instead. Nowadays, there is often little difference in price between the two types. Commercially, they are used as a veneer.

Mahogany (American) Brazilian mahogany
● *price rating* **££**

Grows throughout Central and South America and is usually named according to its country of origin. The properties of the timber depend, to some extent, on its origin – the following summary refers to Brazilian mahogany (now the most widely available) and compares it with the original Honduras mahogany. The colour of Brazilian mahogany is more variable than Honduras mahogany ranging from a rich mellow brown to a deep rich red. The timber usually has a uniform medium texture but the grain varies from straight to interlocked.

Mahogany is very strong (for its weight) and easy to work but some timbers may need heavy sanding to remove woolliness and produce a smooth surface. It takes glues, nails and screws well and can be given an excellent finish with stains and polish. It is naturally durable outdoors.

It can be used for furniture, high-class internal and external joinery and for flooring. Commercially, it is used as a veneer.

Obeche
● *price rating* **££**

Grows in West Africa. The sapwood and heartwood are similar in colour – both vary from a creamy white to a pale straw colour. The timber has an even fine texture but some boards may have an interlocked grain – similar to some mahoganies. Quarter-sawn boards may have a faint stripe.

Obeche is light in weight, fairly soft and not as strong as European redwood. It is very easy to work but is liable to crumble unless sharp tools are used. It can be glued, takes nails and screws well and absorbs stain very readily. For a high-class finish, its open grain should be filled before it is polished or varnished. The timber may contain holes produced by worms that die when the tree is converted.

Obeche can be used in drawer and frame construction for 'whitewood' furniture and in interior joinery. Commercially, it is used as one of the thicker inner layers in plywood.

Sapele
● *price rating* **£££**

Grows in West Africa. The sapwood is totally different in colour from the heartwood which is a typical mahogany colour – reddish brown. The timber has a pronounced regular stripe particularly when it is quarter-sawn and a clear cedar-like odour. It has a fairly close texture and an interlocked grain.

Sapele is stronger than African or American mahogany, generally works well (though the interlocked grain can occasionally cause problems), can be glued and takes nails and screws. It can be stained and polished very well and it is moderately durable outdoors.

Sapele can be used for making furniture, cabinets, and for panelling, flooring and joinery. Commercially, it is used as a veneer.

Teak
● *price rating* **£££££**

Grows in India and Burma. The timber has a greenish brown colour which darkens with age to a brown or dark brown colour which sometimes has a dark brown figuring. Teak from Burma generally has a straight grain whereas that from India has a more wavy grain. It has a coarse uneven texture, looks dull and feels oily.

Teak is strong, has variable working qualities, tends to blunt cutting tools, takes nails and screws reasonably well, can be glued and can be given a good finish with stains and polishes. Teak contains a natural oil which makes it very resistant to decay. It also resists acids and fire reasonably well.

Because of its high resistance to acids, fire and rot, teak can be used in wet conditions for garden furniture, draining boards, duck-boards and so on. It can also be used for furniture, wood block flooring and high-class joinery. Commercially, it is now seen mostly as veneer.

Utile
● *price rating* **£££**

Grows in many parts of tropical Africa. The sapwood is different in colour from the heartwood which is a reddish brown and is similar to sapele (a related species). Like sapele, the timber has a broad stripe (more irregular than with sapele) and an interlocked grain. It has a more open texture than sapele.

Utile is similar in strength to American mahogany, works well but blunts cutting edges slightly, glues well, can be stained and, after the open pores have been filled, will polish well.

Utile can be used for making furniture, cabinets, and for panelling, flooring and joinery. Commercially, it is used as a veneer.

Walnut (African)
● *price rating* **£££**

Grows in Cameroons, Gabon, Ghana, Nigeria and Zaire. Unlike European walnut, which is now almost unobtainable, it is not a true walnut but is similar in appearance having a mid brown colour with dark stripes and a lustrous surface. It is, in fact, related to African mahogany and, like this wood, usually has an interlocked grain.

The timber is reasonably strong, works fairly easily, though sharp tools should be used to avoid tearing the grain. It is easy to nail but care must be taken to avoid splitting and can be rather difficult to finish – though filling followed by sanding can produce a very smooth surface.

It can be used as an alternative to European walnut for panelling, furniture and joinery. Commercially, it is used as a veneer.

Man-made boards

One of the main limitations of natural wood is its size – for example, if you want to make a table top, you will probably have to glue planks edge to edge and this is not easy. Man-made boards – blockboard, chipboard, hardboard, laminboard and plywood – come in large sheet sizes. These boards are all different in their character and properties. The Table should help you decide whether to use a man-made board instead of natural wood for a particular job.

Choosing man-made boards for use outside requires a great deal of care. All man-made boards contain glues (or resins) and only some of these will stand up to the weather – use only those boards which specifically say 'exterior' grade.

Storing man-made boards also requires care – keep them indoors laid flat.

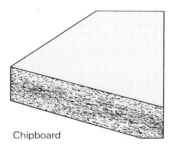

Chipboard

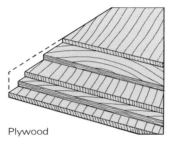

Plywood

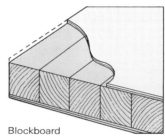

Blockboard

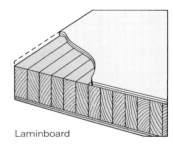

Laminboard

COMPARISON OF MAN-MADE BOARDS

	blockboard	chipboard	hardboard	laminboard	plywood	European redwood
resistance to warping	good	very good	may buckle when moisture content increases*	good	good, can twist	moderate
screw holding	good, except in end grain of core	fairly poor, but not a major problem	not recommended	good, except in end grain of core	good, including edges	good, except in end grain; care needed near edges
finishing the faces	prime before painting; core joints and gaps can show through veneers with high-gloss finish	for painting, use boards with fine-particle faces; apply a filling primer unless using factory-primed board	prime before painting, unless using sealed board	prime before painting	prime before painting	prime before painting; use knotting on knots
gluing the edges	good, except on end grain of core	fairly good on all edges	not recommended	good, except on end grain of core	fairly good on all edges	good, except on end grain
stiffness	good in one direction, fair in the other	poor in both directions	poor in both directions	very good in one direction, fair in the other	good in both directions	very good in one direction, poor in the other
thicknesses available	12 to 25mm	4 to 40mm	2 to 12mm	12 and 18mm	3 to 24mm	up to 75mm
most common thicknesses	12 to 25mm	12, 18, 22, 24mm	3.2, 4.8, 6.4mm	12 and 18mm	4 to 18mm	up to 75mm
sizes readily available	1525×1525mm 1220×2440mm 1525×3050mm	from 1220× 2440mm to 1830 ×3680mm	from 610×910mm to 1220×3660mm	1525×1525mm 1220×2440mm 1525×3050mm	1220×1220mm to 1525×3660mm	up to 225mm wide up to 6.3m long
most common sizes	1220×2440mm	1220×2440mm	1220×2440mm	1220×2440mm	1220×1220mm, 1525×1525mm, 1220×2440mm	up to 225mm wide 1.8 to 3.6m long

*You can avoid this by thoroughly wetting the back face two days before use

Chipboard

Chipboard is made by gluing together small resin-coated particles of softwood under heat and pressure. The particles usually lie parallel to each other and to the surface of the board. It is one of the boards known to the trade as particle boards.

Graded density is the most common type of chipboard – it has large particles in the middle graduating to smaller particles packed together at the surface of the board. This means that it has smooth strong faces. Three-layer chipboard is similar but has three distinct layers – large particles sandwiched between outer layers of small particles. Single-layer chipboard has roughly the same size large particles throughout.

Most chipboard should not be used outside but there are special exterior grades available and a water-resistant grade made with special resins – this can be used indoors in damp conditions but not outside. An extra strong type of chipboard (more densely packed particles) has tongued-and-grooved edges and can be used for flooring. Normal chipboard (often called standard chipboard) is sold with sanded faces but you can buy chipboard with sealed faces – ready for painting – or with faces covered with a wood veneer or plastic. The most widely available wood finishes are mahogany, oak and teak. Plastic-covered chipboard is generally not as strong as normal chipboard.

Working with chipboard

Cutting Chipboard can be cut with the usual woodworking tools. However, its high resin (glue) content means that it blunts tools more rapidly than solid timber and other man-made boards. Veneered boards should always be scored on both surfaces with a marking knife before they are sawn to reduce the risk of chipping the surface veneer.

Fixing Pins, nails and screws can be fixed through chipboard but, as a rule, they should not be driven into the edge. If you need to attach something to the edge of chipboard use the special fixings available or alternatively attach a solid wood lipping to the board – see drawings below – and screw things, such as hinges, into this. Chipboard screws, with twin threads, are quicker and easier to use than normal screws and provide more grip. Chipboard takes glue well on its faces and fairly well on its edges.

Joints can be made in chipboard using the methods described for natural timber. However, there is little advantage in doing this since without the grain strength of natural timber, the strength of a chipboard joint depends solely on the glue. The best way of joining chipboard is to use glued battens at the corners or special plastic dowelling blocks – these are particularly useful when joints may have to be dismantled.

Finishing Chipboard can be finished with paint, varnish or plastic laminate. Wood veneered chipboard is usually varnished or polished. Before painting standard chipboard, fill any cut edges and sand them smooth. A normal wood primer should be used before undercoats or gloss paints. Sealed chipboard does not need priming. Standard chipboard can be treated with a coloured or wood stain and then polyurethane varnish.

Chipboard can be edged with a strip of softwood or hardwood – known as lipping – glued or pinned to the edge. Use lipping which is slightly wider than the thickness of the board and plane it down to size after fixing. Plastic strips can also be used for edging. These normally have a lip and a matching groove should be cut along the edge of the chipboard and the plastic stripping then glued and pressed into the groove. Many wood veneered chipboards are sold in a range of widths – usually in imperial sizes from 6 to 48in – with edges which are already finished with a thin strip of wood veneer. Iron-on edging strips are also available. These edging strips can vary in grain, colour, and surface finish so they need to be chosen carefully to match the existing veneer. Edging strips have a tendency to come off if the finished board is used in a warm position – over a radiator, say.

FIXINGS TO CHIPBOARD

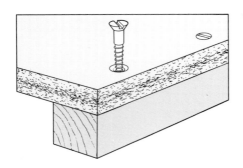

Always screw through chipboard

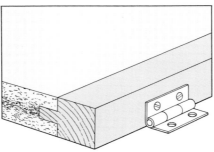

Screw hinges to solid wood lipping

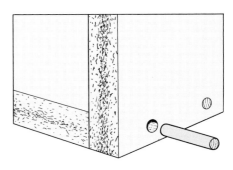

A through dowelled joint

Plywood

Plywood is made of thin sheets of wood joined together with various grades of glue. The thin sheets (veneers) are usually peeled from around a log, so they can be obtained in very large sizes. The grain in alternate sheets runs along and across the board which means that plywood behaves more uniformly than natural wood. Plywood always has an odd number of veneers to create a balance of glued surfaces and keep twisting and warping to a minimum. The grains of the surface veneers always run in the same direction. The thinnest boards are 3-ply; a thicker board might simply have thicker layers, or it might be a multi-ply with up to 11 layers.

Plywood is a remarkably versatile material and can be used to make virtually anything. It can be used outdoors to make Wendy houses, paddling pools, garden furniture, sheds and so on and indoors it can be used to make anything from shelves to wardrobes. On a grander scale, it can be used as a building material for houses, roofs, ceilings, extensions, stairs and walls.

Grades

Plywood is graded according to the quality of the surface veneers and the type of glue. It is imported from many countries and there are many different coding and grading systems.

Surface quality

The three basic grades are:

A veneer perfect – no markings or knots
B veneer has small knots and markings and may have joints
BB veneer has plugs to replace large dead knots and faults, discolouration, small knots and joints.

The grades are written B/BB indicating the grades of *each* side of the boards. Grade BB can be used for painting but for staining or varnishing you need grade B or, better still, grade A.

Glues

Plywood is made with different glues for *interior* and *exterior* use. Sometimes plywood is sold simply as interior or exterior grade but, in fact, four different types of glue are used:

WBP (Weather and Boil Proof) The glue should withstand cold and boiling water, wet and dry heat and any weather conditions. The plywood should stay glued for at least 25 years. Unfortunately, it does not follow that the board as a whole is weatherproof – the wood may not stand long exposure and the surface veneer may weaken and discolour

BR (Boil Resistant) The glue should withstand boiling water and exposure to the weather, but will deteriorate after prolonged exposure to severe conditions. The glue should withstand cold water for prolonged periods. This plywood can be used indoors in damp situations

MR (Moisture and moderately Weather Resistant) The glue should withstand weathering for a short time. It should withstand cold water for long periods and hot water for short periods but it will deteriorate quickly under boiling water. Another useful plywood for damp places

INT (Interior) The glue will not withstand damp conditions and it should be used only indoors.

Types of plywood

Most plywoods can be grouped as either timber ply or veneered ply. Timber ply is made of one timber throughout and therefore each type has its own individual properties and characteristics. Veneered ply generally has one veneered surface and a redwood reverse surface but the internal layers may be a completely different type of wood. Veneered plywoods can be very similar in their properties – they may simply differ in appearance and cost.

Some of the more common plywoods are listed below together with their main properties and suggested uses. The cost of plywood can vary enormously from shop to shop and from type to type. A rough guide to prices is also given – a ££ rated plywood generally costs around twice the price of one rated £ and so on. The exact price will, of course, depend on the availability of the woods.

Beech INT, B/B, £ Very tough but will twist unless firmly fixed and supported. Must be stored flat.

Birch INT, WBP, B/B, B/BB, £ Very strong. Must be stacked carefully to prevent twisting and distortion. A good quality edge can be achieved with care. Commonly used for drawer bottoms.

European redwood WBP, B/B, £ The surface darkens with age. Tends to be rather coarse and it is difficult to achieve a good quality edge.

Gaboon WBP, B/B, £ Lighter and less strong than birch but is unlikely to twist. The surface can be finished easily but it is difficult to achieve a good quality edge. Used mainly in furniture.

Mahogany and Utile WBP, B/BB, ££ Good quality plywood. Stable if well stacked. A good edge can be achieved with care. Mainly used for fitted and free-standing furniture.

Marine grade ply WBP, ££ to £££ Used mainly for boat building.

Red or white meranti MR, WBP, B/BB, £ Utility plywood used for constructional work. The surface is usually painted. The MR type is a cheap plywood for interior constructional use.

Veneered plywoods ££ to £££. Afrormosia, African walnut, teak, oak and sapele are the most widely available veneers.

Special finishes

Many special surface finishes can be obtained including plywood covered by plastic laminate or metal and plywood which has been primed, painted, textured, varnished, treated with preservative or covered with stone aggregate.

Tongue and grooved plywood can also be obtained for flooring.

Working with plywood

Bending Plywood bends most easily at right angles to the direction of the grain of the surface veneers. Thin plywoods can be bent without wetting or steaming. Thicker curved sections can be built up by bending and gluing thin plywoods together. If the plywood has to be dampened to bend it, make sure that it is completely dry before gluing.

Cutting Before cutting, the surfaces should be scored on both sides with a marking knife to reduce the likelihood of chipping the surface veneers. Thin plywoods – 1 to 6mm – can be cut easily with a tenon saw; thicker plywoods – 6 to 12mm – should be cut with a panel saw (or a power saw). The saw should always cut through any decorative surface – when using an electric jigsaw the plywood must be cut with the backing surface uppermost (jigsaws cut on the *up* stroke).

When drilling, place a piece of softwood beneath the plywood to prevent chipping as the drill bursts through.

The edges of plywood can usually be planed fairly easily as long as the plane is used from the corners to the middle to prevent splitting.

Fixing Plywood can be glued and takes nails, pins and screws well.

When using glue, for maximum stability make sure that the grains of the surfaces to be glued lie in the same direction. Roughen the surfaces to provide a good key for the glue, spread the glue evenly and bring the boards together applying an even pressure. Use a waterproof glue for exterior work.

Always drill a pilot hole for screws and pins to reduce the likelihood of surface veneers tearing and lifting. Use screw caps to prevent screw heads sinking into the veneer. Plywood will often split if pins or screws are driven into the edge.

Finishing Plywood can be finished with paint, varnish or plastic laminate. Both surfaces of the plywood should be finished in the same way to avoid distortion. Plywood can be edged with softwood, hardwood, metal or plastic stripping – all are best fixed with glue. Edges can also be filled and painted.

Surfaces for painting should be clean, smooth and free from grease. Edges should be smoothed and filled – an oil-based wood filler will probably produce the best finish. Plywood for use indoors can be primed with an ordinary wood primer, but for outdoor use an aluminium wood primer is preferable.

Two or more clear coats of polyurethane varnish produce a good finish – all coats, bar the final one, may have to be rubbed down with wire wool. Wax polish can be used to achieve a very fine finish. Plywood, especially birch, can be stained before varnishing – plain colours are very effective.

Blockboard and laminboard

Blockboard and laminboard are similar – both have a core of wood strips sandwiched between veneers. The strips all run one way, so that the boards are as stiff as natural wood in that direction. The veneers are at right angles to the strips, so that the boards are stiffer than natural wood in the other direction.

In blockboard – pine, say – the core strips are softwood and may be glued together and to the veneers or they may simply be glued to the veneers. The softwood strips may be glued end to end but there may be the occasional gap between strips. The veneers are usually birch though other, more decorative, veneers are also available.

Laminboard is basically a more refined form of blockboard. The wood strips are smaller – never more than 9mm wide – and are a higher density wood (both softwoods and hardwoods are used). The strips are always glued together and the boards are constructed with more care, so that cut edges should never show holes or gaps. Laminboard is heavier than blockboard and has a

smoother surface – the unevenness of the larger blockboard strips can cause ripples on the surface of the board. Like blockboard, you can get boards with decorative outer veneers.

Neither blockboard nor laminboard are available with WBP glues, so they should not be used outside. The face quality of the boards is graded – like plywood – and the most widely available grade is BB (birch-faced).

Birch-faced blockboard and birch-faced laminboard often have two sheets of veneer on each surface – these are known as 5-ply boards. With mahogany-faced blockboard the grain often runs parallel to the strips. African walnut, oak and teak-faced blockboards often have the decorative veneer on one face only.

Blockboard and laminboard are useful for very wide shelves, furniture, doors and table or work tops. Laminboard can also be used for cabinet work.

Blockboard is widely available – as standard-sized sheets or cut to size – and is about the same price as plywood. Laminboard is much less available.

Working with blockboard and laminboard

Cutting The boards can be cut with the usual woodworking tools though care is needed when the end grain is smoothed – it tends to split at the edges. Always try to make sure that the core strips run along the longest dimension.

Fixing The boards can generally be glued and take screws well along two edges and on the surfaces but the end grain of the core does not take screws well and is difficult to glue securely.

Finishing Blockboard can be finished with paint, varnish or plastic laminate. Because of its better quality and higher cost, laminboard is usually varnished. To prevent uneven surface tensions leading to the boards warping, both surfaces must be treated in the same way. Both boards can be edged by lippings either glued or pinned on. Softwood lippings can be used if the boards are to be painted; an appropriate hardwood lipping can be used with veneered boards.

Hardboard

Hardboard is a fibre building board made by taking softwood (less the bark and knots), pulping it and then hot-pressing it into thin sheets. Hardboard is not very stiff and is generally used as a covering for framework. There are many different types of hardboard – some are produced by variations in the manufacturing process or materials, others are basically 'ordinary' hardboard covered with a special finish.

Standard One surface is smooth, the other has a rough mesh texture. Available in thicknesses from 2 to 12mm, most common 3.2mm and 4.8mm (often called 5mm). Board sizes range from 1220×610mm to 3660×1220mm. Can be used for floor covering, door panels, fitted furniture, toys and drawer bases.

Tempered A water-resistant board made by impregnating it with oil. Available in thicknesses from 2 to 12mm, most common 3.2mm and 5mm. Board sizes range from 1220×610m to 3660×1220mm. Can be used instead of standard hardboard where water-resistant qualities are an advantage. Particularly suitable for floor covering, bench tops, and general outdoor use.

Medium A softer board than standard hardboard. Available with matt, silky or hard shiny surfaces. Usually available in 6.5, 9 and 12mm thicknesses. Board sizes range from 1220×610mm to 3660×1220mm. Can be used for lining walls, ceilings and partitions. Some grades are suitable for exterior use. It is soft enough to be used as a notice-board.

Double faced Both surfaces of the hardboard have a fine sealed smooth surface. Usually available in 4, 6, 9, 10.3 and 12mm thicknesses. Usual board size 2745×1220mm. Can be used for making furniture and toys.

Perforated 'pegboard' Pegboard is single-faced hardboard; other perforated boards are usually double faced. Perforated board is punched with holes or slats at regular intervals. These may be simple or complicated. It can be obtained with a painted surface. Usually available in 3.2, 5 and 6.5mm thicknesses. Board sizes from 910 × 610mm to 2440×1220mm. It is usually used in conjunction with special clips for hanging tools, kitchen equipment, or as a decorative panelling.

Enamel finish Plain, embossed, tiled or painted surfaces are available in various colours with a matt or gloss finish. The boards are usually 3.2mm thick and either 1830×1220mm or 2440×1220mm. Can be used for panelling baths, walls, ceilings and as a splashback.

Moulded finish These boards usually have a raised pattern on one surface, are generally 3.2mm thick and often have to be specially ordered.

Plastic finish These boards are faced with pvc or melamine. Pvc-finished boards may be plain patterned or wood grained. Unlike plywood covered by plastic laminate, these boards will not stand harsh treatment. Usually 3.2mm thick and either 1830×1220mm or 2440×1220mm. Can be used for sliding doors, splashbacks and wall and bath panels.

Working with hardboard

Bending Hardboard can be bent by pinning one edge of the board and bending the board bit by bit, pinning it as you go. The bend must be supported.

If you want to make a bend with a small radius, soak the board in warm water for two to three hours, then stack it under cover (to prevent evaporation) for a further 24 hours. The boards can then be fixed to supports, or bent and temporarily secured around a former and allowed to dry – this will give you an unsupported shape. Make the radius of the former smaller than the eventual radius you want from the hardboard to allow for any spring back in the board.

Cutting Hardboard can be cut easily with a tenon saw. Cut it from the smooth side and support the ends to prevent the board breaking or tearing. Take care when sawing – if the saw jumps out of the cut it will permanently scratch the surface. If the hardboard has a painted or laminated surface, this should be scored with a marking knife before the board is cut on the waste side.

Rough cut edges of hardboard can be smoothed with conventional woodworking tools – with a plane or a trimming tool followed by rubbing down with abrasive paper.

Fixing In general, hardboard should be stored flat and care should be taken to avoid damaging its edges and corners. Hardboard can be fixed to a framework by glue, nails, pins or screws. Before fixing, manufacturers recommend a number of special treatments to reduce the likelihood of it buckling through a change in moisture content after fixing. In most cases this simply means standing the boards separately on edge in the room where they are to be used – 48 hours for medium hardboard and 72 hours for standard and tempered hardboard. Air must be allowed to circulate freely around the boards. But if you want to use standard or tempered hardboard in a new building (a home extension, say), outside or in damp rooms such as bathrooms or kitchens, it should be conditioned by washing the mesh surface of each 2440×1220mm sheet with a litre of water. The boards should then be placed back to back and laid flat for 48 hours (standard boards) or 72 hours (tempered boards). The boards should be fixed immediately after conditioning.

Apart from tempered boards, all hardboards can be glued on either side. If you want to glue the smooth side roughen it first with abrasive paper.

If you use ordinary nails, pins or screws to fix hardboard they may rust unless they are painted. Hardboard pins, which are specially designed with a coppered finish and diamond-shaped heads, fix hardboard neatly and are rustproof.

Finishing Hardboard is usually finished by painting or wallpapering it. Indoors, apply a coat of hardboard primer or diluted emulsion paint (1 litre of water to 4 litres of emulsion) first; outdoors, use an aluminium-based wood primer.

Saws for wood

A saw is a piece of toughened steel with teeth cut into one edge and a wooden or plastic handle. In some form or other, saws have been one of the principal woodcutting tools for thousands of years. The different types of saw for different jobs can roughly be divided into three main groups:
● saws for cutting *along* the grain of wood – rip saws
● saws for cutting *across* the grain of wood – cross-cut saws
● saws for cutting *curves* or special shapes, such as bow-saws and fret saws. There are also special purpose saws for cutting wood while it is still on the tree – pruning saws, for example.

Saws differ in the size and shape of the blade, and the size, shape and number of teeth they have. **Rip** teeth, which are designed for cutting down the grain of wood, work like small chisels. The front edge of each tooth is more or less perpendicular to the saw edge and the back edge slopes at about 30 degrees. If saws with teeth like this are used to cut across wood grain, they tend to tear the fibres and leave a jagged edge. Rip teeth are generally *straight-sharpened* – the tip of each tooth is perpendicular to the cutting line. **Cross-cut** teeth, which are designed for cutting across wood grain, generally slope back rather more and are usually *cross-sharpened* – the teeth are sharpened at an angle to the saw so that the outside edge of each tooth is pointed. Cross-cut teeth tend to cut through the wood fibres rather like a knife. **Fleam** teeth slope back even more than cross-cut ones and have symmetrical points.

Saw teeth are usually *set* – teeth are bent slightly outwards from the blade, alternately in each direction, so that the width of the slot cut by the saw is greater than the width of the blade. This prevents the saw jamming in the slot when cutting and lets you change the direction of the cut slightly during sawing. An even set is essential: saws which are badly set tend to wander from the cutting line.

For years, saw blades have been made from hardened steel which has been tempered to reduce the hardness (and increase the toughness) so that the blade wears well but is still soft enough to be sharpened with a file. More recently, however, saws have been introduced which have 'hardpoint' teeth – the tips of the teeth are hardened to reduce wear. Saws with hardpoint teeth can have several times the life of a conventional saw, but they cannot be sharpened by conventional methods and they are much more easily damaged when they meet a nail in their path.

There are, confusingly, two systems for describing the number of teeth a saw has – both are still based on imperial measurements. The first method records the number of complete teeth in an inch length of blade. The second method states the number of tooth points in an inch, starting on a point and including this in the count. The two methods can be confusing since a saw with eight points per inch actually has seven teeth per inch. The second method is the most widely used and the terminology is often shortened to talk about an eight-point saw, for example. Saws with large teeth generally cut faster but leave a rougher edge than saws with small teeth.

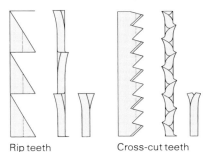

The rip teeth on the left have three teeth to the inch and four points. The cross-cut teeth on the right have nine teeth to the inch and ten points

Rip teeth   Cross-cut teeth

Types of saw

The saws used for cutting straight lines in large or thick pieces of wood are known as handsaws. For more accurate work – such as making joints – you use a back-saw. The saws used for cutting curves and holes are quite different.

Handsaws

The word handsaw is a generic term covering the three main types of saw which are similar in appearance – cross-cut saw, panel saw and rip saw. All three have a thin flexible saw blade which is deeper at the shoulder (handle) end than at the toe end. The back of the blade is often skewed, and the whole blade can

be taper-ground (thicker on the blade edge than on the top edge and thicker at the handle end than at the toe end). These saws generally come in blade lengths of 20 to 26in – the smaller ones are panel saws and the larger ones generally rip saws.

Rip saws are used for cutting along the grain of the timber. They have fairly coarse teeth (about five points) and are especially useful for cutting large or thick pieces of wood.

Cross-cut saws have teeth designed for cutting fairly thick timber across the grain. They usually have seven or eight points per inch.

Panel saws vary considerably. They are designed for cutting panels of man-made boards such as plywood and chipboard. Often the teeth are similar to those on cross-cut saws, but smaller (about nine to eleven points). Sometimes panel saws have cross-cut teeth which are straight-sharpened (like a rip saw). A panel saw is often the only handsaw you need since it can be used to cut both with and across the grain of wood (though it does both jobs more slowly than the individual rip and cross-cut saws) and it can also be used to cut man-made panels which both rip and cross-cut saws have difficulty coping with.

Using a handsaw is quite simple – it should be gripped with the index finger pointing down the blade and pressure should be applied (not too heavily) on the forward stroke only. Keep the saw at an angle of around 60 degrees to the wood when rip cutting and rather less when cutting panels and cross-cutting. When cutting thin panels make sure that the panel is well supported on both sides of the sawing line and take care when finishing a cut. Avoid any situation (such as cutting wood between two supports) where the wood will tend to sag and jam the saw blade near the end of a cut, or possibly even split or tear the wood.

Backsaws

Saws which have a rigid brass, steel or sometimes even plastic back along the top edge of the blade are covered by another generic term – backsaw. The back keeps the saw blade rigid, but also means that it cannot pass completely through the wood. The main difference between the two saws in this group – tenon saw and dovetail saw – is simply one of size.

Tenon saws are designed for cutting tenons but can be used to cut most woodworking joints, thin sheet material and accurate angles when used with some kind of mitring device. Most people choose one with a blade around 10 to 12in long with about 15 points. The depth of the blade is important if you want to use it with a mitre box – around 75mm is usually sufficient. The material of the back is not important provided the blade is held rigidly, though some people would say that the heavier it is, the better. Brass-backed saws tend to be the most expensive. The saws usually have cross-cut teeth which are straight-sharpened.

Dovetail saws are for all practical purposes smaller versions of tenon saws. They can be used where you need a fine, but not very deep, cut such as making a dovetail joint. The blades are typically eight inches long and the saw has around 20 points but the teeth are not set.

There are also very small backsaws which usually have a simple turned handle and are used mainly for very fine work or model making. They are rarely used by the handyman.

When cutting, try to keep the saw blade at right angles to the wood (always do this when cutting mitres or squaring off the wood) unless you are making a joint – such as a stopped dovetail – where this is not possible. You can cut the wood both with and across the grain. Holding the wood firmly when you are using a backsaw is usually less of a problem than when you are using a handsaw – the wood is generally smaller and for most joints it can be held in a vice.

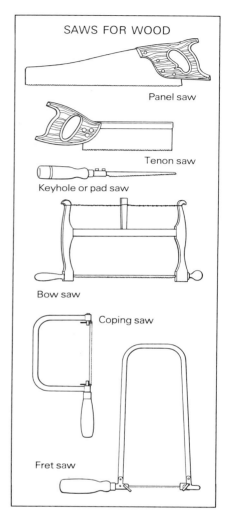

SAWS FOR WOOD

Panel saw

Tenon saw

Keyhole or pad saw

Bow saw

Coping saw

Fret saw

USING A HANDSAW

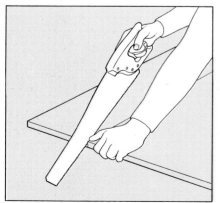

Guide the blade carefully with your thumb when starting the cut. Keep to the waste side of the cutting line

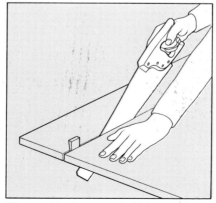

When making long cuts, hold the wood open with a wedge to reduce the likelihood of the saw jamming

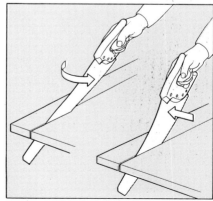

Twist the blade slightly to correct any wandering: bend it slightly if you need to bring it back to right angles with the surface

Curve-cutting saws

There are three main narrow-bladed hand saws used for cutting curves in wood – the bow saw, the coping saw and the fret saw. A keyhole saw may also be used.

Bow saws are used for cutting gentle curves. They have a wooden frame with the blade tensioned by a twisted string. The blade can be twisted through 360 degrees – so it can be turned to follow curves – and cuts on the forward stroke.

Coping saws are perhaps the most useful of the curve-cutting saws. They are similar in shape to a large junior hacksaw, have a round wooden handle and a narrow blade which can swivel through 360 degrees and cuts on the forward stroke. The blade of a coping saw is tensioned by turning the handle. The main limitation of a coping saw is its frame – it can only saw as far into wood as the frame is deep. When making an enclosed cut in wood, drill a hole into the wood and then thread the blade through the hole before fitting it into the frame. When following a curve, you should stop every so often to turn the blade, rather than merely moving the whole frame but make sure when you do this that the blade does not become twisted.

Fret saws are used for cutting very tight curves and for fine work, especially on thin wood such as plywood. A fret saw blade is very narrow and is positioned with its teeth facing towards the handle. The spring of the frame holds it taut. Unlike most saws, fret saws are generally used with their blades vertical.

Keyhole saws (or padsaws) are not easy to use and are generally used as a last resort when nothing else is suitable – for making enclosed cuts in a large panel for instance. The blades cut on the backward stroke and pressure should not be applied on the forward (downward) stroke otherwise the blade is likely to bend. As with coping saws, you start cutting by drilling a hole in the wood and then inserting the saw blade.

USING A TENON SAW

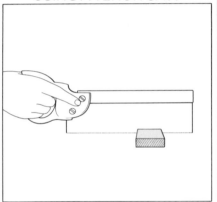

Guide the saw with your index finger and use the full length of the blade

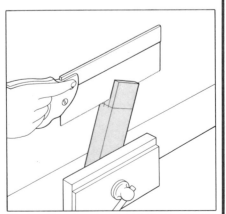

Start cutting at an angle so that you can see the cutting lines clearly

SAWING SHAPES AND HOLES

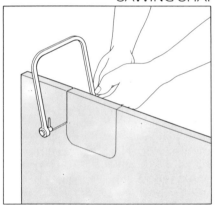

When using a coping saw, start sawing downwards with the frame at a slight angle

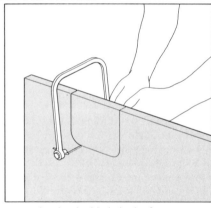

. . . and twist the blade in the frame to continue the curve

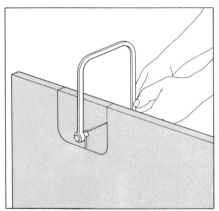

Finish the cut with the blade pointing upwards. Make sure that at all times the blade is aligned correctly at each end of the frame

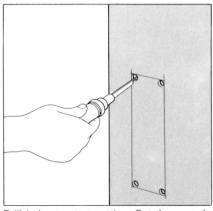

Drill holes to start cutting. Cut downwards applying pressure to the backward stroke. Repeat on the other side, then cut across the top and bottom

Buying a saw

There are several things you can do to prevent disappointment when buying a saw in a shop:

● look at the **type of handle**. Make sure that it feels comfortable in your hand and that the saw has a reasonable balance. Check that the grain of wooden handles runs along the thin parts of the handle, not across it (wood generally breaks along the grain). Avoid hollow plastic handles made by gluing two halves together – this type of plastic handle often has a tendency to separate (nipping your fingers when you use it) and may break if the saw is dropped

● check the **set** of the teeth for accuracy and evenness by holding the saw up to your eye and looking along the cutting edge. Any significant irregularities are usually obvious

● examine the **sharpening** of the teeth carefully. Some saws are not sharpened at all. You can tell if a saw has been sharpened by looking for the tell-tale file or grinding marks. Run your finger lightly along the edge to check whether the saw feels reasonably sharp. Some of the newer saws are sharpened by grinding rather than filing – these tend to be much sharper initially. Saws which have been ground usually have rounded roots to their teeth

● check the **coating** on the saw. Most saws have a lacquer coating on them when new, mainly to prevent them going rusty before they are sold. This rapidly disappears in use. However, some saws have a PTFE coating which is hard wearing and will protect the saw against rusting. A PTFE coating can make a new saw seem slightly less sharp than you would expect as it covers the tips of the teeth. This quickly wears off in use.

● think about whether you want a **hardpoint** saw. Hardened teeth may have bluish tips.

Powered saws

The two main types of power saw – circular saws and jigsaws – are dealt with in more detail on pages 121 and 122.

Circular saws can be used for long straight cuts. They are particularly useful for rip sawing – though most d-i-y saws will not cut wood more than about 40mm thick – and cutting up boards.

Jigsaws can be used for making straight cuts, cutting curves and for rip or crosscutting (though they are somewhat slow for cutting with the grain). They are much safer to use than circular saws. Jigsaws are not suitable for making joints but they can be used for many of the jobs where you would normally use a backsaw, coping saw, bow-saw or padsaw.

CUTTING A HOLE WITH A FRET SAW

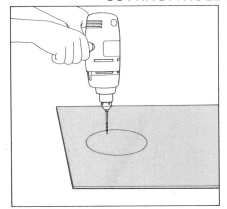

Drill a hole about 6mm in diameter just to the waste side of the circle. Thread the saw blade through and re-attach the frame. Remember to face the teeth downwards

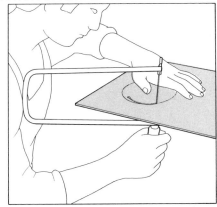

Make sure that the wood is held securely so that it cannot vibrate and start sawing away from the hole with the blade vertical. Approach the cutting line gradually

SAW SHARPENING

Nearly all handsaws and most backsaws (except those with hardpoint teeth) can be sharpened with a small triangular saw file – about 150mm long for handsaws, about 75 to 100mm for backsaws. The blades of bow saws, coping saws, fret saws and keyhole saws are usually discarded when they become blunt.

To sharpen a saw, grip the blade securely just below the teeth along the whole of its length to stop the blade chattering when you sharpen it. You can do this by placing wooden battens either side of the blade and gripping the saw plus battens in a vice. On some saws, it may make sharpening easier if you remove the handle. Level off the worn teeth with a few even smooth strokes of a file along the top of the teeth. Start sharpening at the handle end of the saw with the file in the V-groove in front of the tooth's cutting edge. File every alternate tooth which is pointing away from you, at 90 degrees to the blade for straight-sharpened teeth, and at 60 degrees to the blade for cross-sharpened teeth. Keep the file horizontal, or pointing slightly upwards. Use just enough strokes to bring the tooth to a point. When you reach the toe end of the blade, reverse the saw and repeat the sharpening process on the remaining teeth.

The teeth must then be set. The easiest way to do this is to use a saw set which bends each tooth a controlled predetermined amount. The saw blade should be clamped higher in its blocks before setting.

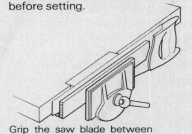

Grip the saw blade between wood battens

Planes

Planes are basically tools for shaping wood to leave it flat and, in most cases, smooth. Originally, most planes were made of wood. Nowadays, most of these have been superseded by metal planes which divide into several different types:
● conventional **bench** planes which are used mainly for smoothing wood with the grain – jack plane, jointer plane and smoothing plane

● **replaceable-blade** planes are used mainly for smoothing but can sometimes perform additional tasks such as rebating
● **small** planes which are used mainly for smoothing the end grain of wood – a block plane, for instance
● **special purpose** planes which are usually used for making special shapes – bullnose (or shoulder) plane, compass plane, plough plane and rebate plane.

Bench planes

The main difference between the three bench planes is the length of the sole plate and this determines how accurately wood can be planed flat and straight – in theory, the longer the better. The jointer plane is just less than 600mm long, the jack plane from 350 to just less than 400mm and the smoothing plane about 230mm. Jointer planes are not very widely used and of the other two the jack plane probably offers the best compromise of properties.

The blade on a bench plane does not usually cover the full width of the plane so it cannot be used for trimming close to an edge. The blade is screwed to a cap iron and inserted bevel side down. The cap iron is clamped with its edge just behind the cutting edge – the optimum distance setting varies somewhat with the type of wood and the shaving thickness, but is typically 1 to 1.5mm. The cap iron breaks the shaving immediately it is cut and this gives a smoother surface and makes the wood less likely to split. The blade and cap iron are held into the plane body at an angle of 60 degrees to the sole plate by means of the wedge iron. The depth of cut can be adjusted by turning a small knob, which governs how far the blade protrudes from the sole plate. Finally, the blade can be aligned so that it cuts evenly over its whole width by using an adjusting lever. To make sure that the blade is set correctly, look along the sole plate from the front end and move the lever until the blade protrudes evenly.

When using a bench plane, always make sure that the wood is held firmly. When planing with the grain, try to make a continuous cut along the whole length

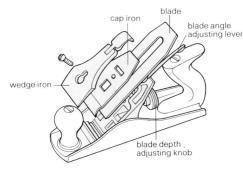

A typical bench plane

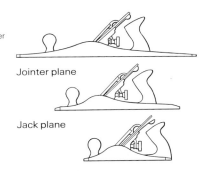

Jointer plane

Jack plane

Smoothing plane

of the timber. Apply pressure to the front of the plane when you start the stroke and the back of the plane when you finish it. When planing end grain, cut from each side towards the middle. It is possible to cut off one corner first and plane towards it, but if you take off too much with a stroke, the wood is likely to split on the far side. When planing thin

edges or chamfers, guide the plane with your fingers, so that the same portion of plane blade is used over the whole cut.

At frequent intervals when using the plane (and also before storing it), clean out all shavings and sawdust. Never rest a plane on its sole plate, always rest it on its side, and store it by hanging it up in a dry place.

USING A BENCH PLANE

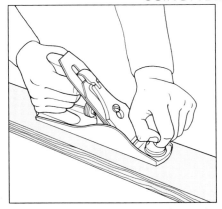

When planing long pieces of wood along the grain, keep an even downwards pressure on the plane except at the beginning and end of the stroke

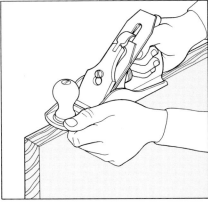

When planing edges, use your thumb to hold down the plane and use your fingers as a guide

Replaceable-blade planes

These are designed mainly for people who do not have the facilities for sharpening blades or who simply prefer the convenience of replaceable blades. A replaceable-blade plane can do any job a bench plane can do and it can do some others as well. It is usually slightly longer than a smoothing plane and narrower.

The blade is the full width of the plane, which means that the plane can be used to plane right up to an edge – cleaning up the shoulder of a tenon, for example. A guide fence is often supplied, so that the plane can be used for rebating. The models made by different manufacturers vary slightly, but typically the blade is held in by a clamp which functions in a similar way to the cap iron on a bench plane. A knurled knob provides control of the shaving thickness by adjusting the blade protrusion from the sole, and the plane also has some form of blade-tilting control.

One major advantage of replaceable-blade planes is the number of different

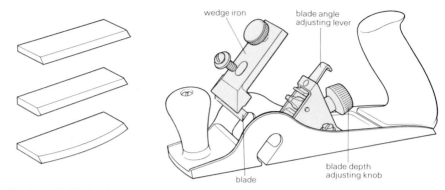

Replaceable-blade plane. Blades from the top: standard straight blade; special blade for laminates; curved blade for wide timber

types of blade which can be used. Besides the standard straight blade, there are curved blades which can be used for planing timber wider than the blade – the curve prevents digging in at the blade edges. There are also special-purpose blades which have been ground to a more obtuse angle so that the blade tends to scrape rather than shave the material being planed. This sort of blade

is particularly useful on harder materials such as plastic laminate (or possibly chipboard) and has a much longer life than a standard plane blade. Replaceable blades *can* be resharpened if required but a special holder is needed to grip the blade.

Using a replaceable-blade plane requires much the same techniques as a bench plane.

Block plane

This is smaller and narrower than a bench plane and is particularly useful for smaller work and for trimming the end grain. The facilities offered by different designs vary but all block planes differ from bench planes in two ways:
● the blade is held, bevel uppermost, at

30 degrees to the sole plate
● there is no cap iron. This is not necessary when planing end grain. Some planes have a knurled screw to hold the blade in position. With these, setting the shaving thickness and blade tilt is a matter of trial and error. The better block planes have separate adjustments for

both and often have an adjustable slot in the sole plate for the blade. This can be used to produce a similar effect to the cap iron on a bench plane.

The plane is usually held with one hand for chamfering or planing with the grain, and with two hands when trimming end grain.

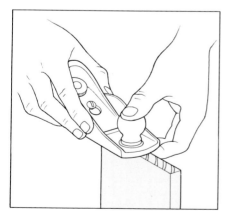

When using a block plane, work from each edge towards the centre using your fingers as a guide

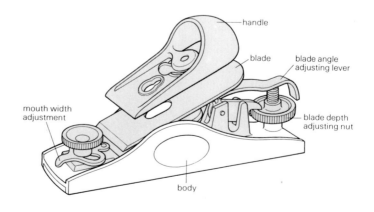

Block plane

Special-purpose planes

The work done by some of these planes can now be done more easily, more accurately, and often more cheaply by using a powered router.

The **rebate** plane can be used for making rebates (steps) along the grain in lengths of timber. A replaceable blade plane can also be used for this.

The **plough** plane can also cut rebates, but its main use is for cutting grooves in a length of timber – in the side of a drawer in order to retain the base of the drawer, for instance.

The **combination** plane can do everything that a plough plane can and can also cut special shapes – tongues and grooves and curves, for example.

The **shoulder** plane is a small plane which has a blade the same width as the sole plate (about 25mm). It is used for cleaning tenons and shoulders. Some versions have a detachable front portion (*bullnose* plane) so that the blade can cut right up to an internal corner – useful for cleaning dried glue from joints.

The **compass** plane is something like a bench plane with a flexible sole plate, which can be adjusted to the contours of regular, large radius, convex or concave curves. It requires considerable setting up and is not easy to use.

SPECIAL-PURPOSE PLANES

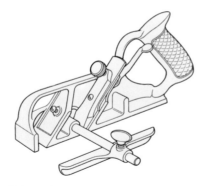
Rebate plane

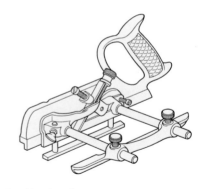
Combination plane

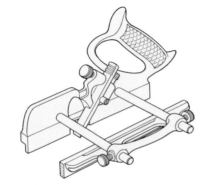
Plough plane

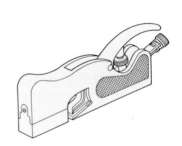
Shoulder plane

WORKING WITH SPECIAL-PURPOSE PLANES

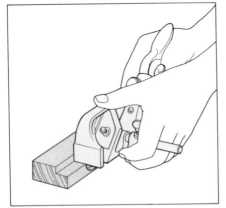

Rebate plane Keep the plane correctly positioned, particularly when starting the stroke. Guide the front of the plane with your hand and keep the fence pressed firmly against the edge of the wood. Make sure you keep the plane upright

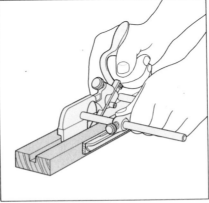

Plough plane Make sure the guide fence is secure. Grip the fence with your left hand and press inwards when cutting

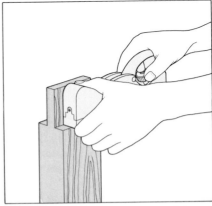

Shoulder plane Keep the plane upright and pressed well into the corner of the shoulder or tenon. Work in from the edges to avoid splitting the wood

Spokeshaves

Spokeshaves are the traditional tools for planing curves. Most spokeshaves are made of metal. The type you need depends on the curves you want to smooth. One type has a flat base for finishing convex curves and the other has a concave base for concave curves. Two patterns are available which differ in their blade settings – on one the blade is set by trial and error, on the other the blade tilt and protrusion can be adjusted accurately. The latter is preferable.

Spokeshaves are fairly easy to use on softwoods but are more difficult to use on many hardwoods – they have a tendency to dig in because of the lack of blade support. When using a spokeshave, always plane *with* the grain.

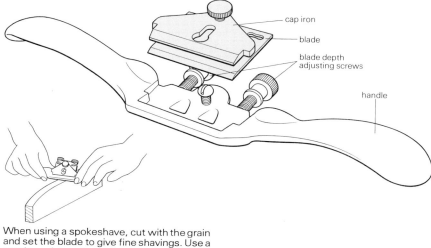

cap iron
blade
blade depth adjusting screws
handle

When using a spokeshave, cut with the grain and set the blade to give fine shavings. Use a gentle wrist action when cutting shallow curves

SHARPENING PLANES (AND CHISELS)

Flat plane blades – called plane irons – and chisels are fairly easy to sharpen; tools with curved blades are more tricky. All blades have two angles – a grinding angle of 25 degrees and a sharpening (honing) angle of 30 degrees. New plane blades come with the 25 degree bevel ground on the front edge, but need to be sharpened before they are used.

For sharpening blades you usually need an oilstone. There are three grades commonly available – coarse, medium and fine. Coarse stones are used for regrinding a blade. For sharpening it you need a medium or fine stone. Combination stones (with two sides of different grades) are also available. Oilstones should be kept in a suitable box which has wooden end pieces which are slightly shallower than the stone – to prevent a blade being damaged when it runs off the edge of the stone. The box should be securely fixed to a workbench (or something similar) when the stone is being used. Oil the stone lightly before use and clean it frequently by wiping it with a soft cloth or tissue.

To resharpen an undamaged blade, hold it at an angle of 30 degrees to the stone (bevel side down) and rub it backwards and forwards along the length of the stone until a burr (sometimes called a wire edge) builds up along its edge. Reverse the blade, lay it flat on the stone and rub it backwards and forwards a few times to either remove the wire edge or bend it back. If it does not fall off, repeat the honing process applying slightly less pressure, until you get an edge which cuts paper cleanly. When sharpening blades which are wider than the stone, hold the blade at an angle so that the whole edge rests on the stone.

The sharpening angle is very important and a honing guide should be used to help maintain the correct angle. Although 30 degrees is normally the optimum angle, it is better to increase this to about 38 degrees when planing man-made boards such as chipboard and plastic laminates.

If a blade is damaged – if it has nicks in it, has been mistreated or has rounded corners – it will need regrinding. A coarse oilstone can be used, with the blade held at 25 degrees, but a grinding wheel is much quicker. Make sure that the blade is held squarely, securely and at the correct angle. Apply minimal pressure to avoid overheating (if this happens the tip of the blade will turn blue) and move the blade from side to side to ensure even grinding. Wheels tend to give a hollow-ground edge as the grinding surface is circular. You can get round this problem by using the side of the grinding wheel.

After regrinding, use a medium grit oilstone for a few strokes to speed up the final honing on a fine stone.

There are a few special sharpening tools available which have a bonded fibre wheel covered with a fine abrasive paste. These are capable of giving an edge somewhat superior to an oilstone, but are unlikely to be used by the handyman.

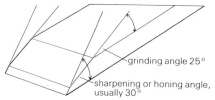

grinding angle 25°
sharpening or honing angle, usually 30°

Grinding or sharpening angles of a chisel or plane blade

Chisels

Chisels are almost essential tools for serious woodworking jobs like making joints and cutting recesses. They are also useful tools for cutting out parts of rotting woodwork. All chisels have a flat steel blade with a wooden or plastic handle and have a cutting edge on the end of the blade. Similar woodworking tools with rounded blades are known as gouges.

Types of chisel

The **bevel-edge** chisel is the most common type of chisel. As its name suggests, its upper edges are bevelled (have sloping sides) so that it can undercut or cut sideways into the corner of an acute angle. The **paring** chisel has a long thin blade which is usually bevel-edged. It can be used for cleaning out deep holes or long slots in wood where other chisels cannot reach. It should never be used as a lever, only for paring off wood. The blade of a **firmer** chisel is rectangular in cross-section but otherwise it is similar to the bevel-edge chisel. The **mortise** chisel has a thick, rectangular section blade and a strong handle. It is designed specifically for cutting mortise joints in which the chisel is subjected to hammering and bending.

In theory, a firmer chisel is supposed to be stronger than a bevel-edge chisel and a mortise chisel should be stronger still. In practice, the strength of a chisel depends on the design of the blade, particularly the shoulder and tang, and on the type and heat treatment of the steel used. To satisfy the British Standard for chisels, the blade must be hardened to within 25mm of the shoulder, and must also be able to pass certain bending tests. There are now one or two brands of bevel-edge chisel which are sufficiently well designed and so well made that they can quite easily be used for mortising without any likelihood of damage. So it seems that a good set of bevel-edge chisels is all you need.

New chisels are not usually sharpened. To get a cutting edge, first make sure that the back of the chisel is flat by rubbing it across an oilstone until an even polished surface is obtained. Then hone the edge using the technique described for a plane iron. The sharpening angle of a chisel is very critical; a variation of only 3 degrees can make as much

CHISELS

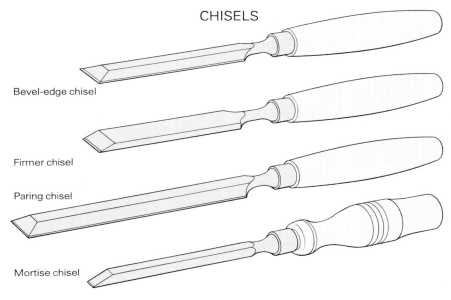

Bevel-edge chisel

Firmer chisel

Paring chisel

Mortise chisel

difference to the life of the blade as the total variation in blade quality of most of the brands on the market. For good quality chisels on softwood, the best grinding angle is around 30 degrees. On hardwoods, this figure should be increased to around 35 degrees. Increasing the angle means that more force is required to use the chisel. On the other hand, decreasing the angle will increase wear. Even a good chisel will blunt rapidly with a honing angle less than about 27 degrees.

Chisels are used for a wide variety of jobs and, like screwdrivers, they tend to be used for some rather unorthodox tasks – often to their detriment. Their main intended uses are:
● removing wood when making joints such as housings, lap joints, mortises and dovetails
● paring, or removing thin slivers from

GOUGES

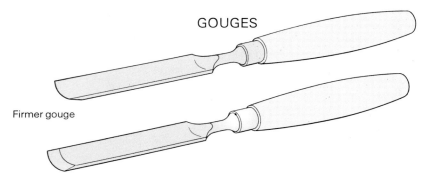

Firmer gouge

Scribing gouge

the edge of a piece of wood, often across the grain.

For paring, you use a chisel with its bevel upwards. Always make sure that you keep both hands behind the cutting edge – one hand on the handle and the other over the top of the blade. And always secure your workpiece firmly. Make sure that if the chisel slips it will not cause damage to you or the wood.

When removing wood from a mortise, you generally drive a chisel into the wood with a mallet. When you do this, start the cut well on the waste side of the wood, with the flat side of the blade nearest the cutting line. If you start the cut on the line, the wedge shape of the blade tip will drive the blade past it when the chisel is driven in. Moreover, the

tendency to use the edge of the wood as a fulcrum when levering out the waste wood will bruise the edge of the wood left and create an unsightly joint. When most of the waste wood has been removed, clean up to the line by paring away the remaining wood.

Buying chisels

For most jobs you need only four chisels ranging in size from 6 to 25mm. But you need to choose them with care.

Handles are made of either wood or plastic. If you choose chisels with wooden handles, go for those made of close-grained wood such as box (this is usually marked on the packaging) and

make sure that the ferrules are securely fitted. Plastic handles can generally be hit with a hammer when a mallet is not available – the likelihood of significant damage is very much less than with wood. Check that the handle feels comfortable to hold (for both horizontal and vertical chiselling) and that it is securely attached to the blade.

Blades should be flat and properly ground. Make sure that they are not thin at the blade shoulder (this is the weakest point on many chisels). A blade which has a slight taper on it (thinner at the blade end than at the shoulder) is also worth looking for. Chisel cutting edges are easily damaged so properly fitting blade guards are very useful.

USING A CHISEL

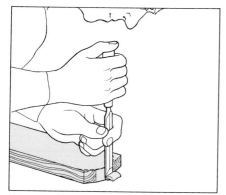

When paring, place the workpiece on scrap timber, keep the chisel upright pressing down with your thumb. Keep your head above the chisel . . .

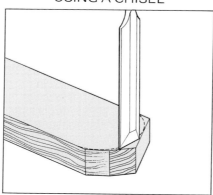

. . . start cutting at the corner of the wood and work inwards towards the cutting line, taking off finer and finer shavings

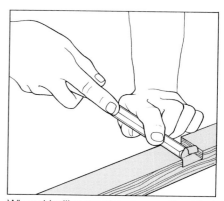

When chiselling out a housing, use the chisel pointing slightly upwards from both sides to remove most of the wood. Then use the chisel horizontally

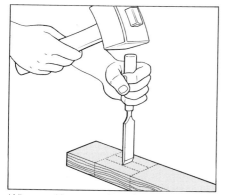

When making a mortise, choose the correct size of chisel and drive it into the centre of the waste removing about 5mm deep wedge of wood

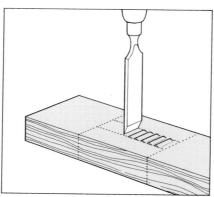

Make successive cuts on both sides of the wood to within 3mm of the ends and remove the waste

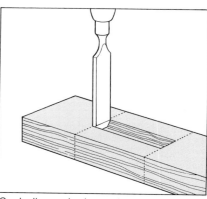

Gradually work down through the wood finally cleaning up the ends with the chisel held vertically

Making holes in wood

If you want to make large holes in wood, you will probably need some kind of saw. For making small holes, you need a drill (or a brace) and a bit. You can buy many different sizes and shapes of bit – some designed for hand drills, some for braces and some for electric drills. All cutting bits are driven in a rotary motion.

Hand drill This has a small, hand or key-tightened, three-jaw chuck (usually about 6.5mm capacity) driven by hand at fairly slow speed through a simple bevel gear. Most have a side handle and a top (or pressure) handle so that you can keep the drill steady while you turn the driving handle. The chuck is designed to take bits which have straight round shanks. Hand drills are used mainly for making holes in wood, glass and soft masonry. They are much slower to use than a power drill but can be easier to control and can be used when a supply of electricity is unavailable. When choosing a hand drill, make sure that its gear teeth are evenly spaced and have an involute profile – a tooth on one wheel should always be in contact with a tooth on the

other wheel when you turn the handle and the load should be transferred smoothly from one tooth to the next.

Breast drill This is basically a larger version of a hand drill and is usually used horizontally. It has a curved metal piece at the top end of the pressure handle against which you push with your chest to increase the load on the drill. Most breast drills have two different gearings to provide different speed ranges. The chuck is usually tightened by hand and has a larger capacity than a hand drill – up to 13mm. A breast drill takes much the same cutting bits as a hand drill.

Brace This has a two-jaw chuck specially designed for gripping the tapered square section ends of specialised bits but it will also take straight shanks. The chuck is turned by sweeping a cranked handle round and round. This means that it has a fairly slow rotational speed, but can provide a relatively high torque. It is used principally for drilling holes in wood up to about 50mm in diameter. Screwdriver bits are also available.

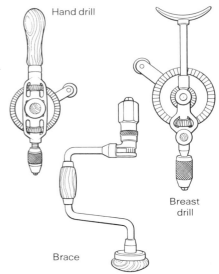

The brace takes auger bits, screwdriver bits and other special bits with a tapered square shank

Electric drill This has a chuck driven by an electric motor. It can be used with twist drills, flat bits and some auger bits. For drilling holes accurately, you may need to use a drill stand.

HOLE DRILLING BITS

Twist drills These are by far the most widely used bits for drilling holes up to around 13mm in diameter. Twist drills are made of either a low alloy steel or high speed steel. The former can be used for drilling holes in wood, or soft metals such as aluminium and copper. High speed steel drills are necessary for harder materials. A few cheaper twist drills do not have a properly-formed land. These should not be used on harder materials but can be used quite successfully on wood.

The tip angle is usually ground to 120 degrees, but more obtuse angles are necessary when drilling thin materials, or when a flatter-bottomed hole is required. Standard twist drills should not be used on materials which are thinner than the radius of the drill.

The ideal speed of rotation of a twist drill depends both on the material and the size of hole. Fairly high speeds (around 3000rpm) can be used for drilling holes in wood up to about 10mm in diameter or holes in steel up to 6.5mm. Lower speeds are necessary for larger diameters than these.

Dowel bits These are used for making flat-

bottomed holes in wood - when making dowelled joints for example. The bit is designed for use in hand or power drills and has a point in the centre so that it can be positioned much more accurately than a twist drill.

Auger bits These are used for making holes greater than 6.5mm in diameter in wood and are designed for use in a brace. They have a standard tapered square shank and a spur in the centre of the cutting edge. The spur has a tapered thread cut into it which draws the bit into the wood as it is turned. The tips of the blade have wings which cut the circular outline of the hole and then the blade shaves away the wood. The two designs – the Jennings pattern and the solid centre type – can be used interchangeably. Both are fast and accurate, but expensive. Another type of bit – the centre bit – is slightly cheaper but it takes a fair amount of skill to prevent it wandering when making deep holes.

When using an auger (or centre) bit, do not drill right through the wood. When the spur breaks through the underside, remove the bit and drill from the opposite side. More pres-

sure is needed in the final stages of a cut as the thread on the spur loses its grip. Auger bits can be sharpened using a small flat file or a needle file. Sharpen the inside of the wing removing just sufficient metal from the leading edge to make it sharp. Similarly file the blades following the original angle making sure that the blades remain even.

Spade bits (or flat bits) These are used in power drills for making holes larger than 6.5mm in diameter in wood. They have an unthreaded spur to aid accurate location on the workpiece. The bit should never be used to drill right through wood from one side – as soon as the point of the spur penetrates the wood, take the bit out and drill from the opposite side. Most bits can be used at a fairly high speed but care is needed to keep the shank of the bit central in the hole. Spade bits are fairly easy to sharpen with a small flat or triangular slip-stone provided care is taken to follow the original angle. The centre spur should be sharpened evenly.

Forstner bits Different shank shapes are available depending on whether they are to be used in a brace or a power drill. These bits,

Power tools

Power tools take much of the effort out of working with wood. But they need an electrical supply and are too bulky for some jobs.

The electric drill is the most popular power tool: it can be used in its basic form for making holes or fitted with attachments. Sometimes, however, it is inconvenient to use attachments and this is when integral tools have an advantage. The three most common ones are the orbital sander, circular saw and jigsaw.

Electric drills

An electric drill is basically a motor which drives a chuck through a series of gears. The motor shaft spins on bearings and turns a fan which blows air over the motor windings to keep them cool. The gears turn the high motor speed into a much lower chuck speed and so increase the available torque.

There are two main body shapes. One has a handle on the end of the drill body – this allows you to apply pressure directly behind the drill bit but, because you are holding the drill at the end of the body, it is difficult to hold the drill steady and horizontal when you are not actually pushing on it. It is also fairly difficult to control the drill if it jams in use. The second body shape has a handle below the body. This sort of drill is easier to handle and better balanced but it is more difficult with the handle below the body to apply a steady pressure. In particular, care must be taken when drilling horizontally with small diameter bits to avoid the tendency to bend the drill bit and break it.

Most drills have a chuck capacity of either 10mm or 13mm. Some chucks are deliberately made so that very small drill bits (generally 0.5mm or less) cannot be gripped. Drills with larger chucks often have a more powerful motor – though this is not always the case.

Manufacturers often advertise the power of their drills in watts input. Unfortunately this stated power is not always a guide to how much power one gets out of a drill. It is often a good deal less – up to 40 per cent in some cases. The curves on the graph show how the power output and the efficiency of a drill

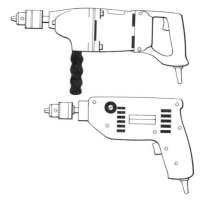

Electric drills – the two main shapes

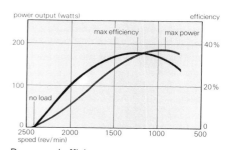

Power and efficiency graph

---

which are not very common, are used mainly for drilling accurate flat-bottomed blind holes in wood, usually greater than 10mm in diameter. They require more pressure to use than auger bits and have a very small central spur for locating the hole.

Expansive bits These are very useful for drilling holes in wood between about 25mm and 80mm in diameter. But they are expensive and can be used only in a brace. The bits have a threaded centre spur and a movable blade which is clamped in position to give the hole diameter wanted. In principle they work like an adjustable centre bit with only one winged cutting blade. They can be sharpened by a technique similar to that described for auger bits but the blade can be removed.

Hole saws These are saws formed into a circle with a twist drill – usually 6.5mm in diameter – at the centre of an arbor. The twist drill makes a pilot hole and keeps the saw blade positioned correctly. The saws can be bought singly, or in sets. A hole saw can be used on most thin sheet materials such as plywood, plastic laminate and softer metals such as copper, aluminium and mild steel. The most common saw diameters available are from 25 to 65mm. The depth of cut varies with the brand of saw, but is typically 6 to

20mm. Saws with fine teeth and a small depth penetration are best for metals and laminates: saws with coarser teeth and capable of deeper cuts are better for wood. A hole saw should be used at a slow speed and needs a comparatively large torque. Most electric drills do not have a slow enough speed to be used successfully with large saws – 38mm in diameter is the maximum size for wood and even less for metals.

Countersink bits These are not actually used for making holes but are used for chamfering the edges of holes drilled in most materials so that countersunk head screws can be screwed into the hole and left with the screw head flush with the surface. Low alloy steel and high speed steel versions are available with an included angle of either 90 degrees or 60 degrees. The 90 degree version can be used for most purposes and is the type usually found in the shops. The 60 degree version should be used when brass woodscrews are used with sockets. Countersink bits cannot be sharpened.

Combination drill bits These can be used to drill a pilot hole and a countersunk clearance hole for woodscrews in one operation. They save time but tend to be less robust than most twist drills.

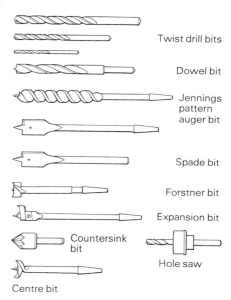

Twist drill bits

Dowel bit

Jennings pattern auger bit

Spade bit

Forstner bit

Expansion bit

Countersink bit

Hole saw

Centre bit

change as it slows down in use.

Efficiency is the output power expressed as a percentage of the input power. The difference between the input and output is lost as heat, which is why a drill needs a fan to keep the motor cool. Starting in the bottom left corner of the graph (no load) a drill initially becomes more powerful and more efficient as it is slowed down – the harder you press, the harder it works. But there comes a point when the efficiency reaches a maximum and then starts to decrease. If still more pressure is applied, the power output will continue to increase but, because the efficiency is now dropping, it too will reach a peak and then fall away. From then on the drill is doing less and less useful work, and will eventually stop altogether. It is also producing more and more heat, and, since the cooling fan is going more slowly, the motor will overheat. If a drill is run for too long like this, it burns out.

Speed

Most drills have a basic free-running speed in the range 2800 to 3500rpm for drilling holes in most materials (wood, for example) and for attachments. But for drilling metal, glass and other hard materials, a lower speed is sometimes preferable.

Some drills have a mechanical gearbox between the motor and the chuck to give a choice of two speeds. The high speed is usually between 2800 to 3500rpm and the low speed from 800 to 1200rpm. As the motor is still running at the same speed irrespective of which speed is chosen, the lower speed produces a greater torque at the chuck than the higher speed (a two to threefold increase) and the power output stays approximately the same.

Some two-speed drills have an electrical speed change which effectively cuts the average voltage going to the motor. The low speed on this sort of drill at around 1500 to 2200rpm is generally higher than the low speed on those with a gearbox and the torque stays about the same irrespective of whether the high or low speed is being used. Obviously this type of speed change is not as useful as the gearbox type but it is much cheaper and how much of a limitation it is in practice will depend on the power of the drill. Some drills have both a mechanical and an electrical change to give a total of four speeds.

A few drills have an electronic variable speed control which is operated by either the trigger switch or a dial. There are two types. The first type is really a variation of the electrical speed change on some two-speed drills – the average voltage going to the motor depends on the position of the trigger or dial control. In most cases, the voltage can be varied up to half the mains value and then the full mains voltage switches in. So, in theory, there is a range of speeds which cannot be used. The second type of control is much more useful. This also varies the voltage going to the motor but, in addition, it detects the load on the drill and increases the voltage as the load increases. This means that the speed of the drill chuck stays almost constant until the maximum power of the drill is reached. So, with this type of speed control, it is possible to set a very low speed (say 200rpm) for drilling with a hole saw or glass drill bit and the drill will keep the speed more or less constant as the pressure on the drill bit varies.

Hammer action

Rotary drilling – either by hand or with an electric drill – is good enough for making holes in softer materials like wood and common bricks. But for hard materials like concrete, a hammering action is better. A drill with a hammer facility vibrates the chuck along its axis – the chuck moves in and out very quickly as it goes round – so that hard particles in the path of the drill bit are broken before being cleared away by the rotary action of the drill. A special type of masonry drill bit must be used when the hammer action is employed. The hammer action is used for drilling hard masonry; nothing else.

Choosing a drill

Before buying a drill, think what you will be using it for.

Two-speed or variable-speed drills cost a little more than single-speed drills but most people find the different speeds well worth paying for.

If you want a drill to drive attachments, look at the attachments available for the drill you have in mind and think about the power these attachments will need to drive them. Many attachments fit only one brand of drill, though some drills, particularly continental ones, have a standard collar size which allows some interchange of attachments between brands. If you have (or will need) several attachments, think about how easily the

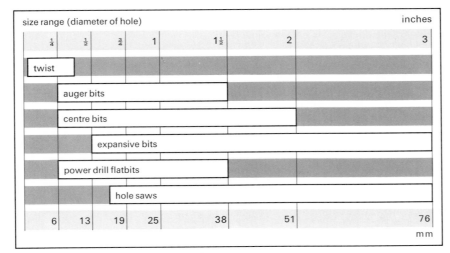

Use this table to choose the bit you need

attachments can be changed. In some circumstances an integral power tool (an orbital sander, jigsaw or circular saw, perhaps) would be a better buy. If you only want to drill holes in wood and other soft materials, you are unlikely to have many problems with reliability and most drills have plenty of power for this sort of use. But frequent use with circular saw or lathe attachments is a different matter. Circular sawing puts heavy loads on the motor which could lead to it overheating. A drill with a thermal (or overload) cut-out prevents excessive overheating and consequent damage to the motor by cutting off the power. Face plate turning especially on a lathe attachment, will severely test the chuck bearings. For both jobs you need a drill with plenty of power.

Consider whether you are likely to need the hammer facility. Hammer drills are a good way of making holes in hard masonry but they have limitations – they may not conquer the very hard concrete found in lintels.

Attachments for drills which produce a mechanical reduction in speed, electronic speed control, or hammer action are available but these are more costly and generally less convenient to use than drills with the facilities already fitted.

There are two types of electrical safety connections used on drills – they can be earthed or double-insulated. Drills with metal cases are usually earthed and can only be used with three-core flex and a three-pin plug. Double-insulated drills are now much more common. They usually have a plastic body, so that the motor is isolated electrically from the case. They need only two-core flex, but should still be run from a fused plug.

Circular saws

These can be integral tools or attachments for an electric drill (drill manufacturers usually make attachments to fit their own brand of drill only). The saws are measured by their blade diameter – generally, the larger the blade, the more powerful the motor needed to run it. Circular saws are generally sold fitted with a combination blade but many

OWNING AN ELECTRIC DRILL

Using a drill is largely a matter of common sense. Always keep the flex well out of the way of the drill bit or attachment, particularly when using attachments such as hedgecutters and circular saws. Make sure that you hold the drill squarely when drilling and do not exert excessive pressure, particularly when cutting soft materials like aluminium which are likely to clog the drill bit. When drilling through metals, be careful when the drill bit breaks through. When using very small drill bits be careful not to break them.

Drills are fairly reliable tools but they need to be looked after – either have them serviced at regular intervals or check them yourself. Clean out the drill carefully, removing all dust and grime. Regrease the gearbox and check the carbon brushes. If excessive sparking occurs on the commutator, check that the brushes are not too short (if they are, replace them), and clean the commutator with a clean tissue dipped in white spirit or meths. If there is any unevenness of the commutator or loose connections, have it examined professionally. Oil or grease any bearings before reassembly.

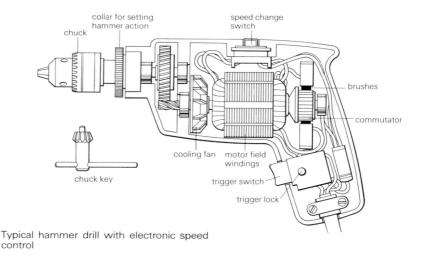

Typical hammer drill with electronic speed control

other special -purpose blades – plywood blades, cross-cutting blades, flooring blades and tungsten carbide tipped blades, for instance – are also available. Most circular saws have guards fitted, but the saws can still cause serious injury and they require great care in use.

Circular saws are particularly useful for sawing long lengths of timber up to 40mm thick and for cutting up manmade boards (plywood, chipboard and so on). But they cannot be used for cutting a curve with a small radius. They have an upward cutting action. As the blade cuts, the saw rests on its soleplate

and the blade passes through a slot in this. The soleplate can be moved up and down to adjust the depth of cut and can often be tilted so that the blade cuts at an angle (45 degrees maximum).

When using a circular saw do not try to push the saw through the wood too quickly – this will make the motor labour and overheat and the saw may eventually stall – though some have a slipclutch to prevent this. If the saw does not cut well or binds on the wood, make sure that the blade is not blunt and that the teeth are set correctly (bent alternately to one side and the other).

USING POWER TOOLS

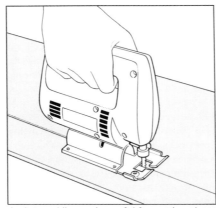

A circular saw attachment is very useful for rip sawing long pieces of wood and for cutting up man-made boards

An integral jigsaw is useful for cutting sheet materials up to 35mm thick. Cuts on the up stroke. Use gentle pressure, do not let the blade slow down or jam

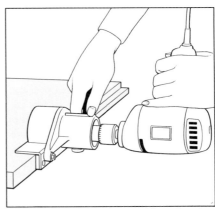

Rebating attachment for moulding, chamfering and slotting the edges of wood. Keep the guide firmly in position and move steadily along the wood

Saw attachments which have a separate bearing for the blade (that is the saw does not bolt directly on to the drill) can be better and more convenient to use than those which do not.

Jigsaws

If you usually buy timber already cut and planed to size, then a jigsaw will probably be more useful than a circular saw. As with circular saws, you can buy a jigsaw attachment to fit on to an electric drill or an integral tool complete with its own motor.

Apart from the motor, the main part of a jigsaw is the ram assembly into which the blade is fitted and held in place with a screw (a screwdriver or Allen key is needed for replacing blades and tightening the screw). The ram assembly is moved up and down by the offset pin and the bridge slider at about 3000 strokes a minute. The short blade (about 50mm cutting length) vibrates up and down in a slot in the soleplate, which holds the material being cut. Some jigsaws have a blade roller guide to support the blade – this needs adjusting and lubricating. The saw blade cuts on the upstroke, so dust and the ragged edge appear on top of the material being cut – this must be remembered when a jigsaw is used on materials, like plastic laminate, which are likely to chip. Jigsaws generally have their motor

cooling fans directed to blow away dust from the line of cut.

One major advantage a jigsaw has over a circular saw is its safety – even if you touched the blade while it was running you would be unlikely to suffer serious injury. It is also more versatile – it can be used to cut curves and enclosed cuts (a cut-out for a handle, say). But, the jigsaw is somewhat slower to use than a circular saw, especially for rip sawing, and does not usually have a guide fence, though either saw could be guided along a batten clamped to the surface of, say, a board. Some attachments tend to be rather unbalanced and buying an integral jigsaw, which is usually more compact and easier to use may be the best solution for many people.

Two-speed and variable-speed jigsaws are available but for the average handyman it is doubtful whether their advantage (the slower speed is to reduce vibration and blade blunting when cutting hard materials, like sheet metal) is worth the extra cost.

Orbital sanders

These attachments or integral tools will take a lot of the fatigue out of the job of finishing woodwork. An orbital sander is basically a rectangular pad which you cover with abrasive paper – usually

aluminium oxide (carborundum) or silicon carbide paper, as glass-paper is generally not tough enough. The abrasive paper is driven round in small orbits – each grain on the abrasive paper travels in a very small circle but the pad itself does not rotate. To produce a smooth surface a fine grade paper is required.

When using an orbital sander avoid the temptation to apply excessive pressure – if you do the sander tends to vibrate more than the sanding sheet. For very fine work it may be advisable to finish the job by hand using a very fine paper and sanding only in the direction of the wood grain. An orbital sander can also be used for providing a key on old paintwork before you paint it.

Attachments and accessories

Listed below are some of the more popular attachments and accessories you can buy to fit on to an electric drill. The list is by no means exhaustive and some of the tools included – lathe and hedgetrimmer, in particular – can also be bought as integral tools. When choosing between an integral tool and an attachment, it is worth bearing in mind that all attachments work from a drill which can usually be locked in the **ON** position, whereas integral tools usually have a 'deadman's' ON/OFF switch.

Rotary (disc) sander Various types of attachments are available which fit directly into the drill chuck. The commonest is the disc sander which uses a circular sanding disc mounted on a flexible rubber backing pad and arbor. These should always be used with the drill at an angle to the workpiece. They are fast and useful for removing paintwork, but tend to sand unevenly and care needs to be taken to avoid ridges forming when sanding softer materials.

Flexible drive shaft This allows a drill fitted in a drill stand to drive a chuck-mounted attachment some distance away from the work area. It can be used for buffing and polishing and for drilling small holes. Unfortunately, flexible shafts cannot transmit much torque and tend to break easily if the chuck jams.

Vertical drilling stand This is useful for drilling very accurate holes. Drilling stands are usually designed for a particular brand of drill – one manufacturer's drilling stand will not fit any other manufacturer's drill. Before buying, try a drill in the stand and check that it is rigidly supported and that play (both sideways and vertical) in the stand is minimal. If you buy a drilling stand, a machine vice to hold the workpiece rigidly is also worth buying. A few drilling stands can take a milling table which with special cutters enables you to do milling, rebating and even mortising.

Horizontal drilling stand This can be screwed or clamped to a bench and holds a drill rigidly so that it can be used with accessories such as grinding wheels and buffing wheels. Guides and tool rests are sometimes available to make sharpening tools, such as chisels and plane blades, a more simple operation. When sanding or grinding, always make sure that the grinding wheel or sanding disc is moving downwards or towards you.

Lathe This attachment is really for a dedicated woodworker who wants to make things like chair legs, egg cups and rounders bats. Lathes usually have the facility for face plate turning (making a wooden bowl by clamping the wood to the face plate, say) up to diameters of around 150mm, but turning big articles can damage the chuck bearings of some drills. Centre turning (chair legs say, where the wood is held at both ends of the lathe) is generally more successful. A two-speed drill is advisable. Prices vary considerably between manufacturers.

Milling attachment This can be used for rebating, grooving (at distances up to about 25mm from the edge of the timber) and chamfering or moulding the edges of wood. It is much quicker to use and more accurate than any type of hand plane. Power routers are also available which have the advantage of being able to cut housings and grooves at any position in a piece of wood.

Saw table This is a useful addition to a power tool kit if you do much circular sawing. The circular saw is held rigidly underneath the table with the blade and guard protruding through. This allows you to have both hands free to guide the wood. If you intend to go this far, however, it may well be worth considering the convenience of buying a complete integral saw table.

Hedgetrimmer Powered hedgetrimmers take some of the tediousness out of cutting hedges and could lead to a better, denser hedge. Attachments are easy to use and cut well. A small single-speed drill is the best type to use – bigger drills tend to be bulky and heavy making the trimmer difficult to use. If you have a large drill and a lot of hedge to trim, an integral tool is a better buy.

POWER TOOLS AND ACCESSORIES

Top row From the left: integral circular saw, integral jigsaw, integral orbital sander, sanding discs and backing pad, vertical drill stand

Bottom row. From the left: circular saw attachment, jigsaw attachment, sander attachment, wire brushes, flexible drive shaft

Measuring and marking wood

Nearly all woodworking jobs involve measuring and marking of one kind or another. The sort of tool you need depends on the distance to be measured, the accuracy wanted and how often the job is likely to be repeated. The importance of accurate measurement and marking out cannot be over emphasised. Often any inaccuracy introduced at this stage of the work cannot be ironed out later and will be reflected in the quality of the finished job. The rule is to measure twice and to mark once but after each marking, check again. A few seconds spent on this stage may save hours of reconstruction or adaptation later.

Measurements and markings on timber are usually made by referring to one edge or face of the wood. To achieve accuracy the wood must be thoroughly prepared so that it has either one or two smooth flat edges or faces (depending on the job). Start by selecting the widest surface which is most free from blemishes and which has the most attractive figure or grain. Plane this surface until it is smooth, then check it for flatness along its length using a straight-edge. Next check the surface for *winding* by placing two parallel hardwood strips across the timber near to each end. Sight from one end – any twisting should be clearly visible because the length of the hardwood strips will highlight any small differences. Small surfaces can be checked by eye. Continue planing and checking until the surface is flat in all directions. This is now the face side and should be marked lightly by drawing an extended loop with a pencil. Make one part of the loop border on the best edge of the wood.

The next task is to plane the best edge until it is straight and square to the face side – use a try-square to check it. Then make a pencil mark on this edge rather like an inverted V so that it touches the end of the loop on the face side.

The wood should now have a smooth flat edge and a smooth flat face and is ready for marking out. All subsequent measurements and markings must be made from either the face side or the face edge.

Measuring tools

The most popular measuring tool is a retractable steel rule. Most are cheap, versatile, easy to use and widely available. They are generally accurate to within 1mm which is good enough for cutting wood to size. But they cannot be used as a straight-edge for marking out as well as for measuring. For this you need a rigid rule.

Rigid rules

A metre stick is probably the cheapest accurate rigid rule. These are pieces of wood, plastic or aluminium alloy a metre long marked with measuring scales. Their size makes them cumbersome to carry around and sometimes awkward to use. Smaller rigid rules – ordinary 300mm wood or plastic rulers – can be used for rough measurements up to their length: never use a 300mm rule to measure lengths over 300mm accurately. Aluminium alloy and plastic rules can be more durable than wood ones and are less prone to problems caused by changing humidity. Plastic and wood rules are likely to be damaged by using them as a guide for a trimming knife.

Rigid steel rules are for making accurate measurements. They come in a number of lengths, normally 150mm, 300mm, 600mm and 1 metre. They can be used as a straight-edge for assessing flatness and as a guide for a trimming knife. The cheaper ones often rust and their scales become difficult to read unless they are cleaned with a fine grade waterproof silicon carbide paper. Expensive ones are often either chromium plated or made of stainless steel.

Folding rules

The traditional woodworking rule is the one metre folding rule made of boxwood. This rule combines stiffness with portability. Before buying, check the hinges to make sure they are not loose and that the rule remains flat when it is unfolded. Those with a bevelled edge to reduce parallax error are best. Synthetic and metal folding rules are also avail-

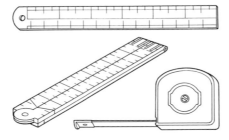

The three most useful measuring tools: rigid rule, folding rule and retractable rule

able. These are more robust than wood ones but neither type should be used as a guide for a trimming knife.

Retractable rules

Retractable steel pocket rules have flexible steel tapes which coil up inside a small storage compartment. The tapes are usually marked in metres, centimetres and millimetres and come in various lengths – generally between two metres and three and a half metres. The tapes are usually either 6 or 12mm in width though wider ones – 16 to 20mm – are also available.

The zero end of the tape has a right-angled steel clip attached to it. This gives some protection to the end of the tape, stops the tape vanishing inside the case and acts as a retaining clip when measuring. The clip should be fitted so that it can slide about 1mm along the tape (the thickness of the steel clip) to expand the tape slightly for external measurements and to contract it for internal ones.

The storage compartments are generally either plastic or steel and contain a coiled spring to help the tape retract after use. With some rules, the tape has to be pushed back into the case – the spring acts as a sort of guide. With others, the spring pulls the tape back into the case – many of these have a tape lock so that any length of tape can be held out of the case. Tape locks are particularly useful when making measurements in poor light conditions or in awkward positions when it is difficult to read the tape.

The shape of the case is important when making internal measurements. Some retractable rules have square cases marked for length and are much more accurate than those in round cases. Some rules have a clear plastic window on top of the case through which you can see the scale and so read off the measurement.

There are a number of things you should avoid doing with any retractable steel rule:
● do not pull hard on the tape around sharp corners – it may break or split
● do not let the tape hook smack into the mouth of the case when it retracts – slow it down by hand
● do not use a steel rule next to bare electrical wires or connections
● do not pull on the tape when it reaches the end of its length
● do not use a steel tape in wet conditions – water may get into the case and cause the tape to rust and the mechanism to seize. If you have to use a steel tape in damp conditions, make sure that you dry it afterwards and wipe it over lightly with an oily rag.

If you suspect the accuracy of a measuring tool, you could ask your local Trading Standards Office to check it.

Home-made rules

For some jobs it is possible to make your own rules from pieces of wood or card. For example, when you want to measure a particular length many times a straight piece of wood can be used as a rule though it should not be stored for future use as a change in its moisture content will change its dimensions. As another example, a set of marks or measurements can be accurately transferred from one place to another by copying them on to a piece of card or paper. As a simple extension of this idea, complex curves or joints can be drawn on card, cut out and then used as a jig or template to ensure that every time the shape is marked out it will be identical.

Marking out

The positions for cuts, holes and so on in wood are usually marked with a pencil, with a knife or with a pin attached to a gauge.

Lines for cutting can be marked with a hard pencil (2H) but the pencil must be kept sharp. Pencils are also very useful for making other marks on wood to remind you which piece you want to keep; which edges are to be joined, and so on. For this, a small range of pencils is a useful asset – say a soft pencil, B or 2B, and two or three different coloured pencils. Any type of system of marking can be used as long as you make sure that each mark always has the same meaning. One such system might be:
● a pencilled arrow to show the side of a line for cutting
● a coloured pencil cross hatching to mark areas that are waste (wood to be cut away)
● pencilled letters on each end or edge where a joint is to be made: A–A, B–B and so on
● pencilled words to indicate the use of each piece of timber – for example, top, bottom, leg, rail.
All these marks must be drawn clearly but lightly as they may have to be removed when the job is finished.

A marking knife can mark closer to the rule or straight-edge than a pencil and actually cuts the surface fibres of the timber. Cutting the surface fibres helps to prevent chipping when the wood is subsequently cut with a saw – it is essential when cutting veneered chipboard to prevent the the surface veneer flaking along the cut. A special woodworking marking knife generally has a forged carbon steel blade with a riveted hardwood handle. The blade, which is angled to make it easy to use, should be kept razor sharp. A trimming knife can be used as an alternative.

Dividing distances

The simplest way to divide distances is by straightforward use of a rule or dividers – the latter should be set to the required measurement against a rule and then walked across the material using a swivelling motion. Each point will mark off the required distance. But occasionally you will be faced with pieces of wood which are an awkward size to divide simply – for example, you might want to divide a 67mm width into four equal parts. To do this, hold a rule across the board at an angle so that the zero end of the rule coincides with one side of the board and the 100mm end, say, coincides with the other side. Mark off where the 25, 50 and 75mm graduations occur to give four equal parts.

Marking and testing angles

The most widely used tool for marking right angles on wood is the try-square. For marking other angles, a sliding bevel or mitre square can be used. The sliding bevel can be adjusted to any angle – including a right angle; the mitre square is fixed at 45 degrees. A combination square can be used to mark right angles and 45 degree angles. All these tools can be used for *checking* angles and corners.

Try-square This is a tool for marking right angles and checking their accuracy. The traditional try-square has a steel blade and a wood stock – usually ebony, beech or rosewood – with a brass edging strip. Nowadays, many try-squares have plastic stocks – these are a better choice if the try-square is likely to be used and left in damp conditions. Many different sizes are available varying from around 100mm to 300mm. Before using a try-square, test its squareness by holding the stock against a straight-edge and marking a line on it. Reverse the blade, hold the other edge of the stock firmly against the straight-edge and check that the edge of the blade coincides exactly with the line marked. Any error in squareness is doubled and should be fairly easy to see.

When using a try-square for marking a right angle, make sure that the stock is held firmly against the face side or face edge. When checking squareness, hold the wood up to the light with the try-square firmly against the face side. Light coming under the blade will show up any unevenness.

TOOLS FOR MEASURING ANGLES

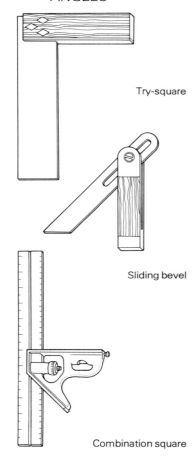

Try-square

Sliding bevel

Combination square

Square template This is a useful device for marking wood which you want to cut through. It is basically an elongated L-shaped piece of beech or rosewood, about 150mm long. When a piece of wood is put in the L, two adjacent sides can be marked.

Squaring rod It is almost impossible to check the squareness of a large rectangular framework – the framework for a built-in wardrobe, say – accurately with a try-square. To do this you need a squaring rod – a length of wood with one end sharpened to a chisel edge. To square a framework, the chisel edge should be pushed into one corner of the frame with the squaring rod held across the diagonal and the opposite corner should be marked on the rod. The rod should then be placed across the other diagonal and the framework adjusted until both diagonals are equal.

Sliding bevel This has a steel blade passing through the end of a stock of ebony, beech or rosewood. The steel blade has a slot cut along half its length which allows it to slide through the stock and to be locked at any required angle. To mark a particular angle, the blade angle should be adjusted with a protractor. A sliding bevel can be used for marking dovetail joints.

Mitre square This has an ebony, beech or rosewood stock with a brass strip down each side of it. A blade set at 45 degrees extends through the stock in each direction. Mitre squares can be used for marking and testing angles of 45 degrees.

Mitre template (or block) This can be used for making mitres across small pieces of wood – for picture framing, say. It is often made of beech or boxwood, about 100mm to 150mm long and L-shaped. It usually has two slots at 45 degrees and one at 90 degrees. You hold the wood in the crook of the 'L' and use one of the slots to guide your saw.

Mitre box This is similar to a mitre block but U-shaped. It usually has two sets of 45 degree slots but rarely a 90 degree one. An advantage is that the saw is guided on both sides of the wood.

Combination square This can be used for marking right angles, checking internal and external right angles and marking 45 degree mitres. It is more accurate than a try-square but it is also more cumbersome to use. The metal stock generally has three slots and locking screws to hold a graduated blade. The blade can be fitted in any one of the three slots and locked at any length.

Marking and testing circles and curves

There are two basic tools for marking out circles and curves – compasses and dividers. Both can be used for most woodworking jobs – rounding the ends of boards and cutting small holes, for example – but dividers cut through the surface fibres of the wood and so have an advantage when the curve or circle is to be sawn later. Dividers also remain sharp. To avoid marking wood noticeably with the centre point, use the tools lightly. On plastic and other hard surfaces, glue a small piece of card where the centre point will go. If necessary this can be removed afterwards.

For marking curves and circles which have radii larger than dividers and compasses can stretch to, you can make a simple beam compass from a length of wood, a bradawl and a scriber or pencil. To do this, bore a series of holes through a straight piece of hardwood, push the bradawl through a hole at one end and use this as a pivot. Push a pencil or scriber through one of the other holes and use this to mark the curve. A piece of string with a drawing pin attached to one end and a pencil or scriber to the other, can also be used to mark out circles and curves.

Dinner plates, ashtrays, pennies and so on are also useful for marking circles.

A piece of string can also be used to mark out an ellipse. First draw a rectangle with dimensions the same as the major and minor axes of the ellipse you want to draw. Quarter the rectangle by drawing a horizontal line and a vertical line joining the mid points of opposite sides. Set a pair of dividers or compasses to half of the length of the rectangle. Place one point on the bottom of the vertical line quartering the rectangle and make two marks near opposite ends of the horizontal line. Fix a pin at each mark and attach a length of string between the pins so that the centre of the string just reaches the bottom of the vertical lines when it is taut. Place a pencil against the string and draw an ellipse by keeping the string taut all the time.

Jigs

If you want to make the same joint many times, you should use a jig to mark it out. Various types can either be made yourself or bought. Metal jigs are preferable when durability is essential. The following three examples are typical of the sort of thing you can devise.

For dovetail joints Use a right-angled piece of metal with two tapers cut out of it (1 in 7 and 1 in 6, say) so that when the jig is held firmly against the dovetail marks on the end grain of the wood, tapered lines can be drawn on the face side.

For comb or finger joints Use a right-angled piece of metal similar to the dovetail jig with parallel cut-outs rather than tapered ones.

For dowel joints Use a metal jig which can be clipped on to each side of the two pieces of wood which are to be joined together. The simplest way to do this is to take a rectangular piece of metal and cut a small slot at the mid-point of one edge. The metal should then be folded at right angles in opposite directions to create two lugs. A similar pair of lugs should then be made on an adjacent edge. Holes can then be drilled through the metal plate for the position of the dowels.

JIGS FOR JOINTS

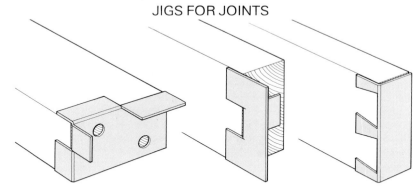

From the left: a *dowel jig* can be made quite simply from a flat piece of metal – it makes the accurate location of the holes for dowelled joints a simple task. A *finger* jig and a *dovetail* jig are useful when you have many joints to cut

Gauges

Three main types of gauge are used for marking timber – marking gauges, cutting gauges and mortise gauges. Each is used to make one or more parallel lines before cutting.

All three tools should be held and used in the same way with the stem and stock gripped in the right hand and with your thumb on the stock. Hold the stock along the face edge of the timber with the blade or pin in the stock angled in such a way so that it follows the stock. Then either push the pin away from you or pull it towards you. Make sure that the stock is firmly against the timber at all times. Use the gauge lightly at first and then make a firmer stroke to produce a more clear mark.

Marking gauge This is the most basic of the three gauges. It has a stem with a pin set in one end and a stock which can be moved along the stem and secured by a thumbscrew.

To set the gauge, you release the thumbscrew, hold a rule against the stock and slide the stock along the stem until the required measurement is in line with the pin. Then tighten the thumbscrew carefully without moving the stock and finally, check the setting with a rule and if necessary readjust.

Marking gauges are mainly used for preparing timber by marking it to uniform width and thickness. They can also be used for setting out rebates and for marking various joints.

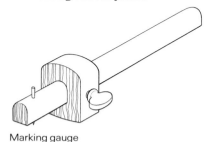

Marking gauge

Cutting gauge This is similar to the marking gauge but has a cutting blade instead of a pin. It should be adjusted in exactly the same way as a marking gauge. The cutting blade can be removed and honed sharp and is usually held in place by a brass wedge. Because a cutting gauge has a blade instead of a pin, it is particularly useful for marking across boards – the cut will prevent chipping when the board is subsequently sawn. A cutting gauge can also be used to cut through thin materials such as plywood, plastic and veneer.

Mortise gauge This is used for marking out mortises and tenons for jointing. The stem has two pins – one can be thought of as being similar to the pin on a marking gauge, the other is attached to a movable brass strip which in turn is attached to a screw thread and a thumbscrew. By turning the thumbscrew the pins can be moved apart. The stock of rosewood or beech is held in position by a set screw which needs a screwdriver to release and tighten it.

To set the gauge, first release the set screw on the stock. If this is not done, the brass slide will not move and the tool may be damaged. Next turn the thumbscrew and adjust the distance between the pins until it is correct. Now adjust the stock, tighten the set screw and check the measurements. Both mortises and tenons are marked with the gauge at the same setting.

Basic woodworking joints

Nowadays, it is possible to build almost any piece of furniture without being able to tell a dovetail from a bridle joint or ever touching a chisel. But if you want to work wood or if your interest is in repairing, restoring or reproducing traditional furniture, you will need to know the purposes of cut joints and the way to make them.

Cutting traditional joints is work for hand tools; the right ones, correctly used without rushing.

The tools you need

The tools required are few and mostly unsophisticated. Jigs, which can save time setting out when the same joint must be repeated several times, are available. But they are limited in the size of work-piece that can be accommodated and require much the same level of concentration in use as tools used freehand. You can also make your own jigs.

A basic setting and marking out kit consists of a try square (for angles other than 90° use a sliding bevel), a pencil and a marking knife, a straight-edged rule (preferably stainless steel) and marking and mortise gauges.

The four basic tools for making joints are a saw, a chisel, a mallet and a plane. You do not need to use all four for every joint. For some joints you need only use a saw – usually a tenon saw, but fine cabinet work may call for a dovetail saw, which is similar, but smaller. Even finer work – on small drawers and boxes or on models, say – may need a gents saw, which has a straight handle and very small teeth. A coping saw is useful for cutting out the waste between dovetails and pins.

Many joints require chisels – the most satisfactory type for general use is the bevel-edge chisel, in widths from 6.5mm upwards. A block or smoothing plane is needed to level the surfaces of the joint after it has been assembled. Rebate, moulding and plough planes could also be used to make the work easier. A router makes a better job of smoothing and levelling the bottom of housings than a chisel.

Joints

The naming of joints is not always consistent: some are called one thing by one craftsman and something else by another. Where alternative names are common, both are given.

A joint is a fixed junction between two or more pieces of wood: it should not be flexible. The simplest is the butt joint, in which two surfaces are brought together in the same plane and joined with glue or mechanical devices, such as pins or screws, or a combination of both. A dowelled joint is basically a butt joint secured with glued-in wooden pins – dowels.

Dowelled joints

Once you have learned how to drill truly vertical holes which are accurately centred (there are many jigs that take the skill element out of this) you will find that a dowelled joint is an excellent multi-purpose joint.

Whether the joint is through dowelled – made with the dowel holes drilled right through one component into the joining one, leaving the dowel ends exposed – or made with blind holes in the mating faces so that the dowels are hidden, certain basic rules are vital to success.

First, the mating faces must fit as closely together as possible. This is a matter of accurate marking, sawing and smoothing with a plane.

Second, the dowel holes must be exactly aligned. In the case of a through dowel joint, this is no problem; the parts can be clamped and drilled as one. To help drill holes vertically you can use a try square stood, blade up, on the work surface and used to 'sight' the drill. Or, better still, use a drill stand. Ensuring

that the holes align in both components is a matter of marking centre lines accurately with a gauge and remembering to mark which are the face sides and edges of the parts.

Third, only as much adhesive as is needed to bond the dowels in the holes and the faces to each other should be used. If the bottom of a dowel hole is filled with glue and the dowel is forced in, the effect is like a piston. The glue, under pressure, seeks to escape – in delicate work this could split the wood. To avoid the piston effect, the dowels should be tapered to assist entry into the hole and grooved along their length to let surplus glue escape. The holes should be slightly countersunk in the mating faces.

Though you can buy a length of dowelling and cut your own, it is probably best to buy pre-cut dowels, which are available in standard sizes from 6mm (diameter) by 25mm (length) to 10mm by 38mm, ready-grooved.

Dowels can be used to join framing battens or to join boards edge-to-edge, edge-to-face or end-to-face. When using dowelled joints for framing, always use two or more dowels to ensure accurate alignment of the components and a rigid joint. You can substitute dowel joints for mortise-and-tenon joints. In carcase construction, dowelled joints can substitute for dovetail joints though they are not as strong.

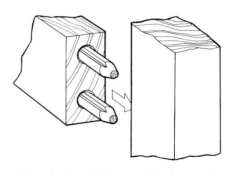

When the dowel holes are 'blind', taper the dowels and cut a groove along them

Lap and halving joints

Full-lap joints and half-lap (also called halving) joints are used for all kinds of framing in furniture and in structural timber work. They are used at corners, T-junctions and where battens or timbers cross and are usually pinned or screwed (as well as glued) together.

The joints are usually made at right angles and may be used for wood of the same, or differing thickness. In the latter case, a joint with one face level is produced. The joints are often covered on at least one side by cladding but may be sometimes visible in simple structures, like wooden bunk beds.

Full-lap joint This joint can be used only with wood of differing thicknesses – the thicker piece being at least twice as thick as the thinner. Typically a full-lap joint could be used to join a thin cross rail, laid face up, to a side rail on edge. As the name suggests, the joint is made where the cross rail overlaps by cutting away the upper edge of the side rail and letting it in, to its full thickness – see below.

Halving joint The half-lap or halving is

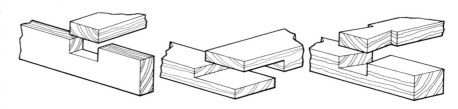

From the left: a full-lap joint, a half-lap (or halving) joint – and this particular one is a corner half-lap joint – and a dovetail halving joint

used to join two pieces of wood of the same thickness. It is basically the same as the full-lap joint except that the cut-outs are made in both pieces to half of their thickness (hence the name). This produces a joint flush on both faces – or edges, since it can be made with the components flat or on edge. Details of this joint are on the next page.

Dovetail halving This is a stronger variation of the half lap. It is basically a T-joint in which the cross rail end is cut as described for a half-lap and then the

halved projection is cut again from both corners back to the shoulder line at an angle, to produce a fan-like dovetail shape. A taper of 1 in 6 should be used in softwood, 1 in 8 in hardwood. With the dovetail placed on the face or edge of the side rail, the halving in that rail should be marked out to fit and cut.

The dovetail halving is much stronger than a square cut halving and can be used where there is a pull along the length of the cross rail, or where the side rail might tend to splay under pressure on its ends.

MAKING A FULL-LAP JOINT

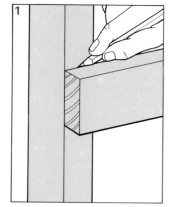
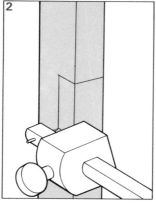
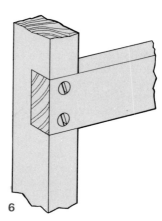
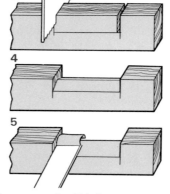

1 The first step in setting out a full-lap joint – a thin cross rail to a side rail on edge, for example – is to mark the width of the cross rail on the edge of the side rail. Then these marks should be squared down both sides of the rail by using a try square.
2 A marking gauge set to the thickness of the cross rail should be used with its head firmly against the upper (face) edge of the rail to mark the depth of the cut-out on both sides.
3 Next, make saw cuts in the edge of the side rail down to the gauge lines. Keep the saw on

the waste side of the cross rail width (or shoulder) lines with its blade vertical to the work surface and moving horizontally through it. Work the saw forward, rather than at a downward angle. You can make one or more extra cuts in the waste to make chiselling it away simpler.
4 To take out the waste, work with a chisel, bevel-up, from each side of the rail so that you form a central ridge, sloping down to the gauge lines on either side. Then pare this ridge away down almost level with the gauge

lines.
5 Finally, with the chisel flat-side-up, level the bottom of the cut-out and smooth it off. If you have a router, you can use it to level off the bottom of the cut-out – it makes a better job than a chisel.
6 The cross rail should now be a snug fit, with its face flush with the side rail shoulders. A lap joint at the end of a side rail does not call for the use of a chisel – saw the shoulder line, then saw from the end of the rail to meet it at 90 degrees.

MAKING A HALVING JOINT

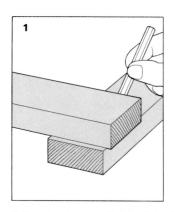
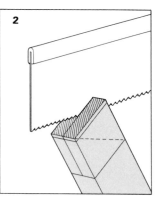
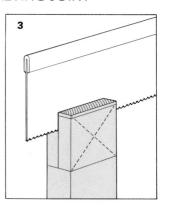
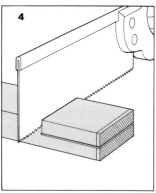

1 To set out a cross halving joint the face of the lower component and the back of the upper should be marked with the width of the cut-out, the marks again being squared on to the edges. A mortise gauge set to half the wood thickness should be used to mark the edges – hold the gauge head against the face of the lower and the back of the upper component.

For a T-halving, the cut-out at the end of the cross rail can be made with a saw alone; for a corner halving, both components should be sawn. In both cases, the shoulder lines should be marked further from the ends than the width of the rail – an extra 2mm is enough. The overhanging excess can be planed off after assembly.

2 To saw a halving (and to saw tenons and bridles) clamp the rail in a vice at about 30 degrees to the vertical, with the end pointing away from the saw, edge upwards. Keeping the saw travel horizontal and the blade vertical, make a cut down to the shoulder – again remember to keep your saw on the waste side. Turn the wood and repeat the cut on the other edge.

3 Now position the rail vertically and square the two cuts down to the shoulder.

4 Turn the rail flat and make another cut across the shoulder to free the waste.

Rebate and housing joints

A rebate joint, at its simplest, is a slightly stronger version of a butt joint – it provides contact between the mating components in two planes instead of one. It is one of the few joints that can be cut effectively in chipboard. A rebate is formed by removing a square or rectangular section across the end or along the edge of a piece of wood.

Rebate joint

In the simplest type of rebate joint, the rebate is normally cut to half the wood thickness, leaving a projecting tongue equal to the thickness of the other, square-cut component. This type of rebate joint is often used on the tops of bookcases and shelf units where the top rests on and between the top ends of the sides. It may also be used for joining drawer fronts to and between the sides.

The joints are usually reinforced with pins, driven through the overlap in pairs at opposing angles – this is called dovetail nailing.

The rebate is usually cut with a rebate plane. This has a width guide and depth stop and cleans the vertical edge of the cut as it is used. Short rebates – in a board end, for example – can be cut with a saw but care is needed.

Bare-faced halving This is another type of rebate joint often used for fixing shelves in bookcases. The shelves have rebated ends with the projecting tongue fitting into horizontal slots in the inner faces of the bookcase sides. The joint is made shoulder-up for strength. This joint may also be used in drawers; a rebated back may be housed between the sides, or a front may have housings for the rebated ends of the sides.

Housing joints

Not all housing joints are rebated, but whether they are or not, they fall in two categories: the through housing, in which the construction is visible at both back and front edges of the joint; and the stopped housing which from the front edge appears to be a simple butt joint.

Through housing This is a simple joint to set out and cut. The shoulder lines of the

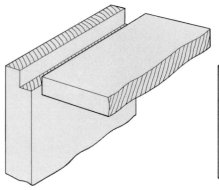

A rebate joint – usually reinforced with pins driven through the overlap

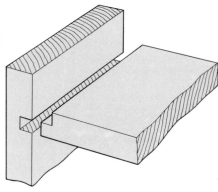

A bare-faced halving joint – sometimes called a shouldered housing joint

housing (the thickness of the board to be housed apart) should be marked across the inner face of the board and squared over the edges. The depth of the housing – between one third and half the thickness – should be marked with a gauge. Then shoulders should be sawn and the waste removed with a chisel – again work from each edge towards the centre. Finish the bottom of the housing with a router or a paring chisel.

Stopped housing In this joint the cut should be taken only part way across the board, stopping about 20mm from the front edge. The end of the board to fit into it should be cut at the front corner to accommodate the 'stop'.

Mark shoulder lines across the inner face as far as the stop and on the back edge. Gauge the depth on the back edge too. To allow room to work the saw, the first 50mm of the housing back from the stop should be cut out with the chisel – used with its bevel down. Then saw shoulders, and chisel out the remaining waste and finish the bottom of the housing with the router.

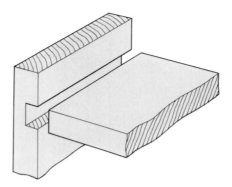

Through housing joint

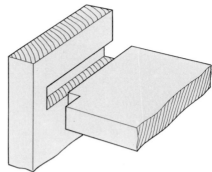

Stopped housing joint

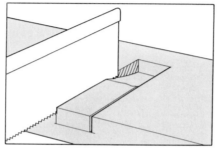

To get a saw into a stopped housing joint you will have to chop out wood near the stop first

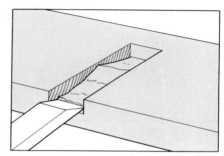

Once the saw cuts have been made, chisel out the waste and finish with a router

Tongued-and-grooved joints

A loose tongued-and-grooved joint may be used to join boards – either natural wood or manufactured boards – edge to edge. Grooves should be cut with a plough plane in the mating edges of both boards and a strip of plywood or hardwood (just the right thickness to fit snugly) should be cut to fit into the grooves. The edges of the boards and the strip of wood should be glued and the whole assembly clamped until the glue sets. Make the tongue strip slightly narrower than the combined depth of the grooves.

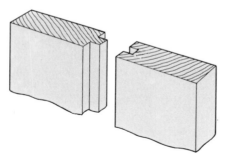

The usual type of tongued-and-grooved joint which is often used on wall cladding and floorboards

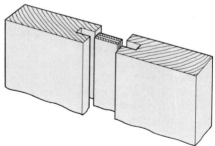

A loose or slip tongued-and-grooved joint which can be used to join boards edge to edge

Mortise-and-tenon joints

The mortise-and-tenon joint is used in structural timber work and framing as well as in high quality furniture and cabinet work.

The mortise is a rectangular slot or recess cut in one piece of wood. The tenon is a projecting tongue cut on the end of a cross rail, which locates in the mortise. There are a great many variations on the basic joint. It may be used with wood of similar or differing thickness and as a through or stopped joint – the latter is a stub tenon joint.

The mortise is usually made with the rail 'on edge', but the joint can be used with the rail face up – as in a cabinet drawer rail. In this case a double tenon joint is made.

MAKING A THROUGH MORTISE-AND-TENON

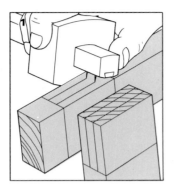 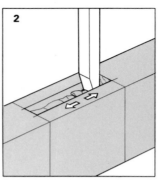 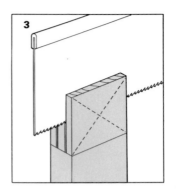 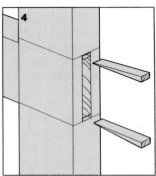

1 The initial setting out of a through mortise-and-tenon joint is the same as for any other framing joint. Mark the width of the rail square across the face of the stile, and mark the width of the stile across the face of the rail, leaving an allowance for the tenon to project 2mm beyond the open end of the mortise before finishing. Square the marks round both edges and the backs of both pieces.

Choose a chisel which is about one third of the width of the stile – the thickness of the tenon should be about one third of the thickness of the rail and the mortise must not exceed one third of the width of the stile edge – and set the two points of a mortise gauge to the width of the cutting edge of the chisel. With the gauge head against the face side of the stile, centre the points on one side and mark the mortise width. Repeat on the other edge. With the gauge at the same setting, mark the edges and end of the rail.

2 Cut out the mortise with the chisel (and mallet), working from the centre of the mortise to each end mark in turn. Keep the bevel-face of the chisel towards the end marks and chop out about half the width of the stile. Turn the work over and chop from the other edge, but stop just short of the ends. When the bulk of the waste has been removed, turn the chisel so that its bevel-side faces into the mortise and square the ends. You can remove a lot of the waste from a large mortise by drilling a series of holes before using the chisel.

3 The tenon is cut with a saw, in the same way as described for a half-lap joint.

4 The joint of a through mortise-and-tenon can be tightened by driving wedges into the end of the tenon. Taper the top and bottom edges of the mortise inwards slightly from the open side to create a dovetailing effect.

Stopped mortise-and-tenon

A stopped mortise is cut from one edge only and should not be deeper than two-thirds of the stile width. A stub tenon should be about 2mm shorter than the mortise depth, so that the end does not touch the bottom of the mortise.

You can tighten a stopped mortise-and-tenon by fitting dowels at right angles through the mortise and the tenon. If the dowel holes are made slightly nearer the shoulders of the tenon than those through the mortise, the joint will be tightened as they are driven in.

Haunched mortise-and-tenon

The ordinary through or stopped mortise-and-tenon joint is used for T-joints. Where the joint is made at a corner – say, the junction of a chair seat rail and the top of a leg – a variation called a haunched mortise-and-tenon is used. The haunch stops any tendency the joint has to twist.

The tenon should be cut to the full width of the rail, then about three-quarters of the length of the tenon should be cut out from its top edge, down for about one-third of its width, leaving a rectangular projection on top of the main tenon. This is the haunch. If the haunch is cut at a slope from the top of the shoulder to the top edge of the tenon it becomes a secret haunch. Cut the mortise to take the full length of the tenon but only the two-thirds width. Then groove the mating face of the stile (or leg) from the end down to the top of the mortise to accept the haunch. With the secret haunch, the groove should slope inwards from the top, so that the haunch is concealed.

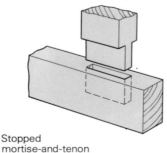

Stopped
mortise-and-tenon

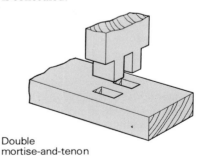

Double
mortise-and-tenon

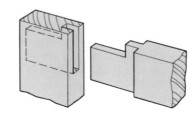

Haunched mortise-and-tenon

Secret haunched mortise-and-tenon

Dovetail joints

There are a number of different joints which use the dovetail principle. The joint which exploits this most fully is the multiple dovetail and pin joint, which is usually found in high quality cabinet and drawer construction. It is the strongest of all corner joints.

Extreme accuracy in setting out and cutting is called for in making a dovetail joint, but it is by no means beyond the capabilities of the beginner. Dovetail jigs are available to aid marking out where many joints have to be cut – or you can make your own jig.

Other dovetail joints Apart from the through dovetail, there are two main variants of this joint – the lap dovetail and the secret or mitre dovetail. They are both rather too difficult for the beginner to tackle.

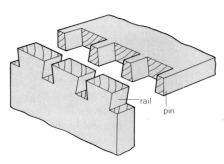

Through dovetail joint

MAKING A THROUGH DOVETAIL

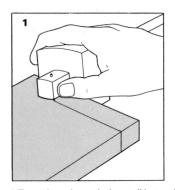
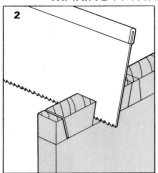
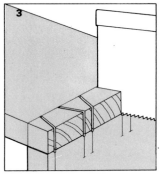
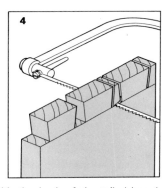

1 To make a through dovetail in two boards of the same thickness, first square the ends of each. Then, with a marking gauge held with its head against the board ends, square the shoulder lines on all faces and edges.

The dovetails should be cut in the end of one board and the pins in the other – it is usual to have a half-pin at each edge of the joint. Draw in the tails on the face of the board with a pencil and sliding bevel. In softwood, set the bevel to give a 1 in 6 slope in towards the shoulders; in hardwood, make the slope 1 in 8. The width of the tails at their shoulders should be 1½ times the width of the widest part of the pins.

2 Use a dovetail (or tenon) saw to cut the tails down to their shoulders.

3 With the end of the other board accurately aligned with the back of the tailed board, place the saw in each cut in turn and draw it back to mark the pin ends. Square the marks back to the shoulders on both faces.

4 Cut the pins keeping the tenon saw on the waste side. Most of the waste wood can be cut out with a coping saw. The gaps between the dovetails and the pins should be finally made true by using a chisel.

Reports in Handyman Which?

Materials		Planes	Nov 1971 and		Aug 1977 and
Man-made boards	Feb 1973 and		Nov 1975		Nov 1979
	Feb 1978	Saws – general purpose	Feb 1973	Drill attachments	Feb 1976 and
Veneered chipboard	Feb 1973	– hand	May 1975 and		May 1976
Wood	May 1972 and		May 1979	Jigsaws	Nov 1977
	Feb 1978	Screwdrivers	May 1974 and	Orbital sanders	Feb 1978 and
			Nov 1980		Nov 1980
Hand tools		Trimming knives	Nov 1977		
Braces and bits	Feb 1980	Trimming (shaping) tools	Nov 1979	**Miscellaneous**	
Chisels	Nov 1975	Vices (and workbenches)	May 1979	Polyurethane varnishes	Nov 1972 and
Clamps	Feb 1978				Nov 1981
Hand drills	Nov 1972 and	**Power tools**		Starting a tool kit	Nov 1971
	Feb 1980	Bandsaws	May 1980	Tools and equipment –	
Marking tools	Nov 1980	Circular saws	Nov 1978	hire or buy?	Feb 1978
Measuring tools	May 1978	Electric drills	Feb 1976,	Workbenches	May 1976

Making a sewing box

The sewing box is built in three parts – a box (plus lid), a sliding tray and a base. By varying the construction it could easily be turned into a side table or by padding and covering the top into a stool.

The difficult parts of the job are cutting through the box to form the lid, mitring the corners and rebating. You could get a timber merchant to cut the rebates for you or simply nail the plywood top and bottom on to the sides – but it will show. You could also vary the joints – using butt joints or even dovetails, for example.

The box can be finished by staining and varnishing it, painting it or covering it with cloth.

CUTTING LIST		length (mm)	width (mm)	thickness (mm)	material
1	Two box sides	500*	145	12	softwood
2	Two small box sides	400*	145	12	softwood
3	Top and bottom	475*	380*	4	plywood
4	Two tray sides	375*	40	8	softwood
5	Four tray sides and division	250*	40	8	softwood
6	Tray bottom	250*	375*	4	plywood
7	Two runners	500*	5	10	softwood
8	Material board	500*	400*	12	fibreboard
9	Lid padding	500*	400*	12	foam rubber
10	Two base sides	525*	45	40	softwood
11	Two small base sides	425*	45	40	softwood
12	Base bottom	500*	400*	4	plywood
13	Two lid beads	500*	as required	6	half-round beading
14	Two lid beads	400*	as required	6	half-round beading

Extras: four Queen Anne legs (150mm), pva glue, 25mm and 10mm pins, Velcro, cloth
*before finishing – actual size smaller: see illustration

Box Cut the sides (**1**) and (**2**) from the lengths of timber, as far as possible leaving out any defects such as knots and splits, and leaving ample waste at each end.

Mark the best face and edge of each side – these will form the outside of the box.

Mark the rebates in the top and bottom edges of each side (for the top and bottom) and cut them out with a rebate plane.

Cut the mitres at each end of the sides using a deep mitre box. Or, cut the sides to length, mark across the inside face with a gauge set to the thickness of the timber and plane off the triangle of waste to form the mitre.

Glue and pin the sides together to form a box – keep the pins at least 40mm in from the top and bottom edges. Before the glue sets, square up the box by making the diagonals the same. Once it has dried, clean any excess glue from inside the box and the rebates.

Carefully glue and pin the plywood (**3**) into the rebates top and bottom and clean up the outside of the box.

Select the best top surface and gauge a line all the way around the box to form the 40mm deep lid. Saw through the box – start in one corner – then clean up the sawn edges, cut out the hinge sinkings and fix the hinges in position. Mitre, glue and pin 6mm half round beading (**13** and **14**) around the top edge of the box and clean up the box ready for finishing.

Tray Cut out the tray sides (**4** and **5**) and mitre, glue and pin them together as outlined for the box. When the glue is dry, clean off any excess from the joints.

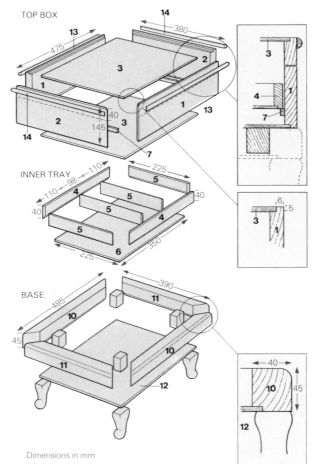

TOP BOX

INNER TRAY

BASE

Dimensions in mm

Cut the divisions (**5**) to the correct length, shape their top edge and glue and pin them in the tray – make sure they are fixed flush with the bottom of the tray. Glue and pin the plywood (**6**) on the bottom of the tray, allowing the excess plywood to overhang the edge of the tray evenly before smoothing it to size with a plane.

Rub down the tray with abrasive paper. Pin two thin strips of timber (**7**) to the inside of the bottom of the box to act as tray runners.

Lid Cut a piece of 12mm fibreboard (**8**) to fit inside the lid allowing room at each side for the cloth covering to be turned around the edge. Glue foam rubber (**9**) to the face of the fibreboard and cover the fibreboard and foam with a piece of material gluing it in place on the back. After the box is finished the upholstery can be glued in place or held in place with Velcro pads. The simplest form of lid restraint is a thin cord attached to the lid and box.

Base Cut the timbers that make up the frame (**10** and **11**), choose and mark the better faces and edges – for the top and outside – and the length as before. Cut out rebates in their inner bottom edges, check that the opposite sides are the same length, then glue and pin the frame together, making sure that it is square. Glue and pin the plywood (**12**) into the rebates.

Round off the top outside edge of the frame where it projects in front of the face of the box and screw the Queen Anne legs on to the underside of the frame.

Glue four timber blocks to the bottom of the box to provide feet for it to sit on the plywood bottom of the base frame.

Making a hi-fi stack

The hi-fi stack is designed to accommodate records or cassettes in the bottom, an amplifier (150mm high), a tuner (100mm high) and a cassette deck (150mm high) on shelves in a compartment above, and a record deck on top.

Hi-fi equipment varies a lot in size – most electronic units which are designed for stacking will fit into a stack which is 450mm wide but the height needed by each unit varies from brand to brand. So check the height of your equipment and any clearance it needs before designing your stack. Altering the stack to suit individual requirements should be fairly simple. But you should avoid making it so tall that it becomes unstable – record decks need a stable base to function properly. The stack here has a back to aid rigidity – but this is not necessary for small stacks. If you want to accommo-

CUTTING LIST	length (mm)	width (mm)	thickness (mm)	material
1 Two sides	850	380	18	veneered chipboard
2 Top	450	380	18	veneered chipboard
3 Shelf	450	330	18	veneered chipboard
4 Bottom	450	350	18	veneered chipboard
5 Back	450	380	18	veneered chipboard
6 Top front rail	450	25	18	veneered chipboard
7 Plinth	450	50	18	veneered chipboard
8 Top back rail	486	75	18	softwood or veneered chipboard
9 Back board	490	75	18	softwood or veneered chipboard

Extras: approximately 18 chipboard (or Twinfast) screws and 15 jointing blocks

date more units than allowed in this stack, think about removing the record storage area from the stack or fitting it on to a projecting plinth.

The stack outlined below is made from veneered chipboard held together by screws, battens and jointing blocks. This method of construction allows you to modify the stack if you change your hi-fi equipment. Veneered chipboard is usually sold in standard lengths, widths and thicknesses, so you need to design your stack to use the standard panels as economically as possible.

Cut the panels to size starting with the longest – if you make a mistake with one of the long panels, you can always recut it to use as a smaller panel. Score the veneer with a sharp knife before sawing and try to cut the edges straight and square.

Clamp together all panels of the same size – use G-clamps – and smooth off the edges with a plane. Plane from the corners towards the centre of each edge.

Iron on veneer edging strips to cover all the cut edges. When the edging strips have cooled and dried, trim all the edges flush with the panels either with a chisel or with abrasive paper and a sanding block. Finally, rub down all the surfaces of the panels taking care not to rub through the veneers.

Set out on the inside faces of the side panels (**1**), the positions of the top (**2**), the shelf (**3**), and the bottom (**4**). Glue and screw the top front rail (**6**) on to the front underside edge of the top. The rail should be set back about 5mm from the edge of the top. Make sure that the screws do not project through the top. Glue and pin the plinth (**7**) on to the front edge of the bottom (**4**). Make sure that the top of the plinth is flush with the top surfaces of the bottom panel.

Mark out, bore and countersink (on the underside) holes in the bottom panel (**4**) for screwing it to the back panel (**5**).

Screw the jointing blocks on to the side panels (**1**). Do not forget to

set the blocks back away from the top rails and the plinth. Place the top in position on the side panel and mark the positions of the jointing blocks. Repeat for the shelf and bottom panel. The joints will fit better if you leave a small gap between the parts of the jointing blocks (see inset) so that when you screw them together the wood surfaces touch a little before the blocks. Check that when the top, shelf and bottom are placed in position they fit properly.

Lay all the panels on the floor ready for assembly. Raise the top and one side panel on to their front edges and lightly screw up the blocks. Then fix the shelf and bottom panels in place on the side panel. Raise the second side panel into place and join it to the top, shelf and bottom panels.

To fix the back panel (**5**) in place, make sure that it fits in between the sides and mark the position of the shelf on the panel. Remove the panel and bore and countersink screw holes so that it can be fixed to the shelf. Replace the back panel, screw through the bottom and then through the panel into the shelf.

Fix the jointing blocks on to the top back rail (**8**) and to the top (**2**) and sides (**1**) and (**5**). This rail is not always necessary, or a rail of similar size to the top front rail could be glued and screwed in position.

The back board (**9**) can be screwed on and the hi-fi stack is then ready for finishing.

First stage of construction – from the front

Second stage of construction – from the rear

jointing block

Dimensions in mm

Making a built-in wardrobe

This built-in wardrobe can be used as a model for you to adapt to fit your own requirements. It has a double hanging unit and a single large storage unit with shelves (this could be used as a hanging unit) with three single smaller storage units above.

The main front frame has been designed in softwood, the dividers, sides and bottom in either chipboard or blockboard (though a veneer finish board could be used) and the doors are large sheets of veneered (or melamime covered) chipboard laid on to and overlapping the front frame.

Before starting to design a wardrobe to suit your room, take all the measurements carefully – looking for walls that lean, bow or are not square. Do not be tempted into making the wardrobe a tight fit – you may need to level it once it is complete. Instead, leave small gaps all round – 15mm overall in width and height – and cover these later with beading.

CUTTING LIST	length (mm)	width (mm)	thickness (mm)	material
1 Top rail	1490	70	19	softwood
2 Long mid rail	965	70	19	softwood
3 Bottom rail	1490	95	19	softwood
4 Three vertical members	2300	70	19	softwood
5 Short vertical member	470	70	19	softwood
6 Short mid rail	525	70	19	softwood
7 Three top cupboard doors	382	425	16	melamine-covered or veneered chipboard
8 Three main doors	1720	450	16	melamine-covered or veneered chipboard
9 Floor support batten	1500	19	19	softwood
10 Two end panels	2205	600	19	blockboard or chipboard
11 Wardrobe divider	2205	600	19	blockboard or chipboard
12 Top cupboard divider	430	600	19	blockboard or chipboard
13 Large top cupboard shelf	935	600	19	blockboard or chipboard
14 Small top cupboard shelf	495	600	19	blockboard or chipboard
15 Wardrobe floor	1450	600	19	blockboard or chipboard
16 Shelf support battens	5000 (total)	19	19	softwood
17 Floor support	1500	78	19	softwood

Set out the overall width of the wardrobe on the bottom rail (**3**) of the front frame and divide this equally for each cupboard. Use one of the vertical members (**4**) in the same way to mark where the top and mid rails (**1** and **2**) are to go. Transfer these markings to all three vertical frame members, the top rail (**1**) and the mid rail (**2**). The two smaller pieces of framework (**5** and **6**) can now be marked.

The frame is joined together with traditional mortise-and-tenon joints. When the joints have been cut, the frame should be assembled and checked for squareness. With the frame flat on the floor, cut and fix the doors (**7** and **8**). Remove them for final fitting later.

To support the floor (**15**), screw a batten (**9**) to the inside of the bottom rail (**3**) – the thickness of the floor from the top of the rail. And screw another batten (**17**) to the floor to support it at the back.

The vertical dividers (**11**) and end panels (**10**) should now be cut to size and fixed in place. These panels stretch from the inside of the frame to the rear wall and from the wardrobe floor to the top of the unit. Make dowelled butt joints to fix them to the wardrobe floor and use jointing blocks to fix them to the inside of the frame. Do not use jointing blocks for the joint to the

wardrobe floor – they will make the inside of the wardrobe difficult to keep clean. The horizontal divider between the larger bottom part of the wardrobe and the three upper cupboards is made in two pieces. These are fitted using support battens screwed to the sides (**10**) and wardrobe divider (**11**). The two shelves (**13** and **14**) are also fixed in place with battens and the top cupboard divider (**12**) is butt joined (with dowels) to the shelf (**13**) and fixed to the frame with jointing blocks.

Now refix the doors using flush hinges which can be screwed straight on to the door and the frame. The three large doors will need four hinges each; the small doors need two.

Nylon catches should be used (top and bottom) to keep the doors closed and door handles attached. Metal tubing with flanges at each end (or wood blocks drilled to take the tube) screwed in position can be used as a hanging bar.

Shelves can be put into the single large unit using battens.

The wardrobe unit should now be levelled – using small wedges as necessary – and any gap between the top and the ceiling covered with hardboard. Beading around all the outside edges of the frame will produce a neat finish.

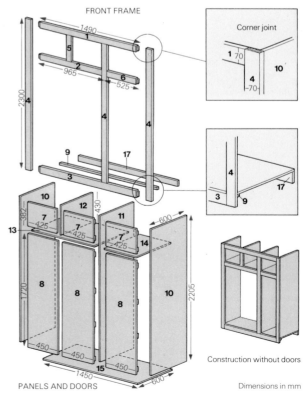

FRONT FRAME

Corner joint

Construction without doors

PANELS AND DOORS

Dimensions in mm

CHAPTER FOUR

FIXINGS

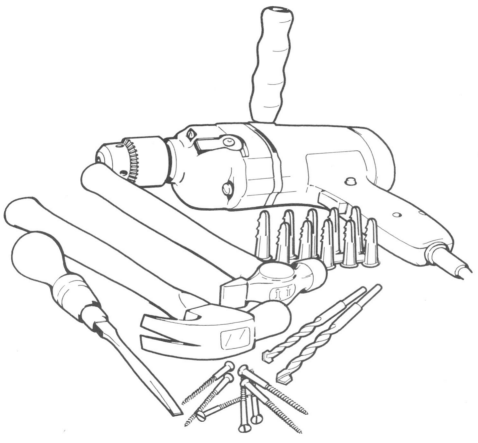

Fixing one thing to another – putting a picture hook on a wall, attaching architrave around a door opening or putting up kitchen cupboards, for example – is one of the most common d-i-y jobs.

There are three basic ways of fixing things together – using nails, screws or glue. Sometimes it does not matter too much which of the methods you choose, but there are occasions when the correct decision can make all the difference between something being firmly fixed and being a persistent problem.

In most cases you have the choice between using nails or screws. The main things which should determine which is the most suitable are strength, appearance and the materials being joined.

A screw will always give a stronger joint than the equivalent-sized nail because its thread can grip the material it is driven into better than the shank of a nail. However, there are nails with shanks specially designed for extra grip and putting nails in at an angle also increases grip. In general, if the two surfaces being joined are likely to pull apart, then screws are better than nails. If the surfaces are trying to slide over each other, nails are usually satisfactory.

Screws give a neater finish and tend to damage the material they are put into less than nails.

Using adhesives as a fixing technique has advantages over using nails or screws – apart from surface preparation no special tools are required, joints are usually invisible, and adhesives can be used to fix things in places where it is impossible to swing a hammer or turn a screwdriver. Used correctly, modern adhesives are very good, though expensive compared with nails and screws. Never use adhesives to fix things which have to carry a load – always screw wall brackets on to a wall, do not glue them. Most glued joints have to be supported until the glue has set. Adhesives are often combined with nails or screws to give a stronger joint.

Using nails is the cheapest way to fix things together, it is also the quickest, and the only tool needed is a hammer. Nailing was principally designed for fixing softwoods together and for fixing things like felt to softwoods. Nails can be used with hardwoods too as long as a guidance hole is pre-drilled but, by and large, hardwoods are better fixed with screws. Special nails are available for fixing into soft masonry.

Banging in a nail is a simple, basic handyman job. Selecting the correct nail, however, is rather more difficult – you may have a choice of head style, shank grippers, shank section and finishes. Some nails have flat heads for fixing things like felt and upholstery; some have much smaller heads which are designed to bury into the surface they are fixing; some have shanks designed to resist movement; and some have shanks which are oval in section to reduce splitting. The finish becomes important where corrosion resistance is essential.

The rule when using nails is to attach the lighter material to the heavier one (thinner to the thicker). The size of nail depends on the thicknesses of the materials being joined.

Using screws is rather more complicated than using nails. There is an even wider variety of screw styles with choices of length to thickness ratios (called gauge), materials, finishes, head styles and slot styles. Screws need more complicated tools too. They should be inserted into pre-drilled holes – which may mean using three different drill bits – and you may also need a variety of screwdriver blade styles and sizes.

Screws do have one major advantage over nails and glues – all screwed fixings can be unscrewed and dismantled quite easily, although the holes will remain.

Adhesives

Adhesives can be either used in the initial construction of joints – making joints in wood, for instance – or for repairing things.

When you use an adhesive in constructional work, choose one which has been specifically formulated for the job. For example, when you make woodworking joints which will have to withstand very wet conditions, you should use a *resorcinol formaldehyde* glue. In slightly less wet conditions a *urea formaldehyde* glue could be used instead.

When you use an adhesive for repairing things you are less likely to be able to find one which has been specifically formulated for the materials being joined. As a result glues used in repair work are less likely to give such good results.

Adhesives have a number of specific advantages over other methods of fixing:
● there is no need to make holes for fixings – this is time-consuming and can weaken the materials being joined

● when using glue for joining wood there is no need to learn how to make complicated joints
● glue can be used to fix fragile things which might be damaged by other methods of fixing
● it is possible to use glue in awkward positions where there is insufficient access for screwing and nailing
● mechanical fixings are often difficult to hide successfully, whereas glued joints can be almost invisible.

But gluing has its disadvantages too:
● although using glue is quick and easy, it may take a long time to set properly – often things which have been glued are too delicate to move or use for over 24 hours
● it is not easy to dismantle a glued joint
● some kinds of wood joint, particularly butt joints involving end grain wood, are unlikely to be very strong
● some glues will not stand large variations in temperature and humidity without weakening.

Which adhesive?

Nowadays most adhesives are synthetic resins and fall into one of three main groups – elastomeric, thermoplastic or thermosetting.

Elastomeric adhesives are based on natural or synthetic rubbers and set when the solvent they contain evaporates. They are weakened by heating or on contact with their solvent.

Thermoplastic adhesives are generally water-based and are often white in the pot and dry clear. Thermoplastics set by water (or solvent) evaporation and may be softened if they again come into contact with water (or their solvent).

Thermosetting adhesives change chemically when they set. The setting process usually involves a hardener (which is sometimes water).

It is also possible to buy **natural** glues – either *animal* or *fish* glues – and a type known as 'super glue' which is based on **cyanoacrylates**.

Many adhesives claim to stick a range of things. Most glues can be used on wood. Natural glues and solvent-based synthetic resins (mainly the elastomeric glues) also claim to stick glass, metal, leather, fabric and some plastics. Thermoplastic pva adhesives claim to stick almost anything apart from pvc, polythene and rubber. Thermosetting epoxy adhesives claim to stick china, glass, metal, leather, rubber and some plastics. The Table below lists widely available types of adhesives and should help you choose which one to use.

CHOOSING A GLUE

	use for:	about the glue
NATURAL **Animal**	wood	inferior to and less convenient than thermoplastic pva
CYANOACRYLATE **'Super glue'**	general purpose and repairing but not for porous materials like wood and un-glazed ceramics	very expensive – though generally only small quantities are required. Clear adhesive perhaps best used where all others have failed. WARNING: sticks skin very well, avoid contact with skin or eyes at all costs. Do not attempt to tear glue away from the skin. Consult doctor in severe cases
ELASTOMERIC **Synthetic rubber resin –** contact adhesives	for sticking sheet material to base surfaces – plastic laminate to wood or carpet to floor, for example	suitable for large areas. Should be spread on to both surfaces to be joined and the solvent allowed to evaporate until the surfaces become tacky. The surfaces should then be joined. Two major types – one type permits positioning when joined, the other does not. Joints must be clamped. Large quantities of solvent are lost to atmosphere – this requires good ventilation and naked flames (including gas pilot lights) must be avoided. Surplus cannot be washed off with water (try petrol before glue dries, instructions may give further advice)
Rubber latex	soft fabrics, carpets and other textiles, soft leather, cardboard, paper	gives a very flexible bond, dries clear, surplus can be washed off with water before it dries
THERMOPLASTIC **Cellulose** – clear plastic (other clear polymers also available)	hard plastics, ornaments, china, models	hardens by evaporation of the solvent. Joints take longer to dry where the solvent cannot escape – on metals, for example. Makes clear joints but once hard can be brittle. Surplus cannot be washed off with water (try acetone)
Polyvinyl acetate (pva) – milky white polymer in solution, different formulations with different uses	very good for wood, also suitable for paper, cardboard, expanded polystyrene, carpets, canvas, leather	cheap for large areas, surplus can be washed off with water while wet. Important to select brand for specific purpose
THERMOSETTING **Casein** – resorcinol formaldehyde or urea formaldehyde	specifically for wood	supplied in powder form for mixing with water. Can be used in damp and lower temperature conditions. The resorcinol types are particularly water resistant. All joints must be clamped until the glue hardens and any surplus glue must be washed off with water while it is still soft. The dried glue is slightly yellow in colour and may leave stains on decorative hardwoods
Epoxy – two-pack with different formulations for different setting times	general purpose, woods, metals, plastics (except polythene)	the contents of two different tubes have to be pre-mixed to initiate a chemical reaction immediately before use (use a match and mix on a piece of waste material). Expensive to use for large areas. Not suitable for damp materials although waterproof. Application of slight heat may speed drying of some brands – check instructions. Surplus cannot be washed off with water (try cellulose thinners or meths)

Using glue

Before using a glue, read any instructions and precautions which come with it. With most glues, once you open the container the glue inside starts to deteriorate slowly.

Epoxy glues – which you have to mix – have a limited life before they set too hard to use. Fast-setting (often advertised as *five-minute*) epoxy glues have to be used immediately but ordinary epoxy glues generally remain usable for one to two hours. Powder and water-mix casein glues should stay usable for three to four hours. With many contact adhesives, once the surfaces are put together they cannot be adjusted.

Where possible, always allow a minimum of 24 hours before putting any load on a joint. Allow even longer if you are using the glue under low temperatures or damp conditions. The following hints apply to most glues:

● always make sure that the surfaces to be joined are clean and dry. Grease must be avoided – use a solvent degreasing agent if any is present. Any wood stored outside should be brought into the house and allowed to stand for at least two days before bonding

● clean off any old glue by sanding or scraping with a knife

● support the glued joint until it is dry. If possible clamp the joint

● where possible, use glues (and allow glued joints to dry) in warm dry conditions – not in a damp cold shed

● always spread the glue as evenly as possible over the entire surface to be joined – not just a blob here and there

● never use your finger to spread the glue: use a wooden spatula instead – some glues are difficult to remove from skin (like elastomers), some irritate (like thermosetting resins) and some are dangerous (like cyanoacrylate glues)

● never use too much glue – a thin film gives a stronger bond than a thick one

● when gluing the end grain of wood, spread the glue on to both surfaces, allow it to dry and then spread on a second coat for making the joint. Any sanding, sawing or planing should be done immediately before gluing, particularly on oily woods such as teak. If you want to treat wood with preserva-

tive, do it two days before gluing. If the wood is already treated with preservative, sand it down immediately before gluing

● in damp conditions, use resorcinol formaldehyde glues for wood and either epoxy or cyanoacrylate glues for other materials. Pre-condition woodwork by leaving it for a few days in the damp environment before gluing

● if glue has to withstand high temperatures in use, choose a thermosetting glue – others may soften when heated. With thermosetting resins (and natural glues), the warmer the temperature, the faster the glue will set and the stronger the bond will be. The converse holds at low temperatures and some may not set properly. Thermoplastic and elastomeric glues will not set at high temperatures

● avoid using thermoplastic and elastomeric glues for making joints which are likely to be under permanent load

● avoid trying to fill gaps with glue. If you have to, use thermosetting resins rather than runny cellulose and pva glues.

Fixing plastic laminates

Laminates can be glued to most flat, dry, slightly rough (to provide a key for the glue) surfaces – man-made boards, for example. Because of their excellent wear, heat and stain resistance, they are often used on kitchen work surfaces. Textured laminates have excellent heat resistance, glossy laminates show scratches more readily than matt ones and dark plain colours show scratches more than light ones or patterns. In general, patterned laminates show wear quicker than plain-coloured ones.

Cutting

Plastic laminate can be cut with a hand or a power saw, with hand shears, or by scoring the decorative surface with a trimming knife (fitted with a special blade) or special laminate scoring tool and then breaking the laminate by hand.

If you use a handsaw – tenon saw, for example – work with the laminate sheet decorative side up, support it over its

entire length as near to the cutting line as possible and use the saw at a shallow angle. Cut the laminate slightly oversize to allow for trimming later. If you use a scoring tool, use a straight-edge as a guide and cut through the decorative layer into the brown underlay. Then hold a piece of wood along the cut line and lift the offcut to snap it off.

Gluing

Laminates are usually stuck down with a contact adhesive – one which allows some minor adjustments after positioning is easier to use than one which forms a firm bond immediately on contact. Around sinks a thermosetting resin adhesive would be a good choice. Clean the back of the laminate and the surface to be covered, spread the adhesive evenly on both surfaces and allow it to dry a little. Putting the laminate on to the surface in exactly the right position first time is quite difficult. To help, you can

either lay strips of wood over the surface and place the laminate on top of these; then work from one end, removing the strips and pressing down the laminate. Or you can stick drawing pins around the edges of the surface to be covered and use these as guides – press the laminate on to the surface working from the centre outwards.

Trimming and finishing

Once the glue is dry – allow at least half an hour – you can trim off the overhangs. For this, you can use a file, a plane, a trimming tool or a special laminate edge trimmer. In general, work from the corners of the laminate to the centre of the side and keep the tool moving straight along the edge – never upwards.

You can make your own edging strips from the laminate or use a special edging strip. Allow a slight overhang at the top and bottom and trim the top (with a file, say) at an angle of 45 degrees.

Nails and nailing

Nailing is quick, requires little or no preparation, gives a permanent joint, needs only the simplest tools, and is a cheap method of fixing or joining things together.

Nails are most frequently associated with woodworking but they are also used for roofing (fixing waterproof felt to roof timbers), upholstery (fixing layers of material to the base frame), masonry and many other specialist tasks. The reference Table on page 143 lists the most common names under which nails are sold, the most widely available sizes and the uses for which they are recommended.

The most common nails are manufactured from mild steel wire and are used in woodworking. They may be either circular in section with a flat circular head (called **round wire nails**) or oval with an oval head for driving into the wood surface (called **oval brad head**). Mild steel nails are fairly soft and may bend if they are not driven in squarely. They also rust in damp conditions unless they are protected by a coat of paint and are incompatible with woods such as oak and some other hardwoods – a chemical reaction takes place which produces a blue stain in the wood and this will streak when it is dam-

pened. For purposes such as these, galvanised – zinc plated – nails are available which are not a lot more expensive than ordinary nails. These can be recognised by their dull grey finish. For better protection against damp and corrosion, aluminium, brass, copper, zinc and silicon-bronze nails are available. These nails are, however, quite expensive and often more difficult to find in the shops.

The cheapest nails are called **cut** nails because they have been stamped from sheet steel.

Other nails available include **panel pins** which are small, thin nails with particularly small heads which can be punched unobtrusively below the wood surface. These can be bought with a copper-plated finish making them suitable for fitting hardboard panels (do not confuse them with hardboard nails which have a *square* cross-section) and tongued-and-grooved matchboarding in areas susceptible to condensation, like kitchens and bathrooms. **Masonry nails** are made of harder steel and can be hammered into the softer types of concrete, stone and other masonry. Also fairly easy to buy are **upholstery** nails with many different decorative finishes.

Buying nails

The size of a nail is usually expressed as its length. Nails are usually sold in imperial sizes but metric ones are gradually being introduced – in most cases the metric sizes are very close to their imperial equivalents. The thickness of a nail is generally related to its length but a few types are available in different thicknesses for the same length. Obviously, the thicker the nail the stronger and the better it should be gripped by the wood. But nails which are too thick could split the wood, especially if they are hammered in too close to the end.

Nails are normally sold loose and by weight – usually ½lb or 1lb or ½kg or 1kg at a time. When you have decided how many you need for a particular job look at the reference Table on page 143 to see how many nails there are in ½kg. Small nails and pins are often sold in quantities of 50g. If you want very few nails, prepacks may be your best choice. Buying in pre-packs is generally more expensive than bulk buying but does reduce the likelihood of you mixing together various sizes of nail and keeps them labelled and clean. If you do not pack bulk-bought wire nails carefully they

will soon corrode and they can be very difficult to sort through once the sizes are mixed.

How to nail

As a rule-of-thumb when joining something very thin to something much thicker, use a nail 2½ to 3 times longer than the thickness of the thinner material. When the thicknesses are more nearly equal, use a nail long enough to penetrate through the thinner material and half to three-quarters of the way through the thicker one.

Starting a nail can be sometimes quite difficult. When nailing into wood, a series of rapid light blows is usually sufficient to get a nail started. If the nail is awkward to hold with your fingers, use chewing gum or putty to hold it in place while you make the first few blows. Try to avoid hitting the wood – this will permanently damage its surface. In some circumstances it could be worthwhile nailing through two layers of cardboard and ripping the cardboard away just before delivering the final few blows.

Nailing into wood will always cause compression and stress in the wood un-

less a pilot hole is drilled. When nailing close to the end of a piece of wood, use oval nails with the longer side parallel to the grain. Better still cut the wood over-length, nail it in place and then trim it to length. Splitting along the grain is always a problem when nailing softwoods. At the first sign of it happening remove the nail and try using a thinner one. If this does not solve the problem, drill a pilot hole or, where appropriate, stagger the nails to reduce the stress within the grain structure. Bending is the only other problem you are likely to encounter. Altering the direction in which you hit the nail may drive it in successfully but if it does not, remove the nail *before* it is too late and substitute another.

Nails which are designed to be hammered flush with (or below) the wood surface are best finished off with a punch. This is simply a hardened steel rod which is flat at both ends but tapers towards the end which you put on the nail head. Punches are specified by the diameter of their tip: a 1.5mm punch is satisfactory for panel pins and a 10mm punch for large (150mm) oval brad heads. Special hollow-faced punches are available for small-topped pins.

Nailing into masonry

When nailing directly into masonry, much harder blows are required than for wood and the nail can be held in position with a pair of pliers.

Masonry nails and hammers are both hard and there is always a risk of bits of metal flying off the nail or hammer. To use masonry nails safely you should:

● wear safety goggles

● use a hammer you can control – one which is not too heavy nor too light

● make sure that the hammer face is smooth and clean

● strike the nail squarely with the middle of the hammer face

● never try to hammer in a nail which has broken – remove it with pincers

● use a piece of steel between the hammer and the nail when nailing in awkward positions where you cannot be sure of hitting the nail head squarely

● stop hammering if a masonry nail strikes a particularly hard piece of aggregate in concrete and begins to bend – pull it out (this may be difficult and is likely to remove plaster on plastered walls) and start a fresh hole with a new nail at least 20mm away.

When fixing things to a wall, use masonry nails which are long enough to penetrate at least 20mm beyond the plaster (usually 16mm thick) and into the major wall material. Increase the length of the nail when nailing into softer interior wall materials such as breeze or lightweight concrete blocks. Avoid nailing things like coat hooks and curtain rails directly to a wall. Use masonry nails

to fix a batten to the wall first and then fix the other things to this batten.

Hammers

A hammer (or special nail gun) should always be used for knocking in nails – they are specially designed for comfort and convenience and are much safer to use than other flat-edged implements. The steel of a hammer head is specially heat treated to make the striking face hard enough to stop it being damaged when it strikes a nail but not so hard that it becomes brittle and liable to shatter.

There are many different kinds of hammer. Some are designed for particular purposes such as bricklaying, panel-beating, stonework and upholstery. The two most common general-purpose hammers are basically designed for woodworking.

The **curved claw** hammer is designed for general-purpose woodworking and carpentry. The most common size is 16oz though 20 and 24oz hammers are also available. (The weight refers to the weight of the head.) Its weight makes it a quick, though tiring, tool to use and it is particularly useful for driving in long nails. It also has a hardened claw which is invaluable for pulling out nails and pins. The handles of curved claw hammers may be ash, glass fibre, hickory or steel. Glass fibre and steel-handled hammers usually have rubber hand grips.

The **cross-pein** (*Warrington* or *joiners*) hammer was designed for joinery and cabinet making. Standard sizes are 4, 6,

10, 12, 14 and 16oz. The smallest size is sometimes called a pin or tack hammer. The hardened cross-pein (the tapered wedge end) is for starting small pins and tacks and for finishing off nails in awkwardly-shaped mouldings. Hemispherical peins, with a ball instead of a tapered wedge end, are also available and although they are generally better balanced they are much less useful for general-purpose woodwork.

From the left: curved claw hammer for general woodwork and carpentry; cross-pein (Warrington or joiners) hammer for joinery and cabinet making; hemispherical pein hammer

Caution

When you are nailing, plugging or anchoring things to walls, do not forget that walls (solid or hollow) often conceal pipes and cables. Try to figure out where they are likely to be – cables, for example, generally run vertically up to a wall socket and down to light switches. Unless you are confident that there are no cables where you are working, it is worth insulating yourself from both your tools and the ground by using a power drill with an all-plastic body or a hammer with a rubber sleeve on the handle and by wearing rubber-soled shoes.

HINTS FOR NAILING

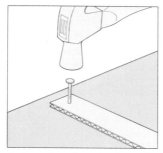

A piece of cardboard reduces the likelihood of damage to a wood surface. Rip the cardboard away to drive the nail home

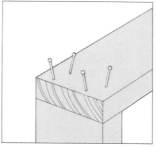

Stagger the nails to avoid splitting the wood; drive the nails in at an angle for greater strength

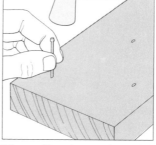

When nailing close to the end of a piece of wood, use oval nails with their longer side along the grain

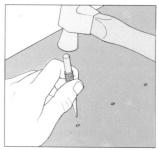

Use a punch to knock nails below a wood surface – a hollow-faced punch is useful for nails with small heads

NAIL INFORMATION

Types of nail	common lengths in	finish	how many a kg	uses	comments
WOODWORKING					
 **cut clasp nail**	1½ to 4	m	290×2in	carpentry and joinery; fixing to masonry	fairly unlikely to split wood; strong grip, difficult to remove; rare
 **cut floor brad**	2	m	260×2in	fixing floorboards to joists	fairly unlikely to split wood; may be difficult to start; rare
 **hardboard panel pin; soldier head pin**	½ to 1½ D(1)	d	4000×¾in	fixing hardboard or thin plywood	head easily driven below surface; not very strong grip
 **lath nail**	¾ to 1¼, D	g,m	1150×1¼in	fixing lathes (thin battens) as a base for plaster	similar to round wire nail (see below); rare
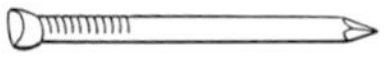 **oval brad head; oval wire nail**	1 to 6	g,m	470×2in	carpentry and joinery	unlikely to split wood; head easily punched in; used instead of cut floor brads; also available with lost head
 **panel pin**	½ to 3, D	b, c, d g,m	3000×1in	cabinet making; fixing moulding; reinforced glued joints	head easily punched in; similar to lost head round wire nail
 **plasterboard nail (jagged shank**	1¼ or 1½	g,m	570×1½in	fixing plasterboard or other man-made boards	jagged shank prevents nail being pulled out, rare
 **ringed shank nail (annular)**	1⅝ to 3, D	m	230×2½in	fixing man-made boards	rings allow boards to be pulled together; jagged shank prevents nail being pulled out; rare
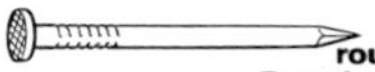 **round wire nail; round plain head nail, French nail spike (over 5in)**	1 to 6, D	g,m	340×2in	rough carpentry	may split wood; also available with lost head (rare) similar to panel pin
 **veneer pin; moulding pin, finishing pin**	½ to 1	b,m	8000×¾in	cabinet making; fixing small mouldings and veneer	similar to panel pin but thinner shank
MISCELLANEOUS					
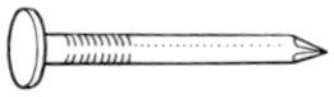 **clout or slate nail**	½ to 2, D	a, c, g, m,s,z	570×1½in	fixing roofing felt; fencing; fixing slates	cut clout or cut slate nail also available, but rare
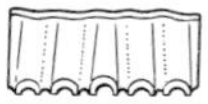 **corrugated fastener; wiggle nail**	½ to 1 (2)	m	(3)	rough carpentry; mitred or butt joints	not very strong joints
 **cut brad; blued cut bill, lino brad, sprig**	½ or ⅝	b,c,m	4500×⅝in	fixing lino; glazing; picture backs	like a headless cut tack
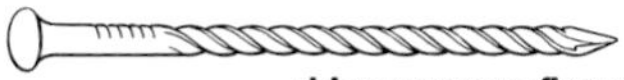 **drive screw; roofing nail**	2½ to 4½	g	50×4in	fixing corrugated sheet materials to wood	threaded shank gives good grip; usually used with special washers; rare
 **escutcheon pin; brass pin**	⅝ or ¾	b	3000×⅝in	fixing small metal fittings to wood	escutcheon is a keyhole cover
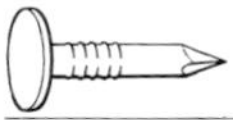 **felt nail; extra large head clout nail**	½ to 1	g	580×¾in	fixing roofing felt; chair webbing	—
 **masonry nail**	⅞ to 4, D	g,m	(3)	fixing to masonry	see page 142
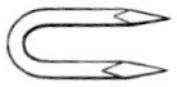 **staple**	½ to 2	g,m	1800×¾in	fixing wire to wood; rough carpentry	also available with covering of insulation fibre for fixing wire
 **twisted shank nail (spring head shown)**	2½	g,m	140×2½in	fixing sheet materials to wood; fixing man-made boards	spring head for use without washer; twisted shank gives good grip; rare; also available without spring head, sometimes called screw nail; rare
UPHOLSTERY AND CARPET					
 **drugget pin**	⅝ to 1	b	(3)	carpets	carpet nail similar but without raised nipple; rare
 **gimp pin**	⅜ to 1	b,e	9000×½in	fixing braid (gimp) to upholstered wood	cut gimp pin also available
 **tack; improved (shown) or fine**	¼ to 1	g,m	3500×⅝in	fixing fabric or webbing to wood frame; laying carpets	improved type have two small lugs under large head
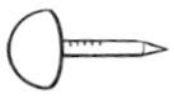 **upholstery nail; chair**	½ to ¾	b,e	(3)	decorative upholstery	—

(1) Square shank ¾in only, 3,500×¾in per kg
(2) Depth given; widths vary
(3) Normally sold in packets, by number

KEY TO COMMON SIZES:
D = available in different thicknesses

KEY TO MATERIALS AND FINISH:
a = aluminium, b = brassed, c = copper, d = coppered, e = enamelled, g = galvanised, m = mild steel, s = silicon-bronze, z = zinc

Buying a hammer

A 16oz curved claw and a 4oz cross-pein make a useful pair of basic hammers. The comfort and balance of a hammer are generally a matter of personal preference, so before buying one make sure you like the feel of it. In particular, try different types of handle. Make sure that the hammer is well finished, paying particular attention to the security of the head and the smoothness of the striking face – cheaper hammers sometimes have a slightly domed face and some may also be slightly pitted or dented. All these things make driving nails more difficult.

Pulling out nails

Any nail which begins to bend severely as you are hammering it in will have to be removed. The two most convenient ways of doing this are with a claw hammer or a pair of pincers.

In terms of leverage and overall performance a claw hammer is the better tool, but pincers are fairly effective at gripping and removing nails so long as they have been manufactured to a satisfactory standard. Pincers also have a considerable advantage over a claw hammer in terms of accessibility. They can grip a nail which has been driven close to a corner and are easier to work under the head of a nail driven into the wood surface. The hardness of the jaw edges is the most important factor in deciding whether a pair of pincers is well made but this is not easy to check. However, you should look at the edges of the jaws to make sure they meet all along and try out the pivot to make sure it is not too stiff.

When you try to lever out a nail you put a considerable downward force on the wood surface. This can cause damage. If this matters, slide a piece of plywood or something similar under the point at which the hammer or pincers pivot – to spread the load.

Some pincers have a tack lifter at the end of one handle. This is a V slot designed for sliding under tack heads. Tacks are easy to pull out because their shanks taper sharply and the tack lifter on pincers will probably do the job. Nevertheless, they are not as good for removing tacks as a purpose-designed tack lifter which has a curved head and gives slightly better leverage. But even with a purpose-designed tack lifter you are unlikely to be able to lift ordinary nails and you would not be able to lift headless pins or brads as the V is too wide.

THREE WAYS OF PULLING OUT NAILS

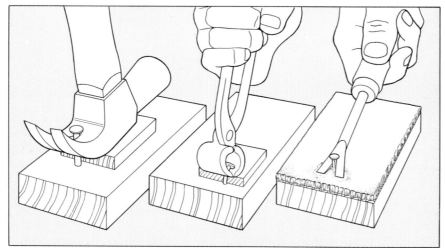

From the left: when using a claw hammer, put a scrap of wood under the hammer to avoid damaging the surface below; pincers are useful for pulling out nails which are too awkward for claw hammer to cope with; tack lifters cannot be used for headless nails or pins but are ideal tools for pulling tacks out of carpets

FITTING A NEW HANDLE

In time, the head of a hammer may loosen a little on the handle. At the first sign of this happening, the handle should be replaced. Replacement handles for most hammers can be bought from tool shops and are supplied complete with wedges – the diagrams show how to fit the replacement. Some all-steel cross-pein hammers have a handle which is permanently joined to the head.

Make two saw cuts in the top of the handle

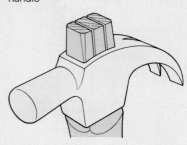

Fit the hammer head on the handle and saw off the end if necessary

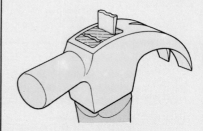

Drive wedges into the saw cuts to hold the head securely

Fixing with screws

Screws are often the best way of fastening things together. The other two common methods – nailing and gluing – are often quicker and require less preparatory work but both produce a permanent joint which cannot readily be dismantled again, and neither method of fixing is likely to produce the strength and abuse resistance that screwed joints have.

About screws

Choosing the right screw for the job can be quite complicated as there are variations in materials, plated finishes, head styles, sizes and thread types.

In addition to different head styles there are two basic head **slot** styles – the traditional *slotted-head* style and the so-called *cross-head* style. Unfortunately, there are three cross-head styles which can be difficult to identify. The most common one – Pozidriv – is found mainly on wood screws. The recently introduced Supadriv is similar and is said to give more grip between the screw and screwdriver, though in practice with wood screws the difference is not significant. The third style, known as Phillips, is found mainly on machine and self-tapping screws.

Traditional slotted-head screws are turned by means of a single slot into which a screwdriver blade should fit snugly. Because the slot size varies with the screw, a range of screwdrivers is needed to cope with all the different sizes of screws likely to be used. In practice, a screwdriver of the wrong size is often used and, if it is too small, the blade can easily slip or ride out of the slot and gouge into adjacent woodwork.

Cross-head screws have the advantage that they are easier to start turning than conventional screws and are easier to turn when it is impossible to make sure that the screwdriver blade and the screw head are exactly in line. Another advantage of the Pozidriv system is that only three screwdriver points are needed to cover all sizes of screw. (No 2 size is the most common.) Pozidriv screwdrivers can also be used for Supadriv screws but Phillips screws need their own screwdriver.

Cross-head screws do have disadvantages – if their slots become filled with paint (as often happens on door hinges) you will have great difficulty in cleaning them out sufficiently well to get the screwdriver blade in, whereas a conventional slotted-head can easily be cleaned with a trimming knife or hacksaw blade.

Most screws designed for use in wood have a **thread** which extends approximately 60 per cent of the way from the tip to the head leaving a portion of blank slightly bigger shank. Any screws found which have threads extending over their full length should be looked at closely. They may be either self-tapping screws designed for fastening metal – these are likely to be bright plated – or Twinfast screws designed for use in chipboard but useful for general woodworking.

Types of head

The two basic head shapes are **round-head** and **countersunk** and both are available with cross-head or slotted drives.

Round-head screws are used mainly for holding thin materials which cannot take countersunk screws. This generally means fixing metal things to wood in positions where the shape and appearance of the head is hidden or does not matter. With this head you need to drill only a clearance hole and a pilot hole.

Countersunk screws are shaped so that their heads can be sunk into the surface of the top material you are fixing. They are less obtrusive than round-head screws and must be used where a bulky head cannot be tolerated – such as fixing hinges. Besides needing to drill a clearance hole and a pilot hole, you may have to make a tapered hole for the head with a countersink bit – particularly when fixing metal or hardwoods. With softwoods, tightening the screw to pull the head into the wood may be enough.

TYPES OF SCREW

From the left: slotted head, Phillips cross head; Pozidriv cross head; Supadriv – similar to the Pozidriv but has a different internal angle in the recess

Countersunk head

Screw with domed head

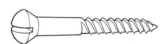
Raised-countersunk head

Self-tapping screw

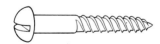
Round-head

Twinfast screw

Reports in Handyman Which?

Adhesives	1981
Fixing to walls	Feb 1974
Glues for wood	Aug 1976
Nailing	Nov 1976
Screws for wood	Feb 1973
	and Nov 1980
Screwdrivers	May 1974
	and Nov 1980

A third type of screw known as a **raised countersunk** is a sort of combination of the other two. They are used for fixing door handles and other visible hardware. They do not stick out too far but still keep the end of the screwdriver away from the hardware.

Countersunk screws of both types can be used with **cup washers** to protect the wood under the head or to avoid having to make a countersunk hole.

Materials and finish
The most widely used material for screws is mild steel. It is quite a weak metal and rusts easily.

When using screws which are likely to get damp, choose those which are plated with a corrosion-resistant finish such as cadmium, sheradized or bright zinc plated. Or better still, use screws made of a non-rusting metal like aluminium alloy, brass or stainless steel. These last three types are expensive; aluminium alloy and brass screws are particularly weak and sometimes break when screwing them into hardwood – the secret is to put in a mild steel screw first.

There are a few other important things to consider when selecting screw finishes:

● when fixing metal things beware of chemical interaction between the metal and the screw finish. Interaction between steel and aluminium alloy is particularly common and the resulting corrosion may make the screws jam. Wherever possible choose screws with the same metal finish as the metal being fixed

● untreated mild steel screws will react chemically with some hardwoods – particularly afrormosia, idigbo and oak – causing discolouration of the wood. Use brass or stainless steel screws instead

● occasionally the appearance of the screw head is of paramount importance. Brass and steel screws plated with chrome or nickel (both shiny) and Pozidriv and Supadrive screws with a bright zinc finish are all available. Chrome-plated screws with domed heads are av-

ailable for fixing mirror and bathroom fittings – the domed head is actually separate from the screw head and has to be screwed into a tiny threaded hole in the screw head once the screw is fitted.

Screw sizes
In addition to *length* (measured from the point of the screw to the surface the screw is driven into, not always the overall length), the diameter or *gauge* needs to be specified too. The gauge indicates the diameter of the screw and the bigger numbers indicate bigger sizes.

Buying screws
When buying screws the specification is listed in this order: gauge, length (in inches), material, head style, special thread (if any), type of finish or coating (if any). For example *8 × 1¼ steel Pozidriv countersunk head Twinfast wood screw, bright zinc plated.* In practice, this is usually abbreviated to 'Inch and a half zinc-plated Twistfast eights'.

Screws are priced by popularity as well as size – so it might be cheaper to buy the size *bigger* than the one you think you want. It is worth checking the GKN price list before you buy.

Screws can be bought in bulk in boxes containing 100 or 200 screws (less popular sizes and types are sometimes available in boxes of 50) from builders' merchants or large ironmongers. The more popular sizes are supplied in 200s rather than 100s. You can also buy them loose, again usually from builders' merchants or large ironmongers, counted out from the boxes but this is a more

expensive way to buy screws. Most expensive of all, however, are small pre-packs.

It is useful to keep a basic stock of screws around the house and to buy special screws as and when you want them. A basic stock might be one box (100 or 200) each of the following sizes of countersunk Supadriv steel screws: 6 × ¾, 8 × 1, 8 × 1½, 10 × 2.

Using screws
When you put in a screw you usually have to drill a clearance hole and a pilot hole. The length and diameter of these holes will depend on the screw size – see Table below. Drill the pilot hole in the thing you are fixing to – make it a little bit shorter than the length of the screw. Drill a shorter, wider clearance hole in the thing you are fixing. Make sure that the clearance hole is deep enough to avoid the wide part of the shank – between the thread and the head – being forced into the small pilot hole. Normally the clearance hole should pass right through the fitting or uppermost material. Finally, if appropriate, countersink the top of the clearance hole. When using small screws, a bradawl (a small hand-held spiked instrument rather like a pointed screwdriver) can be used for making the pilot hole.

When putting in a lot of countersunk screws of the same size, you can avoid changing the drill bit three times by using a combination screwsink which is a combination of all three drills necessary for putting in a countersunk screw. These bits are difficult to buy.

DRILL SIZES FOR CLEARANCE AND PILOT HOLES

gauge	clearance drill	pilot drill – hardwood ordinary	Twinfast	pilot drill – softwood ordinary	Twinfast
	mm	mm	mm	mm	mm
2	2.5	bradawl	bradawl	bradawl	bradawl
4	3.0	1.5	2.0	bradawl	1.0
6	4.0	2.0	2.5	1.5	1.5
8	4.5	2.5	3.0	2.0	2.0
10	5.0	2.5	3.0	2.0	2.5
12	6.0	3.0	3.5	2.5	2.5

A few tips

● Do not drive screws in near the ends or edges of a piece of wood – it may split
● try not to drive screws into end grain – this does not give as much grip as driving across the grain
● with ordinary threads, do not drive the screw in so far that the wide part of the shank is forced into the small pilot hole. If you do this in hardwood or a wallplug, you may break the screw; if you do it in the edge of chipboard or plywood, you may split the board
● it is often a good idea to lubricate screws lightly with wax or grease before putting them in, especially with hardwoods. It makes driving and removing the screws much easier, helps prevent corrosion and hardly affects the grip of the screw at all
● when putting brass or aluminium screws into hardwoods, put a steel screw in first to open out the pilot hole
● occasionally, access for putting in a screw is very limited and while long-bladed screwdrivers should reach into most positions you may not be able to get your fingers in to hold the screw. Special screw-holding screwdrivers are available but a piece of rubber tubing over the end of the screwdriver usually works just as well. Other materials such as sticky tape, chewing gum, putty and plasticine work too but are more fiddly to get right. Magnetizing the screwdriver blade only works for steel screws.

SCREWDRIVERS

An ordinary screwdriver has a plastic or wooden handle fixed permanently to a steel blade which has its end shaped to fit into a slotted or cross-head screw, **Ordinary** screwdrivers can be difficult to use one handed and can cause blisters. With a **ratchet** screwdriver you do not need to release your grip on its handle when using it – it has a ratchet mechanism which can be adjusted to screw up, to unscrew, or can be locked so that the screwdriver acts like an ordinary one. A **spiral ratchet** screwdriver allows you to drive in screws by just pumping on the handle. Most come with a selection of interchangeable blades. These two ratchet screwdrivers should be easier on the hands than an ordinary one. A spiral ratchet may save time when you have a lot of screws to put in but do not expect to get the screws in as tightly as you would with an ordinary screwdriver. A 400mm long spiral ratchet should drive 12 gauge 2in screws into softwood and 10 gauge 1½in screws into beech. A ratchet screwdriver saves little time.

If you want a Pozidriv screwdriver, make sure that it is marked as such – it may say Pozidriv on its shaft and should be marked with its point size too. The most common No 2 fits screw gauges 5 to 10; No 1 fits smaller screws – gauges 1 to 4; and No 3 fits larger screws – gauges over 10. With unmarked cross-head screwdrivers it is best to assume that they are designed to fit Phillips cross-head screws though most work well with Pozidriv and Supadriv screws too.

Slotted screwdrivers are very unlikely to carry any useful size marking on them. And as there is such a wide range of screw slot sizes, it is quite likely that even with a collection of four slotted screwdrivers with blade widths of 2.5mm (electricians), 4.5mm, 6.5mm and 9.5mm, you will still come across screws where the screwdriver tip fits so sloppily in the screw slot that it rides out of the slot when you apply large turning forces. So, if you have a particular size of slotted screw that you prefer to use (or intend to use extensively), take one of the screws to the shop and select a screwdriver with a tip that fits well. Check the condition of the point as well – make sure that it has clean sharp corners and has been cut squarely to the shaft. Where you have a choice, choose the screwdriver with the thickest blade.

You can improve the point of a new screwdriver and retrieve even a badly damaged one with a grindstone. Try to get the end and the faces flat with a good sharp corner between the end and each face. Take care when using a powered grindstone – if the metal gets too hot, the blade will lose its temper and the point will then be too soft. **Wear goggles to protect your eyes.**

Handle shapes fall into three categories – cabinet, engineer's and shapes specially designed by individual screwdriver manufacturers. The handle shape, its size, and what it is made of all affect how tightly the screw can be turned. For most woodworking, larger handles are best – they let you apply most torque and are generally most comfortable. If you are likely to use the screwdriver when your hands are greasy – when repairing the car say – then a plastic fluted engineer's screwdriver should be easy to wipe clean afterwards. (But thin handles on engineer's screwdrivers can become uncomfortable if they are used for a long time.) Always check the finish of a plastic handle and avoid rough moulding seams.

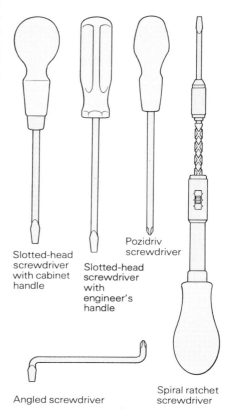

Slotted-head screwdriver with cabinet handle

Slotted-head screwdriver with engineer's handle

Pozidriv screwdriver

Angled screwdriver

Spiral ratchet screwdriver

Fixing things to solid walls

How you should fix things to walls depends on the type of wall you want to fix to and whether the fixing will have to take heavy loads. Ordinary screws and nails are suitable only for soft fibrous materials like wood – nails usually bend when they are hammered into a brick wall and screws either will not go in at all, or go in but do not grip well enough to sustain any load. Masonry nails can be used in brickwork – see page 142.

The usual technique for fixing things to walls is to make a hole in the wall, fill it with a plugging compound or a wallplug and then drive a screw into this: the wallplug expands as the screw is driven in. This works well for solid walls, but if the wall is hollow – plasterboard walls and lath and plaster walls – the fixing has to be made *through* the wall with a hollow-wall fastener – usually an anchor or a toggle.

Making holes in walls

There are basically four ways of making holes in a wall:
● by hand with a Rawltool – you hold the tool against the wall and hit the end with a hammer while rotating the tool
● with a masonry drill bit in a brace, breast drill or small hand drill
● with a masonry drill bit in an electric drill set at either high or low speed
● with an electric hammer drill fitted with a special type of masonry drill. The hammer drill vibrates the masonry drill in and out as it turns.

The Table below shows how these methods compare in different types of wall material. Clinker blocks are used for building internal walls and have now largely replaced breeze blocks; they are fairly soft. Hard bricks, or engineering bricks, are much stronger, harder and more moisture-repellent than common house bricks.

Masonry drills

Masonry drills look like twist drills – see page 250 – but do not have lands on the fluted section and their cutting tip is made of tungsten carbide, which is very hard and resistant to abrasion. When you use the drill you must withdraw it regularly, particularly when drilling holes deeper than the length of the flutes.

Masonry drills come in numbered sizes linked to the use of screws and the traditional fibre wallplugs. Some masonry drills are meant for rotary drilling with hand drills and ordinary electric drills; others are designed for impact drilling with a hammer drill. The latter are difficult to resharpen and this job should be left to a professional; some manufacturers offer a resharpening service for a minimal charge. Those drills designed for rotary drilling can be resharpened with a special grinding wheel (green grit wheel) and although the job is easier than with twist drills it is still a bit tricky.

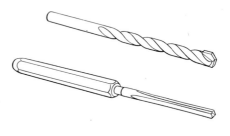

Top: a masonry drill – has a tungsten carbide cutting tip Bottom: Rawltool

Wallplugs

Any type of screw can be used to fix things in masonry as long as a suitable wallplug is used as well. Originally, wallplugs were made only from fibrous material which was fairly difficult to drive screws into and gripped the sides of the hole poorly, often turning with the screw. Nowadays, many wallplugs are moulded from plastic and nylon. Metal ones are available too.

All wallplugs are used in much the same way – you drill a clearance hole in the wall to fit the wallplug, and then drive in an ordinary wood screw. As the screw goes in it forces the plug to expand and grip the sides of the hole. The size of this hole has to be just right for the wallplug – you should have to push it home with your thumb or tap it home with a small hammer. It should not go in too easily or it will not grip the sides of the hole when the screw is turned.

Plug sizes

With some brands of wallplug choosing the size is simple – you use the same size screw as plug as drill – 8 gauge screw in a size 8 plug in a hole drilled with a No 8

DRILLING HOLES IN MASONRY

	clinker block	common brick	hard brick	concrete
Rawltool	☐	◪	■	◪
Small hand drill	☐	☐	■	■
Breast drill	☐	☐	■	◪
Brace	☐	◪	■	◪
Electric drill – high speed	■	◪	■	☐
Electric drill – low speed	◪	☐	■	☐
Electric hammer drill	■	■	☐	◪

Key
■ impossible to make holes by this method
◪ very difficult to drill holes
☐ quite difficult to drill holes

◪ method good enough for most jobs
■ easy to make lots of holes

masonry drill. Most plugs, however, can accommodate a range of screw gauges – 4 to 8, 6 to 10, 10 to 14, for example. So by careful selection, two different sizes of masonry bit and wallplug should be enough to cope with almost all jobs. There are two problems with doing this though. It may mean drilling wider holes than would otherwise be necessary – a plug suitable for screw gauges 4 to 8 must always be drilled with a No 8 masonry drill. And because many wall-plugs are a standard length, it means you may have to drill deeper holes than you need for small screws – a No 4 screw is normally shorter than a No 8. One way of overcoming this latter problem is to drill the hole just a little deeper than the length of the screw and then cut the wallplug to size with a sharp knife (or pair of secateurs). If you have to cut a tapered wallplug, cut off the narrow bottom rather than the top (so it grips in the hole better). If on tapping the wallplug home you find that the hole is just too short, trim off the protruding plastic with a sharp trimming knife.

The exact size of masonry drill used can affect the security of the fixing and the use of metric and inch sizes as alternatives can cause problems – a No 12 drill, for example, is bigger than a 6mm drill but smaller than a 7mm one. When you have a choice of size, a small one will give a better fixing but increases the risk of breaking the screw.

DRILL SIZE CONVERSIONS

drill number	diameter in	mm
6	5/32	4
8	3/16	4.8
10	7/32	5.6
12	1/4	6.4
14	9/32	7.1
16	5/16	7.9
18	11/32	8.7
20	3/8	9.5

Plastic wallplugs
The two main types of plastic wallplug – moulded and extruded – need slightly different techniques to use them.
Extruded plugs are always straight – the whole length of the plug is uniform in

shape and size. When using this type of plug there are two very important precautions to take. First, make sure that the whole length of the plug is sunk into solid masonry – if the plug is flush with a plastered or tiled surface, the expansion as you put in the screws can cause cracking. Secondly, do not drive the screw in so far that the shank is forced into the plug – it will get very tight and may snap. So for such plugs the hole must be drilled sufficiently deep to accommodate both the screw shank (unthreaded portion) and the plug length. Some sort of punch (often the tip of the screw) is required to insert the plug sufficiently deep in the hole.

Moulded plugs can be much more convenient to use. Many have a recess at the top to accommodate part of a counter-sunk screw head and a wide enough hole beneath this to accommodate the screw shank. The bottom portion of the plug has a tapering hole – tapering more sharply than the threaded portion of a screw so that the plug will expand out to grip the sides of the hole as the screw is driven home. This means that these plugs do not have to be pushed deeply into the hole to avoid cracking or to get the best grip. Many have a small lip around the top to stop them disappearing down a hole that is too large. With some of these plugs whether a screw can go in without causing expansion around its shank depends on the size of the screw.

Often the security of a wallplug depends on the material of the wall. The most successful way of overcoming problem walls is to use a big screw in a plug that is not designed to take bigger ones and to use more screws and longer screws and plugs.

Plugging compounds
Plugging compounds can be used to fill large or badly-drilled holes that would not hold a wallplug. You mix the powder to a paste with water, fill the hole, make a hole for the screw and drive it in. The compound should set almost at once.

It is possible to use an ordinary crack-filling compound instead of a wallplug in an irregular hole as long as the hole is not

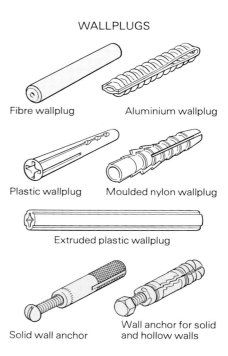

WALLPLUGS

Fibre wallplug

Aluminium wallplug

Plastic wallplug

Moulded nylon wallplug

Extruded plastic wallplug

Solid wall anchor

Wall anchor for solid and hollow walls

The solid wall anchor (bottom left) works rather like a wallplug – tightening the screw forces the anchor apart. With the other anchor, as you tighten the screw it squeezes the body, making it fatter

too wide, and as long as the screw will not have to bear heavy loads. If possible, add a little fibrous material such as glass fibre strands, glass wool insulation material or plastic non-rotting fibre to the mix and pack it tightly into the hole. Once the filler starts to harden, drive in the screw by hand. Leave the screw for several days to give the filler time to set hard. Ordinary steel screws may corrode in the filler – use non-corroding screws or paint them first.

Solid wall anchors
Occasionally interior walls are too crumbly to support a conventional wallplug where a load-bearing screw is needed. The solution to this problem is to use a solid wall anchor. For the most common type you drill a single large clearance hole, insert an integral anchor and bolt and tighten the bolt. The action of tightening the bolt draws a nut through the anchor expanding it so that it grips into the sides of the hole.

Fixing to hollow walls

In most modern houses, plasterboard walls and hollow hardboard doors are common fixing problems. In older houses you may come across lath and plaster walls (plaster on a base of wooden strips). With these walls it is possible to get a secure fixing by using mechanical devices which go through a hole in the wall and then spread out behind it to bear the load behind the surface as well as in the hole. However, even this type of fixing will not take heavy loads if the wall will not bear it. For heavy loads it is best to locate the base wood framework to which the plasterboard has been attached and screw directly into this. The framework can usually be found by plunging a bradawl through the plaster skimmed plasterboard. Plasterboard panels are 1220mm wide and the wood frame is behind each vertical seam – so once you have found one vertical frame locating the rest should be easy.

The fixings for hollow walls are generally called anchors and toggles though a few wallplugs will do the job too. Two things determine which type of device you should use – the depth of cavity you have for fixing into and the thickness of the

board material. Most fittings need a minimum cavity depth of 25 to 30mm, some need 50mm and above. With a wallplug you may be able to fix into a 10mm cavity. Anchors can generally cope with board thicknesses between 3 and 12mm though some can cope with nearly 20mm. Toggles can be bought to cope with board thicknesses up to nearly 75mm. If you want to take down something you have fixed, a few devices will stay where they are when the screw is removed but most drop into the cavity and are lost.

All these fixings need a clearance hole passing right through to the cavity. The hole must be just large enough to accommodate the various bits that have to pass through it. Usually this means that the hole is too large to grip the plug and prevent it turning.

Some of these fixings can be used on ceilings too, but attempt to find the ceiling joists (closer together than on walls) first. On ceilings these fixings can take only very light loads – even a hanging plant pot is better suspended from the hidden wooden framing.

SPECIAL WALLPLUG cheap; gets some grip from expanding within the panel but most of the grip comes from the legs which expand to grip back of the panel – check the size needed for your thickness of board; remains in the hole when the screw is removed

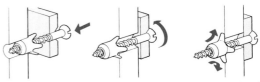

PLASTIC TOGGLE cheap; anchor squeezes through hole then spreads out and grips the back of the board as the screw is tightened; toggle lost when screw removed

COLLAPSIBLE ANCHOR cheap; the sides (metal or plastic) collapse as the screw is tightened; anchor remains in hole when the screw is removed

RUBBER ANCHOR expensive but comes complete with plated bolt; the body is made of rubber and as the screw is tightened the body gets squeezed and bulges; can be removed and reused

GRAVITY TOGGLE expensive but comes complete with plated bolt; the arm drops down when it gets through the hole; toggle lost when bolt removed

SPRING TOGGLE expensive but comes complete with plated bolt; the arms fly apart when they get through the hole; toggle lost when bolt removed

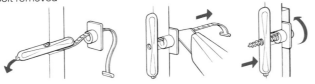

NYLON STRAP TOGGLE expensive; the strap pulls the arm back to the wall; the serrations should then hold the arm as the screw is driven in

CHAPTER FIVE

BUILDING

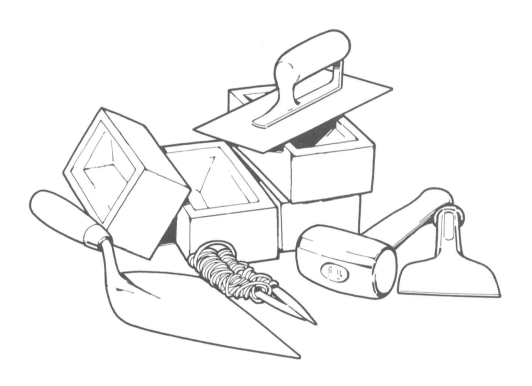

Basic building rules and regulations

There are several rules and regulations governing buildings which aim to ensure that land and buildings are developed in the public interest and buildings are safely constructed.

The two main rules governing building, altering and the use of houses (in England and Wales) are the Town and Country Planning Acts and Building Regulations. Both are administered by your local authority (though not usually by the same department) and are quite different from one another. Most work needs **Building Regulations** approval, but if this is granted, it does not mean that **planning permission** is automatically given – you have to make a separate application for this. Before starting work always check whether you need Building Regulations approval, planning permission or both. In Scotland, the rules and procedures are different.

Planning permission

The Town and County Planning Act of 1971 requires planning permission to be obtained from the local authority for most types of development before work starts. For planning permission purposes development is considered as:

● **building work** – such as a house extension or garage
● **change in use** – such as dividing a house into flats or starting to run a business from a house
● **other work** – such as a hardstanding for a car or putting up a fence.

Work which affects only the inside of a building, such as knocking two rooms into one, is not considered development and so does not require planning permission (but Building Regulations approval is very often required). Work which does not materially affect the external appearance of a building, such as repointing brickwork and general repairs and maintenance, are not considered as development.

Permitted development

Some work is classified as 'permitted development' and can be carried out without planning permission, provided the work meets certain conditions on size and location. Some of these conditions may be varied in the near future.

The enlargement of a house by an extension, for example, is permitted as long as the total addition to the original house is not more than 50 cubic metres or one tenth of the volume of the original house (up to a maximum of 115 cubic metres) whichever is the greater. The volume of the original house is calculated from the external measurements of the house (including the roof) as originally built, or as it stood on 1st July 1948. The enlargement must not be higher than the highest part of the roof of the original house and no part of the enlargement should project beyond the building line (usually defined by a wall of the original house) which faces the road. These rules also apply to the construction of a detached garage within the vicinity of a house.

If a proposed enlargement falls outside any of these conditions, planning permission must be obtained before work starts. If the enlargement is for occupation as a separate dwelling, planning permission is also required.

Loft conversions are normally allowed without planning permission since the only likely addition to the volume of the house is a dormer window.

Small buildings such as garden sheds and greenhouses are permitted as long as they are not more than four metres high with a ridged roof (two sloping sides) or three metres high with a non-ridged roof. In addition, they must not project beyond the front of the house nor in total cover more than half of the grounds.

Porches also come within permitted development provided the floor area of the porch is not more than two square metres; no part is higher than three metres above the ground level; and no part is less than two metres from any boundary between the garden and a road or public footpath.

Planning permission may be required for central heating oil storage tanks, gates, fences and walls, hardstanding for cars and access roads or paths if they exceed their permitted development size and location. If the proposed work will be near a road junction or intersection and likely to obscure a motorist's view, planning permission should be sought even if the work comes within the permitted development limit. The Department of the Environment leaflet – *Planning Permission: A Guide for Householders*, available free from your local planning department gives further details.

Making your application

Normally, to apply for permission you need to fill in four copies of the application form available from the planning department of your local authority. A standard form drawn up by the Department of the Environment is used by many local authorities. If the work is being carried out by a builder or being supervised by an architect, they can make the application on your behalf.

If you do not know whether you need to apply, or are unsure of any details, a preliminary discussion with the planning authority can save time later when the actual application is made. Some authorities issue guidance notes detailing the drawing and documents that are required with the application. You will need to send in detailed scale drawings along with the application form which asks for details of the proposed work.

Your local authority's reply

When you have made your application, the local authority will consider things like how well the proposed work will fit in with the surrounding style of architecture. They will then send you a decision notice of approval or rejection, usually within five to eight weeks of applying. If the application is rejected, the local authority should give their reasons for refusal. Permission may be granted subject to conditions, such as using materials which match the existing building so that the overall appearance is preserved. The local authority should also give reasons for any conditions they impose. If you consider that the refusal or conditions imposed are unreasonable, you can appeal to the Department of the Environment (or Welsh Office if you live in Wales) within six months of receiving the decision notice. An appeal can also be made if the local authority fails to give a decision notice in time (usually two months). Further information is available from the Department of the Environment booklet called *Planning Appeals: A Guide to Procedure.*

The local authority can serve an **enforcement notice** if work is carried out which exceeds the permitted development limit without planning permission, or if work carried out is not in accordance with the approved plans. The enforcement notice can require the work to be returned to its original state.

Other problems

The planning permission obtained when the house was originally built may restrict development which would normally be allowed as permitted development, such as putting up fences and walls on an open-plan housing estate.

A building registered as being of special architectural or historical interest will need *listed building consent* from the local authority even if the work is within the permitted development limit.

In some areas – conservation areas for example – the local authority will limit the types of development that can be carried out by serving an *Article 4 direction* on the owners and occupiers of affected buildings. In this case, planning permission may be needed for fairly small works, even though the work would normally be allowed under permitted development.

Some properties, especially Victorian and Edwardian houses, may have a *restrictive covenant* in the title deeds of the property. This can prohibit or limit carrying out many types of work – the conversion of a house into flats, for instance.

The mortgage of a property often restricts any modifications without the consent of the building society.

WHICH ALTERATIONS OR ADDITIONS NEED PERMISSION OR APPROVAL?

Garages do not need planning permission if they do not exceed the permitted development limit but permission may be needed for new access to a garage.
Garages need Building Regulations approval, though detached garages of less than 30 sq m are exempt from some regulations.

Sheds and greenhouses and other small buildings do not usually require planning permission. But there is a restriction placed on their size, location and on the total area of your garden you can cover with them.
Some sheds are exempt from some of the Building Regulations so long as they are detached and have an area of less than 30 sq m.

Loft conversions generally fall within the permitted development limit and so do not need planning permission (they do in Scotland).
They do require Building Regulations approval.

Porches generally do not need planning permission so long as they are not more than 3 m high, and do not exceed 2 sq m in area. In addition, no part of the porch should be less than 2 m from the boundary between your garden and any road or public footpath. (Front porches need permission in Scotland.)
Building Regulations approval is required — to make sure that damp cannot be transmitted from the porch to the house, for example.

Fences and walls do not need planning permission provided that no part of the fence or wall is higher than 1 m where it runs along the boundary between a house and a road. In other parts of the garden, the fence or wall may be up to 2 m high as long as it does not obscure a motorist's view from a road. There may be other planning restrictions on fences and walls affecting your house — the original granting of planning permission on an open-plan estate, for example.
Fences and garden walls are not covered by the Building Regulations.

General repairs and maintenance such as painting, repointing or replacing a few slates do not require planning permission except where there are other restrictions such as listed building consent.
Building Regulations approval is not needed.

Oil storage tanks do not need planning permission so long as the tank is in your garden, has a capacity of 3,500 litres or less, no part is higher than 3 m above ground, it does not project in front of any part of a house which faces a highway (the one shown needs permission) and as long as it does not obstruct a motorist's view.
Oil storage tanks are not covered by the Building Regulations.

Extensions require planning permission if they exceed the permitted development limit. (The one at the side of the house needs permission because it is attached to a wall of the original house facing a road — see opposite page. The extension at the rear probably does not.)
All extensions require Building Regulations approval.

Paths and driveways from your house to a road need planning permission. You will also need the consent of the Highways Authority if the path or driveway needs to cross a pavement or footpath along the road.
They do not need Building Regulations approval.

Internal alterations such as knocking two rooms into one or converting a bedroom into a bathroom do not require planning permission unless you are converting a house into flats.
Most internal alterations require Building Regulations approval — to make sure that structural alterations are carried out safely and meet fire restrictions, for example.

Building Regulations

The Building Regulations apply to England and Wales with the exception of Inner London where the London Building (Construction) by-laws operate. Scotland and N. Ireland also have their own Building Regulations. The regulations are to protect public health and safety by assuring minimum standards for the construction and alteration of buildings. The regulations are administered by local authority Building Control Officers (District Surveyors in the London Boroughs).

The regulations are written in legal language and are not easy for the layman to understand. Copies of the regulations can be consulted in local authority offices or in many public libraries. They are also available from HMSO.

What is covered?

Building Regulations approval must be sought from the local authority before starting any building work (including the installation of fittings such as WCs), structural alterations or extensions to existing buildings or before making a material change in use of a building or part of building. A material change in use can be work like converting a barn into a house, a house into flats or an integral garage into a living room. To obtain Building Regulations approval, notice of intention to build and drawings have to be submitted to the local authority before work starts.

The things covered by Building Regulations include:

● whether materials to be used in construction are adequate for the job
● preparation of the site before construction
● the protection of ground floors and walls from damp, and their weather resistance
● structural stability
● fire precautions and means of escape in case of fire
● thermal and sound insulation
● the construction of stairs, ramps, balustrades and vehicle barriers
● refuse disposal in flats
● the open space required outside habitable rooms
● the heights of rooms, and ventilation
● the structure of flues, fireplaces and chimneys, and installation of heating appliances (including cookers) which produce smoke or gases
● drains, sewers, cesspools and WCs
● in Scotland, electrical wiring.

The regulations apply to most buildings – some industrial and agricultural buildings are exempt. Some buildings such as detached garages and carports (not exceeding 30sq m in floor area) are partially exempt from the Building Regulations. They do not have to comply with all the requirements, though drawings and particulars still have to be submitted to the local authority for approval. Some small detached single-storey buildings are exempt such as sheds and greenhouses with a floor area of not more than 30sq m and volume not more than 30cu m, at least two metres from any residential building in the same grounds and without fittings such as a WC or a heater which needs a flue or chimney.

What the regulations say

Some of the regulations lay down specific requirements or standards. Others allow some degree of flexibility by demanding a particular performance requirement or standard – for example the regulations say *any wall shall be so constructed as not to transmit moisture from the ground to the inside of the building or to any part of the building which will be adversely affected*. The regulations then give one method of construction which, if followed, will meet the standard required and will be 'deemed-to-satisfy' the regulations. Other methods of construction or materials may however be used to suit particular circumstances, provided they meet the performance standard and are approved by the Building Control Officer. Certain materials and methods of construction are deemed-to-satisfy the Building Regulations if they conform to a British Standard (BS) or to a British Standard Code of Practice (CP).

When planning an extension or removing a wall to enlarge a room, the relevant parts of the Building Regulations have to be taken into account. The regulations can affect the design, size, siting and materials of construction. The regulations are more severe in the case of habitable rooms such as bedrooms and sitting rooms. For example, the conversion of an integral garage into a bedroom or drawing room would be allowed under planning permission, but the conversion would need approval under Building Regulations for things like preventing damp rising, and sound and thermal insulation.

General repairs and maintenance do not need Building Regulations approval as long as no structural work is involved.

Some of the regulations may be relaxed if requested.

Making your application

To avoid possible delays when applying, and to clarify whether approval is required or not, a preliminary discussion with the Building Control Officer (District Surveyor in Inner London) can be very helpful. You should make an appointment by telephone as Building Control Officers are often out on site inspecting building work.

Two copies of the formal notification for Building Regulations approval along with two copies of the drawings need to be deposited with the local authority for approval. They can be deposited on your behalf by an architect or builder. The actual number, type and scale of drawings varies with the type of job. All applications have to be accompanied by a reasonable estimate of the cost of the work together with the relevant fee. Some authorities issue *guidance notes* on what is required, though the Building Control Officer will advise. The drawings should use metric measurements (like the current versions of the Building Regulations).

Your local authority's reply

The local authority must approve or reject your plans within five weeks unless the time is extended (usually an extra three weeks) by written agreement. Where there is doubt as to what is intended on the application form or drawings, the applicant can be asked to clarify the proposals. When the Building Control Officer is satisfied that the work will not contravene the regulations if carried out following the plans and specification, he will recommend approval and a notice of approval will be sent to the applicant.

The local authority may send you, or the builder, a set of postcards to send to the Building Control Officer as notification of certain stages of the work as required in the regulations – 24 hours notice before covering foundation excavations, foundations, dpcs, any material laid over site, and drains or private sewers. Notice must also be given not more than seven days after laying drains and private sewers, and completion of the work. If these notifications are not made, the local authority can require you to cut into or pull down any work to see if the regulations have been contravened. If the local authority does not issue cards it is still your responsibility to give the required notice.

Where work is carried out contrary to the regulations, the local authority can serve notice on the building owner requiring the work to be removed or altered. If this is not carried out, the local authority can alter the work themselves and charge the owner the cost. Notice to alter or remove contravening work can only be served within 12 months of completing the work.

If the proposed work involves building over an existing public sewer, consent must also be obtained from the local authority (they may have plans of the drains and sewers of your property). The Building Regulations deal only with the removal of waste, soil and surfac water from a house. Where proposed work will involve the plumbing in of appliances or altering the plumbing system of a house, the work must conform to the water supply undertaking's by-laws or regulations.

Hiring a builder

Sometimes your skills and experience may not be enough to cope with the building work you want to do – when knocking large holes in load-bearing walls, perhaps – or you may simply not have enough time available to do it all yourself. In these circumstances you may ask a local builder to take on all or part of the work.

Finding a builder

The names of local builders can be found in telephone directories and local newspapers. Not all builders are willing to work on relatively small jobs such as knocking two rooms into one; some even consider extensions too small.

The best way to find a reliable builder is by personal recommendation from someone who has recently employed the builder. Then you can find out how well the builder cleared up, how good he was at timekeeping and how well the work was done. Lists of builders who specialise in particular types of work, such as extensions, can be obtained from regional offices of the Federation of Master Builders and the National Federation of Building Trades Employers. The Building Control Section of your local authority may also have lists. Building Control Officers and local architects may have a good idea of the quality of the work done by local builders.

Whichever builder you choose, it is a good idea to ask to see some of his recent work. If you are employing a specialist package firm to see the job through from design to the actual building, make sure you see work done by the builder who is actually going to do your job. Specialist firms may have several sub-contracted builders working for them.

Getting quotes

You should get at least three quotes for a job – prices can easily vary by over a factor of two, even for small jobs such as removing a partition wall. Check the VAT situation before accepting any quote.

Give the builders who come to quote a clear idea of what you want done, preferably give them a detailed sketch plan. For large jobs such as an extension, they may not be able to give a realistic quote until they have detailed drawings of the construction.

You should allow the builders about a month to send their quotes to you. You will receive either an estimate or a quotation. An *estimate* is a guide to the price that will be charged when the job is finished – it may turn out to be more or less. A *quotation* is a fixed price which the builder offers to do the work for – though there may be provision for variation due to unforeseen problems.

For large jobs, it is a good idea to ask the builder to draw up a **schedule list** (an architect will normally do this and ask the builder to fill it in). This list sets out each stage of the work and may include entries like: building a blockwork wall, plastering, supplying and fitting a bath and so on. Some items may be marked as *prime cost*. Usually, this is an approximate price set aside to cover the cost of a fitting; when you have eventually decided on which fitting (a bath, for instance) you want, you will be charged the actual price. Make sure you know who is buying the fittings – you do not want the builder turning up expecting you to have bought the bath ready for him to install when you thought he was buying it.

Start and finish dates

If you want all the work done within a certain time, ask the builder for a time schedule stating when the work will start and finish. But be wary: jobs often take longer than builders estimate. Find out from the builder how much of the work is going to be sub-contracted. Delays can often be caused by plasterers or electricians not turning up on time for instance. With jobs which involve lots of different trades, you might be better off using a firm of builders who can carry out most of the work themselves.

Reports in Handyman Which?

Concrete

Concrete is an easy-to-use, versatile and inexpensive building material. You can buy the raw materials for mixing your own or buy ready-mixed concrete for immediate use. Few special tools are required when using concrete – many can be made and specialised equipment such as mixers can be hired.

What is concrete?

Concrete is a conglomerate mineral mixture made up of aggregates bound together by a matrix of cement paste. Cement – more properly Portland cement – is a man-made mineral powder which reacts with water to form a dense, stone-like mass. Most **aggregates** are natural stone in the form of gravel, natural sand or crushed stone. Aggregates are classified as *coarse* or *fine* depending on whether or not they are retained on a 5mm sieve: most ordinary concretes contain both fine and coarse aggregates. In mixes suitable for most d-i-y work, the proportions are very roughly one part fine to two parts coarse.

Mortar, strictly defined, is a concrete containing only fine aggregates. In practice, the word mortar usually refers to a mix specifically intended for bedding bricks, blocks or stone – see page 165 – or one used for rendering.

How concrete works

When the dry ingredients of concrete are mixed with water, the cement begins to react with the water (a process known as hydration) to produce a sort of glue which holds the individual cement particles together and adheres to the surface of the aggregate. Cement paste also sticks tenaciously to iron or steel – so reinforcement or fixings hold well when embedded in concrete or mortar but cement paste or concrete should never be allowed to harden on tools or equipment. The cement-water reaction is irreversible – it starts immediately the two come into contact and continues more or less indefinitely as long as free water is present.

In practice, more water is required to produce a workable mix than is needed for the cement hydration process. When concrete dries out, this excess water is lost by evaporation leaving minute voids which weaken the concrete. This is taken into account in the mixes recommended for different jobs – see page 158. Adding more water to a mix that has already started to stiffen will not reverse or slow down the stiffening process: it will simply weaken the finished concrete or mortar. Concrete must not be allowed to dry out too rapidly, especially in the first few days.

Factors affecting hardening

The reaction between cement and water depends on the presence of heat – a mix will become unworkable faster on a hot summer's day than in cool weather.

The reaction can also be affected by certain chemicals. On one hand, impurities – especially organic acids – in the mixing water or in unwashed sand or ballast can seriously affect the strength of concrete. On the other hand, *admixtures* are made specially to prolong workability or otherwise modify the properties of a fresh mix.

Even with a retarding admixture, fresh concrete will lose its fluidity and become impossible to place or compact properly after a few hours. In this *green* state, the surface can be given various finishing treatments to improve its appearance or to provide a mechanical key for rendering, plastering or screeding.

Strength continues to develop for a considerable period after the green stage. For example, in ordinary weather conditions, an *in situ* concrete drive will not be ready for use until seven to ten days after laying, and a ground slab or floor will not be strong enough to walk on for three or four days.

Mixing your own

The basic materials used for making concrete are Portland cement, aggregates and water. Admixtures and pigments may also be used occasionally to modify concrete's working properties or alter its appearance.

Portland cement

There are several kinds of Portland cement made in the UK, but only a few are relevant to the do-it-yourselfer. Most of them are available from builders' merchants and some from d-i-y and garden shops.

All Portland cements are subject to **air-setting** – cement in unopened bags will harden through moisture in the air penetrating the walls of the paper bags. Once this happens the cement is useless and should be thrown away. As a rule, you should order only as much cement as you need for a week at a time and store bags under cover and clear of the ground or floor. Tightly stack the bags so that air cannot circulate between them, and use the oldest bags first.

Dry cement powder is normally harmless but the alkali released when it is mixed with water can cause skin irritation which may be severe in some cases. Wash off any fresh concrete or mortar that gets on your skin. If cement or fresh concrete gets in your eyes, wash it out immediately with clean water and seek medical attention.

Ordinary Portland cement (OPC) is suitable for most jobs. All OPC made in the UK must meet the requirements of British Standard BS12, and in any particular part of the country you should not find much variation in price from one supplier to the next. It is generally packaged in 50kg bags but you may find smaller quantities – down to 5kg – for repairs or other small jobs.

White Portland cement can be used in masonry or rendering mortars, for home-made garden paving slabs and wall blocks or for any other jobs where the grey colour of OPC is undesirable. White Portland cement is about double the price of OPC.

Masonry cement is a Portland cement which contains additives to increase the plasticity and water-retentiveness of masonry and rendering mortars. It is grey in colour and a bit more expensive than OPC. It should not be used in concrete.

Sulphate-resisting Portland cement may be necessary where concrete is exposed to sulphates in solution – see page 162. You should not use it without expert advice on mixes. It is marginally more expensive than OPC.

Aggregates

Aggregates can be obtained from builders' merchants but, for large quantities, it is often cheaper to go direct to the original supplier – consult your Yellow Pages under headings such as *Sand and gravel suppliers* or *Quarries*. Use the type of aggregate you find cheapest and most readily available.

Aggregates may be sold and priced by the tonne (1000kg) or by the cubic metre (occasionally by the cubic yard). Many builders' merchants will supply small quantities of aggregates in heavy-gauge polythene bags – an expensive way to buy but easy to store and convenient for small jobs.

Coarse aggregates are those retained on a 5mm sieve and are normally graded from 5mm to a stated maximum particle size. For most *in situ* concrete, specify a 20mm maximum; when laying concrete less than 50mm thick, or producing homemade blocks or flags, order 10mm maximum. Any aggregates with a 40mm maximum may be used in foundations.

Fine aggregates are those less than 5mm and are generally described as sand. For concrete work – including floor screeds – use only washed *concreting* (or *sharp*) sand. Builders', bricklayers' or soft sand is too fine for concrete. Totally avoid unwashed pit sand – it generally contains impurities that affect the quality of the concrete.

All-in aggregates are commonly called ballast and contain both coarse and fine material, usually (but not always) in naturally occurring proportions. All-in aggregates may be poorly graded – avoid using them when the strength of the concrete is important. Some suppliers can provide *combined* or *reconstituted* all-in ballast, blended from separate stockpiles; choose this if you can get it. Never use unwashed pit ballast.

Special aggregates include single-sized gravels and crushed stone of various types and colours. They can be used in concrete which is to be washed and brushed at the green stage to expose an aggregate decorative finish, or they can be tamped into the surface of fresh concrete. They are also useful when making garden blocks or flags. Good sources of supply are garden centres, stone merchants and even masons. Pits and quarries are likely to supply lorry-loads only.

Aggregates can be stored indefinitely but to minimise waste and contamination by dirt, they should be stored on a hard surface or on a sheet of polythene spread on the ground. Keep piles of different-sized aggregates well separated. Ordinary concrete aggregates do not need covering to protect them from rain – any excess water will drain quickly through the pile. Fine builders' or bricklayers' sand will not drain so readily. However if the materials are to be stored for some time, it is a good idea to put a sheet of polythene over them to deter children and animals.

Special aggregates such as single-sized gravel or crushed stone chippings are best stored in heavy polythene bags: they are expensive and waste is costly.

Water

Use the mains supply when possible. Most water which is fit to drink is fit for mixing concrete with, but this is not an infallible rule – water from moorland streams may be perfectly drinkable yet contain too much organic acid for concrete mixing.

Pigments and admixtures

Pigments and admixtures for concrete and mortar are available from builders' merchants and sometimes from other shops.

Pigments provide a way of making coloured concrete but many are not colour-stable and in time and through the action of weather they will fade – usually unevenly. Even stable pigments require very careful proportioning with other materials to avoid individual mixer loads coming out slightly different in shade or intensity. Such accuracy is difficult to achieve on a small scale.

Admixtures can be useful for modifying the properties of fresh concrete or mortar. Dosages can be critical when mixing small batches. Do not use admixtures unnecessarily and always follow the manufacturer's instructions precisely.

Dry-bagged mixes

Dry-bagged mixes contain accurately proportioned amounts of cement and aggregates. To use them you just add water and mix. They are more expensive, volume for volume, than materials bought separately but save time and trouble and are very convenient for small jobs such as repairs, concreting in a clothes pole and so on. Several dry-bagged mixes are available from builders' merchants and many other retail outlets – make sure you buy the right one for the job: do not use a masonry mortar mix for repairing concrete or a 1:3 cement to sand mix for laying bricks. The cement and sand in dry-bagged mixes is likely to settle to the bottom during handling, so use the whole bag at once and mix it thoroughly.

Sometimes you can buy damp sand or ballast packed in polythene bags with a small inner bag of cement. The proportions of the contents are often not indicated and moisture in the aggregates may find its way into the inner cement bag – through a puncture, say – leading to the cement hardening. Prices are generally lower than for the usual type of dry mix.

Ready-mixed concrete

Ready-mixed concrete is available in most areas. Suppliers are listed in the Yellow Pages under headings such as *Ready-mixed concrete*. If you need a lot of concrete in a short time ready-mix is the practical answer – but everything must be ready when the mixer truck arrives: you have about two hours (if you ask for the mix to be retarded you might have three or at most four hours, depending on the weather) to handle, place, compact and finish the job. Your time limit for using the concrete starts the moment it comes out of the mixer.

Small quantities of ready-mixed concrete tend to be expensive. Suppliers may use a sliding-scale surcharge for less than a full truck load – often based on a fixed amount for each cubic metre of unused capacity. You may also have to pay a mileage-based delivery charge. Not all suppliers make these surcharges – so it pays to shop around. If you have access to a borrowed or hired truck you may be able to collect small loads direct from a nearby ready-mix depot.

When ordering ready-mixed concrete you should:
- give the supplier a clear specification of the mix required, including workability and special requirements such as admixtures
- arrange date and time of delivery
- give the supplier clear directions and discuss access arrangements
- order in plenty of time – no later than the morning of the day before delivery – and try to avoid rush hours.

Try to arrange things so that the mixer truck discharges the concrete where you want to lay it – into a foundation trench or into the formwork for a garage base slab or drive, say. But bear in mind that a typical mixer truck is 2.5m wide, 8m long and weighs 20 to 24 tonnes. If you have to barrow the concrete into place, specify concrete with a high workability. Ask for large loads of mix to be retarded for two hours: this will keep the mix workable for an extra hour or two, but after that the concrete will tend to go off quite fast. Workability can also be prolonged, especially on a hot or dry day, by laying a sheet of polythene over the pile of concrete.

Concrete mixes

The strength and durability of concrete which has been properly mixed and laid depends to a large extent on its cement content: the richer the mix, the stronger and more durable it is. The three basic mixes which cover the majority of jobs are given below both for ready-mixed concrete and for mixing it yourself. When ordering ready-mix, all you have to do with some depots is to quote the mix number – C7P, C20P or C30P – together with the type of cement (Ordinary Portland), maximum aggregate size (normally 20mm), workability (high) and any special requirements. Not all depots are familiar with these standard mix designations, which are fairly new, so the mix quantities per cubic metre are given in case you need to quote them when ordering.

The proportions by volume for mixing your own concrete are also given – these have been approximated on the safe side, so by careful measurement they should give the same quality of concrete as the equivalent ready-mix. These mixes supersede the older 1:3:6, 1:2:4 and 1:1½:3 mixes and assume loose cement and damp sand or aggregate.

C7P mix This is a relatively low-strength mix suitable for foundations, blinding or oversite concrete under suspended timber floors, or for concreting in fence posts, clothes poles and so on. Use it in place of 1:3:6.
British Standard specification (kg to give approximately 1 cubic metre of concrete) cement 210, fine aggregate 800, coarse aggregate 1140.
Batching by bucketful 1 bucket loose cement, 3 buckets damp sand, 4 buckets coarse aggregate *or* 1 bucket cement, 5¼ buckets all-in aggregate.
Yield per bag of cement approximately 210 litres; approximately 4.2 50kg bags of cement needed per cubic metre of concrete.

C20P mix This is a good all-round mix, especially for ground slabs and floors and paths of 75mm or greater thickness. Use it in place of 1:2:4. Do not use it for garage drives, carport floors or hardstandings – see page 165.
BS specification (kg per cu m approx) cement 300, fine aggregate 700, coarse aggregate 1170.
Batching by bucketful 1 bucket loose cement, 1¾ buckets damp sand, 2½ buckets coarse aggregate *or* 1 bucket cement, 3¾ buckets all-in aggregate. If possible, use separate aggregates for this mix.
Yield per bag of cement approximately 170 litres; approximately 6 bags of cement per cubic metre of concrete.

C30P mix This is a relatively strong mix suitable for paths or patios under 75mm thick or for home-made blocks and paving slabs. Use in place of 1:1½:3.
BS specification (kg per cu m approx) cement 380, fine aggregate 620, coarse aggregate 1190.
Batching by bucketful 1 bucket loose cement, 1¼ buckets damp sand, 2¼ buckets coarse aggregate. The use of all-in aggregates should be avoided for this grade of concrete. If you must, use 1 bucket cement and 2¾ buckets all-in aggregate, but avoid unwashed material.
Yield per bag of cement approximately 130 litres; approximately 7.6 bags of cement per cubic metre of concrete.

Special mixes Mixes other than the three given may be required from time to time – see page 162 for foundations and page 165 for garage drives and hardstandings.

Building mortar For bedding concrete paving slabs. Use 1 part ordinary Portland cement to 5 parts concreting (sharp) sand.

Other mortars See pages 165 and 169 for mortar mixes for laying bricks and blocks.

Estimating materials

The yields given for the three main mixes are for finished concrete. When calculating the volume required, remember that excavations for foundations, ground slabs and so on are rarely accurate, so err on the generous side.

For foundations and other fairly deep work, multiply width by depth by length to get the volume.

For fairly large, thin areas such as floors and drives, it is easier to work out the area first in square metres. Rectangles are simple: length times width. So are triangles: base times height (measured at right angles to the base) divided by two.

Irregular areas with straight sides can be dealt with simply by dividing them up into rectangles and triangles, working out the area of each and adding up the total. Really irregular areas are best handled by sketching them out to scale on squared paper and counting the squares – you can average out the part-squares or count them as full squares and leave the extra as an allowance for waste. Once you have the area to be concreted, multiply it by the thickness of the layer required. Alternatively you can use the ready-reckoner chart below: this gives the volume of concrete needed and the quantities of individual materials.

USING THE READY-RECKONER

Start by locating the area to be concreted on the left-hand scales. Then read straight across to the sloping line corresponding to the required thickness, and down to the volume scale at the bottom – this will give you the amount of compacted concrete required, whether ready-mixed or mixed yourself.

Having found the volume, either from the chart or by calculation, quantities of cement and aggregates required for mixing your own concrete can be found by reading on down the chart to the scales for one of the three basic mixes given on the opposite page. These give the amount of cement (in bags) and the quantities of either separate coarse and fine aggregates or all-in aggregates (in tonnes).

Wastage has not been taken into account – add 10 per cent when ordering ready-mix; when ordering separate materials, add 10 per cent to the cement and round up the aggregates to the next whole or half tonne.

A working example Suppose you are concreting a rectangular ground slab 4m wide by 5m long on a good, sound base. Multiplication will give you the area – 20 sq m. A thickness of 100mm will be sufficient, and the appropriate mix is C20P (unless the slab is to be used for parking vehicles). Starting from 20 on the area scale, read across to the 100mm thickness line and down to the volume scale: the concrete required is 2 cu m.

Using ready-mix, add 10 per cent for wastage, giving a total of 2.2 cu m.

When mixing it yourself, read down the chart from the 2 cu m volume mark to the scales for C20P concrete to determine the materials needed. The cement required is 12 bags: add 10 per cent for wastage to give 13.2 bags (13 bags should be enough if you are careful). Read down to the aggregate scales: the quantities required are just under 1.5 tonnes of sand and 2.5 tonnes of coarse aggregate, or just under 4 tonnes of all-in aggregates. Round up and order 2 tonnes of sand and 3 tonnes of coarse aggregates or 4.5 tonnes of all-in aggregates.

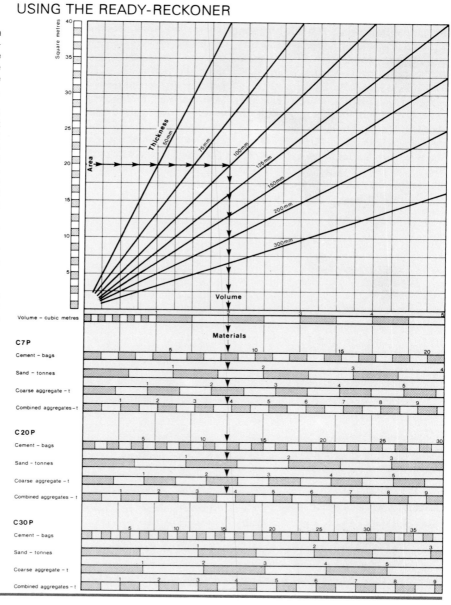

Laying concrete

The first job is to approximately set out the work area – allow about half a metre extra on all sides. Then clear all vegetation, organic material and loose topsoil and roughly level the site.

To start detailed setting-out you need to establish one datum for setting out lines and one for levels. The line of a wall – say a house or boundary wall – is convenient for a horizontal datum; levels can be taken from the damp-proof course of the house or the bed joint of a course of bricks.

The tools needed for setting lines and levels are a long, accurate tape measure (a 15m linen or builder's steel tape); a straight-edge; a 2m pocket retractable steel tape; a 1m spirit level with tubes for both level and plumb; a plumb-line; and plenty of good string. A home-made wooden builder's square is also useful – basically a right-angled triangle with sides in the proportions 3 : 4 : 5 – 1.5m by 2.0m by 2.5m, say. Wood or steel reinforcing rods can be used for setting out pegs.

Setting lines

To lay out a rectangular area such as a garage slab, you need to establish a base line with pegs and string – make sure the pegs are well outside the intended working area so they can be used right through the job.

Set up the two right-angle lines the same way, again with the pegs outside the job. Finally, measure out the two right-angle lines and set up the remaining line parallel to the base line. To check the squareness, measure the diagonals – they should be the same.

For walls and foundations set up profile boards astride the centre lines, again outside the work. A profile board is a U-shaped wooden frame with two verticals and a crossbar. Using a plumb-line, mark the centre line of the wall on the crossbar. Then measure out from the centre line to the width of the wall itself, and then out again to the width of the foundations. Finally, saw notches for each of the lines you have measured. These will locate stringlines as and when they are needed. The profiles can stay in place throughout the work.

A PROFILE BOARD

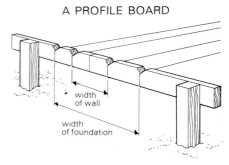

width of wall

width of foundation

A profile board for a wall. The strings indicate the width of the wall and the width of the foundations

SETTING LINES

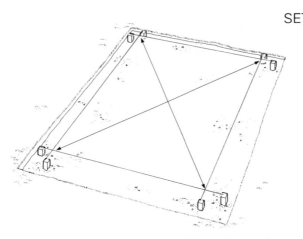

When setting lines for a rectangular slab, make sure that you drive in the pegs well outside the area to be concreted. Measure the diagonals to make sure it is square

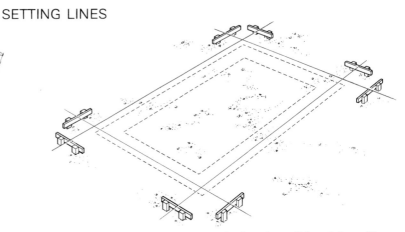

Using profile boards to set out the lines for wall foundations. The drawing does not show all the strings in position. The coloured lines indicate the centres of the walls

Setting levels and falls

Start by establishing a *prime datum* by driving in a peg to the desired level and take all subsequent levels from this. A straight-edge and spirit level can be used over fairly short distances but over large distances use a length of clear plastic flexible tubing (a chemist or home-brewing supplier is a good source) filled with water with its ends turned up. Tie or tape one end to the datum stake, tie the other end loosely to the stake being set, and adjust the tube or add more water until the level is even with the top of the datum stake making sure there are no bubbles in the tube. The water-tube level is accurate over any distance and can be used around corners or obstacles.

To set out a constant slope you need to use boning rods – simple timber tees with cross-pieces exactly 90 degrees to the stems. You need a set of three identical tees. Drive pegs to the required level at either end of the area to be concreted. Hold a boning rod on the top of each end peg and then set intermediate pegs using the third boning rod by sighting along the tops of the three. You can also use boning rods to set pegs outside the initial two. Short slopes can be set with a straight-edge and spirit level by placing a shim under one end of the straight-edge.

Batching and mixing concrete

Accurate proportioning of materials and thorough mixing are essential for making good concrete. When batching by the bucketful, use heavy-duty plastic, rubber or metal buckets of the same size – a three gallon bucket which holds a third of a bag of loose cement is a useful size. Never use the same bucket (or shovel) for cement as you use for aggregates.

One bucket of cement to the required number of buckets of aggregate gives a handy-sized batch and just enough for an ordinary small power mixer. Mark the aggregate buckets with heavy-duty self-adhesive plastic tape for the fractions.

Mixing by hand

Hand mixing is fairly hard work. Mix the materials on a hard, smooth surface – an existing concrete drive or yard or a sheet of plywood, for instance.

Start by measuring out the aggregates into compact heaps. Then form a crater in the middle of the heap and add the cement. Turn the heap methodically until the whole pile is uniform in colour. When using pre-packaged dry mix, follow the same procedure using a whole bag of mix at a time. Next make a crater in the heap of dry material and add some of the water. Bring the dry material to the water with a shovel and keep mixing and adding water as necessary until the whole pile is uniform in colour and consistency and just sufficiently workable to use. The amount of water depends on how much moisture is already in the aggregates – generally something between a third and a half of a bucket to a bucket of cement gives the right consis-

tency. To test the workability, pat the pile a couple of times with a trowel or the back of a shovel and draw the tool across it with a fair amount of pressure. The surface should be close-knit and smooth and water should not ooze out.

Mixing by machine

For large jobs you should consider hiring a petrol or diesel mixer – either from a specialist hire firm or from a local builder. Electric mixers are also available but they are usually fairly small.

If you buy a second-hand mixer or hire one from a small builder, make sure all the safety guards are in place and ask for a demonstration so that you are thoroughly familiar with its operation. Make sure that an electric mixer is a 110 volt machine with a centre-earthed transformer.

A useful size is the so-called half-bag mixer – a 100 litre machine, formerly known as a 3½/5 mixer. Smaller mortar mixers are also available but they are really too small to be very useful.

Once on site, the mixer should be firmly blocked up absolutely level. If the mixer is not large enough to discharge directly into a barrow, use a banker board of plywood or other hard material, so you can tip the load on to it for shovelling into the barrow. Small mixers can be blocked up high enough to discharge directly into a barrow but make sure the mixer is very stable.

Start mixing by adding half of the coarse aggregate, then approximately half the water, then the sand. Mix for a short time, then add the cement and finally the rest of the coarse aggregate and enough water so that the mix falls cleanly off the blades in the drum without being soupy. When inspecting the mix, always look obliquely into the drum, not straight in. Do not overload the mixer, do not mix too long (two minutes is enough), and do not leave it empty for long without cleaning it. If you have to be away from the mixer for a while, leave it running with some aggregate and water (no cement) for the next batch but keep children well away. Never put a shovel, a hand or anything else into the drum while it is revolving.

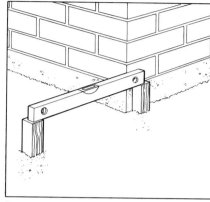

From the *prime datum* – often a peg driven in to the level of the dpc of a house – a spirit level can be used for setting subsequent levels

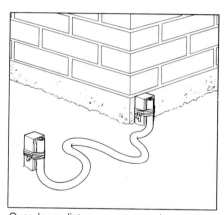

Over long distances or around corners, a clear plastic tube is useful for setting levels. Watch out for bubbles – these can lead to false levels

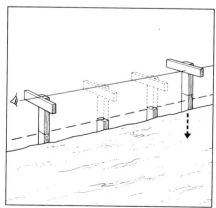

Boning rods are useful for setting out constant slopes. You will need helpers to hold the rods and sight along them while you drive in the pegs

Cleaning up

At the end of a working session clean all tools thoroughly by washing and scrubbing them with a wire brush – stubborn patches of hardened concrete can be rubbed down with a piece of brick. Run the mixer for about fifteen minutes with a small load of aggregate and water to scour it, and clear any stubborn accumulations with a scraper and wire brush. Clean the outside of the mixer as well. Make sure nothing gets into drains.

Laying the concrete

Concrete should always be **compacted** thoroughly to close any voids and drive out any trapped air. Pay particular attention to edges and corners close to formwork – ram the concrete well in with the end of a length of timber.

For deep sections such as trenched foundations, either place the concrete in layers of not more than 200mm thickness and compact with a home-made punner, or use a hired poker vibrator. Deep narrow sections, such as infill for the voids in hollow concrete blocks, can be compacted with a length of steel rod 12 to 20mm in diameter.

Ground slabs or *in situ* paving should be compacted with a *tamping beam* – a length of timber on edge. Small widths such as coal bunker bases or paths can be tamped with a length of 50 by 100mm timber; for larger areas, or thicknesses of 100mm or more, use a heavier timber such as 50 by 150mm, fitted with handles. When tamping a flat slab, spread the concrete evenly to a level about 10 to 15 per cent higher than the depth of the formwork.

Concrete should be **finished** so that the surface is close-knit and not porous.

If the concrete is to be covered with some other material such as vinyl or ceramic tiles, the surface should have a sandpaper texture, obtained by using a wood float, to provide a key. The same goes for the surface of a footing or foundation on which bricks or blocks will be laid with mortar. Floors for garages, garden sheds, and so on, should be fairly smooth for easy cleaning; a rougher texture is better for drives and paths.

Proper **curing** is essential. Cover all exposed concrete with polythene sheeting or damp hessian as soon as it has hardened sufficiently not to be marked. Leave the covering in place for three or four days (if you use hessian or sacking make sure that it is kept damp). You should never lay concrete outdoors when frost is likely. But if you are caught out, protect the concrete with a blanket of straw or earth over the curing sheet.

Foundations

The simplest way to construct a foundation for a wall is to dig a trench and fill it with concrete to just below the finished ground level.

For a simple brick or concrete block garden wall it is usually necessary only to go down about 300mm below finished ground level or to firm, sound soil, whichever is deeper. The footing should be at least 250mm deep, and at least twice as wide as the wall thickness (including piers or pilasters). Set your level pegs to one side of the trench to start with, and drive further pegs in the trench itself using a spirit level and straightedge to transfer the levels. Leave the pegs in the trench as guides for the surface level.

For a more substantial structure such as an extension to the house, foundations will need to be deeper, normally at least 900mm to one metre but sometimes deeper still depending on the soil conditions. Traditionally, deep foundations are constructed as strip footings in the bottom of the trench, with brickwork or blockwork below ground level. The footing should be at least 300mm thick and at least twice as wide as the masonry

work. But this is an awkward method – the sides of the trench may require shoring and the backfilling material will have to be thoroughly compacted. The alternative is to fill the trench with concrete to two or three courses of bricks, or one course of blocks, below ground level. The trench can be narrower, since it will not be necessary to work in it – 450mm is typical. Shoring should not be necessary if you concrete as soon as the trench is finished, and no backfilling is involved.

Normally a straightforward C7P mix with 20mm or 40mm maximum-size aggregate is suitable for all foundations.

However, some soils (particularly clay or reclaimed land) and ground water contain sulphates which will attack concrete made with ordinary Portland cement. Your local Building Control Officer or District Surveyor will be able to advise you on whether sulphates are likely to be present. If so, you need to use a special mix made with sulphate-resisting cement – seek advice from the Cement and Concrete Association (see page 315).

Foundation concrete should be thoroughly compacted – use a punner and compact in layers of not more than 200mm depth.

WALL FOUNDATIONS

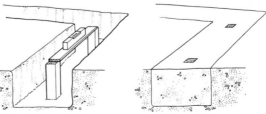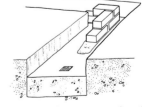

Left: establishing the surface level for the concrete foundation of a garden wall by driving in pegs along the trench. *Middle*: the pegs can be left in place but be careful not to drive them in further when compacting the concrete.
Right: using a narrow trench for the foundations of an extension

Laying a ground slab

Ground slabs of any size from a coal-bunker base to a garage floor can be constructed in simple timber formwork.

Preparation and setting out

After stripping the topsoil, level the subsoil and compact it thoroughly with a roller or rammer. Dig out any soft spots and fill them with sound, hard material. On soft clay or peaty soils, or where the soil is not consistent over the whole area, lay a sub-base of hoggin, clean well-broken hardcore, broken stone or well-burnt clinker. A thickness of 50mm should be sufficient for a small slab such as a garden shed floor; otherwise 75mm is adequate. The sub-base should extend at least 150mm beyond the slab edge to provide a firm surface for pegging out the formwork.

The thickness of the slab itself will depend on its size, intended use and soil conditions. For a small garden shed or greenhouse 75mm should be sufficient; for heavier uses, such as a workshop or garage floor, increase the thickness to 100mm. Add a further 25 to 50mm on soft clays or peaty soil.

Small slabs do not usually need elaborate setting out – it is often perfectly satisfactory to do the setting out as you prepare the site and sub-base and construct the formwork; otherwise follow the procedures on page 160. If the slab abuts the house, make sure the surface level is at least 150mm below the house dpc. If the slab is exposed, it should be given a slight fall away from the house so rain-water will flow away: 1 in 60 should be sufficient. Make the formwork of 25mm thick timber set on edge and nailed to 50 by 50mm pegs driven firmly into the sub-base. The depth of the formwork should be equal to the thickness of the finished slab and the pegs should not project above the top of the forms. Corner joints should be tightly butted and any longitudinal joints should have a length of the same timber on the outside.

LAYING A GROUND SLAB

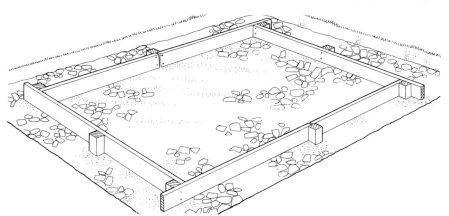

The formwork timber should be 25mm thick and as deep as the slab required

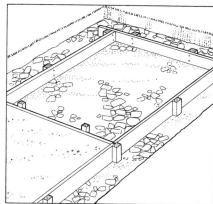

Making a butt joint

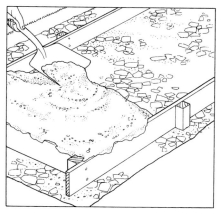

Let the concrete slide off your shovel

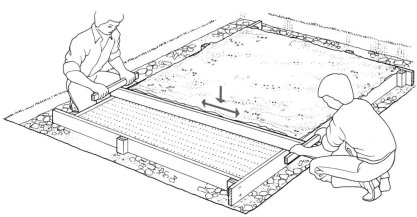

Drop a timber tamping beam on to the concrete surface to compact it

Joints

The slab can be concreted in one piece without joints as long as its length is not more than twice its width, does not exceed 40 times the slab thickness – 3m for a 75mm slab, 4m for 100mm one – and is not more than 4m. Otherwise the area should be divided into two or more bays with joints between, keeping the bays as nearly square as possible and approximately equal in size.

If joints are required in the slab, provision should be made for them in the formwork. If you are not in a hurry and are mixing your own concrete, a plain cold butt joint is sufficient. Concrete shrinks slightly in its early life and the joint will open enough to allow for any subsequent thermal expansion. Place a timber stop-end across the formwork, using the same depth and thickness of timber as for the side forms; fixings should be designed so that the stop-end can be easily removed. Concrete one bay, give it a couple of days to harden, remove the stop-end and concrete the adjoining bay.

The alternative if you want to concrete the whole slab in one go, is to fix a stop-end fairly lightly in place and place a full-depth filler strip of softwood 10 to 12mm thick against the face. Concrete right up to the filler strip, and within 50mm or so of the back of the stop-end, compacting thoroughly. Then remove the stop-end, leaving the filler in place, and concrete in the remaining gap.

If the slab abuts an existing wall or foundation, form an expansion joint between the two with a strip of thick bituminous felt fixed to the existing structure. Follow the same procedure if it is necessary to concrete around a drainage gully or inspection chamber.

Laying the concrete

Unless the slab is going to be used for parking a car, use C20P concrete with 20mm maximum-sized aggregate.

When placing the concrete in the formwork, try not to drop it in; this is likely to cause uneven compaction. Let the concrete slide off the shovel or out of the barrow. When using ready-mix for larger jobs, it may be possible to place the concrete direct from the mixer truck's delivery chute.

Spread the concrete evenly with a rake to a level about 10 to 15mm proud of the formwork: you can tack-nail strips of 12mm timber to the tops of the forms and screed the surface off level with a board before removing the strips.

Compaction can begin as soon as enough concrete has been placed – a 500mm run is sufficient. Use a dropping movement with a timber tamping beam – see page 162 – advancing the tamper about 25mm at a time; do not drag or scrape the tamper over the surface.

Tamp thoroughly, making two or three passes. If the concrete goes right down to the level of the formwork on the first pass it is probably under-compacted – add some extra material and retamp. Finally, make a sawing pass, working the timber back and forth along the top of the formwork to remove any excess.

Finishing

If you want a fairly rough surface, the concrete can be left as it is after the first sawing pass with the tamper. Otherwise make a second finishing pass, advancing the beam slowly to give a finer texture which can be left or further finished.

Finishing with a wood float will give a texture which varies with the age of the concrete and the floating technique. If the concrete is fairly fresh, a wood float will give a roughish texture which can be attractive if done as a series of overlapping fishscale strokes; a similar result can be achieved with the back of a shovel. Floating when the concrete has partly hardened will give a sandpaper texture. A similar texture can be obtained with a soft-bristle broom.

For a really smooth, tight finish, start by wood-floating and then go back with a steel trowel when the concrete has hardened a bit more: timing is pretty much a matter of trial and error. A steel-trowelled finish is liable to be slippery when wet and if the trowelling is overdone the surface is likely to keep on producing dust. Never use a steel-trowelled finish if an additional covering such as tiles is to be applied.

At the other end of the scale, an outdoor slab can be given a coarse corduroy finish with a stiff yard broom. When used across the slab in the direction of a surface fall, this will aid rain-water run-off.

Finally, to give an exposed-aggregate finish first produce a soft-brushed finish. Then, when the concrete has hardened sufficiently to prevent the coarse particles from being dislodged, use a combination of washing and brushing to remove the fine material from the surface, leaving the coarse aggregate slightly proud of the surface and washing away the cement-sand-water slurry. An alternative, if you want to use a particularly attractive but expensive coarse aggregate, is to use ordinary aggregate for the slab itself and tamp the selected aggregate into the surface; then wash and brush after an hour or so. The special aggregate should be fairly large – about 20mm – and of a roughly cubical shape rather than flaky.

Cure the concrete under plastic sheeting or damp hessian for from three days to a week – a week to ten days in chilly weather – and protect it against frost if necessary. The slab can be walked on at the end of the curing period, but avoid heavier loads for a few days more.

Concrete paths

Concrete paths can be laid in exactly the same way as a ground slab. A sub-base of special material is not usually necessary so long as soft spots are well filled and compacted. A 75mm thickness is adequate, but it is advisable to use a C30P mix. Curves can be shaped by cutting halfway through the formwork timbers at intervals and soaking the timber before fixing it in place. The 1:2 rule for bay proportions can be ignored so long as joints are spaced at intervals of no more than about 2m, but on soft ground it is advisable to form dummy joints between the real ones by pressing a triangular strip of timber or a length of T-iron into the surface at regular intervals. This will weaken the slab so that if it does crack it will crack at the grooves rather than randomly.

Drives and hardstandings

The chief difference between building a concrete drive or hardstanding (including a carport floor) which will be used by cars and building an ordinary ground slab is the choice of concrete mix. The combination of de-icing salts picked up by cars from public roads and a cycle of freeze-thaw can cause surface spalling of concrete which is unsightly at best and at worse can affect the structural strength of a slab. To resist this the concrete should be richer and more durable than the C20P normally used for ground slabs, and it should be air-entrained. Ask for a special mix containing a minimum of 380kg/m^3 of cement and an entrained air content of 4½ per cent; maximum aggregate size should be 20mm as for other ground slabs. Producing air-entrained concrete yourself is not a practical proposition at the moment. If the use of ready-mixed concrete is impracti-cal or uneconomic, ask the Cement and Concrete Association for advice. Never use less than a C30P mix.

The thickness of slabs for drives and hardstandings should be at least 100mm and at least 75mm of well-compacted sub-base should be provided under the slab itself unless it is to be laid over an existing drive of concrete or well-compacted material. On soft clay or peaty soils increase both the sub-base and the slab thickness by a further 25mm at least. If commercial vehicles are to use the slab, add a further 50mm.

A width of 2m is just adequate for a private car but 2½m is preferable. Joints should be evenly spaced at intervals of about 3m, and a crosswise fall of approx-imately 1 in 40 should be incorporated: a stiff-broomed transverse surface finish or an exposed-aggregate finish is best.

If the drive is on a fairly steep slope, concrete *up* the slope and watch for bulges in the level below the compacting beam – use the lowest workability you can safely get away with, and if bulges do occur go back and retamp them when the concrete has stiffened a little.

If the drive adjoins an existing build-ing or garden wall on one or both sides there will not be room enough to use a tamping beam across the slab and the alternate bay method will have to be used. Set stop-ends across the width at normal joint position or a bit closer and peg them down solidly. Concrete alter-nate bays using the tamper across the stop-ends rather than the sides of the formwork, parallel to the wall. After a couple of days remove the stop-ends and concrete the remaining bays, working to the level of the already-completed slabs.

Keep cars off the slab for 10 days if possible, 14 days in cool or chilly weath-er or if a heavy vehicle is involved. Leave the formwork in place during this period.

Mortar mixes

Mortar can be thought of as a gap-filling glue which evens out slight irregularities in size and shape between bricks and blocks, provides a uniform bed, enables loads to be distri-buted uniformly and prevents the penetration of water through brickwork.

The colour of mortar can be changed by using various coloured sands or coarse brick dust. Dry-mixed coloured mortar is also available.

There are two basic types of mortar: **cement** mortar (ce-ment and sand) and **gauged** mortar (cement, lime and sand). The higher the cement content, the more durable, stronger, less flexible and more likely to shrink the mortar is. A strong mortar does not bond well to bricks and may develop cracks.

Mortars with a high lime content are less rigid and, there-fore, more capable of accommodating thermal and other movements. But too much lime delays the setting of the mortar. Plasticiser air entrainment agents can be added to the sand or cement in gauged mortars as a substitute for lime to improve workability. These additives must be used strictly in accordance with the manufacturers' instructions.

With clay bricks, for internal walls use a 1:2:8–9 (cement: lime : sand) or a 1:7–8 (cement : sand and plasticizer) or a 1:6 (masonry cement : sand) mortar mix. If the wall is non-load bearing, alter these proportions to 1:3:10–12, 1:8 and 1:7 respectively. For the inner leaf of a cavity wall and for most external walls between the dpc and eaves, use a 1:1:5–6 or a 1:5–6 or a 1:4½ mix; for free-standing or retaining walls, use 1:½:4½ or 1:4 or 1:3. Different mixes may be needed for calcium silicate bricks.

Dry-mixed mortar can be obtained from builders' mer-chants – add water, mix and it is ready for immediate use. Special powders are normally also available which can be added to the dry mix to produce various colours. Dry-mixed mortar saves a lot of time and trouble, and ensures that you have the correct mix proportions and consistent strength, colour and workability. Standard pack sizes are 20 and 40kg. As a ready reckoner, 20kg is enough to lay 80 bricks.

Mixing mortar

Mortar must be mixed with care – by hand or by machine. You should never make more mortar than you can use in about two hours and in hot weather the mortar will start to set more quickly, so you should make even less.

To ensure the correct proportions, use buckets or a gauge box – a solid open top box of suitable dimensions. The sand should be damp – if it is dry (or really wet) reduce the amount you put in by about one-sixth and turn over the dry mixture with a shovel until it appears evenly graded and consistent in colour. Then make a hole in the middle of the dry-mix heap, pour clean water into the hole, gradually push the outside of the heap into the hole, and mix with the water. Add more water as the mixing continues until the mortar has a plastic consistency. If you add too much water the bricks will swim in the wall and mortar will run down the face of the brickwork. If you add too little, the mortar will be too dry and unworkable. Experience will quickly show the correct wetness.

Bricks and bricklaying

The great majority of the bricks made in Great Britain are clay bricks, made from clay or shale and hardened by firing. Their appearance and properties vary widely depending on the nature of the raw material and the method of manufacture. There are also calcium silicate bricks, made from sand or crushed flint and hardened under steam pressure, and concrete bricks. Calcium silicate and concrete bricks, however, represent only a few per cent of the national output and are not readily available in all areas.

A brick is essentially a building unit that can be conveniently manipulated with one hand. The size of this standard unit in Great Britain is 225×112.5×75mm. This size represents the space occupied by the brick and one adjacent mortar joint: 10mm must be subtracted from each of the dimensions to arrive at the actual *brick* dimensions. Variations of a few millimetres from the standard dimensions are to be expected, and it is one of the functions of the mortar joints to accommodate such variations.

Bricks are usually described according to variety, quality and type. Bricks of any one variety made by different manufacturers may differ in quality.

The variety tells you what the brick is used for:
● **common** bricks are suitable for general building work but having no special claim to give an attractive appearance
● **facing** bricks are specially made or selected to give an attractive appearance, and various strengths
● **engineering** bricks have a dense and strong semi-vitreous body conforming to defined limits of absorption and strength. You are unlikely to have anything to do with engineering bricks unless you happen to have a house which has two or three courses of dpc bricks (which are similar in appearance) in place of the more usual slates or bituminous felt damp-proof course. For an extension to such a house it may be convenient to use the same type of dpc bricks.

The quality tells you about durability:
● **special** quality bricks are durable even when used in situations of extreme exposure where the structure may become saturated and be frozen – retaining walls, parapets and paving, for example
● **ordinary** quality bricks are suitable for the external face of a building. They should be protected when used in vulnerable positions, such as parapets and garden walls. They are not suitable for window sills
● **internal** quality bricks are suitable for internal use only.

The three types define the physical form:
● **solid** bricks are the ones most people are familiar with. In spite of the name, they may contain a few holes or a frog (a depression in one face)
● **perforated** bricks have a lot of small holes or a few large ones running vertically through the bricks. They are classified as *solid* if the perforations do not exceed 25 per cent of the total volume

● **standard special** shapes (not to be confused with special quality) are generally used where a particular decorative effect is wanted or for finishing the tops of walls.

TYPES OF BRICK

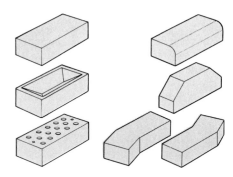

On the left – from the top: solid brick, without frog, solid brick with frog, perforated brick. On the right – from the top: bullnose stretcher, double cant brick, two angle bricks

Brick names

The names of bricks are confusing – the colour, place of origin and method of manufacture may all be included in the name: Leicester red wirecut facing is an example. Many of the bricks made in Great Britain are Flettons, which owing to the large scale of production and hence the moderate price, are sold over a wide area. Both common and facing varieties of Fletton are made and both are of ordinary quality.

The natural colours of fired clay bricks include blue (Blue Staffs, for example), brown, pinkish (Flettons), red (perhaps the most typical clay brick colour), yellow (London Stocks) and white. Red bricks are produced in most areas, white ones are made from chalky clay (including gault clay from the South-east) and yellow bricks often from brickearth and chalk found in Kent and Essex.

The variety of raw materials, methods of firing, the use of additives and surface treatment by sanding or texturing produce the wide range of bricks available. Textures vary from coarse, to smooth, sandcreased to combed and stippled.

Choosing the right brick

Looking at buildings in the neighbourhood should give you some idea of the **quality** of the bricks available from your local works. Local builders or bricklayers may also be willing to talk about their experience with them.

If you have an old house it may not be possible to match the bricks exactly. Many smaller brickworks closed down in 1939 and never reopened. If this is your situation, and you do not like what the local builders' merchant stocks, a visit to the Brick Advisory Centre may help.

The properties of bricks, as measured by tests, are not important to the d-i-y builder. Any brick sold in this country will be **strong** enough for any one or two storey building you are likely to want to build. Bricks may be dense or porous, but this has little to do with getting *watertight* brickwork. If a wall leaks, it is nearly always due to faulty joints.

The main thing to consider is **durability** – this depends on the bricks and on where they are used. Brickwork can absorb any water which either falls as rain or washes over its surface. Some areas of brickwork are likely to absorb more water than others – vertical brickwork absorbs less water than similar brickwork which is horizontal or inclined and parts in contact with the soil absorb more than other parts.

Traditionally, *solid* brick walls – single or one and half bricks thick – were considered sufficiently rain resistant in many areas of the country. In coastal and other severely exposed areas, brickwork was often rendered or tile hung for additional protection.

Over the last 50 years or so *cavity* walls have become much more widely used. They offer a more certain protection against rain penetration and also provide better thermal insulation. A cavity wall is designed on the assumption that water will sometimes penetrate the outer leaf of brickwork (just over 100mm thick) so precautions are taken to ensure that moisture does not transfer to the inner leaf.

Clay bricks of ordinary quality are good enough for all ordinary work. But when you want to use bricks for paving, building external steps, window sills, or for the tops of parapets or free-standing walls and other areas which are particularly exposed to rain, special quality bricks should be used. This is because ordinary quality bricks may be damaged by frost when they are saturated or may contain enough soluble salts to damage the mortar. Many bricks (particularly ordinary quality ones) contain some soluble salts, mostly calcium sulphate (gypsum) and under *very* wet conditions enough of it may find its way into the mortar to cause a chemical action (sulphate attack) on the set cement so that the mortar ultimately becomes soft.

Buying bricks

Large quantities of bricks can be obtained direct from the manufacturer: smaller quantities from builders' merchants and brick manufacturers' agents. Both sources of supply can deliver, but you may have to wait for unusual bricks.

Manufacturers usually sell bricks direct by the thousand and may not be willing to sell you less than a full load – perhaps 2,500. If you want less than this, you could try splitting a load with a neighbour. If you try to buy relatively few bricks direct from the manufacturer, you may find that transport costs make the delivery uneconomical. Try to buy bricks from a manufacturer who is as near your home as possible. If you want to buy bricks to match existing brick-

work, you should show the supplier some of the original bricks. If this is not possible, take samples home to compare with your existing brickwork.

Always arrange to be around when the bricks are delivered and try to make a clean space for them as near as possible to where you will be working (but remember the lorry will need access and not all drives are designed to take the weight of a laden lorry). Make sure that the bricks are not thrown off the lorry on to muddy ground.

Store loose bricks on a clean dry base and cover them with waterproof sheeting. Do not allow them to become saturated by rain before use – using saturated bricks can lead to efflorescence in the brickwork, delay in drying out, and an increased risk of frost attack on both bricks and mortar. When working outdoors, cover newly-laid brickwork overnight.

Blocks

In a few places, hollow clay blocks are made. The commonest size is 300mm long, 225mm high and 100mm wide (including mortar). Wider and narrower blocks are also made.

More important to the d-i-y builder, and more available, are concrete blocks measuring $450 \times 225 \times 100$mm (including mortar). These may be dense concrete – useful for exterior work; or light-weight concrete – suitable only for internal work, but giving good insulation in the inner leaf of a cavity wall. The big units can be awkward to handle, but walls are built more quickly than with standard bricks.

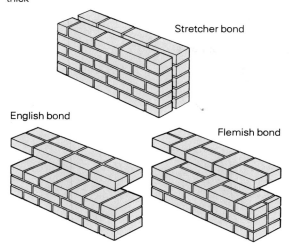

POPULAR BRICK BONDS

Bricks should be laid so that the vertical mortar joints do not coincide from layer to layer. The pattern used to achieve this is known as the bonding pattern. Stretcher bonds are useful for half brick garden walls up to 1m high and for cavity walls. English and Flemish bonds are used for brickwork 225mm thick

Stretcher bond

English bond

Flemish bond

Laying bricks

The following three pages should give you some idea of what is involved in laying and looking after brickwork. They will not tell you all you need to know for building a complete house but should enable you to tackle a home extension, patch up holes in walls and construct garden walls. If you have an ambitious project in view, consider attending a further education class in bricklaying.

Setting out

Smear a very thin layer of mortar on the concrete foundations and then scratch the required position of the brickwork into the smear of mortar – use a long straight piece of wood as a guide for the top of a trowel. If the brickwork is to have a 90 degree corner, start laying bricks there. Extend the brickwork about four or five bricks in each direction and then raise the wall about seven or eight bricks at the corner falling in steps to one brick at the furthest points from the corner. Use a bricklayer's level to make sure that the brickwork is true and vertical: adjust if necessary. Repeat this operation at each corner and then lay the bottom course of bricks to link the corner constructions. Set up the gauge rods and line at the outside top edge of the next course of bricks. The wall is now ready to be filled in.

The basic laying technique

Before trying to lay bricks, watch a craftsman at work to get an idea of the techniques involved. Start by laying a bed of mortar about 10mm thick on the foundation concrete or course of bricks and use the point of the trowel to make a V-shaped groove in the middle of the mortar bed. When a brick is placed in position this groove will allow any mortar at the edges of the bed which is thicker than 10mm to move to the middle of the bed. Ideally, you should not make the V-shaped groove but unless the mortar is very plastic, bringing the brick to the line on a full bed will be hard work if you do not. Until you gain experience you should not try to work with a bed of mortar any longer than three to five bricks, and be prepared to use an even shorter bed in warm weather. 'Butter' one end of a brick with mortar and place it in position against the last brick with its top outside edge touching the guide line so that the mortar bed is about 10mm thick and the joints between bricks are perpendicular to it. Tap the brick into position with the wooden handle of the trowel. Clean off surplus mortar from both faces of the wall, leaving the joint flush with the bricks. You can continue laying bricks for another three to four hours before finishing the mortar joints.

CUTTING BRICKS

Place the brick on its side on a firm but soft surface – a bed of sand or loose soil – position a bolster on the brick and strike the bolster with a hammer. It is usually necessary to strike the brick on opposite faces to complete the cut. Do not try to cut bricks with a trowel – this needs a lot of skill.

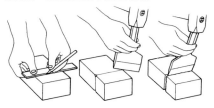

Damp-proof courses

Damp-proof courses provide a physical barrier to stop damp rising from the ground. They are necessary just above ground level in external walls; as a cavity wall tray between internal and external walls; under sills, at jambs and lintels, parapets and thresholds; and where brickwork abuts roofs – usually as flashings. Dpc bricks, bituminous felt and slate are usually used for horizontal damp-proof courses; bituminous felt is also used for vertical dpcs. Further details of the choice and use of dpcs can be found in the Brick Development Association Practical Note 6.

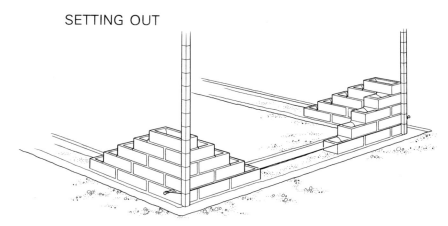

SETTING OUT

Smear a thin layer of mortar on to the foundation concrete and use the point of the trowel to make a V-shaped groove.

Start laying bricks at a corner extending about four or five bricks away from the corner in each direction and building up the corner.

Then fill in the brickwork using gauge rods and line set along the top edge of each course of bricks

Brick dpcs should consist of two or three courses of dpc bricks laid half bonded and bedded in 1:0–¼:3 (cement : lime : sand) mortar with the top course at the level of a bed joint dpc.

A slate dpc inserted at ground level to prevent moisture rising should consist of two or three courses of slates half bonded and bedded in 1:0–¼:3 mortar. The slates must project beyond the face of the brickwork by about 6mm (not be finished flush with the brickwork) and must not be covered with mortar.

Bituminous felt, plastic and polymer dpc materials in horizontal ground level dpcs should be bedded in 1:0–¼:3 mortar and lapped by 100mm at joints and at inter-

nal and external angles. They must project clear of the brickwork face and must not finish flush with the brickwork nor be covered by mortar (any mortar covering felt or slate dpcs will provide a bridge for moisture to rise into the brickwork).

Brick and slate horizontal dpcs are not suitable for preventing the downward movement of moisture in the upper parts of a building. Bituminous felt, plastic and polymer dpc materials can be used for forming dpc cavity trays over window and door openings. A vertical dpc must be provided where the cavity is closed – at door and window reveals, for example. Bituminous felt, plastic and polymer dpc materials or two courses of half bonded slates are suitable – both need bedding in 1:0–¼:3 mortar.

THE BASIC BRICKLAYING TECHNIQUE

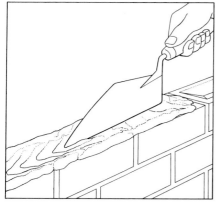

Lay a bed of mortar on the last course of brickwork and make a V-shaped groove in the middle of the bed

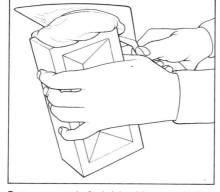

Butter one end of a brick with mortar before laying it on the previously-laid bed

Tap the brick into position. The top of the brick should be level with the guide line

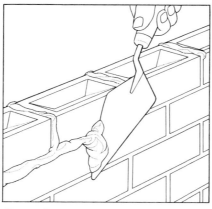

Clean off any surplus mortar leaving the joints flush with the surface of the wall

Bricklaying tools

A bricklayer's trowel is the most important tool. Start by choosing the largest trowel that feels comfortable in your hand but do not choose a 'full size' trowel if it feels too heavy and cumbersome. A bricklayer normally uses a 300mm trowel; you may find a 250mm one more convenient. The smallest trowel is a *pointing* trowel.

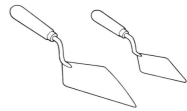

A bricklayer's level is important for checking that the brickwork is being constructed level and true.

A bolster (which is basically a wide chisel) and a **club hammer** are essential for cutting bricks.

A guide line made from a length of fine line with some means of temporarily fixing it to the brickwork is necessary for making sure that long lengths of brickwork are constructed level and true.

A gauge rod is useful for making sure that the height of each course of bricks (plus mortar) is consistent between courses and regular along each course. Two gauge rods can be used as temporary supports for a guide line. To make one, determine the average height of the bricks and mark a series of brick heights (allowing 10mm bed joints) on a piece of wood which is as long as the height of the brick wall to be built. Secure a gauge rod vertically at each end of the wall and use the course marks as reference points for securing the line. The line should be tied to the positions which correspond to the outside top edge of the bricks in the next course.

A mortar board about 600mm square is useful for holding bedding mortar. Support it on bricks as the wall rises.

A hawk is for holding mortar, usually when pointing. A rough hawk can be made by attaching a handle at right angles to an odd piece of scrap plywood or chipboard, say 225 to 300mm square.

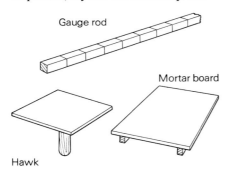

Gauge rod

Mortar board

Hawk

Jointing, joint finishing and repointing

To ensure the durability of brickwork the joints must be filled completely with mortar. The finished shape of the mortar joint will affect the appearance of the finished brickwork. Generally, brickwork joints are *finished* by striking, raking or ironing the mortar while it is still green. *Pointing* consists of raking out the mortar in the joint to a depth of 10 to 20mm and then refilling the joint with fresh mortar. This is usually done on existing brickwork.

Joint finishes When choosing a type of joint finish take account of whereabouts in the building the brickwork is, how exposed it is and where you live. Recessed joints form a horizontal shelf and allow water to lie on them and soak into the brickwork. They are not suitable for high exposure and should only be used with special quality bricks.

There are four popular joint finishes:
● **flush** joints can be rubbed with coarse material (sacking, for instance) to produce a rustic finish when used with rustic bricks, or given a smooth even-surface, with regularly-shaped bricks

● **weather struck** joints are recessed at the top with a pointing trowel to help rainwater run off the brickwork and to produce a shadow line

● **ironed (bucket handle or hose)** joints are grooved by running a piece of round metal rod (a bucket handle, say) along the face of the mortar before it sets hard – they provide a slight shadowing effect

● **recessed (or rake)** joints have a rectangular section raked out (with a Frenchman or a trowel) to produce a deep, bold shadowing effect. They should be used externally only with special quality bricks.

Pointing When it is impracticable to gain the desired visual effect with a joint finish, you may have to resort to pointing. However, this should be done as a last resort – jointing is not only cheaper but disturbs the mortar far less.

Repointing Well-built brickwork generally requires little maintenance. However, as a building ages, the mortar joints may start to show slight decay because of ingress of water through a faulty damp-proof course; incorrect proportioning of the original bedding mortar mix; frost damage due to use of unsuitable mortars; sulphate attack; the building suffering through permanently damp walls; water damage from plumbing leaks – faulty guttering and so on; or through structural movement.

Before starting any repointing the cause of the water damage should be sought out and put right. Repointing should not be done in frosty weather but the brickwork should be damp.

First carefully scrape clean the joints, removing all lichen and moss. Work from the top left-hand corner, across and downwards. Then use a timber dog or similar tool to rake out first the vertical and then the horizontal joints to a minimum depth of 10mm, maximum 20mm. Make sure that the recess formed is left square and brush out all dust and loose particles. If the brickwork is dry, dampen the raked out joint using an old flat distemper brush dipped in clean water. If this is not done, the brickwork will extract the water from the pointing mix too quickly and the resulting joint will be weak and liable to crumble. The brickwork should *not* be soaked.

Fill the joints using a dotter (a small pointing trowel), mixing small amounts of mortar at a time and pressing it into the vertical joints before the horizontal ones. Fill only a few joints at a time. The joints should be raked out and prepared – use a soft brush to remove loose material – as each batch of mortar is used.

Under normal conditions of exposure a 1:1:6 (cement: lime: sand) mixture is generally acceptable. For softer facing bricks, a 1:2:9 mixture is used.

JOINT FINISHES

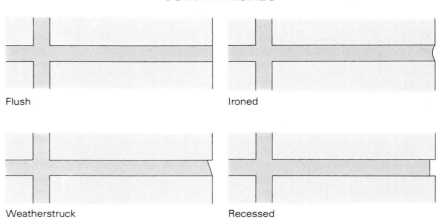

Flush

Ironed

Weatherstruck

Recessed

Making holes in brick walls

Making a small hole in brickwork – to fit an air brick, say – is a fairly simple task. Even fitting a small serving hatch should not present too many problems. But cutting out large holes for doors and windows can be more difficult – you need to think about what the wall supports, how to support the wall (and whatever it supports) while you cut the hole, and what size lintel to use. The next three pages give details of what is involved and should enable you to decide whether you can cope with doing the job. These pages should not be taken as a complete how-to-do-it guide, particularly for making large holes. Most experienced handymen should be able to cut a hole about a metre wide, provided the hole is not near the corner of the building, or another hole, or immediately beneath a floor supported by the wall. Anything wider is really a job for an experienced builder. If in doubt call in a builder.

Establishing the load

As well as having to think about supporting brickwork above an opening, you should also consider whether the wall supports the floor of the room above or even part of the roof.

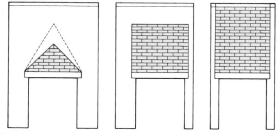

The three drawings show the areas of wall which are at risk of collapse when cutting a hole in the wall.

When the widths of the remaining walls or piers are greater than half the span of the opening, assume that the wall load is within the shaded 45 degree *triangle*. A lintel will have to support the weight of all the brickwork, floor loads or whatever which fall within this 45 degree triangle. (In complicated situations you also need to consider a proportion of the loads which fall between 45 and 60 degrees – the dotted line.)

When one of the remaining walls or piers is less than half the span of the opening, assume that the wall load is within the *square* which has sides equal to the span.

When both of the remaining walls or piers are less than half the span of the opening, assume that the wall load extends right to the top of the wall and is a *rectangle*.

If there are no floors, roofs or any other parts of the building bearing directly on these areas of brickwork, you need only think about supporting the weight of the brickwork itself. But relatively few walls are like this in practice. The drawings on the next page show how other loads may play a part.

What size lintel?

To support the load previously taken by the brickwork, it is necessary to insert a lintel – either a rolled steel joist or a reinforced concrete lintel. The size of the lintel required will depend on the load it has to support. To calculate this, you need to work out what volume of wall and areas of roof and floor the lintel will have to support and multiply them by the **unit loads** – brickwork weighs from about 1250kg to over 2,000kg a cubic metre depending on the bricks and a pitched roof or a floor above the opening will produce a load of about 200kg a square metre. To this you must add an allowance for people, furniture and so on.

With this information an expert – either at a builders' merchant, a building surveyor or your local authority, say – should be able to advise on the type and size of lintel.

The bearings for the lintels must be carefully levelled. For spans up to 1.5m, the lintel must be built about 110mm into the wall on each side of the opening. For wider spans, increase the bearing to about 200mm and, if the lintel is to carry heavy loads, insert a hard stone or pre-cast concrete pad beneath the lintel embedded in mortar to spread the load.

Supporting the structure

Two things need to be considered: supporting the *brickwork* enclosed by the triangle, square or rectangle above the opening and supporting any *other parts* of the building – floors or roof, say – which bear directly on the opening.

When no other parts of the building bear directly on the opening, it is possible to cut a narrow hole – say up to two bricks wide – without supporting the wall above: this needs care. But under no circumstances disturb the existing structure – it is almost impossible to return dropped brickwork to its original position. The only satisfactory remedy is to take down the disturbed brickwork (which can be identified by cracking) and to rebuild it. In some circumstances it might be more convenient to remove the brickwork in the triangle above the opening – the self-corbelling effect of the remaining brickwork which will support the wall above is then obvious.

When you want to make larger openings or when a floor or roof, say, exerts a

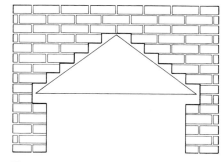

The self-corbelling effect of brickwork supporting the wall above the opening

load on the brickwork above the opening, you will have to provide temporary support while the work is in hand, until a supporting lintel is inserted.

The temporary support is usually provided by adjustable props resting on something firm, preferably solid internal floors and firm ground outside when dealing with an external wall. Hollow timber floors are not always adequate – it is often necessary to remove the floorboards and position the props between the floor joists so that they push against a firm base. The load should be spread by standing the props on lengths of timber about 150mm wide by around 40mm thick. In upstairs rooms the load should be spread by laying the timber across a number of floor joists. It may be necessary to support the floor by inserting props at ground floor level. The adjustable props should be about 900mm apart on both sides of the wall and about 600mm from the wall. These props are used to support temporary beams placed immediately under the floor or roof at right angles to the structural members and parallel to the wall to be disturbed. Once the props are in position they are gradually tightened – in turn – until the whole of the floor or roof weight is carried by the props.

The next job is to support the brickwork which is to be left above the opening. To do this you have to cut out a few bricks about 600mm apart above the position for the opening and insert needles (about 150×100mm timbers) through the small holes left in the wall. The needles will have to be supported with adjustable props, as before. The props should not be placed more than 600mm from either side of the wall.

Provided everything is well supported, it should now be safe to take out the brickwork to form the required opening. This must be done carefully. Take out the first brick at the centre of the opening about one third of the way down from the top by loosening the mortar around it – either by drilling the mortar with a masonry drill or by cutting it away with a hammer and chisel. Surrounding bricks can then be loosened carefully with the hammer and chisel working to-

wards the sides and downwards to the bottom. The opening is finished by taking away the remaining bricks working upwards and outwards leaving the top two or three courses until later. Unwanted parts of bricks will then have to be cut away and the sides of the opening trimmed. Sometimes a brick will fall out and have to be replaced. Finally, the last two or three courses at the top are removed carefully and the sides trimmed. If any bricks above the opening have been disturbed, they should be cut out and replaced as soon as possible. If the wall is an external cavity wall, try to stop debris falling into the cavity.

RECOGNISING SUPPORTING WALLS

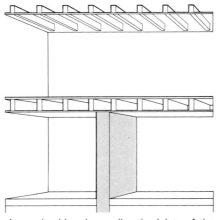

A non load-bearing wall – the joists of the floor above the wall run parallel to the wall and the wall does not support the floor

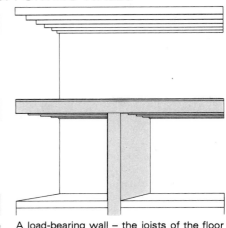

A load-bearing wall – the joists of the floor above the wall are at right angles to the wall and rest on it – the floor will need support

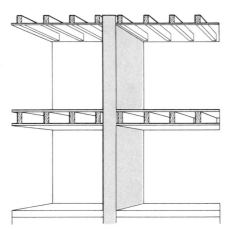

Non load-bearing wall – the floor joists, and ceiling joists above the first-floor wall run parallel to the wall

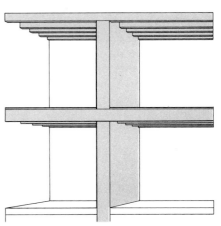

Load-bearing wall – the floor joists and the ceiling joists run at right angles to the wall. Both need supporting

SUPPORTING A WALL

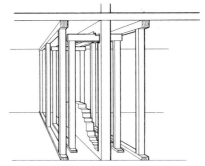

Temporary support for a wall – note the support for the floor (or ceiling) above the wall and the needles supporting the wall

Fitting and replacing air bricks

Air bricks provide under-floor ventilation in homes with suspended timber ground floors. They are essential if damp and rot are to be kept at bay. Occasionally it becomes necessary to replace a broken one or fit a new one to improve ventilation. Air bricks usually measure 215mm by 140 or 215mm and fit neatly into existing brickwork.

When replacing an air brick or inserting one in an existing brick wall, remove the old brick (or bricks) by drilling out the mortar joints with a masonry drill or by cutting away the mortar with a hammer and chisel. There is no need to support the brickwork above for such a small hole. However, the work should be carried out carefully, especially if bricks have to be cut away, to avoid disturbing surrounding brickwork. The air brick should be bedded with matching mortar and the joint finished to match. If the wall has a cavity, use roofing slates to form a duct sealing the cavity and letting air from outside pass directly into the building. This is particularly important when the cavity contains insulating material.

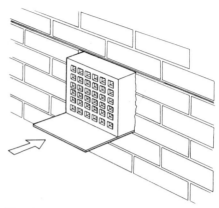

Use slates to seal a cavity wall

Fitting an extractor fan

To make the hole in the wall follow the procedure described under *Fitting and replacing air bricks*. The instructions which accompany the extractor fan should indicate the size of hole and the method of fixing the fan. The easiest way to make the hole is to drill or cut out the joints of a brick, remove it and then extend the size of the hole by gently knocking bricks out. Finally saw or chisel through remaining whole bricks – as necessary – to form a hole of the required size and shape. Install the extractor fan and make good mortar joints and plaster to match the existing finishes.

Putting in a serving hatch

Always try to plan the position for an opening for a serving hatch so that as few bricks as possible have to be removed, or cut, taking into account the size of opening required.

For putting in a small serving hatch, follow the procedure described for *Fitting and replacing air bricks* and for *Fitting an extractor fan*.

When making a large opening, remove the bricks or blocks at the top of the opening very carefully. Prop up the brickwork above the opening if you have any doubts about the ability of the brickwork to support itself. Once you have made the hole, place the serving hatch in position and insert wooden wedges around it to hold the frame firm. Push the wedges in so that they end up below the finished surface of both sides of the wall and check that the frame is square by using a spirit level. Finally, fill the gaps around the frame with bricklaying mortar and finish with plaster to match the existing walls. If the frame fits tightly into the hole you can plug and screw it to the sides of the opening in the brickwork instead of using wedges. The screw heads should be countersunk and filled to match the finish of the serving hatch.

You will have to insert a lintel above the hatch if it is more than about 450mm wide and does not have a top rail strong enough to bear the brickwork above.

Making holes for doors and windows

Follow the procedure described for *Putting in a serving hatch* – a lintel is almost certain to be required. If the door or window is to be built into an external wall, a dpc tray over the lintel is necessary – see page 168.

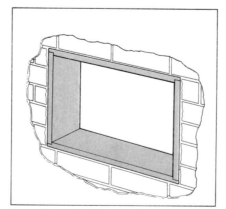

A small hatch without a lintel. If you use wedges to hold the hatch, the hole cut should be about 10 to 12mm larger all round than the hatch

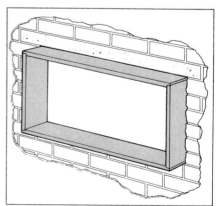

If you use plugs and screws, make the hatch fit tightly into the hole. A large hatch will need a supporting lintel inserted into the brickwork

Removing a fireplace

Before starting to remove a fireplace make sure that it is not an integral part of the chimney breast structure. If it is, you will probably have to seek professional advice, or help, to remove it. Most fireplaces are simply fixed on to the chimney breast and can be removed without creating any structural problems. A typical fireplace – see drawing – usually has two separate parts: a hearth, and a surround (precast briquette, glazed tiles, metal or stone). It may also have a separate mantelshelf.

Taking a fireplace out is generally fairly simple but it needs some brute force and is a messy job – have the chimney swept, remove carpets and as much furniture as possible (cover up the rest), keep the door in the room shut when you are working, wear old clothes, tie a handkerchief over your mouth and nose and wear goggles, particularly when you are chipping at brickwork or plaster. If there is a gas pipe sticking up through the hearth, or out through the surround, have it removed by a gas fitter.

Taking the fireplace out

Remove the grate from the fireplace. If it is fixed in, use a hammer and cold chisel to chip it out from the sides. Now tackle the hearth and surround. In most cases the surround stands directly on the hearth – so it will have to be removed first.

Fireplace surrounds are generally

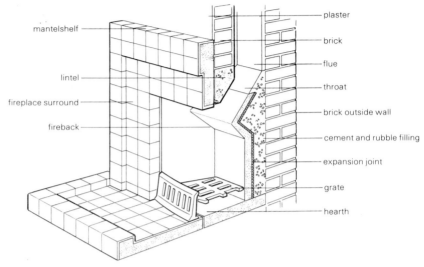

The anatomy of a fireplace with the terminology used

plaster
brick
flue
throat
brick outside wall
cement and rubble filling
expansion joint
grate
hearth

mantelshelf
lintel
fireplace surround
fireback

nailed or screwed to the brickwork with either four or six fixing lugs (two down either side and sometimes two at the top). These lugs are usually metal plates cast into the surround, fixed to the brickwork structure and plastered over.

If there is a separate mantelshelf, this may also be attached to the wall with lugs, but marble and stone shelves may be cemented in. Remove the mantelshelf before the surround. If the shelf is cemented in, loosen it carefully using a hammer and cold chisel until you can

lever it out. If the mantelshelf is fixed by lugs, treat them in the same way as the lugs on the surround.

The first step in removing the surround is to chip away all the plaster around the perimeter of the two sides and top to expose the fixing lugs. Try to unscrew any screws in the lugs or yank out nails with a claw hammer. If you cannot do either, knock the fixings sideways until they are loosened. Have a helper holding the surround while you do this to prevent it toppling over. If the

REMOVING A FIREPLACE

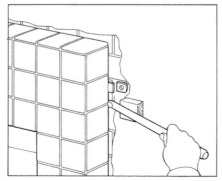

Remove the screws or cut through the fixings (lugs) before levering the surround away from the wall. There may be four or six fixing lugs

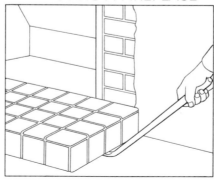

To remove the hearth, cut into the bed of mortar below it using a hammer and chisel, then gently prise up the slab with a crowbar

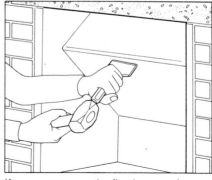

If you want to use the fireplace as a feature, you will have to tidy up by removing the fireback, smoke shelf and so on

surround is tightly held use a crowbar to release it. The surround can be removed independently of the throat lintel which forms the flue throat and also supports the brickwork over the fireplace opening and the fireback, grate and back boiler and so on. Tiles, marble or stone slabs stuck directly on to the brickwork can be prised off with a cold chisel and any separate metal frame covering the gap between the surround and the opening should be removed – the fixing lugs for this are usually inside the fireplace.

The hearth slab will probably be fixed in place on a bed of mortar. To remove it, break the mortar joint by cutting into the bed with a hammer and chisel and then prise the slab up and lift it clear.

To tidy up, remove the fireback by chipping away the mortar which holds it. Take out any loose rubble, the throat restrictor (if there is one) and any smoke shelf. Finally, brush out all the loose bits.

Closing up the opening

You can board over the hole leaving the chimney breast flat or you can block the chimney off leaving a recess – for shelves, say. But the most permanent, and a safer way of dealing with the opening is to use bricks or blocks to fill it in.

When an existing fireplace chimney is sealed the chimney flue must always be permanently ventilated. The chimney should be left open at the top, though sometimes it is advisable to install a hood to prevent rain getting in, and a perma-nent ventilator at the bottom of the flue – either inside or outside the building. If the chimney is not ventilated, moisture will collect inside the flue and damp patches may appear on the face of the chimney breast inside the house.

Bricking the opening Remove the half bricks left around the fireplace and key in new bricks or blocks to the existing brickwork. Clean up the brickwork with a stiff brush and put in an airbrick just above skirting board level. Use a spirit level to check that each row of blocks or bricks is level and a straight-edge to make sure that the wall is not bulging. Use the spirit level to check that the wall is vertical. When the mortar has set, plaster over the brickwork and install a ventilator grill over the air brick.

Boarding the opening Cut and square the edges of the plaster around the hole. Work out what thickness board and how much is needed to cover the hole and to leave the board flush with the plaster. Plywood or tongued-and-grooved boarding fixed to a softwood frame can be used, but if the chimney is shared with another fireplace which is still in use, use plasterboard or incom-bustible materials. Cut the board to fit as close to the plaster as possible and fit in a small plaster or metal ventilator just above skirting board level. Use wall filler to fill in small gaps around the edges of the board.

Leaving a recess There are many ways of finishing off and leaving a recess, includ-ing leaving the bricks bare. Whatever you do make sure that you do not disturb the lintel and, if you share the chimney with the house next door, make sure that you do not remove too much from the back of the fireplace. Fit a ventilated roof to the recess, strong enough to hold anything that falls down the chimney.

Covering the hearth Smooth over the floor where the hearth was using a 3:1 sand and cement screed.

Removing the whole chimney breast

A fireplace chimney breast extends from its foundations all the way up to the flue pot. It is often an integral part of the house and sometimes the house next door as well – so you cannot simply cut it out without taking precautions to ensure that the remaining part of the house is structurally stable. Seek professional ad-vice before starting this sort of job. The following notes do not tell you how to do it – they simply state what the problem is.

The most satisfactory approach from a structural point of view is to take down the entire chimney breast from the ground floor all the way up to the chim-ney pot and make good brickwork, walls, floors, roof and so on. Obviously, this cannot be done if the chimney is shared with the house next door without the consent of your neighbours.

The alternative approach is to take half the chimney breast away but this immediately raises the problem of struc-tural instability. When taking a fireplace and chimney breast away at ground floor level, you have to think about how you can support the upper floor(s) and the roof chimney structure. It is sometimes possible to do this satisfactorily but each house has to be considered on its indi-vidual merits. It is usually quite safe to take down the upper part of a chimney – say removing it down to roof level and perhaps even removing the chimney breast in the bedroom while leaving the ground floor fireplace. But even this cannot be done if the chimney is shared.

CLOSING THE OPENING

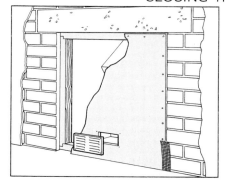

When boarding up the opening, use a soft-wood frame of timber and insert a ventilator – into either the front or back of the chimney

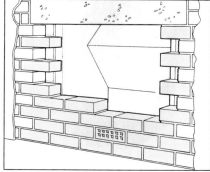

New brickwork should be bonded into the existing brickwork by removing the half bricks left around the fireplace – as shown

Plastering

Plaster is usually applied to walls to cover up the unevenness of the brickwork and to provide a flat surface for painting or wallpapering. It can also improve the sound and heat insulation and fire resistance of a wall.

There are two main types of plaster – **gypsum plaster** and **cement-based plaster**. Gypsum plasters should only be used indoors – if they are used in damp conditions they may fall off the wall. Cement-based plasters (usually called renders) are often used on the outside of a building for weather-proofing but they can also be used inside, especially as part of treatment for damp.

Plasters are further divided into undercoat and finishing plasters.

Undercoat plasters should be applied fairly thickly – up to about 10mm, and built up in layers – to cover any unevenness of the wall. The wall will absorb water from the plaster and if it does this too quickly, the plaster will crack. So there are several types of plaster, each designed to cope with a particular absorption rate. A thick undercoat plaster helps to even out the difference in water absorbance between the bricks and the mortar – so that the finish plaster should dry out evenly.

Finish plasters should be applied thinly – up to about 3mm over an undercoat plaster, or about 5mm thick directly on to plasterboard. Finish plaster can be worked to give a finish which is smooth enough for painting.

Types of plaster

There are many different types of plaster, designed to suit different surfaces, but only a limited number are widely available. Most of the plasters readily available are **lightweight** and contain minerals like perlite or vermiculite to make them easier to use.

Carlite is the most widely available brand of lightweight gypsum plaster. *Carlite Browning* is an undercoat plaster suitable for use on fairly absorbent surfaces, like ordinary building bricks and lightweight blocks. Before using it on old brickwork, rake out the mortar joints to a depth of about 6mm and brush the wall down well to provide a key for the plaster. Then dampen the wall slightly. Apply about a 10mm thickness of plaster built up in layers – two, say. For very absorbent walls (on which Carlite Browning will crack) you should use the less widely available *Carlite Browning HSB* (high-suction background) or seal the wall with a pva bonding agent before using Carlite Browning. *Carlite Bonding* is an undercoat plaster for use on dense surfaces that absorb little water, such as plasterboard and engineering bricks. On plasterboard use a depth of 8mm. You may find this plaster sold in small bags for repairs. *Carlite Finish* is the finish plaster for use on the Carlite undercoat plasters. Use it thinly – about 2mm.

Sirapite is a non-lightweight gypsum finish plaster. It is used mainly on cement/sand undercoats. It sets slightly harder than most other gypsum plasters and is slightly more brittle. Because it sets slowly, it can be worked to a very smooth finish suitable for painting. Once mixed, Sirapite sets in two stages – about 15 minutes after mixing, the plaster becomes too stiff to use but it can be resoftened by adding a little more water and mixing it again (called retempering). This should not be done more than about 30 minutes after mixing otherwise the plaster will not set correctly. Sirapite is sold under other brand names in small bags for patching and repair work.

Thistle plasters are the more traditional non-lightweight gypsum plasters. *Thistle Browning* is an undercoat plaster for use on surfaces such as brickwork and lightweight blocks. When used on brickwork it should be mixed with three parts of plastering sand (sharp sand) by volume. *Thistle Finish* is a finish plaster for use on cement/sand undercoats, on Thistle Browning (or on plasterboard). It needs to be mixed with water only. *Thistle Board Finish* is a finish plaster developed specially for single coat work on plasterboard. Since the plaster should be applied only 5mm thick, the plasterboard joins should be flush.

Cement-based plasters are mixes of cement, sharp sand and lime. The most common mix for indoor brickwork is 1 : 1 : 6 (parts of cement to lime to sand by volume).

Buying plaster

Large quantities of plaster (50kg bags) can be bought from builders' merchants. Most will sell a single bag if they have one in store. Some hardware and d-i-y shops sell small bags of plaster (2.5 to 10kg) for patching and repair work.

Plaster is heavy and bulky and can mess up the boot of your car. Builders' merchants will usually deliver it – for an extra charge of typically 10 per cent. Delivery may be free for orders above a certain amount.

Because gypsum plaster can deteriorate if it's stored for more than about two months, many builders' merchants order at frequent intervals and 50kg bags should be stamped with a date of manufacture. This allows the builders' merchant to sell stocks in rotation. Lightweight cement-based plasters deteriorate after about six months. If you do not use all of a bag of plaster, store it in a sealed polythene bag.

Plastering tools

The basic plastering tool is the trowel. For plastering near corners use an *angle trowel*. There are two types – one for internal angles and one for external angles. For producing the final smooth finish use a *finishing trowel*. This can also be used to apply the plaster. It has a thin, slightly flexible steel blade measuring about 100mm by 200mm with a very slight curvature across its face. Choose one with its handle smoothly riveted to the blade. For applying undercoat plaster over a large area, you can use a *float* made from knot-free softwood or plastic, or a *floating trowel*.

For holding the reserve of mixed plaster, use a wooden board known as a *spot board*. For carrying a reserve of plaster to the working area use a *hawk*. This is usually a square sheet of roughened aluminium measuring about 300mm by 300mm with a detachable wooden handle. You can make your own from a piece of chipboard, plywood or hardboard.

To level off wet plaster, use a *rule* – a softwood batten about 10mm thick and 50mm wide.

How to plaster

Because finishing coats are applied thinly, the background undercoat should be applied true and flat. This can be achieved fairly easily by using *screeds* which are basically depth guides. The simplest are wooden battens about 15mm wide and as thick as the plaster undercoat – about 10mm – fixed temporarily to the wall with nails. They should be fixed vertically and small wooden wedges can be inserted between the battens and the wall to make sure that the screeds are in line with each other. When plastering a fairly large area, set the screeds about 400mm apart.

Fill the area between the screeds with undercoat plaster, built up in layers until the final coat is just above the screeds. Then, while it is still wet, level off the plaster by running the rule along the screeds. Remove the screeds when the plaster has set and fill the gaps. Small areas of damaged plaster can be replastered in a similar way by using the surrounding plaster as a guide for the rule.

Mixing the plaster

Mix up a cupful of plaster and see how long it takes to go too stiff to work with. Less than about half an hour means you probably need to buy fresh plaster. This test should be modified for Sirapite.

You can mix plaster in a plastic bucket or bowl. Always use fresh tap water and add the plaster to the water, stirring until the mix reaches a thick creamy consistency. The mix should be just thick enough so that it doesn't fall off the mixing stick. Remove any lumps and make sure that the plaster in the bottom and sides of the bucket is well mixed in. At first, do not try to mix up more than about one-third of a bucketful of plaster – about 2 litres of water.

Tip the plaster on to a dampened spot board. Scrape a lump of plaster about the size of your fist on to the hawk using the face of a trowel. To get the plaster from the hawk to the trowel, tip the hawk towards you and in one movement, push the plaster upwards off the hawk with the face of the trowel. Right-

handed people should hold the hawk in the left hand and the trowel in the right hand.

Putting on the undercoat

The undercoat should be built up in at least two layers, applying the second layer while the layer underneath is still damp but firm. Start applying the first layer at the bottom of region 1 – see drawing. (Left-handed people should start at the bottom of region 9.) Push the plaster firmly against the wall and move the trowel upwards steadily keeping the blade of the trowel at an angle of about 45 degrees to the wall. When coming to the end of the stroke, flatten the trowel off slightly. Do not work right up against the screeds – try to keep them clean.

Reload the trowel and apply the plaster starting at the bottom of region 2. Work up towards region 1 and move the trowel in an arc to one side where the two regions meet. Never flatten the trowel completely on the plaster. Apply the plaster in the sequence shown.

When the first layer starts to go stiff, scratch it to provide a key for the next layer which should be put on in the same sequence. While this final layer is still damp and soft, place a clean, slightly dampened rule at right angles to the screeds and work upwards moving the rule from side to side in a sawing action. Fill in any hollows left and rule off again. Leave the plaster to set for about two hours, remove the screeds and fill the

PLASTERING A WALL

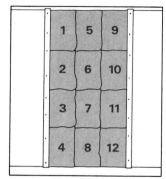

Right-handed people should start plastering at the bottom of region 1 and work in the sequence shown.

Push the trowel against the wall at an angle of about 45 degrees, flattening off slightly at the end of each stroke

Use a dampened rule running along the screeds to remove any excess plaster. Work upwards using a sawing action

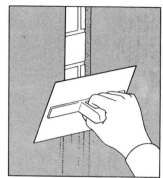

Finally, remove the screeds and fill in the gaps. Do this about two hours after plastering the surface

gaps. Once the surface has set stiff, scratch it with a piece of wire or a nail to provide a good key for the finish coat.

Never try to put on stiff plaster and do not try to resoften it by adding more water otherwise it will not set correctly.

Putting on the finishing coat

Controlling the thickness of the plaster is the main problem when applying a finishing coat. Starting off on a flat background (plasterboard or a screeded undercoat) makes the job easier.

Apply the finishing coat using the same sequence and with the same technique as described for the undercoat. Avoid pressing against the wall with the trowel – this produces a rippled effect. The plaster should just flow out of the trowel. When a strip (regions 1 to 4 say) is complete, smooth the plaster off by lightly running the trowel from the bottom to the top holding it at an angle of about 20 degrees to the wall. Do this once or twice – resist the temptation to try and achieve a perfect finish. Plaster the other strips and fill small hollows with very small amounts of plaster.

The plaster should be smoothed off when it just starts to go stiff. To check whether it is ready, touch it with your finger – if it sticks, it is not ready. Smooth off with a damp clean trowel, running it from bottom to top holding it at an angle of about 20 degrees to the wall. By pushing fairly hard at this stage, any high spots can be levelled off.

After another 20 to 30 minutes the plaster will be quite firm and can be finally smoothed off. Dampen the plaster slightly using a large paint brush and again run the trowel from bottom to top over the whole of the plastered area.

Plasterboard

Plasterboard is gypsum plaster sandwiched between two sheets of heavy duty lining paper.

Plastering grade boards have grey-coloured paper on both sides. They are used as a base for plastering over since they provide a ready-made flat background and cut down the drying out time of a plaster undercoat (new plaster can take several months to dry out fully). *Thistle Baseboard* is 9.7mm thick, 917mm wide with square edges and comes in lengths of about 1200mm. *Gyproc Lath* is narrower, 406mm wide, 12.7mm or 9.5mm thick with rounded edges and comes in lengths around 1200mm. Both types of board are used mainly for ceilings as the relatively small size of these boards allows them to take up movement of the timber joists to which they are attached and this reduces the chances of cracking at the joins between the boards. If the boards are fixed flush, only a single 5mm coat of plaster is needed. In some cases an undercoat of Carlite Bonding followed by Carlite Finish is required. Plastering grade boards are not all that widely available.

Dry lining boards (Gyproc wallboards) have ivory-coloured paper on one side and a grey backing paper on the other side. The ivory-coloured paper is intended for decorating directly with paint, wallpaper or textured wallcoating. Dry lining boards are much more widely available than plastering grade boards – and are frequently used for ceilings, especially in new houses, where the ivory coloured side is covered with textured wallcoating. The grey-coloured side can be used as a base for plastering, but there is a greater risk of cracking at the joins. Never attempt to plaster the ivory side – the plaster will fall off in time. The boards most frequently stocked in builders' merchants are 2400mm by 1200mm and 1800mm by 900mm in 12.7 or 9.5mm thickness with square or tapered edges. Tapered-edge boards form a shallow groove when butted together. This groove has to be filled by bedding in strengthening tape with joint filler and smoothing over with joint finish to give a smooth flush surface ready for painting.

Fixing plasterboards to ceilings

The easiest way to replace old lath and plaster is to use plasterboards. The thinner 9.5mm boards should be used only when the ceiling joists are less than 400mm apart, the 12.7mm thick boards can be used on joists up to 600mm apart. The boards should be arranged in a staggered pattern with the long edges of the boards at right angles to the joists. Noggins must be fixed between the joists to support the edges of the boards.

Use galvanised plasterboard nails to fix the boards – 30mm nails for 9.5mm boards and 40mm nails for 12.7mm boards – driven in until the paper surface of the board just starts to dimple. Avoid tearing the lining paper by nailing too hard. The nails should be spaced about 150mm apart along each joist and noggin but make sure that the nails are no less than 15mm from the edges of the boards. Nailing the boards takes two people – one to hold the board while the other starts nailing at the centre of the board and works outwards.

Plan the position of each board carefully – it helps to mark the position of each board on the joists. Plasterboards can be cut fairly easily with a trimming knife by scoring deeply through the lining paper on the side that is going to face the room. The board can then be broken over a straight-edge and the backing paper cut with a knife.

Fixing plasterboards to walls

The easiest way to fix plasterboards to walls is to first fix wooden battens – not less than 25mm wide and 20mm deep – to the wall and then nail the plasterboards to these. Fix the boards vertically with the battens spaced the same distance apart as ceiling joists. It helps if you fix horizontal battens about 25mm above floor level and about 25mm below ceiling height. The vertical battens can then be fixed in line using small wooden wedges between the wall and the battens. Extra battens can be fixed to the wall to support anything that is too heavy for the plasterboard – such as wall units.

All the plasterboard sheets must be positioned so that all joints lie along the battens. Cut the boards about 25mm shorter than the floor-to-ceiling height and lift them into position so that they press against the ceiling before nailing. Nail at least every 150mm along every batten. Where walls may suffer from damp, use vacuum-impregnated timber.

CHAPTER SIX

FLOORS

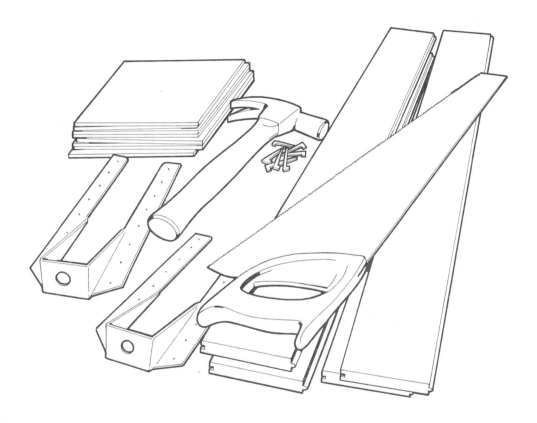

The majority of older houses in Britain have suspended timber floors (also known as hollow floors) in the ground floor rooms. However, during and after the Second World War, timber became scarce and restrictions were placed on its use and availability, so other forms of construction were employed. The solid floor was introduced as a suitable and economic alternative at ground level.

Suspended timber ground floors

A suspended timber ground floor consists of a number of timber boards – usually tongued-and-grooved – or sheets of man-made board such as chipboard or plywood, laid over and

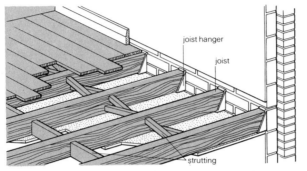

Suspended timber upper floor. This drawing shows joist hangers and the two types of strutting used – solid and herringbone

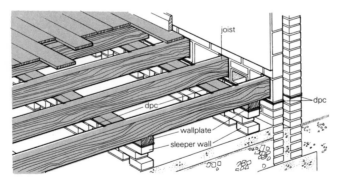

Suspended timber ground floor. Note the position of the dpcs

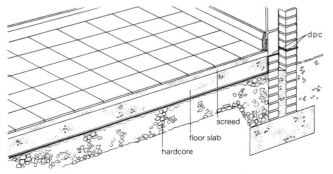

Solid ground floor finished with vinyl tiles on the floor screed.

supported by timber joists. The joists are roughly 400mm apart and are supported by 100mm × 50mm timber wallplates which are in turn supported by the main walls of the building, or by sleeper walls built up from a layer of concrete beneath the house, or by a combination of the two. To prevent the timber floor from absorbing any moisture, the wallplates are bedded on top of a suitable damp-proof course.

Suspended timber upper floors

Like suspended ground floors, upper floors consist of timber boards or sheets of man-made board laid over and supported by timber joists. Suspended timber floors which are not at ground level are often called single floors because the joists bridge a single span – they run from wall to wall.

As it is not possible to give additional support to upper floors by using sleeper walls, the joists of single floors are bigger than those of hollow ground floors and usually bridge the narrowest span – often across the narrowest part of the room. If the joists bridge spans greater than 4.5m, timber or steel cross-members (called binders) may be used to give intermediate support. Joists in a single floor tend to flex so rows of struts may be laid across the floor between the joists to make the floor stiffer.

The ends of the joists may be built into the walls, or supported by joist hangers built into or fixed on to the face of the wall. If the joist end is built into the wall, this part should be treated with preservative to protect it from decay.

The ceiling of the room underneath the floor is usually plasterboard, insulation board or tiles fixed to the underside of the joists. It may have a plaster 'skim' finish.

Solid ground floors

The cross-section of a solid floor consists of a number of layers of different materials – hardcore, blinding, damp-proof membrane, floor slab and screed.

The first layer is 100 to 150mm of consolidated **hardcore** composed of crushed stone and clean broken bricks. This is to level out any unevenness in the ground caused by the excavation and to provide a firm and level base for the floor slab.

A 50mm thick layer of fine ash, sand or weak mix concrete is laid over the hardcore to bind the surface. This **blinding** will also give a smooth even surface for laying the damp-proof membrane on. The damp-proof membrane should never be laid directly on to the hardcore – its sharp corners could puncture the membrane.

The **damp-proof membrane** may be placed above or below the floor slab. In the latter case, the dpm will keep the floor slab free from moisture. A wide range of materials are suitable as dpms: hot and cold poured bitumen, asphalt, epoxy pitch compounds and 1000 gauge polythene sheeting.

The **floor slab** (concrete) can vary in thickness from 100 to 150mm and have one or two layers of mesh reinforcement, depending on the area of the floor and its intended use. The concrete slab may have a cement **screed** laid over its surface, depending on what type of floor finish is to be used.

Restoring old wood floors

The floors of older houses often fall into poor repair through a lack of maintenance, through uneven wear, and as a result of decay and insect attack. The most common problems likely to be encountered are:

● a worn floor surface – usually unevenly – by abrasion from feet and furniture
● gaps between boards, split boards, and irregular and uneven floor surfaces caused by shrinkage
● gaps between boards and split boards from previous inferior repair work
● broken or split boards as a result of misuse
● split and broken boards through weakness due to insect or fungal attack.

Removing and replacing floorboards

It is often necessary to remove floorboards when installing or repairing central heating pipes, plumbing pipes and electrical wiring. You may also need to remove old, broken floorboards to repair the floor. The first thing to do is to turn off your electricity – just in case you cut through a cable. Then mark out carefully the area of flooring which is to be removed. The lines marking the area should run down the joints between the boards, across one end of the boards as close to the edge of a joist as possible (the first joist) and across the other end of the boards along the centre of a joist.

If none of the boards is loose, starting to lift the boards by cutting across the first one is the most difficult part of the operation. A floorboard saw will make the job easier. If you do not have one, bore a number of small holes close together along the line of the intended saw cut near the first joist. This will form a starter slot which is long enough to allow a padsaw blade to be inserted. Cut the board along the line as close to the edge of the joist as possible. If the floor is made of tongued-and-grooved boards, repeat the procedure along both edges of the board (along the board length) to remove the tongues – these would otherwise prevent easy removal of the board. Next insert a bolster chisel into the saw cut, lever up the end of the board and place a small piece of timber underneath the board across the gap in the floor. Raise the board and saw through the other end immediately over the centre of a joist (the second joist). When an end joint falls in the area to be removed, the board can be lifted at this point. Further boards can be lifted with ease – simply cut across the boards along the edge of the first joist, raise them and cut across the other end in line with the centre of the second joist.

When replacing the boards, screw a small batten on to the side of the first joist to support the ends of the boards.

If you are replacing the old boards with new ones, cut the new ones longer than the boards taken out – by half the width of a joist – and provide support for the ends of the new boards by cutting back the remaining boards to the centre of the first joist. But be careful – you need to use a chisel and this could be damaged if it comes into contact with the nails – you should remove the nails before attempting to cut back the boards.

Finally the old (or new) boards should be either nailed or screwed in place. If you think you may need to remove the boards again for access, or if hammering could damage the ceiling below, use screws to secure the boards in position.

Strengthening and replacing floor joists

The floor joists of older houses often sag under load and sometimes the floor becomes springy. These are symptoms of defects which are often caused by:
● overloading the floor
● joists which are too small for their span
● failure of the strutting in single floors
● collapsed sleeper walls
● weakening of the joists as a result of attack by woodworm or decay.
These problems can generally be put right by strengthening the floor joists but eradicate any woodworm or rot first.

REMOVING FLOORBOARDS

Make room for a padsaw by boring a number of small holes close together along the intended line of the saw cut

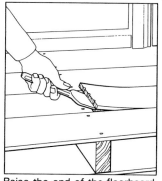

Raise the end of the floorboard by inserting a bolster chisel into the saw cut and using this as a lever

Support the end of the raised floorboard with a piece of wood – it must bridge the gap in the floor. Saw off the other end.

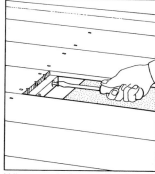

When replacing a floorboard, screw a batten on to the joist to support the end of the floorboard

Strengthening floor joists

A joist which is too small to support the loads it has to bear, or one which has been weakened – by woodworm attack, say – can be strengthened by attaching another new strong piece of timber to it. Attach the new joist to the existing one by bolts or by bolts and timber connectors. When fastening the two together, make sure that the new joist does not project above the level of the old joist – if it does, it will prevent you replacing the floor properly. In an unboarded loft it does not matter if the new joist projects above the existing ones. In a single floor, if the new joist projects below the existing ones, it could damage the ceiling.

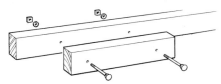

Strengthening a weakened joist

Replacing ground floor joists

Removing a floor joist in a ground floor is easier than removing one in a single floor: in a single floor the joists are invariably built into the main walls but in a ground floor they are nailed on top of wallplates.

Before you can start work on the joists, remove all the flooring and floorboards around them. This is quite a laborious task when you are faced with a large floor. The job can be shortened by sawing across the floorboards along the edges of the two joists adjacent to the area you want to remove. If you want to replace only part of a ground floor joist, remove only those floorboards above that section of the joist and between the two adjacent sleeper walls.

The next job is to cut the new joist to length, place it in position on the wallplates and nail it to them. Make sure that the replacement joist is exactly the same depth as the existing joists, otherwise it will produce an uneven base on which to lay the floorboards.

When replacing part of the joist, remove the defective section by sawing across the joist between the two adjacent wallplates. Cut the replacement joist long enough to overlap the ends of the existing joist and to rest on top of the two wallplates. Manoeuvre the joist into position and nail it down on to the wallplates and into the existing joist ends.

Before replacing the floorboards, screw lengths of batten to the side of the two adjacent joists – flush with the top edges. The floorboards can then be nailed or screwed to these battens.

Replacing floor joists in single floors

Remove the floorboards as necessary to expose the floor joists to be replaced. Then remove the corresponding area of the ceiling below. If you take a lot of care over replacing the joist, it may be possible to do it without removing the ceiling.

But if the ceiling is constructed from plasterboard, you should expect it to suffer damage.

Next remove the floor joist by sawing through the joist at an angle – this will let you extract the ends of the joist from the walls.

Cut the new joist to length – the distance between the two supporting walls plus the amount the timber can be inserted into *one* of the holes in the walls. (This should be at least 150mm – roughly 115mm of brickwork and 50mm of cavity.) Next, push one end of the new joist into one of the holes. Make sure that you push it as far as it will go. It should then be possible to insert the other end of the joist into the hole in the opposite wall. Adjust the position of the joist so that its weight (and the loads the joist will have to take) is supported equally between both walls. Failure to do this may result in one end of the joist coming adrift from the wall.

Older houses often have solid walls and for these the sliding method of inserting the joist – described above – is not practical. With solid walls you will have to chase out the wall above the hole to allow the joist to drop down on to the brickwork. Alternatively, you could brick up the holes and fix two joist hangers into or on to the face of the wall – then simply cut the joist to length and drop it into position on the hangers.

Finally replace the floorboards and ceiling.

REPLACING FLOOR JOISTS

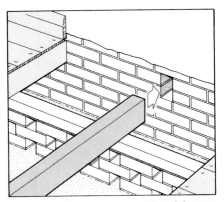

When inserting a new ground floor joist, use pieces of slate to pack it up to the level of the other joists

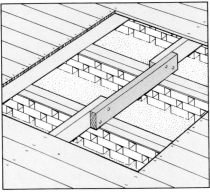

Bolt on a new section of joist as shown – allow good overlap between old and new

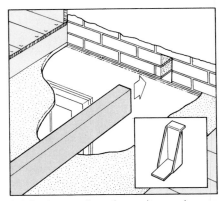

A joist hanger (insert) may be used as an alternative way of supporting the end of a joist

Putting in a solid floor

Suspended timber floors in ground floor rooms of older houses are subject to rot or woodworm attack, especially if the house was built without a damp-proof course or with an inadequate one (many cheaper old cottages were built with tar-sand dpcs which are no longer effective). Many of these houses were also built with brick-on-earth floors in kitchens and larders; these are often damp and may have become uneven through settlement. Either type may be replaced, in most cases, with a solid concrete floor – a straightforward job for a moderately confident do-it-yourselfer. A solid floor is also the simplest and most economic choice for a new extension.

What you need

A cross-section of a solid concrete floor is described on page 180.

For a sub-base use one of the following materials: hoggin (sandy clay), broken stone, well-burnt clinker or crushed clean hardcore. For deeper fill, such as when replacing a suspended floor, rejects (oversized stones from a gravel pit) or clean building rubble may be used. When replacing a suspended timber floor the fill needs to be fairly thick, but under an extension floor it needs only to be thick enough to replace stripped topsoil and to bring the level up to that desired. The existing soil under a brick-on-earth floor is normally adequate for a sub-base.

For binding use a layer of sand or hoggin spread over the hardcore.

For a damp-proof membrane use 1000 gauge polythene or Bituthene sheet. If you put the damp-proof membrane (dpm) under the main floor slab it will allow you to use a bonded floor screed which will, in turn, minimize the risk of subsequent failure. The dpm should be continuous with tightly interfolded and lapped joints and should link up with the damp-proof course in the walls; if there is no dpc as such, or if an injected dpc has been used, carry the dpm up the walls behind the skirting boards.

For a floor slab use C20P concrete, medium workability, with 20mm maximum-sized coarse aggregate – see page 158. Use a thickness of at least 100mm.

For a screed use a layer of sand-cement mortar, trowelled or floated to a smooth, level finish. If the screed is to be bonded to the floor slab concrete, the thickness should be 40mm; if the damp-proof membrane is to be located between the slab and the screed, the thickness should not be less than 60mm – this will allow pipes and cables to be buried in the screed without harming the dpm.

Replacing a suspended ground floor

Replacing a suspended floor with a solid one is generally a fairly straightforward job. However, if the depth of fill required exceeds about 600mm, or if there is a marked variation in the fill depth across the floor area, do not use a solid floor. If your house is on clay soil consult your local Building Control Officer before putting in a solid floor.

When the need arises to put a solid floor in a ground floor room, it is a good idea to replace all the ground floors at the same time, even if the floors in other rooms are in good condition: otherwise the remaining area may need improved underfloor ventilation. Again, ask a surveyor or a Building Control Officer.

Laying the foundations
Remove all timber including wallplates and sills and break up any intermediate sleeper walls or supporting pillars. If there is any sign of organic growth on the underfloor soil, sterilize it with Jeyes fluid or something similar.

Check with water, gas and electricity authorities about any special treatment of underfloor service pipes: a gas pipe on the mains side of the meter, for example, is the property of the Gas Region. Attend to any necessary electrical rewiring – run any underfloor wires through conduit. Central heating and hot water pipes should be lagged.

Put in the fill material (hardcore) layer by layer and compact it thoroughly between layers. When using building rubble, bed each layer – including the bottom one – in a layer of hoggin: break up any large pieces with a sledgehammer to avoid leaving large air pockets. When the fill reaches the level required, break up any rough patches or sharp corners with a sledgehammer and then blind the surface with sand or hoggin.

PREPARING FOR A SOLID FLOOR

The hardcore foundation for a solid floor must be laid in layers and well compacted. Break up any large pieces to avoid leaving air pockets

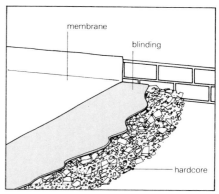

The damp-proof membrane should be laid on top of a layer of sand or hoggin, carried well up the wall and tucked neatly into corners

Spread the damp-proof membrane sheeting carefully, smoothing out any wrinkles and lapping and taping joints. Carry the dpm sheeting well up the wall (it can be trimmed later) but make sure it is well tucked into corners; otherwise voids will be left when the slab is laid.

Laying the floor slab

Before starting the floor slab, mark out the level of the top at several points around the room. Unlike laying an outdoor ground slab – see page 163 – you will not be working to formwork, so you will need to check against these level references as you go.

Lay concrete in strips as wide as you can conveniently compact with a length of 50×100mm timber – about 1200mm is a reasonable width. Spread the concrete with a rake to about 15mm above the desired level and tamp thoroughly. Start in the corners of the room, working around the walls first and then filling in the centre working towards a doorway. Check levels with a straight-edge and spirit level: ignore minor variations as they will be taken out by the screed.

As soon as the concrete has hardened enough to walk on (if you put a sheet of ply over the top of it you can walk on this after a few hours) brush the surface with a stiff broom while washing it down with a sprinkling rose on a watering can. This will remove fine material from the surface and leave it ready for a bonded

screed. Cure the slab under plastic sheeting for three or four days.

Laying the screed

This last step is crucial to the success of the floor, so take care with it. The screed mix depends on the final floorcovering. For carpet, lino or vinyl floor tiles, use 1 part loose cement to 2⅔ parts (clean, washed) damp concreting (sharp) sand. For rigid concrete terrazzo or quarry tiles, use 1 part loose cement to 3⅓ parts damp concreting sand. Do not use bricklayers' (builders' or soft) sand. If possible, use a machine to mix the screed: a pan-type mixer is preferable to the ordinary tilting-drum type. When mixing by hand, make sure the materials are mixed dry at least three times before adding water: all the sand particles should be completely coated with cement paste before use.

Getting the water content right is the crucial step in preparing a good screed mix: if it is too wet, the levels will be difficult to control; if it is too dry, it will be impossible to compact the screed sufficiently. To check the mix, press a ball of it in your hand. With a good mix only a drop or two of water will be squeezed out and the mix should hold together in a ball when your hand is opened again – it should not crumble.

To bond the screed to the main floor slab, the surface of the slab must be absolutely clean. If the slab was not

roughened by brushing it before it hardened (as described above) it will have to be mechanically roughened to expose the aggregate. Recheck levels and establish level references around the walls.

The first step in actually laying the screed is to dampen the floor with water and brush in a cement-water grout, about the consistency of double cream. A bonding compound can be added to the grout. Styrene-butadiene rubber (sbr) compounds can be used anywhere but polyvinyl acetate (pva) bonding agents should not be used where the floor is likely to get wet.

Do not grout too much of the floor at once – the area you can cover with the screed in twenty minutes is enough. Use a spirit level and straight-edge to set up screeding rails in strips of well-compacted screed mix: timber battens will do but lengths of angle or T-iron are better. Spread the screeding material 5 to 7mm above the required level and tamp really thoroughly: use a flat-bottomed punner, a roller or a timber tamping beam. Be careful not to disturb the level of the screeding rails during compaction. When the screeding material has been thoroughly compacted, remove any excess material by moving the tamping beam in a sawing motion across the screeding rails. If there is no excess, you have used too little screed; add more material, compact and strike off again.

Finish the surface with a wood float as you proceed. Remove the screeding rails as the work advances, filling in the depressions with well compacted and floated screed material. Work in strips around the room but remember to end up near the door out of the room.

As soon as the screed has hardened enough for you to walk on it, spread plastic sheeting over the surface and leave it in place for at least four days.

Replacing a brick-on-earth floor

When replacing a damp or uneven brick-on-earth floor, follow the procedure given for replacing a timber floor but be prepared to dig out some sub-base material to preserve existing levels. The same technique can be used to lower the floor of an old cottage with a low ceiling,

LAYING THE SLAB

Start laying the concrete solid floor in the corners of the room. Spread the concrete evenly with rake to about 15mm above its final level

Tamp the concrete thoroughly but remember to check levels using a spirit level and a straight-edge – minor level variations can be ignored

provided that in lowering the floor you do not undercut the wall foundations or go below ground level and the dpc.

New floors for extensions

Some types of extension, such as lightweight sunrooms, conservatories or kitchen extensions, require only a plain ground slab – see page 163; the only difference is that you will need a damp-proof membrane under the slab and probably a screed (not essential if you can directly finish the concrete to the required surface during construction). The dpm should be laid so that it comes up around the edges of the slab.

If the extension is substantial enough to require strip or trench-fill foundations, build the walls up to dpc level. Prepare the soil between the foundations exactly as for a ground slab: some filling will probably be needed. Lay a dpm as a *tray* linking into the dpc of the walls. Construct the floor slab as for an outdoor ground slab – using the walls as formwork and exposing the aggregate during finishing. Lay the screed when the extension is finished.

Putting the floor into use

When an impervious flooring material such as vinyl tiles, lino or carpet bonded with adhesive is to be used, allow the floor to dry out thoroughly before covering it. Otherwise the floor covering is likely to lift. The Building Research Establishment recommends a drying period of one month for each 25mm of floor thickness: for a 100mm slab with a 40mm screed this means nearly six months before adhesive-bonded flooring can be laid (mortar-bedded concrete or quarry tiles can be laid after a couple of weeks). The drying-out time can be reduced by placing the damp-proof membrane between the slab and the screed, but this increases the risk of screed failure; in any case the thicker screed required (at least 60mm) means waiting two and a half to three months.

A well-laid screed of good mix proportions should be strong enough for use within a couple of weeks of laying. Meanwhile, sheets of plywood or hardboard laid over the surface will protect it. During the drying-out period do not drag furniture over the surface and support furniture on feet clear of the floor. Open-textured rugs or matting can be used to protect the surface from foot traffic. Minor damage which cannot be covered with a self-levelling compound can be made good with mortar.

LAYING THE SCREED

Dampen the floor and brush in cement-water grout – this should be about the consistency of double cream

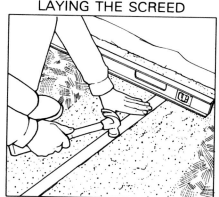

Timber battens can be used as screeding rails. These should be laid in strips of well-compacted screed mix

Spread the screed 5 to 7mm above its final level and tamp it thoroughly – a flat-bottomed punner is used here

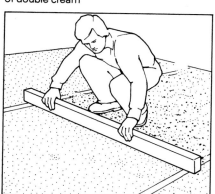

To remove excess screed, use a sawing action with a tamping beam resting on the screeding rails

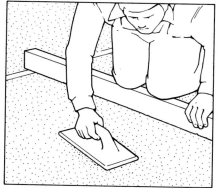

Use a wood float to give the surface a smooth finish and remove the screeding rails as you proceed

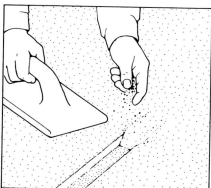

Depressions left by removing the screeding rails should be filled with well-compacted screed mix and levelled

Laying a chipboard floor

A wide range of flooring grade of chip-boards is available: ask a local timber merchant for information about the variations in surface finish, edge finish – and the size of sheets available. The sheet used most widely measures 1220×2440mm and is 18mm thick. It has either a square or tongued-and-grooved edge – the latter is the better of the two for flooring. Sheets of tongued-and-grooved chipboard are also available in widths which are likely to pass through the opening in a loft.

When replacing a suspended floor, the first job is to strip off all the original flooring and clean off the joists. The centre of the joists in houses are usually just over 405mm apart – convenient for laying 1220×2440mm sheets.

The next step is to provide support for the edges of the chipboard sheets by inserting noggins between the joists around the perimeter of the floor. If square-edge boards are used, it is necessary to insert noggins over the central part of the floor wherever the edge of a sheet will be unsupported.

The joins in the floor should be staggered to provide a stiff floor. The easiest and most economic way of doing this is to start every other row with a half sheet of chipboard and then use full sheets to fill in the rest of the floor area. Square-edged sheets should run with their longest edge along the joist. Tongued-and-grooved sheets should run with their longest edge across the joists.

When starting to lay the sheets, make sure that the joints between sheets will run along the centre of the supports (or joists) and will fit tight to one another. The sheet can be fixed either with lost head nails or with countersunk screws. Calculate the length of nail or screw needed by multiplying the thickness of the chipboard by 2½. Insert the fixings in a regular pattern from 200 to 300mm apart around all the edges of the sheets and from 400 to 500mm apart along the intermediate joists.

Think about access panels and traps in the floor for things like water taps and central heating pipes. These are best built into the floor when it is being laid – though small traps can be cut out afterwards with a padsaw. Position access panels so that two edges are supported by joists. Then fix noggins across the joists to support the other two edges. When the trap is cut out after the floor has been laid, screw a batten to each joist and insert noggins between them to support all four edges of the trap. Access panels and traps should be screwed in position so that they can be removed.

Once the floor is down, punch all the nails 2 to 3mm below the floor and make sure that all screws are sunk into the chipboard.

LAYING A CHIPBOARD FLOOR

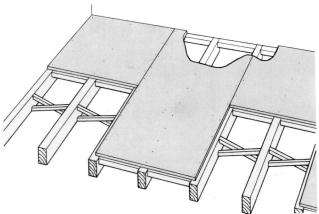

Square-edged flooring chipboard laid along the joists – note the staggered joints. The drawing shows 1220 x 2440mm chipboard laid along joists which are just over 600mm apart

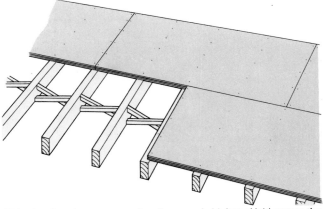

This drawing shows tongued-and-grooved chipboard laid across the joists, which are again 600mm apart – 405mm is more likely in practice

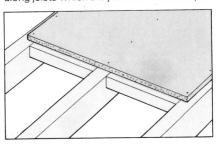

Noggins used to support the edges of square-edged chipboard

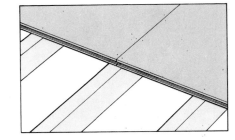

The joints of tongued-and-grooved sheets of chipboard do not need additional support

Stairs

A staircase should be designed to allow safe and easy movement from one level of a house to another. So:
● it should be of sound construction
● the angle of the stair should not be too shallow or too steep
● the length of each flight should not be excessive
● each step should have the same *rise* and *going*
● each step should be parallel and of a uniform width which is adequate for the use of the stairs.
● there should be sufficient headroom above the stair to allow unimpeded passage
● it should have handrails to assist people ascending and descending the stair; handrails should also be provided along with balusters to protect open sides of the stair
● it should be well lit.

Stair construction

A staircase has three major components – strings, treads and risers. The whole assembly is held together by wedges and glue blocks.

The **strings** are the main structural members which run up each side of the treads and risers, from the lower floor or landing to the *trimming joist* on the upper floor or landing.

The **treads** are the horizontal parts of the stair you step on when ascending and descending it.

The vertical member between each tread is called a **riser**. The riser closes the opening between the treads and lends support to the stair as a whole.

The steps formed by the treads and risers are tongued-and-grooved together, fixed to the strings and held in position by wedges.

A **closed-string** staircase has its steps housed into grooves cut in the inside faces of the strings. The tops of the strings are straight.

An **open-string** staircase has the tops of the strings cut away following the shape of the steps. Many homes have a staircase which is a combination of the two styles – a closed string along a wall and an open string on the other side.

The stair is held in position by screwing it to the wall through the wall string below the level of the treads and risers; by screwing it to the trimming joist at the top; and by screwing timbers to the floor and strings at the bottom of the stair.

Staircases with at least one open string can usually be repaired from above. Those with two closed strings – staircases between two walls, say – usually have to be repaired from below.

Reports in Handyman Which?

Flooring   May 1976

STAIR CONSTRUCTION

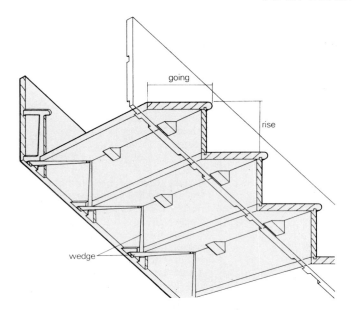

A staircase viewed from beneath showing wedges, glue blocks and housings for the treads and risers. Some stairs have an extra support running along the underneath of the stairs

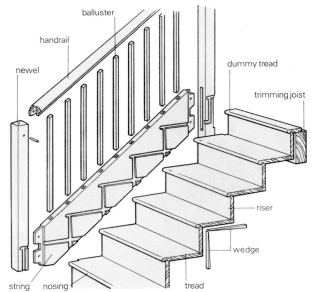

An exploded view of a typical staircase showing details of the haunched tenon joints between the strings and the newels

Curing defects

The main defects found in timber stairs are: worn treads and nosings, creaking steps and loose, cracked and broken balusters and handrails.

Worn treads are often the result of leaving the stair uncovered – no carpet. The wear is usually on the edge of the nosing. Repair is simple – cut out the worn section and splice in a new section. The section of timber removed should be about 50mm wide so that the replacement can be glued and screwed securely to the existing tread and riser.

Creaking steps may be caused by a number of things. The most common are loose or missing glue blocks, loose wedges, and a defective joint between a tread and the bottom of a riser. Staircases over 900mm wide often creak because the centres of the wide steps are not supported well enough. To identify the cause (or causes) of the problem, examine the underside of the staircase.

First check all the glue blocks to make sure that they are in position and securely fixed to both the tread and the riser. Replace any loose or missing glue blocks with new ones. There should be at least three glue blocks underneath each tread.

Now check all the wedges to see if they have worked loose as a result of shrinkage. Any loose wedges should be glued and rewedged. Sometimes it is necessary to recut the wedges so that you can hammer them further in.

When it is impossible to gain access to the underside of the stair to carry out repairs to loose or missing glue blocks, it is often possible to eliminate the creaking by driving screws down through the tread into the top of the riser.

Occasionally the joint between the tread and the bottom of a riser comes apart. This can be fixed by driving screws up through the underside of the tread into the riser – three equally-spaced screws are usually sufficient to prevent the joint from coming apart again.

Missing, broken or loose handrails are extremely dangerous and should receive immediate attention.

Small cracks in handrails can be repaired by squeezing glue into the crack and clamping the parts together in position. With large cracks and breaks it may be necessary to insert a length of dowel as well. When it is necessary to replace a section of a handrail, fix the new length to the existing handrail either by splicing them together and using dowels or by joining them together with handrail bolts and dowels.

Cracked and broken balusters can be repaired by gluing them together or by splicing them together with new timber. Obtaining replacements for the decorative balusters often found on older staircases can be quite difficult. So, it may be necessary to repair even the most badly damaged baluster. New ones can be made but this is expensive.

REPAIRS TO STAIRS

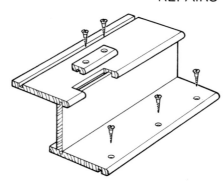

Nosing can be repaired by inserting a new section. Screwing a tread to a riser may stop squeaks

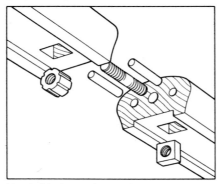

Handrail bolts can be used to connect a new section of handrail. The dowels stop the rail rotating around the bolt

---

STAIRCASE TERMS

The terms below are used when discussing stairs but may differ from area to area.

Apron A board used to cover the edge of the floor or landing and to provide a neat finish to the side of the trimming joist.

Balusters The vertical members which run between the string and the handrail. They provide support for the handrail and protect the open side of the stair.

Balustrade The combination of string, newels, balusters and handrail forming the side of the staircase.

Flight A continuous run of steps from floor to floor, landing to landing or floor to landing.

Glue blocks Small triangular pieces of timber that are glued in the corner of the tread and riser underneath the stairs.

Going The distance between the face of two consecutive risers.

Handrail A rail at the side of a staircase to help people ascend and descend safely.

Landing A small platform between two flights to allow a change of direction in the staircase.

Newel A large timber member at the ends of the string which supports the handrail.

Nosing The moulded front edge of a tread which projects over the face of the riser below it.

Rise The distance between the tops of two adjacent treads.

Riser The vertical member in a step.

Step A combination of tread and riser.

String The vertical member on the side of the staircase that supports the treads and risers.

Total going The distance between the faces of the top and bottom risers or the edges of the top and bottom nosings.

Total rise The distance between the finished floor or landing levels through which the staircase rises.

Tread The horizontal member in a step.

Flooring

Although carpet is a very popular floorcovering for living rooms and bedrooms, there are many other flooring materials which may be more suitable for other rooms. Each type has its own particular properties – how hard-wearing it is, stain and dust resistance, ease of laying and so on.

To see a flooring material to its best advantage it must be laid on a sub-floor which is sound and flat.

Linoleum is available in either tile or sheet form. It is generally very hard-wearing, though it does not take kindly to much water getting down cracks – in the tiles, say – and underneath it. Linoleum is a bit difficult to handle and lay, and comes in a restricted range of not very exciting colours. It is now rarely laid in private houses.

Cushioned vinyl sheet is probably the most popular type of sheet flooring used today. It consists of a printed pattern sandwiched between a vinyl backing layer below and a thin clear vinyl wear layer on top. Beneath the backing layer is a layer of soft foam – to make the material softer to walk on, and to take up slight irregularities in the sub-floor. Many bright patterns and colours (including embossed effects) are available. The material is generally a good choice for bathrooms and kitchens – though it is important not to let water get down between seams. It cannot tolerate very hot things, such as lighted cigarettes and hot coals from a solid-fuel boiler, and it is not very suitable for rooms with underfloor central heating. Because the wear layer above the printed pattern is very thin, its life is relatively short (five years or so).

Unbacked vinyl usually comes in printed sheet form, with a clear wear layer above the pattern. It shares most of the other characteristics of cushioned vinyl, too – except that it is less comfortable to walk on, and may be more slippery when wet. It should tolerate underfloor heating.

Solid vinyl almost always comes in tile form. The wear layer extends the full thickness of the material – so durability is much better than the two vinyls above, though it is not as comfortable as cushioned vinyl, and is more slippery when wet. A range of plain and mottled colours is available. Some brands are self-adhesive, which makes laying easier.

Vinyl asbestos tiles are like solid vinyl tiles, but contain a much greater proportion of filler material; have little flexibility; and on a less than perfect sub-floor may be more prone to cracking. However, they are tolerant to water spillages, and can even cope with slightly damp sub-floors. Underfloor heating can soften the tiles if it is hot.

Clay tiles are usually either glazed ceramic floor tiles or clay floor quarry tiles. Glazed ceramic tiles are available in a range of patterns, colours and shapes. Quarries come in a limited range of red and brown shades, the tiles are square and are usually rougher in shape and finish than glazed ceramics.

Clay tiles are extremely durable, but are noisy and cold underfoot and slippery when wet, unless special slip-resistant ones are used. A damp-proof course may not be needed – but it is still a good idea.

Cork tiles are very comfortable, but not very durable. For kitchens and bathrooms, it is probably best to use un-finished tiles. These have to be sanded and then sealed with coats of polyurethane sealer – this will prevent water getting down between the tiles. Pre-finished tiles are easier to lay, but do not have this advantage. Cork tiles covered with a thin vinyl wear layer are also available but these are less durable.

Wood makes a very attractive and fairly comfortable floor. Wood generally has good durability, though it is not very tolerant to water. Perhaps the most popular type for domestic use is the *wood mosaic panel* – small strips of wood built up in a basket-weave pattern to form a panel about 18in square and stuck to a bitumen felt backing. *Overlay strip* flooring looks like superior, narrow floorboards. *Blocks* can be laid in the traditional herringbone parquet flooring pattern. Most wood flooring is solid hardwood – some types have a thin hardwood layer bonded to a plywood backing. Even these types are unlikely to wear away with normal domestic use.

Sheet or tile?

With vinyl flooring there is often a choice between sheet or tiles. Both types have advantages and disadvantages.

Sheet flooring is available in widths up to 12ft (for imperial sizes) or 4m (for metric), so whole floors can usually be covered without unsightly joins. A wide range of patterns is available – some of them imitating tiles. Wide sheet flooring is rather difficult to get home, and to lay – though specially flexible, foldable, types are available. A mistake in cutting to size can prove very expensive and with irregular shapes a lot of material may be wasted.

Tiles are relatively easy to lay, and mistakes in cutting usually waste only a single tile. The odd tile which gets damaged in use can be replaced. But the range of patterns and colours may not be so great, and there are many cracks, through which dirt and water can seep.

Laying flooring

Preparation of the sub-floor which is to receive the floor covering is vitally important. Aim for a perfectly dry, level firm base.

Wooden sub-floors Go over the surface carefully, nailing or screwing down loose boards, and then smoothing the surface – with hand tools if the boards are reasonably level; with a power floor sander if the boards are very uneven.

Unless the floor is then very flat, with no gaps between the boards, it should be covered with sheets of hardboard, laid rough side up (unless the floor covering manufacturer recommends smooth side up) and nailed all over at 150mm intervals with ring-shank or annular nails (or hardboard nails). For ceramic tiles, use chipboard or 9mm plywood.

Solid sub-floors Slight rising damp can be held at bay by coating the floor with an epoxy pitch waterproofer: for badly damp floors, the only real remedy is to dig it up and to relay it incorporating a damp-proof membrane.

Slightly uneven solid floors can be levelled off using a self-levelling compound (or underlayment). A badly bumpy floor will need to be relaid.

Sheet flooring

A couple of days before laying sheet vinyl put it in the room you want to lay it in. Then loose-lay the floor covering, leaving it overlapping at joints and up the wall. The vinyl will probably shrink and after a week or two, it can be trimmed to fit the room. It is possible to crease the material into the edges at the walls, and cut along the crease with a sharp trimming knife, but an easier method is shown in the diagrams.

If you have to have joints between sheets, cut through both thicknesses as they overlap using a sharp knife against a steel straight-edge. Then remove the waste from both the bottom and top sheets, and the cut edges should butt together perfectly. With patterned material, this technique will work only if the material has a selvedge or 'trimming edge', otherwise you will ruin the continuity of the pattern.

Some sheet vinyl is designed to be loose-laid – and it is hardly worth sticking down the cheapest printed vinyls. Other types should be stuck down all over using if possible the adhesive recommended by the manufacturer. Smooth out the sheet as you lay – 'ironing' it with a sand-filled bag may help.

For fitting flooring round complicated obstructions, it may be useful to make a paper template first.

Tiles

Vinyl and cork tiles It is usual to start laying tiles from the middle of the room: this way, it is easier to cope with the inevitable irregular edges. Start by laying a tight string from the middle of one wall to the middle of the opposite wall; repeat with the other two walls. Loose-lay some tiles along one string from wall to wall, starting where the strings cross and butt the tiles up closely. Aim to have a nearly full-size tile at both edges: shift the tiles along the string and remove one if necessary to achieve this. Repeat along the other string. When you are satisfied with the layout, start sticking the tiles down, following the manufacturer's instructions and adhesive recommendations. Cut tiles to fit along edges – for complicated shapes, make a template.

Unfinished cork tiles need sanding (hand sanding should be sufficient), carefully wiping clean to get rid of all the dust, and then sealing – with a polyurethane seal, for example.

Wood mosaic tiles Most wood mosaic tiles or panels can be set out and stuck down using the procedure described for vinyl tiles: panels can be cut with a fine-toothed saw. One type of panel has tongued-and-grooved edges – these should be loose-laid on an underlay of cork (on wood floors, a hardboard underlay may not be necessary).

In most cases, a small expansion gap has to be left round the edges of the room: this can be filled in with a cork strip, or covered with beading.

Wood strip overlay Wood strip is tongued-and-grooved. On timber sub-floors, it can be secret nailed (you nail through the tongue of one piece, so that the groove of the next hides the nail).

The bottoms of doors usually have to be cut to allow for the extra thickness of the overlay. Tapered fillets, called 'diminishing strips', can be fitted to make a neat join in doorways.

Clay tiles Ceramic tiles can be laid using modern thin-bed adhesives. The technique is much the same as wall tiling, though it is better not to use a notched adhesive spreader. Ordinary tile cutters can be used, though a masonry disc in an electric drill may be easier. A grouting joint has to be left, but as floor tiles rarely have spacer lugs, you will have to improvise.

Quarry tiles are usually laid on a thick (15mm) bed of mortar cement.

LAYING FLOORING

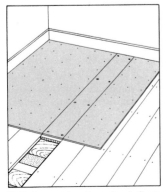

Nail down a hardboard sub-floor (150mm between nails). Cut and screw down separate strips for access to pipes and so on

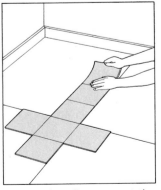

When laying tiles, start at the middle of the room and loose lay some of the tiles before sticking them down

To mark sheets make a mark as shown, pull the flooring from the wall and use a batten to mark the cutting line

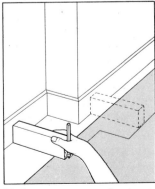

Mark corners – near fireplaces, say – first by using a pencil at the end of a batten and pushing it around the wall

CHAPTER SEVEN

ROOFS

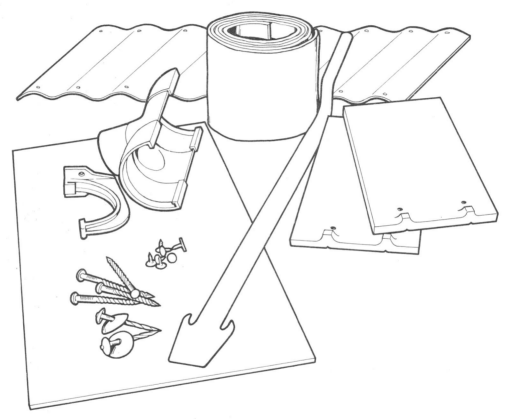

The roofs of houses, garages and extensions are generally either flat, lean-to or pitched. The differences in construction are discussed below.

Flat roof This type of roof is very simple to construct and is often used on small extensions and garages. A flat roof basically consists of a series of timber rafters supporting boarding (or chipboard) covered with layers of bituminous felt bonded together to make the roof waterproof. The rafters are supported at each end on wall plates and the roof is built at a slight angle so that rain-water can run off into a gutter.

Lean-to roof This is the simplest kind of pitched roof and is often known as a monopitch roof. It is widely used on conservatories, verandahs, porches and garages built against the side wall of a house. If the roof is tiled, rafters run up the roof and support boards or tiling battens placed across the rafters; if the roof is covered with corrugated sheets, purlins are fixed longitudinally. Both types of roof are supported at the foot by a timber wall plate and at the head by another timber plate fixed to the wall of the main building.

Pitched roof Most house roofs are pitched at an angle on both sides of a central ridge. This sort of roof has rafters running from the wall plates on either side of the roof to the ridge. Purlins are used to give additional support to the rafters and are themselves often supported on load-bearing internal walls. If a roof has a very small span, it may not have purlins. The ceiling joists act as cross ties to stop the weight of the roof covering (which bears on the rafters) thrusting the exterior walls outwards. Binders are placed across the ceiling joists and are suspended from hangers.

As an alternative to this traditional construction, the roof may have prefabricated roof trusses erected without a ridge. Each rafter section is formed using special gang-nail plates and braced with longitudinal binders and diagonal braces.

TYPES OF ROOF CONSTRUCTION

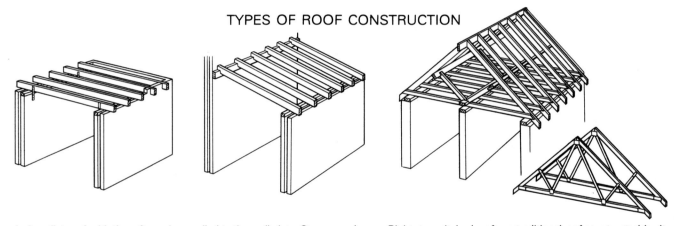

Left: a flat roof with the rafters skew nailed to the wall plate. Straps are used to fix the rafters to the brickwork. Middle: a lean-to roof with the rafters at one end let into a timber wall plate bolted to the house. Right: two pitched roofs – a traditional roof constructed *in situ* and a modern factory-built trussed roof section

SAFETY WARNINGS

Repairing a roof or chimney stack can be a hazardous business for you – because you are working off the ground – and for others below who may be injured by falling tiles, tools and so on.

You can work at roof level – repairing barge boards, fascia boards and soffit boards – and gain access to the roof by using a ladder. It should extend at least three rungs above gutter level and should be tied securely to a hook screwed into the fascia board or exposed rafter ends. However it is usually much safer – particularly when working on high roofs – to work off scaffolding tied securely to the building.

Never attempt to walk directly on the covering of a pitched roof: it may be slippery due to moss growing on it; the battens supporting it may be rotten; the valley boards may be rotten beneath the covering; and you may damage the roof. Always lay a ladder or crawling board across the roof – this should have a stout hook on one end which you can hook over the ridge of the roof. Always make sure that tools and materials are secure so that they cannot slide down the face of the roof on to passers-by. Take similar precautions when working on a slate roof from inside the loft. It is a good idea to station someone outside to make sure that nobody strays into the danger zone.

When walking across a flat roof never assume that the underlying boarding is sound. Try not to walk on the stone chips in hot weather – your weight may be enough to make any sharp-edged chips puncture the layers of felt and bitumen.

Repairing a flat roof

All roof faults should be attended to immediately they are noticed. If not, the damage to the fabric of the roof will rapidly get worse and worse, turning a minor repair into a major one. This is particularly true for flat roofs.

The waterproof covering is usually three layers of bituminous felt laid on the roof boarding. The first layer is attached with clout nails. The two subsequent layers are bonded to the one beneath using either bitumastic (also called cold mastic and mastic bitumen) which is applied cold or a bitumen-based solid compound which has to be turned into a liquid by heating it before it can be applied. The bituminous material is poured on to the underlying felt and spread evenly. The second layer of felt is bedded into the bitumen compound, another layer of bitumen compound is applied and more felt. The compound hardens when it cools. All joints are overlapped rather than butted and are arranged so that the joints in each layer do not coincide. A final covering of stone chippings is spread over the roof and bonded to the felt with a chipping compound. The chippings reflect solar rays which would otherwise cause the felt and bitumen to degrade and fail prematurely.

The joint between the house wall and the roof is sealed with a flashing of felt mortared into the wall and stuck to the roof felt.

If a felt-covered flat roof starts to leak, it could be an isolated problem with most of the roof still in good condition or it could be the first sign that the whole covering is on its last legs and will soon need replacing. The first thing to do is to inspect the surface of the roof closely. It is often difficult to pinpoint the exact point of failure of a flat roof – any water which has penetrated the felt covering may have run some way along the roof timbers before finding its way between joints in the boards and appearing on the ceiling below.

If moisture has got beneath a section of the roof, the felt covering may have bubbled and burst through the action of

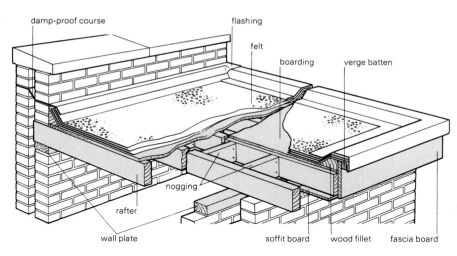

The drawing above shows a typical flat roof. The wall plates measure about 100 × 50mm: the house wall plate is fixed in place with rag bolts, the others are bedded into mortar on top of the walls. The rafters (also 100 × 50mm) are about 450mm apart and are nailed to the side wall plate and are usually nailed and half lapped into the house wall plate. The noggings are approximately 600mm apart. End rafters are nailed to the noggings so that the rafters overlap the ends of the roof. Fascia boards are nailed to the projecting ends of the rafters, and soffit boards to the projecting underside

heat expanding the moisture. In this case, a simple repair may be all that is needed – cut the bubble and open it out to allow all the trapped moisture to evaporate. Brush a layer of cold bitumastic compound on to the boards of the roof and then fold the edges of the bubble back into place and bed them into the compound. Spread a layer of bitumastic compound over the surface and spread a layer of chippings on top of it.

But, if the surface is showing signs of general failure, you have two options:
● completely strip and recover the roof, or
● apply a waterproof covering all over the surface.

Stripping and recovering

This can be done professionally – usually by a roofing contractor – or you can do it yourself. Contractors nearly always use a hot bonding method; if you are doing it yourself, a cold bonding method is much simpler.

First, block off any gutter outlets with old rags, then remove any defective flashings (materials used to weatherproof a junction – usually between a roof and a wall) and the old roofing felt. Flashings in good condition can be folded upwards away from the roofing felt. Inspect the wood surface, repair and replace boards and rafters as necessary, plane down any raised board edges and punch down any protruding nail heads.

Sweep the roof clean and start laying the new felt at the centre of the gutter edge. Roofing felt consists of two or three layers of fibrous material which is impregnated with, and bonded together by, a liquid bitumen. Before fitting new felt consult your local Building Control Officer – the types of felt which can be used on a flat roof are controlled by the Building Regulations. Allow an overlap at the gutter edge and fix the strip of felt to the roof at roughly 150mm intervals in both directions: nail from the centre of the felt outwards. Lay and nail down the rest of the first layer overlapping the strips by about 50mm.

DEALING WITH THE ROOF EDGES

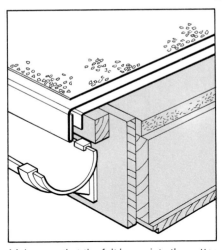

Make sure that the felt hangs into the gutter so that rain-water will not run down the fascia. The batten positions the edge of the felt over the gutter

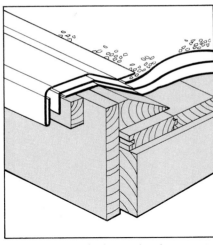

A wood fillet can be inserted at the verge to prevent rain-water running off the roof. The verge felt is fixed after the main roofing felt

The roofing felt should be cut just short of the top of the wood fillet so that the flashing felt overlaps it and forms a watertight joint

At any exposed edges, cut the first layer of felt flush with the inside edge of the verge batten.

If the verge has a triangular fillet of wood inserted to prevent rain-water running off the edge of the roof, this technique may have to be modified – see drawing above.

At the junction of the flat roof with a house wall there should be a triangular fillet of wood – if there is not, put one in. The felt should be cut just short of the top of the fillet. Any corners on the roof surface should be overlapped – cut paper templates before cutting the felt.

At the gutter fascia cut a piece of felt about 250mm wide, nail it to the gutter fascia about 20mm from the top, fold it up over itself and stick it to the felt on top of the roof. Make sure that the folded felt is big enough to sit well inside the gutter when you replace it – so that all the rain-water shed by the roof goes into the gutter and does not dribble on to the gutter fascia board. Strips about 250mm wide are usually big enough but it is better to allow too much than too little. Some roofs have a wood batten attached to the gutter fascia to hold the felt over the gutter fixings and into the gutter.

The second layer of felt on the roof should be laid so that it butts against these gutter fascia strips.

Start the first strip of the second layer alongside any exposed edge making sure that the overlaps in the first and second layers do not coincide – they must be at least 50mm apart. Clean the roof, spread the cold bitumastic compound, lay the felt on top of it and tread it down to fix it in place. Completely cover the roof. Repeat the whole process, starting the third layer at least 50mm away from an overlap in the second layer.

Felt for the verge batten should now be cut – lengths about 1.2m long by 350mm wide should be fixed to the batten in a manner similar to that described for gutters (folding it up, over, and on to the flat roof and gluing it in place). Overlap lengths of verge felting by 50mm.

Fold down existing flashings or lay new felt ones. Flashing felt should be laid in lengths about 1.2m long by about 300mm wide. The top should be tucked into the brickwork joint and held in place by wedging other pieces of felt into the mortar joint. The joint should then be repointed – see page 170 – and the bottom of the flashing should be glued firmly to the roof surface.

Finally, spread more bitumastic and sprinkle stone chippings evenly over the roof.

Applying a waterproof seal

Block gutter outlets and brush the surface of the roof to remove loose chippings. Use a mastic seal on any splits or cracks. Coat the roof with a bitumastic solution containing a reinforcing mesh and apply a further coat of a thicker bitumastic compound over the top. When this is dry, apply a final coat of solution and spread chippings.

OVERLAPPING FELT

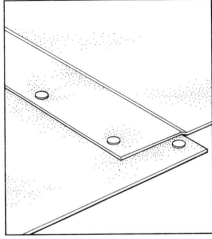

The lengths of felt laid on the roof should overlap by about 50mm and should be nailed to the roof boarding every 150mm or so

Repairing a lean-to roof

Lots of different types of materials can be used to cover a lean-to roof. The most suitable choice largely depends on the intended use of the space underneath.

Conservatories, carports and covered ways are often covered with corrugated translucent plastic sheets which allow natural light through. They are easy to fix; light in weight, making them easy to lift and manoeuvre; and require a relatively small supporting framework. The sheets are available in a variety of colours, profiles and lengths and weights.

Lean-to garages and sheds are often covered with corrugated sheets made of asbestos or galvanised iron. The latter is usually only used when the roof is out of sight. Asbestos sheet is often used because it is fireproof. But it is heavy, needs a strong structure to support it and is also relatively fragile – it needs careful handling when new to avoid damaging it and with age it becomes brittle and easily broken. **Never** attempt to walk directly on an asbestos roof – always use a crawling board.

Leaking roofs

Water dripping from the underside of a lean-to roof covered with plastic, asbestos or galvanised iron sheeting does not necessarily mean that the roof is leaking – the drips may be due to condensation. But if the drips only occur when it is raining, a leak is the likely cause. Three

areas of a lean-to roof are particularly troublesome – flashings, around fixings and at overlaps.

The joint between a lean-to roof and the house (or building) is sealed with a flashing strip. If this joint leaks, make sure the flashing strip is securely fixed to the house and to the corrugations of the roofing sheets. If the flashing is loose in the brickwork, it should be rewedged and repointed. If it is torn or split, it is usually simpler to replace the strip than to waterproof it. A flashing kit – which sticks to both roof and wall – is easier to use than conventional flashings.

Each roofing sheet is fastened to the roof timbers by nails or screws through holes drilled in the ridges of the sheet. A rubber or plastic washer beneath the head of each fixing stops rain-water getting through. With age, these washers sometimes become brittle and split, allowing water to run down the fixing. The only cure is to remove the fixing and replace the washer.

Each roofing sheet should overlap its neighbour by two corrugations. If plastic roofing sheets are not adequately supported, they will eventually bow and no longer mate sufficiently well with their neighbours to retain watertight joints. This can only be cured by introducing more supports.

Galvanised iron sheets will eventually rust unless they are given a protective covering of a bitumastic-based paint. Once a sheet has perforated through rust the only permanent cure is to replace the

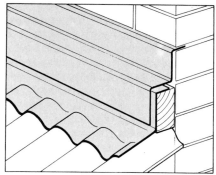

Some flashing strips are specially made to cope with the problem of sealing a corrugated roof to a wall

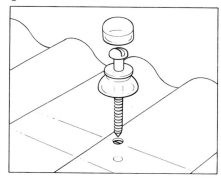

Fix corrugated sheets through the ridges not the valleys, even though this is more difficult – driving fixings through the valleys can lead to leaks

sheet with a new one. Temporary repairs can be made with a bitumastic sealer.

Asbestos becomes brittle with age and will split if it is knocked. Again bitumastic sealer can be used for a temporary repair.

Repairing pitched roofs

The timber rafters of most pitched roofs measure 100×50mm. On roofs less than about 30 years old, the rafters are covered with roofing felt – a type called *reinforced* (it has a layer of hessian cloth bonded into it) comes in rolls 20m long by 1m wide. The felt is often fixed to the rafters with 11 SWG galvanised felt nails 20mm long which have large heads. Each strip of felt should dip slightly be-

tween the rafters, overlap the next one further down the roof by at least 150mm, and the bottom strip should overlap the fascia so that it pokes into the gutter. On exposed roofs the rafters might be covered with wooden boards (called *sarking*) to give extra protection.

Battens are nailed over the felt across the rafters. The size of the battens depends on the type of roof covering to be

used and how close the rafters are together: 38×19mm timber is usually adequate. The battens should be treated with preservative and fixed with 50 or 65mm nails – if steel ones are used they should be the galvanised type. Roofs covered with sarking need counter battens – lengths of 38×6mm timber – nailed parallel to the rafters before the main battens are fixed.

The most common materials used to clad pitched roofs are slates, tiles (plain or interlocking) and shingles.

Slates and plain tiles are overlapped so that each row overlaps the one below and the vertical joins in each row are staggered. They are nailed to the battens – perferably with aluminium, copper or silicon-bronze nails – usually with two nails to each tile or slate. The amount of overlap needed depends on the pitch of the roof – more overlap is needed for shallow roofs. The *head lap* is the amount the tiles overlap the row-but-one beneath. The *side lap* is the distance from the side of a slate to the vertical gap between the slates in the row directly beneath. The *gauge* is the length of the slate or tile exposed on the roof and is the same as the distance between the battens – see drawings opposite.

Slates

Natural slates, usually a blue-black colour, were used on many older houses built around the turn of the century. Simulated slates made of asbestos cement or concrete are becoming popular on new houses and as replacements on

ROOFING MATERIALS

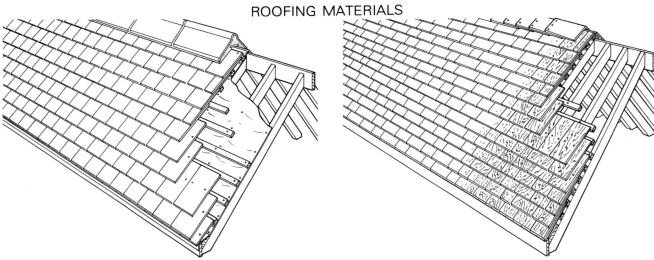

Slates Many older houses have slate roofs – most will not have the covering of roofing felt shown in the drawing unless the roof has been renovated in recent years. The slate may be centre-nailed (as shown) or head-nailed

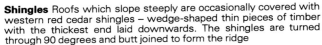

Shingles Roofs which slope steeply are occasionally covered with western red cedar shingles – wedge-shaped thin pieces of timber with the thickest end laid downwards. The shingles are turned through 90 degrees and butt joined to form the ridge

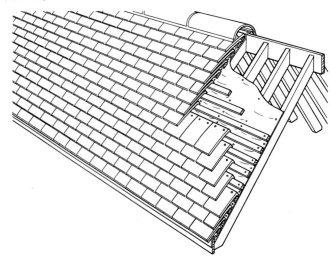

Plain tiles Roofs covered with plain tiles are very easy to lay and repair. The tiles simply hook over the battens and should be nailed in exposed positions – at the end, say – and every fourth or fifth row on the main part of the roof

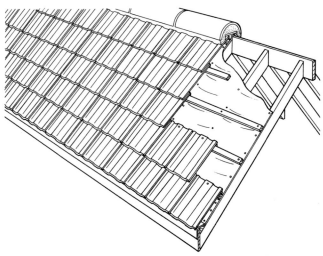

Interlocking tiles There are many different types and the sort you need depends on the pitch of the roof. Nowadays, most are made from concrete: in the past many were clay – these may be difficult to match

LAYING ROOF COVERINGS

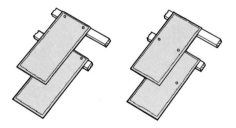

Slates may be head-nailed (left) or centre-nailed (right) – the holes are traditionally made with a slater's hammer

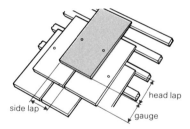

The terms used in describing slate and tile coverings are illustrated above. Shallow roofs need the largest side and head laps

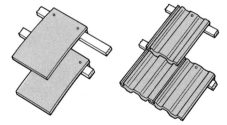

Tiles With interlocking tiles (right) the gauge equals the length minus the head lap. With plain tiles (left) divide this distance by two

older existing properties.

Slates come in many different sizes, usually from 250×150mm to 650×400mm, and every one needs nailing to the battens – the holes can be made with an electric drill fitted with a masonry bit. There are two positions for the nail holes.

Head-nailed slates have holes so that the head comes more-or-less flush with the top of a batten. Slates can be laid on roofs with a pitch as low as 20 degrees. A 25 degree roof using 500×300mm tiles needs a head lap of 115 to 125mm so the gauge is about 190mm.

Centre-nailed slates have holes further down but not exactly central so that the head of the slate sits on the bottom edge of the batten, to make room for the nail from the slate above. The pitch can be the same as for head-nailed slates but the head lap can be about 25mm less.

Head-nailed slates are more likely to lift in wind than centre-nailed ones, more are needed over the roof area and the nails are less easy to get at than on centre-nailed slates. But centre-nailed slates need more care when fixing them.

Tiles

Traditionally, tiles were made of clay but since the end of the Second World War most have been made of concrete. Most houses are now roofed with interlocking concrete tiles but plain tiles are still available. Matching ridge or valley tiles are also available.

Plain tiles Some plain tiles are nailed to the battens but most have small projections – called nibs – as well which hook over the battens. Usually nailing every fourth or fifth row on the main part of the roof and exposed tiles – a couple of rows at the ridge and eaves, and the tiles at the verges – is enough. For plain clay tiles the pitch must be at least 40 degrees and the side and head laps at least 65mm. Tiles used to be about 265×165mm, so the gauge is about 100mm. These tiles are very slightly curved.

Interlocking tiles With these tiles the sides of the tile overlap each other so only one layer is needed. There are many different types depending on the pitch of the roof: most cope with pitches of 30 degrees, some with pitches less than 20 degrees. The sizes vary but 380×230mm is fairly common. The lap needs to be about 100mm for a 30 degree pitch but the gauge is large – about 280mm for a 380mm tile.

Shingles

Shingles are a kind of wooden tile often made from western red cedar – a wood which weathers to a silver-grey colour. They are used on roofs and for cladding walls which need extra warmth and weather protection and are also more common on steep roofs where their visual appearance can be best displayed. The tiles are usually about 350mm long and taper from 8mm to 1.5mm. They are available in a variety of widths.

Leaking roofs

The first sign that something is wrong with a roof is usually a damp patch on the ceiling below. Do not assume that the damp patch is directly below the roof defect – water may have travelled along the roofing felt before finding a way through or may have travelled along the underside of the roof before dripping off a rafter.

To find out what the problem is, look at the outside of the roof for obvious signs of damage – like slipped or missing slates or tiles. Then look more carefully (binoculars will help) for broken or cracked ones. The problem may be the ridge or hip tiles and the mortar between them. If you cannot see anything wrong, the flashings or valleys may be at fault.

Loose slates Slates usually slip because the nails holding them have corroded and can no longer support the weight of the slate. Sometimes it is possible to carefully ease the slate back to its proper position. You may be able to do this from inside the loft space by drilling a small hole near the top of the slate and then wiring it to an adjacent batten. Or you can slip a strip of lead, copper or zinc (called a *tingle*) underneath the slate and feed it under the slate to appear above a batten. Then fold this end of the tingle down over the batten and the other end up over the slate. If one slate is loose, others may also be about to slip – check this by gently tugging any suspect ones.

Cracked or damaged slates It can be quite difficult to tell whether a slate is leaking because of damage or deterioration – isolated small pieces missing from corners are not a serious problem but large pieces missing, cracks, splits or flaking due to deterioration with age can let in water.

Cracked or split slates can be repaired temporarily by sealing the break with a mastic. But the only permanent cure is to replace the defective slate. This can be a fiddly job since it is not usually possible to gain access to the nail securing the slate. The best way to remove the slate is by pushing a slate ripper under the slate, hooking it over the nail and then giving it a sharp jerk to break the nail. The faulty slate should then be eased out carefully. The new slate is held in place using a tingle measuring about 230×25mm nailed to a batten between the exposed slates. Slide the new slate into place and bend the tingle up round the slate to fix it in position. Make sure that the bottom edge of the new slate lines up with existing slates.

Loose tiles High winds may dislodge tiles or the nibs which hook over the battens may be damaged and no longer able to hold the tile in place. If the tile has simply been dislodged, it can be carefully pushed back into position so that the nibs hook over the batten. It may be necessary to lift the adjacent tiles slightly

to ease movement. But if the nibs are broken, the tile will have to be replaced or wired in place like a slate. To get the old tile out, wedge up adjacent tiles so that you can slip whatever nibs remain over the batten. If the old tile is nailed, rock it from side to side or, if necessary, use a slate ripper to get it out. Fitting new tiles is usually fairly easy – work from the eaves upwards when fitting more than one and use 30mm nails to secure them.

If you notice any flaking tiles while you are on the roof, replace these too – they may be porous.

Loose ridge tiles Carefully prise the loose tiles free and scrape away all remaining loose and crumbly mortar. Replace the ridge tiles on to a bed of weak mortar – one part cement, three parts of soft sand plus a plasticiser added to the water. If you use a mix which is too strong, it will be stronger than the tile and if movement occurs the tile will crack rather than the mortar. Point all the joints with the same mix.

Loose shingles Loose shingles can be slipped back in position and carefully nailed in place. If there is a general deterioration of the shingles (rot, for example) the only real cure is to replace them. When recovering with anything other than shingles, consider the structural implications carefully – tiles are much heavier than shingles and the roof may not have been designed to cope with a higher loading.

Roof sealants

If the roof covering has started to deteriorate overall and will need replacing fairly soon, you could consider having the roof cladding covered with a plastic coating. This treatment is becoming increasingly popular due to the high cost of reroofing a house. But remember that this is a treatment for a defective roof **not** a cure. The coatings are available in a variety of colours and roofs so treated can be very conspicuous.

Roof repairers

Working on a roof is dangerous. You should only attempt it if you have a head for heights and use well secured proper climbing ladders. Otherwise, ask at least three firms to look at your roof, tell you what is wrong with it, what they think needs doing and to provide you with a written estimate. The contractor really needs to climb up to the roof to check its condition and may need to go into your loft.

To compare the estimates, find out exactly what is included – are all materials included? Who has to clear away the mess after the work is finished? And so on. Check whether the contractor is promising to make the roof *waterproof* or simply to replace slates or tiles. If possible ask the contractor to specify, in writing, that the work will conform to British Standard Code of Practice, *CP* 142.

REPLACING OR REFIXING SLATES

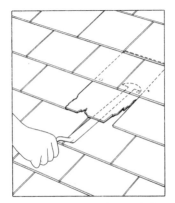

Slide the slate ripper beneath the slate, hook it over the nail and give it a sharp tug

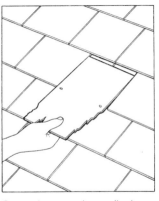

Once the securing nails have been broken, the damaged slate can be removed

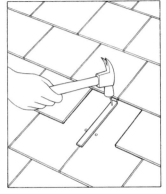

Nail a 'tingle' – a strip of lead, say – to a batten between the exposed slates

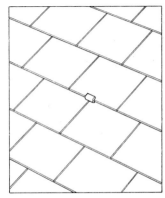

Line up the bottom of the new slate with existing slates and bend the tingle

Repairing chimneys

Chimney stacks are often neglected because of their relative inaccessibility. But they are sited in an exposed position and suffer badly from the ravages of the weather. Neglect often allows relatively minor defects to become more severe and often dangerous. Even if you feel unable to repair a chimney yourself, it is worthwhile periodically carrying out an inspection so that if any deterioration is detected you can employ a builder or roofing specialist to put it right before it gets worse. Periodic inspections can be carried out quite easily using a pair of binoculars and looking at the chimney from a number of vantage points around the house so that all elevations are viewed.

Minor repairs to a chimney can often be carried out using ladders for access. Use a conventional ladder to reach gutter level and a roof ladder hooked over the ridge and laid across the face of the roof for access to the chimney. Place sacks of rags or straw between the ladder and the roof covering to prevent damage.

Never attempt to carry out major repairs – such as replacing pots or areas of brickwork – working off ladders. Erect a proper scaffold around the stack.

Insecure or damaged pots Pots are secured to the stack by a cement flaunching. If the flaunching has cracked or broken away from the stack, it should be removed and replaced – a partial repair is liable to crack at the joints between the old and new material. To replace the pot, the flaunching will have to be removed – use a club hammer and bolster to break it. Lower the old pot to the ground on a rope – chimney pots are very heavy. Then clean away the top of the stack with a wire brush and, if necessary, repoint the top course of brickwork.

Make up a new cement flaunching from one part cement to three parts sharp sand. Wet the brickwork on top of the stack and the bottom of the new pot, place the pot in position then build up the new flaunching to about 75mm deep around the pot. Trowel it smooth so that

it slopes away from the pot in all directions – to throw rain away.

Defective pointing Defective joints should be raked out to a depth of about 20mm and all powdery material brushed away. Damp the brickwork before repointing with a mixture of one part cement to three or four parts soft sand with a plasticiser added to the water. The mixture should be just moist enough to be plastic. Apply it with a pointing towel and press it firmly into the joint. Finally, smooth it off.

Defective flashing This defect will allow rain-water to run down the stack into the roof space and beyond. So look at the stack inside the roof space in your periodic inspections.

There are two major defects which occur with traditional lead flashing:
● the joint into the masonry may be loose, allowing water to run down the back of it. To remedy this fault, rake out the masonry joint and rewedge the lead flashing using strips of lead driven into the joint with a blunt chisel. Then repoint the joint
● the lead may have aged and developed small splits. A temporary repair can be effected by cleaning and drying the whole area and then spreading a bituminous mastic over the split.

To carry out a permanent repair you will have to completely replace the flashing. This can be done with sheets of lead, zinc, aluminium alloy, a rigid bitumin-based material or with a purpose-made self-adhesive foil-backed flashing strip.

Replacement is fairly simple. First remove the lower layers of roof cladding (slates, tiles, and so on) to expose the edges of the flashing. Remove the old flashing with a cold chisel and rake out the mortar from the flashing joint to a depth of about 20 to 25mm. Shape the new flashing to match the old – use a sliding bevel to measure the angles. Wet the brickwork, place the new flashing in position and wedge it in the flashing joint. Replace the roof cladding and repoint the flashing joint.

Lead commands a high price as scrap, so it is worth taking defective flashing (assuming it is lead) to your local scrap metal merchant.

Flashing is used to seal most joints between roofs and walls and where roofs meet – at the valley junction between roofs, for example. Sometimes it is called a different name – the metal sheets or roofing felt used to seal the junction between the side of a roof and a wall are often called soakers and are covered with a layer of mortar. Replacement of most flashing is fairly easy and requires only a common sense approach – the existing flashing should be examined and a similar replacement made.

Linings

Smoke or fumes leaking out of a chimney – stained brickwork and damaged mortar in need of repointing along the line of a chimney on an outside wall are typical signs – indicate that the lining inside the flue is defective.

Replacing or installing a sectional fireclay liner is practical only for very large chimneys and, even then, involves breaking into the chimney. A more practical solution is to employ a specialist contractor to line the flue with insulating concrete poured around an inflatable tube blown up inside the flue.

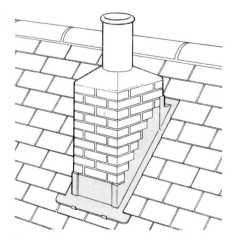

Use the old flashing as a template when cutting out the new. Finish off the brickwork with weather-struck joints

Gutter boards

All roofs, apart from thatched ones, have wooden boards protecting the ends of the rafters called *fascia* boards and *soffit* boards (collectively *gutter* boards).

Fascia boards are flat boards nailed vertically to the ends of the rafters and usually hold the gutter. On modern houses they are often used in conjunction with a soffit (which often fits into a groove in the back of the fascia) to form a boxed *eave*. Many soffits are made of softwood; recent ones may be asbestos.

The gutter is often positioned very close to the fascia boards and unless it is removed the fascia boards are difficult to paint properly when carrying out routine exterior decorating. Consequently fascia boards are often left unprotected and rapidly rot. In extreme cases the timber could be so badly weakened that the gutter starts to fall down.

When repairing rotten gutter boards, you should replace them completely rather than introduce a patch – when buying, allow an extra 150mm on each length. The old gutter boards can be ripped off with a crowbar and cold chisel and all the old nails removed. The joists and rafter ends should be lined up – by cutting excess off or adding packing – before the new boards are nailed in place. Check the alignment of the joists by tying a string around the joists at each end of the roof and, using a spirit level, put wood packing under one of the outer joists until the string is level. Now cut away the wood on joists projecting below the string and add packing to those which do not touch it until the joists are level.

Fit the new soffit boards – nail them through the joists and make joints at the joists (use a 45 degree mitre). The soffits should fit tightly against the wall. Use a similar technique for aligning the ends of the joists or rafters to take the fascias. The ends of the joists or rafters should be in line with the inner edge of the tongue on the soffits. Make sure that joints in the fascias are not on the same joist or rafter as the soffit joints. Protect all boards with preservative before finally fixing them in position.

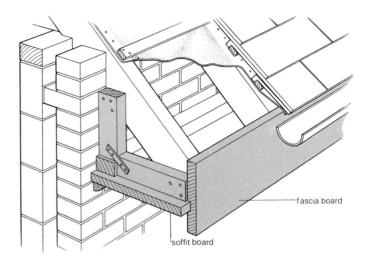

f fascia board

soffit board

The rafters are notched slightly to fit over the wall plate. The bricks in the outer leaf are turned to close the cavity and the brickwork made up to the level of the roofing felt

BARGE BOARDS

The fairly substantial pieces of timber which form the facings at the gable end of roofs and which cover and protect the end of the wall plate, ridge and tile battens are known as barge boards. Because they are very exposed and often very high, they may not be painted as frequently as they should be and consequently suffer from rot.

Replacement is straightforward but can be awkward because of their size and position. You can replace them with wooden boards (suitably shaped) or with a plastic substitute. Plastic barge boards have many advantages: they are light in relation to wood, self coloured (usually white) and so need no painting, and they will not rot. Plastic barge boards can be sawn and nailed just like wood.

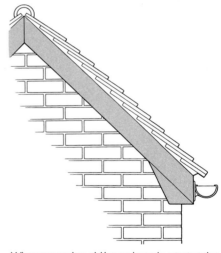

When removing old barge boards, start at the bottom and work upwards. Buy new boards to match the old ones

Reports in Handyman Which?

REPAIRING GUTTER BOARDS

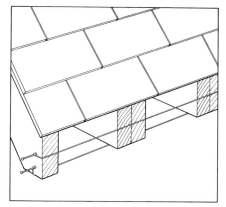

Check the alignment of the rafter ends and the underside of the joists with taughtly-tied string and a spirit level. Use wood packing or a saw to adjust

Attach the soffit boards first. The boards may have to be shaped to fit snugly against the house wall and all butt joints should be angled

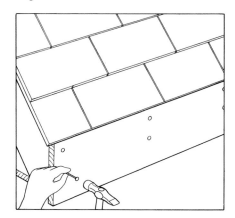

Attach the fascia boards with one or two galvanised nails into each rafter end and a nail directly below into the soffit boards

GUTTERS

Gutters collect rain-water shed by the tiles and lead it away to drains and soakaways.

Very early gutters and associated pipework were made from lead. This was later almost universally replaced by cast iron and again over the last twenty years or so this has totally changed to plastic which is easy to cut and secure, light to carry and support, and needs no maintenance. Aluminium guttering is also available from specialist firms who make the guttering on site.

Cast iron guttering is generally fairly durable but it can rust and is rather brittle. It should be protected with a coat of gloss paint on the outside and a covering of bitumastic paint on the inside. If corrosion has perforated the metal, you can make a temporary repair using a hessian-reinforced mastic or even glass fibre.

The joints in cast iron guttering are made by placing putty between the pieces of pipe or gutter and then clamping them together using a small nut and bolt. In time these joints can fail but they can be repaired by unscrewing the nut and bolt, scraping the jointing surfaces clean, spreading a mastic jointing compound across the surfaces and finally clamping the two sections together.

Cast iron work in bad condition should be replaced by one of the more modern materials. It is generally wise to replace all the old cast iron guttering – new plastic gutters cannot be joined to old cast iron ones. A variety of shapes and supports for plastic gutters and pipes are available to suit most houses. Always support plastic guttering at regular intervals – as specified by the manufacturer – otherwise it can bow and sag and water may overflow.

All guttering should be inspected periodically to make sure that it has not become blocked by leaves or silt washed from the roof. Use a trowel to get the rubbish out. If the trouble occurs frequently, it is worth fixing guards into the gutters. You can buy these or use pieces of wire or plastic netting bent to a half-round shape and jammed in the guttering so that they spring out and hold themselves in place. A down spout can be unblocked by pushing a long stick down it – you may have to undo some of the joints and reseal them again afterwards.

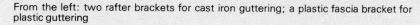
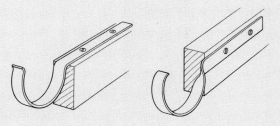

From the left: two rafter brackets for cast iron guttering; a plastic fascia bracket for plastic guttering

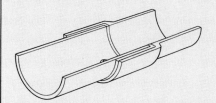
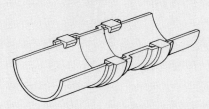

Typical joint in cast iron guttering　　　Typical joint in plastic guttering

Working off the ground

When repairing a roof or decorating – either the inside or outside of a house – you need equipment for gaining access to the areas you want to work on. Outside, particularly if you have a long job to tackle – replacing a roof covering, say – you might consider erecting scaffolding. But for other jobs you will probably use either an extension ladder or a platform tower, or both. Inside, step-ladders are more useful.

Step-ladders

Painting a ceiling by standing on the floor and using a roller fitted with an extension handle is safe but very tiring. By getting yourself off the ground – say 600mm or so – the job should become much less strenuous. A pair of step-ladders allows you to stand at various heights without ever needing to over-stretch.

There are three main types:
● **platform** step-ladders which generally have five or more steps and are over a metre or so high with a large working platform as the top step.

● **traditional** step-ladders are like platform step-ladders but do not have a platform. They are sometimes called painters' or swing-back step-ladders.

● **convertible** step-ladders which can be used as a step-ladder or opened out into a straight ladder for using against a wall.

Most of these ladders are either aluminium or steel and wood. Aluminium ones are by far the lightest.

Platform step-ladders are fairly easy to put up but convertible ones are more tricky – when they are extended the catch holding the top section of the ladder in place should be checked to make sure it is engaged, and the ladder must be put up the right way round.

When choosing a platform step-ladder, look for one which has a guard rail which is 0.6m or more above the platform and which does not interfere with you standing on the platform. Choose a ladder without any obvious finger-traps and one with wide, flat comfortable treads.

MULTI-PURPOSE LADDER

One type of step-ladder can be used as a straight ladder, a stair ladder, a raised working surface and as a straight ladder in the stand-off position – shown

PLATFORM STEP-LADDERS

Wood step-ladder   Aluminium step-ladder   Tubular steel with wood steps

CONVERTIBLE STEP-LADDER

Some go from steps to a straight ladder by sliding one half over the other; others have to be swung through 180 degrees

Platform towers and extension ladders

For decorating outdoors and for access to roofs or gutters you will need an extension ladder or a platform tower. Both have their pros and cons:

● extension ladders may not be as convenient or as comfortable to work from as platform towers (which have working platforms measuring about 1.2m square) but they are easier to move about and put up and are much cheaper to buy. However, both can be hired and some platform towers have wheels which enable them to be manoeuvred over hard flat ground

● platform towers should be safer than ladders and are more versatile – they can be used for decorating indoors

● platform towers dismantle readily but take up more storage room than a ladder and unless the frame is galvanised it will need painting from time to time. Extension ladders are normally made of wood or aluminium and require little or no maintenance.

Platform towers

Most platform towers are built up from pairs of H-shaped frames each one being about 600mm high and either 600mm or 1.2m across. Each successive pair of frames goes at right angles to the one underneath, so when only 1.2m wide frames are used a platform tower with a platform measuring 1.2m square is built, but when 600mm and 1.2m wide frames are alternated, one with a platform measuring 600mm by 1.2m is built. Square platform towers can be built up much higher than oblong ones without additional support – about 3.6m high as opposed to 1.8m or so. But oblong ones can be used in more confined situations. A platform tower also has diagonal braces to keep it rigid, boards for the platform, and corner posts and handrails to stop you falling off. Some platform towers go up to 4.8m in height.

Platform towers are generally fairly simple to build. With a rope and a hook to help you get the H-frames off the ground, one person could build most 3.6m platform towers in about a quarter of an hour. But it is much easier if a second person helps.

Extension ladders

Most extension ladders sold to do-it-yourselfers have two sections and extend to around seven metres – enough to get to the top of most modern houses. Choose one which is a little over one metre longer than you want your feet to go.

Two mechanisms are used for extending ladders. With the push-up type, the top section can be pushed along the bottom one and held in place with either fixed or hinged hooks. This type of ladder has to be laid flat on the ground to get an extension of more than about two metres. Rope-operated ladders can be extended while they are against the wall but they are more expensive than push-up ones and are generally not sold in the smaller sizes.

Two materials are widely used – wood and aluminium. Aluminium ladders are generally lighter than wooden ones and should last longer. Choose one with rungs which are flat on top.

PLATFORM TOWERS

A conventional platform tower built from 1200 x 600mm H-frames

Some have castors for ease of transportation – on this type you tighten the screw to lock the wheel when the tower is in use

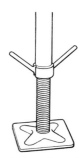

Some have a jacking base for coping with uneven or sloping ground, or steps

On level, even ground, most platform towers use a base plate to spread the load and reduce the likelihood of sinking in

Ladder accessories

A wide range of ladder accessories can be bought including:

● cripples for securing a horizontal plank between two ladders. Choose those which can take a guard rail

● platforms which increase the rung area and make standing towards the top of a ladder much less uncomfortable on the feet

● stand-offs which hold the top of a ladder away from a wall and provide access to gutters and windows which might otherwise create a problem

● special feet which improve the grip of ordinary ladder feet.

LADDER ACCESSORIES

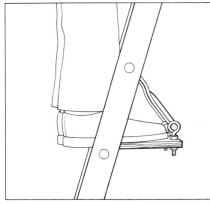

Ladder platform

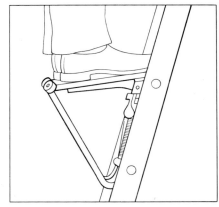

Ladder platform

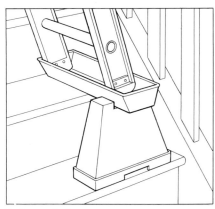

Stairway platform

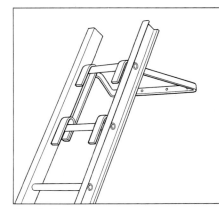

Stand off

EXTENSION LADDERS

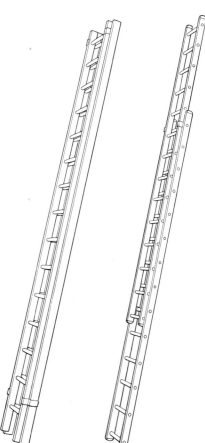

Wood   Aluminium

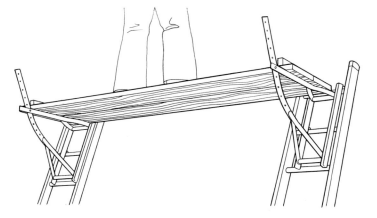

A pair of cripples allows you to construct a large working platform between two ladders leaning against a wall by using planks. Note there is no rear guard

Avoiding an accident

Working off the ground is dangerous: falls and associated ladder accidents account for many deaths each year plus thousands of broken limbs and minor injuries.

When using an **extension ladder**:

● make sure that its feet are placed on a flat, secure non-slippery base

● on slopes, make sure the feet of the ladder are level and properly secured

● on soft ground always put the feet of the ladder on a plank or something similar and secure them

● lean the ladder against the wall at an angle of 75 degrees (the distance of the ladder feet from the wall should be approximately one quarter of the height of the ladder up the wall)

● make sure that you position it sensibly – the ladder should not lean to one side and should not be in front of a front door that is likely to be opened and it should go well above the level at which you want to stand or get off

● always face the ladder when climbing or descending it

● never attempt to extend an extension ladder when you are on it and always check that supporting hooks are properly engaged

● where possible, tie the top of the ladder to something secure and never rest the top against something weak or likely to give way

● never go up a ladder in a high wind

● do not stretch upwards, lean to one side or be tempted to step away from the ladder when painting

● always keep one hand on a rung – use a bag or rope to carry things – and never drop things to the ground.

Finally, if after a little practice you are still frightened of going up the ladder, do not force yourself to go up it, instead use a platform tower or hire a professional decorator or roof repairer.

Like ladders, **platform towers** must always be used sensibly. You should:

● build the tower on a firm surface. If the ground is soft use boards to spread the load and prevent sinking

● make sure that the first frames are level before building higher and make sure each section is securely fitted to those beneath

● not build very high platform towers without securing them first

● always climb inside the main frame and use a rope or bag to take things up so that you always have both hands free for climbing

● never use a ladder or steps on top of the platform and never leave the platform tower unattended for long periods with the boards on

● never let children play on the tower – keep them away at all times.

PUTTING UP AN EXTENSION LADDER

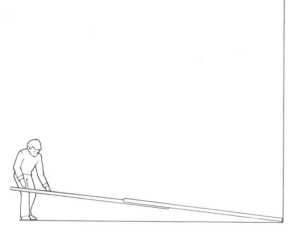

Putting up a ladder by yourself is risky. Start by jamming the bottom of the ladder against the wall, then move towards the wall pushing the ladder upright – as shown. When the ladder is upright, walk the bottom out. This job is much easier if you have a helper to hold the bottom of the ladder instead of using the wall. The helper *must* keep the end of the ladder firmly on the ground to stop the ladder going out of control as you push the ladder upright

Loft insulation

The main objective of improving insulation is usually to reduce fuel bills. Therefore, it is important to compare the cost of installing the insulation with the likely savings – to work out whether it is cost-effective compared with, say, putting the same amount of money in a building society. Insulation does, of course, have other benefits – notably increasing comfort and reducing condensation. Some forms of insulation may increase the value of the house.

Although more heat will be lost through the walls in most houses, the roof is the first place to start. It is possible to put insulating material on the underside of the roof itself, but unless you intend to use the loft space for an extra room, it is usual to add the insulation to the floor of the loft – or, to the ceilings of the rooms immediately below. The two main kinds of loft insulation: blanket, and loose-fill.

Blanket insulation

Blanket materials are sold in rolls which are usually 400mm wide. The two main materials used are glass fibre and mineral wool, of which glass fibre is the more common. Laying the roll is quite simple: you lay the roll between two joists and unroll it. The tricky bit is getting it up in the loft space to start with. The roll is slightly wider than most modern joist spacing – you let it curl slightly up the sides. Some old houses have joists somewhat closer together – so unless you can get wider rolls (1.2m widths are sold) and cut them up with a panel saw, you will have a much greater overlap. An alternative is to lay it *across* the joists. Blanket materials are sold in 75mm and 100mm thicknesses. It is probably worth fitting the greater thickness if fuel prices

continue to rise rapidly.

Laying blanket insulation is hard and dirty work and the insulation itself can irritate the skin: wear a simple face mask and rubber gloves. The blanket can be used to insulate the top and sides of cold water tanks if they are not already insulated, but insulation should not be laid *under* the tank. The loft space will be colder when it is insulated and the heat coming through the ceiling under the tank will help prevent it freezing in cold weather. Otherwise blanket should be laid on all exposed floor space right up to the eaves, but space at the eaves should be left for ventilation.

Loose-fill materials

The most common d-i-y loose-fill material is vermiculite, though it is possible to get polystyrene granules and loose mineral wool. Loose-fill materials are sold in bags and you empty out the bag between the joists, spreading the fill out to the depth you want. The practical limit to this depth is the depth of the joists (usually 100mm). This is equivalent to about 75mm of blanket insulation. Laying vermiculite takes longer than laying blanket and it can be dusty. You need to be careful at the edges of the loft to prevent the granules falling down the cavity in the walls. Loose-fill materials can blow about in the loft and may need some attention from time to time.

A more recent form of loose-fill insulation is cellulose fibre which is usually blown in by an installer, though d-i-y brands are becoming available. Cellulose fibre is basically recycled paper and it is important that it has a fire-retardant added. This may be corrosive to exposed metal and may affect light fittings, so these need to be protected.

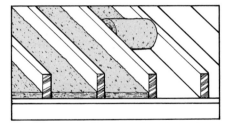

Mats of glass fibre or mineral wool are unrolled between the joists. Alternatively it can be laid across the joists

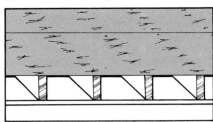

Rolls of aluminium foil are laid between or, as here, across the joists with the shiny side down to reflect the heat

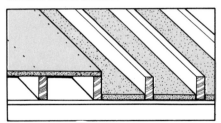

Sheets of fibreboard or expanded polystyrene are laid between or across the joists

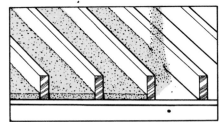

Granules of vermiculite or expanded polystyrene are spread evenly between the joists. Draughts can cause quite a bit of movement

Grants for loft insulation At the time this book went to press it was possible to get a grant from your local authority to help with the cost of installing loft insulation. The grant covers two-thirds of the cost (up to a maximum) of laying the equivalent of about 75mm of glass fibre blanket provided that there is no insulation already in the loft and provided that you use an *approved* material – you get a list of approved materials when you apply for a grant.

CHAPTER EIGHT

DOORS AND WINDOWS

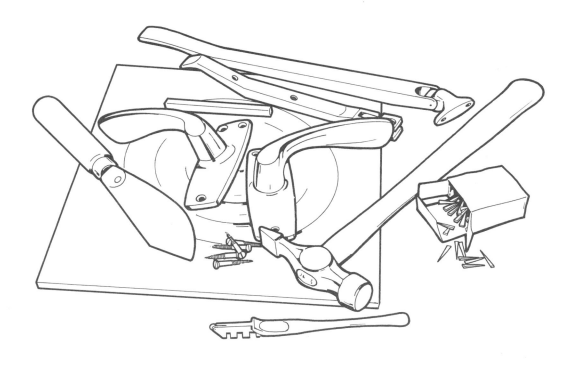

Doors

Doors come in a wide range of different styles, types and sizes. Many are designed mainly for their appearance using different materials, period styles, surface finishes and colours. Others are designed for a specific purpose – external doors which have to be burglar-proof and bear the brunt of the weather, internal doors and fire doors, for example. Most are wooden but you can get metal, plastic and all-glass ones too. You can also get doors that slide or fold.

Wooden doors

There are four common types of hinged, wooden door:

● **panel** doors have a moderately substantial timber frame enclosing a number of inset panels of timber, plywood or glass

● **flush** doors have a light framework of timber covered on each side with a single skin of sheet material such as plywood or hardboard

● **boarded** doors have a timber frame inset with a single panel of matchboarding

● **louvred** doors have a timber frame inset with canted horizontal timber slats spaced to allow for ventilation through the door.

External doors should be manufactured from materials capable of withstanding the ravages of the elements – usually hardwood or exterior plywood. Internal doors are usually made from much less durable materials – softwoods and hardboard, for instance.

Fire doors are built to withstand the effects of fire for periods of half, one or two hours depending on where the door is to be used. You may have to fit one to comply with the Building Regulations – for example if you build a garage on to your house, any door connecting the house to the garage must have at least half an hour's fire resistance. A *fire-resisting* door should protect against smoke as well as checking the movement of the fire. The doors are commonly referred to by their fire performance – a 30/30 door or a 30/20 door, for instance. The first figure tells you the door's stability in a fire and the second its resistance to penetration by flames. The 30/20 door is also known as a half hour *fire-check* door. Fire-resisting doors are usually flush doors formerly with plasterboard or asbestos cores but nowadays increasingly with flaxboard or chipboard cores.

Panel doors

These doors have a timber framework, usually softwood, enclosing one or more panels. They are available in a wide range of styles, including traditional and period designs.

The framework consists of two stiles running vertically up the door and three or more rails running horizontally across the door. The stiles and rails are usually joined together with mortise-and-tenon joints, however there is a trend towards replacing these by dowel joints. The inside edges of the frame are grooved to take the sides of the panels and may be decorated with a moulding.

Glass panels are housed in rebates and held in place by either wood beads or putty.

External framed-and-panelled doors should be made from timber which is naturally durable and able to stand up to the weather. Or they should be treated with a wood preservative. Plywood panels should be of exterior quality.

The stiles are generally about 100mm wide, so most locks will fit. A centre rail provides extra strength and is convenient for mounting letter plates. (However, letter plates should not be let into fire-resisting doors without the testing authority's approval.)

Some flush doors are made to resemble panelled doors – they have a moulded fibreboard facing to give the panelled effect.

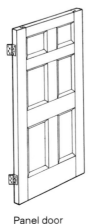

Panel door

Flush door

Ledged-and-braced door

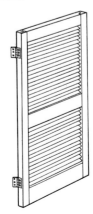

Louvred door

Flush doors

A flush door consists of a light timber frame covered on both sides with some form of sheet material. A core may be used to increase the rigidity of the two panels – called *facing* or *skins* – and to keep them apart. The frame is made from quite small sections of timber, usually 38×38mm – and is butt jointed and fastened together with glue and corrugated fasteners or staples.

Many different types of facings are used – from cheap hardboard to expensive hand-cut veneers on carefully-selected plywood. Facings can be unfinished, prepared for painting, or covered with a veneer.

To give a neat finish to the vertical edges of the door and to protect the edges of the panels, a narrow strip of timber is fastened to the door by a tongue and groove, or by gluing and pinning. This is known as a *lipping*. It is essential on external doors – to prevent water getting under the facings – and makes it easier to keep a neat edge when you have to plane off a little to make the door fit. On veneered doors the lipping is the same timber as the face veneer.

As the timber frame is often fairly flimsy, extra pieces of timber have to be built into the door for fixing locks and door handles. The extra material is called a *lock block*. Some doors have lock blocks on each side, others have only one – so you have to be careful when hanging the door to make sure you fix the hinges to the correct edge of the door. New doors should have a stamp on one edge showing the location of the lock block. On some very lightly-built doors, blocks are also provided to assist when fixing the hinges, and external doors have blocks and wide rails for fixing letter plates – find out exactly where these are before buying the door.

Boarded doors

There are two common types of boarded door in use today – ledged-and-braced doors and framed, ledged-and-braced doors.

The **ledged-and-braced** door is suitable for garden sheds and gates. It is made up of a number of boards fastened together with ledges across the back and braced to prevent it distorting.

The **framed, ledged-and-braced** door is used in situations where strength is required but the physical appearance of the door is not of prime importance – garage doors, stormdoors, outbuildings and gates are examples. The door consists of a frame held together with mortise-and-tenon joints. Diagonal braces are inserted inside the frame to prevent the door sagging and a panel of matchboarding runs from the top to the bottom of the door. The bottom rail is 30 to 40mm above the bottom of the door to help make fitting easy over uneven ground and to lessen the risk of the door being severely weakened by rot. As these doors are usually manufactured from softwood, they should be painted regularly or treated with a water repellant stain to reduce the rate of deterioration – particularly when the door is in an exposed situation.

DOOR FRAME CONSTRUCTION

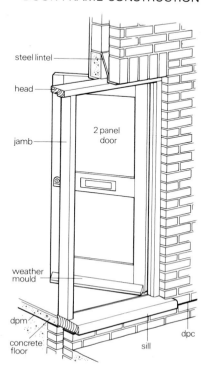

A door frame set into a cavity wall. Note the level of the damp-proof course – below the frame

Louvred doors

A louvred door may be used when ventilation is needed through the door or when this type of decorative appearance is wanted.

The door consists of a light timber frame of stiles and rails containing a quantity of horizontal slats called *louvres*. The louvres are set at an angle, overlapping each other in such a way to leave an airspace between them. On some doors, the louvred effect is produced by using triangular slats or a moulded panel – these will not provide ventilation.

Other types of hinged door

All-glass doors are made of a specially toughened glass which cannot be cut once it is made, so you should measure your door frame carefully and make sure that it is square before you buy one. They can be ordered made-to-measure or bought in a standard size – 1981×762mm or 1981×838mm, for example.

Aluminium external doors may provide a useful way of replacing a badly-rotted wooden door. But they are expensive and may suffer from condensation on the frame.

Buying doors

You may find doors quoted in either metric or imperial sizes. The most common internal door size is 1981×762mm (6ft 6in×2ft 6in). External doors might be 50mm taller and 50 or 75mm wider. External doors are usually 44mm thick; internal ones are normally 35mm, especially the cheaper ones.

If your door frame does not take a standard-size door, you will have to either buy the nearest size above and cut the door to fit or have one specially made. The door should be up to 4mm less than the frame in height and width. With most panel doors, you can cut off up to 20mm all round; with most flush doors you should not cut off anything.

Doors are usually sold by d-i-y shops, builders' merchants, timber merchants and joinery stockists.

Hanging a new door

The first job is to remove the existing door from the frame without damaging the frame or the hinge sinkings – do this very carefully, using small wood wedges to take the weight of the door.

Carefully check that the jambs of the door frame are firmly fixed and reasonably straight. If the frame is loose, it should be refixed before hanging the door. If the stops are loose, they can be removed and refixed later when the door has been hung and latched. Any twist or excessive bend in the frame will hinder and complicate successfully hanging the door. Check that the hinge side of the door frame is more-or-less vertical – use a spirit level. It is not quite so important for the other side to be vertical – you can shape the door to fit.

Check the location of the lock block and hinge blocks. With panel doors it may be necessary to cut off the horns on

the ends of the stiles – use a tenon saw. The horns protect the corners of the door, until it is ready to be hung. For external doors, coat cut surfaces with preservative – unless the wood is naturally durable.

Hold the door in position to see how well it fits in the door frame. The best way of doing this is to push the door against the hanging side of the top of the frame and to support the door in this position with the wedges.

Mark the position of the door on the frame, transferring the position of the hinges on the frame on to the door. Remove the door and then transfer the measurements to the door itself. Remember to subtract about $1\frac{1}{2}$ to 2mm for clearance all round – to allow for painting the door and to leave a sufficient gap at the bottom for the door to clear carpets and uneven floors. When cutting off

a lot, manoeuvre the door so that the amount to be removed can be shared between both sides and the top and bottom but if you cut anything off the hinge side, make sure that it is still vertical.

Plane the edges of the door to the lines previously marked out – if you have to cut off a lot, try sawing first. On the top and bottom rails, work from the ends inwards. Always make sure that you do not take off so much material that you affect the intended appearance of the door. If the amount you want to remove from a flush door is greater than the thickness of the lipping, remove the lipping, take off the required amount from the door, and replace the lipping. This needs a lot of care. If it looks as though you will have to plane off a large amount of timber from one stile of a panel door, readjust the door so that equal amounts can be planed off both stiles – this will

Try the new door into the frame opening by pushing it against the top of the frame

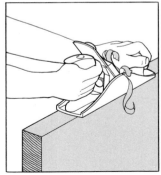

Plane the edges of the door to the lines previously marked on the door – or use a saw

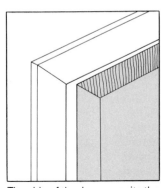

The side of the door opposite the hinge may be bevelled so that it closes easily

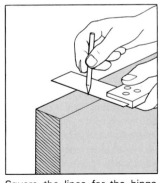

Square the lines for the hinge positions across the edge of the door – use a try square

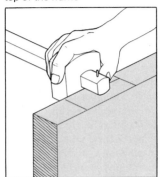

A marking gauge is useful for marking out the width (shown) and depth of the hinge recesses

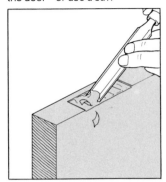

Cut out the hinge recesses with a broad (30 to 35mm) chisel and a mallet

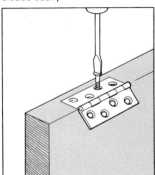

Fix each hinge to the door with one screw through one of the central screw holes

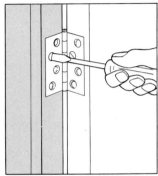

Wedge the door in position and fix it to the frame with one screw into each hinge

give the door a balanced appearance.

To allow the door to close easily, the swinging side – opposite the hinge – may be bevelled a small amount on the closing edge.

Check that the door fits into the frame with the required amount of clearance.

Place the door in the frame with the gaps at the top and bottom. Hold it in place with the two wedges and square the lines of the existing hinge recesses on to the edge of the door. Check that the marks made earlier are still correct before you do this. If you do not intend to reuse the original hinges, or identical replacements, you will need to make new hinge positions on the frame as well as on the door. Use large hinges rather than small ones.

Square the lines across the edge of the door. Mark out the width and depth lines for the hinge recesses – make sure that the knuckles of the hinges are just clear of the edge of the door. The best tool for this job is a marking gauge.

Cut out the recesses for the hinges in the door with a broad chisel and mallet, making the recesses as deep as the hinges themselves. Check the fit of the hinges in the recesses on the door and the frame.

Position the hinges in the appropriate recesses in the frame and mark the centre screw holes. Remove the hinges and use a bradawl or drill to make holes of sufficient size for starting the screws.

Locate the hinges in the door recesses and fix them in position with one centre screw. Using a rule as a straight-edge, check that the hinge pins are parallel to the edge of the door. Insert the remaining screws into the hinges.

Hold the door in position against the frame – by using wedges (and a helper). Locate the top hinge into the recess in the frame and insert the screw into the previously made hole. Repeat this operation with the bottom hinge.

Try the door to see if it swings easily and closes properly without catching the frame at any point. If it does not and there is sufficient clearance all round, you have probably recessed the hinges too much or too little - so you will either have to take off more or pack the recesses (with bits of cardboard, for example).

When everything looks satisfactory, put the remaining screws into the hinges.

Tools and materials for the job
Tools Brace and drill bit, bradawl, hammer, mallet, marking gauge, pencil and rule, plane, saw, screwdriver, try square, wood chisel (25 to 35mm)

Materials Two or three cast butt hinges (100mm), 30mm countersunk wood screws (8 or 10 gauge), two large wood wedges and some small wood wedges, door.

WEATHERBOARDS AND SILLS

Weatherboards
Weatherboards are designed to throw out from the face of the door any rainwater that runs down the door when it is raining.

There are two basic types of weatherboard (though many more individual designs). The traditional weatherboard is basically a flat piece of timber with bevelled edges screwed or nailed across the face of the bottom rail of the door.

Modern weatherboards are substantial pieces of timber moulded into a suitable shape and are often known as weathermoulds. These may be either attached on to the face of the bottom rail or tongued-and-grooved in place. They have a drip groove to stop water creeping under the weathermould.

Traditional weatherboards are the most vulnerable to damage. They may break away from the face of the door quite easily due to their flimsy shape. Both types are likely to decay if they are left unprotected – they should be painted or varnished.

Door sills
Door sills (sometimes called thresholds) serve three purposes:

● they provide a weathertight finish at the base of the door

● they assist the weatherboard in directing water away from the face of the door and from the face of the house

● they form a solid edge to the floor construction in the door opening.

Nowadays, it is common practice to build a door frame with an integral sill. The most suitable woods are the durable hardwoods such as oak and teak but these are expensive and other, cheaper, woods such as keruing may also be used.

There are a number of different door sill designs. The most usual arrangement is to have a rebated sill (to take the door) and a water bar to stop the water getting in under the sill. Some doors use a different arrangement with the sill sealed on its underside with mastic and fitted with a draught excluder instead of a rebate.

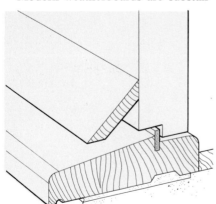

A traditional weatherboard and door sill – note the water bar inserted into the sill and the shaped door bottom

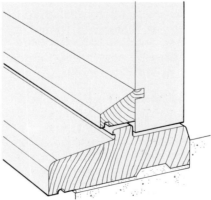

A modern weathermould tongued-and-grooved into the bottom of the door. Note the flat door bottom

DOOR HINGES

Butt hinges These are available in pressed steel, cast steel, brass and cast brass in sizes ranging from 50mm to 100mm, for fitting internal or external doors and wardrobe or cupboard doors but not fire doors. For fitting details see page 210.

Rising butt hinges Sometimes it is useful if a door raises itself as it opens so that it can clear things like carpets. Rising butt hinges are designed to do this. They are usually made from cast steel, in right and left handed sets. The top end of the hinge pin is open ended and as long as the hinge is fixed on to the frame with the knuckle (or the pin) clear of the frame, the door can be removed by lifting it off the pins.

Rising butt hinges are fixed in a manner similar to that described for butt hinges. But the following additional points should be considered:
● doors fitted with this type of hinge tend to be self-closing owing to the weight of the door on the spiral seating of the hinge

● the hinges must be accurately located on the door and the frame, otherwise only one hinge may be resting on its spiral seating – fit one hinge and then the other.
● to allow the door to close without catching the frame, the top back corner of the frame must be tapered.

Strap hinges These are sturdier than T-hinges and are ideal for garage doors and large heavy gates. This sort of hinge is held in place by screws and a coach bolt. It has an open pin so the door can be removed from the frame – by taking off the upper pin cup – without having to unfasten the hinge from the door.

T-hinges These hinges are made from sheet steel and black japanned to protect them from corrosion. They are lightly built and suitable for use on ledged-and-braced doors and gates. Framed, ledged-and-braced doors may be hung on T-hinges or on standard butt hinges.

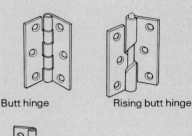

Butt hinge   Rising butt hinge

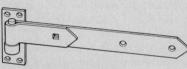

T-hinge

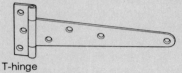

Strap hinge – hook and ride

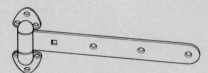

Strap hinge – with reversible cups

DOOR FURNITURE

Doors need something for you to open and close them with – usually a handle of some sort – and something to keep them in the closed position once they have been shut. On external doors the retaining device is usually a lock. On internal doors, including cupboard and wardrobe doors, a number of different devices can be used.

Ball catches These are basically a casing containing a spring-loaded ball or roller which holds the door closed when it engages with a striking plate (keep) in the door frame. They are simple to fix – insert the catch into a prebored hole in the door and hold it in position with screws.

Lever handles These are used to open latches fixed in doors. They work by rotating a square metal spindle which passes through the door and the latch. Lever handles come in a variety of shapes and finishes – including anodised aluminium and brass – see next page for fitting. Door knobs work in a similar way.

Spring latches These hold a door more firmly than ball catches. To open the spring latch a lever handle or knob is required. See next page for fitting details.

Thumb latches These are the traditional latches for ledged-and-braced doors and garden gates.

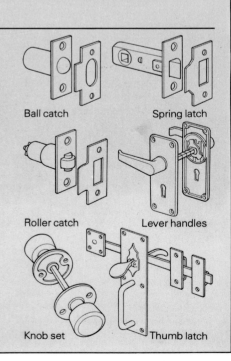

Ball catch   Spring latch

Roller catch   Lever handles

Knob set   Thumb latch

Fitting lever door handles (or a spring latch)

Details of the locks available for external doors and how to fit them can be found starting on page 234. The details here refer mainly to internal doors. First read the manufacturer's instructions noting the sizes of fixing holes and where they should be positioned.

Find the centre of the door edge and mark it. Decide how far above the ground you want the handle. Measure the required height on the door and mark it across the centre line on the door edge. Transfer the height line around on to the two faces of the door. Measure in from the edge of the door the distance recommended by the manufacturer for the centre hole of the latch spindle.

Bore holes into the edge of the door for the latch and into the face of the door for the spindle. Where possible bore the spindle hole from both sides to prevent the bit from breaking through and damaging the face of the door.

Insert the latch in the hole and mark around the face plate with a sharp knife or pencil. Remove the latch from the door. With a sharp chisel cut out the housing for the face plate of the latch. Be careful not to go too deep. Replace the latch and screw it in place.

Push the spindle into the latch and put one lever handle on to the spindle. Ensure that the handle is parallel to the edge of the door then screw it in position. Repeat with the other handle – with very thin doors it may be necessary to shorten the spindle. Check the working of the handles – they should return to the horizontal position freely on release.

Close the door carefully and mark the position of the latch on the frame. Measure back from the edge of the rebate in the frame the distance the latch face is set back from the face of the door.

Put the striking plate on the frame in the correct position and mark around it with a sharp knife or pencil.

Cut out a deep hole to take the latch and a shallower one so that the striking plate can be sunk flush with the door frame. Screw the striking plate in position and check that the latch engages properly when you close the door.

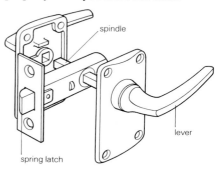

A mortise latch and lever handles.

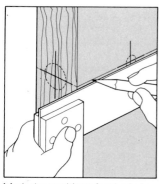

Mark the positions for the holes for latch and handle spindle on the door

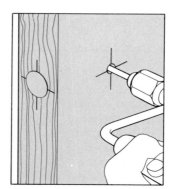

Bore the spindle hole from both sides of the door – to stop the bit damaging the door face

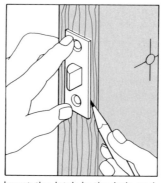

Insert the latch in the hole and mark around the face plate with a pencil or sharp knife

Chisel out the housing for the face plate, replace the latch (and plate) and screw it in

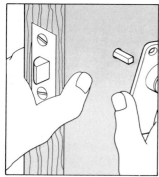

Screw on the lever handles making sure that they are parallel to the edge of the door

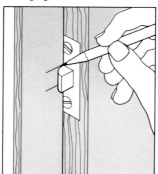

Close the door so that you can transfer the position of the latch on to the frame

Position the striking plate on the door frame and mark around it with a pencil or knife

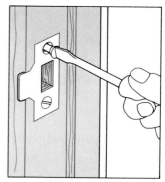

Cut out the hole for the striking plate (and latch) so that it is flush with the frame

213

Door problems

During normal use or even during hanging, a door and its frame may develop several defects. The most common ones are discussed on these two pages with an explanation of their cause and an outline of how to cure them.

A binding door

If the hinge side of a door comes into contact with the frame before the door is fully closed, it is probably because the hinges have been sunk too far into the door or frame. A door in this condition is said to be hinge bound. A door may also become hinge bound if the screws project out of their countersinks and stop the hinge closing fully.

This problem can be cured either by packing out the hinge in its sinking – use materials such as sandpaper, card, cardboard or hardboard – or by driving the screw fully home. In the latter case new screws which are shorter than the original ones may be the best solution.

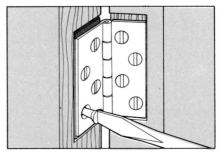
Insert packing beneath the hinges to cure a hinge bound door. Always leave the screw slots vertical

A sticking door

Occasionally a door may stick when it comes into contact with the frame through too much paint on the door and frame, or in the case of external doors, because the wood has swollen.

The simplest solution is to plane off a sufficient amount of wood to allow the door to close freely. Take the wood off the door, not off the frame – it is much easier. The door may have to be removed to get at the top and bottom. Take care not to overdo planing down external doors that are damp. The door will shrink when it dries out and if too much is taken off, a large gap will be left.

When a door which has to pass over an uneven floor catches the floor over the high spots, you should locate the problem places on the floor, put sandpaper over them and pass the door over the sandpaper a few times.

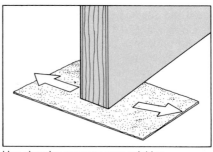
Use abrasive paper to stop sticking

A sagging door

Doors usually sag because the hinges have been pulled out of the frame or door edge, or because the hinges have been strained. Hinges often work loose when a door is hinge bound. To resecure the hinges you can:
● use longer screws
● use thicker screws – size 10s instead of 8s, for example, so long as the hinges have holes large enough to accommodate them
● insert pieces of dowel into the screw holes before putting the screws back in.

A problem with strained hinges usually means that the hinges were not big enough – a pair of 75mm hinges will generally hold an internal door but a heavy external one may need three 100mm hinges.

With boarded and panel doors the swinging (lock) stile – the one opposite the hinges – may drop so that the door bottom catches on the floor as you open it. This sag in the frame can usually be attributed to one of two causes.

Loose joints In framed doors – panel and boarded – the joints occasionally work loose. To resecure them, cut new wedges for the ends of the tenons and bore two holes through the stile and the tenons to take pieces of dowel. Glue the wedges and dowel firmly in place. If the tenon is broken in the mortise hole, bore two holes down the tenon into the rail and glue pieces of dowel in place to strengthen the joint.

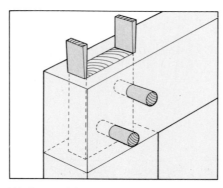
Wedges and dowels to retighten a joint

Poor bracing Framed ledged-and-braced doors need to be braced. A door that is not adequately braced – because its braces are at too shallow an angle, say – has no braces, or has its braces the wrong way round, will sag. Braces should have their lowest point at the swinging stile.

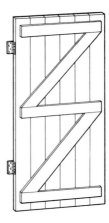
A ledged-and-braced door with adequate bracing. This door has its hinges on the left hand side

A twisted or bowed door

Twisting, bowing and warping can be caused by uneven heating around the house – a very warm room on one side of a door with a cold hall on the other side, say. Or by turning up the heating in a new house before the building has had a chance to dry out slowly. To cure the problem, the door must be bent in the opposite direction.

If the swinging side of the door is warped, you could try forcing it back into shape and jamming it closed with wedges driven between the door and frame. Leave the door closed for a few days. Otherwise you could clamp a stout piece of timber to either side of the door and insert packing pieces to reverse the distortion. Use G-clamps and take care to avoid damaging the door. It is a good idea to put timber packing under the G-clamps to prevent their indenting the door surface. The clamps and timber

should be left in place for at least a couple of days.

If a door is bowed on the hinge side, it could be forced back into line and kept there by fitting an extra hinge in the middle of the side.

If the above methods are unsuccessful or impractical – you should not try bending doors which have glass panels – you could try to reduce the effect of the distortion by one of the following two methods.

If the door frame has loose stops, these can be removed and replaced in a new position that allows the door to enter further into the frame, thereby concealing some of the distortion.

Warping can also be made less obvious by moving the hinge in the opposite corner to the twist. Do this by removing the screws in the hinge, plugging them with timber and rescrewing the hinge further forward in the frame.

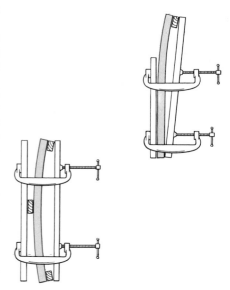

Top: removing a twist in a door – in this case one of the top corners is twisted. Bottom: straightening a bent door

A loose door frame

A door frame may work loose and come away from the wall if it has been misused or was inadequately fixed. Curing the problem is generally fairly simple.

Remove the door and remove the architrave from the loose side of the frame. Clear away any loose plaster and broken brick from behind the frame. You will probably find some packing – bits of plywood or hardboard, for example – which was inserted when the door and frame were originally hung. Replace this behind the frame so that when the frame is refixed it will be vertical, and can be secured firmly to the wall behind.

Use a masonry drill to bore holes through the frame into the wall – a depth of about 60mm in the wall should be sufficient. Plug the holes in the wall and screw back the frame – see page 148 for details of wall fixings. Before replacing the architrave make sure that the frame is straight and free from twist. Finally, refix the architrave and rehang the door.

You can also use the procedure outlined above when hanging a new door into a badly distorted or tapering frame. In this situation you will have to adjust the packing behind the frame (you may need to add more) to remove the distortion or taper.

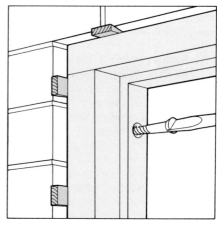

Repacking a loose door frame

A rotten door frame

Door frames usually rot at the bottom. Repair means carefully sawing away the rotten wood at least 50mm above the rot – this may mean as much as 600mm above the rot you can see – and splicing in a new section of frame.

First saw off the base of the frame above the rotten section – *cut 1*. Saw half way across the frame at least 50mm above the first cut – *cut 2*. The further apart these two cuts are, the better the

rigidity of the splice. Carefully chisel away the waste between *cut 1* and *cut 2*.

Cut a new section of timber to fit into the frame and check the accuracy of fit. The better the fit, the more likely you are to achieve a good repair.

Paint the new section of timber with a wood preservative and then a primer. Fix it in position using at least two screws into the existing frame. If the new section is very long, it may need fixing to the brickwork – use long screws and plugs.

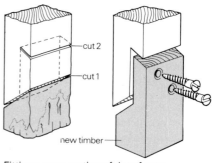

Fitting a new section of door frame

Windows

Windows provide nearly all the natural light which enters a house and are important sources of ventilation. They are usually designed to be compatible with the architectural style of the house.

Light Too much sunlight coming in can mean extremely hot rooms on bright sunny days and can lead to problems with furniture – fabric and wood – fading. Too little, on the other hand, means dark dismal rooms, particularly in winter. As a general rule, the area of window in a room should be approximately one seventh of the floor area of the room.

Ventilation Adequate ventilation should be provided by the inclusion of opening windows. The area of opening should be at least one twentieth of the floor area of the room.

Insulation Although glass is a good insulator, the thinness of window panes – from 3 to 6mm in most cases – compared with the 300mm or so thickness of house walls, means that about 20 per cent of the heat lost from the house goes out of the windows. This heat loss can be reduced by using thicker glass or by installing double glazing. Either method will improve noise insulation too.

Window construction

As well as satisfying the demands for light, ventilation and insulation, windows should be constructed so that they: can be opened and closed easily; are easy to clean, inside and outside; and are weatherproof.

A window usually consists of a main frame around the window itself which in turn consists of fixed *lights* and opening *sashes* (or *casements*). The number of fixed lights and opening sashes can be varied by adding vertical *mullions* and horizontal *transoms* to the main frame. And the fixed lights and sashes may also be sub-divided into smaller panes of glass by using *glazing bars*.

A casement window, for example, is made up of two basic parts – a frame and an opening window. The frame is built from two vertical jambs, a sill and a head. Additional fixed or opening windows may be formed by inserting horizontal transoms and vertical mullions into the frame. The window is made up from two stiles, a top rail and a bottom rail. Additional glass panels may be formed by inserting glazing bars into the window.

A variety of materials and combinations of materials are used in the manufacture of windows today.

Timber is the most common. Windows designed for painting are made of softwood; those designed for sealing or varnishing are hardwood. Hardwood may also be used for sills in softwood frames as it is more durable than softwood.

Aluminium alloy is becoming increasingly popular, particularly in double-glazed units and it is available with a variety of anodized coloured coatings, including white. Some aluminium alloy windows are fixed into a timber sub-frame – usually a hardwood.

Steel with a galvanised coating to protect it from corrosion was particularly popular in the 1930s but is now less widely used. The steel frames are usually fixed into timber sub-frames.

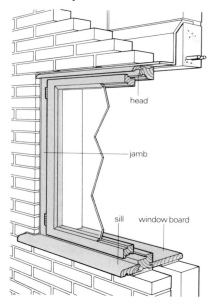

A timber stormproof window – with one opening window. The frame does not have any mullions or transoms

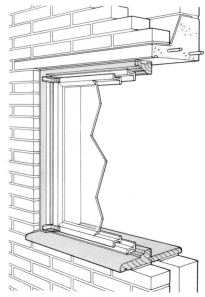

A metal window fixed into a timber sub-frame. Again the frame does not have any mullions or transoms

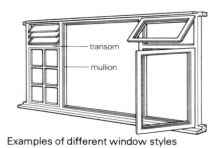

Examples of different window styles

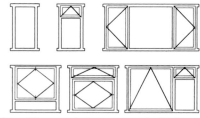

How different windows open: the V-shapes indicate hinges; the diamonds, pivots

Types of window

The different window types and styles are usually available in a range of sizes. The most common types are:

● **standard casement windows**, which are the most widely used type today. They are available off the shelf in a wide range of shapes and sizes, from the major timber window manufacturers and builders' merchants. Because of the versatility of this design, a variety of formats can be created by insetting mullions, transoms, and top and side hung opening windows

● **double hung vertical sliding sash windows**, which are very sophisticated in design combining a large area of glass with slim timber sections. An arrangement of cords, weights and pulleys is used to counterbalance the weight of the sash and so make the windows easier to open and close. Double hung sliding sash windows have, over the years, proved their reliability. The main causes of complaint – rattling and sticking – were a result of the window's designer making an allowance for the thickness of the paint film. If paint is over zealously applied the windows tend to stick. On the other hand, if the designer leaves a large gap around the window for the paint film, the window may rattle. Modern exterior stain finishes overcome this problem – they do not build up on the window – and so modern sash windows can be built to much closer tolerances without sticking or rattling. This type of window is still very popular today – it provides excellent control over ventilation and can be double glazed. In a modern version the weights and pulleys are replaced by a pair of spiral sash balances. These balances remove the necessity for the jambs to be built up to form the pockets for the weights – instead smaller solid jambs are used

● **horizontal or vertical pivot hung windows**, which originated in Scandinavia. This type of window is useful for situations when a large clear sash is wanted yet provision must be made for the cleaning of both sides of the window from the inside – a roof window in a loft conversion, say. The window may be pivoted horizontally or vertically – the horizontal pivot is the more popular.

The most common variations are:

● **bow windows**, which are Georgian in style and are curved – they bow out, hence their name. This type of window usually contains lots of small glass panels formed by using glazing bars to produce flat glazing areas instead of curved ones. The window may curve within the thickness of the wall or, as is more common, project out from the face of the house. Projecting windows have a small flat roof which is usually covered with lead

● **bay windows**, which vary a great deal in plan and elevation. The types most commonly found are semi-circular, segmental, splayed, and square on plan. The bay may provide a window for the ground floor only, or it may extend up to the top of the house. The shape of the roof above the bay varies – from flat roofs to some form of pitched roof which is similar in style to the main roof.

Metal windows

Metal windows are manufactured from mild steel and coated with a layer of zinc to protect them against corrosion when fixed. The sections are welded at the corners to form a frame. This frame has pre-bored countersunk holes (in the web of the section) so that it can be screwed directly into a brick wall or on to a timber or pressed steel sub-frame.

A metal frame fixed on to a timber sub-frame produces a window which is fairly easy to maintain. If corrosion becomes excessive, the window can be removed from the sub-frame and replaced with a new one. If the sub-frame starts to rot, the window frame can be removed and the sub-frame repaired or replaced.

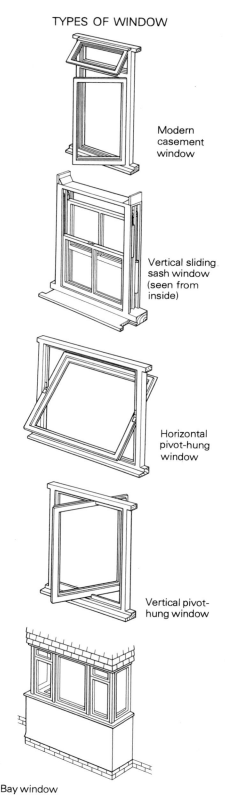

TYPES OF WINDOW

Modern casement window

Vertical sliding sash window (seen from inside)

Horizontal pivot-hung window

Vertical pivot-hung window

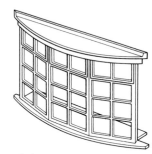

Bow window

Bay window

Repairing window frames and sills

Problems with windows often go unnoticed until it is time to decorate. Then loose joints, rotten rails and rotten frames become all too obvious. Most window repairs are fairly simple and well within the capabilities of the average handyman. With most frame and sill repairs, it is best to take the frame out of the window opening but some can be effected – on a temporary basis, at least – with the frame in place. The jobs outlined on the next five pages may not cover your own particular situation exactly but should give you some idea of what is involved and where to start.

Windows are fixed to the brickwork surrounding them in a number of ways:
● with fixing cramps screwed to the window frame and buried into the mortar between the bricks
● by building the 'horns' on the ends of the sill and frame head into the brickwork
● by driving screws or nails into wooden plugs held between the bricks
● by driving screws into plugged holes in the brickwork.

If you are taking the old frame out for repair, you will want to cause as little damage as possible to the old frame and should plan the job to take into account how you intend to replace it. When taking out an old frame to fit a new one, you can go about the job in a more vigorous and much quicker manner.

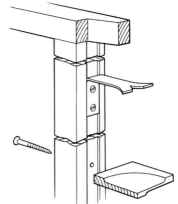

FIXING A WINDOW FRAME

The methods commonly used to fix window frames into brickwork – with cramps, plugs and screws or by the horns

Removing a window frame – for repair

Unscrew any opening window in the frame and reclaim any hinges and stays that might be reusable. If the frame has fixed lights, remove them if possible and save the glass for reuse. Glass left in place will hinder the safe removal of the window.

Use an old cold chisel or some similar implement to scrape and chisel away the mastic and mortar around the edge of the frame. Then insert a thin hacksaw blade between the frame and the brickwork and run it down the side of the frame until you find the fixings. Wrap the blade in cloth to protect your hand (or use a padsaw handle) and cut through the fixings.

Use a plugging chisel carefully to cut away the mortar joints around the brickwork holding in the horns. Remove the brick or bricks and save them (you will want to replace them later). Rake out the mortar bed under the window sill.

The frame should now be free so you can gently knock it out of the opening with a mallet or a hammer and a piece of wood held so that it protects the frame. It may be necessary to remove the window board before you can get the frame out.

Putting the old frame back
Before you start taking the frame out, you must decide how the frame is to be refixed. The choices are: to build in the horns or cut them off; to use screws or nails driven into wooden plugs in the brickwork; or to use screws driven into plugged holes bored into the brickwork.

This sequence of operations deals with a window that has horns built into the brickwork and is held in position with wooden plugs and screws.

If the existing plugs are loose, refix

REMOVING A WINDOW FRAME FOR REPAIR

Cut through the fixings holding the frame in place – a padsaw handle is being used to grip the hacksaw blade

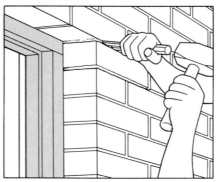

Use a plugging chisel to cut out the bricks and free the horns of the window. The bricks can be reused

Knock out the frame with a mallet (as shown) or a hammer – with a piece of wood between the frame and hammer head

Removing a window frame – to replace

Unscrew any opening windows in the frame and reclaim any hinges and stays which you could possibly use again. Carefully remove any glass in the fixed lights. You may be able to use this again too – for garden cloches at least.

Cut through the sill, transom and head of the frame twice. Make the cuts at an angle so that the material can be easily removed from between the jambs – see drawing. It may be necessary to remove the window board while you are doing this. If you do not remove it, take care to avoid damaging the internal reveals (and the window board itself).

Use a crowbar carefully to lever out the jambs from the sides of the window opening and then clear away from the opening any loose mortar, projecting

nails and plugs. The opening can now be covered over temporarily if necessary to await the fixing of the new frame. In many circumstances, a polythene sheet will provide satisfactory cover but when security is a problem use plywood.

CUTTING OUT AN OLD FRAME

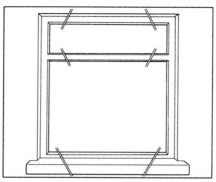

Make two cuts through the sill, transom and head of the frame at an angle – as shown – to make it easier to remove the wood between the cuts

Lever out the jambs using a crowbar. Note the window board has been removed to avoid damaging it when making the saw cuts

them into the brickwork or replace them with new ones. If the frame was held in position by fixing cramps, it may be necessary to cut new holes into the mortar between the bricks.

Check the fit of the frame in the opening and if everything is satisfactory lay a bed of mortar for the sill to rest on. You can shave off bits of the frame with a trimming tool or plane and pack out areas where the fit is poor. Any areas of bare woodwork exposed (and any new woodwork put in during the repair) should be treated with a preservative and primed before the frame is fixed.

Place the frame into position in the opening, hold it there making sure that it is square, and screw through the frame into the timber plugs. It may make the job easier if the frame is pre-bored – mark the location of the holes on to the frame when you try it in position.

Replace the bricks into the wall around the hole cut for the horns. If the bricks are damaged replace them. Point the mortar bed under the sill – see *Building* starting on page 151 for details of mortars. Replace the glass into the fixed lights and rehang the windows.

Fill the gap between the frame and the

brickwork with mortar to within 10mm of the outside edge of the frame. When the mortar has set (and possibly shrunk) fill the remainder of the gap with a non-setting mastic. Finally repaint the frame.

Reports in Handyman Which?

Doors

Doors	Aug 1977

Windows and glass

D-i-y double glazing	Nov 1977 and
	Nov 1973
Glass	Nov 1977
Putting in a window pane	Nov 1971
Replacing a sash cord	Feb 1973

REPLACING THE FRAME

After checking that the frame fits, lay a bed of mortar for the window sill to sit on

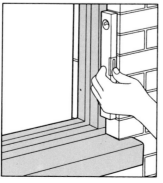

Use a spirit level to check that the frame is vertical and is not twisted

Screw through pre-bored holes in the frame into the plugs in the brickwork

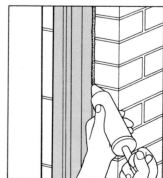

Apply mastic around the outside of the frame to seal and weatherproof the joint

Putting in a new window frame

When buying a new frame or having one specially made, make sure it is slightly smaller than the size of the opening. A slightly smaller frame is easier to locate in the opening and to adjust so that it is straight and vertical.

Fitting a new frame into an existing opening is basically the same as fitting a repaired frame. However:

● if the frame is smaller than the opening, insert packing between the frame and the brickwork. If the gap is too big to be covered by a mastic strip, a piece of timber – a quadrant mould, say – should be fitted around the edge of the frame

● if the original window was cut out, do not bother to cut away the brickwork to take the horns on the new frame – cut them off

● the new frame will probably be primed when you buy it – give it another coat of primer before you fix it. If the frame is bare wood – one specially made, say – treat it liberally with a wood preservative before priming it.

Damp-proof course

On modern buildings a damp-proof course will be found when the window is removed. The dpc is a strip of waterproof material that separates the two leaves of the cavity wall and stops moisture crossing from the outside leaf to the inside leaf around the window.

Do not remove a sound dpc. It should be refixed around the window frame when the window is replaced.

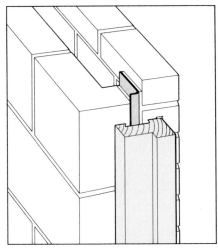

The dpc around a window (or door) frame is usually laid into a wide groove in the back of the frame

Replacing a wooden window sill

It is possible to replace a wooden window sill without removing the frame but the quality of the job, the strength and weathertightness of the window in the long term, and the life of the window may not be very great. To replace a wooden window sill properly, you should remove the window frame.

. . . by removing the frame

Before starting to remove the frame buy a replacement sill from your local timber merchant. If you have an unusual window, you may need to have one made specially. Choose a durable hardwood in preference to softwood. Use the old sill as a pattern to mark out the new one – the length of the sill and the size and position of the mortise holes.

Cut the old sill away from the frame. This can be done by cutting across the sill alongside the jambs and mullions (if there are any). The remaining wood around the tenons can be chopped off with a chisel but you must be careful – nails may have been used for fixing the sill to the frame. Remove any nails in the jambs and mullions. Cut out the mortises in the new sill.

If any of the tenons are rotten, you should splice in a replacement. To do this with a jamb, cut a slot out of the jamb along the line of the original tenon. This slot should be the same thickness as the original tenon and at least as long. Now cut a piece of wood the same width and thickness as the tenon but much longer – its length should be equal to that of the original tenon and the extra length of the newly-cut slot. This piece of wood will form a new tenon when it is glued and screwed in the slot.

Treat the mortises and tenons with preservative, paint them with primer and assemble the frame. Wedge and nail the mortise and tenon joints. Finally, treat all bare woodwork with preservative and paint the edges of the frame with primer.

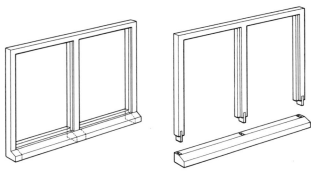

A rotten sill can be cut out – make the cuts alongside the jambs and mullions. If the tenons are rotten, replacement 'tongues' should be spliced in

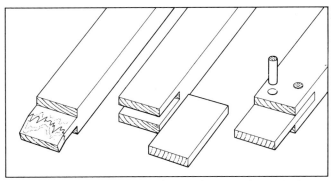

To splice in a new tenon, cut a slot out of the jamb (or mullion) along the line of the original tenon. Cut a 'tongue' to fit and dowel and glue it in place

REDUCING DRAUGHTS

Badly-fitting doors and windows can give rise to considerable heat loss and the draughts they produce can be uncomfortable. Fortunately, they can be dealt with cheaply and easily. It is important not to stop all draughts – gas-burning appliances, open fires and people need a constant supply of fresh air, and adequate ventilation will also help keep down condensation.

Door bottoms There are various types of draught excluder used to seal the gap between a door and the floor. **Plain strips** have a flexible seal attached to the door by a strip of wood or plastic. The seal is always in contact with the floor. **Hinged and parallel** draught excluders last longer – the seal is kept off the floor until the door closes. **Threshold** draught excluders fit on the floor, so they can be difficult to fit if the floor is uneven or not made of wood. **Round doors and windows** The simplest way of draught proofing round doors and windows is to use **plastic foam strip.** It is self-adhesive and sticks to the frame to fill any gaps. It is not very durable but is cheap. Metal or plastic **weather-strip** is more durable and particularly suitable for draught proofing front doors. **Rigid or flexible** draught excluders cover the gap rather than filling it and are quite noticeable.

DOOR BOTTOMS

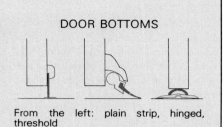

From the left: plain strip, hinged, threshold

ROUND DOORS AND WINDOWS

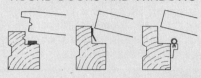

From the left: plastic foam strip, weather-strip, flexible (or rigid) strip

. . . with the frame in place

Very carefully remove the opening windows, fixed lights and window board. These will be reused later.

Cut across the sill as close to the jambs as possible and after most of the sill has been removed, carefully cut away the timber around the joints, taking care not to damage the jambs. Cut away the tenons from the bottom of the jambs.

Clean off the opening and remove any mortar bed left on the brickwork where the sill has been.

Cut the new length of sill to fit in between the brickwork. Prime it and the ends of the jambs. Make sure that the new sill has a groove (throating) beneath the front edge – this prevents rain-water running back.

Manoeuvre the sill into position and insert packing between the sill and the brickwork to push the sill as tightly as possible against the jambs. You may have to cut away the timber rebate of the sill to let the sill pass under the jambs.

Fix the sill in position using either screws or nails driven diagonally through the jambs. Screws are best: countersink the screw holes and cover the screw heads with a stopping to finish the job.

Pack the mortar under the sill, pushing it as far towards the back of the sill as possible. Replace the mastic joint around the frame.

Glue pieces of timber into the gaps in the joints between the jambs and the sill. (Use a water-resistant glue.) When they have set tightly in place, clean off the excess timber using a chisel and preserve and prime all exposed new wood.

Finally, replace the window board, windows, fixed lights and fasteners. If the window has a concrete or stone sub-sill, it may be easier to insert the sill in two pieces – the main part of the sill and a lath to form the rebate between the two jambs. The lath may be glued and screwed in position between the jambs. Alternatively, the sill could be made deeper and the jambs cut off square to fit into the housing in the sill.

Cut across the old sill close to the jambs – after removing the window board

Trim off the tenons from the bottom of the jambs and any transoms

Slide in the new sill – and shape the bottoms of the jambs and transoms as necessary

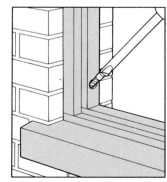

Fix the sill to the jambs by driving screws (countersunk) through the jambs into the sill

Repairing and replacing concrete sills

Minor defects such as cracks and chips can be repaired, but sills with major defects – a bad break or crumbling concrete, say – may have to be removed and replaced with a sill cast *in situ* or a new pre-made sill.

Repairing a cracked sill

The crack should be cleaned out and all the loose material removed. The crack can then be filled with a thin cement-based filler, or a branded product – see page 24 for details of filling cracks in brickwork and concrete.

Repairing a broken or chipped sill

A sill with some part broken off can be repaired by reforming the missing part of the sill with concrete.

The first task is to build a mould around the sill to support the material used to repair the damaged part. The best way to do this is to make a timber box around the sill and to hold it in position by using temporary timber supports nailed on to the brickwork. The damaged part of the sill should be cut back to sound concrete – use a bolster – before spreading the new concrete. The formwork should be left in position for a few days to allow the concrete to set.

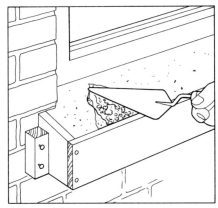

When repairing bits broken off the edge or corner of a concrete sill, use wood framework nailed to the wall

Resurfacing an old concrete sill

If a concrete sill is flaking, it is often better to resurface the whole sill rather than to try to repair a small area.

Use a hammer and bolster to chip away the surface of the old sill – take off 30 to 50mm. Hold a batten against the front edge of the sill, dampen the exposed surface and lay a mortar mix over the whole sill. Push the mortar well into cracks. Remove the batten and slope the mortar on the surface of the sill so that rain-water will run off. Round the outer edge slightly and smooth the surface.

Building a new sill

It is often possible to concrete a new sill *in situ* without too much trouble.

The first step is to remove the existing sill from the wall and to clear out the opening – remove all the rubble and dirt.

Now you will have to make a timber box to act as a mould for the new sill. This box should fit snugly against the wall around the opening and must be fixed securely in position – use stout pieces of timber fixed temporarily to the brickwork along both outer ends of the box and beneath it. Fix the box on to its supports with nails or screws but do not knock nails fully home. The sill must have a groove (or throating) in its under side. This can be formed by pinning a length of thick cord – such as washing line or sash cord – to the inside bottom of the box. It can then be removed after the concrete has set.

Place a few short lengths of steel in the box to act as reinforcement – two lengths about 6mm in diameter and 50 to 100mm shorter than the sill should be satisfactory. Care must also be taken to ensure that the lengths of steel do not get too close to the edge of the concrete and show on the finished surface.

Fill the box with a concrete mix of one part cement, two parts sand and one part fine aggregate. Give the sill a downwards slope before the concrete sets fully. Finally after one or two days the mould box can be carefully removed.

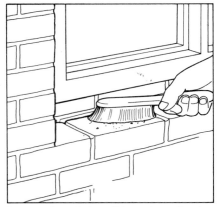

Remove the existing sill from the wall, using a hammer and bolster, and clear away all the rubble and dirt

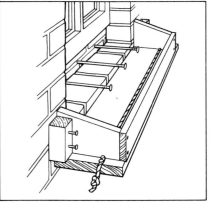

Two lengths of steel rod about 6mm in diameter or large nails (shown) should be used as reinforcement

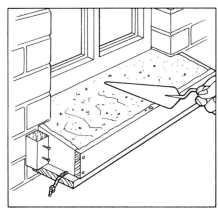

Fill the box with the concrete mix – slide it into the corners and smooth the surface. Give the concrete a downwards slope

Replacing sash cords

Tools and materials

Hammer
Pincers
Screwdriver
Rule
Pencil
Chisel
Knife
A long-tailed mouse (see text)
Waxed damp-proof sash cord or rot-resistant man-made fibre cord
25mm clout nails
Oval brads

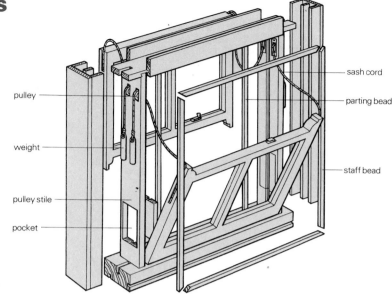

A traditional vertical hung sliding sash window with pulleys, cords and weights used to counterbalance the weight of the sash. Modern sash windows use spiral sash balances

On a sash window the sash cord' and timber sashes need regular maintenance and care to keep the window in good working order. If a cord breaks and some of the other cords show signs of wear, it is advisable to replace all the cords.

Remove the curtains and clear a large area around the window for you to work in. Assemble all the necessary tools and materials. Lower both sashes to the bottom of the box frame.

To remove the sashes from the frame you need to remove the beads holding the sashes in position. Do this with care as you will need to use them again later. First remove the staff bead – this runs up the jambs of the window and across the head. It is held in position either with pins or with nails and can be levered away from the jamb with a broad chisel. Start levering the bead in the middle of its length.

When the beads have been removed, the inner sash is held in position by its own weight and by the sash cords. Lean the top of the sash away from the frame and carefully cut the cords with a knife. Keep hold of each cord as you cut it and gently lower the weight to the bottom of the box frame. When both cords have been cut, the sash can be removed. Put it somewhere safe.

A pair of beads – called parting beads – lie between the two sashes to keep them apart. These will have to be removed to take out the outer sash. Again do this carefully by levering them out of their grooves with a broad chisel. Start at one end of the bead and work towards the other end. Cut the cords and remove the outer sash.

You can get access to the weights inside the box frame through a small pocket at the bottom of the pulley stiles. A small wooden cover is let into the timber forming the pulley stiles. To remove this cover undo the small screw holding it in place and carefully lever the cover out.

To remove the weights, carefully raise them inside the box frame and draw them out – bottom end first. The two

Carefully lever off the staff bead starting at the centre of its length – use a broad chisel

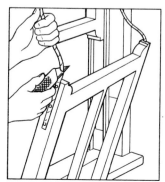

Lean the top of the inner sash away from the frame and cut the cords with a knife

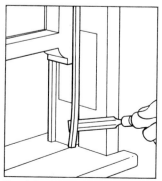

Carefully lever off the parting bead starting at the bottom and working upwards

Open the pockets at the bottom of the pulley stiles and remove the weights – bottom end first

weights in each side should be separated by a thin strip of timber called a wagtail. Do not try to remove it or damage it – you can get at the weights by moving the wagtail aside. The wagtail keeps the two weights apart and so prevents them banging into each other when the sashes are moved up and down.

Mark out the lengths of cord needed. Do this carefully as cord is expensive and waste should be avoided. For the window to work properly the lengths of cord should be such that, when the sash is in the lowered position, the weight should be at the top of the box frame and when the sash is in the raised position the weight should not quite rest on the bottom of the box. The sash cord will need to be fixed on to the sash below the centre of the pulley for approximately 100mm. Mark this distance down from the top of each sash and square it across the edge. Measure the distance from the bottom of the sash to the cord line and mark this measurement up from the sill on each jamb. This line on the jamb is the lowest point that the end of the sash cord on the sash stile will reach. The two sashes may be different sizes, so care must be taken to ensure the correct measurement is marked for each sash. If a man-made rope cord is used, make allowance for the cord stretching.

The next step is to insert the sash cord through the pulleys and pockets. To do this you need a 'long tailed mouse' – a small bent piece of lead fastened to a long piece of string. Insert the mouse over the pulley and allow it to fall to the bottom of the pocket. Tie the sash cord to the end of the mouse's tail and pull the mouse and cord through the pocket. The weight can now be tied to the cord – see drawing for the knot to use – and put back in the pocket. The weight will go back easier if you pull on the cord a little.

Now you can cut the cord to length. Pull the weight up as far as it will go to the pulley and hold it in this position. Cut the sash cord off at the length line marked across the jamb. Tie a figure of eight knot in the end of the cord and lower the weight. The knot will prevent the cord slipping back through the pulley. Repeat the operation on the remain-

REPLACING THE WEIGHTS

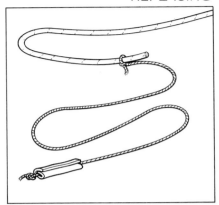
Tie the tail of the 'mouse' on to the sash cords and use the mouse to feed the sash cords over the pulleys

The sash cords should be tied to the weights using the non-slip knot shown above

ing weights. (The outer weights should be inserted into the frame first.) Replace the pockets and screw them in position.

While the window is stripped down, it is advisable to sand off the paintwork and repaint the frame and sashes – this is a difficult and very often unsuccessful job when the window is assembled. Examine the sashes to see if their joints are sound.

Replace the sashes in the frame starting with the outer one. Pull down the sash cord and nail it into the sash cord groove on the edge of the sash. The end of the cord should be nailed on the length line marked on the edge of the sash. Use clout nails – their large heads give a secure fixing. When both sides of the sash have been fixed to the cord, place it in its proper position and check that it can rise to the top of the frame.

Replace the parting beads – if they are damaged they should be replaced with new ones – and refit the inside sash.

Replace the staff bead – use oval brads to nail it in position. Again renew it if it is damaged. Check that both sashes rise and lower without any difficulty.

Fixing a loose corner joint on a sash

Sashes may develop loose joints when they get old, particularly if they are gummed up with paint and stick in the frame. A sash in this condition is not only awkward to operate easily, it can also be dangerous. Loose joints can be fixed in

one of two ways – either by refastening the tenon in the mortise, or by attaching a metal plate to the side of the sash to strengthen and stiffen the joint.

To refix the joint you will have to remove the sash from the frame. Hold the sash in suitably-sized sash cramps and bore two holes through the tenons that are loose. Next bore two holes down the tenons, making sure that the holes penetrate well into the rail. Glue pieces of dowel into the holes – 5mm dowel should be satisfactory and use a waterproof adhesive. The dowels will go into holes bored through the tenons more easily if they are tapered at one end. You will have difficulty forcing tightly-fitting dowels into the blind holes down the tenons unless the dowels have a groove cut down their edges.

When the glue has dried the sash can be removed from the cramps and the dowels cleaned off ready for the sash to be replaced in the frame.

The second method is to screw a metal plate on to the face of the sash. This is less successful and looks ugly, but it can be achieved without the sash being removed from the frame. To clamp the joint, it is necessary to insert two hardwood wedges between the edge of the sash and the frame. The metal plate can then be screwed in position and the wedges removed. If the angle plate is bright steel, give it protective coats of paint to stop it corroding.

Glass

Most of the glass sold is for replacing broken windows or for installing new ones. The sort of glass you need for this is usually known as flat glass or, sometimes, **window glass**.

For those places where there is a high risk of breakage – such as internal doors and low-level glazing – it is essential to use one of the special sorts of **safety glass**.

As well as these two types of glass, there are many **other sorts** of glass for use in windows and doors, many of which are designed to achieve some kind of special effect.

Window glass

Until a few years ago, there were two main types of glass sold for putting in windows: sheet glass and plate glass.

Sheet glass was made by drawing molten glass up a tall tower and breaking it off in sheets at the top. The surface of sheet glass is 'fire finished' and perfectly smooth, but its thickness varies and the two surfaces may not be exactly parallel. This means that panes of sheet glass will tend to distort objects that are seen through them and the distortion will vary as the observer moves. The traditional way of expressing the size of sheet glass was by its weight (in ounces) for each square foot of sheet. The common sizes were 18oz, 24oz and 32oz.

Plate glass was made by a quite different process where the glass was first cast and then ground and polished to make the two surfaces smooth and flat. This meant that plate glass was free of distortions and stronger than sheet glass, but its method of manufacture made it rather expensive. Sizes for plate glass were traditionally expressed by thickness – in fractions of an inch. Common sizes were $\frac{1}{8}$in, $\frac{1}{4}$in and $\frac{1}{2}$in.

In 1959, a completely new method of making glass was invented involving floating the molten glass on liquid tin while it cools. The resulting **float** glass has both the lack of distortion of plate glass and the smooth surface finish of sheet glass. Not surprisingly, float glass has almost entirely replaced sheet and plate glass, though some low-quality sheet glass is still made for use in greenhouses. This **horticultural** glass is about half the price of normal glass and is often sold in standard sizes to fit greenhouses. It is not suitable for use in windows.

As well as the method of manufacture changing, the method of quoting glass sizes has changed, too. All glass is now sold according to its thickness in millimetres – common sizes are 3mm, 4mm, 5mm, 6mm and 10mm (equivalent to 24oz, 32oz, $\frac{1}{16}$in, $\frac{1}{4}$in and $\frac{3}{8}$in).

Which size? The thickness of glass you need for a window depends on the size and shape of the window, the likely wind loading and the likelihood of breakage. With small or very sheltered windows, 3mm glass can be used but, for most windows, 4mm is the best choice. Larger windows will need 6mm or even 10mm glass. For windows at risk you should use at least 6mm – or one of the safety glasses (see below). Glass for patio doors should be 6mm or 10mm; glass for picture framing can be 3mm or even 2mm. The price of window glass is proportional to its thickness – so expect to pay twice as much for 10mm as for 5mm – but prices can vary widely. Sizes up to 6mm should be readily available in glass merchants, though you may have to order 10mm and above.

Safety glass

Ordinary glass breaks into very sharp pieces. Safety glass is designed so that it is less likely to break and when it does so the consequences are less serious. There are three types: toughened, laminated and wired.

Most **toughened** glass (sometimes called tempered glass) is produced by special heat treatment of ordinary (annealed) glass and when it breaks, it crazes into lots of tiny fragments. Because the surface of toughened glass is very hard, it is not possible to cut it, make holes in it or carry out any 'edge working' once it has been toughened. Ordering toughened glass may take a few weeks and you can expect to pay about twice the price of the equivalent size of ordinary glass. Toughened glass is up to five times stronger than ordinary glass and can be used for internal doors, door side panels, low-level glazing, balustrades and shower screens and because it is heat resistant, it is ideal for table tops.

In **laminated** glass, two or more panes of ordinary glass are interleaved with a layer or layers of plastic. When laminated glass breaks, the glass sticks to the plastic layers and so is much less of a hazard than ordinary glass. It is possible to make laminated glass that is extremely tough, and in the home, it can be used for the same risk areas as toughened glass, but has the advantage that it provides added security since it is extremely difficult to penetrate, even when broken. You will probably have to order laminated glass – expect to pay around twice the price of ordinary glass. It is possible to cut and shape laminated glass, but it is a skilled job which is probably best left to the glass merchant.

The third type of safety glass – **wired** glass – is made by fusing together two layers of glass with a welded wire mesh sandwiched between them. Unlike the plastic layer in laminated glass, the wire mesh does not make the glass any less likely to break but it does hold the glass pieces together when it does. Its main use is to act as a barrier against flames and smoke in the event of a fire – it has a one-hour fire rating. It can also be used for skylights where ordinary glass could constitute a hazard for those below. The usual thickness for Georgian wired glass is 6mm (Georgian wired glass has a mesh of small squares as opposed to the chicken wire type). For rough cast wired glass, which provides a degree of privacy, you can expect to pay slightly more than ordinary 6mm glass; for polished wired glass, which is clear, you can expect to pay at least twice as much. Wired glass can be cut, but again it is probably a job best left to a glass merchant.

Other sorts of glass

There are many other sorts of glass, apart from window glass and safety glass, which can be used in the home although some of them are designed with industrial or commercial uses more in mind.

Patterned glass is produced by passing molten glass over a textured roller which imparts its pattern to one side of the glass; the other side is usually smooth. There is a wide range of patterns available, including a number which are available in tinted versions – blue, green and amber, for example. Patterned glass serves two main purposes: to provide a degree of privacy and to provide decoration. The degree of privacy depends on the amount that the light passing through the glass is diffused, which varies with the pattern. The common sizes of patterned glass are 4mm and 6mm, and prices for ordinary white patterned glass are only a little more than similar sizes of flat glass; tinted glass is roughly twice as expensive. It is possible to get patterned glass toughened – for use as room dividers, kitchen screens, shower screens or in all-glass doors.

Diffuse reflection glass Glass reflects about 10 per cent of the light falling on it. Sometimes, this reflection can be a nuisance – the reflection of a window or table lamp in the glass of a picture frame, for example. Diffuse reflection glass has a slightly textured surface and can be used to overcome this problem. It's readily available in 2mm thicknesses and costs about twice as much as float glass.

Solar control glass A room that faces south can get very hot when the sun is shining into it, and furniture can be damaged by direct sunlight. Solar control glasses cut down the amount of solar heat radiation passing through the glass without reducing too much the amount of light passing through – though they do cut down glare. These glasses are often tinted and some have a surface coating. Most are available in toughened or laminated versions and for use in both single and double glazing units. A common solar control glass is 'Antisun' float glass which is body tinted grey or bronze and comes in a range of thicknesses; 6mm 'Antisun' costs twice as much as ordinary 6mm float. As well as being used in windows and doors, this can be used effectively for glass shelves, table tops or for silvering as a tinted mirror. Another solar control glass you may find is 'Spectrafloat' which has a metallic layer just below the surface. The 6mm size is a little cheaper than 6mm 'Antisun'. Another way of cutting down solar radiation is to apply a self-adhesive plastic film to an existing window pane. As well as cutting down solar radiation (and reducing heat loss) this film has a safety advantage in that the film will hold the pane together if it breaks.

Mirrors At its simplest, a mirror is a piece of 6mm glass with silvering on the back. The silvering is usually covered with layers of copper and backing paint to protect it. It is possible to get any piece of glass silvered, but it is probably simplest to buy a mirror ready-made. 'Verity' mirrors are made by a number of manufacturers to standards laid down by the Glass Advisory Council. They are made in only four standard sizes: 760×440mm; 1200×360mm; 1520×440mm and 1200×600mm.

Decorative glass Glass can be stained, engraved or treated in other ways to provide unusual decorative effects. It is worth investigating glass merchants to see what they offer. You can even have glass with your own coat of arms. One effect, often used in pseudo-Georgian windows is *bullion* glass which comes in a range of sizes to fit different size windows and costs about five times as much as ordinary 4mm glass.

Buying glass

Glass is sold by some builders' merchants and also by some do-it-yourself and hardware shops. But the main place to buy glass is from **glass merchants** – sometimes known as **glaziers** if they offer an installation service as well as selling glass.

Compared with other types of shop, glass merchants are cheaper – though prices still vary from one to another – and have a much wider range of types of glass in stock. In addition, they offer a number of helpful services:

● **advice** on the types and sizes of glass to use for different jobs. In general, this advice is likely to be sound

● **cutting** glass to your dimensions without charge. It is essential that you give correct dimensions – cutting thin slivers off a pane is not easy and, of course, there is not much you can do with a pane that is too small

● **edge working** by smoothing rough edges or giving edges a polished effect. They usually charge for this and for shaping or bevelling the edges of a piece of glass. Sometimes, you may want a hole cut in a pane – for an extractor fan, say – and a glass merchant can do this for you, too. This may be free if you're buying the glass at the same time

● **delivering** glass in specially-designed vans which protect the glass in transit. The amount glass merchants charge for this depends on the distance they have to come and the size of the order. If you live fairly close and are buying a reasonable quantity, delivery will probably be free

● **disposal** of broken glass. One of the problems of replacing a broken window is getting rid of the broken glass. Some glass merchants will take this for you – they sell it back to the glass manufacturers since broken glass (known as *cullet*) is an important ingredient in the glass-making process.

Buying glass from a glass merchant can be a strange experience. Although many have a 'shop' where different types of glass are on display and where you give your order, some are large warehouses full of glass where you have to find someone who might serve you. It is probably best not to take small children when shopping for glass.

Working with glass

The key to successful working with glass is confidence. If you know what you are doing and treat glass with the proper respect, there should be no problems; if you are careless or uncertain, you will break it.

Normally, it makes sense to get a glass merchant to cut glass to the exact size when you buy it and perhaps to cut any holes and smooth the edges, but there will still be occasions when you will need to know how to cut a straight line, how to cut a circle, how to drill holes and how to finish edges.

Safety note When working with glass, it is important to wear protective clothes: the main areas that need protecting are hands, wrists, eyes and feet. Hands and wrists can be protected with gauntlets – alternatively, wear thick gloves and wrist bands. For eyes (particularly when drilling), wear proper eye protectors. Dropping a jagged piece of glass on to your foot can be nasty – so wear strong shoes.

Cutting straight lines

Glass is cut by scoring a line along the surface with a glass cutter and then applying pressure on either side of the score line to make a clean break. The glass itself should be clean and free from cracks and notches and the surface it is cut on should be flat, even and padded – with felt, old carpet or layers of newspaper. Patterned glass should always be cut on the flat side.

Most glass cutters have a small hardened steel wheel to make the score – some have six wheels, which are used in turn as they go blunt. More expensive glass cutters have diamond cutters: these should last indefinitely and you will need a diamond for harder high-silica glass. Before use, a glass cutter should be 'wetted' with light oil or paraffin.

The line should be scored with one continuous firm stroke, pulling the cutter towards you. The cutter is held in the hand rather like a pencil and at an angle of about 60 degrees to the glass. It is essential to use a straight-edge or T-square to keep the line straight. Too much pressure can cause the glass to flake.

The glass can now be broken – by placing a straight wooden lath or other straight edge under the score and applying light but firm pressure on either side of the score. Another method is to tap the underside of the score lightly with the back of the glass cutter and snap the glass apart by holding it at one edge on either side of the score and flexing downwards. This method is particularly useful when cutting only a thin strip off a pane. With a *very thin* strip, it is necessary to nibble the strip off after making the score using pliers, pincers or the slots in the handles of most glass cutters. These slots – usually for two or three different thicknesses of glass – are known as a breaker rack.

After the glass has been broken, the edge can be smoothed with the smooth side of an oilstone moistened with water. Fine glasspaper can also be used, but it must be wrapped round a support block for safety.

Cutting holes

If you want to make a large circle in a pane of glass – to take an extractor fan, perhaps – you will need a different sort of glass cutter: a beam compass (or circle) cutter. This consists of a pivot with a rubber suction pad, an adjustable beam and a cutter on the end of the beam.

As with straight line cutting, the first thing to do is to score the glass, having first set the cutter to the radius you want. The pivot with its sucker should be supported with one hand while the other applies gentle pressure to make an even continuous score. Tap the glass lightly underneath to open the score. Once you have a neat circle, make several straight line scores within the circle – going right to the edge but not beyond – until there is a good crosshatched pattern. Tap the glass lightly on the back, tapping more heavily towards the centre of the circle until some of the glass falls out. Go on

CUTTING A STRAIGHT LINE

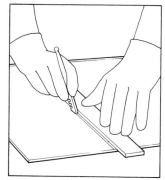
Make a score by running the cutter along a straight-edge. When using a wheeled cutter, make sure that the wheel rotates

Lubricate the score with white spirit, place a wooden lath beneath the glass and apply even pressure to both sides

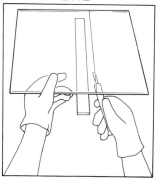
Alternatively, tap the underside of the score lightly with the back of the glass cutter then flex the glass downwards

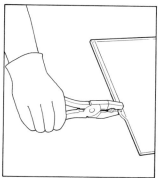
Very thin strips are difficult to break off – use pliers or a breaker rack to nibble them away. Finish off with an oilstone

CUTTING A CIRCLE

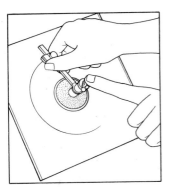

Apply an even pressure and make a continuous score. If you want to cut a hole, score a second circle inside the first

Crosshatch the inner circle with scores about 5 to 10mm apart and make radial scores to the outer circle

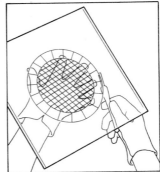

Supporting the glass, gently tap the underside to knock out the centre

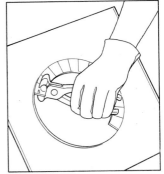

Use a breaker rack to nibble out the remaining pieces of glass or use pincers – as shown

tapping – or use a breaker rack to remove the remaining pieces. Finally, smooth the cut edge with fine glasspaper wrapped round something circular – a screwdriver handle, say.

When cutting a hole near the edge of a pane of glass, it is better to cut the hole first and cut the pane to size afterwards.

Circular glass cutters can also be used for cutting discs of glass. To do this, tangential lines are scored to the scored circle and the pieces broken off as with straight line cutting. The finished disc will need a considerable amount of smoothing to get it perfectly round.

Drilling holes

To drill holes in glass, a special glass bit should be used – these are often shaped like a spear. Masonry drills should **not** be used: they are likely to shatter the glass.

Once the position of the hole has been decided, put a ring of putty or plasticine around it to form a well and fill this with a small amount of lubricant – water, paraffin or white spirit. The glass should be well supported on the back with several layers of newspaper.

The main problem is starting the hole

DRILLING A HOLE

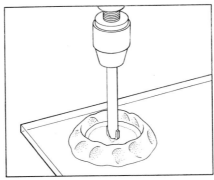

Fill the well around the drill bit with a lubricant – water, turps or paraffin, say. Support the glass on newspaper

in exactly the right place as the drill bit will tend to skid across the glass. Use a slow speed to start the hole, preferably with the drill mounted in a drill stand. Light pressure should be maintained and the speed kept down to prevent the drill bit overheating. Reduce the pressure as the bit comes to the end of the hole.

When drilling mirrors, start the hole from the back – to make a clean cut through the silvering – and once the drill point makes a pinhole on the other side, turn the mirror over and finish off from the front.

When drilling holes in bottles, fill the bottle with sand and rest it in a bed of sand to hold it in position. Stop drilling from time to time to lubricate the drill bit or the hole.

If all this sounds like too much bother, get a glass merchant to drill the holes for you. Unless you are drilling a large number of holes, this will not be very expensive.

Double glazing

As its name suggests, double glazing is a matter of having two panes of glass rather than one. There are three main reasons for fitting double glazing to your windows: to reduce the amount of heat getting out; to reduce the amount of noise getting in and to increase comfort for people in the room or house – mainly by cutting down draughts.

Reducing heat loss Around 20 to 25 per cent of the heat loss from a house is through the windows. Double glazing can reduce this by up to a half because of the layer of still air between the two panes, which acts as an insulator. The optimum thickness for this air gap is about 20mm. Double glazing is not normally cost effective unless it is a do-it-

yourself installation.

Cutting down noise Double glazing may not, on its own, solve a noise problem but where the noise is getting in through the windows – traffic noise is an obvious example – double glazing can be very effective. The thickness of air gap needed is quite large. The normal recommendation is for an air gap of between 100mm and 200mm – practical considerations rule out gaps any larger than this. This size of air gap still provides effective heat insulation.

Increasing comfort One of the effects of a single-glazed window is to create a pool of 'cold' near the window. In addition, the cold inside surface of the window will create draughts. Because the inside pane of a double-glazed window is warmer, both these effects are reduced and more of the room becomes comfortable to sit in.

Another important effect of double glazing is to reduce condensation. Because condensation is caused by warm moist air meeting a colder surface, the warmer inside pane of double glazing will reduce it or eliminate it altogether. However, condensation can occur on the inside of the *outer* pane if the air gap is not properly sealed from the room. This can be reduced by 'venting' the air gap to the outside with holes drilled through the window frame.

Types of double glazing

The type of double glazing which is most suitable will depend on whether it is being installed for heat or noise, the type of window being double glazed (wooden casement, metal casement or sliding wooden sash) and the amount of money available.

There are two main types of double glazing: sealed units and secondary windows.

Sealed units A sealed unit *replaces* the existing pane of glass. It consists of two sheets of glass permanently sealed together around the edges with an air gap between them. The thickness of the air gap is between 6mm and 12mm, which means that sealed units are not the best choice for noise insulation. The thickness of the panes of glass varies, too – usually from 3mm up to 10mm. The size to use depends on the size of the window and its vulnerability to damage. Sealed units are available with one of the panes made from patterned or wired glass or with solar control or toughened glass. They can be bought from glass mer-

chants or directly from the manufacturers.

Because they replace the existing pane, sealed units are suitable for all types of windows. They are sold in standard sizes; non-standard sizes can be made to measure – take the dimensions very accurately.

There are two main shapes of sealed unit: **spaced** units where the two panes of glass are the same size and **stepped** units where the inner pane is smaller than the outer one. A stepped unit is used where there is insufficient width in the rebate to take the thickness of a spaced unit.

The two big advantages of sealed units are that they do not suffer from condensation between the panes and that they are inconspicuous.

Secondary windows These use the existing window pane as the outer pane of the double glazing.

The simplest form of secondary window is **plastic film**, similar to the film used to wrap food, stretched across the window and stuck in position with double-sided adhesive tape. This method is not really suitable for metal-frame windows as the air gap would be too small. Plastic film can be unsightly and can be easily damaged but it is

cheap, easy to fit and good for preventing condensation.

The most common method of do-it-yourself double glazing is **plastic channel** where a pane of glass is fixed to the window by a U-shaped channel which fits all round the pane and is held to the window by clips. Again, it is not really a suitable method for metal windows. For sash windows plastic channel is fixed to the inside of one pane and the outside of the other, so that the two sashes can still slide. The size of air gap achieved is about 25mm, depending on the thickness of the window. Plastic channel is cheap, fairly unobtrusive and easy to fit. It is also easy to remove. Because the panes are fitted to the opening parts of the window, ventilation is not a problem.

With **sliding** double glazing, a track with two channels is fitted all the way round the reveal. The *simple* systems have two or more pieces of glass – with smoothed edges – sliding in the track; sliding *panel* systems have the glass mounted in rigid frames. Because the track can be some way from the existing window, this type is a good choice for noise insulation and is suitable for all types of windows – there are vertical sliding versions for sliding sash windows. Sliding types are fairly noticeable and can be poor for condensation. Simple systems are easy to fit; sliding panel systems, which are fairly expensive, can be more complicated.

The other main type is **fixed** or **hinged panels**. With these, the glass is mounted in a rigid frame of aluminium or plastic with a seal which is fitted to the outer wooden frame of the window. On non-opening windows, the panels are *fixed* – with clips or slotted channel. On opening casements, the panels are *hinged* along one side with clips on the other (small panels can be fitted for top-opening casements). If wanted for noise insulation, the panels can be mounted on a sub-frame mounted in the window reveal away from the existing window. This type of double glazing is fairly noticeable but is fairly easy to fit. It is more expensive than plastic channel but cheaper than sliding panels and it is the type that most professional installers fit.

WHERE TO FIT

Plastic channel double glazing can be fitted to the inside or outside (**1**) of a window – usually on the opening part. Fixed or hinged panels are usually fitted to the inside of the window frame (**2**) but they can be fitted to the reveal (**3**). Sliding double glazing is fitted to the reveal (**4**)

Replacing a window pane

It is possible to repair a window temporarily by using a sheet of polythene fixed to the inside of the window with adhesive tape or nailed lightly on with battens. But sooner or later, you will have to replace the glass. How you do this depends on whether the window is wooden or metal.

Removing the old glass Most of the glass pieces (which will be sharp) should pull out easily. If the glass is held in by putty, this will have to be chopped out with a screwdriver or old chisel or with a *glazier's hacking knife*. With wooden windows, the old glass will probably have been held in place with glazing *sprigs* – these should be removed and discarded. If the glass was held in place with beading, this should be removed carefully by prising it up at the centre of the longest sides. Glass in metal windows is held in place with metal clips. These should be removed carefully and saved for reuse – mark their position on the window as you take them out. When all the putty has been removed, brush out all the dust and debris and apply a coat of primer – wood or metal, as applicable.

Measuring up It is important to measure the rebate accurately so that the glass is the right size. Take at least three measurements in each direction to the nearest millimetre. If these are slightly different (by a few millimetres), do not worry – use the smallest size. The piece of glass you want is **3mm less** in either direction

than your measurements – to allow for slight movements in the frame. Check the window for squareness by measuring the diagonals. If it is badly out (or opposite sides are very different), you will have to make a template out of card to take with you to the glass merchant. You will also have to do this if the window is an unusual shape.

Buying the glass Take the old glass with you for the glass merchant to dispose of – it is not a good idea to put it in the dustbin. When replacing patterned glass, it helps if you can show the glass merchant the exact pattern you are replacing – make a note of which way the pattern runs. Buy the thickness of glass appropriate to the vulnerability and size of the window. The glass merchant will probably sell the other things you need: linseed oil putty and glazing sprigs for wooden windows; metal casement putty for metal windows.

Fitting the new pane First make a check that the new pane *is* the right size. Knead a ball of putty in your hands until it is soft and pliable – hard linseed oil putty can be softened by adding more linseed oil. Press a continuous layer about 3 to 5mm thick all the way round the rebate with your thumb pressing it well into place. Lift the new pane of glass carefully into place, bottom first, allowing an expansion gap at the bottom, about the thickness of a matchstick. Push the glass, gently but firmly, against the putty: press at the edges, never at the centre. This

should push some of the putty out, but leave about 2 to 3mm behind the glass all the way round. Now hammer the sprigs into the window so that one edge holds the glass in place – use a glazier's hacking knife (or the edge of an old firmer chisel) to tap the sprigs home by sliding it along the surface of the glass. Using a hammer is likely to break the glass. When all the sprigs are in place (or clips replaced with metal windows), run another layer of putty on the outside of the glass and finish it off at an angle to allow water to run off: the best tool for this is a putty knife. The corners should be mitred – look at your other windows to get the angles right. Any putty which has been squeezed out on the inside of the window should be cleaned up, too, leaving a slight angle to allow condensation to run off. When fitting or replacing wooden beading on the outside, you need less putty between it and the glass and the beading should be held in place with panel pins. Remember to prime new beading before it is fitted.

Finishing off When the putty is neatly finished, run over it with a moistened paint brush to make sure that it adheres firmly to the glass. It has to be left for a week or two before it can be painted – if you paint it too soon or too late, the paint will crack. Carry the paint line just over the edge of the putty to prevent water getting in. Putty smears on the window pane can be removed with a cloth moistened with methylated spirit.

REPLACING A WINDOW PANE

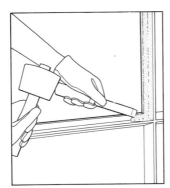
Chop out the old putty

Push new putty into the rebate

Tap in the glazing sprigs

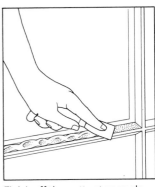
Finish off the putty at an angle

CHAPTER NINE

SECURITY

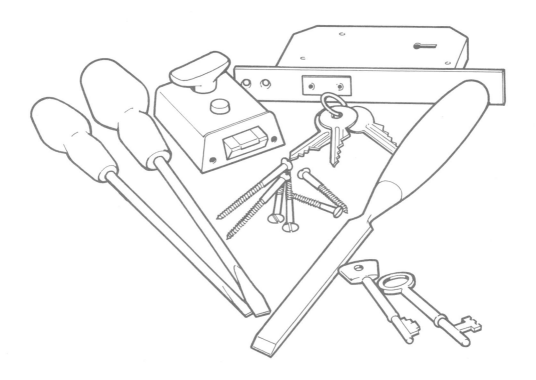

Protecting your home against a professional burglar is very difficult and if you often have a lot of jewellery, small valuables or money in your home, it may be worth investing in a safe or burglar alarm as well as good locks. But most burglaries are carried out by opportunists who are likely to be deterred by even a modest show of security in particularly vulnerable places. The drawing opposite shows these places and suggests possible solutions. Burglars often get in through ground floor windows – by breaking the glass and reaching in to undo the catch. Specific details of locks, bolts and catches recommended for doors and windows are given later, but first some general advice.

Basic precautions

If you have to leave your house empty, following the precautions listed below may further deter burglars.

When you are going out

- always lock up all external doors, windows and fanlights
- take keys out of locks and put them somewhere else (this can make it more difficult for a thief to plan an escape route if he has forced his way in). In particular, do not leave a key under the doormat or hanging by a string inside the letter-flap
- in the evening, leave a light on – preferably not the hall or bathroom light. Close the curtains. An automatic time switch can be fitted to lights. Leaving a radio on can help too
- a dog may deter thieves – if possible, do not lock him up in one room. Fit dog or cat flaps away from any locks or bolts.

When you are away for some time

- do not let everyone know that you are going to leave the house empty, but do tell the police
- stop all deliveries in advance – particularly milk and newspapers – and, if possible, ask a neighbour to make sure letters are properly pushed through the letter-flap (temporarily remove any internal letter-boxes or baskets). It is possible to have the telephone disconnected temporarily
- do not close the curtains
- try to arrange for a neighbour to come in occasionally and switch lights on and off in the evening
- lock up and do not leave any windows open
- take all valuables to the bank.

When you buy a house

On moving to a new home, find out whether any of its locks have registered keys. If so, it is worth asking the lock company if they know how many keys have been issued so that you can make sure that they are all accounted for. If not, change the lock. A lock on a final exit door (the last door to be locked as the house is left – normally the front door) which does not have registered keys should be changed too.

Advice on house security

Further advice on how to secure a house most effectively against burglars can be obtained from various sources. The addresses of the associations listed below can be found at the end of the book.

Crime Prevention Officer (CPO) Part of the police service and can be contacted through your local police station (not every police station has a CPO permanently attached but they can arrange for one to help). A CPO will be prepared to come to look at your house and give free advice on improving security and may know about particular risks in your neighbourhood.

Insurance company All insurance companies have their own burglary insurance surveyors who will assess houses and valuables for insurance purposes. They may be prepared to advice on security, particularly if you have a lot of valuables.

Locksmith A specialist shop selling locks may have a locksmith. The locksmiths' trade organisation is listed at the back of the book.

National Supervisory Council for Intruder Alarms This is an inspectorate of burglar alarm systems installed to BS 4737 by approved installers. They have a list of NSCIA approved installers available.

British Security Industry Association A trade association which can help with names and addresses of lock manufacturers, burglar alarm companies and so on.

Glossary

automatically deadlocking the action of a plunger which may be incorporated in, or with, a springbolt to ensure that the springbolt cannot be forced back when the door is shut
bolt part of the lock which keeps the door shut. When moved, it goes into the staple or striking plate
cylinder the casing for a lock mechanism,
usually pin tumbler; many rim locks have cylinders
deadbolt a bolt which usually can be moved only by the action of a key, so it cannot be pushed back into the lock
deadlockable means that a springbolt can be turned into a deadbolt, usually by an extra turn of the key
escutcheon a plate which fits around and
protects the keyhole
fore-end the end plate joined to the lock body. An outer fore-end may be fitted over the fore-end
key differs the number of variations of keys for any one lock design
latch see springbolt
length of lock the horizontal length of the lock including the fore-end and outer fore-

WAYS TO IMPROVE YOUR HOME SECURITY

1 Fit a lock to the garage – for example, a close-shackle padlock fitted through a strong hasp and staple. Fit a lock to any connecting door between house and garage. If possible, chain ladders to something fixed or, at least, together

10 Fit locks to all external doors – not forgetting the back door

9 Fit a lock to the skylight, if accessible from, for example, drainpipes

8 Fit locks to upstairs windows which may be reached from drainpipes, flat roofs and so on

7 Fit a lock to a garden shed window, or reinforce it with metal bars or Georgian wired glass

6 Fit a lock to the door of a garden shed – for example, a close-shackle padlock fitted through a strong hasp and staple. Lock away do-it-yourself tools

2 Fit locks to all ground floor windows – particularly those out of sight of neighbours or passers-by. Lock casement and fanlight (transom) windows to prevent the casement fastener being undone by reaching in through broken glass. Lock sliding sashes and prevent louvred glass being removed from the frame. Window-mounted extractor fans should only be fitted to fixed windows or those with locks

3 Fit a lock with a deadbolt, or a deadlockable lock, to the front door. A night latch should not be relied on as the sole method of securing an external door

4 Fit a porch light and a door chain. If the door is a solid one, fit a door viewer. The lock should be well away from the letter-flap

5 Fit bolts to the top and bottom of French windows. (Fit special locks to sliding patio windows or doors)

Reports in Handyman Which?

Securing your home May 1977 and 1981

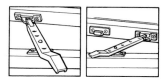

Left: cockspur handle

Right: fanlight stay

Far right: casement stay

The drawing above shows some of the parts of the house which are most vulnerable to thieves

---

end, if any, but excluding the bolt
lever lock a lock with moving levers in its mechanism (detainers are similar to levers)
mortise lock a lock mortised into the stile of a door
nightlatch a rim lock with a springbolt operated by a knob indoors and a key outside. It has a snib which can be used to deadlock the bolt from indoors, but it is not deadlockable from outside

pin tumbler lock a lock with moving pin tumblers in its mechanism. Disc tumblers are similar
rim lock a lock mounted on the inner face of a door
springbolt often called latch – a spring-operated bolt, moved by a handle, knob or key

staple the housing fitted to the door frame into which the bolt of a rim lock is shot
stile a door's vertical frame member, at the opening edge
striking plate the flat plate mortised into the door frame into which the bolt of a mortise lock is thrown. A **box striking plate** has a box surrounding the hole for the bolt throw – the distance moved by the bolt.

Securing doors

Burglars may attack a door in many ways. The most common method, and the simplest, is to break open the door with a jemmy or something similar. Other methods include reaching in through broken glass to undo the latch, slipping the night-latch by pushing back the bolt and, occasionally, picking the lock.

Locks for final exit doors
Doors which can be protected by locks and bolts from the inside can be made more secure than the final exit door which can be locked only from the outside as you leave the house. A lock for a final exit door will be more secure if it has either a deadbolt or is automatically deadlocking with a deadlockable handle or has a latch which is deadlockable from the outside. It should also be strong enough to resist being forced with a jemmy or something similar and the bolt should be reinforced against attack with a saw.

A lever lock should have at least five levers and a pin (or disc). Tumbler locks should have at least five pins or disc tumblers. The number of levers may be stamped on the lock fore-end but if in doubt, ask a locksmith. Not all five lever locks or five pin tumbler locks have mechanisms which produce a large number of key differs (more than 1000, say). Again, if in doubt, ask a locksmith how many differs there are.

Buying the right lock

Before buying a lock, check in which direction the door opens – it may be left or right-handed. Many locks will fit or can be adapted to fit both sorts but with a few locks, the model needed depends on the direction the door opens.

Some manufacturers have a scheme for registering the keys of their locks. Extra keys can be usually obtained only from the manufacturer and against the registered authorised signature. No blanks are issued to key-cutting companies. Some locks have a microswitch facility (shunt lock) which is a special switch incorporated into a lock so that it can be part of a burglar alarm circuit.

For mortise locks, the thickness of the door's stile is important – it should be at least 45mm and preferably 50mm. The stile should also be at least as wide as the length of the lock – usually 63mm but some locks need stiles around 75mm wide. It is possible to buy locks which are suitable for stiles narrower than 63mm.

Most mortise locks are provided with

Locks approved to the British Standard on Thief-Resistant Locks (BS 3621) – this number should be stamped on the lock – meet at least these basic requirements. Both mortise and rim locks are approved to BS 3621, but no nightlatches.

It is a waste of time fitting good quality locks to weak doors and door frames – they must be sufficiently strong and fit well enough to resist forcing. Before fitting a lock, check that both door and frame are sound and that the hinges are not worn. There should be no more than a 3mm gap between the edge of the door and the frame. The overall construction of a door also affects its strength. Generally:
- hardwood doors are stronger than softwood doors and solid wood doors are stronger than panelled. Given the same stile thickness, wood panels in doors are better than glazed panels. However, a glazed panelled door with 50mm thick stiles may be more secure than a wood panelled door with thin stiles (under 45mm) – particularly if the panels are rebated or are plywood
- framed, ledged and braced doors (tongued-and-grooved boards with horizontal, vertical and perhaps diagonal bracing) are less secure than most panelled doors
- flush doors (which have hollow cores usually filled with some material other than wood) should generally not be used as external doors – they are not strong enough.

TYPES OF DOOR LOCK

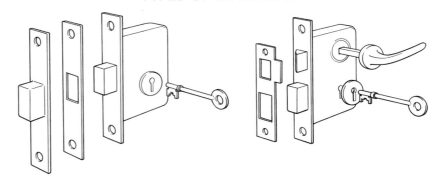

Mortise deadlock

Sash lock (a mortise lock with a handle)

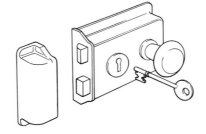

Rim lock

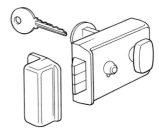

Rim lock with cylinder nightlatch

escutcheons to protect the door around the keyhole. Flaps fitted to escutcheons help keep grit and dust out of the lock and provide privacy.

A rim lock can be used for doors with thin stiles less than 45mm which are unsuitable for mortise locks. Most rim locks cannot be fitted to doors with stiles thicker than 63mm.

Rim locks generally have knobs or handles fitted on the inside; mortise locks with just one bolt are usually operated by the turn of the key. Two-bolt locks – those which incorporate a spring-bolt as well as a deadbolt – normally have holes for handles to be fitted. These have to be bought separately.

Sliding doors need a different sort of lock from conventional doors – one with a claw or hook bolt. There are both mortise and rim versions.

Lock maintenance

About every six months locks should be lubricated. With a cylinder or lever lock put some powdered or flaked graphite on the key, insert the key in the hole and turn it back and forth. Lightly grease or oil visible moving parts such as bolts and handles. Window locks with a single universal key may also be oiled. When cleaning the outside of a lock, make sure that nothing gets into the key mechanism.

If a lock is sticking, test it first by turning the key so that the bolt is thrown with the door open. If it works all right, it may be that the lock and striking plate or staple have got out of alignment. Check the door and frame for warping.

Keep keys free from dust and debris – some types may not operate locks when they get dirty.

Other locks and bolts for external doors

Bolts Bolts can be used to provide extra security on external doors – fit one to both top and bottom of the door. Barrel, padbolts and tower bolts can be screwed to the surface of a door. Each has a long bolt which is generally shot into a staple (a hoop of metal) fixed to the door

frame. Always choose a bolt with a heavy duty staple and long fixing screws. Alternatively, the bolt may be shot into the sill, floor, or top of the door frame.

The bolts are neither key-operated nor deadlocking and so may be easily undone if access is possible. If you want to use one near glass, choose a padbolt – these can be secured by a padlock.

Flush bolts are similar to barrel and tower bolts, except that they are designed to be mortised into the edge or face of a door. They are useful where a concealed bolt is needed – in the edge of French windows, for example.

Locking bolts These are fitted to the inside face of a door and can be operated from indoors only. They can be a useful supplement to existing door locks and will resist some forcing. Some models are available for metal doors as well as wooden ones.

The bolt may be thrown into a staple or striking plate (and locked) by means of a key, or by a knob, lever or switch. Locking bolts are generally unlocked by a key but since they are operated from indoors it is not usual to have more than a few key differs. They should only be used on well-fitting doors and should be positioned near the centre of the door.

To fit a locking bolt, you simply screw the lock to the door – rebating the edge of the door is necessary to take the fore-end of the lock – and rebate the frame to take the staple or striking plate. For further details see *Fitting a rim lock*.

Mortise rack bolts These can be mortised into the edge of a wooden door and should be fitted so that the key is on the inside face. They are inconspicuous when fitted and will resist some forcing. The deadbolt is operated by a key and enters a striking plate mortised into the door frame. Each model usually has one universal key only. Many mortise rack bolts can be unlocked without a key – this type should not be used next to glass (which can be broken).

You should fit mortise rack bolts to both the top and the bottom of a door: on French windows, fit four – not just two on the opening leaf. To do this you

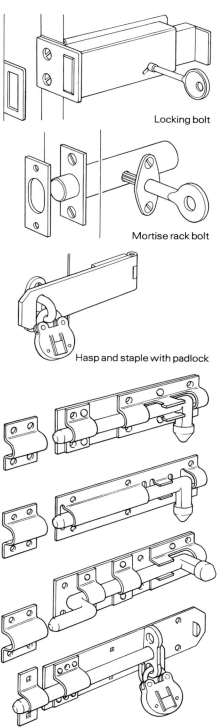

OTHER LOCKS AND BOLTS

Locking bolt

Mortise rack bolt

Hasp and staple with padlock

Four types of surface-mounted bolts. From the top: tower bolt, barrel bolt, skew bolt and pad bolt

have to cut a mortise in the edge of a door in a similar manner to that described for *Fitting a mortise deadlock* – see page 239 – but in this case the hole for the key should not be drilled right through the door.

Padlocks These can be used with a hasp and staple (together often called a padlock bar) to lock garden sheds, garages and so on. The hasp is fitted to the door or gate and the staple to the frame. The padlock locks the two together. Choose a heavy duty hasp and staple with fixing screws which are concealed when the padlock is in place. Use a closeshackle padlock which has the hoop (shackle) close to the body of the lock.

Other security devices for doors

Hinge bolts (sometimes called dog bolts) These provide protection against forcing (or even removal) of a wooden door from the hinge side, particularly doors which open outwards. The bolt enters the striking plate when the door is closed. They should be fitted to the top and the bottom of a door, close to the

hinges. The bolt is usually mortised into the hinge edge of the door, but it may be surface mounted. The striking plate is rebated into the frame in a similar way to a mortise lock.

Door chains These prevent a door being opened more than a small amount (the chain is about 200mm long). Door bars are similar. A locking chain has a key-operated lock which can be operated from outside. Key-operated door chains should not be regarded as a substitute for a secure lock for a final exit door.

When fitting a door chain, position it close to the centre of the door and close to the edge – to prevent marking the door when it is opened. The actual fixing is simple – the chain receiving plate should be screwed to the door and the chain holding plate to the frame.

Door viewers These allow you to see outside the door without opening it. Different models have different angles of vision – normally between 150 and 175 degrees. Choose one with as wide an angle as possible. Some models are made to fit different door thicknesses.

A door viewer should be fitted centrally in the door at eye-level and should be used in conjunction with a porch light.

The correct drill size is very important for secure fitting.

DOOR SECURITY FITTINGS

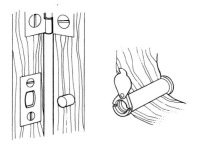

Hinge bolt (or dog bolt)   Wide-angle viewer

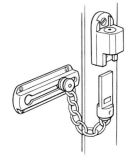

Door chain – available with or without the locking mechanism shown

Securing windows

Traditional catches for fastening sliding sash, casement and fanlight (transom) windows do not give much protection against forcing or slipping the catch from outside. Also, in many cases, the catch can be easily undone if a burglar puts his hand in through nearby broken glass or an open fanlight. Window locks are designed to prevent this happening.

The Table on page 238 lists common types of lock for metal and wooden casement, fanlight and sash windows and also tells you what each type is intended to do. Windows and frames vary a lot, so check that the lock fits your frame type and size. If necessary, take measurements or a sketch to the shop. Your local CPO may also be able to help.

Fitting window locks

Most of the types are shown opposite.

The method of fitting window locks varies from type to type, from brand to brand and is different for metal and wooden windows. Many are fitted simply by screwing the lock body to the window, but some are mortised in. Striking plates may have to be mortised into the frame, or holes (sometimes tapped ones) made in the frame to take the

lock's bolt. Always make sure that you drill holes of the right size – sloppy fitting locks are not secure.

The window and its frame should be sound as some locks could be ineffective on ill-fitting windows. Drill out or burr over the slots of fixing screws which are still accessible when the lock is locked.

The Table on page 238 indicates the **type of fitting** for each lock, **where to fit** it and what sort of **frame material** it is suitable for.

Keys

Most window locks are opened by keys – one which does not have a key will not be much use next to glass which can be broken. Keys are generally not needed for locking – this is usually done by pushing a lever or some other part of the lock.

Window locks seldom have key differs – instead there is one universal key which fits all locks of the same model. Often the key is sold separately, so that you can have one key which will operate the locks on a number of your windows. Some brands have interchangeable keys for a number of different locks.

The Table indicates the **locking method** and whether there are likely to be **key differs** for each type of lock. Some locks – in particular mortise rack bolts – can be unlocked by using a tool other than their key.

Ventilation

With some locks it is possible to leave windows locked open to provide **ventilation** while you are out for a short while. It is probably best to lock windows closed when your house is going to be empty for any length of time.

This sort of lock can also be used to secure upstairs windows in homes with children – to reduce the likelihood of them opening the windows and falling.

Appearance

The Table indicates how **obtrusive** the locks appear when seen from indoors and how **noticeable** they are **from outside** – which might put a burglar off.

Security

A really determined or fairly skilled burglar could probably defeat most of the usual window locks. The Table gives a verdict on the **security** of each type of lock based on the likely attack of an opportunist unskilled burglar.

Problem windows

Certain types of window are particularly difficult to secure satisfactorily without taking extreme measures. All problem windows can be made secure by fitting a metal grille or bars across them. Thick laminated glass can be used in some windows but it is expensive.

Wired glass does not provide much protection against break-ins and the security value of double glazing is doubtful.

French windows These should have a good overlap between the two sides (called *leaves*). Fit mortise rack bolts or lockable bolts top and bottom to both leaves of wooden-framed French windows. Shoot the bolts upwards and downwards into something solid which will resist forcing. Use lockable bolts on metal-framed windows.

Leaded lights The only effective way to protect these is to fit a metal grille or bars behind the window.

Louvred windows Some are now made with the glass secured in the frame. If not, glue the glass into both sides of the frame using a glue such as Araldite. Even so, louvred windows are not really secure and if they are in a vulnerable place – the ground floor at the back of the house, say – they may need further protection with a metal grille or bars.

Sliding windows and patio doors There are specially made locks available for these: make sure that the lock fits the window or door (not all locks fit all sections of the window or door frame).

WINDOW LOCKS

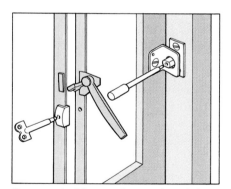

Casement lock for metal or wooden windows

Cockspur stop

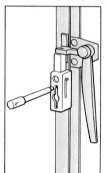

Dual screw

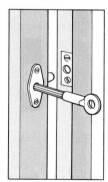

Locking bolt

Mortise rack bolt

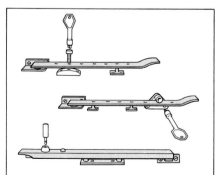

Casement stay locks

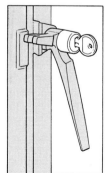

Locking handle

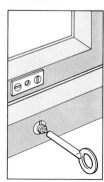

Dual screw (sash)

Sash lock

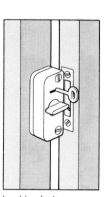

Sliding window lock

Window locks

	what they do	type of fitting	where to fit	frame material	locking method	key differs?	ventilation possible?	obtrusive indoors?	noticeable from outside?	security
Locks for casement and fanlight (transom) windows										
casement lock	locks casement/fanlight to frame	screw to surface; drill hole for bolt (use tap for metal frames)	near centre	models for both	key	perhaps	no	yes	yes	generally good, but some models may be unlocked by a tool other than key
casement stay screw/stop	prevents casement/fanlight stay being lifted	screw to frame or fit to stay	stay	models for both	key	no	yes, but see comments on security	no	no	not secure against burglars when locked in open position
cockspur stop	prevents cockspur handle being lifted	screw to frame	below handle	usually metal	manually locked; unlocked by key	no	small amount only	yes	yes	good, providing cockspur handle cannot be removed
dual screw	locks casement/fanlight to frame	drill through casement; fit striking plate	top and bottom of large window; one centrally for small windows	wood	key	no	no	no	not very	good, but window and frame should fit closely; fit two to a window
locking bolt	locks casement/fanlight to frame	screw to surface; fit staple or striking plate	near centre, if possible	models for both	often manually locked; unlocked by key	perhaps	no	yes	yes	generally good but window and frame should fit closely; some models may be unlocked by tool other than key
mortise rack bolt	locks casement/fanlight to frame	mortise into casement edge; fit striking plate	top and bottom of large window; one centrally for small windows	wood	usually key	no	no	no	no	less effective for windows than for doors but can be well concealed; fit four to french windows
substitute catch	replaces existing catch	as existing catch	as existing catch	models for both	key	perhaps	not usually	as normal catch	as normal catch	security depends on brand; some manufacturers are now supplying locking window catches as extras with new windows
Locks for sliding sash windows										
acorn stop	restricts movement of sliding sashes	drill into upper sash; screw protective plate to lower sash	one either side no higher than 100mm above lower sash	wood	key	no	yes	no	no	can be secure if two stops fitted on a window
dual screw	prevents movement of sliding sashes	drill through lower sash into upper	one either side no higher than 100mm above lower sash	wood	key	no	no	no	not very	good, but sashes should fit closely; fit two to a window
sash lock	restricts movement of sliding sashes	screw to surface; fit staple or striking plate	one either side on lower sash	wood	key	perhaps	yes	yes	yes	sashes must fit well if lock is to be secure
sliding window lock	restricts movement of horizontally sliding sashes	screw or clamp to surface; drill hole for bolt	at bottom where sashes meet	models for both	key	perhaps	yes	yes	no	can be secure, but choice of lock depends on size of frame

Fitting a mortise deadlock

Tools needed
brace and bits
bradawl
chisel and mallet
combination square
(optional)
padsaw
(or hacksaw blade)
pencil and rule
screwdriver

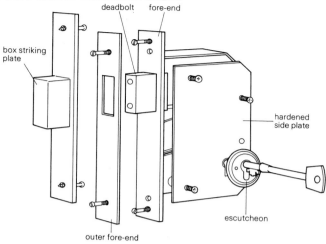

deadbolt fore-end
box striking plate
hardened side plate
escutcheon
outer fore-end

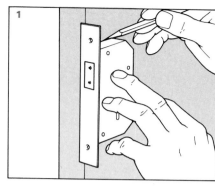

1 Decide where you want to place the lock: this is normally at the centre of the door edge but, if you want to put it somewhere else make sure that the stile is adequate. If the lock has a hardened side plate, fit this to the lock body. Hold the lock against the door

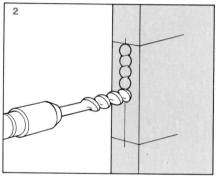

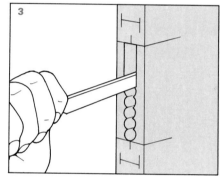

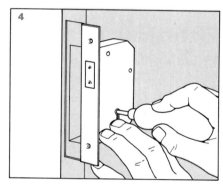

edge and mark the top and bottom of the lock body on the edge of the door. Continue the lines along the length of the lock on both faces of the door. (If the lock manufacturer provides a template use this.) 2 On the edge of the door, draw a vertical line midway be-

tween the two marked horizontal lines. Carefully measure the thickness of the lock body and then mark an auger bit of the same diameter with the length of the lock by using an elastic band or piece of tape twisted around it. Drill a series of holes close together

along the vertical line. 3 Chisel away remaining wood to make a squared-off hole. Fit the lock body into the hole and mark around the fore-end. 4 Chisel away the wood inside the outline to the depth of the fore-end(s) so that the outer fore-end lies flush with the edge of

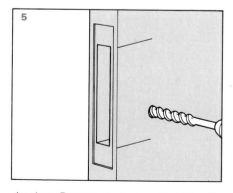

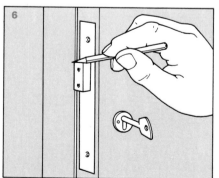

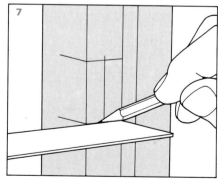

the door. Remove the lock and hold it, with the outer fore-end in place, against the door and use a bradawl to mark the position of the keyhole. 5 Drill the keyhole through the door, making sure that it goes through horizontally (at right angles to the door). Then either drill

another hole below this and chisel out the waste or use a padsaw or hacksaw blade to cut out enough wood to enable the key to pass through. (For a two-bolt lock, drill a hole for the handle spindle to pass through in the same way.) Fit the lock, using fixing screws,

through the fore-end(s). Try the key from both sides to make sure that it works. Screw the escutcheons with covers (if any) over the keyhole on both sides of the door – have the key in place when you do this. 6 Standing indoors, turn the key so that the bolt is

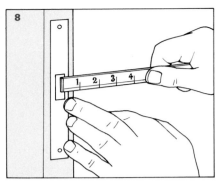

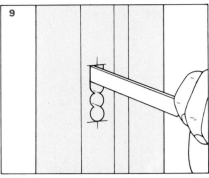

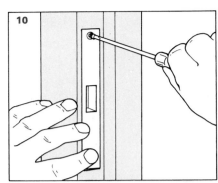

thrown and close the door as far as possible. Mark the top and bottom of the bolt on the door frame. (For a two-bolt lock, mark the top of the upper bolt and the bottom of the lower one.) **7** Use a combination square to continue these lines to the frame where the box will

fit. **8** Measure the distance from the vertical centre of the bolt to the outer face of the door. Draw a vertical line on the frame between the two marked horizontals at the same distance from the rebate edge. **9** Cut a mortise to the depth of the box (or throw of

the bolt) in the same way described for the lock body. **10** Fit the box of the striking plate into the hole and mark round the outside of the plate. Chisel away wood to the depth of the plate and screw it flush with the edge of the frame.

Fitting a mortise deadlock with a dual-profile cylinder

Fitting a mortise deadlock with a cylinder is very similar to fitting a mortise deadlock without one with the modifications shown below.

The tools needed are exactly the same as for fitting a mortise deadlock without a cylinder. If you need to replace the cylinder, make sure that the replacement matches your brand of lock.

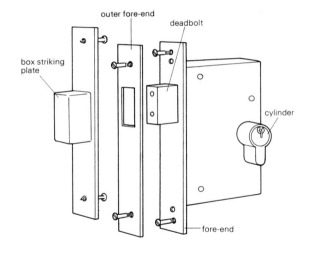

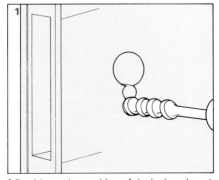

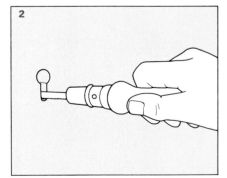

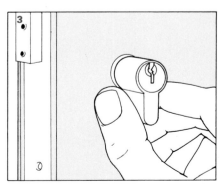

1 Decide on the position of the lock and mark it on the door as described for fitting a lock without a cylinder. Cut out a mortise for the lock body as described in steps 2 to 5 for a lock without a cylinder leaving off the outer fore-end, if any. Use the template provided

and drill a hole halfway through the door from the inside face (for the rotating cam on the cylinder). Use the template and drill hole(s) for the cylinder. **2** Chisel or use a padsaw or a hacksaw blade to enlarge the hole to the correct size for the cylinder. **3** Install the

cylinder in the lock and screw in the cylinder retaining screw through the edge of the door. Fit outer fore-end and escutcheons as with mortise lock without cylinder. Fit striking plate as described in stages 7 to 10 for a lock without a cylinder.

Fitting a rim cylinder nightlatch

Tools needed
brace and bits
bradawl
chisel and mallet
combination square
pencil and rule
screwdriver

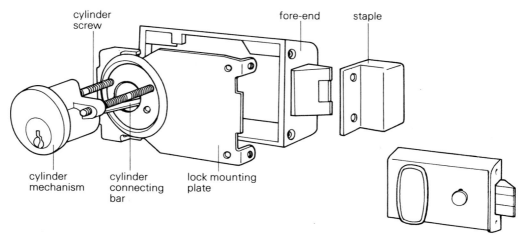

cylinder screw

fore-end

staple

cylinder mechanism

cylinder connecting bar

lock mounting plate

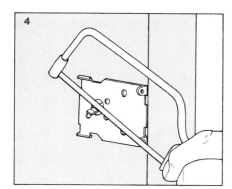

1 Decide where you want to position the lock – a rim lock is always fitted to the inside face of a door. If you have (or are fitting) a mortise lock as well, position the rim lock at shoulder height. If not, position it halfway up the door edge. Check that the lock is suitable for your

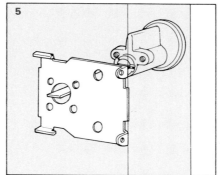

door – it depends on whether your door is left or right-handed. Use the template, if provided, to mark the position of the cylinder hole. If there is no template, measure the distance between the fore-end and the centre of the cylinder keyhole. Mark this at

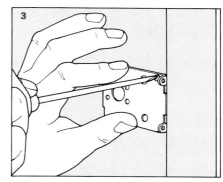

the required height on the inner face of the door. Drill the hole(s) for the cylinder as described in the instructions with the lock (different cylinders require different sizes and shapes of holes). **2** Place the cylinder and retaining ring through the hole from the out-

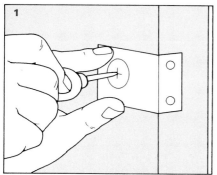

side. Hold the lock mounting plate in position against the inner face of the door and mark the positions of the fixing screws with a bradawl. **3** Fix the mounting plate to the door. **4** Measure the projection of the cylinder connecting bar and screws beyond the mounting

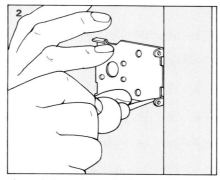

plate on the inside and adjust their length as necessary. (This will probably be described in the instructions for the lock.) **5** Refit the cylinder in the hole and tighten the connecting screws which pass through the mounting plate. Make sure that the keyhole slot is

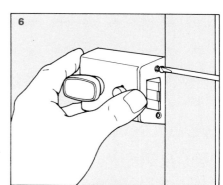

positioned correctly – check with the manufacturer's instructions – and do not tighten the screws too much as this may distort the mounting plate. Check that the key operation is smooth. **6** If the fore-end has to be rebated into the edge of the door, position the lock

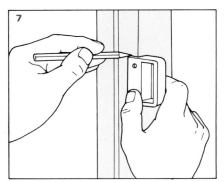

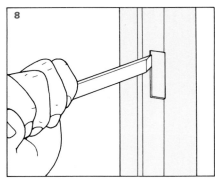

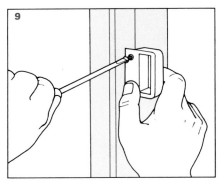

body against the mounting plate and mark the top and bottom of the fore-end on the edge of the door. Measure the width of the fore-end and mark a vertical line this distance from the inner face of the door. Chisel away wood within this outline to the thickness of

the fore-end. Screw the lock body to the door. Check the operation of the lock with the key before tightening all the screws. The case fixing screws are inserted through the holes on the inside end of the lock case. **7** Standing indoors, close the door with the

bolt(s) in the withdrawn position. Hold the staple against the frame so that it is aligned with the lock body. Mark the top and bottom of the staple and its depth on the door frame. **8** Chisel away the frame to form a rebate for the staple. **9** Screw the staple to the frame.

Fitting a rim lock

Surface-mounted rim locks – such as the one shown alongside – are not really regarded as security locks. But they are very easy to fit and are often found on greenhouses, workshops and so on. The tools you need to fit one include: a bradawl (or a long pointed tool such as a pair of compasses), a brace and auger bit, a chisel (or padsaw), and a screwdriver.

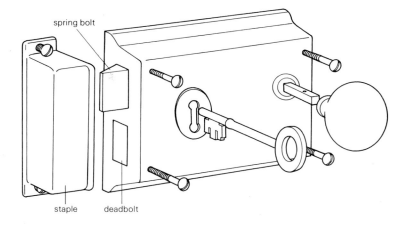

spring bolt

staple   deadbolt

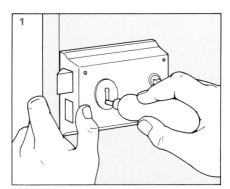

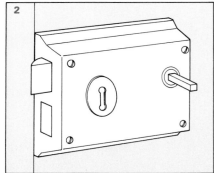

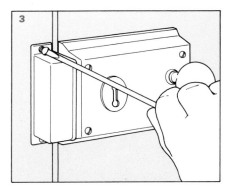

1 Mark the position of the handle and keyhole with a bradawl and bore the holes. For the keyhole drill more holes vertically below the initial one and take out the waste with a chisel, or use a padsaw. Position the lock body against the door with the handle

bar and key in place and mark the positions for the lock body screws. Screw the lock body to the door. **2** Check the length of the handle bar – cut off any excess using a hacksaw – and fit the handles. **3** Close the door, mark the position for the staple on the

door frame and, holding the staple in position make sure that the spring latch and bolt will run in and out of the staple without catching. If necessary, recess the staple or lock slightly to get a smooth action. Use long screws for fixing the staple.

CHAPTER TEN

METALWORKING

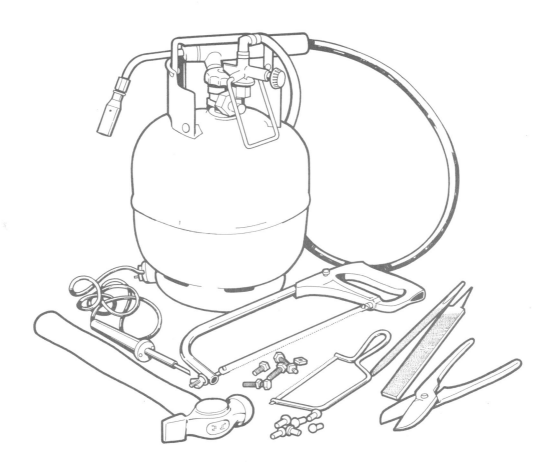

Many of the techniques for cutting, bending and joining metal are fairly simple and well within the capabilities of most do-it-yourselfers. Welding is an exception: a good deal of skill is required to do it well – an outline of the tools and techniques starts on page 257. But before you can start working with metal you should know something of the metals themselves.

Metals are usually grouped as ferrous or non-ferrous according to whether they contain iron.

Ferrous metals such as cast iron, wrought iron and mild and alloy steels contain iron. They are often found around the home. For example, central heating boilers, basin brackets and metal gutters are made of *cast iron*; architectural ironwork – garden gates and ornamental screens, for instance – are usually *wrought iron*; car body panels, metal hinges and shelf brackets are usually *mild steel*; cold chisels and leaf springs are *medium carbon steel*; coil springs, wood chisels, files, drills and knives are *high carbon steel*; and sinks, kitchen ware and cutlery, and some water pipes are *stainless steel*.

You can buy most ferrous metals in plate, sheet or strip form, as round, hexagonal or square bars, threaded rod (studding) and as tubes of various shapes. Cast iron is the exception – it comes only as the finished product.

Galvanized steel is steel that has been dipped in molten zinc to give it a thin corrosion-resistant outer coating.

Non-ferrous metals such as aluminium and its alloys and brass, copper, lead and zinc do not contain iron.

Aluminium alloys are available as sheets, strips, round and square bars, tubes, and relatively complicated extrusions – often found in aluminium doors and window frames. Brass is available as sheets, wire, tubes and as solid bars – round, hexagon shaped or threaded. Copper is normally available as sheets (often rolled up), as tubes and as wire. Lead is usually available only as pipes or rolled sheets. Zinc is usually available only as sheets which may be flat or rolled up.

Small quantities of all these metals are often available from builders' merchants, plumbers' merchants, hardware shops, ironmongers and small engineering works.

COMMON NON-FERROUS METALS

	properties	uses
Aluminium alloy	lightweight, soft, ductile, low tensile strength, corrosion resistant	window and patio door frames, car cylinder heads, toys, kettles, saucepans, tent poles, step-ladders and general repairs
Brass	stronger than copper, corrosion resistant	electrical components, screws, taps, radiator valves and other water fittings, often nickel or chromium plated
Copper	soft, ductile, relatively low tensile strength, corrosion resistant	electrical conductors, water and central heating pipes, hot water cylinders, ornamental decoration
Lead	soft, ductile, very low tensile strength, high corrosion resistance	waterproof flashings around chimneys and roofing valleys and as a base for solder and alloys
Zinc	soft, ductile, low tensile strength, corrosion resistant	waterproof flashings around chimneys and roofing valleys and as a protective coating on steel (galvanized steel)
Zinc alloy	low ductility, moderate tensile strength, corrosion resistant	diecastings for door furniture (often copper plated), motor car and washing machine components, and toys

Key to the terms used under **properties**. Some other common properties are also explained.

Compressive strength is the ability to withstand a pushing or squeezing load without collapsing

Elasticity is the ability of a metal to bend or stretch when a load is applied but to return to its original shape when the load is removed. If a metal is excessively bent or loaded, its elastic limit may be exceeded and it will acquire a permanent set

Hardness is the ability to resist scratching or indentation by another hard material

Impact strength is the ability to withstand an impact or sudden shock and is often called *toughness*

Plasticity is the ability of a metal to bend or twist under load and to retain its new form when the load is removed. When the deforming load is a *tensile* one, the material is said to be *ductile*. When the deforming load is a *compressive* one, as in hammering, the material is said to be *malleable*

Shear strength is the ability to withstand off-set loads, or transverse slicing actions

Tensile strength is the ability of the metal to withstand a pulling or stretching load without breaking

Cutting metal

There are many ways of cutting metal – straight cuts can be made with a saw or snips, bits cut away with a cold chisel or file, holes made with a drill, and special shapes cut with taps and dies and with tools such as tank cutters.

Handsaws

The teeth of ordinary handsaws used for woodworking are too soft to cut metal. All-purpose saws can be used for cutting metal but their teeth are usually too thick and too coarse to make them an ideal tool when much work has to be done.

There is a range of handsaws which are specially designed for cutting metal. These include:

● hacksaws
● junior hacksaws
● padsaws
● sheetsaws.

Because cutting metal can blunt a saw blade very quickly, each type has a disposable blade.

Hacksaw This is the basic saw for cutting metal. It consists of a frame which holds a blade under tension. The frame is generally adjustable so that it can accommodate blades of different lengths – normally 250 or 300mm. The blade is held by angled pegs – one at each end of the frame – and is brought under tension by turning a wing nut and threaded adjuster at one end of the frame. Two and a half to three turns of the wing nut usually gives the right tension.

With most hacksaws, the blade can be mounted at an angle to its normal position – usually at right angles but a few saws allow other positions too. This can be useful when sawing long strips or when space is limited.

The frame imposes two limitations on what can be done with a hacksaw: a clearance of 100 to 125mm above the workpiece is necessary before sawing can start, and after the cut has gone down about 100mm the frame stops any further travel. For these reasons, hacksaws are generally used for straightforward cutting jobs on pipes, bars and sections. They are not really suitable for cutting sheets of metal into anything other than narrow strips of at the most 100mm wide.

Always fit the blade in a hacksaw with its teeth pointing away from you. Start the cut on the waste side of the material making a suitable allowance for the metal which will be sawn away by the blade and for filing the cut smooth when it is complete.

Hold the job in a vice with the cutting line between you and the blade, so that you can see it at all times. Start sawing with the blade cutting along the largest length of surface possible. Use pressure on the forward stroke only and keep your left hand on top of the saw frame at the front (vice versa for left-handed people). Use smooth long strokes of the saw blade and never use any pressure on the return stroke. When cutting awkward shapes:

● be prepared to turn the metal around so that you are always cutting through the longest length of surface possible. When cutting through pipes, in particular, make sure you turn the pipe around as the cut progresses – never rip right through it

● stop large thin sheets vibrating by clamping pieces of wood near the cutting line or by using a finer blade

● clamp a piece of wood beneath the cutting line on very thin sheets and cut through both.

Junior hacksaw This is smaller than a hacksaw and is useful in confined spaces or for intricate work. It takes a smaller – 150mm – blade held at a fixed angle and usually at a set tension. Junior hacksaw blades are fairly easily kinked, become blunt quickly and are not really suitable for hard steel.

Padsaw This is a pad handle clamped over one end of a hacksaw blade: a good grip is very important. It is not necessary

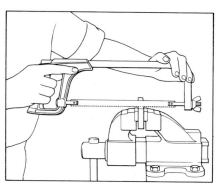
Use long smooth strokes and apply pressure on the forward stroke only

SAWS FOR CUTTING METAL

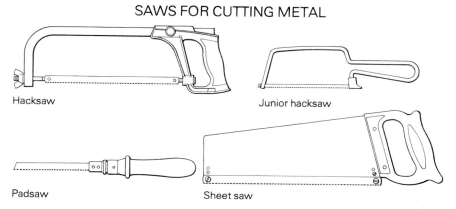
Hacksaw

Junior hacksaw

Padsaw

Sheet saw

to use a whole hacksaw blade, so a padsaw is a useful way of using up broken but still sharp blades. The blade teeth should face towards you and the cut is made on the pull stroke. Padsaws are normally only used in confined spaces – to cut off the head of a corroded bolt, for instance. They can be used, with care and a lot of effort, to cut sheet metal if nothing else is available.

Sheetsaw This saw is designed for use on large sheets of metal. It uses a hacksaw blade fixed across the bottom edge of a much broader, stiffer blade which is slightly thinner than the hacksaw blade. It can be used to saw across metal sheets and down to any depth. It is not as good as a hacksaw for many other jobs and not always easy to use.

Hacksaw blades

Hacksaw blades are usually made from one of two sorts of steel – low alloy steel or high speed steel. Low alloy steel blades tend to blunt quicker than high speed steel ones.

Blades are normally available in two lengths – 250mm and 300mm – and with a variety of teeth per inch (called *coarseness*). Blades with 14, 18, 24 and 32 tpi are commonly available: the coarseness to use depends on the thickness and type of metal being cut. Blades with 18 and 24

tpi are for general use; 32 tpi for cutting sheet metal and thin-walled tubes (copper pipe); and 14 tpi is useful for cutting a soft metal like aluminium because the blade is less likely to become clogged.

The coarseness of the blade usually determines its *set*. Coarse blades usually have teeth bent each way alternately; fine blades have a wavy set – the whole cutting edge of the blade is a wavy shape. The set enables a saw to cut a slot slightly wider than the body of the blade and so reduces the likelihood of the saw jamming.

Hacksaw blades are hardened to make their teeth last longer. Four different types of blade are available.

A **flexible** blade is only hardened along the row of teeth, the back of the blade is left soft. This allows the blade to spring back if it is bent a little; if it is bent too far, it will not spring back. It may be possible to bend it straight again but the hardened portion containing the teeth may crack.

An **all-hard** blade is hardened throughout the blade but has the area around the fixing holes softened to prevent it cracking. This type of blade is very stiff. If it is bent a little, it will spring back; if it is bent too far, it will snap. All-hard blades tend to be used in machines or by professional metal workers.

A **spring-temper** blade is heat treated so that it can be bent a long way and still spring back straight – rather like a flat spring. Spring-temper blades are not very common.

A **bimetal** blade is made up of two pieces of metal – hence its name. A narrow strip of hard metal with teeth is welded on to a wide softer strip which forms the back.

All-hard blades tend to break fairly easily – if the handle of the saw is not lined up exactly with the cut, say. Flexible blades can be bent a long way without breaking but getting them perfectly straight again can be difficult. Bimetal blades are a compromise between these two extremes and are least likely to be damaged when sawing.

Hacksaw blades – tpi for various metals

14 on thick sections, 18 on thin ones
- Aluminium
- Brass
- Copper
- Duralumin
- Mild steel
- Cast iron*

18 on thick sections, 24 on thin ones
- Alloy steels*
- Medium angle steel
- Tubing steel

24 on thick sections, 32 on thin ones
- Light angle steel
- Tubing and conduit

*use a high-speed steel blade

Snips

Sheet metal can be cut to size by using snips or shears rather like scissors are used to cut paper. Snips usually have plain handles – like pliers – so that you can grip them tightly and cut thick material. Some snips have bow handles – like scissors – so that you can control them easily and use them quickly, but since bow handles cannot be gripped as tightly as plain ones, these snips are more suitable for use on thin materials. Snips with bow handles are often called *shears*. Both types are mainly for trimming small sheets of metal rather than for tackling large sheets.

There are three main types of blade: straight, curved and universal. **Straight** blades are quite deep but thin and can be

used for cutting straight lines or trimming round the outside of a piece of sheet. **Curved** blades are also deep and thin and can be used to cut inside curves. **Universal** blades are a compromise. They are straight but much less deep than the others and this means that they can be used to cut inside curves as well as straight lines and outside curves.

The handles of snips may be in line with the blades or cranked out of line. Snips with cranked handles and universal blades can be used to cut inside curves in large sheets, but they can cut in one direction only – according to which way they are cranked; left-handed snips have to be used clockwise, right-handed snips anti-clockwise.

Snips are available in a variety of sizes

SNIPS

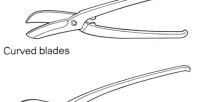

Universal blades

Curved blades

Cranked handles (and universal blades)

from about 150mm to 350mm in overall length. Their length gives a rough guide to the leverage you can obtain with them when cutting – the larger snips are for cutting thick or tough sheet. For general use, a 250mm pair of snips with plain handles in line and with a universal blade

should suffice.

When using snips try to:
● cut as near to the pivot as possible. This gives better leverage and reduces the risk of forcing the blades apart
● avoid closing the blades completely. If you do, the snips will leave a nick in the

edge of the sheet every time
● keep the pivot of the snips oiled and tight – rivets can be tightened by using a hammer, carefully.
The cut edge left by snips is often sharp and jagged and should be smoothed with a file.

Cold chisels

Cold chisels are useful tools for cutting things apart quickly when the accuracy of the cut and the finish left are of no importance – like removing rusted bolts. However, special cold chisels can be used for shaping metals precisely.

All cold chisels are basically pieces of hardened steel with a cutting edge ground on one end. You hit the other end – the head – with a heavy hammer to make the cutting edge (chisel) cut. The most useful sort is the ordinary flat chisel. For cutting grooves, a cross-cut chisel is needed; for circular grooves or for producing a round finish on an internal corner, you need a round nose or half-round nose chisel; and for getting a sharp internal corner or for cutting V-grooves, a diamond-point chisel is needed.

Cold chisels are specified by their cutting width and length and sometimes by the thickness of the bar they are made from as well. The most useful range of

flat chisels is from 150mm to 250mm long and 13mm to 25mm across. A good compromise size is 200mm by about 20mm. Choose chisels which taper gradually towards the point so that they can be resharpened several times without appreciably thickening the point.

Using a cold chisel
Cold chisels may appear to be very robust but you should take lots of care when using one. In particular:
● use a heavy hammer in a controlled manner rather than raining down lots of blows with a light one. A club hammer is best
● when the head of the chisel starts to spread (called mushroom) after a little use, trim it back to shape with a file or grinder. Otherwise, fragments may break off and fly about and cause injury
● support the job firmly to avoid wasting a lot of effort
● keep the edge of the chisel sharp. This can be done by using a grinding wheel

COLD CHISELS

Flat chisel

Diamond-point chisel

Cross-cut chisel

Half-round nose chisel

but avoid getting the chisel too hot, and so softening it. Alternatively, a file can be used but it is a slow job and can damage the file
● do not use a chisel on, or very near, the jaws of a vice or other hard metal
● do not attempt to heat treat a chisel to make it harder – it might become dangerously brittle.

Files

Files can be used to shape metal, to remove sharp edges and for sharpening things like saws. They are lengths of hardened steel with rows of tiny teeth cut into some or all of the faces. Files come in different shapes and sizes and with different types of teeth for particular tasks – large coarse teeth are suitable for rough shaping or fast removal of soft metal, since they do not clog up easily. Small fine teeth are suitable for smoothing edges when a good finish is required.

The teeth of a file are described by its cut. A single-cut file has sharp parallel ridges which run the full width of the file but at an angle to it. This type of file is good for sharpening tools. A double-cut

file has two crossed sets of ridges giving small individual, diamond-shaped teeth. It removes metal more quickly than a single-cut file.

The file grade is a measure of the size and spacing of the teeth. Dead smooth files have the finest teeth followed by smooth, second-cut, bastard and rough. The different grades might have slightly differently-shaped teeth and the size of the teeth increases with the size of the file, as well as with the grade. A second-cut file will be suitable for most purposes; coarser grades are better for removing metal – particularly soft metals – quickly; finer ones are better for finishing hard metals.

The most common shapes of file are rectangular, round, half-round, square

FILE TEETH AND GRADES

Rough-rasp

Double-cut

Single-cut

Rough-dreadnought

and triangular. Not all cuts and grades are available in each shape.

Flat files are rectangular in section, with double-cut faces and single-cut edges, and get narrower towards the point. Thin, more pointed versions with fine teeth are used for cutting keys and known as *warding* files.

Hand files are similar to flat files but get thinner towards the point, not narrower, and have one edge with no teeth making them useful for widening a slot without deepening it as well. A very narrow hand file is known as a *pillar* file.

Round files are for use on concave surfaces and holes and are usually single-cut. Small ones are often called *rat tails*.

Half-round files have a double-cut flat face and a single or double-cut round face.

Square files are for cutting slots and getting into square corners. They have four double-cut faces.

Triangular (or three-square) files have three double-cut faces which are the same width. *Knife* files are similar but have one narrower single-cut face.

Saw files are usually triangular and are single-cut. A *mill saw* file is flat with one or both edges rounded and is useful for sharpening axes and saws with large teeth.

FILE SHAPES

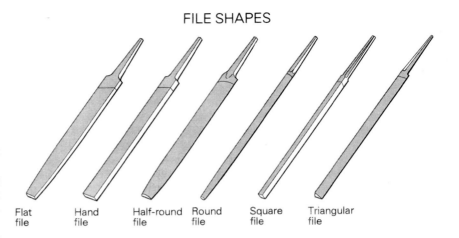

| Flat file | Hand file | Half-round file | Round file | Square file | Triangular file |

The most common shapes of files are shown above. Not all the cuts and grades possible – see page 247 – are available in each shape

Very small files called *needle* files are used for precision work. They have their own integral handle instead of a tang and the cutting point is usually only about 75mm long and 3 to 6mm wide.

Using files

Files are very hard and tend to be brittle so they should never be abused:
● never use a file as a hammer or lever – it could snap dangerously
● treat a file with care, do not let it get rusty or rattle around in a tool box – both things will blunt the teeth
● never use a file without a handle and always use handles with ferrules. The tang of a file is very sharp and could dig into your hand or body. To fit a handle, grip the file in a vice and knock the handle on to the tang with a mallet. Make a hole in the handle first if it has not got one
● clean out teeth clogged with metal or dirt by stroking a *file card* across the file. File cards are wire brushes with short, hard bristles.

MEASURING AND MARKING TOOLS

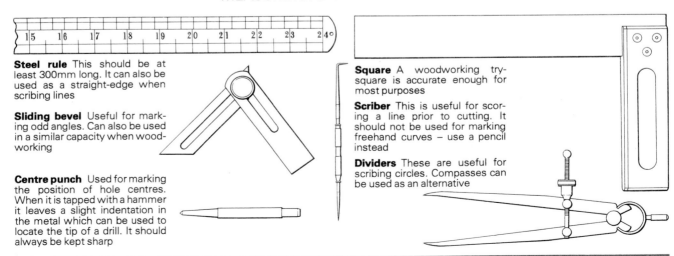

Steel rule This should be at least 300mm long. It can also be used as a straight-edge when scribing lines

Sliding bevel Useful for marking odd angles. Can also be used in a similar capacity when woodworking

Centre punch Used for marking the position of hole centres. When it is tapped with a hammer it leaves a slight indentation in the metal which can be used to locate the tip of a drill. It should always be kept sharp

Square A woodworking try-square is accurate enough for most purposes

Scriber This is useful for scoring a line prior to cutting. It should not be used for marking freehand curves – use a pencil instead

Dividers These are useful for scribing circles. Compasses can be used as an alternative

Cutting shapes in sheet metal

There are a number of occasions when you may need to cut tight curves or holes in sheets of metal or in tanks – when installing a new cold water cistern, for example. Quite a few different tools are available to cope with this type of job. The main ones are sheet metal cutters and nibblers, sheet metal punches, hole saws, and tank cutters.

Sheet metal cutters and nibblers can be used for cutting irregular shapes and for cutting up big sheets but they cannot cut holes less than 25 to 50mm across. The other tools mainly make round holes and to use them you start by drilling a small pilot hole.

Sheet metal cutters work by cutting a very narrow strip of metal (the width of the blade) out of the sheet, leaving a slot. When you squeeze the handles of the tool together, the cutting blade shears the sheet between two anvils, rolling the waste material up in a coil as you push the tool forward a bite at a time. Because they take only a little bite, they can be manoeuvred to follow quite tight curves. But as the handles provide a very limited amount of leverage, most sheet metal cutters do not work too well on thick, tough metals. Sheet metal cutters can also be used on other materials like plastic laminates.

Nibblers work in a slightly different way – the cutter moves up and down perpendicular to the sheet, takes a very small bite out of the sheet, then advances and takes another bite. Many nibblers are operated by hand but some can be attached to an electric drill. When you use nibblers you can change direction very easily and cut quickly but it is difficult to get a completely straight edge. When using either nibblers or sheet cutters a strip of metal is lost – always cut on the waste side of your marking out line.

Sheet metal punches have three parts – a *punch* which makes the hole, a *die* which supports the metal on the other side, and a *bolt*. They are easy to use and cut very clean holes but access is needed from both sides of the material being worked on.

To use a sheet metal punch, you drill a pilot hole for the bolt, pass it through the die, through the hole drilled in the sheet, and then screw it into a threaded hole in the punch. By tightening the bolt (usually with an Allen key), the punch is slowly pulled through the sheet into the die leaving a very neat hole. They are available in a variety of sizes and shapes but they are not suitable for curved surfaces, since the die tends to flatten the area around the hole.

Hole saws usually look rather like a piece of a saw blade bent into a circle, with a drill bit at the centre of the circle – see page 119 for details. The hole cut by a hole saw is not as clean as one made by a punch but hole saws need access from one side only and can be used on curved surfaces.

Most hole saws are a fixed size – the stated size may be the size of the hole it cuts or the size of the pipe fitting or conduit the hole is meant to take. There are also multiple saws available which have a number of blades – you simply remove those which are not required.

Tank cutters are mostly rather like hole saws. They also turn about a central twist drill and cut a circular channel at a set distance from it. But they should be turned more slowly than a hole saw – in a carpenter's brace – and usually have a single cutting edge. The distance of the bit from the drill can be adjusted. They are designed for cutting large holes in thin sheet metal. Some will cut holes up to 200mm in diameter, though 100mm is more common. If the blade is kept sharp, they can be used successfully on plastic laminate.

A tank cutter is quite easy to use once you get the knack – the cutting bit should be directly below the brace handle or should lag slightly behind it – but it is hard work. Be careful when the bit starts to break through and do not force it. If necessary, reverse the direction of rotation by turning the bit backwards. This type of tank cutter can be sharpened on a grinding wheel.

Another type of tank cutter is more like a metal punch. It has a cutting handle attached to the cutting head. To use it, you drill a hole in the metal, pass the pivot (or clamping) bolt through the cutting head, through the hole in the metal, and screw it into the support block. The bolt should then be retightened and the process repeated until the cutter breaks through. This type of tank cutter can be used in confined spaces but access is needed from both sides, and it is not suitable for curved surfaces.

TOOLS FOR CUTTING SHEET METAL

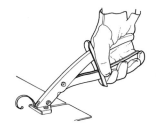
Sheet metal cutter

Nibbler

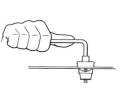
Sheet metal punch

Hole saw

Tank cutter

Making small holes in metal

Most small holes – up to about 10mm – in metal are cut with **twist drills**. These can also be used for making small holes in many other materials, including wood and plastic laminates. Twist drills can be bought individually or in sets containing from around four up to about 13 drills of different sizes. Twist drills are designed for use in either hand drills or power drills. How suitable they are for making holes in different materials depends mainly on the material of the drill itself and how well the drill has been made and sharpened – mainly the shape of its point and its hole clearance.

Drill materials

Many inexpensive twist drills are made of *carbon steel*. These are quite adequate for making holes in soft metals, wood and plastics but they will blunt quickly on hard metals and may not cut through some metals at all. *Chrome-vanadium steel* drills are next in price – these will cut through hard metals but are brittle and the smaller-sized drills snap fairly easily. *High-speed steel* drills are the most expensive and are essential for harder materials.

Drill points

The most suitable *point angle* for a drill depends on the material you want to use it for. When making a hole right through a piece of wood, the drill can splinter the wood as it comes out of the other side, so you need a drill with a sharp point – say about 60 degrees. On the other hand, when drilling through thin sheet metal, a large point angle of, say, 130 degrees is desirable so that the whole drill gets a chance to start drilling before the point breaks through the metal sheet. A point angle of about 118 degrees is correct for mild steel and a reasonable compromise for everything else.

It is also important for a drill to have a symmetrical point, otherwise the drill may wobble and make holes larger than required. If a drill does not have a symmetrical point, it will also be more difficult to start the hole.

Hole clearance

The *cutting edge* should be straight and sharp and have adequate *lip clearance*. If the lip clearance is too small, the drill will tend to rub instead of cutting. If it is too large, the cutting edge will be weak and may chip or break when drilling tough materials.

When drilling deep holes, the main part of the drill should not rub against the sides of the hole – this will cause unnecessary drag which, in turn, can lead to the drill overheating. To overcome this, drills should have *lands* – these stand out from the main body of the drill and are the only parts that come into contact with the sides of the hole. The distance the lands stand out from the body is called the *body clearance*.

Drills should have *flutes* for carrying the swarf away from the cutting edge which are deep enough to do their job efficiently but not too deep so that they weaken the drill. The surface of the flutes should be smooth.

Buying drills

You can check all the things mentioned above by simply looking at the drill and its packaging before you buy it. It is worthwhile doing this – some cheaper drills have no points, some have no cutting edges, some have no lip clearance and some have no body clearance. These things matter much more when drilling metal than when drilling wood. When buying a set of twist drills, check every drill in the set, particularly the smaller ones.

Most drills are known as *jobber* length – they will drill holes up to 10 times the diameter of the drill. For deeper holes, *long series* or *extra length* drills are available. For drilling in confined space, short drills called *stub* drills are available. These special drills are usually sold singly, whereas jobbers drills are normally sold in sets.

Sharpening drills

Twist drills can be sharpened free hand on a power grinder or by using a sharpening guide – basically a jig to hold a drill in position against the side of a grinding wheel. The jig can be adjusted to provide different point angles. Hand sharpening guides are also available for using with abrasive paper. Purpose-built power sharpeners generally produce just one sharpening angle. If you do not need to sharpen drills often, it is worthwhile finding a shop to do the job for you. Smaller drills could even be replaced.

Using drills

Standard twist drills should not be used on materials thinner than the radius of the drill, as they tend to dig into the edge of the hole. Cutting lubricants, such as white spirit, are necessary on some harder metals, but aluminium, brass, cast iron and mild steel can be drilled without one – though using a lubricant may speed up the job and make the drill stay sharper longer. Lubricants are not needed for wood and plastics.

The ideal speed of rotation of a twist drill depends on the material you are trying to cut and the size of the hole. When using a twist drill in a power drill, make sure that you select the correct speed for the size of drill bit – if you use too fast a speed, the tip of the drill will overheat and become weakened. Fairly high speeds (around 3000rpm) can be used for drilling wood up to about 10mm and steel up to 6.5mm. Use lower speeds for larger diameters.

ANATOMY OF A TWIST DRILL

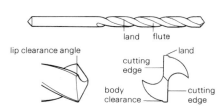

land   flute

lip clearance angle   land

cutting edge

body clearance   cutting edge

Taps and dies

Screw threads can be cut by hand using taps and dies. A tap cuts an internal thread – to make a nut, say – and a die cuts an external thread on a piece of bar, usually to make a bolt. This technique can be extended from making nuts and bolts to cutting threads on almost any piece of suitably-shaped metal.

Taps For cutting a thread from scratch, three taps are needed:

● a **taper** tap to start the thread. This is tapered for approximately two thirds of its length

● an **intermediate** (or second) tap to follow the taper tap. This is tapered for approximately the first third of its length and it continues and extends the thread started by the taper tap

● a **plug** (or bottoming) tap is the final tap. It is parallel along its length except for a small-angled lead. A plug tap is used only when tapping blind holes. For holes passing right through the metal, only the taper and intermediate taps are needed.

To use a tap, a hole of the correct size has to be made first – you will need tables

to look this up in. Taps have square heads which should be gripped in a tap wrench. The tap needs to be held perfectly square to the surface – and the squareness checked regularly. Turn the tap a quarter of a turn at a time and then turn it back. If you try to take too large 'bites' the tap will break – getting broken taps out of blind holes is not easy. When tapping a hole in aluminium, lubricate the tap with paraffin; use a light oil lubricant when working on bronze, copper and steel. A lubricant is unnecessary for brass and cast iron.

Dies Two types of die are normally used for cutting new threads – circular split dies and pipe-thread dies.

Circular split dies have a limited range of adjustments and usually come in sizes below 13mm. When using one of these, you should be particularly careful to make sure that the die is perfectly square to the bar being threaded when you start.

Pipe-thread dies are circular dies fitted with a guide bush to make sure that the die is square to the bar.

With both types of die, chamfer the end of the bar before cutting the thread.

TAPS AND DIES

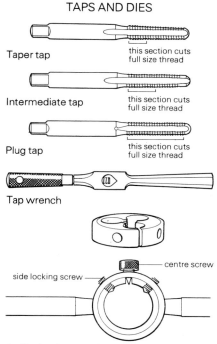

Taper tap — this section cuts full size thread

Intermediate tap — this section cuts full size thread

Plug tap — this section cuts full size thread

Tap wrench

side locking screw — centre screw

A die (top) is used in a special die holder (bottom). You run the loose die down the thread and tighten it (with the grub screws on either side of the central screw) progressively. The central screw loosens the die

Reclaiming damaged threads

If the thread on a stud – on the cylinder head of a motor car, for example – gets damaged, it can often be reclaimed by using a nut as a die. You can also clean corroded studs – on bits of equipment which have been dismantled for some time, perhaps before reassembling them.

It is important for you to do this when reassembling car parts which need tightening to a specific torque.

Use a nut which would fit the undamaged stud, and saw a slot through one side of it. Then push a screwdriver blade into the slot to stretch the nut open. It should now be possible to screw the nut over the damaged portion of thread and

on to good thread. Squeeze the nut together using a pair of pliers or mole wrench and, still maintaining your grip on the nut, screw it back over the damaged thread reforming it in the process. With a very badly damaged thread the nut may have to be closed bit by bit and run over the thread on the stud a number of times.

RECLAIMING THREADS

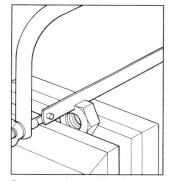

Saw through one side of a nut

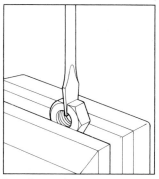

Open it out with a screwdriver

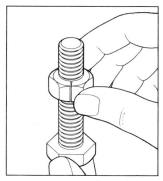

Run it down the damaged thread

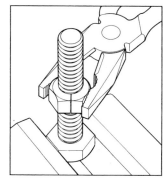

Tighten the nut progressively

Joining metal

There are six main ways of joining metal – with screws (self-tapping screws and nuts and bolts) or rivets, or by soldering, brazing, welding, or gluing. The most appropriate method to use depends mainly on how strong the joint will have to be and the materials being joined, but other factors – listed below – should also be taken into account.

	easily dismantled?	special skill required?	heat necessary?	likelihood of damage to nearby parts?	inherently watertight?
screws	yes	no	no	no	no
rivets	fairly	no	not usually	no	no
soldering	yes	some	yes	yes	yes
brazing	no	yes	yes	yes	yes
welding	no	yes – a lot	yes	yes	yes
gluing	no	no	sometimes	when using heat to cure joint	not always

Screws and bolts

Screws work by pulling tightly together the pieces of metal being joined.

Machine screws pass through a hole in one piece of metal and screw into a matching thread already cut in the other piece, or pass through both pieces and screw into a matching nut.

Bolts are larger machine screws but they are only threaded along part of their length.

Nuts and bolts are very easy to use and provide a good strong joint. A hole slightly larger than the bolt diameter should be drilled through the parts to be joined, the bolt passed through the hole and a nut screwed on to the protruding thread by hand. The bolt should then be held and the nut tightened using a suitable spanner. A washer placed between the nut and the metals being joined spreads the load and avoids damage.

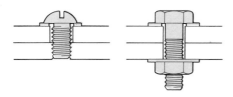

Left, a machine screw passes through the hole in the top piece of metal into a matching thread; right, a bolt needs a nut to screw into

Screw threads and sizes

Screws, bolts and nuts come in a wide variety of shapes and sizes, in most cases specified by their diameter and thread type. The *diameter* of a bolt determines what size hole it will go through, the *thread* type determines what nut will fit it and the *head* size determines what spanner is needed. There are sometimes two versions of a thread available – fine and coarse. A fine thread screws in less quickly than a coarse thread but it is able to exert a greater clamping force for a given tightening torque than its coarse equivalent.

Most nuts and bolts used nowadays have one of the four threads recognised by the International Standards Organisation (ISO). All four use the same shape of thread but three have inch dimensions, called *Unified* (either *UNC* or *UNF*) or *ISO Inch* and the fourth is metric – *ISO Metric*. All have both coarse and fine versions. The coarse metric thread is usually given the name *Metric* – as it is the most common.

A number of other screw threads, now officially obsolete, are still found – *British Standard Whitworth* (BSW), *British Standard Fine* (BSF) and *British Association* (BA). In America there are *American National Coarse* (ANC) and *American National Fine* (ANF).

All these types of nut and bolt are different though one or two can be interchanged.

BA screws are found on radio and TV equipment, particularly if it is old. The sizes are numbered from 0 BA (largest) to 10 BA. Odd numbered sizes are least common and most sizes are 6mm or less in diameter.

BS (BSW and BSF) bolts are bigger – from ¼in diameter upwards – and are known by their diameters stated in fractions of an inch. They are generally found on old equipment.

Unified nuts and bolts sometimes have identifying marks. The hexagonal head of a bolt may have a circular recess on the top, or a line of little circles indented on one of the six flat sides. The nut may have a similar row of circles, or a groove running round one of its two faces. Sizes smaller than ¼in are numbered so that the larger bolts carry the higher number; over ¼in the bolts are called by their actual size. Unified bolts can be found on British cars and domestic appliances.

Metric bolts cover a whole range of sizes and are marked with an M and the diameter in millimetres – M10 for example. Bolts larger than M5 have M or ISOM marked on the head.

Both ISO bolts – Unified and Metric –

SCREWS, BOLTS, NUTS AND WASHERS

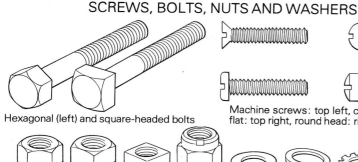

Hexagonal (left) and square-headed bolts

Machine screws: top left, countersunk: left, flat: top right, round head: right, raised head

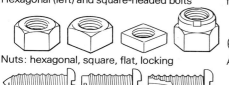

Nuts: hexagonal, square, flat, locking

A selection of washers

Self-tapping screws: left, AB thread-forming; centre B thread forming; right, thread cutting

Spring steel fasteners

have hexagonal heads that increase in fractions of an inch or whole numbers of millimetres from one of the flat sides to the one directly opposite. This is often known as the width across flats (A/F) and the spanners which fit these bolts are often labelled with this dimension. Do not confuse the bolt diameter with the head size – a M8 bolt (8mm thread) with a 13mm head takes a 13mm spanner.

Spanners for BA and BS bolts are labelled with the same name as the screw thread.

Self-tapping screws

A self-tapping screw is by virtue of its shape able to cut or form its own thread in metal as it is driven in. Self-tapping screws are most commonly used for joining sheet metal.

There are two basic types: thread-forming and thread-cutting. Both types need a pilot hole – the diameter of this hole depends on the gauge of the screw and, to a lesser extent, on the metal and its thickness. The Table below gives the pilot drill sizes necessary for joining thin sheet metal (18 to 22 swg) and thicker metal (14 swg) with the most common type of self-tapping screws.

As the **thread-forming** type is driven into the pilot hole, the hardened thread deforms the sides of the hole and forms a matching thread. This type of screw should not be used on brittle materials but is suitable for most metals. Two

PILOT DRILL SIZES

Screw gauge	thin sheet metal mm	thicker sheet metal mm
4	2.0	2.5
6	2.5	3.0
8	3.0	3.5
10	3.5	4.0
12	4.0	4.5

types of thread-forming screw are available, known as AB and B. The pointed end of AB means that it can be used with a slightly smaller pilot hole.

When the **thread-cutting** type is driven into the pilot hole, the hardened thread cuts its own matching thread. This type can be used on brittle materials. The two main types of thread-cutting screws are known as BT and Y. The cutting edge of type BT is a nicked-out groove in the end of its shank. Type Y has a broken thread which allows it to cut along more of the length of the shank.

The most common type of self-tapping screw available is the thread-forming type AB. Many different head shapes can be found but the slotted pan head is the most common. The most common sizes and gauges are 10mm to 25mm and 4 to 10 gauge though self-tapping screws can be found in lengths up to 50mm and in gauges from 2 to 14. Plated screws are also available – mostly nickel or zinc. This should protect the screws against rust in service.

Spring steel fasteners

It is quite common for manufacturers, particularly in the motor industry, to use spring steel fasteners for joining sheet metal components. These are used in preference to self-tapping screws because they allow the holes in the components being joined to be slightly out of line. They are also known as spire or speed nuts. They are useful for coping with over-large pilot holes and for joining thin sheet metal. The fasteners are often used with sheet metal screws which look similar to self-tapping screws but do not have a cutting edge.

Riveting

Riveting is a method for making permanent joints. A rivet is basically a short metal rod with a head on one end. The head may be domed or countersunk. To make a joint, a clearance hole is drilled in the pieces to be joined, the rivet is inserted through the holes, the head supported, and the other end hammered to form a second head. Rivets are available in soft iron, mild steel, copper, brass, aluminium and aluminium alloys. This type of rivet is strong but to use it access is needed to both sides of the pieces of metal being joined. Another type of rivet known as a blind rivet, is essentially a short metal tube – and requires access to one side of the joint only. The rivet is passed through clearance holes, as be-

From the left: standard rivet and two types of blind rivet

fore, but is set from one side using a special tool. Blind rivets are particularly useful for fixing things to hollow objects.

Blind riveting

Most of the special tools required to set blind rivets look rather like pliers with two handles that have to be squeezed together. Some have a nozzle, some do not. With a nozzle it is easier to use the tool in awkward corners or recesses. The other fairly common tool for setting blind rivets is known as a lazy tong and is operated by pushing it. Lazy tongs tend to be rather larger than plier riveters and should be used only when working on things which are strong enough to withstand pushing and firm and rigid enough not to move.

The basic principle of blind riveting is the same for all the different types of tool – a rivet containing a mandrel is put in the hole, the special tool grips the end of the mandrel and the far end of the rivet is deformed by pulling the mandrel through it. Once the rivet is set the mandrel snaps off and is withdrawn with the special tool and then ejected.

The size of a rivet is defined by its diameter and its length. The **diameter** of a rivet determines the size of the hole that has to be drilled. (The drill size should be slightly bigger.) Different diameter rivets have different diameter mandrels, and riveters have spare nozzles or swivelling turrets on their heads to cope with these different sizes. The

most common rivet diameter is 3mm; 4mm rivets are also fairly easy to buy, but 5mm are more difficult.

The **length** of the rivet needed depends on the total thickness (the *grip*) of the metals being joined. A rivet that is too long for the grip of the joint will need more effort to set it and will probably produce an untidy joint, but it will be strong. A rivet that is too short may not spread sufficiently to make a secure joint. When riveting soft materials allow enough room for a washer. Rivets made by different manufacturers vary slightly in length. In most cases with 3 and 4mm diameter rivets *short* ones have a maximum grip around 3mm, *medium* ones around 6mm and *long* ones around 10mm.

Blind rivets are usually made of aluminium alloy but mild steel rivets are also available – usually in large quantities. Steel rivets are stronger than aluminium ones and, while it is possible to make structural load-bearing joints with either type, both are normally used for cosmetic joints – where the rivets have to withstand light loads only – and for jobs such as holding wings or sills of cars in place prior to welding or brazing. For a load-bearing joint, make sure that the diameter of the rivets is not less than the thickness of the thickest material being joined. This may mean using 5mm rivets – for these lazy tongs, which require much less effort than the plier-type riveting tools, are the most sensible

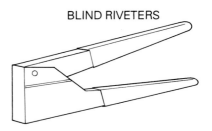

Plier-type riveter without nozzle

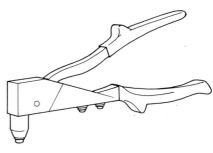

Plier-type riveter with nozzle and spares

choice: but they are expensive and awkward to use.

Threaded rivets

Threaded blind rivets leave behind a rivet which can take a screw. To set these, use a reusable mandrel screwed into the rivet. Grip the mandrel with a riveter (a special nozzle is required) and set the rivet in much the same way as an ordinary blind rivet but do not break the mandrel – unscrew it from the rivet.

HOW BLIND RIVETING WORKS

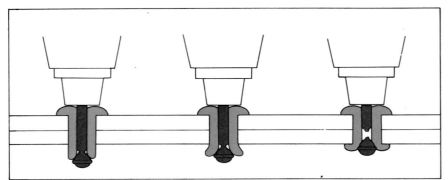

There are three stages in setting a blind rivet. Left: the rivet is put in the hole and the riveter's jaws grip the mandrel. Middle: the

mandrel is drawn through the rivet deforming the end. Right: the mandrel breaks and is withdrawn

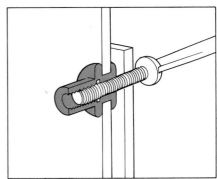

Once a threaded rivet has been set you can drive screws into it – to hold fixings, say

Soldering

Metals can be joined together by soldering, using an alloy (the solder) as a kind of glue. The basic technique is to heat the surfaces to be joined and then feed the molten solder between them. Both surfaces need to be clean – the appropriate flux will keep them clean and help the solder stick properly. The flux prevents the surfaces oxidising at the temperatures involved in soldering.

Soft solder This is sometimes called Tinman's solder and consists of an alloy of lead and tin which melts at a fairly low temperature and runs easily into fine gaps in a hot joint. It comes as a wire which, for electrical work, has the flux incorporated in it – called "multicore".

Flux can also be bought by itself in tins. Plumber's solder is different – it is meant for filling large gaps and is used for lead pipe joints. Ordinary soft solder is used for electrical joints and for situations when a good seal is more important than strength. The temperatures required are easily reached with a blowlamp or an electric soldering iron.

Soft-soldered joints can be made most easily in brass, copper and zinc but mild steel, galvanized steel and lead may also be soldered without difficulty. Stainless steel can be soft soldered using tin-lead solders but special fluxes which are free from chlorides should be used - you can usually buy this sort of flux from plumbers' merchants who stock stainless steel

water pipe.

Aluminium may be soft soldered but special solder is required as well as special flux.

Silver solder This is usually made of copper, zinc and silver. Some types contain cadmium too, but this can give off poisonous fumes and should be used with great care. Silver solder melts quite suddenly at fairly high temperatures and is useful for small-scale work where heating the metal too much has to be avoided – a blowlamp will usually give enough heat. It is very expensive and strong and is often used where its appearance matters, but it should not be used on very loose joints.

Making a soft-soldered joint

Thoroughly clean the surfaces to be joined by using a wire brush or emery paper to remove scale, old paint or corrosion and by using white spirit or paraffin to remove oil and grease. Cover the clean joint with flux and heat it until it reaches a temperature slightly above the melting point of the solder being used. Apply flux. When the solder is now applied it should melt immediately and run into the joint. If the solder does not run freely, the joint is probably too cool and needs further heating. Solder will not run freely on dirty surfaces.

Remove the heat source and allow the joint to cool. As the joint cools, the

molten solder solidifies and forms a solid joint. Do not disturb it until the solder has properly solidified – well after the solder loses its shine – otherwise a poor joint could result.

When using a soldering iron as a heat source, it should be *tinned* before use for the first time (and again when it gets dirty) and it is advisable to tin both parts of the joint too. To do this, clean up the bit by filing it to reveal bright clean metal. Warm it a little and dip it in flux. Then warm up the iron and spread solder over the surface. Keep the bit clean and tinned by wiping it occasionally on a damp rag when it is hot. Do not knock electric soldering irons to remove excess solder from the bit.

To tin the parts of a joint, clean them as before – try not to touch them – and put flux on at once. Heat up a tinned soldering iron, hold it against one piece of the joint area and rub it around so that the whole area reaches the required temperature. Put a dab of solder on the tip of the iron and spread it thinly over the joint surface. Wipe off any blobs of solder and make sure that the area is clean and evenly covered. Repeat this on the other part of the joint, bring the two parts together with a little flux in between and use the soldering iron to reheat the whole joint until the solder melts together and makes a joint. It may be necessary to add a little extra solder to the joint – not to the iron.

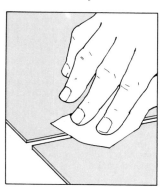
Clean the surfaces

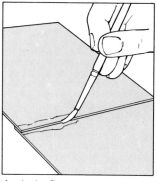
Apply the flux

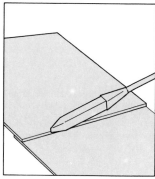
Warm the joint

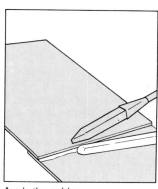
Apply the solder

THE TOOLS FOR SOLDERING

The heat sources normally used for soldering are the electric soldering iron and the gas blowlamp. The once popular traditional soldering iron is now rarely used.

When deciding which tool to use you should remember that it is a waste of time trying to solder with a tool that is not powerful enough for the job. Equally well, one which is too powerful may heat up the solder too much and weaken the joint. For very delicate electrical work, you will most likely need to use an electric soldering iron. Some gas blowlamps can do this job well too. For bigger electrical jobs and for soldering jewellery and model making, you can use a blowlamp which takes a fine or an extra fine burner – a flame which is quite hot but not too big or diffuse is needed – or one of the more powerful soldering irons. For plumbing work – soldering copper pipes – a gas blowlamp is the most sensible choice. For soldering large lumps of metal (or brazing), you need a powerful blowlamp. You should also think about the following points:

● the temperature the solder and joint have to reach – ordinary solder melts at about 250°C and this temperature must be maintained in the joint all the time it is being made

● the thermal size of the joint and its immediate surroundings – a large joint will need a larger source of heat to enable it to reach the required temperature and when soldering metals, such as copper, which are very good conductors of heat, a steady supply of heat is needed to keep the temperature high

● the position of the joint – if the joint is near temperature sensitive electronic components like transistors, it is wise to insert a heat sink between the joint and the component to mop up the heat used in soldering and so prevent it from travelling. A mass of metal is the usual heat sink and a good heavy pair of pliers will often do the trick. On the other hand if the joint has a large surface area and is exposed to the air, it may radiate the heat away too quickly. This can be overcome by enclosing the joint in a temporary brick hearth, or by burying part of it in a bed of ashes. Never lay the joint on a good conducting surface.

Traditional iron This is a thick steel rod with an insulating handle on one end and a heavy copper bit screwed on to the other end. The bit is heated in a fire or flame – over a gas stove, say – and acts as a reservoir of heat: the larger the thermal size of the joint, the larger the bit has to be. Traditional irons tend to be cumbersome and are not really suitable for delicate jobs or for use in a confined space. Even the largest irons have a relatively small thermal capacity.

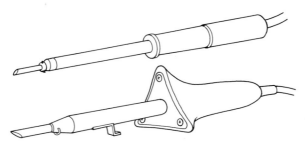

Electric irons These use a small built-in electric element as a source of heat and a variety of powers (wattages) are available. Electric irons tend to be less cumbersome than traditional irons and are easy to use in confined spaces or on delicate objects. However, they can be used only where there is a suitable power supply. Small electric irons may have thermostatic control switches; these are ideal for small electrical work.

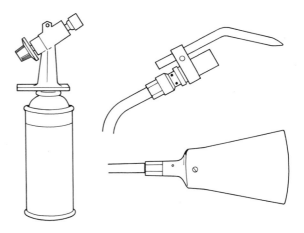

Blowlamps These are capable of providing a lot of heat, so they need to be used with extra care to avoid damaging the workpiece or burning the solder. They are normally used in one of two ways.

The flame may be played directly on the joint. This method is useful for large joints which are unlikely to be damaged by excess heat and for making a lot of joints quickly – joining central heating pipes, say. This method can also be used for making small or delicate repairs to large objects by using the blowlamp to pre-warm the object to just below the required temperature and then using a smaller, more easily controlled, iron to effect the repair.

A blowlamp can also be used with a soldering bit attached. A variety of sizes is available. In this form a blowlamp is rather like a traditional iron with a constant supply of heat – the bit is heated by the flame from the blowlamp playing on its back.

Brazing

Brazing uses alloys of copper and zinc which melt at much higher temperatures (700 to 800°C) than solder and give stronger joints. A special flux or a borax paste is needed. Braze (or bronze) welding uses the same sort of alloy but instead of running it into the joint a fillet is built up on the surface. If the joint is small, it may be possible to reach the tempera-ture required with a gas blowlamp, by playing the flame directly on the joint. If this is not successful, a more powerful heat source is needed.

A brazing attachment is available for use with an arc welder. This usually takes the form of two carbon rods fixed in a hand-held clamp. An arc is created be-tween the tips of the two rods and the resulting flame is used to heat the joint.

This source is both powerful and fierce, so it is advisable to practise this method before attempting to use it for a repair.

Oxy-acetylene welding equipment is frequently used for brazing – the heat is easily controlled by using the appropriate size nozzle and the torch is easy to manipulate. Unfortunately, these advantages tend to be outweighed by the difficulty in getting hold of the gases.

Welding

Welding is a technique for joining two pieces of metal together by melting a small area of each piece on either side of the joint and allowing them to flow together. A third piece of a similar metal – a *filler* – is often melted into a groove in the joint. The filler – as a thin rod or wire – may also be used to form a bead on the surface of a joint or a fillet between two pieces of metal at an angle.

Welding is necessary only when strong joints are needed. It requires considerable skill and can be hazardous. The manufacturers of welding equipment often produce booklets telling you how to do it and comprehensive books on the subject are also available. If you want to do it properly, think about taking an adult education course.

Welding needs a very steady hand and practice – a small area of metal must be maintained at the right temperature. If the temperature is too low, the weld will crack apart when it is jarred; if the temperature is too high, too much of the join will be melted and in thin materials a hole will appear. If the filler is fed too fast, blobs will form; if too slow, the weld will be uneven and have weaknesses.

The parts to be joined have to be heated to their melting point along the joint, so powerful heat sources have to be used. The two systems most readily available are gas welding and electric arc welding.

Gas welding

In oxy-acetylene welding, acetylene gas is burnt at the nozzle of a hand-held torch. The intensity of the flame, and hence its temperature, is controlled by adjusting the proportions of oxygen and acetylene gases within the torch. A range of torch nozzles are available. Another form of gas welding is oxy-LPG welding. This is similar to oxy-acetylene welding except that butane or propane gases are used as the fuel gas instead of acetylene.

Gas welding can be used on a variety of metals – most commonly steel and aluminium – and because it is possible to control the heat output carefully, it is especially suitable for welding thin sheets, such as car body panels.

The main problem with gas welding is getting the gases. Until recently they were available to commercial users only and were supplied in large, heavy metal cylinders which were expensive to buy. Since the gases are stored in these cylinders at high pressure (oxygen at 2000psi and acetylene at 200psi), great care has to be taken in their storage and use. However, it is now possible to rent small, easily-transported metal cylinders (gas bottles) from the gas supplier. These can be exchanged for refilled bottles when empty. But it is still expensive since a substantial deposit has to be made on the bottles. So, unless you are going to do a lot of work over a long period, it is unlikely to be financially worthwhile. A small engineering works will usually do a few joints at relatively low cost.

When welding mild steel with an oxy-acetylene flame, a flux is not needed – the flame has an oxygen-absorbing envelope and any carbon formed will burn in the flame.

Fix the two pieces of metal to be joined in position by using clamps or blind rivets. Select the gas pressures and nozzle size from the data supplied with the equipment. When lighting the torch, always turn on the acetylene and light this first. **Always wear dark-coloured safety glasses which are approved for gas welding**.

Play the flame on to the joint to raise it

WELDING EQUIPMENT

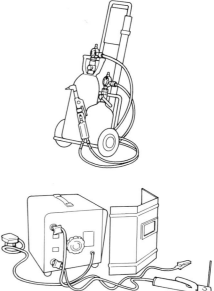

Electric arc welders (bottom) generally operate from a 13-amp socket and as the ultra-violet radiation emitted can damage eyes and skin, a face mask must be used. Gas welders (top) usually run on acetylene and oxygen

to melting point. The joint area looked at through dark safety glasses will at first appear dark (at about 700°C), will then slowly turn orange-red (900°C) and finally appear white (about 1300°C to 1700°C) as the metal melts. When this happens, a pool of molten metal will appear between the parts being joined. Now, slowly move the flame along the joint so that the pool appears to move along the joint. In theory, the pool continually fills with new molten metal from the leading edge of the pool while metal at the back of the pool cools and solidifies. In this way a continuous joint is built up. However, in practice, a filler metal is also used. This is a rod (or wire)

of similar metal which is melted by the flame as it proceeds and is allowed to drip into the pool. This additional metal fills the small gap between the joint. If this were filled by the parent metals, the area around the joint would become thin and weak.

Warning

All welding needs care, with gas welding:

● the gases are stored under high pressure – never bump or drop the containers and control gauges

● when assembling the equipment, under no circumstances use oil or grease on any of the threads

● the flame is small but extremely hot and even brief contact with it can cause serious burns.

Electric arc welding

In this method of welding, an electric arc is formed between the tip of a metal rod and the metal being joined. The intense heat created by the arc causes the metal to melt and fuse.

The high current necessary to produce the arc are supplied by a transformer. The output of this transformer can be varied to increase or decrease the intensity (power) of the arc which means that this welding technique to be used on

MAKING WELDED JOINTS

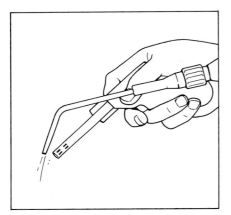

Light the acetylene first. Do not turn on the gas excessively, point the flame away from yourself and make sure that it will not burn anything else

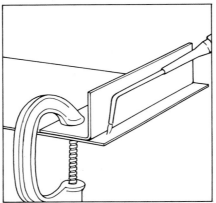

Work from one side of the joint to the other moving the filler rod smoothly; a special technique is used to control the flame

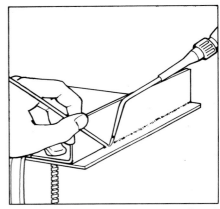

When clamps cannot be used, a series of tack welds – on the wing of a car, say – will keep the joint in position while you weld it

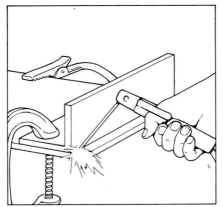

When using an electric arc welder, keep the welding rod at the angles shown in the drawing – about 45 degrees to the vertical and 70 degrees to the horizontal

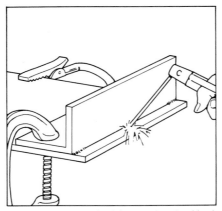

In many instances the joint requires 'tacking' along its length, and either left like this or filled in between the tacks

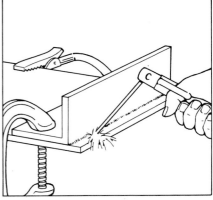

Most electrodes are of the 'touch' type – the electrode and joint can come into contact – so the electrode can be dragged along the joint

a range of material thicknesses. Small welding transformers are readily available which will operate from a 13-amp socket.

The output current controls on transformers may be either stepped or stepless. A *stepped* control has a series of fixed outputs which can be selected individually. The main disadvantage of this system is that one point may not be quite powerful enough and the next incremental point may be too powerful. This is particularly a problem at low powers when welding thin sheet. By contrast a *stepless* control can be set anywhere between the minimum and maximum power of the transformer, so it is easier to select the correct power when welding thin materials. Stepless transformers tend to be more expensive than stepped ones.

A welding transformer comes with two heavy duty cables. One cable is the earth return and this should be clamped to the job. All parts of the job must be electrically in contact with this cable. The other cable is attached to an electrode holder which you hold in your hand. A flux-coated metal rod of suitable size is clamped in this holder.

Start the welding process by striking an arc between the tip of the electrode and the job. This is done by lightly scraping the tip of the electrode across the job until an arc is made. Then guide the tip of the electrode along the joint at a suitable speed. The heat generated by the arc will melt the metal on either side of the joint and will also melt the electrode which will then flow into and fill the joint. The electrode has a flux coating and this will also melt and form a shield between the joint and the atmosphere. When the joint is cool, the flux adhering to the outside of the joint should be chipped away with a hammer.

If the electrode is moved along the joint too quickly, the joint will not have sufficient time to heat up and melt and a weak joint will result. If the electrode is moved along the joint too slowly, too much of the metal around the joint will be melted and holes may appear. This will also happen if too high a power is selected. But, if too low a power is selected, the arc will be difficult to strike.

Warning

The electric arc emits intense ultra-violet radiation which can damage skin and eyes. Anyone using an electric arc welder and anyone nearby must wear a very darkly-tinted screen to view the arc – one conforming to the appropriate British Standard (BS679).

The fumes from the molten flux can be harmful – do not weld in a confined space. Sparks or hot slag from the weld can cause a fire.

Adhesives

Adhesives provide a useful way of making permanent joints between metals. They are particularly suitable for:
● joining two different metals which are considerably different in thickness
● joining thin and relatively weak metals which would be damaged by other joining techniques
● places where a smooth finished joint is necessary
● joining awkwardly-shaped pieces of metal.
When using an adhesive for joining metals, make sure that the surfaces are clean and free from dirt and grease. Avoid using adhesives when the joint will be under constant loads.

Contact adhesives These adhesives should not be used where a strong joint is essential. To make the bond, apply the adhesive to both surfaces and leave them to become tacky. Then hold the two surfaces together – they should bond immediately.

Cyanoacrylate adhesives These adhesives are based on cyanoacrylate esters and produce very strong bonds. They are very easy to use – simply spread a very small amount of glue on one component and hold the other one in contact with it for approximately 10 seconds. Do not use too much glue. Cyanoacrylates harden by reacting with the thin film of water present on most things and if there is too much glue, or too much water, present the result will be a weak joint. Once the parts are pressed together they cannot be repositioned (so there is no need to clamp things) and the joint quickly reaches full strength.

Use cyanoacrylates with care – they form strong bonds with human flesh, so you should avoid getting any on your fingers or in your eyes and should always store them well away from children. If you do have an accident – bond your fingers together, say – plunge the affected parts into hot soapy water as quickly as possible and try to peel the joined surfaces apart as the glue softens. You can use a teaspoon handle as a lever. Do not try to pull the surfaces apart. You can wear polythene gloves when using cyanoacrylates but do not wear rubber ones.

Epoxy resins These adhesives produce strong joints but need a long setting time – often around 24 hours. They usually come in two parts – a resin and a hardener which have to be mixed together immediately before they are applied. A chemical reaction then takes place which produces heat and cures the joint. The time taken to cure the joint can be shortened by warming it.

Epoxy resins tend to be brittle when set and should not be used for joints which are liable to be flexed in use.

Bending metal

The technique for bending is much the same for most metals but they may require different pre-treatment. Thin sheets of mild steel can be bent cold, thicker ones may need to be at red heat before they can be bent easily.

Non-ferrous metals – copper, brass and aluminium alloys – are supplied in different *tempers* (degrees of hardness). Annealed (soft) and half-hard tempers of copper and brass can be bent cold without problems. Hard tempers of these metals may need annealing – heating the metal until it is a dull red colour and either allowing it to cool slowly in air or plunging it into cold water to cool it quickly. Bending the metal will reharden it and it may be necessary to repeat the treatment with thick metal or complicated bends.

'Commercially pure' aluminium may be bent without prior annealing. Aluminium alloys such as H9 (used for window frames and so on) and H15 (called Duralumin) are usually supplied in a heat-treated condition. These can be bent to some extent without cracking but they are rather springy. They may be annealed to make them more ductile but will lose a lot of strength in the process. Since aluminium alloys do not become red hot on heating it is difficult to judge

the annealing temperature. As a guide, you can place a matchstick on the surface of the metal – it should just char – or coat the metal with a thin film of soap and continue heating until the soap turns black. The metal should be allowed to cool in air after annealing.

Some metals are very difficult to bend – high-speed steel, for example will not bend readily at temperatures below white heat – and some, like cast iron, are too brittle.

The first step is to mark the position of the bend. Think about this carefully when making complex bends as the distance from a set point, say the end of the metal, will be greater on the outside of a bend than on the inside – roughly by the thickness of the metal itself. So if the inside distance is the important one, make a mark along the inside and bend to that, but if the outside distance matters, make a mark on the outside and allow for the stretching that will take place. This stretching of the outside and compression of the inside of a bend also means that the metal will become slightly thinner around the bend and its edges will tend to taper – a strip of metal will be wider on the inside of the bend than on the outside.

The metal to be bent should be firmly

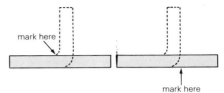

When bending complex shapes, think carefully about marking out

held in a vice. Sheet metal should be adequately supported on both sides by using wood or metal bending formers. The metal can then be bent along its length by using light blows from a soft-handled hammer. When bending very soft metals, a piece of wood between the hammer and the metal will avoid hammer marks on the metal. Use light hammer blows and hit as near to the bend as possible. If the metal needs excessive force to bend it, then it will have to be bent hot. When using formers, allow for some spring back of the metal by using a former with a slightly smaller radius than you want in the metal.

Special tools are available to help you bend soft or half-hard copper water pipes without the tube wrinkling or flattening – see drawing below. For other tubes a well-packed filling of dry sand may be used.

BENDING SHEETS AND PIPES

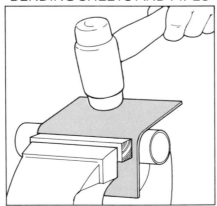

Use wood battens to grip the metal. Work from one side to the other raining down light hammer blows to bend the sheet smoothly and progressively

A metal pipe can be used to form a smooth bend. Remember to strike the sheet of metal as near to the bend as possible.

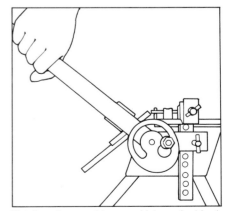

Pipe bending machines – which can be hired – make the job of bending plumbing pipes a simple one. See also the chapter on *Plumbing*

CHAPTER ELEVEN

PLUMBING

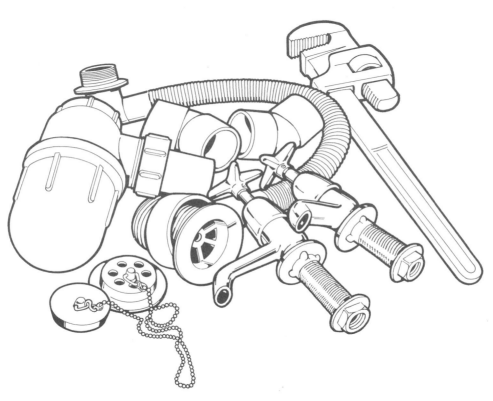

Doing your own plumbing work can save you a lot of money and simple plumbing jobs do not require a great deal of knowledge or skill. A beginner should be able to cope with straightforward jobs, like replacing a tap washer or plumbing in a basin and an average handyman should be able to tackle more complicated jobs, such as plumbing in a separate shower. But you should think twice before trying to tackle very complicated jobs. Working on a plumbing system can be dirty work – especially if you have to lift the floorboards or work in a dusty loft – and it can be fairly strenuous.

There are two main parts to a household plumbing system – the water supply system and the waste system. The **water supply** system is a set of pipes and fittings which carries clean water to baths, basins, WCs and so on. The **waste** system is another set of pipes which carries used water away to drains and sewers. In an old house, or one with many plumbing fittings, the pipework may seem very confusing, but basic plumbing systems are really quite simple. Before starting work on your plumbing system, trace all the pipework carefully so that you know where each pipe leads and what it does.

Water supply

A household plumbing system basically starts at the water supply undertaking's (either a water authority or a company) stopcock. This is usually situated outside the boundary of the property about 750mm below ground under a small metal cover, probably in the pavement. **Most water supply undertakings' stopcocks** need a special key to turn them on and off. The stopcock controls the flow of water between the water supply undertaking's water main and the household water supply. The pipe which carries water from the stopcock to the house is known as a service pipe and the responsibility for maintaining it lies with the householder. Before 1939, service pipes were usually lead or steel; nowadays they are often copper, or polythene. Many service pipes slope upwards slightly from the water supply undertaking's stopcock to the house but should always be at least 750mm below ground. Once inside the house, the pipe (now called a rising main) can be protected against freezing by running it along an inside wall. In houses with suspended floors it may be necessary to give the pipe additional frost protection by wrapping it in polystyrene pipe lagging bound with several layers of glass fibre wrap.

There are two basic systems for moving water about the house from the rising main to places where it is wanted – indirect and direct.

Indirect plumbing systems

In an indirect system, the primary purpose of the rising main is to feed water into a cold water cistern (often, wrongly, called a tank) which is usually situated in the loft. Most of the taps and other plumbing fittings in the house will get their water supply from this cistern, which is kept topped up from the rising main through a ballvalve. However, at least one tap – usually the cold water tap in the kitchen – has to be supplied direct from the rising main to provide a supply of pure (or *potable*) water for drinking and cooking.

Depending on the local water byelaws, one, two or more fittings may be made direct to the rising main – one for an outside water tap, and one for a cold water supply to a washing machine or dishwasher, say.

Most indirect plumbing systems have two pipes (often called draw-off pipes) taking water out of the cistern. One pipe

INDIRECT PLUMBING SYSTEM

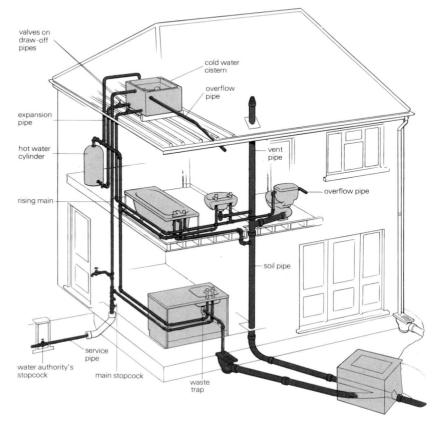

valves on draw-off pipes

cold water cistern

overflow pipe

expansion pipe

hot water cylinder

rising main

vent pipe

overflow pipe

soil pipe

service pipe

water authority's stopcock

main stopcock

waste trap

This house, with the indirect plumbing system, has a single-stack waste system.

feeds WCs and cold water taps in bath-rooms and any other rooms where there are basins. The other feeds a hot water cylinder where the water is stored and heated – for example, by an electric immersion heater. Plumbing systems may have extra draw-off pipes for some types of bidet or shower or to make pipe runs to some fittings more convenient.

Hot water taps draw their water from a pipe connected to the top of the hot water cylinder – again, bidet and shower installations may need their own, indi-vidual, connections. The hot water cylin-der will also have an expansion pipe (leading back to the cold water cistern) to allow for expansion of the water as it heats up, and to provide a safety vent if

the water should start boiling.

To carry out work on a plumbing sys-tem, or to stop a leak or burst, different parts of the system need to be isolated and drained of water. In theory, only one stopcock or valve is really necessary in a system. This should be as near as pos-sible to the point where the main service pipe enters the house to enable the whole house to be isolated from the water supply. Two drain cocks are needed – one just above the main stop-cock to drain the rising main and any branch pipes connected to it, and the other as low down as possible on the pipe feeding the hot water cylinder to drain the cylinder. Pipes feeding hot taps and cold taps connected to the cistern, and

the cold water cistern itself, can be drained by turning the taps on.

In practice, to save having to drain the entire system every time repair work or modifications are carried out, it is better to include more valves, so that some parts of the plumbing system can be isolated from the rest. This usually en-tails having valves on each draw-off from the cistern. It is also possible to fit small isolating valves just before each tap or fitting. There should also be a valve on the pipe feeding the hot water cylinder but not on the outlet pipe from it.

Direct plumbing systems
In a direct plumbing system, all the cold taps, WCs and so on are fed directly from the rising main. If the hot water is heated by a storage hot water cylinder (rather than by instantaneous heaters) this will usually be fed from a small cold water cistern though the cylinder may be fed direct from the rising main.

Which system is best?
An indirect plumbing system has four main advantages. First, and possibly most importantly, because most of the system is isolated from the mains by the cistern, water is less likely to be drawn back into the mains (this is called back-siphonage) so there is much less risk of contamination of the water supply. Sec-ondly, the system operates at constant water pressure so you do not need to worry about variations in the mains water pressure – this is particularly im-portant for some types of shower which need roughly equal pressures of hot and cold water. Thirdly, the water pressure is relatively low which helps to reduce noise and, finally, the cistern provides a reserve supply of water if the mains fails.

A direct plumbing system is a little less complicated and can be cheaper to in-stall than an indirect one. But some of the fittings used may have to be specially designed to lessen the risk of contamina-tion of the mains.

The sort of system you can have will depend on the local water supply undertaking. Nowadays, most prefer an indirect one.

DIRECT PLUMBING SYSTEM

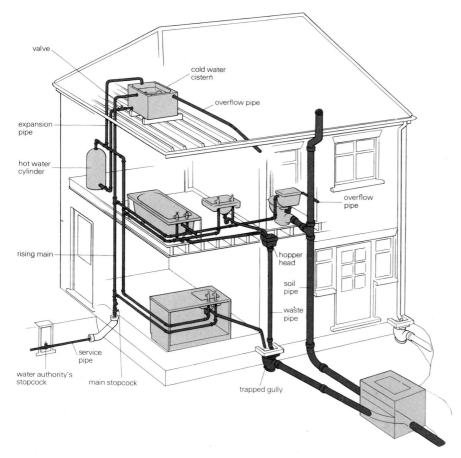

valve
cold water cistern
overflow pipe
expansion pipe
hot water cylinder
rising main
overflow pipe
hopper head
soil pipe
waste pipe
service pipe
water authority's stopcock
main stopcock
trapped gully

This one with a direct plumbing system has a two-pipe waste system. Other plumbing/waste combinations are often found.

The waste system

In modern plumbing systems, the pipes which carry used water away from baths, basins, WCs, bidets and showers have traps – often called U-bends – full of water. The water in these traps prevents smells from the sewers getting into the house – in Victorian times, this 'drain air' was thought to be directly responsible for a number of diseases. Even if this is not the case, smells from sewers are at least unpleasant. On a WC, the water trap is part of the fitting; in other cases, it is part of the outlet pipe.

Single-stack systems

Most houses built since about 1960 have a single-stack waste system. The branch pipes from the U-bend traps, attached to baths, basins, WCs and so on in the upper stories of the house, connect into a single pipe usually 100mm in diameter – called a discharge pipe, soil pipe or soil-stack – which runs vertically down the side of (or through) the house. The top of this pipe should terminate outside the building, not less than 900mm above the level of any opening windows. The bottom is connected directly into the house drainage system – it has no trap in it.

When designing a waste system, care has to be taken to ensure that the water in the traps cannot be sucked out so breaking the seal against smells. This can happen if waste water rushes through the branch pipe leading from the trap (or through other pipes connected to this branch) quickly enough to create sufficient suction to pull the water out of the trap. To guard against unsealing, the top of the soil-stack can be left open. It should, however, be fitted with a cage to stop birds nesting in it and stopping up the open end. (Technically, the length of pipe above the highest branch connection to it is called a vent pipe.) In the single-stack waste system, there need to be other design constraints – the slope, length and diameter of branch pipes, the position of their connections to the soil-stack, and the radius of the bend at the foot of the soil-stack all have to be worked out carefully. Despite all this, the single-stack system is widely used, because it is economical and neat.

WCs at ground-floor level may also be connected to the soil-stack but are more usually connected directly to the drain. Other ground-floor waste pipes will probably discharge over an open gully (or into a back-inlet gully). This is basically a water trap with the top open to the air at ground level and an outlet connected to the house drains. The open gully should be fitted with a grid to prevent leaves and other things blocking it. The waste pipes enter the gully below the level of the grid but above the level of the water in the gully trap either by simply passing through a hole cut in the top of the grid, or by being connected to an inlet forming part of the gully. When this inlet is at the back of the gully (the front of the grid is where the outlet is) it is called a *back-inlet* gully; when the inlet is at the side, it is called, not surprisingly, a *side-inlet* gully. The different forms are simply to make installation easier.

Two-pipe systems

Many older houses have a two-pipe waste system with WCs connected into one vertical *soil* pipe, and other wastes (baths, basins, and bidets) connected into a separate vertical *waste* pipe. This system calls for less careful design of slopes and connections, but the vertical pipes still need to be vented to the air. In the drawing on page 263, the soil pipe is vented by having its open end above the eaves – as in the single-stack system. But the waste pipe is open to the air at first-floor level, and the branch pipes discharge into a funnel – called a *hopper* – fixed to this open end.

An existing two-pipe system can be extended by allowing extra waste pipes to discharge into the hopper head. This is clearly much simpler than having to cut into the side of a vertical waste pipe – particularly a cast-iron one. But in new two-pipe systems installed nowadays, branch waste pipes have to be connected into the side of the main waste pipe in the same way as WCs have to be connected into soil pipes.

In the two-pipe system, the soil pipe is connected directly to the drains, and the waste pipe is connected via a trapped gully.

REGULATIONS

Most plumbing and waste work is covered by regulations designed to ensure that the results of the work are not a danger to health, and do not lead to undue consumption or waste of water.

Building Regulations

The Building Regulations (and their equivalents in Northern Ireland, Scotland and Inner London) control the way waste systems are designed. You should give notice of your plans to do anything to the waste system in your house (apart from straightforward repair or replacement). Ask where you pay rates for information about the person to contact – in England and Wales (outside Inner London) it is the Building Control Officer of your Borough or District Council.

Briefly, the Regulations aim to ensure that waste pipes and traps are of a suitable size, that the ventilating ends of pipes are high enough not to cause a danger to health, and that wastes are designed so that traps remain full of water. In some cases, the proprietary waste products that are available will ensure that you comply with the Regulations.

Water Bye-laws

Because there are differences in the type of water supplied to different areas of the country, each local water supply undertaking issues its own water bye-laws – though these are normally based on the *Model Water Bye-laws*. You should give notice of your plans for any plumbing work before it is started. For the name and address of your local water supply undertaking, look at your last water rate's bill.

The Water Bye-laws cover such things as the size of storage cisterns and the position of inlets, outlets and overflows; the provision of stop taps and drain taps; the protection of pipes against frost damage, corrosion and vibration; and most importantly, the design of the system so that there is no possibility of the water becoming contaminated, particularly by back-siphonage. To make sure that any work complies fully, it is essential to read (and follow) the local water undertaking's bye-laws.

There are quite stiff penalties for ignoring the waste and water regulations.

Pipes and fittings

In the past, plumbing pipes were often iron or lead. Each has its advantages and disadvantages – lead, for example, is easy to bend but it requires skill to join, it is expensive and lead plumbing systems have been a contributory factor towards lead poisoning in soft water areas. Nowadays, most plumbing pipes are copper, though stainless steel and rigid and flexible plastics are sometimes used. Rigid plastic pipe is becoming more common for cold water services in new houses.

Copper pipe

Copper pipe is generally easily available and fairly easy to work with. It comes in various sizes and is sized by its *outside* diameter – 15mm, 22mm and 28mm are the most common sizes (equivalent to ½in, ¾in and 1in *inside* diameter). Main runs and pipes feeding bath taps and the hot water cylinder are usually 22mm pipe. Pipes to all other taps are usually 15mm in diameter. The 28mm size might be used for boiler pipes and sometimes for feeding the hot water cylinder (instead of 22mm pipe).

Copper pipe can be **cut** with a fine-toothed hacksaw, or with a special pipe-cutting tool. Care must be taken when using a hacksaw to cut the end of the pipe exactly square, and the cut must be filed smooth both inside and out. A pipe cutter tends to leave a burr on the inside of the pipe – this should be filed off.

Copper pipe can be **bent** fairly readily but it must be supported during the process or it will kink. Smaller diameters can be bent by hand with the aid of a *bending spring*. This is a stiff metal coil of nearly the same diameter as the inside of the pipe. It is pushed into the pipe around the point where the bend is to be made and supports the pipe during bending.

The spring should be compressed a little – by turning it – before attempting to withdraw it. You need one for each size of copper pipe. Pipe can also be bent using a *bending machine*. Both springs and machines have their advantages and disadvantages.

For simple, small plumbing jobs, bending springs are probably all that you need – with these you can make bends of different radii, make bends near the end of a length of pipe (but with difficulty) and bend pipes up to and including those of 22mm diameter. They are also inexpensive to buy, but require effort to use.

MAKING A COMPRESSION JOINT

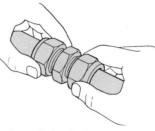

File the end of one piece of pipe smooth, pass the cap nut from the fitting over it, smear the end with an approved jointing paste

and push the olive on to the pipe. Then push the fitting over the end of the pipe.
Prepare the end of the other

piece of pipe in the same way – with jointing paste and an olive – and push this into the fitting.
Tighten the fitting with span-

ners – as shown in the drawing. Do not overtighten: if a small leak appears when the water is turned on, tighten a little more

MAKING A CAPILLARY JOINT (SOLDER-RING TYPE)

Thoroughly clean the outside ends of the pipes, and the inside of the fittings with wire wool until they are bright and shiny.

Using a brush or spatula, smear a small amount of solder flux all round the inside of the fitting and push the fitting and pipes to-

gether so that they overlap.
Carefully heat the joint with a blow-lamp until a ring of solder appears at each end. If you can,

solder *all* the ends of a tee fitting at the same time. Do not disturb the joint until it has cooled. If the joint leaks, reheat it.

For large plumbing jobs involving a lot of bending, a machine is worth having – they are very expensive to buy but can be hired. A machine takes most of the effort out of bending any size of pipe but the radius of the bend is fixed, and it requires practice to get the bend in the right place.

It is also possible to use fittings for altering the direction of a run of pipework but, in general, it is better to make bends as these are cheaper and provide a smoother path for water flow which helps cut down noise.

Fittings for copper pipe

There are two main ways of joining lengths of copper pipe together – with a compression joint which is fitted to the pipes using spanners or with a capillary joint which is soldered on to the pipes.

A **compression** fitting has a screwed body with a nut and sealing ring, called an olive, at each end. To make a joint, the pipe ends are pushed into the body and the nuts are tightened, squashing the olives on to the pipes to form a watertight seal. A special type of compression fitting, known as the manipulative or Type B fitting, should be used for joints underground. With this joint the pipe ends should be expanded, using a steel drift or swaging tool, after the fitting nuts have been passed over them.

With **capillary** fittings, a watertight seal is made by melting solder so that it flows (by capillary action) and fills the small gap between the fitting and the pipe ends which are inserted into it. The type most suitable for the amateur plumber is the *solder-ring* fitting which has its own, built-in, supply of solder – see drawings showing how to make a capillary joint. *End-feed* fittings are similar, but they do not have their own supply of solder. The pipes and fitting should be prepared in the same way as with a solder-ring fitting, and the joint heated. A length of solder wire (enough to go around the end of the fitting) should be melted at the mouth of the fitting and allowed to creep into the gap between pipe and fitting.

There are no strict rules about when to use capillary fittings and when to use compression ones. However:
● compression fittings are more expensive than capillary ones
● compression joints are fairly easy to make but capillary ones require a bit of practice
● compression joints are usually easy to undo and reconnect whereas capillary joints are permanent – they generally have to be sawn apart
● if a compression joint leaks after being made, the leak can usually be stopped by slightly tightening the fitting. A leaking capillary joint often means that the solder has not flowed properly. Reheating the fitting may stop the leak but it is unlikely
● compression joints cannot be made in confined spaces where there is no room to use spanners. On the other hand, there are many places where a blowlamp – necessary for making a capillary joint – cannot be used without the risk of starting a fire or loosening other joints.
● capillary joints are much neater and less obtrusive.

There are many different types of fitting with either capillary or compression joint ends: *straight couplings* for joining two lengths of pipe together in a straight line; *elbows* and *bends* for joining two lengths together at an angle (usually a right angle); *tees* for joining a branch pipe; and *adaptors* for joining pipes to taps. The Chart on page 268 gives more details. Merchants often stock only the most common ones.

Some fittings, such as taps for garden hoses and washing machines, have a **screwed** end. These fittings can have different sizes of screw thread – ½in BSP (British Standard Pipe) is the most common. There are a number of ways of making a watertight joint with these fittings. The simplest is to wrap PTFE tape around the male thread before screwing it into the female part of the fitting. But PTFE tape will not seal large threads – like the ones on immersion heaters – or threads near central heating boilers. For these joints, smear a small amount of jointing paste on to the threads followed by a few strands of hemp (which looks like unravelled string) before screwing the joints together. Screwed fittings

which may need to be undone – tap adaptors, for example – have a washer to make the watertight joints.

Adding to existing pipes

Joining a new pipe to existing old pipework usually means forming a branch – the drawings opposite show how this can be tackled. Before starting, make sure that you have got the correct fittings. In many houses the existing copper pipes are the old *imperial* sizes, rather than the newer *metric* ones. Depending on the size of pipe and type of fitting a special adaptor may be needed to connect a new piece of metric pipe to an imperial system – see Table below. Special adaptors are needed more often for capillary joints (for the capillary action to take place the exact sizes of the tube and fitting are critical) than for compression joints (where slight differences in size can be tolerated).

Unfortunately, it is difficult to tell whether old pipework is imperial or metric just by looking. Equivalent pipe sizes may sound totally different – 15mm metric is the equivalent of ½in imperial – but the actual sizes are, in fact, only slightly different because imperial pipe is described by its *internal* diameter and metric by its *external* diameter.

metric external diameter	imperial internal diameter	adaptor needed? cap-illary	comp-ression
15mm	½in	yes	no
22mm	¾in	yes	yes
28mm	1in	yes	no

There are three different types of imperial-to-metric capillary fittings – though your plumbers' merchant may not stock them all:
● **tees** which have imperial connections on the main ends and metric on the branch – used for taking a new branch off a run of imperial pipe.
● **straight couplers** with imperial one end and metric the other – used for continuing an existing imperial pipe in metric
● **adaptors** one end of which fits into a metric fitting, while the other end forms a fitting for imperial pipe.

ADDING A JOINT (TEE CONNECTOR)

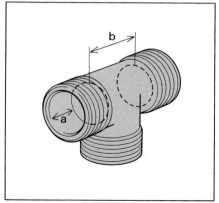

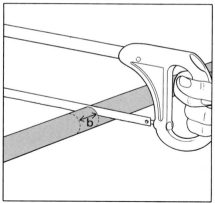

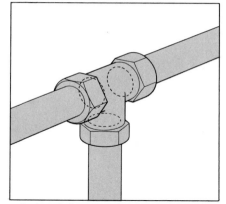

Measure the distances 'a' from the mouths of the tee connector to the pipe stop – the point at which the pipe can no longer be pushed into the fitting. Subtract 2 × a from the overall length to give the distance 'b'.

With a hacksaw, carefully cut the length 'b' from the pipe at the point where you want the branch to start from. To fit the tee connector, it will probably be necessary to remove some pipe clips, so that the pipe can be

pulled and the tee connector slotted into place. Fix the connector, following our instructions for compression or capillary joints. Fit the branch pipe into place. If you are using a capillary fitting, do this before soldering

Lead and stainless steel pipe

New copper pipe can be joined to **lead** pipe by making a proper 'wiped' soldered joint but this is probably best left to a qualified plumber. If your house contains much lead pipe, consider stripping it all out and having a joint made near the main stopcock in the house – this will make it easier to carry out future work.

When copper is expensive or difficult to get, **stainless steel** may be used in domestic plumbing systems – it was used in the 1970s for central heating systems.

Sizes of stainless steel pipe are the same as copper – 15mm, 22mm and 28mm. It can be cut with a hacksaw or pipe cutting tool and bent with a bending machine. It is easier to make joints in stainless steel pipe with compression fittings rather than with capillary fittings.

Flexible plastic pipe

There are two main types of polythene tubes used for water pipes – type 32 (low density) and type 50 (high density). There are also several different classes, depending on the thickness of the tube wall – class D should be used for mains pressure; class C (or D) for pipes from the cold water cistern.

The sizes to use are ⅜in polythene in-

stead of 15mm copper, ½in for 22mm, and 1in for 28mm. Polythene pipe can be cut with a sharp knife or fine hacksaw and bent easily by hand, though it needs supporting frequently with pipe clips. Compression fittings are used for joining polythene pipes but a hollow liner has to be inserted into the pipe to stop it collapsing as the fitting is screwed tight.

Rigid plastic pipe

Rigid plastic tube is currently suitable only for cold water. It is measured by its inside diameter and the usual nominal sizes are ⅜in, ½in and ¾in which can be used instead of 15mm, 22mm and 28mm copper pipe.

Bending rigid plastic pipe is not easy but elbows and bends are fairly cheap to buy. To join pieces of pipe to a fitting, clean the pipe and the inside of the fitting with a cleaning fluid, coat the cleaned surfaces with a solvent weld fluid, bring them together and leave them to set.

Buying hints

When buying your plumbing goods:
● **decide on the material** Nowadays, copper is the natural choice but for large jobs, plastics could work out cheaper. Consider using flexible plastic pipe for outdoor work and for long twisting runs

inside houses
● **plan the system** Always plan to use the fewest fittings and try to stick to simple couplers and tees. Be prepared to modify your plan so that you can make the best use of different materials
● **shop around for prices** List the materials you need and try a number of builders' and plumbers' merchants – prices can vary a lot. Remember to include all the relevant costs – and do not forget that VAT is often extra.

POINTS TO REMEMBER
Care needs to be taken over the following:
● **corrosion** can be a problem when joining different metals to each other, particularly copper and galvanised steel. Water in some areas can attack the brass used for normal compression fittings, making them porous. Your local water supply undertaking should be able to advise you whether this (or other things) is a problem in your area
● **plastic pipes** are more likely to be damaged than copper pipes and may need protective covers in vulnerable situations. Plastic pipe should be kept away from hot water pipes, adequately supported, and room left at the ends to allow for expansion. If you use it for replacing metal pipes, make sure the house electrical earthing system is not affected – in particular, run a separate earth to exposed metal in bathrooms.

PIPE CONNECTIONS

Straight couplings

Used for connecting two pieces of pipe together in a straight line, or a pipe to a fitting.

Both ends equal For connecting two pipes of the same diameter – both 15mm or 22mm, for instance. Compression or capillary types available.

One end reduced For connecting two pipes of different diameters. Rarely used. Compression or capillary available.

Female iron one end For connecting to fittings with a male iron thread. Male iron one end also available. Usually compression joint on the other end.

Flanged tank connector For connecting pipes to water cisterns. Usually compression joint the other end.

Tap adaptor For connecting pipe to a tap – enables the joint to be easily broken – when replacing tap, for example. Compression or capillary types available.

With drain cock To enable part of the plumbing system to be drained of water. Also available as part of a stopcock. Usually compression.

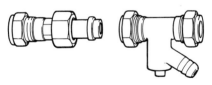

Cross

For connecting four pieces of pipe together – not often used in domestic work.

All ends equal For connecting pipes of the same diameter. Usually compression.

One end bigger To connect three pipes branching out from a single one. Usually compression.

Bends

Used for connecting two pieces of pipe together at an angle, or a pipe to a fitting.

Elbow, both ends equal For taking a run of pipe round a tight 90 degree bend. Compression or capillary.

Elbow, one end reduced For connecting two pipes of dissimilar diameters at 90 degrees. Rarely used. Compression or capillary.

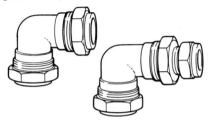

Elbow, female iron one end For connecting to fittings with a male iron thread. Male iron one end also available. Usually a compression joint on the other end.

Slow bend For taking a run of pipe round a corner, where it is important to keep the resistance to water flow low – to reduce noise, for instance. Range of ends available. Usually compression or capillary.

Tap adaptor For connecting pipe to a tap, as with a straight coupling.

Bib tap wall flange Like an elbow with female iron one end, but incorporating a mounting bracket to enable fitting (and therefore a tap) to be fixed to a wall. Usually compression.

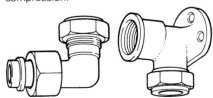

Tees

Used for connecting three pipes together – to connect a branch pipe in the middle of a main pipe run, for example.

Equal tee All ends take the same size pipe. Compression or capillary.

Branch reduced Used when the branch pipe does not need to carry as much water as the main run – when the main run is feeding a bath tap, and the branch pipe a basin tap, for instance. Other combinations of reduced ends also available – used, for example, to enable the main run to have a bend in it. Compression or capillary.

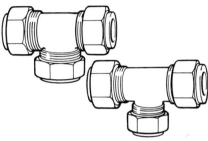

Wall plate tee with female iron connection on branch Used, like a bib tap wall flange elbow for connecting and providing a mechanical mounting for a bib tap. Usually compression. Various patterns with male or female iron connections on one end or branch (but without a wall plate) also available.

Offset tee Combines a tee with an elbow in the branch connection. Usually compression.

Sweep tee A tee with a slow bend in the elbow for reducing resistance to water flow. Has to be fitted so that the direction of the bend is the same as the direction of the water flow. With equal ends, or with one end reduced. Usually compression. Other sweep patterns are also available.

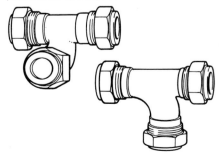

Taps

Taps and valves control the flow of water through pipes. Taps are generally installed at the end of a pipe; valves are used in the middle. Either can be used to cut off the flow of water completely or to reduce it. Manufacturers' catalogues often contain a large range of taps and valves – the main ones are illustrated and described below. The size, shape, appearance and price of a valve is usually determined by the job it has to do. But with taps the price will depend on the 'style' and finish – the choice is often a matter of personal preference. The simplest and cheapest taps are separate hot and cold taps; the various sorts of mixer taps can be much more expensive. Unusual taps can be difficult to find at a discount.

Types of tap

Stop tap or stopcock Ordinary brass tap used for pipes at mains water pressure. Usually has a cross-head handle but also available without a handle (a special key is needed to turn water on and off). Install with the arrow in the direction of water flow. Usually provided with compression fittings. 15mm, 22mm and 28mm sizes commonly available.

Gate valve Ordinary brass tap used for pipes from cistern – when the gate is fully open it does not restrict water flow. Usually has a wheel-type handle and compression fittings. 15mm, 22mm and 28mm sizes commonly available.

Drain tap (or drain cock) Used for draining down plumbing systems – by pushing a hose on to the ribbed end of the spout and undoing the square nut with a spanner. Three types are usually available: an in-line type; incorporated into a stop tap to isolate part of the system whilst the rest is drained (install so that the drain tap is *above* the stop tap); and as part of an elbow bend fitting. The in-line type illustrated on the opposite page is provided with compression fittings but you can also buy drain taps with male BSP threads.

Bib tap Usually brass finish but also available chromium-plated. Has horizontal inlet. Brass taps with a threaded outlet for a hose connector are often used as garden and washing-machine taps. Chromium-plated ones with a plain outlet are sometimes used over sinks. Inlet has ½in (sometimes ⅜in may be necessary) BSP male thread. The tap is often connected to a wall plate elbow fitting for mechanical security.

Sink tap Chromium finish. Has vertical inlet. A back-nut is used to bolt the tap to the deck of a sink so the plumbing connections need provide no mechanical strength. A sink tap should be tall enough to allow buckets to be filled but, before you buy, check that the *spout height* (distance from top of sink to bottom of spout) plus sink depth will be enough. Inlet has ½in BSP male thread – usual pipe fitting is a tap adaptor.

Sink mixer Mixers have separate hot and cold inlets, but a single outlet. Spout outlets can be pushed to either side – to feed two sink bowls or to make it easier to get things in and out of the sink. Usual spout length is 7in – but 9in spouts are better for double-bowl sinks. Most kitchen sinks are fed with cold water direct from the mains and hot water via the cold water cistern. Water bye-laws do not allow the stored hot water to mix with the mains cold water inside a fitting, so sink mixers are usually divided-flow or dual-flow types. Non-divided flow mixers can be used only when the hot and cold supplies both come direct from the mains (ie where the hot water is heated by means of an instantaneous-type water heater) or both come from the cold water cistern (which is unlikely for a kitchen). Tap holes in sinks, and inlets on sink mixers, are usually a standard distance of 7in apart. Tap holes at non-standard distances can be accommodated with mixers having adjustable inlets. Inlets are ½in BSP male threads – other sizes indicate the mixer is probably a continental type, which may not be suitable.

Supatap Bib-type, basin, bath and sink types available – no mixers. Designed so

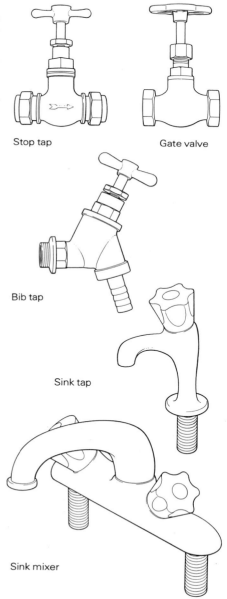

Stop tap

Gate valve

Bib tap

Sink tap

Sink mixer

Five of the most common taps and valves – typical designs shown

that the washer can be changed without turning off the water supply. A special adaptor is needed for connecting hoses – this provides a very secure fixing: the hose cannot blow off the tap. Note when rewashering that there are two half-inch models: type A (discontinued in 1962) takes a ½in diameter washer; type D (current since 1962) takes ⅝in diameter.

Bath and basin tap Separate taps for hot and cold water. Many different patterns are available with different handle designs. The type of handle often determines the price of the tap – ordinary cross-head is usually the cheapest. Check before buying that the handle is easy to grasp. If you want to be able to wash your hands under running water, make sure that the spout is long enough to project well over the edge of the bowl when it is installed. Taps have a vertical inlet with a BSP male thread – ½in for basin taps; ¾in for bath taps. Other sizes indicate continental-type taps.

Bath mixer Does not usually have divided-flow or dual-flow spout and so must be connected to hot and cold supplies either both coming directly from the mains or, more usually, both coming from the cold water cistern. A bath/shower mixer has a shower attachment (the outlet for a shower pipe may be positioned so that the pipe can be exposed or concealed) and a diverter for switching the flow of water from the spout to the shower or vice versa (diverters usually switch the flow to the bath spout automatically when taps are turned off). A *basin mixer* (sometimes called a 4in mixer because the inlets are a standard 4in apart) usually has a pop-up waste – you buy the mixer complete with a basin waste outlet and plug. Taps have vertical inlets with male BSP threads – ½in for basin mixer; ¾in for bath mixer. Other sizes indicate continental-type mixers. The tap holes in baths and bath mixer inlets are usually a standard distance of 7⅛in apart – buy a mixer with adjustable inlets for non-standard distances.

Three-hole basin mixer The hot and

cold taps and the tap spout each fit separate holes in the basin. The connections between the spout and the valves are often flexible to accommodate different hole distances. A three-hole mixer with rigid connections usually has the taps 8in apart with the spout centred between them. A mixer which has taps 8in apart may sometimes be called an 8in mixer – but the connections are not necessarily rigid. Does not usually have a divided-flow or dual-flow spout. Mixer usually comes with pop-up waste. Taps have vertical inlets with ½in BSP threads.

One-hole mixer Available for basins, sinks and bidets. Fits into a standard single tap hole. Spout usually swivels and is not the divided-flow or dual-flow type. Inlets are usually plain-ended 10mm bendable copper and adaptor fittings are needed to attach them to the usual 15mm pipe supplies. The pressure of water from cistern-fed supplies may not

be high enough to give an adequate flow rate. (These are continental-type taps intended for use on direct high-pressure plumbing systems.)

Bidet set Through-rim supply bidets, with spray, use a complicated tap arrangement. The hot and cold tap valves and the mixer body fit into separate holes in the bidet surround. The mixer body has a diverter to direct water to the rim of the bidet or, via a flexible tube, to the spray head in the base of the bidet. The mixer usually has flexible connections and a pop-up waste. A through-rim supply bidet has to satisfy particular regulations – see *Bidet regulations* on page 289. An over-rim bidet can be fitted with single taps, or a 4in basin mixer.

Panel sets The hot and cold tap valves and the tap spout can all be mounted on a false wall or panel. With some panel sets, the bodies of the taps are separate

BATHROOM TAPS

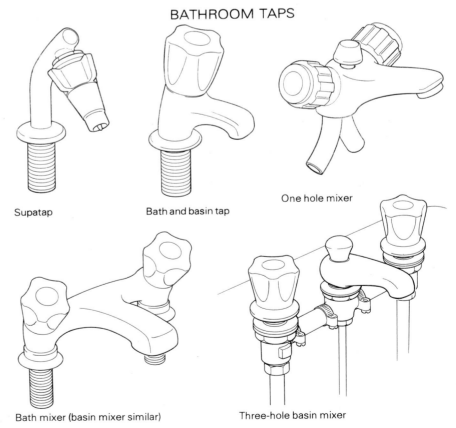

Supatap

Bath and basin tap

One hole mixer

Bath mixer (basin mixer similar)

Three-hole basin mixer

from the spout so that the spout can be mounted for example, on a wall above the basin or bath – and the taps can be mounted wherever is convenient. Bath spouts are available with or without a shower attachment. The connections to and from taps and spout are ½in BSP threads for basin panel sets; ¾in BSP threads for bath panel sets.

Plastic taps Cheaper than normal chromium-plated brass taps: manufacturers also claim that they are cooler to the touch. Some brands come in a range of colours to match sanitaryware. With most brands, only a restricted range of types is available. Plastic taps need extra care when fitting. No jointing paste should be used and no soldering should be done near them – even vapours from soldering fluxes can harm the plastic. The threads can strip easily – be careful when screwing metal nuts on to them.

Lever taps Instead of a tap handle, which has to be turned several times from fully on to fully off, the lever has to be turned through only a quarter of a circle to turn the tap from full on to full off. Sink mixers come with one lever working clockwise and the other anti-clockwise. To get this arrangement with separate taps, a pair has to be ordered. Not often used in homes – but might be useful in a kitchen, or for use by elderly people. Some authorities might not allow their use, because they may give rise to water hammer.

SPECIAL PURPOSE TAPS

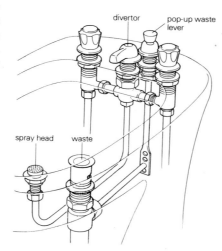

A through-rim supply bidet set

Tap conversion kits
Tap conversion kits make old taps – with ordinary cross-head handles – look more like new ones with shrouded handles. There are two types – one sort simply replaces the handle; the other sort replaces the old spindle assembly as well.

Conversion kits are cheaper than new taps, but they may not look quite as up-to-date. If your old taps are leaking because of a worn washer, kits that replace the spindle assembly will cure this – but replacing the washer would be much cheaper and would involve no more work. A conversion kit will not cure leaks due to worn tap seats.

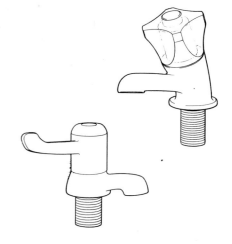

Top: plastic tap. Below: lever tap

Some brands may cut down the flow rate through the tap.

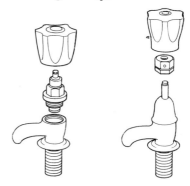

Tap conversion kits: the one on the right simply replaces the handle

---

WHAT THE TERMS MEAN

Adjustable inlets A system on mixer taps (of all sorts) to provide some flexibility in the distance that the inlets are set apart, so that the taps can be used on baths, basins, and so on where the tap holes are not the standard distance apart.

Diverter A lever to divert water through different parts of a fitting – for example, in a bidet set the lever diverts water from a spray in the base of the bidet

to a supply through the rim; in a bath/shower mixer it diverts it from the bath-filling part to the shower head.

Divided-flow The spout of the tap has two completely separate waterways running through it – one for the hot water, one for the cold. In this way, the hot and cold waters do not mix until a short distance after they have left the spout. This prevents contamination of the cold water by the hot water being

siphoned back up the cold water pipe. Sink mixer taps must be of this type.

Dual-flow Same as divided-flow – see above.

Pop-up waste Found on some mixer taps, which come complete with a basin waste outlet and plug. The plug is connected by rods to a lever on the mixer body; operating the lever lifts the plug up and down.

Replacing taps

To replace taps, you will need:
– new taps of the appropriate type
– spanners – probably a basin spanner (or a plumber's adjustable wrench); stillsons, a right-angled adjustable spanner (or a pair of slip-joint pliers)
– plastic washers for seating the taps
– plumbing mastic
– PTFE tape
– possibly new tap connectors of the appropriate pattern
– tap adaptors
– new pieces of pipe
– metric to imperial adaptors.

First, turn off the water supply to the tap to be replaced and open the tap to drain the pipe. If you are replacing upstairs taps, opening downstairs ones may drain a bit more water out of the pipes – in any case, have a bucket handy to catch water leaks when the taps are removed.

Try to undo the back nut holding the tap to the basin (or whatever) and the nut connecting the tap connector to the threaded tap inlet shank. If the connections are stuck, try using penetrating oil or heating the fitting gently. If the back nut will not come loose, it may be possible to take the basin off the wall. If the tap connector nut will not come loose, try undoing any other fitting nearby. As a last resort it may be necessary to saw the pipe off – do this where it is possible

to connect a new joint easily.

The old tap will probably be fixed in a hard setting compound and to remove it from the basin you may need to chip away the hard compound and to loosen the tap by gently knocking it.

Fit the new tap to the basin. Use a plastic washer or non-setting plumbing mastic between the tap and the top of the basin and a plastic washer between the bottom of the basin and the back nut – a ceramic basin may crack if metal taps are screwed directly on to it.

New taps have smaller fixing lugs than old ones (new basins have different tap holes). To prevent new taps from turning in old holes, special *anti-rotational* washers are available if necessary.

To bolt taps to sinks and other fittings with a thin surround, a special washer – a *top-hat* washer – is needed.

New tap shanks are about 13.5mm shorter than old ones. There may be enough slack in the supply pipes to bridge this gap. Otherwise, use a Conex No 74 tap adaptor – this makes the tap shank longer. If you had to cut the pipes when removing the old taps, use a slightly longer piece of new piping. If you are using the old tap adaptors, remember to replace the fibre washer. Before screwing the tap adaptor to the shank, wrap some PTFE tape round the threads.

SPECIAL TOOLS

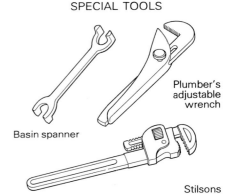

Plumber's adjustable wrench

Basin spanner

Stilsons

HOW A TAP WORKS
The two main types of tap mechanism are shown in the drawings – a rising spindle tap (top drawing) and a non-rising spindle tap. As the handle is turned, the spindle jumper moves towards the washer seat gradually cutting off the flow of water – if the flow stopped quickly, a shock wave might recoil back up the pipe, causing a knocking noise called water hammer. When the washer on the end of the jumper is in contact with the washer seat, the flow stops completely. With rising spindle taps the spindle rises or falls to lift or lower the jumper. With non-rising spindle taps the spindle is threaded and lifts the washer stem itself. Because the washer does not turn on non-rising spindle taps, it should last longer. In addition, the gland is sealed with an 'O' ring which is easier to replace than the gland packing in rising spindle taps.

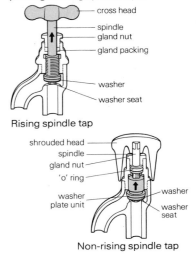

cross head
spindle
gland nut
gland packing
washer
washer seat

Rising spindle tap

shrouded head
spindle
gland nut
'o' ring
washer
plate unit
washer
washer seat

Non-rising spindle tap

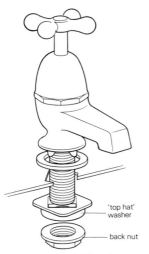

'top hat' washer

back nut

Fitting a tap to a thin sink using a special top-hat washer

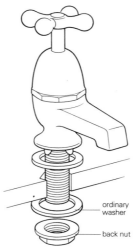

ordinary washer

back nut

Fitting a tap to a thick basin using an ordinary washer

Ballvalves

Ballvalves (sometimes called floatvalves) automatically control the flow of water to cold water and WC cisterns. As the level of water in the cistern rises, the ball which floats on the surface moves a lever which pushes a piston or diaphragm against a water inlet nozzle, thus cutting off the supply of water and preventing the cistern from overflowing.

The most common types of ballvalve are the Portsmouth and the relatively new *diaphragm/equilibrium* type (such as the Torbeck).

Most ballvalves have ½in BSP threaded inlets, usually detachable from the valve body. Inlet lengths vary. In most cases, the inlets are horizontal but some modern WC cisterns have bottom entry inlets.

Ballvalves are designed to work best at particular water pressures – with many patterns, this can be altered by changing the inlet nozzle. For ballvalves fed from the cold water cistern (such as those in a WC), a low pressure (LP) valve is needed – if the cistern is only marginally higher than the ballvalve (for example, on the same floor at the top of an airing cupboard), (a *fullway* valve or nozzle might be necessary. For ballvalves fed by mains water (such as the one in the cold water cistern) a high pressure (HP) type is needed.

Always make sure you use the correct valve. If you use a HP valve when you should have used an LP one, the cistern will fill slowly and noisily; an LP valve used in place of a HP one might not shut off properly.

Noisy filling can be due to a number of causes – besides incorrect pressure valves. Much noise can be reduced by adding a silencer tube, which brings the outlet of the valve below the level of the water in the cistern. Water regulations prevent the use of anything but a collapsible silencer tube – only these will not allow back-siphonage to take place.

Some very old-fashioned types of valve can be particularly noisy, and might be replaced with a modern type – particularly one with an approved silencer tube.

Noise in the pipes may be due to float bounce – ripples on the surface of the water causing the ball to bounce up and down. This may be reduced by fitting a paddle.

Portsmouth By far the most common type of ballvalve. Readily available and easy to get spares
Croydon Old-fashioned. As float falls, lever pulls piston away from nozzle allowing water to flow into cistern down sides of piston

Equilibrium Piston has equal water pressure at either end so it can work under high, and varying pressures. No nozzle required – filling is very fast. Generally most expensive
Garston or BRS Diaphragm type. Small movement of diaphragm is enough to cut off

supply. Fewer moving parts to seize up than other types
Torbeck Brand name for a type of valve like Garston but with the diaphragm balanced as in an equilibrium valve. Comes with an adaptor for high or low pressure supplies

Replacing a ballvalve

Before deciding to replace a ballvalve, consider whether cleaning it, replacing the float or bending the lever will solve your problems – see page 280.

You will need a new ballvalve of the right pressure and size, two right-angled adjustable spanners (or stillsons or slip-joint pliers) and possibly new washers for the inlet shank and for the tap adaptor.

First turn off the water supply and, if necessary, drain the pipe by pushing down on the lever. If you are replacing the ballvalve with another of the same pattern, you probably need only to disconnect the ballvalve at the valve back nut. Hold the valve body steady with the second spanner while undoing the nut. Remove the body complete with lever and float.

If necessary, the valve can be removed by disconnecting the tap adaptor and undoing the nut on the inlet shank outside the cistern. Remove valve complete with inlet shank. If you want to, it may then be possible to undo the valve at the back nut.

Fit new valve, using new washers on the inlet shank and tap adaptor if these have been disturbed. Bend float arm if necessary to get the correct water level.

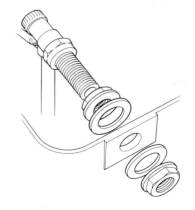

Ballvalve connected to a tap adaptor

Cisterns

What most people call a cold water tank is strictly *a cold water cistern* – the difference is that a tank is a sealed vessel capable of containing water at above atmospheric pressure; a cistern is open to the atmosphere.

Types and sizes

There are three main types of cistern:

● **galvanised steel** These are heavy, relatively expensive, and prone to corrosion. Not a sensible choice for domestic work

● **rigid plastic** One the same size as an old galvanised cistern will make replacement work easier. Rigid plastic can withstand warm water and can be used as a feed-and-expansion cistern in central heating systems

● **flexible plastic** These are generally round and made of polythene. They can be squashed to get them through small loft hatches that rigid cisterns could not pass through. They should not be used as feed-and-expansion cisterns.

Most water authorities require a new cistern to be of 50 gallons (227 litres) *actual capacity* – cisterns which feed only a hot water storage cylinder could be smaller. In use, cisterns are never filled right to the brim so the *nominal capacity* (full to the brim) is more than the actual capacity – 50 gal actual is 70 gal nominal.

To keep the water inside free from contamination, cisterns should have closely-fitting, but not airtight, lids. A suitable lid could be bought or made (it should be a material which is unaffected by condensation and does not support mould).

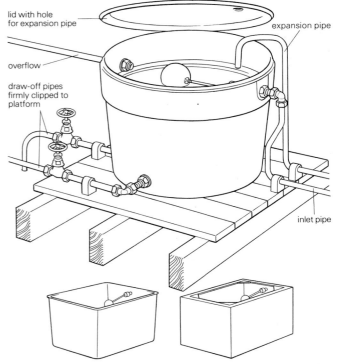

Three cisterns: top, flexible plastic; bottom left, rigid plastic; bottom right, galvanised steel

Fitting a new cistern

Great care should be taken while working in the loft

Turn off the water supply at the mains, empty the old cistern, and bail out the water that remains in the bottom. Detach the old pipes – at the connections to the cistern if possible, particularly if the new cistern is the same shape and size; otherwise, wherever is convenient. The old cistern will have to be left in the roof if it is too big to take out.

A new plastic cistern – flexible or rigid – must be well supported on a firm flat platform.

Pipes should be connected to the cistern using tank connectors – a length of threaded pipe with a compression or capillary joint at one end. Pass the connector through a hole cut in the side of the cistern and hold it in place with nuts. A hole can be made with a hole saw or tank cutter (see page 249) or by making

lots of little holes around the inside of the circumference of the hole you want with a drill, knocking out the ring, and then smoothing out the larger hole with a half-round file. Use plastic washers for sealing – jointing paste must not be used on plastic as it might crack it.

Pipes should be well supported so that the cistern is not taking any of the strain.

Outlets from the cistern should be about 50mm above the base of the cistern. The arm of the ballvalve should be adjusted so that the water surface is about 100mm from the top of the cistern.

Position the overflow pipe so that it

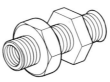

Tank connector

discharges outside the house, in a conspicuous position. It must be at least 22mm in diameter. The overflow pipe should be connected to the cistern about 25mm above the normal water level.

Overhauling an old cistern

If a galvanised cistern is only slightly corroded, it may be possible to stave off having to fit a new one by coating the inside with an approved non-tainting bitumen paint.

The cistern must be emptied and thoroughly dried. If possible, detach the pipes and tank connectors. Completely remove all rust – if at this stage, the cistern is found to be very corroded, it would be wise to replace it, rather than risk it leaking. Otherwise, apply two coats of bitumen, paying particular attention to the edges around the pipe holes. Allow the bitumen to dry well before refilling.

Wastes

Waste pipes and fittings are made almost exclusively from plastic materials nowadays. These are relatively cheap and easy to install.

There are several different brands of pipe and fitting available but, unfortunately, there is little interchangeability between brands, so some detective work may be needed when adding to an existing plastic waste system. If you have a copper waste system which you want to extend or modify, choose the plastic fittings with care – not all brands will fit.

Basins usually have 1¼in nominal diameter pipe; baths and sinks 1½in nominal. WC pipes are usually 4in nominal.

Plastic waste pipes

Plastic pipe is easily cut with a knife or a fine-toothed hacksaw.

There are two methods used for joining. With the **push-fit** system, connectors have rubber sealing rings ('O' rings) which seat into grooves around their inside surfaces. To make a joint, smooth off the ends of the pipes, chamfer the outer surfaces at about 15 degrees and then lubricate them – with water, soap or a special silicone lubricant (soap is satisfactory only if you do not want to move or remake the joint after its initial installation). Finally, push the ends fully into the connector and withdraw the pipe slightly to allow for thermal expansion – consult the manufacturer's instructions.

To make a joint using the **solvent-weld** method, wipe the pipe ends and the inside of the connector with a degreasing cleaner, and coat them with a solvent cement. Then push them together and leave the joint undisturbed for a couple of minutes while the cement sets. Manufacturers sometimes recommend that the joint should not be used for 24 hours.

Some pipe materials are not suitable for solvent-welding, but all can be used with appropriate push-fit connectors. Even in a waste system that is primarily solvent-welded, some push-fit joints may have to be used to allow for thermal expansion when hot water is discharged. Solvent-welding makes a neater joint than push-fit and the connectors are a little cheaper but a little more difficult to install.

Designing wastes

A single-stack waste system must comply with the Building Regulations. Follow these design rules to help you make sure that it does:

1 The bend at the foot of the stack should be at least 200mm radius (proprietary products will probably be designed so)

2 The lowest connection to the stack should be at least 450mm from the bottom of the stack (ground floor wastes are usually connected into yard gullies rather than into the stack and ground floor WCs are usually connected direct to the drain)

3 WC connections must be swept in the direction of flow (proprietary products are designed so). Lengths and slopes are rarely critical

4 Do not make any connections to the stack within 200mm below the connection of a WC branch. (For the bath connection, use an offset – as shown – or a proprietary collar boss)

5 Use 1½in pipe for bath wastes. The lengths and slope are not critical. Use a deep-seal trap

6 Avoid using combined wastes where possible

7 Use 1½in pipe for sink wastes. The length and slope is not critical even if it is

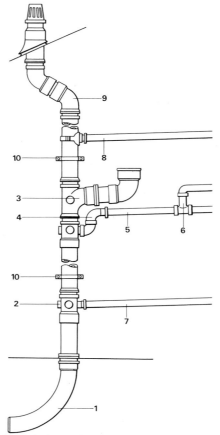

Ten design points – the numbers match those in the text

connected to the stack. Use a deep-seal trap. Some plastic pipes are not suitable for very high temperatures – from automatic washing machines, for instance

8 Use 1¼in pipe for basin wastes. The maximum slope allowed depends on the length of the waste – a standard 92½ degree bend (slope of 40mm per metre run) can be used for a waste up to 1.125m long. Maximum length allowed 1.68m (with slope of 1¼ degrees). If longer runs are essential, connect the trap outlet into 2in pipe, or use special resealing traps. All bends should be at least 75mm radius. Deep-seal trap should be used

9 Any bends in the stack should be above the topmost connection

10 Always use adequate and correctly positioned pipe supports – read the manufacturer's literature carefully.

Buying hints

Follow this plan for buying your waste goods:

● **find out what's available** For all but the simplest alterations, get catalogues of fittings from your local plumbers' merchants

● **decide on the brand to use** Take into account: prices; availability of the different fittings and whether push-fit or solvent-weld joints are to be made.

● **design the system** Plan the system around the components available for the brand you have chosen. When doing work on a single-stack system, follow the design rules carefully

● **shop around for the best prices** List the materials needed and try a few builders' and plumbers' merchants – prices can vary a lot. Remember to include the price of connectors, solvent cleaner and cement, pipe clips and so on. Try to find somewhere that will give refunds on unused fittings.

Extending and modifying existing waste systems

Waste pipes and fittings are less standardised than those for water so it is not possible to give firm rules for altering and adding to existing systems. The best method is to obtain a catalogue of the various bits and pieces available in a particular brand – from a builders' or plumbers' merchant – and to plan the work around the parts listed. Drawings of some of the main fittings available, together with notes on how they are used, are given below.

Alterations which enable pipes to be run into hopper heads or yard gullies are fairly straightforward – ensure that each basin, bath or whatever has its own trap and that waste pipes all slope to the outlet and are of the correct size.

Pipes which have to run into soil stacks are more tricky – slopes, lengths and connections have to be carefully designed to avoid the traps becoming unsealed. Adding waste pipes to a plastic soil stack involves cutting a hole in the stack and solvent-welding an appropriate boss to it. The pipe can then be connected to the boss. The method of fixing the boss varies with the brand – some types can be fixed only if access can be gained to the inside of the pipe. Read the manufacturer's instructions and ask the merchant for advice before buying.

FITTINGS FOR WASTE SYSTEMS

Pipe Different plastics are available: some are not suitable for high-temperature discharges from sinks and washing machines. Support horizontal pipes about every 750mm, vertical pipes about every 1.5m. Basin pipes connected to a single-stack system are restricted to a maximum length of 1.68m unless special precautions are taken (special automatic resealing traps or designing the system with separate ventilation pipes, for instance).

Sockets For joining lengths of plain-ended pipe together. Both solvent-weld and push-fit types are available. Some sockets have a plain end to take another connector instead of a pipe.

Bends For taking runs of 'horizontal' pipe round corners. 90 degree and 135 degree angle bends are most widely available. Waste pipes should slope (but often only slightly) towards the outlet – to connect these to vertical pipes, use 91½ degree or 92½ degree bends. Some bends have a plain end. One manufacturer has adjustable bends in his range.

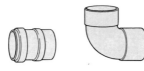

Tees Common angles are 90, 91½, 92½ and 135 degrees. Tees are usually swept in the direction of flow (the tee should be fitted so that the direction of the bend from the branch into the main pipe is the same as the direction of the flow of water). Avoid using tees for joining two waste pipes that then run to a single-stack system – wastes should be connected individually to the stack.

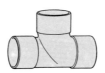

Connectors Various types are available for connecting pipe to different fittings. *Reducers* can be used for joining 1¼in or 1½in pipe to 1½in or 2in pipe. *Copper compression* can be used to connect plastic pipe to existing copper wastes. *BSP screwed thread* can be used to connect pipe to a waste outlet in sinks and so on. Jointing paste must not be used on screw threads, but PTFE tape can be used if necessary.

WC connectors The easiest joint to make to a WC is with a plain-ended connector. This should be dry-jointed to the WC outlet, using a rubber gasket. Various patterns of connector are available with different angles and lengths of plain-ended spigot (depending on the position of the WC pan and the soil pipe to be connected). For particularly awkward joints, a *Multi-kwik* connector can be used –

again, various patterns are available, including one that will cope with slight displacements between the pan outlet and the soil pipe.

Traps P-traps have a horizontal outlet; S-traps have a vertical outlet. Trap inlets usually have BSP threads for connecting directly to waste outlets. Shallow seal traps can be used on wastes discharging into gullies or hopper heads; on single-stack systems deep seal (3in) traps must be used. Deep-seal traps take up more room, and to install one beneath a bath you may need to cut away the floorboards. *Bottle traps* are neater than tubular ones and may be easier to use in tight spaces instead of a deep-seal trap. Special *adjustable* traps are available for repair work to mate with existing pipes. *Bath traps* often come complete with overflow system attached. *Washing machine traps* have an inlet at the side for taking a washing machine outlet hose – the trap replaces the sink trap. In some situations, *automatic resealing traps* may be necessary – for example, for extra-long basin wastes connected to single-stack systems.

P-trap,   S-trap,   bottle

Plumbing first aid

Even if you do not intend to carry out major plumbing works such as putting in a new sink, or laying a drain, the chances are that at some time you will have a plumbing emergency – perhaps a leaking tap, an overflowing cistern or a blocked waste. The advice here is designed to help you to cope, either by fixing the problem or at least by minimising the damage until the plumber comes.

The onset of an emergency is the wrong time to start learning about your plumbing system – you should know how to isolate and drain various parts of your plumbing system *before* trouble strikes so that you can take immediate action if an emergency arises.

Draining down a plumbing system

To carry out repairs to taps, ballvalves and leaking pipes, the water supply to the offending part has to be cut off and the pipes drained of water.

Before trouble strikes Learn the position of all stopcocks and valves and of any drain cocks. Make sure you know which parts of the system they each control. Regularly turn stopcocks and valves on and off to ensure that they are free – if seized, apply penetrating oil and carefully try again.

In an emergency Cut off the water supply to the leaking tap (or whatever) and open all taps on this part of the plumbing system. Turn off any immersion heater or boiler. Attach hoses to any drain cocks on the affected part of the system and open them.

If you are unsure which part of the system is affected, turn off the water at the main stopcock in the house. If the leak is in the section of pipe before this, also turn off the water at the water undertaking's stopcock in the road if you can. This will isolate the leaking pipe which can then be repaired. Then:

● with a *direct* plumbing system, open *all* the cold taps, drain off at any drain cocks on cold water pipes, and flush WCs. If the leak is in the cold water system, it should stop when the taps run dry. If the leak is in the hot water side, isolate the storage cistern supplying the hot water cylinder by turning off the valve in the pipe connecting the two, or the valve at the outlet of the hot water cylinder. Turn off any immersion heater or boiler supplying the cylinder. Open all the hot taps. If there are no valves, simply turn off any water heaters and open the hot

taps – the system will take longer to drain, because the cistern will have to empty as well as the pipes.

Note the hot water cylinder will remain full of water

● with an *indirect* plumbing system, open any taps or valves connected directly to the rising main – probably only the tap over the kitchen sink, but possibly taps feeding washing machines, outside taps and a valve for a downstairs WC as well. Drain off at the drain cock immediately above the stopcock on the rising main. If the leak is in the rising main, or a pipe fed from it, it should stop when the taps run dry. If the leak is further on, isolate the cold water storage cistern. The cistern will have at least two pipes leading from it – one to feed the cold taps and one to feed the hot water cylinder which supplies the hot taps. Trace and close off any valves on both of these pipes and any valve at the outlet of the hot water cylinder. Turn off any water heaters. If both pipes have valves, turn on all the hot and cold taps, and flush WCs. The leak should stop when the taps run dry. If only one pipe has a valve, try turning on the appropriate taps first. If this does not work, turn on the other set of taps – the system will take longer to drain, because the cistern will have to empty as well as the pipes. If there are no valves, open all taps together – again the cistern will have to drain as well.

Note the hot water cylinder will remain full of water

● if the leak is in a hot water cylinder, this will have to be drained. Turn off water heaters. With solid fuel heaters, rake out the fire and allow it to go cold

before draining. Isolate the cylinder from the cold water cistern if possible: if not, cut off the supply to the cylinder by turning off at the main stopcock. Drain the cylinder at the drain cock – usually located on the cold feed of an indirect hot water system or at the boiler on a direct hot water system

● if the leak is in the cold water storage cistern, isolate it by turning off the water at the main stopcock. Drain the cistern by turning on *all* the hot and cold taps (except those fed directly from the rising main). If the leak is in the bottom of the cistern, the last bit of water will have to be bailed out by hand.

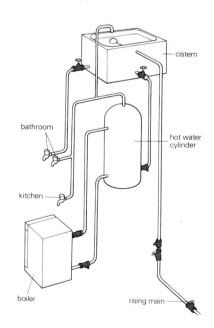

A simplified indirect plumbing system showing the likely positions of the stop valves and drain cocks

Leaking taps

Leaking taps may appear to be more of a nuisance than a full-scale emergency – but leaks can waste a lot of water and should be cured as soon as possible.

Before trouble strikes Know the sort of taps you have – Supataps need different washers to those used on ordinary taps;

rising and non-rising spindle taps use the same washers, but other parts are different; more complicated bidet and mixer taps sets may use special washers. Get together a set of spare parts: ½in and ¾in synthetic rubber washers; spare jumpers for rising-spindle taps; Supatap washers – see page 270; joint washers; gland

'O'-rings for non-rising spindle taps; and washers for mixer tap sets. Know how to isolate and dismantle each tap.

In an emergency Isolate the tap from the rest of the water supply. Turn it on until the water flow stops (not all repairs need the water supply turned off – see below).

Replacing a tap washer

If the tap leaks or continues to run when it is turned off, the washer probably needs replacing. First isolate the tap.

Then on the older cross-head taps with covers, turn the tap on fully and unscrew the cover. If you have to use a wrench, protect the cover by wrapping a cloth round it and prevent the rest of the tap from turning by holding it with another wrench – otherwise you might crack the basin. If the cover will not undo, try penetrating oil, or pour boiling water over it.

Under the cover is a large nut – undo this with a thin open-ended spanner. If the spanner is too thick to fit the gap, the cross-head will have to be taken off so that the cover can be removed completely – it is held on with a grub screw. If it will not lift off, try heat or penetrating oil, or place a wooden wedge between it and the cover and screw the head down on to it.

On shrouded-head taps, take off the head which exposes the nut directly. The head may pull off, or be fixed with a screw in its side, or underneath a small cover at the top.

Undo the nut, and so remove the whole of the tap mechanism. The washer

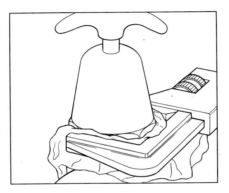
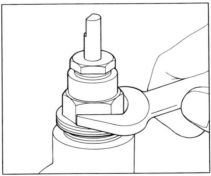

is at the base of this, and may simply pull off or be held on by a nut.

If the nut on a rising spindle tap does not undo, the whole jumper can be replaced. On a non-rising spindle tap, part or all of the works may have to be re-

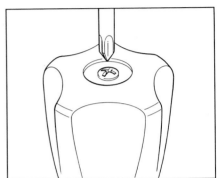
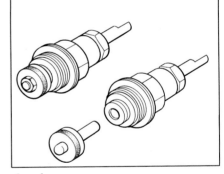

placed.

Leave the tap fully open when reassembling. Replace the joint washer if you have a spare; greasing joints and threads with petroleum jelly will help when the tap needs dismantling again.

Curing a mixer tap leak

If mixer taps leak at the base of the swivel nozzle, the washers here need replacing. There is no need to turn off the water. Remove the nozzle – it may pull off or be held with a grub screw. Replace all the washers found – their position varies with different brands of tap – lubricating them with water or a little petroleum jelly.

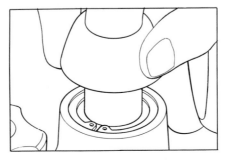
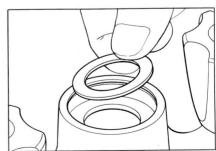

Replacing a worn washer seat

If a tap continues to leak after the washer has been replaced, the *washer seat* is probably worn. The seat can be refaced with a *tap reseating tool*, which may be hired – try a d-i-y tool hire shop or a plumbers' merchant – or a new plastic seat can be inserted into the tap.

Stopping a spindle leaking

If the tap leaks at the top, or round the base of a shrouded head, the *spindle gland* is leaking. There is no need to turn off the water. Take off the shrouded head (or remove completely the easy-clean cover). Try tightening the gland nut slightly. If this does not cure the leak, remove the nut and take out and replace the gland packing. This is generally a simple washer or 'O' ring but on older taps it could be string greased with petroleum jelly.

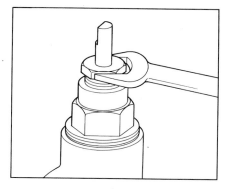
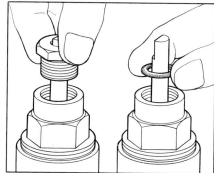

Replacing a Supatap washer

If a Supatap leaks, its washer probably needs replacing. Unlike ordinary taps, there is *no need* to turn off the water. Turn on the tap nozzle slightly, and undo the nut exposed above the finger grip. Continue to open the nozzle until it falls off – the water will then stop flowing. Press the nozzle on a hard surface to free the anti-splash device: lever out the washer/jumper unit, and push home a new one of the same size. Screw the nozzle back in place until it is almost closed, tighten the nut and close the tap fully. If this does not cure the leak, the anti-splash device may need replacing, or the seat refacing – see above.

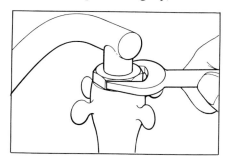
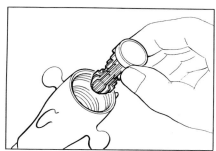

Leaking pipes

Pipes burst usually after freezing-up – so ensure they are all well lagged. In cold weather, drain all outside pipes. If pipes freeze regularly, consider relocating them so that they run in more sheltered places.

Before trouble strikes Make sure you know the easiest and quickest way of draining each bit of pipe. If a pipe freezes, check for bursts *before* it thaws. Keep a supply of filler – an epoxy resin repair kit, say – to make temporary repairs.

In an emergency Drain the pipe quickly to minimise damage. If the leak is from a hot water cylinder, turn off any water heaters: rake out a solid-fuel boiler. Bursts are often due to joints coming undone – remake these if possible.

If a pipe is split, a temporary repair can be made by using an epoxy resin filler, waterproof tape, or even strips of rag soaked in paint. First, hammer the split so that it closes, and then clean and dry off the area around the split. Gently turn the stopcock partly on to keep the water pressure as low as possible.

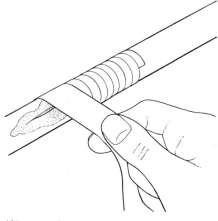

Waterproof tape as a temporary repair

Overflowing cisterns

Water running from a cold water cistern or WC cistern overflow pipe is usually a sign of a sticking or leaking ballvalve, or a ballvalve positioned wrongly. It is important not to let an overflow run for long – not only does it waste water, but it might lead to damp problems.

Before trouble strikes Know how to turn off the water supply to the cisterns. Ensure that the ballvalve can be dismantled – or at least removed from the cistern. Keep spare washers and seats – sizes and types vary depending on the type of valve – and perhaps a spare float or ball. It is a good idea to dismantle and clean ballvalves occasionally.

In an emergency Isolate the offending ballvalve. If the float is a copper ball, check for leaks by holding and shaking it – if it is heavy and splashing noises can be heard, it is leaking. Replace it by a new plastic one (these are much less likely to leak). A temporary repair can be made by emptying out the water, replacing the ball, and fitting a plastic bag round it securely tied to the arm.

If a leaking float is not the cause, the valve should be removed from the inlet pipe and dismantled – the drawings show how three types of valve can be taken to pieces. Corrosion may make dismantling difficult – clean up the valve and apply penetrating oil as necessary. The most likely cause of a leak is a worn washer (or diaphragm in a diaphragm valve). This can be replaced. The valve seat or nozzle may also have worn – with some types of valve these can also be replaced: low-pressure valves have a larger opening in the nozzle than high-pressure ones, so make sure you choose the right sort.

On the other hand, a running overflow may be due simply to dirt or grit in the valve causing it to stick – make sure the nozzle and other waterways are clear, and clean all parts thoroughly before reassembling the valve. A worn split pin may be partly to blame for a leak.

With the valve back in place in the cistern and the water turned on again, check that the level of the water in the cistern is correct – about 50 to 100mm below the overflow outlet (or no higher than the water line level in the cistern if there is one). If the level is not right, gently bend the ball arm – upwards to increase the level, downwards to decrease it. With some diaphragm valves, the ball is moved along the arm to alter the water level.

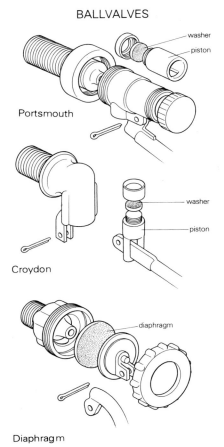

BALLVALVES

washer
piston

Portsmouth

Croydon

washer
piston

diaphragm

Diaphragm

Airlocks

An erratic flow of water from a tap combined with slightly alarming hissing and spluttering noises is a sign of air in the pipe. In bad cases, the flow of water may stop completely.

Before trouble strikes There is little to be done.

In an emergency Connect one end of a hose pipe to the affected tap, and the other to another tap – preferably one fed directly from the mains. Turn on both taps fully, and the pressure of water should drive out the air bubble. If this does not work, drain the system and refill slowly, having first turned on all the taps slightly. If airlocks occur frequently, suspect a partly-blocked pipe or some design fault in the pipe layout.

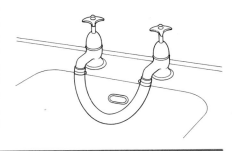

Blocked wastes

If sinks and so on do not empty, there is a blockage somewhere.

Before trouble strikes Know how your waste and drain system is laid out – see pages 262, 263 and 264 and the section on *Drains* starting on page 290. A blockage is often found in the waste trap underneath the sink or the basin affected – make sure the traps are easy to take apart, and clean out regularly.

In an emergency Unblocking wastes is dealt with fully in *Drains* – see page 294.

Planning a bathroom

The easiest course when refitting an old bathroom is to use equipment that is the same shape and size as the old equipment. Then all the pieces will fit in the same positions and the existing plumbing and waste runs can be used. But the opportunity of planning a new bathroom from scratch so that it works better than the old one is usually too good to miss.

Start by deciding what improvements could be made – for example, would a shower plus a bidet be a better idea than a bath? Should the WC be part of the bathroom, or separate from it? Would two wash basins ease the load on the bathroom in the mornings? Or should extra basins be put in some of the bedrooms?

There is an enormous range of bathroom equipment available – some examples are given below and on the next two pages. Some equipment is inexpensive and utilitarian; some unashamedly luxurious; and some is designed to overcome special problems, such as a shortage of space.

Once you have decided what bathroom equipment you would like, cut out scaled down plan shapes of the individual items from a piece of card and put these on a scale plan of the bathroom. Leave sufficient room round each piece of equipment so that it can be used properly – space for elbows at the side of the wash basin and for knees in front of the WC, for example. The recommended sizes of these **activity spaces** for each item of equipment are shown in the drawing. Add scale plans of these activity spaces to your cards. Where two fittings are unlikely to be used at the same time – for example, a WC and a bidet – the activity spaces may overlap without making the bathroom any more awkward to use.

Do not forget to take account of things like windows and central heating radiators. Doors that get in the way could be rehung, or converted into sliding doors. Where possible, arrange equipment in a logical order – WC next to both basin and bidet for example. Bear in mind that it is best to keep water and waste pipe runs short and that they may need to be concealed if they are not to look ugly. WC waste pipes are large and you may need to allow space for them.

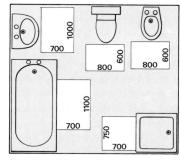

Recommended size of activity spaces

Baths

Baths are made of a variety of materials. Enamelled cast iron, the traditional material, is very heavy (it takes two strong people to move a bath made of it), rigid and hard-wearing, but it has poor resistance to chipping and is expensive. Enamelled pressed steel has much the same properties, but is much lighter, a little less rigid, and relatively cheap. Plastic materials – acrylic or glass reinforced plastics – make a bath that is very light, fairly cheap, and with good resistance to chipping. But the bath needs properly supporting, has poor resistance to chemicals, and will melt if hot things like a cigarette end come into contact with it. The common shapes of bath are listed below.

Plain rectangular bath Cheap; usually 700mm wide and 1700mm long, but other sizes (including the old imperial 5ft 6in) also available.

Rectangular bath with extra features More expensive than the simple type. Different brands have different features: *Handle grips* – usually for holding on to when moving about in the bath; *non-slip base* makes standing in the bath safer; *dipped front* makes it easier to climb in and out; *taps* need not be positioned at the end, but on one side, in a corner or plumbed into the wall; *plug holes* need not be at the end.

Corner bath Usually has an oval bathing area. As well as looking unusual; it might be the answer to some space problems. Like other unusual baths, it is generally made of a plastic material – and may require a greater volume of water than a traditionally-shaped bath.

Double-sized bath For comfort when bathing with a friend; many different shapes are available.

Bath with seat A small, deep bath for sitting in rather than lying down in; some are deep enough to allow the water to come up to shoulder level.

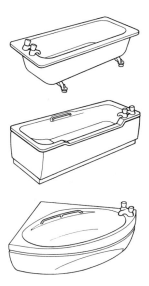

From the top: plain rectangular bath; rectangular bath with, dipped front handle grip and side taps; corner bath

Basins

Most basins are made of vitreous china which has good resistance to chemicals and naked flames but is easily cracked or chipped. Other materials used are glazed earthenware or fireclay and sometimes plastics or enamelled pressed steel.

Pedestal basin The pedestal provides some support for the basin and helps to hide plumbing and waste traps.

Wall-hung basin Can be positioned at any height and leaves the floor clear, but relies completely on the wall for support and does not provide any cover for the plumbing and waste pipes.

Vanity or counter-top basin The basin is mounted in a worktop – either above it, flush with it (perhaps surrounded by a metal trim) or beneath it. Ready-made vanity units are also available. When cutting the hole for the basin, take the dimensions of the actual basin to be used, as these can vary in size by a few

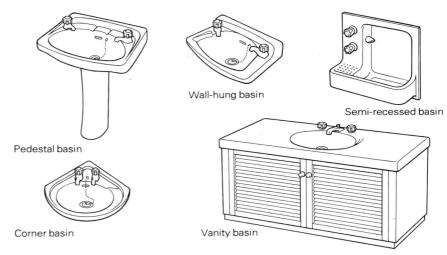

Wall-hung basin

Semi-recessed basin

Pedestal basin

Corner basin

Vanity basin

millimetres. Vanity basins complete with their own surround are also available.

Corner basin Designed for use in confined spaces but often a small conventional basin is a better solution.

Semi-recessed basin Another solution to fitting a basin in a small area. Recesses about 60mm or so into the wall.

WCs

The pan part of a WC is made of vitreous china; the cistern (now almost always a low-level type) may be china or plastic. The waste outlet from the pan may be vertically downwards – *an S-trap* – or nearly horizontal – *a P-trap*. Some WCs have a short horizontal outlet to which a ceramic or plastic connector can be added to convert the outlet into an S-trap, or P-trap – angled if necessary. The standard height of the pan is 405mm, but other heights are available.

Horizontal outlet S-trap P-trap

Washdown pan with standard cistern The most usual type – the contents of the pan are simply washed down the waste pipe by the fo ce of the water from the cistern. Cheap but rather noisy in operation. Cisterns usually come complete with ballvalve – often a high-pressure type. For cisterns fed from a cold water storage cistern, a low-pressure ballvalve is needed. Inlets and overflows are positioned at the sides and can be inter-

changed. The flush handle is also mounted on the side.

Syphonic pan with close-coupled cistern The contents of the pan are sucked out by syphonic action in the trap. Quieter in operation than the washdown type and the pan is also less likely to get soiled. Two types – single-trap and double-trap: double-trap is more efficient and common, but some get blocked more easily; both types cost more than the washdown type. A *close-coupled* cistern is linked directly to the pan – neater than the standard type. Some washdown pans are designed for use with close-coupled cisterns too. The cistern has its inlet and overflow mounted *underneath*, which gives a neater appearance.

Wall-hung WC Keeps the floor clear but does not necessarily allow any flexibility in mounting height. The cistern is usually concealed behind a false wall.

WC with narrow cistern Useful when converting an old-fashioned high-level cistern to a low-level type, or for when space in front of the WC is restricted.

Dual-flush cistern Enables you to flush the pan using either half or the full amount of water. Saves water when using the WC as a urinal (half flush).

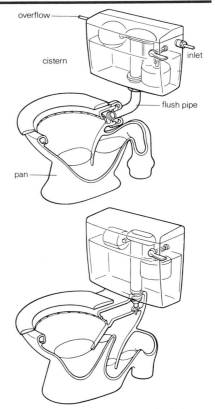

overflow

cistern

inlet

flush pipe

pan

Top: washdown pan with standard cistern. Bottom: double-trap syphonic pan with close-coupled cistern

Bidets

The main purpose of a bidet is for washing the bottom and genitals. It is used by sitting astride it – either facing towards or away from the taps, whichever is more comfortable. It can also be used as a footbath, as a basin for small children, or for soaking clothes.

Over-rim supply The water is supplied to the bowl of the bidet from taps, in exactly the same manner as a wash basin. This type is easier to plumb in but the rim can feel cold when sitting on it.

Through-rim supply Special water valves are needed and the warm water flows round the rim before filling the bowl, to warm it. This type often has a spray fitted to the base of the bowl, which is used for

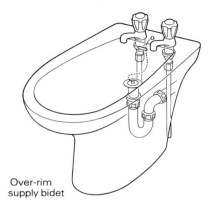

Over-rim supply bidet

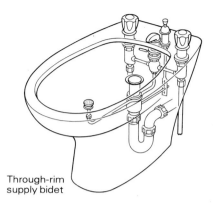

Through-rim supply bidet

douching. Both the bidet and the taps are more expensive than the over-rim type and special plumbing regulations have to be observed, see page 288.

Wall-mounted bidet As with wall-mounted WC, keeps the floor clear, but does not necessarily allow any flexibility in mounting height.

Showers

Taking a shower has a number of advantages over bathing – it is quicker and uses less water. But, depending on the existing plumbing system, some types of shower can be impossible to install without radical alterations. So check what is and is not possible before buying – see *Installing a shower* on page 287.

Some showers have simple *hot* and *cold* valves, like those on an ordinary mixer tap; others use one valve to control the amount of water (the *flow*), and another to control the *temperature*. The flow and temperature may also be controlled by a single tap: or in some cases, only the temperature may be variable. The controls may be *thermostatic*, which keeps the temperature of the spray more stable. Thermostatic controls are easier and safer to use than non-thermostatic.

Whatever the type of shower, the valve part can be connected to the outlet (the rose) by a rigid pipe or flexible hose. A rigid pipe may look neater, but a flexible hose allows the rose to be positioned at different heights to suit different members of the family and to be used for hair washing over a basin or bath. To prevent possible back-siphonage, a flexible hose should be constrained so that the end cannot fall into the bath water.

All types of shower can be mounted over the bath. Some can be mounted

over separate shower trays: these are probably easier to use, but can require much more installation work.

Push-on rubber hose Ends push over existing bath taps. Cheap and no installation required, but water authorities frown on their use.

Bath/shower mixer Easy to install – replaces existing bath taps; relatively inexpensive. Can be used only when hot and cold water come from a storage cistern or with certain instantaneous gas water heaters. Usually non-thermostatic.

Shower mixer – non-thermostatic controls Usually mounted over a separate shower tray: may need a lot of plumbing and waste installation. Some types have *hot* and *cold* valves; others may have *temperature* and *flow* controls.

Shower mixer – thermostatic controls Usually mounted over a separate shower tray: may need a lot of plumbing and waste installation. Usually has *temperature and flow* controls. Quite expensive.

Electric shower heater Can be mounted over a bath or a separate shower tray. Takes its water from the mains cold water supply, so plumbing may be extensive. Water is heated instantaneously as it passes through the heater – the spray may not be as forceful as with a conventional shower. Special electric wiring needed as well as plumbing but an electric shower can be used where a conventional type is impractical.

Push-on rubber hose

Bath/shower mixer

Shower mixer

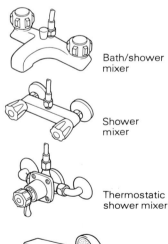

Thermostatic shower mixer

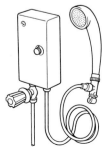

Electric shower heater

Fitting a sink or basin

Before starting to work on the sink or basin, turn off the water and drain the system as necessary.

If you are replacing an old sink or basin with a new one, it is usually much easier to saw off the old supply and waste pipes and the screws securing the fitting rather than trying to undo them. Loosening old, corroded fittings is at best frustrating, and often impossible. Cut the pipes where they are easy to get at – both at this stage and later when the new basin is installed. When the old fitting is off the wall, the taps can usually be removed comparatively easily.

Before starting any plumbing work, make sure the new basin or sink fits properly. Prepare the mountings: for example, fix wall brackets, check the position of a pedestal and drill fixing holes, check the positioning of a sink unit and cut any necessary holes in it for pipes and so on.

Plumbing pipes can usually be manipulated so that they end up exactly where they are wanted. But waste pipes are less amenable – often their slope and position is fairly fixed. So ensure that your proposed position for the new sink or basin enables the waste to be connected properly – it is a good idea to have a catalogue of manufacturer's waste pipes and fittings: many of the fittings have been specially designed to overcome typical installation problems.

Before fixing the new unit into place,

do as much plumbing work to it as possible. First, fix the waste outlet. Ceramic wash basins usually have an overflow built in, and a slotted waste outlet has to be used. To seal this to the basin surface, bed it in using plumbing mastic. Position the waste outlet so that the slot in it coincides with the slot from the overflow in the basin and hold it in place with the washers and back-nut supplied. Do not overtighten or the basin may crack. Remove any excess mastic.

Stainless steel sinks have a hole for an overflow, but the overflow pipe comes with the waste outlet. The plastic washers supplied with sink waste outlets are usually sufficient to seal the outlet and the overflow inlet to the sink surface.

Next fit the taps – see page 272. To make the job of connecting the taps to the supply pipes easier, it is often a good idea to fit 'tails' first. Tails are short lengths of pipe fixed to the taps with tap adaptors. Make the tails a suitable length and shape so that connecting them to the supply pipes, even once the sink or basin is in position, is easy.

With a pedestal wash basin, a common dodge is to cross the supply pipes over behind the pedestal – the pipes stay relatively well hidden, and there are not too many tight bends in the pipes.

Finally, fit the unit into place, making sure that it is secure before connecting the water and waste pipes. A pedestal

basin can be bedded into its pedestal with plumbing mastic; some basins have a special fixing for securing the basin and pedestal together. As usual, ensure that there is no strain on any of the pipes or connections – if there is, refit or rebend the pipes as necessary.

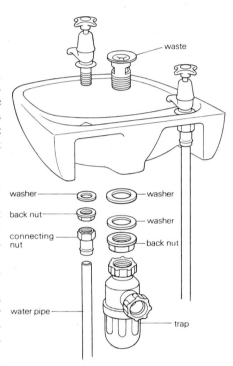

A typical ceramic basin with an integral overflow and slotted waste outlet. It is fitted with tap connectors and a bottle trap

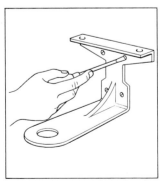

Prepare the mountings for the sink. Position accurately and secure wall brackets firmly to the wall – see the chapter on *Fixings*

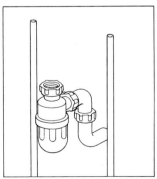

Before fixing the basin in place, do as much of the plumbing work as possible. In particular, fit the waste outlet to the basin

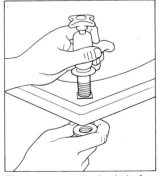

Fit the taps to the basin before you put the basin in position. Fit 'tails' to the taps using tap adaptors

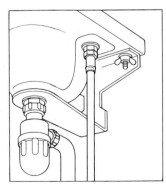

Make sure that the basin is firmly fixed to the wall before connecting it to the water and waste pipes

Fitting a bath

Many of the problems involved in fitting a bath are the same as those involved in fitting a sink or basin – see previous page. The problems of access are often worse so fitting tails to the taps and carefully working out the exact position of the various parts of the waste system is often more important. Before starting to work, turn off the water to the taps and drain the system as necessary.

When replacing an old cast iron bath, it is usually easier to break it up on the spot rather than trying to remove it in one piece. Cover the surface with sacking, old blankets or quilts and protect any nearby ceramic ware. Wear goggles, thick gloves and protective clothing and smash the bath into pieces with a sledge-hammer. Wear protective clothing when you remove the pieces, too. If the bath is being broken up *in situ*, it may not be necessary to disconnect water and waste pipes first – otherwise deal with these in the same way as for removing an old sink.

If you want to remove a cast iron bath in one piece, disconnect the pipes first. Lowering the bath on its adjustable feet may help to release it from the wall and to protect any tiling round the edge of the bath. Strong helpers will be needed to get the bath out of the bathroom.

As with sinks, do as much plumbing work as possible, fitting at least the taps to the bath before fitting the bath in position. It may be easier to fit the waste

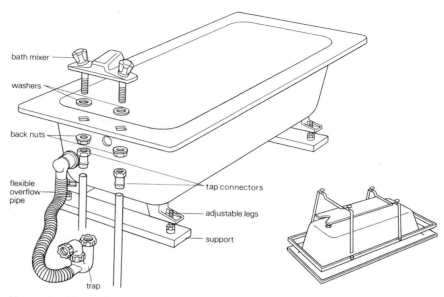

outlet at this stage too. A bath waste outlet usually comes complete with the trap and overflow pipe. Taps and wastes are usually sealed with washers rather than mastic.

Fitting the bath itself can be more difficult than fitting a basin. Steel baths usually have brackets fitted to the bottom – these have adjustable feet to ensure that the bath can be positioned so that the bottom of the bath slopes slightly in the direction of the waste outlet. Plastic baths need a proper supporting cradle to ensure that they do not creak or sag in use. Make sure you get the correct

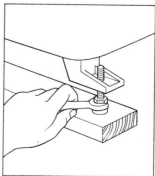

Above: plumbing and waste arrangement for a bath   Right: a cradle for an acrylic bath

cradle for the bath and instructions on how to install it.

With any sort of bath, it is sensible to put boards beneath the levelling feet to spread the load over the floorboards.

Once the bath is properly fixed in place, connect the pipes to the taps (or tap tails – see opposite page – if these are being used) and the waste pipe to the outlet of the trap (if this has already been fitted). It is usually best to start by connecting the tap furthest away (you may need to temporarily disconnect the overflow pipe); then deal with the waste and overflow; then connect the other tap.

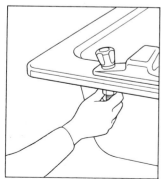

Most baths offer very limited access to their plumbing and waste pipes once the bath is in place. Fit the taps to the bath. . . .

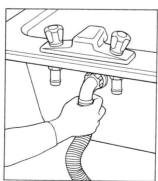

. . . and fit the waste system before fixing the bath in position. Seal the taps and waste with washers

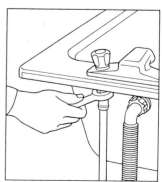

Adjust the feet of a steel bath so that it slopes slightly towards the waste outlet

Finally, fit the supply pipes to the taps (or tap 'tails') and the waste pipe to the outlet of the trap

Fitting a WC

Probably the most difficult part of fitting a new WC in place of an old, existing one is connecting the new pan outlet to the existing soil-pipe opening. Unless the new pan is an exact replica of the old one, the outlet and the opening probably will not coincide. If a low-level cistern is being fitted in place of an old high-level one, the pan will probably have to be sited further out from the wall otherwise the seat will not stay up when it is lifted. Before you buy, try to measure the position, slope and size of the outlet and of the soil-pipe opening. A variety of connectors is available to overcome any problems – probably the most useful is the range of *Multikwik* connectors: there is even one that will allow small offsets between the outlet and opening.

Once the problem of connecting the outlet has been solved, start work by removing the old WC. Cut off the water supply and flush the cistern. Unless the joints undo easily, simply saw off the water supply pipe to the cistern's ballvalve and the flush pipe to the pan. Remove the cistern and its wall brackets – they may need sawing through – see *Fitting a sink or basin*.

To remove the pan, break the top bend of the trap (unless the pan is connected to the soil pipe with a rubber connector) and unscrew or lever the pan from the floor. Then *carefully* chip the rest of the pipe outlet from the soil pipe – tuck a cloth into the outlet first to stop

the debris falling down it.

Try the new pan in place, and ensure that the connector you have is suitable. Make sure too that the pan is level.

Put the pan in place but do not fix it to the floor (and if you are not using a connector with a rubber seal, do not seal the joint between pan outlet and soil pipe). If the cistern is of the close-coupled type, connect this to the pan and then screw the cistern to the wall – use non-corroding screws, and tighten them gently. With a cistern for a wash-down pan, it is probably best to connect the flush pipe to the pan first then the cistern to the flush pipe – make sure that its weight is properly supported until it is firmly screwed to the wall. To ensure correct flushing, the cistern has to be fixed dead level.

Screw the pan to the floor using non-corroding screws with washers and tighten them gently to avoid cracking the pan.

Connect the water supply pipe to the ballvalve inlet with a tap connector. The overflow pipe can be connected to the cistern outlet with a ½in tap connector. Ordinary copper pipe and fittings can be used, but plastic piping and fittings specially made for overflows are available. Overflow outlets should be put in a prominent position so that when they run, the fault can be seen immediately – special bath wastes are available that direct cistern overflows through the bath overflow outlet into the bath.

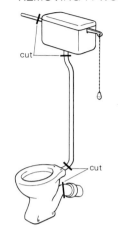

Saw off the pipe and break the pan where shown

Chipping out the rest of the pan

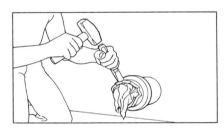

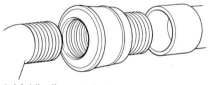

A *Multikwik* connector

Try the new pan in place, making sure that it sits dead level and check the suitability of connectors

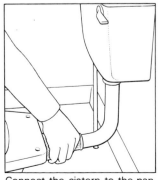

Connect the cistern to the pan. With some WCs it is easier to connect the flush pipe to the pan before the cistern – see text

Screw the pan to the floor using non-corroding screws and washers, tightening them gently to avoid cracking the pan

Use a tap connector to connect the water supply pipe to the ballvalve inlet

Installing a shower

Fitting a shower is essentially no more difficult than installing any other piece of equipment – it usually involves fitting taps or valves, making a branch pipe, running a new waste, and so on. Details of how to do these jobs are given in other parts of this chapter. Before starting any plumbing work, turn off the water and drain the system as necessary – see *Plumbing First Aid*, page 277. But, because a shower is a *mixer* fitting and is usually designed to deliver a forceful spray of water, installation does pose some particular problems – some of these are discussed on this, and the next page. It is best to consider all the potential problems before buying – many of them can be solved by careful choice of shower type.

1 You have a direct plumbing system – see pages 262 and 263.

This can be solved most easily by fitting an electric shower. For this, run a 15mm branch pipe from the nearest point of the cold water supply to the heater. If the control valve is part of the heater unit, the whole thing will have to be mounted inside the showering area. But if the control valve for the shower is separate from the heater – positioned on the inlet to the heater – the control valve can be

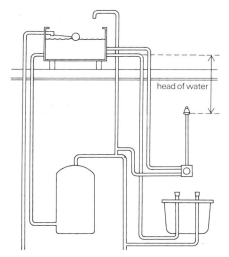

A head of water – measured as shown – of at least 1.5m is usually adequate

mounted within the showering area with the heater unit outside. The heater unit is generally fixed in position by simply screwing it to the wall.

The electrical supply has to be run from a separate fuse at the main fuse box – depending on the wattage of the shower, a supply between 13A and 30A will be needed: most need a 30A supply. It should be switched at the shower end using a special double-pole pull-cord switch of the correct rating.

Other types of shower can be fitted only if an indirect plumbing supply is installed for the shower. Unless the cistern feeding the hot water cylinder is larger than is normal, a new cistern will have to be installed in its place, and a 15mm cold supply pipe run from it to the shower unit. The hot supply can be taken from the existing hot water pipe.

2 The vertical distance from the base of the cold water cistern to the shower rose (called the 'head') is less than about 1.5m

If the head is between about one metre and 1.5m and the hot and cold pipe runs are both reasonably short (in effect, if both the shower and the hot water cylinder are more or less directly underneath the cistern) a shower may be fitted without any extra work, but the force of the spray may be a bit limited. Otherwise, there are three solutions:

● the cistern may be raised to give a sufficient head. Putting the cistern in the loft (if it is not there already) may be sufficient – this will involve lengthening all the pipes that connect to the cistern. If the cistern is already in the loft, there may be enough headroom to mount it on a platform – again, this involves lengthening all the pipes. A cistern full of water is very heavy – so the platform must be constructed very sturdily. Remember to allow enough space above the cistern to give access to the ballvalve – and remember that you should now lag underneath the cistern

● if raising the cistern is not practicable, a shower booster or pump may be fitted

into the hose between the shower valve and the rose. A booster can be used as long as there is a small head between the surface of the water in the cistern and the rose. A shower pump can be used as long as there is some head between the cistern and the control. Boosters and pumps are electrically operated

● an electric shower may be fitted. Since an electric shower usually takes its water supply from a cold water mains pipe, the pipe run may be rather long – but the height of the cistern is unimportant.

3 The cold water flow fluctuates when other taps and so on are turned on. This may result in the spray from a shower becoming uncomfortably, or even dangerously, hot

This problem is most likely to arise when a shower is fitted downstream of other fittings, particularly if the branch pipes to the shower are taken off 15mm pipes, rather than larger ones. If you want to fit a bath/shower mixer, try turning on the existing bath cold tap and then turn on other taps and flush the WC to see if this affects the flow of water from the bath cold tap. The hot water flow can also fluctuate in the same way – this is less dangerous, but still uncomfortable.

The problem can be partly overcome by fitting a thermostatic valve, which will iron out small fluctuations in the hot or cold supply, leaving the temperature and flow reasonably stable. If the hot or cold supply should vary greatly, the shower will shut off – safe, but annoying.

Another solution is to run pipes for the shower alone directly to the hot water cylinder and cold water cistern. No other fittings should be connected to these pipes. In this case, a non-thermostatic shower will do but a thermostatic one would still be safer.

Fitting an electric shower could also solve the problem.

4 A separate shower tray is to be installed

Separate shower trays, usually made of plastic, are generally simple to fix into

place. But most give a fairly small showering area – a better solution is to make
your own by tiling part of the floor
around a raised threshold, though this
clearly involves much more work.

The main problem lies in running the
waste. Since the shower tray is at floor
level, the trap and waste pipe have to be
run entirely underneath the floor. Access to the trap for cleaning will have to
be made – with an upstairs shower, this
would be best made by fitting a small
hatch to the ceiling below. The waste
pipe will have to be run in the direction
of the joists – these will not usually be

deep enough to be cut to allow the waste
pipe to be run across them.

**5 The shower is to be fed from an in-
stantaneous gas-fired heater**
In some cases, this may lead to an erratic
hot water supply. This might be overcome by changing the shower rose or by
having adjustments made to the heater.
But it would be sensible to check with
your gas board and with the shower
manufacturer whether problems are
likely to be encountered.

Right: if the head is inadequate use a booster
pump or move the cold water cistern

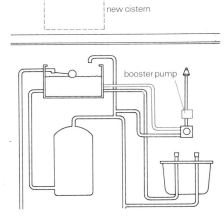

new cistern

booster pump

Fitting a bidet

Over-rim supply bidets are really only
low-level wash basins and they are
plumbed in in exactly the same way. In
most cases, this means taking branch
pipes from the pipes which supply the
other pieces of bathroom equipment. If
the pipes are 22mm, use 22mm to 15mm
reducing tees to make the branch. Before starting work turn the water off and
drain the system as necessary.

Screw the bidet to the floor using brass
screws – special ones that take a covering
cap which conceals the screw can be
bought. Use washers and tighten gently
to ensure the bidet is not cracked. If a
basin mixer is used instead of separate
taps, then both hot and cold supplies
must come from the cold water cistern,
or a divided-flow mixer must be used.

Through-rim supply bidets may or
may not have a spray attachment. Those
that do not can be plumbed in to the

existing bathroom supply pipes in the
same way as an over-rim bidet. The taps
which supply the water to the rim form a
bidet set – this should come with instructions on fitting and with sealing washers.
The inlets to a bidet set are usually compression fittings, so tap adaptors are not
needed. Divided-flow bidet sets are not
available – both hot and cold supplies
must come via the cold water cistern.

Through-rim supply bidets that incorporate a spray or douche have to be
connected to separate supply pipes run
directly from the hot water cylinder and
the cold water cistern. This makes them
more difficult and expensive to install.

The waste outlet from a bidet is made
up in exactly the same way as for a wash
basin – use a slotted waste sealed with
plumbing mastic with a trap connected
to it. In a two-pipe waste system, it can
be fed into a hopper head rather than

connected to the WC's soil stack.

Bidet regulations
When installing a through-rim bidet:
● the bidet must have its own cold water
supply pipe direct from the cold water
cistern. No other pipes or fittings can be
connected to this pipe
● the hot water pipe must be the highest
pipe taken off the hot water cistern. It
too must not have any pipes or other
fittings connected to it.

If the bidet is on the lowest floor of the
house and there are no other plumbing
fittings at a lower level, it may not
be necessary to fulfil these conditions.
But some water undertakings do not
think these conditions are stringent
enough and ban through-rim bidets.

These regulations do not apply to
bidets with a simple over-rim supply,
which are treated like basins.

Fitting an outside tap

Fitting an outside tap follows much the
same lines as plumbing in a washing
machine: a tee has to be fitted to a cold
water pipe; a branch pipe fitted to this;
and a tap fitted to the branch pipe.

Before starting the work tell your local
water authority what you intend to do.
To be an effective supply for a hose pipe
the outside tap should be fitted to the
rising main so that the pressure is high

enough: some authorities may impose
special conditions. You may also have to
pay extra water rates.

First fit the outside tap in place; then
cut or drill a hole in the wall, and run the
new branch pipe from the tap to the
point where you intend to connect it to
the rising main. Then turn off the water,
drain the system and cut the rising main
to fit a tee as described in *Installing an*

automatic washing machine. Make sure
all joints have been properly made before turning the water back on and flush
the pipes thoroughly.

It is a good idea to fit a stopcock into
the branch pipe close to the rising main
and to ensure that the branch pipe slopes
down slightly towards the tap. Then in
cold weather the branch can be drained
of water to prevent it freezing.

Installing an automatic washing machine

Some machines need both hot and cold supplies; others are (or can be converted to) cold-fill only. Cold-fill only machines are clearly easier to plumb in but may be a bit more expensive to run – depending on how you heat your water.

Most machines will cope with a wide range of water pressures but supplies from storage cisterns or hot water cylinders may not give adequate pressure – particularly if the machine is only one floor below the storage cistern.

Hot water may be supplied from a hot water cistern or from a multi-point instantaneous heater, but not from a single-outlet water heater which is not designed to cope with washing machines. There are a variety of special washing machine valves available, most of which have ½in BSP threaded outlets to suit the fittings on most washing machine hoses. As an alternative you can use a standard bib tap with a ½in threaded outlet – see page 269 – and either a ½in to ¾in BSP adaptor, or a ½in hose union adaptor (the plain end of the hose fits over this and is held in place with a Jubilee-type clip). The inlet side of the valve may be ½in BSP. If it is the best way to connect it to the branch pipe is with a wall plate elbow having a 15mm compression fitting on one end – see *Pipes and fittings* on pages 265 to 268. Alternatively, the valve may already have a 15mm compression end.

Another type of valve can be fitted *in-line* in the supply pipes. In-line valves can be used only where the machine hoses reach as far as the supply pipes. There are two main types of in-line valve. With one, you cut a length out of the supply pipes and fit the valve in the same manner as an ordinary tee fitting. With the other – saddle-fitting – type, you drill a small hole in the side of the pipe and bolt the valve body round this. Because of the small diameter of the hole, the machine may fill more slowly. The job of fitting is only a little less difficult than fitting tees and branch pipes.

As with all plumbing, you should tell your local water supply undertaking be-fore you start work. They may have special rules about where the branch pipes to the machine have to run from – for example, they may require that the cold supply comes from the storage cistern – rather than from the rising main, which is generally much easier to arrange.

Water supply

Before starting any plumbing, turn off the water and drain the system as necessary – see page 277.

Unless you use in-line valves, start by fitting tees to nearby hot and cold supply pipes. In many cases, the nearest supply pipes will be those feeding the taps over the kitchen sink – the cold will come from the rising main and the hot from the hot water cylinder.

Use a hacksaw carefully to cut out a section of the supply pipes about 19mm long – the exact length to cut is the length of the body of the tee fitting you are using, less twice the amount by which a pipe will slide into the end of the fitting. Prepare the ends of the pipe and fitting properly – see *Pipes and fittings* on page 265. The supply pipes will need manipulating somewhat in order to get their cut ends into the ends of the tee – remove pipe clips and slacken the taps at the sink, as necessary. Position the tees in place but do not fix them yet.

Cut the branch pipes to length and make bends (or use elbows) in them as necessary to clear any supply pipes or other obstacles. Fit the valves to the other ends of the branch pipes. If the valves have to be fitted first to wall plate elbows, seal this joint with PTFE tape. Ensure the valve is firmly fixed to the wall: if the branch pipes are longer than a metre or so they will need clips.

When the pipes are properly installed there should be no strain on any of the fittings, pipes or pipe clips, and the tees can then be tightened or soldered. Check that any other loosened joints have been retightened before turning on the water again. Flush the system well before use and check carefully for leaks.

Wastes

The outlet from the washing machine could simply discharge into the sink – but the most usual way with machines on the ground floor is to take the waste outside the house into a yard gully.

Plastic waste pipe, suitable for occasional very high temperature discharges should be used. The end of the washing machine outlet hose should hook into the open end of a stand pipe. The diameter of this pipe should be large enough to allow an air gap where the hose enters it; the top is usually about 600mm from the floor – check with the washing machine's instructions.

Fit a suitable trap to the bottom of the stand pipe and lead the pipe out through a hole in the wall and into the yard gully – make sure the open end is below the grating in the gully. An alternative is to fit a special washing machine trap to the kitchen sink and connect the outlet hose to this directly.

If the washing machine is not on the ground floor, providing a waste system can be more tricky. With an old two-pipe system – see page 264 – you might be able to use a convenient hopper head; with a modern plastic single stack system, you could join the waste pipe into the stack. Either way, the waste pipe still needs a trap in it.

INSTALLATION

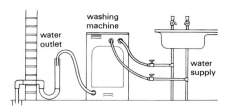

Plumbing in a washing machine (or dishwasher) normally involves providing a supply of cold water (and sometimes hot water) via branch pipes, valves and the machine's inlet hoses and providing a waste outlet to the drains via a trap.

Drains

The underground drain system of a house takes the wastes from soil pipes and yard gullies to the main public sewer (if the house is on mains drainage) or to a septic tank or cesspool (if mains drainage is not available).

The layout of underground drains is rather less standardised than that of above-ground soil and waste pipes and because it is hidden it is a little more difficult to trace.

The simplest form of layout in a house with mains drainage is shown in the drawing alongside. Here there are just two connections to the drain – one at the foot of the soil pipe and one at the foot of the yard gully. There is no trap at the base of a single-stack waste pipe (or at the base of the WC soil pipe in a two-pipe system); the yard gully has a trap incorporated in it and so do pipes carrying waste from fittings other than the WC in a two-pipe system. To gain access to the drains – in order to clear any blockages – there are **inspection chambers** or **manholes**. These are sited near the connection with the soil-stack, where the drain turns a right-angle at the side of the property, and at the boundary of the property.

In most cases, these drains do not carry rain-water – sewers and sewage plants would have to be made much bigger if they did. Instead the rain-water – either from the gutters and rain-water pipes or from surface-water drains in a drive, say –

is carried through a separate set of drains either to a public surface-water drain, or to a **soakaway** in the grounds of the house. A house may have a soakaway even if the foul drains are connected to a main sewer.

A different drain layout is often used when there is a group of houses together. In the example shown in the drawing there is only one connection to the sewer, and from this runs a communal drain through the back gardens of all the properties. The individual house drains are connected to this communal drain. This clearly saves money and effort when several houses are being built at the same time – but because the responsibility for the drain is shared, there can be more headaches for the householders when something goes wrong.

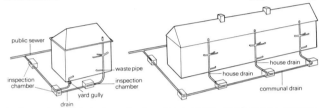

Left: a simple drain layout, showing a single-stack waste system and a yard gully fed from a kitchen sink – note the positions of the inspection chambers. Right: a communal drain system

Inspection chambers

It is clearly important to be able to gain access to all parts of the underground drains. This is usually done by providing inspection chambers at various points. The Building Regulations say that chambers have to be provided: within 12.5m of junctions between drains; where the drain changes direction or gradient; at the beginning of the drain; and at intervals of not more than 90m on long, straight runs. In between the inspection chambers, the drains should be laid in

straight lines.

The usual form of an inspection chamber is the manhole. The sides of the manhole are usually made of brick, often cement-rendered either on the inside or the outside. At the base of the hole are open channels to which the drains are connected and along which the water in the drains runs.

In the drawing, the manhole is at a junction between three drains. The branch drain is connected to the main one with a specially-shaped half-channel

bend which is swept in the direction of the flow of water through the main channel.

The sides of the channels are built up with *benching* – smoothly finished concrete shaped to direct any splashes back into the channels. The top of a manhole is covered with a *manhole cover* – a heavy, cast-iron plate set in a cast-iron frame. If there is a manhole cover within a building it usually has to be screwed down to the frame and the joint sealed with grease.

INSPECTION CHAMBERS AND RODDING POINTS

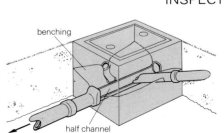

A manhole at the junction of three drains. Note the open (half) channel at the base of the manhole and the benching

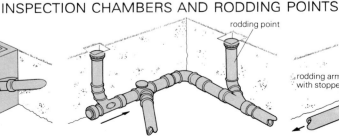

A drain system which uses rodding points at a junction and a bend. Manholes are still needed for better access

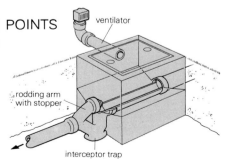

An inspection chamber fitted with an interceptor trap and a rodding arm (which has a stopper)

With modern drain materials, it may not be necessary to have full-scale manholes at all junctions and bends in the drain. Instead, *rodding points* may be used.

A length of pipe with a gentle bend in it is connected at an angle to the drain. The other end of the pipe leads to ground level and is covered with a suitable removable cover. If the drain needs unblocking, the cover is removed and drain rods passed down into the drain. Rodding points are small and neat – unlike large, ugly manhole covers – but manholes may still be needed where better access to the drain is necessary.

In older properties, the inspection chamber at the boundary of the property may have an *interceptor trap* fitted at the outlet of the channel. To gain access to the length of drain between the trap and the main sewer, the trap has its own rodding arm which bypasses the U-bend. The rodding arm is fitted with a stopper (secured with a chain) to prevent the drain water from bypassing the U-bend, too.

This inspection chamber may also be ventilated by means of a short pipe projecting above ground from the side of the chamber. The pipe is usually fitted with a grilled ventilator, behind which is a flap. The theory is that the flap allows fresh air into the drain, but prevents foul air from escaping. Ventilators are probably more of a hindrance than a help and damaged ones can be removed completely rather than repaired. Interceptor traps also give problems – the rodding arm stopper can fall out of place and cause a blockage if it is not suspended by a chain.

Cesspools and septic tanks

There are two methods for dealing with sewage from houses that are not connected to the main sewer.

A cesspool is simply a lined hole in the ground where the sewage collects. In time, the pool becomes full and has to be emptied – either by the local council or by a private firm. Many houses have cesspools as small as 500 gallons: a fam-

ily of four could fill this in as little as a week. Current Building Regulations require a capacity of about 4000 gallons. Modern cesspools may be prefabricated from glassfibre or concrete rings and simply placed into an already excavated hole; old ones would be made of brick, carefully sealed so that the sewage cannot escape and water in the surrounding ground cannot get in.

A septic tank is in effect a small sewage works. In it, the waste is broken down by bacteria until it is liquified and rendered harmless: the resultant liquid can be disposed of into a ditch or stream. Usually two different chambers are needed in a septic tank: in some cases, the second chamber which contains a filter bed can be dispensed with and the half-treated sewage filtered through the sub-soil via land drains.

A well-constructed septic tank should need little maintenance apart from a periodic (say once a year) emptying of sludge. It is important not to use excessive amounts of disinfectant or detergents in the house, otherwise the bacteriological action could be slowed down and the tank clogged up.

Soakaways

Rain-water often drains into a soakaway. This can be a hole in the ground – of one or two cubic metres capacity – filled with rubble. The hole should be lined with bricks laid dry and covered with close-fitting concrete slabs. Rain-water drains into this hole and in time soaks away into the surrounding ground.

Tracing drains

Tracing the layout of a drain system is fairly simple – provided you remember that there should be an inspection chamber at all junctions and bends and that drains should run in straight lines between the chambers.

By pouring water down the various fittings in the house, it should be possible to determine which waste pipe connects to which drain and where each branch drain connects to the main drain. Fluorescent drain dyes can be used as an aid, if necessary. Any drains that do not show water after this test may be connected to a neighbour's drainage system.

A plan with the deeds of the house may also show the layout of the drains; or the local council may know.

REGULATIONS AND RESPONSIBILITIES

Drains laid within the grounds of a house, for that house's use only, are the responsibility of the householder. The length of drain from the boundary of the property to its connection with the public sewer in the road is also the responsibility of the householder.

With a communal drain the responsibility is shared. For those built before about 1937, the local council is responsible – but they can pass on the cost of maintenance and repair of any section of the drain to *all* the individual households connected to the drain.

Communal drains built after 1937 are the responsibility of the householders themselves – so if a blockage occurs, or repairs are needed, to a part of the drain within one house's grounds, all the householders have to pay their share.

If you are connected to such a drain, it

is worth while establishing this common responsibility with the other owners – then if trouble strikes, it can be put right without time-wasting arguments about who is responsible and who should pay. If you are buying a property, clarify the position first.

A drain serving only one property may also run through a neighbouring property. In this case, there should be provision in the deeds of the house allowing access for maintenance and repair.

The main rules governing the construction of drains in England and Wales (not in Inner London) are the Building Regulations. These cover the size of drains, how they have to run, access for cleaning and so on. The Public Health Acts also regulate the provision of drains; with new buildings, the local authority may also be concerned.

DRAIN MATERIALS

For hundreds of years, the traditional material for drains has been short lengths of salt-glazed clay pipes (the glazing helped make the clay watertight). Originally, the joints were made by packing a gasket of tarred hemp into the gap between the spigot end of one pipe and the socket of its neighbour and filling the rest of the gap with clay. The joints were flexible and were able to give a little as the pipeline settled – as a result of ground movement.

But these joints tended to leak, so they were superseded by a cement filling (still with a tarred rope gasket to prevent the cement from falling into the pipeline before it dried). In fact, the whole pipeline was usually bedded on a cement base, with the cement carried up the sides of the pipe (called haunching).

But a rigid pipeline like this is often too brittle, and can break if ground settlement takes place. So modern practice is often to revert to the original idea of flexible joints – and indeed flexible beds and flexible pipes.

The main materials used for house drains are clay, pitch fibre, and PVC.

Clay Modern clay pipes are not always salt-glazed (they are more impervious than they used to be). Socketed pipes are still used, but the sockets and spigots usually have plastic linings and are sealed with a rubber 'O' ring. Plain-ended pipes are also available: these are jointed with a plastic sleeve which slips over both pipe ends; again, sealing rings seal the joint. A large range of clay fittings is available and pipes still come in short lengths. It usually takes a bit of practice to cut them successfully – they have to be cut with a sharp bolster chisel in the same way as bricks: filling the pipe with sand may help to prevent it breaking in the wrong place.

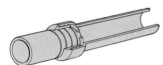

Pitch fibre These pipes are made from waste paper and other fibres soaked in pitch. For drainage work, the pipes usually come with plain ends and are jointed with a plastic sleeve. The sealing rings used are called snap rings – as the

sleeve is pushed into place over the pipe, the ring should suddenly and clearly snap into place. The joints will remain watertight even if the completed pipeline is not dead straight. There is a range of plastic fittings – including ones for jointing pitch fibre to other materials. Pitch pipes come in long lengths, but can be cut easily with a saw.

PVC These are joined in the same way as plastic waste pipes – either by using sockets or sleeves with sealing rings or by solvent welding. A range of fittings is available, including ready-made inspection chamber bases, rodding points, gullies, and fittings to join PVC to other materials. PVC pipes come in even longer lengths than pitch fibre but can also be cut easily.

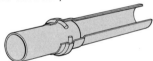

Laying drains

The techniques for bedding drain pipes on the bottom of the trench and for filling in the trench afterwards depend to some extent on the type of soil and the attitude of the local authority.

Clay pipes may be laid directly on the surface of the trench if the soil is suitable (clay or chalk probably would not be). If the pipes are socketed, the trench base will have to be scooped out to take the sockets so that the bottom of the pipe can rest on undisturbed soil. Usually, clay pipes have to be laid on a bed of gravel about 100mm thick and the first lot of soil used to fill in the trench (called backfill) should have all the stones, large lumps of clay and so on removed. In some cases, it may still be necessary to lay clay pipes on a bed of mortar.

Pitch fibre and PVC pipes are usually laid on a 100mm thick bed of gravel.

With PVC, the gravel fill should be continued above the level of the top of the pipeline. The first 300mm or so of backfill again has to be selected soil.

When laying a new drain, the first thing to decide is where the new drain will connect with an existing one. It is usually best to make the connection at an existing inspection chamber – cutting into an existing pipeline to form a new chamber is a bit more tricky. Make sure though that when the drains are laid at the correct level, they can be fed into the inspection chamber. Household drains must have a slope of one in forty (for every 40m run of pipeline, the level at the end farthest from the house has to be 1m lower than the level at the end nearest the house). This slope has been arrived at through trial-and-error as being the right value to make the drain self-

cleansing: if the slope is much shallower, the flow of water would not be fast enough for the solid waste matter to be carried along with it; if the slope is much steeper, the water would tend to flow over the solids.

The level of the bottom of the drainpipe (called the *invert* level) at the inspection-chamber end is often the same as the level of the *top* of the main channel running through the base of the chamber. The level of the drain at the house end should be a minimum of about 300mm below ground level if the drain is being connected to a single-stack waste pipe; a bit less otherwise (though drains should not really be laid any closer than about 600 to 900mm from the surface).

Measuring the difference between these two levels may not be easy, particularly if the two points are a long way from each other, or if the ground between them slopes. It may be possible to refer the depths to a known horizontal line, such as a damp-proof course on the side of a house, or it may be necessary to set horizontal levels using a spirit level.

Unless you are used to cutting clay pipes or can plan the layout of the drain so that no cutting is needed, it will probably be best to use pitch fibre or PVC pipes. Plan the whole layout using a manufacturer's catalogue, which will tell you what radius and angle of bends, depth of gullies and so on are available.

Laying a new drain (though not repairing an existing one) requires Building Regulations approval – before starting work, you should submit plans to your local authority, and get them approved. The Building Control Officer will probably want to see the trench before the drain is laid, the drain after it is laid before it is covered up, and the completed works.

Dig the trench so that it is not too wide – about 500mm – and in a straight line, except at properly-made bends.

If you are able to lay the pipe directly on the bottom of the trench, make sure this is flat, with no large stones or lumps in it, and with holes cut to take any pipe sockets or sleeves. Ensure that the pipe itself will be laid on firm, undisturbed soil – do not use pieces of wood or brick to support the pipe. The Building Control Officer should be able to tell you if the pipe needs to be bedded in and surrounded with loose fill, and whether you can use the soil excavated from the trench itself or whether (as is usual) the fill has to be coarse aggregate. If fill is needed, dig the trench about 100mm deeper than required, lay fill to a depth of 100mm and tamp it down to the correct level and slope.

Lay the pipe, following the manufacturer's instructions for jointing. Often, whole lengths can be jointed on the surface and lowered into the trench.

Joining the new drain to the old one at the inspection chamber end involves breaking a hole in the wall of the chamber and chopping away the benching in the base. Bed the new branch channel (of the same material as the new

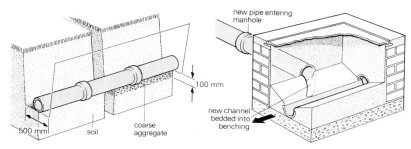

Left: clay pipes can be laid on a flat soil bed (not clay or chalk). Right: pipe laid on a layer of coarse aggregate (gravel)

Joining a new drain to the existing one at an inspection chamber. The new channel is bedded into benching

drain) in cement and sand so that its end discharges over the main channel. Pass the end of the new drain through the hole in the side of the chamber and connect it to the channel following manufacturer's instructions. Build up new benching round the new channel to match the old and finish it off with smooth, sloping sides. The hole in the chamber wall round the new drain should then be filled in with bits of brick mortared into place.

If a new inspection chamber is to be made, the position of the existing drain has to be located and a large hole dug down to it. Be sure to take precautions against the sides collapsing while the chamber is being built. Break into the old drain carefully.

The brick sides of an inspection chamber, and the drain channels and concrete benching should be laid on a thick concrete base.

The old drain will probably be of clay pipes, and it is usually difficult to position the chamber to avoid cutting these. An alternative to cutting is to connect short lengths of PVC or pitch fibre pipe (using proprietary couplings) to the old drain and then lead these into the new inspection chamber.

If the old drain has PVC or pitch fibre pipes, making a new inspection chamber is a bit easier. Before the trench is backfilled (and possibly after), the Building Control Officer will almost certainly want to test the drain to ensure that it is watertight.

In an **air test**, drain stoppers are used to block off the drain – for example, at the entrance to the inspection chamber and at the top of the vent pipe. One of

the drain stoppers has a nipple in it to which a U-tube pressure gauge can be fitted. The drain is then pressurised, usually by blowing down a tube connected to another stopper, until the pressure gauge reads about 100mm of water. To pass, the pressure should not drop below about 75mm within five minutes.

In a **water test**, the drain is stoppered off as before and a length of pipe 1.5m high is connected vertically to the highest point of the drain. This pipe and the drain are filled with water. To pass the test, the amount of water lost from the drain should not exceed 0.05 litres per metre length of the drain over a period of 30 minutes. The water test is more stringent than the air test and can be used to test inspection chambers as well as the drains themselves.

The requirements for passing the test may vary from those given above – the pressure in an air test may be less, and the head of water in a water test may be lower than 1.5m. There are other methods of test, too. A Building Control Officer may carry his own drain-testing equipment; if you hire it, you can do your own tests first.

For backfilling, use aggregate or loose fill first followed by the rest of the materials dug out of the trench. Tamp down in thin layers.

Clearing blockages

If a sink, bath or basin refuses to empty, or empties only slowly, the first thing to do is to check whether the grille of the waste outlet is blocked. If it is not, suspect the trap in the fitting – though if more than one fitting is affected, the blockage is further on in the system.

A drain-cleaning solution can usually be used for clearing a blocked trap – these are caustic and should be used with care. The traditional method is to use a plunger. Block up the overflow, fill the bath or sink with water, grease the rim of the plunger cup, place it over the plug hole and pump up and down on the handle keeping the cup in contact with the surface.

If neither of these methods works the trap itself will have to be cleaned out. Put a bucket under the trap before unscrewing it. Older, metal traps should have an access plug at the bottom: unscrew this with a bar or screwdriver, holding the trap itself securely so that it does not turn. The bottom section of a plastic trap unscrews completely; so does the bottom section of a bottle trap. Poke the blockage clear with a piece of wire – a straightened coat hanger, say. Reassemble the trap, flush through with washing soda, and check for leaks.

If the trap is not blocked, the blockage is further down. If a yard gully is overflowing, the trouble is clearly at that point. Cleaning the grill of grease and dead leaves may be all that is needed, otherwise check the trap in the gully –

this is probably most easily cleaned out by hand (or with a flexible drain rod).

Raising the covers of the inspection chambers in turn, starting with the one nearest the house, will show where the blockage lies – it is in the section of drain between the last chamber that contains water, and the first one that contains none. The problem can usually be solved by **rodding** – unless the chamber which contains waste is the last one before the main sewer in the road, or the chamber which is dry is the one nearest the house. Drain rods are thin, flexible canes that can be screwed together to form a longer rod. They can be hired, and come with a set of different fittings to attach to the business end. Screw a couple of rods together with the corkscrew head on the end and push them down the drain in the direction of the blockage attaching more rods as you go. Be careful to twist the rods in a clockwise direction only, otherwise they may come unscrewed and be lost in the drain. Push against the blockage until it breaks up and clears.

If the chamber nearest the house is dry, the problem lies in the waste pipe to the drain, or whatever length of drain lies between the waste pipe and the inspection chamber. The waste pipe should have access doors in it – these should allow all parts of the pipe to be rodded, or it may be possible to rod at least part of the pipe from the drain end. If all this fails, a drain-cleaning solution may work, or it may be necessary to call

in a specialist drain-cleaning firm.

If the last chamber has water in it, the blockage lies between here and the public sewer in the road – remember that this section of drain is still the responsibility of the householder – or in the interceptor trap, if the chamber has one. If you have not examined your drains before, you may need to probe gently with a drain rod to find out whether there is a trap or not – unless you are willing to feel with your hands. A blocked trap may be freed by plunging (the drain rod set should come with a plunger end) or by hand. If the blockage is further down, it can be rodded through the **rodding point**, once the stopper in the end of the point has been removed: this may be a piece of slate cemented into place, in which case simply break it; or a stone stopper which has to be pulled out. Once free, the drain can be rodded in the normal way – as can a drain without an interceptor trap.

A particular problem with interceptor traps is that the stopper falls out of its own accord and blocks the trap. Since the water can now escape through the rodding eye, the problem is not noticed until the sludge which falls to the bottom of the chamber becomes particularly foul-smelling. Removing the stopper unblocks the trap – but the job can be particularly unpleasant. If the stopper falls out repeatedly, attach a chain to it or replace it with a piece of slate, cut to size and cemented into place.

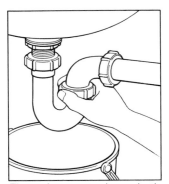
The easiest way to clear a plastic trap is to undo it and poke it clear with a piece of wire

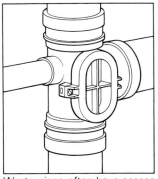
Waste pipes often have access doors which allow all parts of the pipe to be cleared by rodding

If a yard gully is overflowing, clear any debris from the grill and clear out the trap by hand

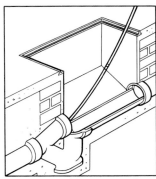
Use the rodding arm of an interceptor trap to clear blockages further down the drain

DAMP, ROT AND WOODWORM

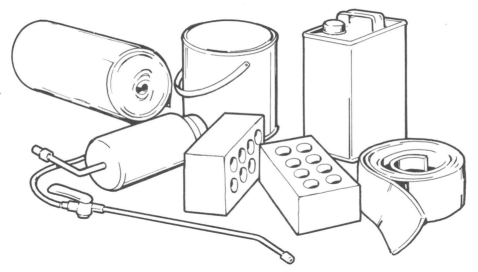

Damp

Dampness in houses can be due to penetrating damp, rising damp or condensation. The treatment for a damp problem depends on which of these three is the cause, so it is important to be able to distinguish between them.

Penetrating damp

As its name suggests, penetrating damp generally occurs when water lands on the outside of a house wall and penetrates through the wall to appear as a damp patch on the inside. It is usually a problem of older houses built without a cavity wall – a wall made of two leaves of brickwork separated by an air cavity – and is often due to some simple defect which results in an unusually large amount of water being deposited on a small area of wall. It is typically associated with leaking gutters or downpipes or leaking water pipes buried in the walls. It may also be associated with a faulty window sill which perhaps lacks a drip channel and so lets water run down on to the wall instead of dripping it clear from the edge of the sill.

Generally, rendering the external face of a wall provides good protection against rain. But if the render is cracked and has pushed away from the brickwork underneath then water can enter through these cracks and collect between the render and the brickwork. And, because the render is basically a waterproof finish, the trapped water will then take the easiest way out – through the wall into the house.

Penetrating damp is more likely to occur in areas of the country where heavy rain is regularly driven on to the face of a wall by strong winds. This is more of a problem in the North and West, especially in Scotland where it is standard practice to render walls to provide an extra barrier.

Penetrating damp problems can occur in cavity walls if the wall ties – plastic or metal strips which provide a structural link between the two skins of brickwork – were incorrectly placed so that they slope downwards to the inner leaf, or if the wall ties were fouled by mortar droppings when the wall was built.

Both can lead to water flowing across the wall tie.

Isolated damp patches on internal walls which are well away from the floor are almost certainly penetrating damp. Damp patches near floor level are more difficult to diagnose: they could be due to any or all three types of dampness. If the damp patches ebb and flow with periods of heavy rain, they are likely to be penetrating damp but they could be one or both of the other types of dampness too.

Rising damp

Rising damp is rather more of a problem: it is more difficult to diagnose and more costly to treat. It is due to the water present in the ground rising up the walls of a house by capillary action. Whether a house is likely to suffer from rising damp depends on the materials used in its construction – in particular, their permeability to water – and whether or not it has a damp-proof course (a non-permeable barrier low down in its walls and often simply referred to as a dpc).

Modern houses are built with fairly porous bricks so you might expect rising damp to be a potential problem. But the cement-based mortar between the bricks is not very permeable to moisture so rising damp is unlikely to occur even when the obligatory dpc has been left out.

Older houses are a totally different story. In these, the mortar between the bricks is based on lime and sand with no cement; cement-based mortar was used to point the mortar courses. Lime/sand mortars are much more permeable than cement-based ones and their permeability almost certainly increases with age, so old houses without a damp-proof course or with one which has deteriorated with age are very susceptible to rising damp.

The most common cause of rising damp in old houses is bridging of the dpc – providing a path for moisture to flow up the wall. This can happen both inside and outside the house.

Soil levels around a house generally rise over the years and

SOME COMMON CAUSES OF PENETRATING DAMP

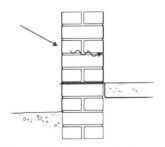

Heavy rain and strong winds can lead to penetrating damp on exposed walls – one solution is to provide extra protection by rendering

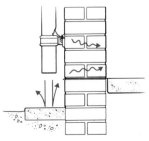

A broken downpipe may direct a large volume of water on to a small area of wall – broken or blocked gutters may also create a problem

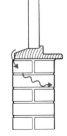

A window sill without a drip channel – or one blocked by paint – may let rain-water run along the underside of the sill on to the wall

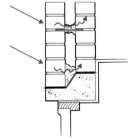

Incorrectly positioned cavity wall ties and mortar droppings inside a cavity wall may lead to damp finding a way across the cavity into the house

SOME COMMON CAUSES OF RISING DAMP

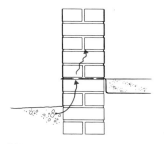  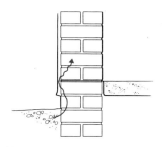 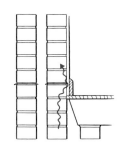

Old dpcs may not provide an effective barrier against rising damp – some slate dpcs go crumbly and soft with age, and bitumen becomes brittle

Soil piled up against a wall (above the level of the dpc) provides a bridge for damp to cross – one of the most common causes of rising damp

If rendering on an outside wall is carried down below the level of the house dpc, it may act as a bridge for damp to cross

Plasterwork inside the house carried down the wall too far may bridge the dpc. This problem is often hidden behind the skirting boards

many houses and their foundations settle. These effects may eventually lead to the level of the ground (or paths) around the house being above the dpc and effectively bridging it. A concrete path around an old house may also have been constructed so that it covers the dpc – again allowing moisture to creep up the wall.

Internal bridging is usually due to plasterwork being carried down the wall too far and again covering the dpc.

The classic symptoms of rising damp are dampness at the base of a wall and a tide-mark about one metre above floor level. The height of the dampness depends on a complicated balance between the amount of moisture feeding into the wall and the rate at which moisture evaporates from it. The higher the evaporation rate, the drier the wall. This rate, in turn, depends on such things as internal and external temperatures and ventilation rates as well as on the amount of moisture carried in the air (humidity) moving across the wall. The height is also subject to some seasonal variation – as soil water 'levels' fall in the summer and rise in the winter so the level of rising damp falls and rises.

The tide-mark created by rising damp is due to the water carrying soluble salts from the soil up the wall. These salts may be hygroscopic – making the problem worse by absorbing moisture from the surrounding air – and they can be very destructive to the plasterwork.

Damp-proof courses All houses built since 1875 should have a dpc (the Public Health Act of that year made the inclusion of one obligatory). Many houses built before that time have a dpc too.

Early damp-proof courses were made of slate. This was followed by bitumen and felt and sometimes lead or copper sheet. Modern damp-proof courses are often thick flexible black polythene sheet. Some kinds of slate do not last well and tend to go soft and crumbly. Bitumen damp-proof courses become very brittle with age but there seems to be no evidence that in this condition they fail to stop rising damp. With all brittle materials however, there is always the possibility

that any settlement which takes place over the years may create cracks in the dpc. But, this will not always lead to rising damp.

Condensation

Air always contains a certain amount of moisture: the exact amount it can hold increases as the temperature rises. At the sort of temperatures found inside a house, air can carry a lot of moisture and when it comes into contact with a cold surface, such as a window, some of this moisture may condense out and appear as droplets of water on the cold surface.

Any part of a house that is colder than the air temperature inside the house – windows and north-facing walls, in particular – is a possible trouble spot for condensation. These rooms where extra water is added to the air – in kitchens and bathrooms – are particularly prone to this problem. Other forms of dampness will push up the moisture content of the air too and can in turn cause condensation problems that would not normally arise.

Condensation is usually worst in the winter months when the air outside a house is cold (so the walls and windows are cold) and when ventilation – which can reduce condensation problems – is kept to a minimum.

COMMON CAUSES OF CONDENSATION

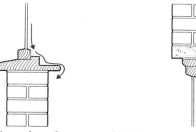 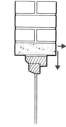

Condensation often forms on windows which are much cooler than the inside air temperature

Lintels can act as a 'cold bridge' between the outside and inside of a house

Which type of damp?

If damp is left untreated, it can lead to many problems. It creates a damp and unhealthy atmosphere and ruins internal decoration. Any woodwork in the house that becomes damp through contact with damp masonry is likely to suffer eventually from wet rot and is susceptible to the much more serious problem of dry rot. Efflorescence on the walls and mould growth on things like furniture and floors can become rampant.

Diagnosis

Generally, the symptoms of **penetrating** damp appear on the exposed walls of a house during periods of sustained rain: the degree of penetration depends on the severity of the rainfall. Penetrating damp patches which appear inside a house are often well defined and, although they tend to disappear in dry weather, they often leave a stain or a line of efflorescence around the area affected. Efflorescence usually appears as a white powdery deposit on the surface of the wall.

Condensation depends on air temperature rather than rainfall and generally occurs in the cold winter months rather than in the summer. It appears on walls inside the house and in those areas which are particularly cold and poorly ventilated – such as the corners of a room, near skirting boards, behind or in cupboards, and on cold bridges – see page 307. Condensation is usually a chronic problem producing diffuse damp patches which in severe cases can support the growth of mould on the wall. Ventilation of the room and extra heating can greatly reduce the extent of condensation, but affect the appearance of rain penetration to a much lesser degree.

Rising damp usually begins at ground floor level and ex-tends to a 'tide-mark' some distance above. Unlike penetrating damp, it does not come and go with the weather but the severity of the problem is subject to some variation with weather and season.

Taking action

Unfortunately, it is not always easy to distinguish penetrating damp from the other causes of dampness and sometimes dampness is a multiple problem. For example, a wall which is wet through penetrating or rising damp becomes susceptible to problems with condensation. So the best course of action is often to look for *all* the possible causes for dampness and to put those right. If dampness appears on a wall:

● the first step is to check for leaking gutters, downpipes or waste pipes that may be feeding water on to the wall

● check window sills for the same reason

● if you have external rendering, check for cracked, loose or crumbly areas above or near the damp patches

● if the wall facing is plain brickwork, inspect the mortar joints – they may need repointing

● try to get rid of any obvious source that may be causing condensation and make sure that enclosed spaces have some ventilation – in particular cupboards under the stairs and larders off the kitchen

● check whether or not the house has a damp-proof course; if it has a suspended wooden floor with ventilation grills set in the wall beneath the floor, the dpc should run in the mortar course at the top or bottom of the grill. At the same time make sure the grills are clear and provide plenty of ventilation for the space beneath the floor

● make sure that any dpc is not being bridged either exter-

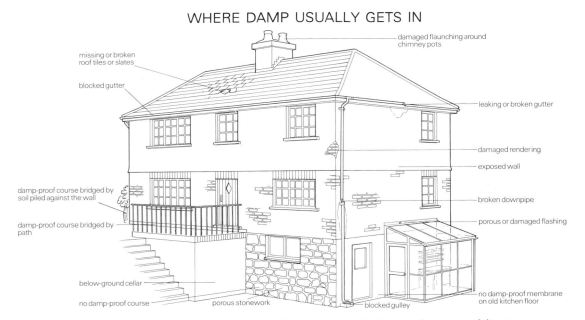

WHERE DAMP USUALLY GETS IN

damaged flaunching around chimney pots

missing or broken roof tiles or slates

blocked gutter

leaking or broken gutter

damaged rendering

exposed wall

damp-proof course bridged by soil piled against the wall

broken downpipe

damp-proof course bridged by path

porous or damaged flashing

below-ground cellar

no damp-proof course

porous stonework

blocked gulley

no damp-proof membrane on old kitchen floor

A good look around the outside of your house – particularly soon after rain – may help diagnose the causes of dampness

nally or internally. To do this you might have to lift a few floorboards and to dig away any soil piled against an outside wall.

If you find any of the above faults, put them right and see if the damp problem goes away within a few months. If it does not, and if the dampness is around the base of a wall you may have rising damp which needs further investigation. At this stage, it might be worthwhile calling in a surveyor or consultant. If the wall is suffering from genuine rising damp, it will be damp through its entire thickness – this may need professional help to demonstrate. A wall suffering from penetrating damp will also be damp through its entire thickness but one suffering from condensation will be damp on the surface and dry beneath.

Damp tests
The most reliable way of finding out the level and extent of dampness in a wall is to drill out samples of the wall using a 9mm masonry drill and to measure their moisture content. The samples should be taken from the mortar courses rather than from the bricks – the mortar is usually wetter than any bricks in contact with it. Material taken from the first 20mm or so should be thrown away and the sample for measurement collected from the centre part of the wall – a wall that is damp on the surface but dry underneath does not have rising damp.

Many ordinary building surveyors investigate dampness with surface-reading electrical moisture meters. These meters can give very high readings if the concentration of salts present is high, even when the wall is not very damp. The readings therefore need careful interpretation and you should make sure that any surveyor you use is aware of this problem. If you have a free survey done by a damp-proofing firm, examine the report with care – rising damp is very difficult to diagnose and some firms err on the safe side by recommending treatment for the problem when it does not exist.

Dealing with penetrating damp

Before you take any remedial action against penetrating damp, you should make sure that the cause of dampness is indeed water penetration and not condensation or rising damp – see opposite page.

Generally, penetrating damp is easier to diagnose when you have cavity walls than when you have solid walls. With cavity walls, visible dampness can be more obviously correlated with rainfall, and drying out afterwards is likely to be more rapid. With solid walls, the greater thickness of masonry tends to smooth out fluctuations with the weather and leads to more diffuse damp patches which can be confused with condensation. Some of the more common faults which result in penetrating damp are mentioned on the opposite page. It helps if you look for these during heavy driving rain so that you can see whether water is being directed on to those walls with a dampness problem. Take this opportunity to look at the areas around doors and windows too.

To confirm a rain penetration problem, trickle water on to the outer leaf of the affected wall across an area about two metres wide and about two or three metres above the position of visible dampness in your house. If the damp patch grows or becomes more distinctly visible within about an hour, penetrating damp is the likely problem.

Occasionally, penetrating damp is caused by leaks in water supply pipes buried in the wall or passing along the cavity. Obviously, in these cases the appearance of damp patches is not correlated with rainfall.

Damp near windows and doors

Rain often penetrates around openings in external walls, such as windows and doors. Unfortunately, the precise cause of the problem can be rather elusive.

First, make sure that visible seals between the frame and wall are intact – they may have been made with a hard-setting material which has deteriorated with age. Small cracks can be blocked with an external wall filler and then primed and painted over; with large cracks the joint should be raked back and then refilled. Non-setting mastic sealants are probably best for this purpose. With windows, you should make sure that the drip channel in the sill is not blocked – by dirt or successive layers of paint. If the problem persists, further examination is necessary.

In **solid** walls, water may penetrate the brickwork round the frame – for example, in a prevailing cross-wind, driving rain may be concentrated on the jamb to one side of a window. A damp problem in this area can be solved by repointing the brickwork followed by local treatment with a surface water repellent.

In **cavity** walls, penetration around door and window openings is usually due to faulty installation of the damp-proof course. Often dampness *over* an opening is due to an accumulation of mortar droppings on the lintel dpc which were allowed to fall down during construction of the brickwork above. The mortar may stop the damp-proof course operating correctly and allow water to cross the cavity.

Water penetration at the *side* of an opening may arise from a badly installed vertical dpc at the cavity closure. Alternatively, the lintel dpc may be incorrectly installed such that it sheds its water too near the window openings – for example, the dpc may not extend sufficiently far beyond the end of the lintel into the cavity.

Penetration at the *bottom* corners of windows is sometimes due to mortar lodged on to the part of the sill which projects into the cavity.

Putting these faults right can be difficult and usually involves removing some brickwork so that you can see what the problem is. Cleaning away simple mortar obstructions is relatively straightforward, but for more complex tasks – such as altering or installing a dpc – you may want to call in a builder.

Damp patches on walls

When damp patches occur on cavity walls well away from door and window openings, the probable causes are splashing or cavity bridges. If there are only one or two areas of dampness, it is worth taking out some of the bricks from the outer leaf so that you can see into the cavity. Provided the mortar is in reasonable condition, you can remove several bricks in a single horizontal run without affecting the structural stability of the wall – but do not overdo it.

To remove the bricks, drill closely-spaced holes in the mortar joints around one brick using a masonry drill, then gently hack away at the remaining mortar with a flat chisel. Carefully remove the bricks in one piece so that they can be replaced later. Make sure that no large pieces of mortar or brick break off and fall into the cavity – these could act as a cavity bridge at some later date.

By using a mirror and torch, you should be able to see for a considerable distance inside the inspection hole – use the mirror for reflecting torch light into the cavity at the same time as for viewing. Sometimes, when you remove the bricks you dislodge the bridge. Inspection of the inner leaf will often reveal whether this was so – for example, you may see staining or a fresh surface on mortar stuck to the inner leaf. A good vantage point for inspection is an outside corner of the house. Bricks removed here give a good view along the cavity without the need for a mirror.

If the dampness is due to a simple mortar or brick obstruction in the cavity, you should be able to dislodge it with a rigid pole or stiff piece of wire. Make sure that any obstruction falls to the foot of the wall, below the dpc.

Widespread dampness

If you cannot identify a simple cause for dampness or if it is widespread, it may be necessary to improve the weather resistance of the external face of the wall. You can do this by covering the wall with cladding, repointing, rendering or by applying a water repellent, paint or clear coating to the outside wall surface. In some circumstances you may have to do a combination of these things.

Cladding

Cladding the outside wall of a house – for example, tile hanging or weatherboarding – offers a virtually foolproof way of preventing penetrating damp. Protection of a wall in this way is expensive but it is easier to do than rendering. However, you must think carefully about the design of protective edge features around windows and doors.

When dealing with solid walls, it may be worthwhile insulating the wall at the same time. There are various systems for applying insulation to the *outside* of a solid wall which can be finished by tile hanging or rendering.

Repointing

If the mortar joints are obviously in poor condition – perhaps crumbling away or with visible cracks – you need to repoint. Rake out the joints to a depth of 10 to 15mm and repoint with fresh mortar, preferably finishing the brickwork with a concave or weather struck joint.

Repointing is a time-consuming job and requires some practice if it is not to look messy. Nevertheless, repointing poor joints is essential and a necessary preliminary to other treatments – such as applying water-proofing solutions or paints. Often, however, it is not necessary to repoint the whole wall – dealing with small areas or even isolated joints may be adequate.

When mortar shows signs of sulphate attack – near old flues, for example – allow the brickwork to dry thoroughly and then repoint with a mortar containing a sulphate-resistant cement. Allow the mortar to cure for at least a month and, assuming that the brickwork is still dry, finish the wall with a coat of water-repellent solution. This treatment should reduce further sulphate attack but it may be necessary at a later date to deal with the problem more thoroughly.

Rendering

Rendering is a technique for coating a wall with a layer of mortar and giving it a textured finish. It generally provides excellent weather protection for exposed brickwork but it can present problems if it is allowed to deteriorate – see page 296.

The choice of materials and the application of a render is a skilled job and is likely to be expensive. Like paint treatments and cladding, it will significantly alter the appearance of your house and may therefore be aesthetically unacceptable. In this respect, you should consult your local authority before proceeding.

Once again, selected areas on the wall can be treated – for example, houses are often designed with render on the first floor only.

If a render is not applied correctly, it can literally be worse than useless. If the render is stronger than the backing brickwork, it will crack. And if this is accompanied by a loss of adhesion over a significant area, water will enter the crack and build up behind the render generating a hydrostatic pressure which may force the water through the wall.

When localised rendering faults are themselves a cause of dampness, it is sometimes possible to remove the defective material only, to prepare the brick surface and the boundaries of the sound mortar, and then to re-render. The match to the old render will nearly always be poor – it can be disguised by painting the whole wall with a masonry paint. Small cracks in render can be stopped and then finished with a masonry paint.

Water repellents

Water repellents for masonry – such as spirit-based silicones – probably provide the most inexpensive and easiest external treatment for penetrating damp and, as they are colourless once dry, they should not seriously affect the appearance of the wall.

These products work by lining the pores of the brickwork with a water-repellent material and so inhibiting capillary absorption of water. They work well – as long as they are applied well.

Application You generally apply water repellents with a brush, working a generous amount on to the areas of brickwork and mortar which need treatment. Use at least the quantity of solution recommended by the manufacturer – a little extra can only improve matters.

With *cavity* walls, most of the water which gets into the cavity has probably passed through fine cracks between the bricks and the mortar – not through the bricks themselves. So, you should concentrate the water repellent on the joints and make a particular point of brushing extra solution along the line separating the bricks and mortar. A useful technique is to dampen the wall with water and allow it to drain for an hour or two before treatment. This will satisfy some of the brick suction, leaving more of the water repellent solution available for the interface cracks.

With *solid* walls, where capillary attraction through the brick pores is also important, you should treat the walls dry. Again pay attention to the joints.

Before treating your wall it is advisable to apply the treatment to a small test area in an inconspicuous position to make sure that the product you intend to use does not affect the appearance of your wall unduly.

Effectiveness Surface water repellents are generally effective for about 10 years before a further application is necessary. The *surface* repellency – seen as an obvious shedding of water – will weather after a short while, but the repellent will remain effective within the pores of the brickwork.

Because these treatments line the brick pores but do not block them completely, the wall can continue to allow water vapour to diffuse through the surface, although at a much reduced rate. The ability of the wall to breathe in this way prevents the build-up of water behind the repellent.

If a repellent treatment is not successful, other measures can be taken later – although it may be necessary to allow the surface of the repellent to weather first.

Small areas Water repellents are often used to treat whole walls but they can be used for the spot treatment of selected areas too. For example, rain penetration around a window frame in a cavity wall may be prevented by treating the area of wall above the frame. This will reduce the volume of water entering the cavity and lessen the problem for the lintel and dpc. However, spot treatment may lead to a patchy appearance, particularly after rain.

Clear coatings

Clear coatings attempt to provide a continuous and impervious film on the surface of the brickwork. They are somewhat more visible than water repellents – many give the wall a varnished look. Clear coatings can seal bricks well, but are likely to be less efficient in bridging cracks. Since clear coatings block the pores of the bricks, they inhibit the movement of water vapour.

Masonry paints

Masonry paints can be used to seal surface brickwork and to bridge narrow cracks, provided the wall is basically sound. Since paints are opaque, deterioration with time can be seen easily and unsealed cracks can be identified. A wide range of paints is available.

The durability of paint obviously depends on the paint itself, how thoroughly the surface of the wall was prepared and how well the paint was applied. When using a masonry paint to reduce penetrating damp, it is of the utmost importance to maintain the integrity of the paint film – cracks will allow water to get in between the paint film and the wall and produce problems similar to those which appear with unsound rendering.

Hiding damp

One of the traditional methods for 'curing' or, more correctly, masking rising damp is to dry line an internal wall, with plasterboard mounted on a batten frame – leaving a ventilated air space between the lining and the wall. This measure can be adopted for penetrating damp too,

but it is expensive and it is much better to cure the problem from outside – if possible. The timber battens used to hold the plasterboard *must* be treated with a wood preservative: and the wall and back of the board should be treated with a fungicide. It is generally advisable to use a vapour check grade of plasterboard. Details of putting up plasterboard are on pages 178 302 and 306.

Cavity wall insulation

Many specialist companies will fill cavity walls with an insulating material to cut down heat loss from your home. Normally, these companies will not fill a wall which shows signs of penetrating damp. Any signs of rain penetration after filling should be reported to the company involved. Even though the cavity fill may itself not be the cause, it will often be necessary to disturb the material in order to diagnose the fault, after which any voids may need to be refilled.

NHBC guarantee

Most houses less than 10 years old are guaranteed against structural defects by the National House Builder's Council. Contact the builder before taking any remedial measures against penetrating damp. If you are not satisfied with the result, approach the NHBC.

Other sources of information

There are a number of useful publications dealing with penetrating damp and related topics. Particularly recommended are:

Department of the Environment Advisory Leaflets
23 Damp-proof courses
27 Rendering outside walls
47 Dampness in buildings
49 Simple lintels
70 Flexible sealing materials
Building Research Establishment Digests
89 Sulphate attack on brickwork
125 Colourless treatments for masonry
196 External rendered finishes
197 Painting walls Part 1: Choice of paint, Part 2: Failures and remedies
These are available from the BRE at Garston, Herts.

Dealing with rising damp

Rising damp can be dealt with in one of two ways. In the first, the problem itself is not cured but its effects are *covered up* by lining the inside wall of the house so that the dampness does not appear on the new surface. In the second, the problem is *cured* by installing a new damp-proof course.

The most satisfactory way of covering up rising damp is by dry lining the wall with plasterboard attached to battens which are fixed to the wall. As when dealing with penetrating damp, the battens must be thoroughly impregnated with a suitable wood preservative and the wall surface and the back of the lining board should be treated with a fungicide. Thermal insulation of the wall is improved by creating the air cavity.

Two other methods for covering rising damp involve stripping off the old plaster and introducing an impervious layer between the wall and new plaster. One method uses a backing of bitumen lathing which should be mechanically fixed to the wall and then plastered over. The other involves applying a rubber/tar or bitumen preparation to the wall and covering this with sand before it sets and finally plastering over this.

All these methods of covering damp reduce evaporation of water from the wall and are likely to drive the damp further up the wall, leading to the acceleration of rot in joinery such as wooden window frames.

DRY LINING A WALL

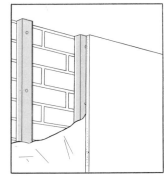

Treat the wall surface thoroughly with a fungicide and nail on battens (which have been treated with preservative)

Use special vapour check plasterboard or staple polythene to the battens before putting on the plasterboards

BITUMEN LATHING

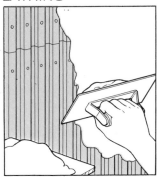

Hack off the old plaster and nail bitumen lathing to the wall. Overlap the strips – about 75mm – and use nails every 150mm

You can plaster over the bitumen lathing immediately but if you want to decorate at once, stick plasterboard to the lathing

Installing a new damp-proof course

There are essentially four ways of introducing a new damp-proof course into an existing wall, but only one of these methods – inserting a new physical membrane (dpc) into the wall – is certain to cure rising damp in all circumstances. This is often referred to as the traditional method. If a new physical membrane is installed properly, there is no way that moisture can penetrate across it. The other methods are: injecting a chemical barrier into the wall; using a technique known as electro-osmosis; and inserting porous tubes in the wall.

Putting in a physical barrier
Any physical membrane introduced into the wall will have to be let into a course of mortar. So, the first problem is deciding which mortar course to use. In older houses suffering from rising damp which have suspended wooden floors, the new dpc should always be installed below floor level and at least 150mm above outside ground level. The dpc should be inserted below the level of any wooden wallplates or joists which are in direct contact with outside walls. If the structure of the house makes this impossible, apply liberal quantities of wood preservative where necessary. Apply wood preservatives as well to any timbers which have become damp.

In houses with solid floors which have a damp-proof floor membrane, the dpc should be inserted as near to the top level of the floor as possible and any remaining gap on the inside wall should be painted with a bituminous-type material. This will protect any wooden skirting boards placed over the gap which are in direct contact with the wall.

Once you have chosen the mortar course in which to insert the damp-proof membrane, the next step is to clear the course on both sides of the wall. Remove any obstructions such as skirting boards, electrical connections or pipes. Then cut through the entire thickness of the mortar course using a tungsten-carbide tipped chainsaw specially designed for the purpose. Insert the damp-proof membrane – usually a flexible black polythene material – and drive wedges into the gap between the brickwork and the membrane until this gap can be back filled with mortar. Do not tackle any more than about one metre of wall at a time to prevent settlement and structural damage as the thickness of the mortar course is removed. Separate lengths of the membrane material should be over-lapped.

The equipment needed for inserting a physical membrane can usually be hired from a tool-hire firm, but you should take great care when using it – chainsaws are potentially dangerous tools and there is always the possibility of cutting through electrical cables or gas or water pipes you did not know about.

There are many firms who specialise in this sort of installation and it may be wiser to call one in rather than to attempt the job yourself. The technique does have its limitations and is the most expensive. It cannot be used on very thick walls or on walls with a loose rubble infill. It can only be used on walls with regular mortar courses – such as brickwork or coursed stone blockwork – not on the random coursed flint walls that are found in various parts of the country.

Chemical injection
Of the non-traditional methods, chemical injection seems to be the most proven and popular alternative. In this system, a chemical water repellent is injected throughout the thickness of the wall to act as a partial or complete moisture barrier and to stop moisture rising from the ground.

Three types of water repellent are in common use: the first consists of a silicone material carried in a white spirit solvent; the second is an aluminium stearate compound also in white spirit; the third is a silicone material using water as the solvent.

The water-based silicone liquid is usually fed into the wall under very low pressure and allowed to diffuse into the structure over quite a long period of time – sometimes a matter of days. The other two fluids do not mix with water so they are pumped into the wall under quite high pressures to displace at least some of the moisture present.

Once the fluids have penetrated the voids or pores in the masonry, various curing processes take place and the pores become lined with a very thin clinging film of water-repellent material. These materials do not completely block the pores – treated pores will stop liquid moisture passing through them but they will not stop moisture vapour. This allows the wall to breathe.

Chemical injection should not be used to stop water which is trying to push through a wall with a substantial pressure behind it. This sort of situation can arise in a basement which is partly below the level of the soil water table.

The efficiency of chemical injection really depends on how well a wall is penetrated by the water-repellent fluid. In practice, it is almost impossible to treat every water carrying pore in a wall successfully and, in general, the wetter the wall is and the less uniform it is, the poorer are the chances of successful treatment. Current evidence suggests that these treatments will be effective enough at coping with the levels of dampness found in ordinary solid brick walls as long as they are properly applied. Current evidence also suggests that chemical injection treatments should have a life-span of 20 years or so and perhaps longer. The firms operating these systems invariably give 20 or 30 year guarantees.

Of all the techniques for damp proofing, chemical injection is the easiest to do yourself and all the necessary pumping equipment can be hired, usually from a tool-hire firm.

Start by drilling holes spaced 100 to 150mm apart at the chosen level in the brickwork or mortar course. Inject each hole in turn, making sure that the fluid spreading from each hole meets up with the fluid spreading from adjacent holes. The depth of the holes depends on the technique being used but the aim should always be to inject each leaf of brickwork thoroughly. With high pressure injection systems, this means a double injection of the standard 225mm double-leaf solid wall – one injection from each side. Each leaf is injected separately with holes about 10mm in diameter drilled just beyond the mid-point of the leaf – about 75mm deep. The two injections can be carried out from one side of the wall by drilling the first leaf, injecting

WAYS OF PUTTING IN A NEW DPC

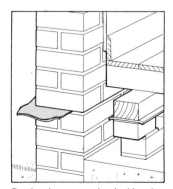

Putting in a new physical barrier involves a lot of hard work – a slot has to be cut in the brickwork for the dpc

Chemical injection using a water-based silicone material being allowed to diffuse into the wall over days

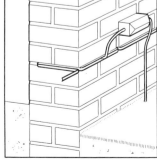

Damp proofing using the electro-osmosis system. Despite technical worries, good results are claimed in use

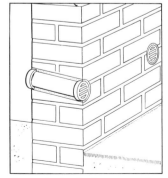

A method of damp proofing using porous tubes set into the wall to increase evaporation of water from the wall

and then drilling the same hole deeper into the second leaf and injecting again. A detailed guide to the installation of chemical damp-proof courses is issued as a Code of Practice by the British Chemical Dampcourse Association.

Electro-osmosis

This is an electrical method of damp-proofing and cannot be installed on a d-i-y basis – a specialist firm must be called in.

There are two types of system. The **active** systems need power to operate them. This is usually taken from the mains supply to the house. The **passive** systems need no electrical power and have been far more widely used because their installation is simple and cheap.

The passive systems are claimed to work on the principle that a damp wall contains an electrical charge and by installing a continuous length of metal conductor in the wall at damp-proof course level and earthing the circuit to the ground via metal earthing rods, the charge is removed and the rising damp driven down. This explanation has been the cause of some controversy in the scientific world as some scientists believe that if the electrical charge or potential is created by the rising damp in the first place, then getting rid of the potential should cause the reverse to happen and

damp to rise even further up the wall.

The active systems do employ a well accepted and easily demonstrated scientific principle – an electrical voltage applied to a wet porous material will cause water to move within the material. However, a question mark still remains as to whether the size of the voltages used in practice are high enough to have a significant effect and whether the same potential will cause water to move in opposite directions in different building materials.

Porous tubes

The use of porous tubes, set in a wall at closely-spaced intervals, to control rising damp is not new – the technique was in use as far back as the 1930s. Any device which increases the evaporation rate from a wall suffering from rising damp must help to reduce the level and severity of the dampness. The question is how much more effective the technique of boring the holes and cementing porous tubes in them is over simply boring holes and leaving them without tubes. It is claimed that the tubes draw moisture to them but whether any soluble salts are drawn into the tubes to block them is less certain.

Replastering

Many firms who treat rising damp insist

on some replastering as part of the treatment and issue a tight specification for replastering work.

Strictly speaking, visibly undamaged plaster containing no hygroscopic salts does not need replacing but plaster is rarely undamaged where genuine rising damp has been at work. Another reason for replastering is that although an effective damp-proof course has been installed, it can take a year or more for the residual dampness in the wall to evaporate away. Something needs to be put on the wall to prevent the residual dampness and salts from appearing again on newly-plastered internal surfaces. For this reason, the type of plastering specified is intended to act as an effective moisture barrier in its own right.

There are two points to bear in mind here: first, the installer's guarantee is likely to become null and void if the plastering specification is not strictly adhered to; second, the new plaster could quite easily mask an ineffective damp-proof course.

Reports in Handyman Which?

PHYSICAL DAMP-PROOF COURSES

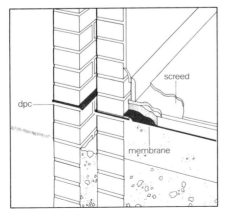

Damp-proof courses in solid floors should be 150mm above outside soil level and to keep floors inside the house dry, a dpm is used under the screed

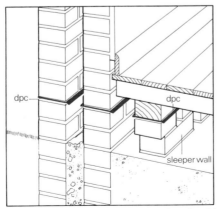

With suspended timber floors, a dpc should be laid beneath the sleeper walls so that the wallplates they support remain dry and are less likely to rot

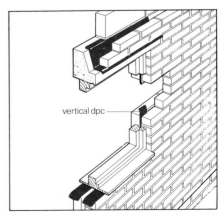

Wherever there is a break in an external wall – for a door or window – a dpc is needed. Typically the dpc is tucked into a groove in the frame and sandwiched between the bricks

Condensation

Condensation creates unpleasant living conditions and can damage the structure of a house. Water vapour will condense out of the air and appear on a surface if there is too much water vapour in the air for the surfaces it is in contact with or, put the other way round, if the temperature of the surface is too low for the air in contact with it.

The maximum amount of water vapour that can be held by air increases dramatically as the temperature of the air increases. Normally, the air inside a house is not saturated with water vapour. In the example on page 308, air at 15°C may contain only half its maximum amount of water vapour (this would mean around 5.4g of water in each kg of dry air

compared with a maximum of 10.7g/kg), but as this air is cooled down it becomes saturated and condensation takes place. The temperature at which saturation occurs – in this case about 5°C – is called the *dewpoint* of the air and this form of condensation is normally referred to as **surface** condensation. It often occurs on the inside surface of walls, and on glass windows and doors. When condensation occurs on a wall it is not always visible – the only indication might be mould.

Condensation can also occur within the thickness of a wall (normally called **interstitial** condensation) and can often go undetected for a long time before any serious damage is observed.

Curing condensation

Unless you understand the causes of condensation and how all the potential cures interplay, you will never be able to deal with the problem effectively. Unfortunately, there are a great many reasons why condensation occurs. In simple terms it depends on four **main factors** – the *thermal insulation* of walls, windows and so on; the amount of *heat* you put into your house; how much *ventilation* you provide; how much *moisture* – from things like baths – you produce.

Basically, to cure condensation you have to warm the affected part of the house or reduce the amount of water vapour in the air, or both. But, in practice, it is not quite as simple as this: you have to get the right balance between the four main factors and, to make things even more difficult to work out, all four are individually quite complicated – see **Secondary questions** in the Table.

You may obtain the solution to a condensation problem by changing one factor but in many situations it may be desirable (or necessary) to change two or more. For example, a condensation problem on the inside surface of an external wall may be remedied by:

● increasing the heat input to the room
● increasing the thermal insulation of the wall
● applying a lightweight lining (insulated or uninsulated) to the inside surface of the wall
● increasing the ventilation of the room.

Before making any decision about which way to solve a condensation problem, consider all the options, taking into account cost and whether the solution will be effective in the short or long term.

THE PARAMETERS AFFECTING CONDENSATION

Main factors	Secondary questions to think about
Thermal insulation	Does your house have a heavyweight structure (plaster on brick or concrete walls, for example) which is slow to warm up and to cool down?
	If so, is there a lightweight lining (plasterboard on timber battens, with vapour check or barrier) over the inside?
	Does your house have a lightweight structure (timber-framed walls, for example) which rapidly warms up and cools down?
Heat input	Do you have a quick response heating system (forced warm air, gas or electric fires) which is used for long periods? Or intermittently each day?
	Do you have a slow response heating system (hot water central heating – not small bore or micro-bore – or open solid fuel fires) which has to be used over long periods and cannot be used successfully intermittently?
Ventilation	Do you have the means to provide a little ventilation in winter?
	Do you have a mechanical extraction system (an extractor fan which can rapidly get rid of steam and water vapour from your kitchen during cooking and washing and from your bathroom, especially if it has a shower)?
	Do you have the means to provide ventilation in summer? (Condensation should not be a problem in summer.)
Moisture production	Do you produce excessive moisture when cooking (by using saucepans without lids, say)?
	Do you produce a lot of moisture when washing and bathing?
	Do you dry clothes in the house? (Tumble driers should be ducted to outside.)
	Do you use flue-less gas or paraffin heaters? (These release water vapour into the air.)
	Does the house have a lot of occupants? (People breathe out water vapour.)

Thermal insulation

If all the other factors remain the same, any improvement in the thermal insulation of your house will result in higher air and surface temperatures and consequently reduce the risk of condensation. (But if improved insulation leads to less heat input, the condensation problem may not be solved.)

Slated or tiled pitched roofs Increasing the insulation on top of the ceiling directly below the roof is generally the easiest improvement to carry out. This is known as providing loft insulation and is also the most cost effective way of insulating your house.

Insulating materials such as mineral wool, preferably about 100mm thick, can be laid between the joists. The insulation must be laid evenly between the joists with no gaps and must be taken down to the eaves to cover the wallhead, whilst ensuring that ventilation openings are not blocked – see also page 206.

As improving the insulation of the ceiling will make the roof space colder, the movement of moist air from the house into the roof space must be kept to a minimum. Gaps in the ceiling – around pipes, pipe ducts and so on – must be sealed as well as possible. The roof (loft) hatch should also be sealed and fitted with a catch to prevent movement. As long as you have had no previous serious problems with condensation in your roof space, the above precautions should be sufficient. However, if condensation occurs, you will have to improve the ventilation in the roof space by providing ventilation openings at the eaves, if they are not already there. Or reduce the moisture content of the air by using extractor fans.

If you insulate your loft, you should also insulate the cold water tank and pipes.

Flat roofs (bitumen felt or metal covered) Although improved insulation may be possible, how it should be done depends on the type of roof. Repair or renewal of existing roofs should be of the over-deck insulated type – see British Standard 5250, 1975, Basic data for the design of buildings: the control of condensation in dwellings.

External walls You can increase the insulation properties of a wall by applying extra insulation material to the inside or outside surface of the wall or within the wall itself. As a d-i-y task, fitting internal linings is the most practical. Cavity wall insulation has to be left to specialist contractors (except when building a new house) and insulating the outside of a wall involves a considerable number of alterations.

A lightweight lining built on to the inside of a masonry wall produces a surface which warms up and cools down considerably faster than the wall itself – so the temperature of the surface directly in contact with the air is more able to keep in step with the air temperature in the house. This will considerably reduce the risk of condensation if your house is intermittently heated – unoccupied during the day with little or no heating on followed by very large moisture and heat inputs during the early evening.

A plasterboard lining is generally sufficient to prevent surface condensation on a cavity wall but insulated plasterboard is preferable for a solid wall. When lining a cavity wall, fill the gap between the plasterboard and the existing wall with insulation – this will improve the thermal insulation without any further loss of floor area.

When you build on a lightweight wall lining you must provide a vapour check to restrict the flow of water vapour through the wall so that interstitial condensation is kept to a minimum. This can be achieved either by using special vapour check board or by stapling a separate sheet of polythene to the timber battens holding the board to the wall. Unfortunately, you should not use this method on dense concrete walls. In this case, a vapour barrier (rather than a vapour check) is essential and this is difficult to provide practically.

You can also improve the condensation resistance of a cavity wall by sticking insulating material directly to the inside surface of the wall (this technique is not suitable for solid walls). The insulating material usually comes in rolls of thin sheet polystyrene which is generally permeable to water vapour, so the risk of interstitial condensation is high.

In cases where condensation problems do not exist, this technique has little or

USING INSULATION TO REDUCE CONDENSATION

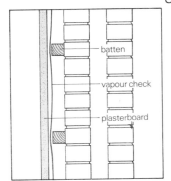

Insulating a cavity wall using plasterboard nailed to timber battens – these should be at least 20mm square

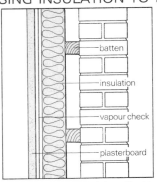

Insulating a solid brick wall with insulated plasterboard – again the battens should be at least 20mm square

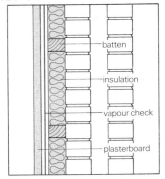

When dry lining a cavity wall it's worthwhile increasing the size of the battens to 50mm, and filling the gap with insulation

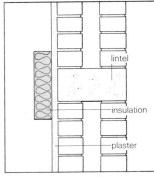

To overcome a cold patch on a wall – caused by a dense concrete lintel, say – stick extruded polystyrene over it

no value, especially if you decorate over the insulation with a vinyl wallpaper, which will then act as a vapour check.

Cold bridges These occur when the thermal insulation of small areas of a wall is considerably lower than the wall which surrounds them. Typical cold bridges are window lintels and solid columns forming part of a wall. Condensation problems on cold bridges can seldom, if ever, be satisfactorily prevented by adjusting the heat input, ventilation or moisture production. So remedial treatment is generally necessary.

The easiest way to overcome a cold patch on a wall is to stick insulation over it. Choose a type of insulation which is *not* permeable to water vapour – use extruded polystyrene not expanded polystyrene such as bead board. It may be possible to hide the insulation in the plaster finish, however in many instances, techniques similar to those described for improving wall insulation will have to be used to obtain a pleasant and satisfactory wall finish.

Windows Condensation on the glass of single glazed windows can be overcome by installing double glazing. However in many cases, condensation will still occur on metal window frames. Double glazing at present is barely cost effective as far as fuel saving is concerned but when window frames have to be replaced then double glazed windows should be considered. Further details can be found on page 228.

Heat input

In a house which is well insulated and has a heating system which supplies a rigidly fixed low amount of heat, the control of a condensation problem is dependent on increasing the ventilation and reducing the moisture production. In practice, it may not be possible to achieve control over condensation and to retain comfort conditions.

Make regular checks to ensure the existing heating system is operating efficiently. Think about installing additional time or temperature controls (or both) to regulate operational efficiency and to obtain maximum fuel saving – the

ON/OFF operation of the heating system could be altered to match the requirements of a heavyweight or a lightweight structure depending on the category your house falls into.

Ventilation

Ventilation of a house is necessary to remove odours from cooking, smoking and so on and to provide air for people to breathe. When you provide ventilation, the outside air which enters has a lower moisture content and so dilutes the moisture content of the air inside the house which in turn reduces the risk of condensation.

Traditionally, fortuitous ventilation through small gaps and cracks around windows and from flues (especially when fires were burning) provided more than enough fresh air. However, many modern houses have better sealed windows, doors and no flues. It is therefore essential to provide adequate means to ventilate a house without excessive heat loss and discomfort from draughts or rain penetration.

Extractor fans These move steam or water vapour from the inside of a house to the outside. They should be fitted in all kitchens.

The fan should have an extract capacity of at least 80 litres/sec (or 300m^3/h). In large kitchens where more space is available, a larger fan should be installed (say one or two sizes up and with speed control). Generally, it should be fitted as high as possible above floor level, though in modern houses with low ceilings, fans may be fitted into the upper part of a window. It should also incorporate a shutter which may be closed to limit the ventilation rate or to prevent unpleasant draughts.

If your house is heated by natural gas or smokeless solid fuel appliances, **you must ensure** that an adequate supply of outside air is available to these appliances, otherwise in a well-sealed house reversal of the flow of flue gases may be serious enough to prove fatal. If in doubt, consult your local Gas Board or Solid Fuel Advisory Service.

Cooker hoods To obtain any appreciable reduction in condensation, cooker hoods must be ducted to the outside. Unfortunately, the design of many cooker hoods leaves a lot to be desired, resulting in condensation within the hood or ducting, and the condensed water dropping on to the cooker. Cleaning the inside of the ductwork may be difficult.

Windows Traditionally, windows could be opened a very small amount at high level to provide ventilation during the winter. With many modern picture windows this is not possible so controllable ventilators at high level are essential.

Secondary windows, although desirable in many ways, can greatly reduce fortuitous ventilation in houses to such an extent that condensation occurs in places previously unaffected. This fortuitous ventilation can be further reduced by blocking existing flues.

Home improvements which reduce ventilation rates may, as a side effect, so upset the balance between the factors affecting condensation that you will have to make further changes to redress the balance. These changes may range from a slight change in your pattern of living to a major building alteration – this will depend on existing conditions.

Weatherstripping, draught sealing In theory, all gaps causing unnecessary ventilation should be sealed to improve insulation. In practice, this will reduce ventilation and, if condensation is a problem, all weatherstripping and gap sealing should be carried out in stages, carefully observing the effect of each stage before proceeding to the next one.

Moisture production

The amount of water vapour present in the inside air determines the dewpoint of that air. So, the amount of steam or water vapour discharged internally should, wherever possible, be kept to a minimum, or extracted quickly to the outside.

If your house is affected by condensation and at the same time you use flueless gas or paraffin appliances, either provide additional ventilation or change the way you heat your house.

UNDERSTANDING CONDENSATION – NOTES FOR THE ENTHUSIAST

The Humidity Graph has been simplified for explanatory purposes. Consider air at a dry bulb temperature of 15°C, when saturated it has a moisture content of 10.7g/kg dry air and this is represented by point A on the saturation curve. Likewise, if air at 15°C contains only half its maximum amount of water vapour (5.35g/kg dry air) this is represented by point B. Cooling this air results in its relative humidity increasing to 100% at point C, known as the dewpoint of this sample of air – 4.8°C.

Dewpoint The temperature at which a sample of moist air becomes saturated.

Moisture content The ratio of the mass of water vapour present in the air to the mass of dry air, usually expressed as grams per kilogram of dry air.

Percentage saturation The ratio (expressed as a percentage) of the actual moisture content to the saturated moisture content of air at the same temperature. When dealing with condensation problems, the percentage saturation of air should always be expressed with the air temperature – x% saturation at y°C.

Vapour pressure The water vapour in the air contributes to the total atmospheric pressure and is expressed in millibars. The vapour pressure in a heated house is higher than the vapour pressure of the outside air, due to the various activities taking place – heating, washing and so on. This difference in vapour pressure causes water vapour to move from inside a house through the walls (when porous to water vapour) to the outside.

Relative humidity The ratio (expressed as a percentage) of the actual vapour pressure to the saturated vapour pressure of air at the same temperature.

For general condensation problems in dwellings, adequate accuracy is obtained by assuming that relative humidity may also be expressed as percentage satura-

tion. Likewise, it is essential to express relative humidity with reference to the air temperature – x% r.h. at y°C.

Measuring relative humidity

To obtain the humidity condition of a sample of air, simultaneous measurements of dry and wet bulb temperatures are made with a sling psychrometer. These readings when transferred to a humidity graph (or Humidity tables) show the physical properties of the air sample. From the Graph, it can be seen that if a sample of air has a dry bulb temperature of 15°C and a

wet bulb temperature of 9.8°C the intersection of the vertical and oblique lines occurs at point B from which its moisture content, relative humidity and so on can be obtained.

Further information

For more detailed information regarding condensation refer to BRE Digest 110 Condensation which is available from HMSO or the Building Research Establishment. Also useful are BRE Digest 108 Standard U-values and BRE Digest 190 Heat losses from dwellings.

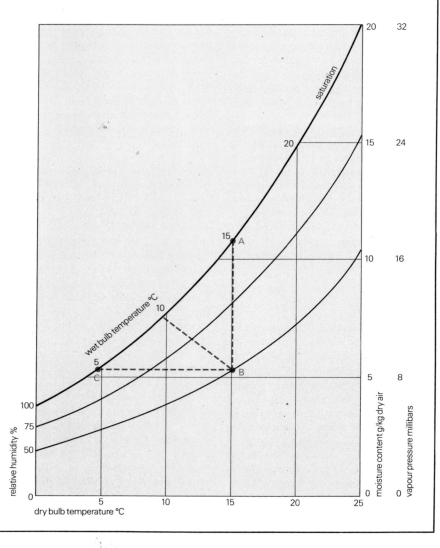

Rot

Timber may decay if it is exposed to persistently damp conditions for a long time – months rather than weeks. Any temporary wetting, from water spilt on a wood floor say, will not set up decay if it is dried out quickly.

Rot usually develops where timber is in contact with damp brickwork or concrete. It is not the moisture itself that causes decay but rather wood-rotting fungi which can grow in the damp wood.

The areas of a house most susceptible to rot are:
● cellars
● bathrooms and lavatories
● solid floors laid directly on concrete and covered with linoleum or vinyl tiles
● conservatories
● window frames, porches and garage doors in houses built since around 1945.

Inspection should begin with a careful examination of the walls outside to see if there are any indications of leaking gutters and downpipes, such as green staining from growths of algae and mosses. Then have another look during a heavy shower of rain to pinpoint the problem areas. If damp is discovered, any internal woodwork in contact with these areas should be carefully inspected.

Rot usually begins in wood that is in direct contact with the outside walls and it may remain undetected until it has reached an advanced stage. Only by taking up the floorboards alongside an external wall is it possible to find out whether the ends of joists in the walls are sound. Leaks from gutters also frequently cause decay in lintels over the windows.

Unsound wood is fairly easy to recognise as it is usually warped and shows signs of its surface collapsing. This becomes more obvious after any damp problems have been solved and the wood has dried out – the decayed areas shrink much more than the sound wood. Any areas of woodwork under suspicion should be prodded with a sharp pointed tool, such as a bradawl or a small screwdriver. The point will slip in easily if the wood is rotten, whereas sound woodwork will resist both insertion and withdrawal.

If decay is suspected in a floor, take up the floorboard which runs alongside the outside wall and prod the ends of the joists below. Prod all round the ends and pay particular attention to the areas where the joists enter the outside wall. In old buildings with cellars the ground floor joists can often be conveniently inspected from below.

Rot should also be suspected in a floor if wide gaps appear between the skirting and the floorboards. The suspicion is confirmed by the development of fungal growths on the surface. Suspect decay in wood block flooring if the blocks tend to become loose or to curl up at the sides.

Rot in window frames and external doors usually occurs at the joints between the lower rails and the upright pieces. It is particularly prevalent when glazing beads (the small strips of wood that fix the glass) have been fixed without external putty.

Types of rot

For practical purposes, decay in house woodwork can be classed as either wet rot or dry rot.

Wet rot is caused by fungi that can only spread as far as the moisture has penetrated and their strands (root-like growths) cannot penetrate brickwork. There are a number of fungi that can cause this type of rot. In floors the most common one is the cellar fungus, *Coniophora puteana* (formerly *C. cerebella*). This makes affected wood darken and leads to cracks forming which mainly run along the grain of the wood. The fungus often forms narrow, dark brown strands on the surface of the wood.

Dry rot is a much more serious type of decay which, in the UK, is caused by the dry rot fungus, *Serpula* (formerly known as *Merulius*) *lacrymans*. Like all other fungi it needs damp conditions to become established but once it gets a hold it forms root-like strands, sometimes as thick as a pencil, which enable it to spread into surrounding less damp timber and to penetrate through walls and masonry. The infection can spread from one room to another and the strands can be found in walls between the plaster and the brickwork. They can also travel through mortar joints seeking out any pieces of timber in the walls.

Wood attacked by dry rot tends to break up into dry brick-shaped pieces and usually has grey, felt-like growths of fungus on its surface. However, if the air around the fungus is very moist, it can form white, fluffy cotton wool-like growths which often have tinges of lilac or yellow on them. When the fungus has been growing for a year or two, it produces fruiting bodies on the surface of the wood or on adjacent brickwork. These are pancake-shaped, or thick brackets with a wrinkled surface that soon becomes a bright, rusty red colour as the spores (seeds) develop. These spores are minute, oval cells about 0.01mm long. They are produced in such abundance that the surrounding surfaces soon become covered with what looks like a fine, rust-coloured dust. When this dust is found on the surface of a floor, it is a sure indication that the dry rot fungus is present somewhere nearby. Sometimes the appearance of the fruiting body is the first indication that dry rot has attacked your timber.

Mould is the least worrying fungal growth that is likely to attack your house. Heavy growths of mildew and dark-coloured moulds may develop as a result of condensation on cold walls. This indicates that there is lack of ventilation and insufficient heating, but it does not mean that the woodwork is decaying.

Dealing with rot

Once the type of rot has been established, repairs should be undertaken as soon as possible. At this stage, it is worth thinking about treating against woodworm too – see page 313. Fortunately, dry rot is much less widespread than wet rot and the latter is much easier to deal with and much less expensive to treat.

Treating wet rot inside houses

First, try to discover the source of the damp and deal with this immediately – see *Damp* starting on page 296. Inadequate ventilation below suspended floors is often the cause of dampness and decay in flooring. This should be improved by inserting galvanised iron air vents measuring about 225mm by 400mm in the outside walls.

Next, carefully examine all the woodwork around the decayed area to find out how far the rot has spread. Sometimes rot does not show on the surface and can only be detected by prodding the wood. It may be necessary to drill into beams and other large timbers to find out whether they are sound in the middle.

All decayed wood should be cut away beyond the last signs of incipient decay. Where damp is likely to persist, or recur – such as skirtings in damp walls in basements, or lintels embedded in solid walls – it is better to replace the decayed wood with an inert material such as concrete. Elsewhere, use replacement timbers that have been treated with a wood preservative. Take the opportunity to treat existing sound timbers exposed during the repair work and any rubbish, particularly bits of wood below floors, should be cleared away.

If the site on which the house is built is damp, and the concrete or soil below the ground floor is also damp, you should take the opportunity when renewing the floor to cover the ground with a screed containing a stout polythene sheeting as a damp-proof membrane – see page 183.

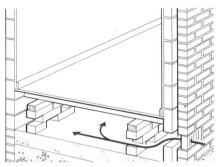

Suspended ground floors need a good circulation of air beneath them to avoid damp and decay – see page 173 for fitting air bricks

Treating wet rot in external joinery

Rot in window frames, external glazed doors and porches has become increasingly prevalent in post-war buildings because:
● the timber used (frequently Baltic Redwood) now contains a fairly high proportion of non-durable sapwood which is highly permeable to moisture
● windows are now often fixed near the external face of buildings, instead of being set deeper into the thickness of the wall

● glazing beads are sometimes used to fix the glass in windows and doors, without external putty.

Wet rot generally starts by rain-water finding its way into the joints between the horizontal and the vertical parts of a window or door frame, making the wood wet and ripe for attack by the fungal spores which enter the joints and set up rot. The organisms that cause decay start to grow into the end grain of the wood. The paint over the joints soon begins to flake off, the wood of the frame becomes

softened and eventually rots away. In severe attacks the glass may fall out of the window or door.

Frames which have been severely attacked must be removed and replaced. But if the attack is spotted early on and the first signs of softening detected (by prodding with a sharp-pointed tool), further progress of the decay can be checked. To do this, drill holes near the joint in both the bottom rail and the vertical pieces, insert plastic valves into these holes and inject a fungicidal wood preservative into the woodwork.

Treating dry rot

An attack of dry rot is generally much more extensive than it appears at first sight. Sometimes when the first visible symptom is a fruiting body on the surface of a skirting board, the actual area affected may be many square metres. To eradicate dry rot it is essential to trace out the full extent of the attack, taking up floorboards and pulling off lath and plaster wallcoverings to find out just how far the fungus has spread into the adjacent brickwork.

As when dealing with wet rot, the source of the initial dampness that enabled the fungus to develop must be found and treated. If ventilation below the floors is poor it must be improved.

All decayed wood that shows signs of attack or growth of fungus should be cut out taking with it a margin of about 450mm of sound wood beyond the last visible signs of attack. If dry rot is found on one side of a wall, the fungus will probably have penetrated to the other side too, so woodwork in the adjoining

room must also be carefully inspected.

After removing all decayed wood, the plaster should be stripped from the walls until no further fungal threads are found on the surface of the brickwork. Then strip off another 300mm or so beyond this as a safety margin. Collect all infected wood and plaster in large polythene bags and either burn it or dispose of it as quickly as possible.

After stripping off the plaster, remove any pieces of wood, such as fixing blocks, which are embedded in the wall. Brush down the surface of the brickwork and take out any loose mortar from the joints. Before replastering the wall, swab down the surface of the brickwork with a fungicide, such as 5 per cent solution in water of sodium orthophenylphenate or sodium pentachlorophenate. These two chemicals may not be readily available in local shops, so it may be easier to buy a proprietary fluid specially formulated for treating infected walls. Apply the fungicide until the surface of the wall is saturated: use either a large brush or a coarse spray from a low pressure sprayer (never use a fine spray). Always wear a face mask and pvc gloves when applying a fungicide.

So far as is possible, new timbers should not be brought into direct contact with the old brickwork – for example, rest the ends of new joists on felt where they enter a wall. As an additional precaution, brickwork around window or door openings should be covered with a layer of zinc oxychloride plaster or paint (ZOC) where it comes into contact with new wooden frames.

All new timber used in repairs should be thoroughly treated with a wood preservative. Give new joinery and flooring two full flowing brush-on coats and stand the ends of joists in a bucket of preservative for at least ten minutes. Sound timber exposed during the work should be brushed over with a preservative to kill any infection that might be on its surface.

The eradication of dry rot can be a major undertaking requiring a knowledge of building construction. A limited outbreak can, however, be dealt with successfully by a skilled d-i-y enthusiast by following the lines laid down above. Further advice on the matter can be obtained from pamphlets published by the Building Research Establishment, and by the British Wood Preserving Association. Should you decide that the

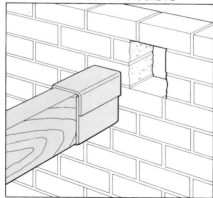

TREATING NEW JOISTS

Covering the ends of new joists

work is beyond your capabilities you can employ a remedial treatment company to undertake the task. In this case, you would be well advised to employ a firm which is a member of The British Wood Preserving Association and one which employs well-trained operatives.

Wood preservatives

There is a wide choice of wood preservatives available and it is important to choose the right one for the job.

Tar oil preservatives (such as creosote) are suitable for preserving fencing and other external woodwork such as half timbering, outhouses, chicken houses and barns. They are cheap and easily applied by brush or spray. However, wood treated with tar oils cannot subsequently be painted, and tar oils have a strong, persistent smell. Tar oil preservatives should not be used for greenhouses – their fumes can damage plants.

Water-borne preservatives consist of salts, which are toxic to fungi and insects, dissolved in water. Wood treated with such preservatives has no smell and once it is dry it can be painted with oil paints or with vinyl emulsions.

Organic solvent preservatives contain chemicals toxic to fungi and insects, dissolved in an organic solvent – usually white spirit. They penetrate dry wood well (better than water-borne types) and once the solvent has evaporated, treated wood can be painted. When freshly applied they have some odour but this disappears. Wood treated with these preservatives gives off flammable vapours: keep all flames or electric sparks away from treated wood until the solvent has completely evaporated – at least two days.

The majority of wood preservatives found in shops are of this type.

Emulsions are mayonnaise-like mixtures of an organic solvent-type preservative with water. They have been developed recently and can be applied thickly, giving a much heavier dose of fungicide to the wood than it is possible to obtain by simply brushing a liquid fungicide on to the surface. Emulsions are especially useful for treating large timbers which cannot be replaced without great cost. For instance, the ends of main beams which have slight wet rot, but which are still amply strong enough to support a floor, can be treated with these emulsions *in situ*.

Applying preservatives

Any timber which is in contact with the ground or which is exposed to persistently wet conditions should have the preservative impregnated deeply into it. Timber that has been treated commercially, either in a pressure cylinder or by prolonged diffusion process, can be purchased from many larger timber merchants. Two well-known treatments of this kind are called Tanalised and Timborised timber.

All other areas of woodwork can be treated by liberally brushing on several flowing coats of preservative. But if you are treating a considerable quantity of timber, it is worthwhile constructing a long, narrow, deep bath and partly filling this with preservative. The pieces of wood for treatment can then be totally immersed for about ten minutes by weighting them down with a metal bar. Carry out all sawing, planing, sanding, cross-cutting, boring or drilling before treatment, so that no untreated wood is exposed by subsequent woodworking. Always follow the preservative's safety warnings and wear rubber gloves when handling freshly-treated timber.

Wood pests

Certain kinds of wood in buildings are liable to be attacked by the larvae (grubs) of wood-boring beetles. By far the most common of these is *Anobium punctatum*, the common furniture beetle. The larvae of this beetle are generally known as woodworm.

These insects naturally inhabit the dead branches of trees and shrubs, but they can also survive and breed in the relatively dry wood of roofs and floors. The beetles can fly for some distance and may get into a roof space from the outside. In towns, infestations most frequently come from old furniture and wickerwork stored in attics and roof spaces.

At one time it was thought that timber had to be old before it could be attacked, but this is not so. Freshly-felled and recently-seasoned wood can also become infested, but the insects breed so slowly that it is usually many years before they cause sufficient damage to be observed.

The holes seen in infested wood are the exit holes made by beetles that have emerged after spending several years as larvae tunnelling in the depths of the wood. It need not be assumed that there is an active infestation just because you see some holes in the wood. It is quite common to find woodwork in old buildings with many holes on the surface but no active insects at all. Small piles of wood dust, called *frass*, on the surface of the wood are a sure indication of recent activity, and fresh clean exit holes also indicate that live beetles have recently emerged. Old holes soon become dirty and dark.

Where to look
A bright electric torch and a large magnifying glass are useful when inspecting woodwork for signs of woodworm damage.

Although the larvae of the common furniture beetle can survive in dry seasoned timber in the roof of a modern house, they thrive best under rather damper conditions, such as the woodwork of cellars, outhouses and barns. Decayed wood is more nutritious for them than sound wood, so they can often be found infesting wood that is already slightly softened by decay. They also find glue a useful source of protein and the older types of plywood made with animal glue or casein are especially susceptible to attack. An infestation can often be traced to old tea chests in an attic, and plywood meter boards in cellars are also a common focus for infestation.

Some timbers, such as pine and oak, have a distinct, darker-

HOUSEHOLD INSECT IDENTIFICATION

By no means all the insects found in buildings are able to attack wood. Only if exit holes or tunnels are found need any anxiety be felt as to the soundness of the wood. The common furniture beetle is by far the most usual pest in buildings in the UK, but other types of beetle may occasionally be found and their recognition is important. Their distinctive features – usually the shape of their exit holes and the type of dust left – and where they are likely to be found are summarised in the following Table.

	where found	timbers attacked	exit holes	bore dust
Bark borer	throughout UK	softwoods on which bark is present	round, 1.2 to 2.0mm across	bun-shaped, dark brown and light brown
Common furniture beetle	throughout UK	sapwood of softwoods and oak; beech; birch; elm; mahogany; plywood	circular, 1.6mm across	tiny lemon-shaped pellets
Death-watch beetle	England, very rare in Ireland or Scotland	old hardwoods – for example oak, partly decayed	circular, about 3mm across	coarse, bun-shaped pellets
House long-horn beetle	W Surrey and NE Hants	seasoned softwoods, mostly in sapwood	oval, about 10 by 6mm	large compact pellets
Powder post beetle Lyctus	throughout UK	sapwood of recently-seasoned oak, ash	circular, about 1.6mm across	fine dust, like talcum powder
Weevils	generally distributed in very damp places	all kinds, but only when decayed by wet rot	not clearly defined, ragged outline	fine pellets

coloured heartwood. This is practically immune from beetle attack, though they may eat away all the pale-coloured, outer sapwood. It is quite common to find old oak beams from which practically all the sapwood has been eaten but which are still strong enough to support the floors. Other woods, such as beech, have no distinct areas of heartwood and sapwood and larvae may eat right through them.

In roofs, damage will always be most severe along the sapwood edges of rafters and joists, and in floors it will be confined to the sapwood portions of the boards and the joists.

The underside of a staircase is another area where infestation quite often becomes established.

Since the beetles always seek bare wood on which to lay their eggs, an infestation can never start on polished surfaces of floors or furniture, though the adult beetles may make their exit holes through such surfaces.

The life cycle of wood boring beetles

After mating, the female beetles lay their eggs on the end grain, or in cracks, crevices and joints of certain kinds of wood. After four of five weeks the eggs hatch and the small larvae bore into the wood, tunnelling and eating their way inside it for several years, during which the internal damage may remain undetected.

When the larvae are fully grown they pupate and emerge as beetles, usually during the summer months. Most of these beetles are sluggish in cool weather but on warm sunny days they can fly quite well.

Treating woodworm

The first thing you have to decide is whether you want to call in a remedial treatment company – of which there are now a great number – or to deal with the problem yourself. Before World War II, very few firms carrying out this type of work existed, and at that time the average builder dealt with these problems quite efficiently, even without the help of modern insecticides.

Nowadays, most building societies refuse to give mortgages unless they have a guarantee from a remedial treatment company that any infestation, however small, has been treated by the operatives of the remedial company.

Roof timbers Remove all objects stored in the roof space. If the rafters have been attacked, examine the joists in the ceiling below carefully – these will probably have been attacked as well. Remove any roof insulating materials from between the joists and clear any dust from the surface of the timbers with a vacuum cleaner. Industrial cleaners are particularly suitable for this job and can be hired. If the edges of the rafters (or joists) are severely tunnelled, the disintegrated portions should be cut away with a draw knife.

The next step is to wet thoroughly the surface of all the exposed timbers with an insecticidal wood preservative. This can be applied with a large brush, but big areas are much quicker to treat by spraying. Use a sprayer with a long lance so that you can reach areas which are not easily accessible, such as the ends of rafters near the eaves. Apply sufficient insecticidal wood preservative to wet all the exposed wood surfaces thoroughly but do not apply so much that it soaks through and stains the ceiling beneath. Always use a coarse spray, never a fine one. Wear a face mask and gloves and do not smoke or have naked flames nearby.

Floor timbers The upper surface of floorboards can be treated easily by brushing or spraying. To treat the joists beneath, take up about every fourth floorboard and use a spray gun to direct the insecticidal wood preservative in all directions wetting as much of the joists as possible.

TREATING A ROOF SPACE

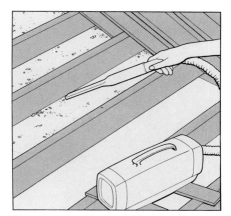

Remove everything stored in the roof space, take up any loft insulation and use a vacuum cleaner to clean away dust

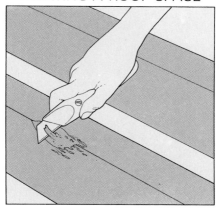

If the edges of the rafters or joists are severely tunnelled, cut away the badly damaged portions with a knife

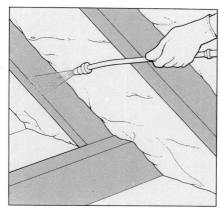

Apply a coarse spray of insecticidal wood preservative. Always follow the safety precautions listed on the product – never have naked flames near

Guarding against woodworm

You can reduce the chances of getting woodworm by:

● never storing in attics or roof spaces any wicker baskets or chairs, plywood boxes, or old furniture that shows traces of woodworm unless it has been thoroughly treated

● applying a preservative or varnish to the surface of floors in attics and other rooms in which bare timbers are exposed

● applying a preservative or varnish to exposed bare wood on the underside of chairs and other furniture, and any plywood backing to furniture.

Treating other wood pests

Woodworm is by far the most common wood pest. Some other pests need similar treatment, others require none at all.

Lyctus Use the procedure outlined for woodworm.

House longhorn beetle This is a rare pest which can cause a lot of damage. Authorities are anxious to know of any outbreak and if you suspect that you have one you should seek expert advice.

Death-watch beetle This is rarely found in modern houses but it is a problem in churches where it is usually associated with fungal decay which may have caused structural damage to the roof. Eradication treatments are similar to those for woodworm but as the insect often penetrates well into the wood it may be necessary to inject the insecticide more deeply. In roof spaces, regular use – every summer, say – of insecticidal smokes for several years should achieve effective control.

Bark borer (*Ernobius mollis*) No treatment is required as this beetle cannot breed in buildings.

Weevils This pest is only found in timber which has already suffered wet rot. Replace the rotten wood with new treated timber to ensure no further attack.

If you can neither carry out treatments yourself nor afford to employ a remedial treatment company, it is possible to reduce the population of beetles in a roof space drastically by suspending strips of plastic impregnated with dichlorvos. This is best done in June when the fumes will kill the emerging beetles. If this treatment is repeated each summer for three or four years the breeding population will be controlled, and with luck almost completely annihilated.

Insecticidal solutions: warning

Most builders' merchants carry stocks of insecticidal wood preservatives specially formulated for the control of wood pests. The precautions set out on the containers should be strictly observed. Most of the products give off flammable vapours and no naked flames should ever be brought near freshly treated timber. Face masks and gloves should be worn when spraying these products in a closed space, such as a roof space. And enough clothing should be worn to keep the insecticides off other parts of the body.

HOW URGENT IS REMEDIAL TREATMENT?

Woodworm The damage caused by woodworm extends fairly slowly and the infestation only spreads when the beetles emerge in early summer. It is usually best to postpone remedial treatment until May or June, when the insects are likely to be nearer the surface of the timber than at other times of the year.

Dry rot If active dry rot is discovered take action quickly – the fungus will continue to spread in all directions until its further growth is checked. If repairs cannot be put in hand immediately, open up and expose the fungus to the air so that the wood can begin to dry out and so check further growth.

Wet rot Because wet rot does not spread as far nor as fast as dry rot, a few weeks delay in dealing with it may not matter much, especially if the wood is beginning to dry out. But it must be eradicated as soon as conveniently possible.

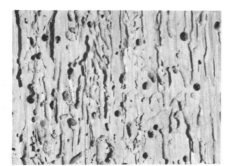
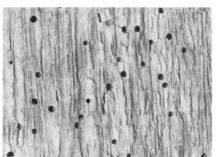

Untreated and treated woodworm

Rot

Useful names and addresses

The Asphalt and Coated Macadam Association, 25 Lower Belgrave Street, London SW1 0LS mainly provide an advisory service to the industry but if you are quoted different specifications by different contractors they will do their best to sort out which one suits your needs.

The Brick Advisory Centre is in the London Building Centre and has samples of many different types of facing bricks, paving bricks and fireplace briquettes.

The British Chemical Dampcourse Association (BCDA), 51 High Street, Broom, Bidford-on-Avon, Warwicks B50 4HL vets specialist damp treatment firms before granting membership. They will investigate complaints against members.

The British Ready Mixed Concrete Association (BRMCA), Shepperton House, Green Lane, Shepperton, Middlesex TW17 8DN set technical standards, give advice to users and will pursue complaints against member firms. They will also provide the name and addresses of ready mix depots covered by their Authorisation scheme.

The British Security Industry Association, 68 St. James's Street, London SW1A 1PH is a trade association which can help with the names and addresses of lock manufacturers and burglar alarm companies.

The British Wood Preserving Association (BWPA), 150 Southampton Row, London WC1B 5AL vets specialist woodworm and rot treatment firms before granting membership. They will investigate complaints against member firms.

The Building Centres in major cities maintain a permanent exhibition of building materials with related literature available to visitors. They will send you literature (for a fee). The London centre is at 26 Store Street, London WC1E 7BT.

The Building Research Establishment (BRE) carries out research and development relevant to the needs of central government and industry in the fields of building and construction. The BRE operates an Advisory Service (a fee is charged for site investigations). For information on damp and building materials contact The Building Research Station, Bucknalls Green, Garston, Watford, Herts. For information on wood, rot and woodworm, contact the Princes Risborough Laboratory, Princes Risborough, Aylesbury, Bucks.

The Cement and Concrete Association, Wexham Springs, Wexham, Slough SL3 6PL is an independent non-profit making organization which provides advice and information to users of Portland cement and concrete. The Association also publish a free booklet on DIY concrete, **Concrete round the house** by Dave Beadle (Publication number 93.006).

The Electrical Contractors Association (ECA), ESCA House, 34 Palace Court, Bayswater, London W2 4HY guarantees that work done by its member firms will conform to the IEE Wiring Regs. Their members work is regularly inspected and the ECA will take up complaints against member firms.

The Federation of Master Builders (FMB), 33 John Street, London WC1N 2BB is a trade association of mainly small and medium-sized building firms and have regional lists of member firms specialising in one type of building. Member firms are not inspected for their standard of workmanship but the FMB operate an arbitration service in disputes. The FMB is introducing a scheme for guaranteeing the work of certain members.

Fidor, Fibre Building Board Development Organisation Ltd., 1 Hanworth Road, Feltham, Middlesex TW13 5AF offer an advisory service on hardboards and other fibre building boards.

The Glass and Glazing Federation, 6 Mount Row, London W1Y 6DY will send you a list of their members in your area with details of the types of glass they handle and the installation services they offer. The Federation also offer advice on any type of flat glass, including mirrors.

The Incorporated Association of Architects and Surveyors (IAAS), Jubilee House, Billing Brook Road, Weston Favell, Northampton have names of building surveyors.

The Institute of Plumbing, Scottish Mutual House, North Street, Hornchurch, Essex RM11 1RU have area lists of members who have satisfied the institute of their experience and competence – send a stamped addressed envelope.

The Master Locksmiths Association (MLA), 7 Hollingsworth Road, Croydon, Surrey CR0 5RP have lists of their members.

The National Association of Plumbing, Heating & Mechanical Services Contractors, 6 Gate Street, London WC2A 3HX can tell you the name of the secretary of your local association who has a list of local members.

The National Federation of Roofing Contractors, 15 Soho Square, London W1V 5FB is a trade organization which inspects the work of firms carefully before admitting them as members and takes up complaints about member firms.

The National Home Enlargement Bureau (NHEB), PO Box 67, High Wycombe, Bucks HP15 6XP is a non-profit making organization which aims to give help on home enlargements. They publish a booklet called **More Room for Living** (60p inc. P & P) and will also send you a list of builders, builders' merchants and insurance brokers in your area.

The National House Building Council (NHBC), 58 Portland Place, London W1N 4BH is a non-profit making body which aims to improve the standards of *new* houses and safeguard their buyers. It operates a 10-year protection scheme for new homes and flats against some defects that occur after building.

The National Inspection Council for Electrical Installation Contracting (NICEIC), 237 Kennington Lane, London SE11 5QJ (Tel. 01 582 7746) maintain a list of approved contractors – available in libraries, Citizens Advice Bureaus and Electricity Board showrooms – whose work should conform to the IEE Wiring Regs. They regularly inspect their members work and will take up complaints against member firms.

The National Supervisory Council for Intruder Alarms (NSCIA), St. Ives House, St. Ives Road, Maidenhead, Berks SL6 1RD have lists of approved installers who install burglar alarms to BS 4737 and have an inspection team covering the whole of the UK.

The Royal Institute of British Architects (RIBA) have a Clients Advisory Service at 66 Portland Place, London W1N 4AD (Tel. 01 323 0687) and have lists of architects who have been through a recognised course of training and abide by a code of professional conduct.

The Royal Institution of Chartered Surveyors (RICS) have an Information Centre at 12 Great George Street, London SW1P 3AD (Tel. 01 222 7000) and have names of building surveyors qualified in building design.

The Timber Research and Development Association (TRADA), Hughenden Valley, High Wycombe, Bucks HP14 4ND will answer simple problems you have about wood and wood-based sheet materials. A charge will be made if investigation is necessary. They will also provide the names of independent consultants who are able to investigate the failure of a woodworm or rot treatment.

Index